THE ABC'S OF RELOADING

SIXTH EDITION

By C. Rodney James
and the Editors of Handloader's Digest

DBI BOOKS
a division of Krause Publications, Inc.

Staff

SENIOR STAFF EDITORS
Harold A. Murtz
Ray Ordorica

PRODUCTION MANAGER
John L. Duoba

EDITORIAL/PRODUCTION ASSISTANT
Karen M. Rasmussen

ELECTRONIC PUBLISHING DIRECTOR
Sheldon L. Factor

ELECTRONIC PUBLISHING MANAGER
Nancy J. Mellem

ELECTRONIC PUBLISHING ASSOCIATE
Laura M. Mielzynski

GRAPHIC DESIGN
John L. Duoba

COVER PHOTOGRAPHY
John Hanusin

MANAGING EDITOR
Pamela J. Johnson

PUBLISHER
Charles T. Hartigan

ABOUT OUR COVERS

In 1993, Lee Precision, the subject of our covers and one of the leaders in handloading tool technology, celebrated their 35th birthday. They honored their tradition of providing the best tools for the best cost by offering the Anniversary Reloading Kit we show here. This complete kit proved so popular that they have kept it in their line.

Everything the handloader needs to reload ammunition, except his choice of dies and the various components, is included. The heart of the kit is the Challenger Press, a sturdy O-frame design with a larger than normal opening angled 30 degrees for maximum hand clearance. Its spent primer catcher really works, in addition to being easy to empty.

Also included is a complete powder handling system. Lee's Perfect Powder Measure is said to be almost as good as a scale because it's so accurate, and it comes with the steel stand. Through excellent design and by using the right nylon material, the measure eliminates cut powder and jerky action of the lever, plus there's no drum binding or powder bridging, and the micrometer adjustment positively locks. Unlike other measures, the adjuster reads directly in cubic centimeters. Just multiply the charge in grains by the cc for one grain and you have the setting.

The Lee Safety Scale is simple yet highly accurate, and very sensitive. It's magnetically damped and has an approach to weight lifter enclosed within its heavy base. The scale's phenolic beam is tough, but like glass, it can't be bent, which means it can never get out of adjustment as long as it's not physically broken. This powder scale is said to be the easiest to use, most accurate and sensitive model made. To help get the powder into the cases, the kit comes with a powder funnel that fits cases from 22- to 45-caliber.

Case preparation tools include a cutter and lock stud to trim your cases, an inside-outside case mouth chamfering tool, a primer pocket cleaner, and a tube of Lee's great sizing lube.

For priming cases, they've included the Lee Auto-Prime along with a set of shellholders for over 115 different cartridges. It's said to be the fastest, most accurate priming tool made. You never touch the primers from the box to the shell. It automatically feeds and installs primers as fast as you can place a shell in the shellholder.

Also included is Lee's new *Modern Reloading*, by Richard Lee. It contains 350 pages of loading data, with the remaining 162 pages devoted to how-to articles on reloading and the various Lee Precision tools. This 512-page data source gives an interesting history of a company that has offered reloaders such good values in innovative, high-quality tools over the last 38 years.

Shown with the Anniversary Reloading Kit are a two-die set of rifle dies that store in the round yellow case and a selection of Lee Factory Crimp Dies. These items are optionally available.

All the handloader needs to begin this fun and money-saving hobby is a set of dies and the various components. It seems to us like a very good way to get set up.

Photo by John Hanusin

ISBN 0-87349-190-4   Library of Congress Catalog #73-91588

Acknowledgements

A number of people helped in the preparation of this book and should receive credit for their efforts. At the top of the list is Mary McGavick, my own personal reference librarian, editor and critic who read it all; Allan Jones of Blount, Inc., who guided me to many facts and away from God knows how many pitfalls; also Dave Davison of CH/4-D Custom Die Co. who did same. Chris Hodgdon of Hodgdon Powder Co., Inc., Dan McDonald from IMR, Ben Amonette at Alliant Techsystems, Bill Falin at Accurate Arms, Mike Larsen from Federal Cartridge Co. and Mike Jordan from Winchester all took time to explain things and answer questions they had undoubtedly heard before. For the others who have helped and whose names I have forgotten, my thanks and apologies.

—C. Rodney James

Contents

Contents

Introduction

THERE ARE AT least five good reasons to begin reloading your own ammunition. First is **economy**. It doesn't take the beginning shooter long to discover that the cost of factory ammunition makes frequent trips to the range almost prohibitive. A pleasant afternoon of target shooting, banging through a half-dozen or more boxes of cartridges, can run past the hundred dollar mark if you use anything other than 22 rimfires. By reloading the empty cases with commercially available bullets, primers and smokeless powder you can reduce the cost of ammunition by about 60 percent. If you cast your own lead alloy bullets, you can save even more since good bullets can be made from scrap alloys that can be bought for very little, or even obtained for free.

The second is **accuracy**. Firearms and ammunition are standardized—more or less—with a range of tolerances, which means that your average gun will function properly with your average commercial ammunition, producing acceptably accurate results. For those who want better than "acceptable," handloading allows you to make custom-crafted ammunition, loaded to draw the maximum degree of accuracy from *your* gun because the cases, powders and bullets are tested by you to produce the best accuracy in your particular gun.

A third reason might be termed **usefulness**. While commercial ammunition may be available in perhaps two or three loadings, handloaded ammunition can extend this to more than a dozen. Low-power, cast-bullet, loads can be made for short-range practice allowing economical shooting with low noise and low recoil. This means not only less wear and tear on your gun, but on you as well. Heavy hunting loads can be fabricated for taking the largest game possible within the limits of a particular rifle or handgun. Light, flat-shooting bullets designed to expand rapidly on small game, can be loaded to turn a deer rifle into a varmint gun for spring and summer varmint shooting—good practice plus enjoyment. Reduced-velocity loads, in turn, can turn a varmint rifle into a good small game rifle that will kill effectively without destroying edible meat. Thus the usefulness of a gun is doubled by simply altering the ammunition.

Necessity, that mother of invention, is a fourth reason to reload. There are any number of older guns, both foreign and domestic, for which commercial ammunition is simply no longer available—cartridges that have fallen prey to the cold-blooded attrition of supply and demand economics. Cartridge cases may be formed by reshaping and trimming similar ones that have acceptably close dimensions. In some instances, the cases you need may be commercially available, but the commercial loadings are not suitable for your gun which, because of its age, may require a lighter load or one of black instead of smokeless powder.

Finally there is the sheer **enjoyment**. Mastering a craft that will improve your shooting is an extension of the shooting sport. You will gain a better understanding of the dynamics involved in the shooting process. Good shooting is far more than simply good aiming. Good aim and proper shooting technique are necessary for hitting what you shoot at, but you will score far more hits if you have a clear understanding of the ammunition in your gun, what it is and is not capable of doing, and why.

Who should reload? This is a question firearms writers hear fairly often. It's not for everyone. The casual shooter satisfied with rimfire ammunition performance, the person who targets his gun once or twice a year, and the person with no time for hobbies will find little use for this avocation. Then there are those who may wish to join the reloading clan, but for reasons of safety shouldn't do it. Those who persist in drinking or smoking while reloading, the chronically careless, the forgetful and accident prone, and those given to dangerous experimentation would best be advised to take up knitting or bowling.

Reloading is far safer than driving a car, but you have to pay attention to what you are doing. Reloading is as safe or as dangerous, as economical or expensive, as simple or complicated as *you* make it.

How do you get started? As an educator facing eager students, champing at the bit to get along with the hands-on part, I began my classes with an apologetic: "Yes, I applaud your enthusiasm, but you should know a little something about what you are going to be doing. Those who don't know have a bad habit of breaking equipment, getting poor results, and having no clue as to why bad things happen. You can't learn from your mistakes unless you can figure out *what* they were and *why* they happened. In order to accomplish this you must have a grasp of the basic dynamics involved." To put it another way: Some people live and learn, others just live, but never as long or as happily.

What kinds of guns are we loading for? This book is designed for shooters of modern guns designed for metallic cartridges using smokeless powder. The bibliographic material in Chapter 12 directs the reloader to what is considered advanced reloading. These resources touch on loading for blackpowder guns, early smokeless guns which may not be up to modern loads or which may have chamber and bore dimensions different from those of current manufacture. It also includes references for custom-bored guns for non-standard wildcat cartridges, and loading for obsolete and non-standard foreign guns. This level of reloading is for the experienced reloader and is not within the scope of a basic manual.

—C. Rodney James

1

Before beginning
any activity, a
solid foundation
is needed to
build upon, and
reloading is no
different. For this
reason, we....

Start with Safety

EVERY BOX OF cartridges, every loading manual, advises that these loadings are for "modern arms in good condition." What is a modern gun? Like any other arbitrary definition it has fuzzy edges. Modern gun designs (such as modern-looking double-action revolvers) were developed in the late 1880s. Modern semi-automatic pistols were on the market by 1900. Bolt-action, 30-caliber rifles intended for high pressure (40,000 to 60,000 p.s.i.) smokeless powder ammunition were in general military use by 1895. Roughly speaking, the era of modern gun making begins around 1886-1900.

The real issue is whether the gun for which you wish to reload can take the pressures of modern ammunition. For instance, a tightly locking Winchester low wall single shot or Stevens target rifle from the last century can be safely used with modern, high-velocity 22 Long Rifle ammunition. To use such ammunition in a light revolver or pistol from the same era will destroy it. Even guns made as recently as the 1920s may not be safe with the high pressures generated by the high-velocity

This reproduction 1874 Sharps rifle (bottom) is made of modern steel (4140 for the receiver and 1195 for the barrel). It is capable of handling modern high pressure 45-70 loadings to 28,000 psi. The Allin "trapdoor" 45-70 Springfield (top) was made in 1888. The receiver is mild steel, case-hardened. The barrel is mild "decarbonized" steel. Its maximum pressure rating, at the time of manufacture, was 25,000 psi. It is *not* a modern gun and must be loaded accordingly.

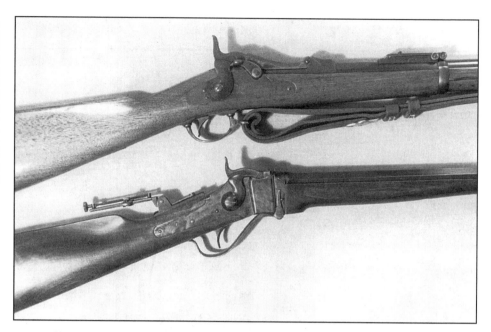

A ninety-four-year-old 32 ACP Colt Model 1903 pocket pistol (bottom) and a Cold-War era 9mm Makarov—both qualify as "modern guns."

loadings. The 22 Long Rifle Reising automatic pistol of that period had a very thin breechblock which regularly splits on the first firing of a high-speed round, so it is to be used with standard velocity ammunition only.

While a modern looking revolver such as the Model 1889 Colt Navy double action looks very like the 38 Special police models that have been in use for over sixty years, it was made for the 38 Long Colt blackpowder cartridge. Some of these early guns will chamber a contemporary smokeless-powder, 38 special cartridge. However, to fire such a loading in one of these old Colts is to court disaster.

Some early smokeless powder guns were by no means as strong as later models chambered for the same cartridge. The

soft steel on U.S. Krag rifles—Models 1892-1896—was not up to the pressure of some heavy smokeless-powder loadings, and those guns began to develop cracks around the bolt locking lug after prolonged use. Krag and early 1903 Springfield rifles were inspected "by eye," the proper color indicating proper heat treatment of barrel and receiver steel. When Springfield receivers started failing with higher pressure loadings, the heat treatment process was improved. This occurred at serial number 800,000.

The Colt Single Action Army revolver (Model 1873) is still being made. The original was a blackpowder gun. The steel was later improved and some internal redesigning was done, making it safe for smokeless loadings. Colt has advised that guns with serial numbers below 160,000 are for blackpowder only!

The U.S. standard 30-06 Springfield cartridge (left) and Russian 7.62x54mm Mosin rifle cartridge are *not* compatible. Some Russian rifles have had chambers recut to take the '06. The smaller-diameter 30-06 has plenty of room to swell and burst in the oversize Russian chamber.

The 30-06 Springfield (left) and 8mm Mauser rounds are close enough in size the Mauser can be fired in a 30-06 chamber. This will happen ONCE! The gun will be wrecked along with the shooter's face by the tremendous pressures generated by an oversize bullet.

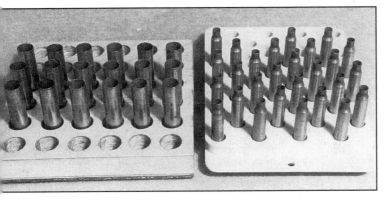

Loading blocks can be homemade from wood (left) or of moulded plastic (right). Loading blocks are *not* merely a convenience, they are a necessity to keep you from double-charging a cartridge case.

Except for serial numbers and a few minor details neither the '03 Springfield nor the Colt SAA has changed in external appearance since their introduction.

Early 38 Colt semi-automatic pistols (Models 1900, 1902, 1903) are chambered for the 38 Colt Automatic cartridge, no longer manufactured. The same cartridge, in terms of dimensions, is still on the market as the 38 Super Auto. This is the old 38 Auto with a much heavier charge of powder. It is poison for the older guns.

The original Model 1895 Winchester lever-action rifle was chambered for the 1903 Springfield's 30-06 cartridge. For some reason this rifle got a reputation as having an action that was stronger than the Springfield when, in fact, it was weaker.

Older guns can be fired quite safely *if* you are aware of their limitations and don't try for "improved" performance. Determining what is and is not a "modern" gun in terms of its strength falls under the COIK limitation. COIK stands for Clear Only If Known. Therefore, defining what is a safe "modern" gun at times requires some knowledge beyond the appearance and the date it was introduced. Thus if the gun you are planning on reloading for is questionable in any way regarding the caliber, its age and/or mechanical condition, have it checked by a competent gunsmith and if you don't like the first answer a second opinion won't hurt.

Occasionally what might be termed "nightmare guns" turn up on the used market. These are standard rifles, often surplus military guns which some amateur gunsmith has attempted to rework into a caliber different from the one it was originally intended to fire. The 6.5mm and 7.7mm Japanese Arisaka and the 7.62mm Russian Mosin-Nagant rifles have been found converted to take the 30-06 Springfield cartridge.

Some were only half converted—the chamber being recut, the barrel left untouched. In the case of the 6.5 rifle, 30-caliber bullets were squeezed down to 25-caliber in the barrel creating tremendous pressures. Some of these rifles, amazingly, held together for a while. The Russian rifle was never intended to take the pressures of the 30-06, and no recutting of the chamber can replace metal at the rear of the chamber which is considerably oversize for the 30-06 cartridge. Case swelling and eventual ruptures are a matter of time. There is no way such a butchered rifle can be made right short of rebarreling. Even then the new caliber should be one which will not give pressures greater than that of the original cartridge. If you plan to shoot and reload for a centerfire rifle *know* what you have—don't guess! If, on firing some commercial ammunition, there is *any* sign of trouble, stop right there. What is a trouble sign? The best quick and easy means is to look at the fired cartridge case. If it looks significantly different from an unfired one, is now swollen or misshapen, with a flattened or pierced primer, take the rifle and case to a good gunsmith for an analysis.

The Loading Process

The loading process is not terribly complicated, though it does involve a number of steps. Each step is there for a reason. It may not be apparent to the beginner, at the outset, why those steps are there. This often seems to be a good excuse to take a shortcut and eliminate a particular step. I was once one of those people. I started reloading cases in what I thought was a very safe manner. Each cartridge case was sized and decapped, just as this book tells you to do. Then I inserted a new primer, also according to the manual. I carefully weighed the powder charge on a good scale (I was assembling precision ammunition) and even weighed bullets to make sure there was no more than $1/2$-grain difference in weight. After weighing the powder charge to an accuracy level of less than $1/10$-grain, I put it directly in the case and immediately seated the bullet.

Everything worked fine with this system until the day I was in the process of loading and someone came to the door. I left a cartridge case sitting on the loading bench, charged with a small charge of fast-burning powder that disappeared in the dark bot-

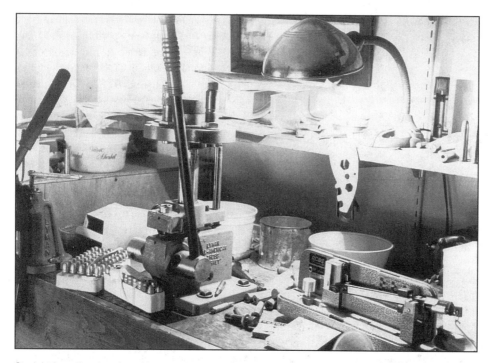

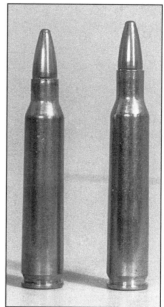

The 223 (left) has a shorter neck than the 222 Magnum.

Straight from the chamber of horrors. Before your loading bench looks like this, it's time to clean up and get organized. With such a mess, it's easy to mistake and/or waste a lot of time puzzling over what's *really* in those various bins and boxes.

All are ready to shoot, except the one in the middle is a 222 Magnum and the rest are 223. If you plan to load similar calibers, extra caution is needed to keep the cases, loaded ammunition and, in some instances, bullets separate.

tom of the cartridge case. After dealing with the visitor, I returned to the bench to continue loading, picking up where I thought I'd left off. I carefully measured out a charge of powder and funneled it in the case. I was wary of accidentally getting two charges in one case so immediately seated a bullet and added the finished cartridge to the box I had been filling.

Two charges is exactly what resulted.

Every instruction manual will warn you not to do this. Use a loading block, a small plastic or wood tray that holds cartridge cases heads down. They cost a couple of bucks, or you can make your own by boring the proper-sized holes through a piece of plank and gluing a flat bottom on it. A loading block is a safety device allowing the reloader a second chance to inspect charged cartridges *before* seating a bullet, because there might be the slight possibility that one of those cartridges got too much powder.

I discovered my error the following weekend while target shooting at a friend's farm. The double-charged case wrecked a nice old Springfield, the purchase price of which would have bought an amazing number of loading blocks. I was very lucky, because the people who had designed and built that Springfield had built-in some good safety features. These saved my eye-sight. Many reloaders owe a lot to those folks who designed and built their guns—people who were smarter than they are.

Everybody who loads will throw double charges. The careful ones won't do it very often and they'll catch their mistakes before they are fired. Once is all it takes to ruin a gun. Once is all it takes to ruin your face, eyesight, hearing, and if you are really unlucky, kill you.

I have never considered myself a particularly lucky person, so I have made it a point to try to be careful. Follow the steps listed in the reloading manuals, all of them in the proper order. They are there for a good reason.

Many reloading accidents stem from simple carelessness, like avoiding steps, taking shortcuts, and not paying attention to your work. Reloading is a solitary activity. Don't try to watch television or chat with friends while you reload. A radio may be played, but softly. Reloading is a simple task requiring concentration and paying attention to details. Close the door to the room where you reload to keep others out, especially children. If there's an interruption, stop at the completion of an operation and then deal with whatever it is. If this isn't possible, back up one step and do it over. Because it is repetitive, reloading can become routine and boring. When it becomes boring is the time to take a break. Never reload when you are tired or ill, because this dulls your concentration.

Handling Materials Safely

My teachers constantly reminded me that neatness counts. I wasn't very neat and it never bothered me too much. In reloading it will be your gun that will tell you, not your teacher. A cluttered, messy reloading area leads to more mistakes. Primers not put away get mixed with the next batch that may be different. Cartridge cases that are similar can be mixed and the wrong one can wind up in the loading press, jamming it, or worse dropped in a box of loaded ammunition of a different caliber. Mismatched ammunition can wreck guns and shooters.

Primers are perhaps the most potentially dangerous components of the reloading hobby. They come packaged in little packets of 100, separated in rows or in individual pockets in a plastic holder. There is a very good reason for this. While modern primers are well sealed there is always the possibility that minute amounts of priming compound can coat an exposed surface of a primer and flake off as dust. If primers are dumped into a can or bottle this dust can accumulate and be detonated, followed by all the primers in that can or bottle, in something

approaching $^{25}/_{1000}$-second. That's faster than most people can let go of a can or bottle. Primers should never be dumped more than 100 at a time and this should be done only in a plastic primer tray. Shaking a can or bottle of primers is not merely tempting fate, but telling fate to go straight to hell. Primer trays should be wiped clean if there is any evidence of residue in them.

The more advanced loading tools are often equipped with automatic primer feeding devices that will occasionally jam. Dealing with such a jam is a delicate process. All primers that can be removed should be taken out before attempting to clear a jam. Problems with feeders are best dealt with via a call or letter to the manufacturer.

When loading using an automatic primer feeder, it is a good idea to wear safety glasses because primers can explode. Aeronautical engineer Edward Murphy came up with a very good set of rules known as "Murphy's Laws" regarding how and why things fail, concluding that they fail at the worst possible time—airplanes when they are flying, guns when they are being fired, primer feeders when they are packed full of primers.

(Text continued on page 14)

The right and wrong way to store primers. Dropping or shaking the bottle could cause the primers inside to detonate with enough violence to remove a good part of your hand. The box is specially designed to keep the primers apart. It is made of soft plastic and paper. If you are careless and leave it open, dropping it will cause no problems beyond a spill.

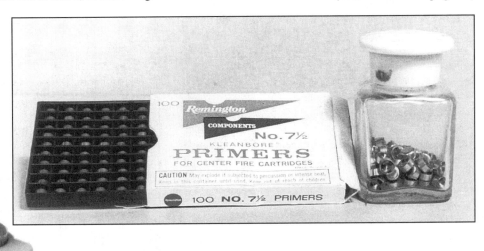

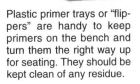

Plastic primer trays or "flippers" are handy to keep primers on the bench and turn them the right way up for seating. They should be kept clean of any residue.

Lead Hazards In the Shooting Sports

by Robert D. Williams, Ph.D.
director, division of toxicology, The Ohio State University Medical Center

LEAD IS AN integral component in the manufacture of ammunition, ranging from a relatively low amount to nearly 100 percent in shot. Lead is also present during bullet casting, reloading, and gun cleaning. Lead interacts with organic matter to produce stable complexes. Specifically, human tissues possess prominent lead-binding characteristics. Thus, with a high degree of accumulation and relatively low turnover in man, concerns over the hazards of lead exposure become apparent in the shooting sports.

Exposure to lead can occur through ingestion, inhalation, and dermal contact. In the general population, the primary route of administration of lead is through ingestion: children eating lead-based paint or drinking water contaminated by lead piping. Individuals involved in shooting sports are exposed to high lead levels through dust inhalation, particularly at indoor and covered outdoor firing ranges, or during bullet casting where *inadequate ventilation* exists. Although firearm instructors constitute an occupational group at higher risk, studies have demonstrated that even recreational use of small bore rifles can produce elevated red blood cell lead concentrations and symptomatic toxicity, following a 6-month indoor-shooting season averaging only 70 minutes per week.

Higher air-lead levels have been measured in firing ranges where powder charges were employed relative to ranges where only air guns were used, which in turn were higher than archery ranges. The use of totally-copper-jacketed or solid-copper ammunition has been proposed to decrease shooting range air-lead levels, since most of the airborne lead is vaporized from bullet surfaces.

Natural sources of lead in the atmosphere represent an insignificant risk: providing lead chiefly in its sulfide form, estimated to be half a billionth of one gram per cubic meter of air. Airborne dust from the environment and gases from the earth's crust contribute to the low "background" atmospheric level. Certain areas of the world contain substantially higher than background levels of lead, e.g. cities in industrialized regions where about 98 percent of airborne lead can be traced to the combustion of leaded gasoline. Air-lead levels averaging 660 micrograms/m3, which are over one hundred million times greater than normal environmental levels, have been measured at some indoor firing ranges. One analysis of firing range dust samples revealed it was composed of 24 to 36 percent lead. Soil lead is also enriched during shooting.

Acute lead poisoning is rare and usually occurs from ingestion of lead in soluble form, not sucking or swallowing a bullet which could lead to chronic poisoning if done long enough. The symptoms of acute poisoning include a sweet metallic taste, salivation, vomiting, and intestinal colic. A large quantity ingested may produce death from cardiovascular collapse. Survivors of acute poisoning frequently develop signs associated with chronic toxicity.

Chronic lead poisoning, or plumbism, is manifest with a variety of symptoms. Initially, the individual is tired and weak due to anemia. Subsequent neurologic problems can develop which encompass irritability, restlessness, convulsions and in severe cases coma. Associated gastrointestinal disorders are constipation and a metallic taste. Neuromuscular symptoms include fatigue and muscle weakness. The most serious effect of lead poisoning which occurs more often in children than adults, is encephalopathy. The early signs of encephalopathy involve clumsiness, irritability, and insomnia which develop because of necrosis of brain tissue. Lead sulfide may appear in the gums and gingiva of toxic individuals as a blue-to-black line of discoloration termed the Burtonian line.

Toxicity from lead absorbed by the lungs and gastrointestinal tract is cumulative. In circulation, it is primarily bound to the red blood cells. Lead accumulates in soft tissues such as liver, kidney and brain. It can remain in the kidneys for 7 years and in bone for 32 years. During steady state, blood tests are considered the best indicator of relatively recent exposure. Urine tests are also employed, although urine lead concentrations tend to fluctuate more over time. Furthermore, hair may be tested to determine long term exposure. Chelating agents are used as a treatment to assist in the removal of lead from the body. In the event lead poisoning is suspected, it is recommended that a primary care or occupational physician be contacted.

Assistance can also be obtained through state health and environmental agencies or local poison control centers. The National Lead Information Center (NLIC) may be contacted for general information regarding household lead at (800) 424-LEAD (5323).

Precautions that reduce lead exposure while involved in shooting sports will result in significantly improved health

Exposure to lead can occur when shooting in indoor ranges. Airborne lead particles are inhaled into the lungs and absorbed into the blood.

and a more enjoyable sport. Foremost attention should be given to the presence of children. The same exposure to a child relative to an adult results in a much higher total body burden of lead due to the reduced size of the child. In 1991, as a result of a large volume of epidemiological data, the Centers for Disease Control revised the recommended concentration of lead it considers dangerous in children from 25 to 10 micrograms per deciliter of blood. A number of studies indicate that high blood-lead concentrations can hinder a child's bone growth and can induce neurological damage. Since most young children place objects in their mouths, most lead poisonings in children occur between 1 and 5 years of age. There also tends to be a higher incidence of child-related lead poisonings during the summer months. Children should be kept at a safe distance from any *enclosed* shooting to avoid breathing airborne lead contaminated dust or soil. Dual cartridge respirators or masks are also advisable. Furthermore, materials which may be laced with lead residue including cartridge cases, bullets, wads, primers, shot, cleaning patches, and cloths should be kept out of reach of children.

While cleaning any firearm, avoid contact with bore-fouling residue from oily cloths or patches, which increase the absorption of lead through the skin. Solvents such as Shooter's Choice Lead Remover or Gunslick Super Solvent effectively remove lead from gun bores. Gloves are recommended as a barrier to absorption during cleanup using this or other products. A detergent containing trisodium phosphate, available at most hardware stores, is effective at solubilizing the lead for proper removal from lead-contaminated areas. Measures should be taken to ensure that all areas, as well as tools and accessories of the loading bench, including presses, dies, scales, gauges, measurers, and funnels are properly cleaned of lead residues. During bullet casting, an adequate amount of ventilation is required. Outside is best since vaporized lead coming off a melting pot will condense on walls and rafters and can be inhaled directly or as dust in cleaning. Smoking and eating is dangerous when handling any

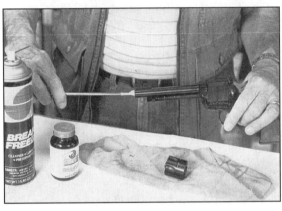

(Above and below) When cleaning firearms, avoid the fouling left on patches. The residue can be absorbed into the skin, so gloves are recommended. Also, be sure to thoroughly wash your hands and the work area when finished.

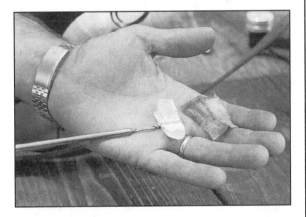

lead-based material because of accidental transfer from hands to mouth. After handling equipment and cleaning the area, hands should be washed.

With adequate precautions, the presence of lead while shooting, reloading or cleaning can be adequately controlled to minimize potential exposure, improving the quality of the sport and the health of each participant. Since toxicity is cumulative, periodic blood tests can provide added assurance for safety.

(Text continued from page 11)

Modern smokeless powder is far safer to handle than gasoline or other flammable solvents, acids or caustic substances such as lye-based drain cleaners. Powder can, however, be mishandled and this leads to trouble. Powder left in a measure or unmarked container can lead to guessing about what it is and a wrong guess can be disastrous. Powder should always be kept in the original container. If for some reason that container is unusable, the powder should be put into a suitable container like a can or plastic bottle, not a glass jar. It should then be *clearly* labeled with a label that will not come off, that covers up whatever the original label was, and will not fade or otherwise become unreadable. Powders should *never* be mixed. This can happen if some is left in a measure and a different powder is poured on top. Such contaminated powder is worthless and should be discarded. Likewise, powders that are in unlabeled containers, from unknown sources, are not worth keeping. Even though they might look like another, you can't really be sure so they should be considered as "unknown" and discarded. It's not worth risking your gun let alone your eyesight, hearing and, yes, your life to experiment for the sake of saving a few dollars of material.

Disposing of such powder is easy, but should be done sensibly. It can be burned outside, on open ground, *in small amounts* of no more than a couple of tablespoons at a time. Far easier is to scatter it on your lawn or flower bed because it adds nitrogen. It will break down in the weather rather quickly. Unexploded primers that have been damaged are best buried after soaking in a lye solution.

Failure to recognize what sort of powder you are dealing with can have disastrous consequences. Recently, a would-be blackpowder shooter bought a new-made blackpowder revolver. The dealer at the gun show didn't have any blackpowder for sale, advising the buyer to come by his shop the following week where he had plenty. The buyer really wanted to try out his new gun that weekend. A helpful neighbor allowed as how he had some old blackpowder shotgun shells. These could be broken down, he figured, the powder extracted and used.

They did that. There was powder in the shells, and it was black in color. Two heads may be better than one, so long as the cooperative effort is not simply a pooling of ignorance. When the gun fired the charge blew off the top strap, blew out the chamber being fired and the chambers on either side. Fortunately no one was seriously injured. A basic ignorance was the fault. With very few exceptions *all* gunpowder is colored black by a graphite coating, including the fast-burning smokeless shotgun powder that was contained in the neighbor's shells. Never guess about powder.

Related accidents with ignorance at their root have been caused by reloaders loading bullets into blank cartridges. Blanks are loaded with a *very* fast burning type of powder that will produce a loud report. If a bullet is loaded on top of such powder, rather than being accelerated down the barrel, the powder burn is so rapid that the bullet has no more than begun to move before the pressure has jumped to a catastrophically high level and the bullet acts like a plug. In essence, this is a bomb. I

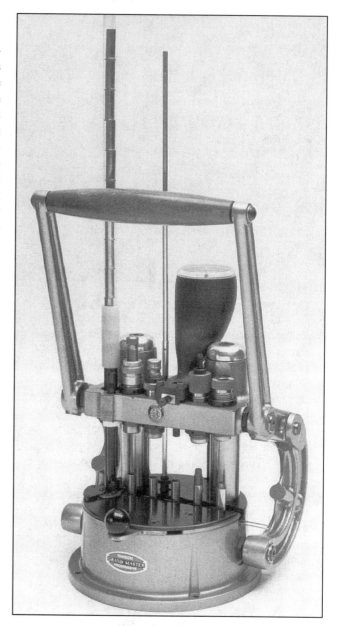

The tall thin tube in the center rear of this progressive reloading press is filled with a stack of primers. If the feeding mechanism jams, the stack can explode if you do not clear it properly. If a jam occurs, read the manual, and if in doubt, call the manufacturer for assistance.

have steel hooks instead of hands because I was holding a bomb when it exploded. No one wants to be near a bomb when it explodes.

Recognizing powder, obviously, is easiest when it is in clearly marked containers. There is, however, an additional point to be made here. Powders are identified by manufacturer, trade name and often numbers. There are powders on the market which are very similar, but *not* the same and can be confused if the reloader does not have a clear understanding of what he is dealing with. The IMR Powder Co. makes a powder called IMR 4831 (formerly made by DuPont). The Hodgdon Powder Co. produces a similar powder called 4831 and is labeled H4831. The IMR powder is much faster burning than Hodgdon's and loading data for H4831 would be very dangerous to use with the IMR propellant. To confuse things a little

Smokeless powder is far safer to store or handle than many common household products. It is highly flammable, but less so than gasoline, petroleum-based cleaning fluids and similar household items.

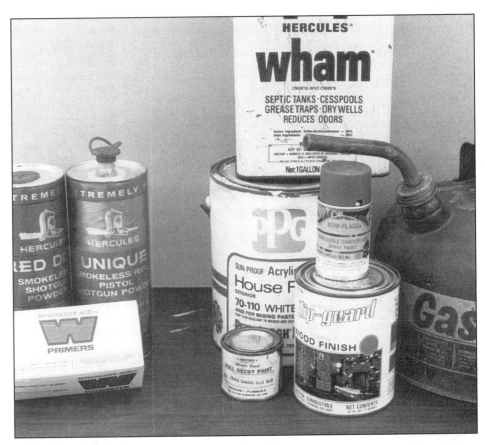

(Below) Powder should be stored in the original container. If for some reason this cannot be done, use a similar container and *mark it clearly* as to the contents.

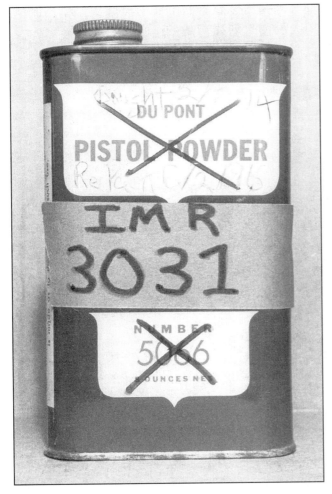

more, both companies market a powder with the designation 4895, IMR 4895 and H4895 respectively. These are very similar in terms of their burning characteristics and are virtually interchangeable.

Loading Data and Loading Manuals

The typical loading manual provides loading data for individual cartridges using a variety of powders and bullets that have been tested and found to be suitable for that particular cartridge. The powder types and charges listed for each cartridge are given as "starting loads" and "maximum loads." Often there will be an "accuracy load" listed that performed particularly well in the firearm that was used for the tests. This data is the result of rigorous testing over long periods of time. It involves the efforts of a number of engineers and technicians using the latest and most sophisticated test equipment available. This loading data brackets the lowest safe pressure and velocity loads up to the highest. Working within this range the reloader can work up a loading that performs best in his gun.

The semi-experienced reloader is occasionally tempted to go beyond the bounds of whatever loading guide he is using and try something else. This is fine if the "something else" is to avail himself of more loading books containing tried and proven data, and not simply guessing on the basis of, "What if I tried 52 grains of_____?" The dangers of exceeding the upper limits of various loadings should, by now, be clear to the reader. There is, though, an apparent danger from going in the opposite direction. A certain amount of press has been given to a phenomenon known as detonation. This involves excessively high pressures generated by *reduced* loads of slow-burning powders—charges

These are *not the same* powders, although the number is identical. Read the powder reference section for further information and *never* guess about the burning characteristics of a powder.

below those recommended by the reloading manuals. Never guess at the burning characteristics of a powder, nor exceed the recommended charges on either end of the loadings recommended in the manuals.

The weight, composition and fit of the bullet in the barrel are factors in the pressure equation. Heavier bullets boost pressures, as do those made of harder material. The size of the bullet also plays a role. The tighter the fit of the bullet in the barrel, the greater the force needed to drive it through.

When using modern components, loading problems are usually simple and straightforward, *if* the reloader keeps in mind

that the changing of any component can affect pressure. These include the type of case (military vs. commercial), the type of primer (pistol vs. rifle vs. the magnum version of either), the make of primer or case, and the lengthening and thickening of the case mouth in bottlenecked cartridges after repeated reloadings. A final consideration is the capacity of the case. The larger it is the lower the pressure, all other things being equal.

All these factors must be carefully weighed in the loading game, particularly when working toward maximum pressure/velocity loadings. At this point, particularly with guns of less than the best design and strongest materials, the gap between a safe

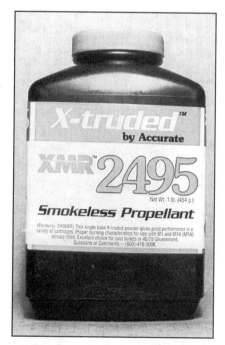

More or less identical, H-4895, IMR-4895 and Accurate's XMR2495 (formerly 2495BR) all have nearly identical burning characteristics. To know the players, you gotta have a program—read the loading manuals!

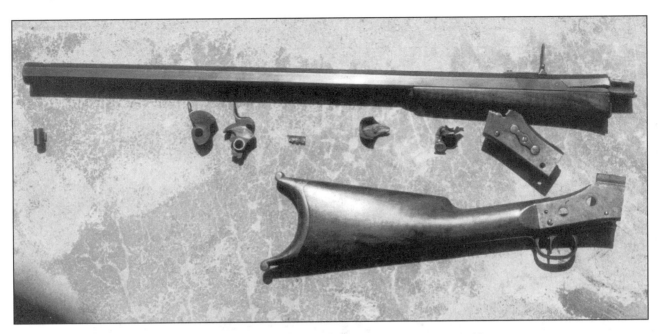

The sad end of a fine old rifle—accidentally overloaded with a double charge. (Photo courtesy of Tom Trevor)

maximum loading and a destroyed gun can be very close, and a slight variation in *one* of the above mentioned pressure factors can lead to a case rupture and disaster. The danger is greatest in what might best be termed the area of "advanced reloading." This takes in the obsolete, the foreign and the wildcat or experimental cartridge. In loading these cartridges, the reloader often finds himself in *terra incognita,* faced with guns whose internal dimensions may vary considerably from book descriptions, and with cartridges that are old or of otherwise doubtful quality. Often a gun may not be clearly marked as to the exact caliber. Rifles chambered for the German 8.15x46R cartridge were a popular "bring-back" following WWII. This cartridge came in *many* case shapes, and the rifles had bore diameters ranging from .313- to 326-inch, with .318 and .323 being the most common. Guns do turn up that have been rechambered for some cartridge other than the one listed in the books or on the barrel. When in doubt, make a chamber cast. The most common problem is that there is often little or no data on loading these cartridges. In such instances even the experienced expert must proceed with extreme caution.

On the subject of published loading data there are a couple of final caveats. Old manuals dating from the early 1950s or before were developed without the benefits of today's modern test equipment. Often the weaknesses of particular guns were not known at the time or if they were, those guns were not being used to an extent great enough to justify their inclusion in the creation of the loading data. Circumstances alter cases and those weak guns may now be in a larger supply, meeting a larger demand. I have seen loading data in manuals dating from the early 1950s that if used with old, low-strength rifles from the 1870s and '80s would very likely take those old rifles apart in one shot. There is now a lot of interest in shooting old cartridge rifles, and the new manuals reflect this interest with data developed especially for them.

There is also the matter of data published in magazines. This is often the work of an individual who has cooked up some handloads that he thinks are pretty good. This is sometimes an amateur working without the benefits of pressure testing equipment. Magazines publish disclaimers to the effect that any loading data published therein is used at the shooters' own risk. It is indeed.

Firearms/ammunition expert and author Philip Sharpe received many letters during his career as a technical editor and advisor for the *American Rifleman* magazine. By his assessment, one of the most dangerous types of reloaders was the "instant expert." This is the person who has read one or perhaps two books on reloading. He has been doing it for a few years and has grown a towering intellect (make that ego) in the process. He has become imbued with an innate savvy of all things firearms related and wants not only to chart new courses in the reloading business, but to share his "discoveries." This is the person who, without the aid of pressure-testing equipment or any form of metallurgical analyses, has decided to start experimenting with improved-performance loads, meaning higher velocities, heavier bullets, more pressure. How does he know his gun can take these higher pressures? Because it's a Remington, Winchester, Mauser, whatever. More correctly he has a kind of simple faith that his guns possess hidden powers because those companies make their guns tough enough that they can't be destroyed. This is nonsense.

There has yet to be a small arm built that can't be wrecked. Firearm and reloading equipment manufacturers are constantly improving their products to make them safer and easier to use. This is good, but I will close this chapter with the recollection of the words of a talented and inventive engineer who made hand-crafted, custom-designed motion picture cameras. When I talked with him, nearly 30 years ago, he was in the process of repairing one of his creations after it had suffered abuse at the hands of a supposedly trained cameraman. "You know," he said, "you can develop and improve a product to the point where it is pretty much foolproof. But you can't make it *damned fool* proof."

When reloading,
only one compo-
nent in the load
chain is reused
over and over. It
all begins with...

The Cartridge Case

THE ORIGINAL PURPOSE of a cartridge was to facilitate quick reloading and serve as a means to keep those loads consistent. The first cartridges contained charges of powder wrapped separately in paper to speed loading and eliminate the powder horn. These appeared in the late 1550s. It became apparent fairly early in the shooting game that breech-loading firearms were a lot more convenient than muzzleloaders. Soldiers especially liked the idea of not having to stand up to load while being shot at, since this interfered with their concentration. Sometimes they would forget where they were in the process, and would load a second powder charge and bullet on top of the first. At least one such soldier tamped more than a dozen loads into his rifle at the Battle of Gettysburg before tossing it away to look for something better to do than try to extract them. Several thousand rifles with multiple unfired loads were picked up after that battle.

Early self-contained cartridge cases were made of paper, cardboard, linen, rubber, collodion, even sausage skin. All

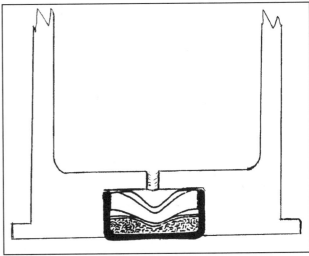

Boxer (above) and Berdan (below) systems are the ones used today.

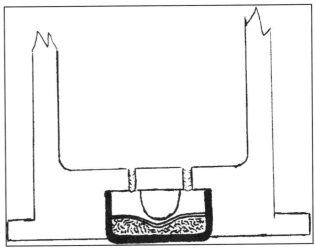

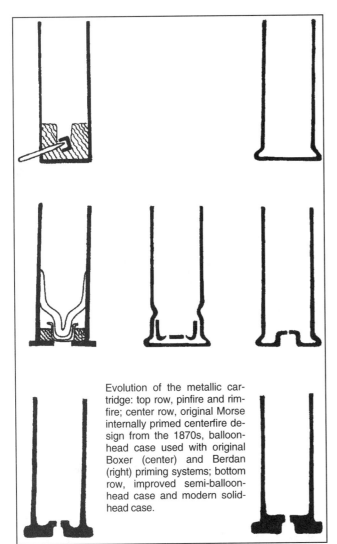

Evolution of the metallic cartridge: top row, pinfire and rimfire; center row, original Morse internally primed centerfire design from the 1870s, balloonhead case used with original Boxer (center) and Berdan (right) priming systems; bottom row, improved semi-balloonhead case and modern solidhead case.

were fired by a separate percussion cap. While they were more or less easy to load, those that went into breech-loading guns still had not solved the breechloader's basic problem of gas leaks. Many attempts were made to deal with the early breechloader's nasty habit of spewing fire and smoke out of the joint between breechblock and barrel into the face of the shooter. The actions also tended to stick and eventually jam when they became encrusted with blackpowder fouling. It was these problems that the metallic cartridge really solved, by closing the breech with a gas-tight seal and containing much of the fouling that wasn't in the barrel. At this point the cartridge became not merely a convenient package-form of ammunition, but an integral part of the firearm. By containing all the gas generated in the firing cycle it made the firearm more efficient. It also made possible the use of heavier charges generating higher pressures than could be used in a non-sealed gun. Finally, it served as a safety device by preventing gases from entering the action and destroying it.

The first commercially successful, completely self-contained metallic cartridge was invented in 1836 by Casimir Lefaucheux in France. The original style had a metal head and cardboard body, much like a shotshell. The primer was fired by a metal pin protruding above the head. The pinfire cartridge, however,

had problems: It was not waterproof, and there was some gas leakage where the pin entered the case; the cartridge had to be properly oriented or "indexed" to enter the breech; if dropped it could accidentally discharge; and it was fairly expensive to produce, though it could be reloaded.

The second advance in cartridge design was the rimfire, developed in 1857 by Horace Smith and Daniel Wesson. It was based on the tiny "cap" cartridges patented around 1845, in France, by Flobert. It consisted of a copper tube closed at one end. The closed end was flattened just enough to create a hollow rim which contained the priming material. The tube was filled with blackpowder and the open end or mouth was crimped to hold a bullet. The cartridge discharged when the rim was crushed at any point on its circumference by a firing pin. No indexing was necessary. The rim also stopped the cartridge from sliding into the barrel. The rimfire was cheaper to manufacture than the pinfire, was less susceptible to accidental discharge and could be made weather and water tight. The first rimfire was the Smith & Wesson Number 1 pistol cartridge, now known as the 22 Short. Rimfire cartridge cases could not be reloaded. During and shortly after the American Civil War, rimfires were made in sizes up to 58-caliber.

Good small designs, when made large, often don't work.

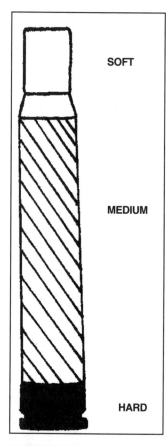

SOFT

MEDIUM

HARD

(Left) The modern brass cartridge is made hard and thick where the greatest amount of support is needed, springy in the body for easy extraction, and soft at the mouth to ensure a good gas-tight seal when fired.

(Right) The parts of the cartridge case.

(Below) The loaded cartridge fits closely, but not *tightly,* in the chamber. The case swells on firing to make a gas-tight seal in the chamber. After firing, the pressure returns to normal and the case springs back to close to its unfired size for easy extraction.

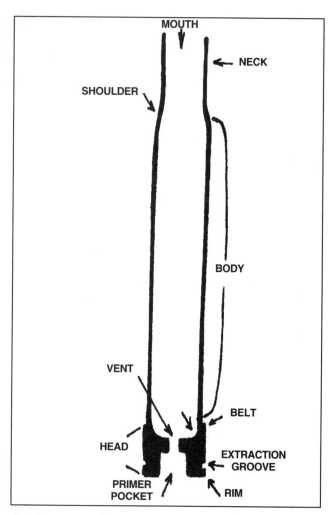

MOUTH

NECK

SHOULDER

BODY

VENT

BELT

HEAD

EXTRACTION GROOVE

PRIMER POCKET

RIM

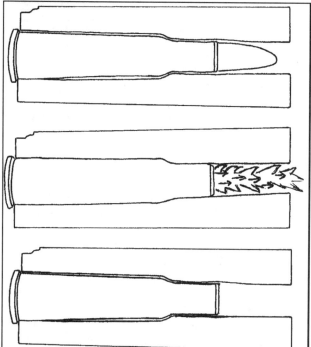

This was the case with the rimfire. The larger sizes had the habit of swelling in the head area when fired if this head was not fully supported by the breech of the gun. Bulged heads jammed revolver cylinders preventing rotation. Solving this problem by making the cartridge head thicker or harder required a very heavy hammer spring to fire it, which made the gun difficult to cock and resulted in an unacceptably heavy trigger pull. In addi-

tion, the amount of powerful priming material in the rims of the bigger cartridges would occasionally blow them off, leaving the tubular body of the case stuck in the chamber.

During and after the American Civil War, dozens if not hundreds of patents were submitted for all sorts of cartridges. One design had the firing pin inside; another was a spinoff of the rimfire, with the entire inside of the base coated with priming compound and held in place by a perforated washer. There were others with heads shaped like champagne bottle bottoms in attempts to overcome the shortcomings of the pin and rimfire designs. The basis of the solution came from George W. Morse who designed a cartridge in 1858 having a solid base with a small, separate primer in the center of the head. The primer fired when crushed against a wire anvil soldered inside the case. Mass production was impractical then, but Morse had overcome the above problems by creating a cartridge that was strong in the head where strength was needed, did not require a heavy firing pin blow to discharge it, did not need to be indexed, was not susceptible to accidental discharge and could be made durable and waterproof.

In the 1870s the first really powerful cartridges were produced, based on the Morse design, with center priming and a reinforced head. The problem to be solved at this point was to come up with a design that was rugged, dependable, and one that lent itself to ease of manufacture. Various folded and composite head systems were tried with limited success. The heart of the problem was to create a reliable, simple-to-manufacture primer. The problem was solved twice—by Hiram Berdan in America, in 1866, and by Edward M. Boxer in England a year later. Berdan reduced the Morse wire to a tiny knob in the primer pocket with the priming material in a simple inverted cup above it. The ignition flame entered the cartridge case through two or three vent holes. Boxer crimped a tiny anvil in the primer cup itself with a space on either side to permit the flame to reach the powder charge through a single vent hole in the cartridge case. These are the two systems in use today. Oddly, the Boxer system became the American standard while the Berdan system found favor in Europe. The Boxer priming system with a single vent hole lends itself to easy removal by a simple punch pin, while the Berdan primer must be levered out with a chisel-type extraction tool.

Why Brass?

Early cartridges were made of copper because it was a soft, easily worked metal that could be formed into complex shapes in punch dies without becoming too brittle and splitting or cracking in the process. It had a high degree of *plasticity*. Among the copper cartridge's merits were that it resisted the corrosion of blackpowder and early corrosive primers; it was strong enough not to crack under the pressure of firing if well supported; and it formed a good gas-tight seal in a gun chamber. Copper's major failing, however, was low *elasticity*. When fired with a heavy charge the copper case had a tendency to stick in the chamber of a gun, particularly if that chamber had become hot and dirty with powder fouling.

Brass, an alloy of copper and zinc, possesses strengths and qualities neither element has separately. Most notable are hardness and elasticity. Modern cartridge brass (70 percent copper, 30 percent zinc) is the ideal metal for cartridges, being capable of being hardened and softened by the application of pressure and heat respectively. Thus, the head can be hardened, the body made semi-elastic and the mouth left relatively soft for a good gas seal. Such a cartridge case swells on firing to make a good gas seal in the chamber. After firing, the case springs back close to its original size, allowing easy extraction from the chamber. By the simple expedient of squeezing a fired cartridge case to its original size in a die and replacing the fired primer with a new one, it can be reused. A brass case may be used dozens of times with conservative loads. It is the most expensive component in the cartridge.

Because brass is relatively expensive, compared to other

All of these rounds are non-reloadable for a variety of reasons. Left to right: The 12mm pinfire could theoretically be reloaded, but no components are available; tiny 230 Morris used a smaller than standard primer (not available), but new cases can be formed from cut-down 22 Hornets; aluminum and steel cases are for one-time use. "Posts" in the aluminum CCI Berdan primer pockets are battered in the first firing. The steel 7.62x39mm and 7.62x54mm Russian military cases are Berdan-primed and difficult to decap, but it can be done. The two darker cases are lacquer coated to make them function through autoloaders. This coating will likely come off in your reloading dies. In short, it's not worth the effort with Boxer brass cases becoming commonly available.

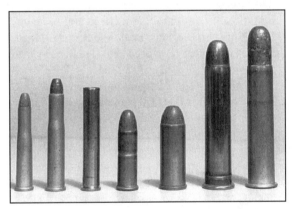

Old copper and soft brass cases from the last century and the early part of this one are a bad bet for reloading. They are often corroded by the blackpowder they contained, by deterioration through exposure to pollutants, or are simply made of poor metal and are too weak for modern smokeless pressures. Examples include, left to right: 22 WCF, 25-20 SS (with a newly made 25-20 case), 38 Long, 45 S&W, and two 45-70s.

All rimfires are essentially non-reloadable. They range from the miniscule 22 BB Cap (far left) to the 52-caliber Spencer round used in the Civil War.

alloys, engineers have been at work to find cheaper materials that will do as well. Steel and aluminum alloy cases have been experimented with since the World War I period. In the last 20 years, advances in metallurgy and coatings have resulted in acceptable quality (for one-time use) steel and aluminum cases. Neither, however, are very suitable for reloading.

In spite of advanced heat-treating techniques, steel cases cannot be made as selectively elastic as those of brass. Steel cases tend to be rather hard and brittle. After a few resizings, the necks split, rendering them useless. To make steel cartridges feed through various autoloading rifle and pistol actions, they are often coated with a varnish-type lubricant to keep them from sticking in the chamber when fired. When resizing these cases, this coating will tend to slough off in the resizing die and thus lose its effectiveness. Steel cases are most often encountered in military ammunition. The most common is the 7.62x39mm cartridge for the SKS and AK-47 rifles. These cartridges, in addition to being made of steel, are Berdan-primed and are thus more difficult to reload. Occasionally some steel-cased ammunition from WWII will turn up in 45 ACP and 30 M-1 Carbine. It is Boxer primed and can be reloaded, but with good quality American brass cartridges in the above calibers now in plentiful supply, attempting to reload this stuff isn't worth the effort. Be careful of shooting this ammunition, because some steel-case cartridges loaded with steel-jacketed bullets have been known to rust together, jumping pressures considerably when fired.

Aluminum cases in handgun calibers are manufactured by CCI as their Blazer line. These use a special Berdan primer, unavailable to reloaders, and are specifically marked NR for non-reloadable. Aluminum suffers some of the same problems as copper with its lack of spring-back, though it can be alloyed and heat-treated to make good cases for low-powered cartridges. Aluminum does not hold up well under resizing and crimping, and the cases frequently split on the first attempt to reload them. It's not worth the effort when good brass cases are available.

The shortcomings of various early types of cases have already been mentioned, but a few points should be added. Pinfire guns and ammunition are totally obsolete; neither were made in this country and there is no reloading equipment or data available for these. Rimfire cases are primed with a wet mixture spun into the hollow rim. Owners of obsolete rimfire guns have a few of options: 1) Search for ammunition through such dealers as The Old Western Scrounger, or large local dealers who may have some in stock; 2) Polish them up and hang them on the wall.

Early centerfire cartridges are usually far too valuable as collectibles to shoot. Old cases, however, are still around and often are the only source of ammunition for some obsolete and foreign guns. Some of these cases are available from specialty suppliers and manufacturers. If vintage cases have been fired with blackpowder they are nearly always badly corroded and not safe. Copper and soft brass cases of the old balloon and semi-balloon-head construction, from the last century, are too weak for use with modern smokeless loadings. Centerfire cases from

The REM-UMC case on the left suffered near total separation due to mercury contamination. This same factor caused the one on the right to pull apart in the resizing die.

Blanks are made of substandard brass and often contain flaws, like the 223 case with the star crimp. This crimp, as with the flutes on the sides of the 30-06 dummy round, weakens the metal. These cases would likely split in the reloading die or in the next firing. In short, don't try to use brass from blanks, grenade launching or dummy rounds.

the 1920s through the 1940s which have been contaminated by mercuric primers are very dangerous and should not be reloaded. This problem will be addressed in the chapter on primers.

Finally, a final word about blank cases. Even with the powder removed, these are not fit for reloading. Blanks are made from substandard cases not capable of meeting pressure and dimension standards for full-power ammunition. Attempting to remove the crimp in such a case usually splits the mouth and it's finished. The same is true for dummy cases which

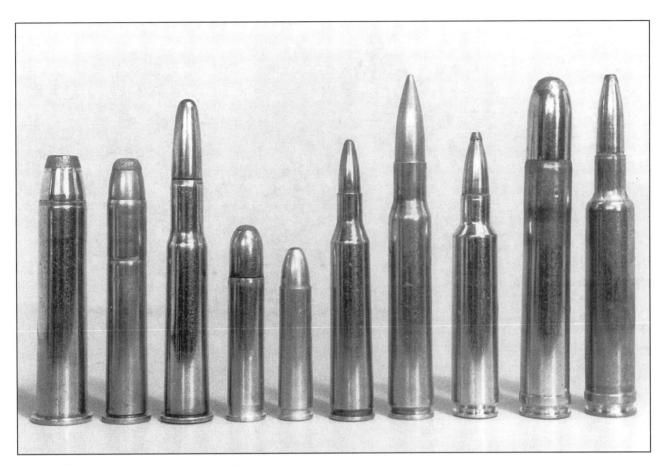

(Above) Basic cartridge case forms include the following variations, left to right: straight-walled rimmed (45-70), straight-tapered (38-55), rimmed bottleneck (30-40 Krag), semi-rimmed straight (351 Winchester SL), rimless straight (30 Carbine), semi-rimmed bottleneck (220 Swift), rimless bottleneck (30-06), rebated head (284 Winchester), straight belted (458 Winchester Magnum) and bottleneck belted (7mm Weatherby Magnum).

Basic cartridge forms for handguns, left to right: straight rimmed (357 Magnum), straight semi-rimmed (38 ACP), straight rimless (45 ACP), semi-rimmed tapered (9mm Luger), rimless bottleneck (30 Mauser), and rebated head (41 Action Express).

contain a bullet and no powder or primer and have flutes in the case body.

The Modern Brass Case

As firearms technology has advanced, guns have become more powerful and sophisticated. Cartridge case design has had to keep pace with this evolution. In reality, cartridges are often designed first and then guns are designed or adapted to fit them.

The basic design of the contemporary centerfire cartridge case can be one of a number of variations. The case can be: 1) straight-walled rimmed. These date from the 19th century, and include the 32 and 38 S&W revolver cartridges, the 45 Colt and the 45-70 rifle. They also include modern cartridges such as the 38 Special, 357 and 44 Magnums; 2) straight-tapered. An effort to improve extraction led to this design. It is now nearly obsolete, the 38-55 being the only current survivor; 3) rimmed bottleneck. These include late 19th century smokeless powder cartridges such as the 30-30 and 30-40, 303 British, and 22 Hornet; 4) semi-rimmed straight. These include currently-made 32 Auto and 38 Super Automatic cartridges. The

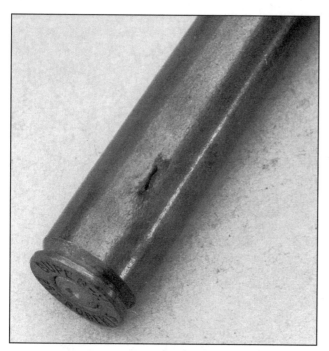

Case failures are not common, but they do happen. The nearer to the case head the rupture, the more serious it is.

This 45 ACP has been so badly battered that it will probably not go into the resizing die. The split in the body of the 22 Hornet probably resulted from too many reloadings. The tiny split on the mouth of the 44 Winchester (center) could be easily overlooked. All are rejects.

semi-rimmed design was to facilitate feeding through box magazines, with a slight rim to keep the cartridge from entering the chamber; 5) semi-rimless bottleneck. Now rare, the 220 Swift is an example; 6) rimless straight. A common example is the 45 ACP; 7) rimless tapered. These are the 9mm Luger and 30 M-1 Carbine; 8) rimless bottleneck. This is an improved smokeless design from the 1890s. Most modern rifle cartridges use this design; 9) rimless belted. This design is used only on high-pressure magnum rifle cartridges such as the 458 Winchester Magnum; 10) rebated head. This one has a rimless head smaller then the body permitting a slightly increased case capacity. Examples are the 284 Winchester and 41 and 50 Action Express.

Case Selection

When buying cartridge cases for reloading, the first thing you want to be sure of is that you have the right one for your gun. Most civilian guns have the caliber marked on the barrel. Military arms, however, are not so marked, at least not very often. When in doubt, have the gun checked out by a good gunsmith. If there is no question about caliber, you want new or once-fired cases from a reputable source, marked with the headstamp of a known manufacturer and not from the "Royal Elbonian Arsenal." Military cases, referred to collectively as "brass," are often sold at bargain prices. Sometimes they are a bargain if they have been fired only once and are not battered up by being run through a machinegun. The best military ammunition bargains are loaded rounds bought in bulk. That way you shoot it first. Military cases do, however, have a few drawbacks. Assuming they are not Berdan primed, they may have been fired with corrosive primers. A wash in hot water and detergent will remove corrosive primer salts after firing.

The main problem with military cases is the crimp holding in the primer. Removing this crimp means a heavy-duty decapping pin and either chamfering the primer pocket or removing the crimp with a primer pocket swage die, as explained in the Chapter 10, "Rifle Cartridge Reloading".

With the exception of new unfired cases in the box, all brass should be given an initial inspection. Bulk, once-fired, military and commercial cases may have loose debris, including primers (live and dead), rattling around inside them which should be removed. Cases should be sorted by manufacturer and kept in separate containers. Although the dimensions for all cases are basically the same, internal dimensions (caused by varying wall and head thickness) and the size of the vent in the primer pocket will vary. Mixed cases will yield different pressures and velocities, giving less accurate shooting. Varying pressures can be dangerous if the load you are using is a maximum one. If, for instance, this load is worked up using one type of case with a fairly thin wall and thus a comparatively large internal capacity, in combination with a small vent, the internal pressure will be significantly lower than one with a thicker wall, smaller capacity and larger vent, which will be *significantly higher*.

Beyond separation by manufacturer, cases should be checked for splits in the neck, corrosion and any anomalies indicating pressure or headspace problems (meaning case stretching) or serious battering in the firing process that would render them unreloadable. Oil, grease, grit and dirt should be removed before reloading.

Reading Headstamps

The headstamp markings of cartridge cases contain valuable information that will prove useful when buying ammunition and empty cases. Commercial makers mark their cases with their name or trademark, the caliber and name of the cartridge, e.g., WW 45-70 Govt. This tells you it was made by Winchester/Western and it is the 45-70 Government cartridge (originally made for the 45-caliber Springfield army rifle).

Markings on cases made for the military contain similar information, and sometimes a two-digit date of manufacture. LC is the Lake City Ordnance Plant; WRA is Winchester Repeating Arms Co.; RA is Remington Arms Co. A stamp of RA 79 indicates the cartridge was made by Remington in 1979. American military cases are not marked by caliber. Early cases made at the Frankford Arsenal in Philadelphia were marked, for instance, F or FA 3 05. This indicates the source and the month of manufacture (March) and the year 1905. This is not ammunition you would want to shoot, especially if it shows any sign of corrosion. American-made military ammunition used corrosive priming into the early 1950s. Different arsenals switched to non-corrosive priming at different times with all being changed over by 1954. Non-corrosive priming will require less cleaning of your gun.

Case Cleaning

Most shooters like to keep their cases shiny and bright. They look better and are easier to find on the ground. Shined cases are less likely to collect dirt and grit and can be easily checked for damage caused by corrosion. Dirty cases can hide flaws that may run deep.

There are two basic methods of case cleaning. The first is a wet process that uses a concentrated, acid-based cleaner that is mixed with water. This must be done in a glass, plastic or stainless steel pan. Warming the pan with the cases in the mixture speeds the process. The cleaned cases must be rinsed to remove all residue and then oven-dried on "warm." Too much heat can ruin the heat-treatment of the cases. Cases should be decapped before wet cleaning.

Dry cleaning is by tumbling the cases in an abrasive cleaning media that's usually made of ground corn cobs or ground walnut shells. This requires a motor-driven tumbler or vibratory tool into which the cases and media are put for cleaning. Once cleaned, cases must be wiped free of dust and any media trapped inside must be removed.

Cartridge Case and Ammunition Storage

"Store in a cool dry place" is good advice for keeping just about anything, but this isn't always possible. Depending on one's paranoia and/or notion of thrift, the decision may be made to buy a large quantity of cases. Sometimes quantity simply accumulates in the form of various loadings, always expanding with the addition of new guns to a shooting battery. Ultimately

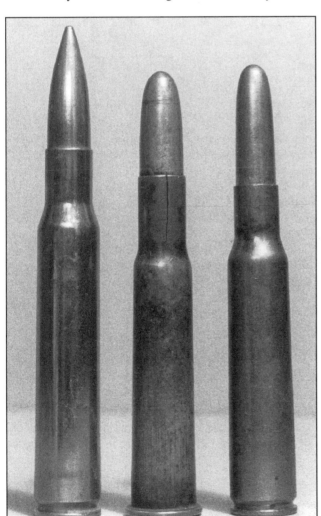

(Above) Manufacturing defects, in this instance what appears to be poor brass, resulted in split necks in these 223 military cartridges.

Season cracking (deterioration through exposure to pollutants in the air) caused this 1904-made 30-40 Krag case (center) to split at the neck. The 7mm Mauser round (right) has hairline cracks in the deep tarnish at the shoulder. The 30-06 (left), made at the Frankford Arsenal in 1905, benefited from the advantages of good storage and is in near-perfect condition.

What headstamps tell you. Commercial ammunition is marked with the caliber and name of the manufacturer, at least in this country. Military ammunition is usually stamped with the code of the arsenal or manufacturer and the date of manufacture. Top row, left to right: a 45-70 current headstamp, pre-WWII commercial Winchester and Remington headstamps (good candidates for being mercuric primed), and an inside-primed military centerfire from the 1880s. R indicates a rifle load, F is the code of Frankford Arsenal, 2 82 indicates it was loaded in February, 1882. Bottom row: a 30-40 Frankford Arsenal round loaded February, 1904, and a Spencer 52-caliber rimfire made by the Sage Ammunition Works.

the questions arise about how long this stuff will last (both cases and finished ammunition) and how do I take care of it?

The shelf life of modern ammunition (both commercial and good handloads) is virtually indefinite *if* kept under ideal conditions—sealed, cool and dry. Most of us don't have this kind of storage. Experts have preached since time immemorial about the avoidance of heat and dampness when storing. Actually, heat and moisture by themselves don't do all that much damage to quality ammunition. Heat does drive off volatiles in lubricants and propellant powders, and to a degree accelerates powder decomposition. Heat and dampness together are most injurious because water absorbs pollutants and heat accelerates chemical reactions between these pollutants and ammunition. The triple threat in airborne pollution consists of acids, ammonia, and sulfur compounds. All occur naturally in the atmosphere in addition to being man-made pollutants. They are also found in a variety of household products.

I have often heard it said that certain metals crystallize and become brittle with age. I put this question to Professor Bryan Wilde, a metallurgist and director of the Fontana Corrosion Center at The Ohio State University. He assured me this was not the case. Cartridge brass *has* a crystalline structure. When exposed to pollutants in the atmosphere, notably ammonia, a breakdown of the alloy begins as the ammonia dissolves the copper. Acids in the atmosphere dissolve the zinc in a process

known as "dezincification." In areas where the metal is stressed, like case necks, shoulders and crimps, the crystal edges are farther apart, thus speeding the breakdown in a process known as season cracking. Season cracking begins as tarnish, gradually turning into deep corrosion which often follows the edges of the crystals, giving the surface a frosted appearance, leading to the impression the metal is changing its structure. This phenomenon was first noted in 19th century ammunition used by the British in India, where it was exposed to the ammonia-rich fumes of cow dung and urine in a hot, humid climate.

Salts, though direct contamination, are another hazard. They occur in perspiration and are a problem mainly because they are hygroscopic—they draw and hold water which combines with the salt to corrode the metal. Sulfur, notably sulfur dioxide (SO_2), causes a tarnish when it combines with lead and copper to form sulfides. When SO_2 combines with water (H_2O) the result is sulfuric acid (H_2SO_4). Lead and lead alloy bullets are subject to damage mainly from acids. These attack lead, causing a hard white oxide crust to form, which, in rimfire ammunition, may make it impossible to chamber. Generally, the powder coating on bullets is not a problem, but it does indicate old or improperly stored ammunition/bullets. Unless the coating is excessive, such ammunition should be safe to shoot.

Pinpointing the *exact* reason why a particular batch of ammunition went bad is a mystery to be solved by an expert metallurgist-detective through chemical analysis and examination of cartridge surfaces with a scanning electron microscope.

Manufacturers continue to come up with better priming, powder, lubricants, case materials, sealants, and packaging. What you buy represents the maker's state of the art combined with his sense of economy at the time the product was made.

Plating cases with nickel and plating or jacketing bullets with copper inhibits corrosion by acid. Non-hygroscopic bullet lubricants keep moisture away from bullets and out of case interiors. Paper boxes absorb moisture but are generally not a problem if kept dry. This boils down to the fact that if the cases/ammunition are in good shape when put away, and if kept dry and cool, they will last for years, probably decades.

A second problem that still crops up is brittle brass. After cartridge brass is formed it gets a final heat treatment called stress relief. This process involves less heat than annealing and is done to bring the brass to the optimum degree of springiness. Occasionally, a batch will get through that is improperly treated. It will perform fine when new, but after a number of years the brass will have returned to its original brittle state. This is exacerbated by the process of firing and resizing. Cases will split and sometimes burst. Any corrosion taking place will hasten this process. One advantage of the old copper cases was that they were less subject to corrosion and stress changes since they were softer to begin with.

Beyond cool and dry there isn't much to be added regarding

Liquid case cleaners contain a mild acid and require no more equipment than a stainless steel, plastic or glass bowl to soak them in. Cases should be decapped before cleaning and either air-dried or oven-dried at no more than 150° Fahrenheit.

Vibrator/tumbler case cleaners use ground corn cobs or ground walnut shells to clean cases through abrasive action. This is probably the best system for cleaning large batches of cases.

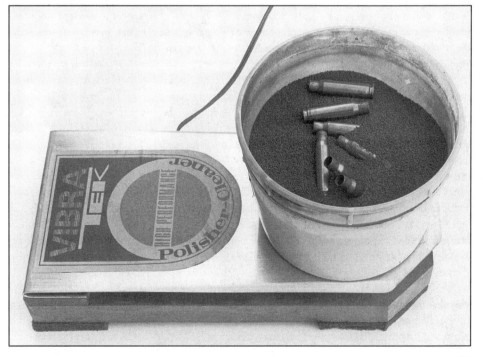

Plastic boxes are good for case storage and do a good job of keeping moisture and pollutants out if they're closed on a dry day and kept closed. The cases should always be identified by maker, caliber and number of times reloaded.

shelf storage. For the longest run the best means is a military ammunition can with a rubber gasket, along with a fresh packet of desiccant. The can should be closed on a dry day and opened as infrequently as possible. If ammunition is stored in a can or tightly sealed cardboard container, don't break the seals (letting in pollutants) to have a look. Second floor rooms are perhaps the best for shelf-stored ammunition, avoiding attic heat and basement moisture. Cartridges should be stored away from cleaning products containing ammonia, bleaches, or acids. If it must be stored in a basement, run a dehumidifier and keep it off the floor. It is a good idea to make periodic checks of shelf-stored ammunition in non-sealed boxes—twice a year is fine—to inspect for case tarnish or a haze of white oxide forming on lead bullets.

To the above might be added a list of dumb things not to do. Slathering a gun with Hoppe's No. 9 may do well to keep it from rusting, but if this is the one kept for home defense the ammonia in the Hoppe's will spread onto the cartridges in the gun and eat right into them. The same is true for any ammonia-bearing solvent cleaner. A rust inhibitor such as WD-40 spray may work preservative magic, but WD-40 is designed to *penetrate* and will do so in the seams between primers and cases, eventually working into the priming compound and neutralizing it. Leaving cartridges in leather belt loops may look nifty, but if the leather has tanning salts or acids in it these will eat into the metal, etching a ring which adds nothing to the looks or strength of the case.

It should not be forgotten that cartridges are interesting and people can't seem to keep their sweaty hands off them. Ask any collector how often he wipes down his collection after showing it to friends. To prevent damage, two suggestions

passed to me by collectors are to treat specimens with a light coat of rust-inhibiting grease or liquid car wax like Rain-Dance. These are the best defense against repeated attacks of finger-borne corrosion. Like the guy at the gas station used to say, "Rust never sleeps."

Case Failures

In the 19th and early 20th century, case failures were an expected hazard. Today, however, the "headless" or "broken" shell extractor, once found in every shooting kit, has gone the way of the stereoscope and flatiron. Yet failures still happen; they have to me and they will to you if you do enough shooting.

The quality of today's metallic cartridge ammunition is superb. Nearly two generations of shooters have grown up since the last corrosive, mercuric-primed, centerfires vanished into the mists of erosive smokeless powder, and not a moment too soon. Case failures these days with new factory centerfire ammunition are virtually nonexistent.

It is in the business of reloading ammunition that most problems occur. Here, the reloader (you) becomes the manufacturer and must become your own quality control expert. In this role you must learn to recognize all the signs that may lead to an accident, and become an expert at "reading" cartridge cases. This is by no means as easy as it might appear, since similar failures may come from a variety of causes. Flattened, cratered and punctured primers, and gas leaks around primers, are generally signs of excessive pressure. Soft primers, stretched primer pockets caused by multiple reloading or a poor fit of the primer, however, can produce signs similar to high pressures. Swelling of the case head, often

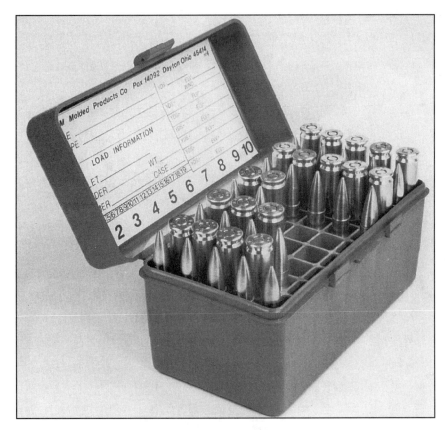

Plastic boxes are best for ammunition storage and usually come with data cards.

accompanied by the brass flowing back into the extractor port are signs of high pressures, but can also be caused by soft, poorly-annealed brass. Splits in cases around the head can indicate excessive headspace, which is a gun problem. Similar splits can also indicate inferior brass that contains oxides and impurities, and is sometimes recognizable by its scaly appearance. Internal corrosion from blackpowder loads or corrosively primed smokeless loads can also produce such splits. Improperly annealed brass, in this instance too hard and brittle, or brass made brittle by mercuric primers, or stressed by excessive resizing, will also show problems. That's a lot to consider in one bite, so let's move a bit slower here.

The old saying that lightning doesn't strike twice in the same place is just as false in cartridge case failures as it is in meteorology. The low overall incidence of case failures might lead to the belief that the one that failed was simply one bad case. Sometimes it is. In my experience, if the problem rests with a defective component, given the consistency in today's ammunition, that problem may run through a case-sized quantity, possibly an entire production lot, or at least until someone in quality control realizes there is a problem and does something about it.

Split Necks

By the same token, if one case from a particular box or purchase-lot that you have been reloading develops a split in the neck, it has become brittle from resizing and the rest of the lot can sometimes be given a longer life by annealing with a propane torch. This is not recommended since this practice will do nothing to correct other problems of wear and tear brought on by long use. About the only instance where annealing makes

economic sense is with very expensive cases of the custom-made variety. A split neck is a common failure and not dangerous to gun or shooter. Discard cases so afflicted. They are not fit to reload.

Body Splits

These are far more dangerous, with the degree of danger increasing in relation to the closeness of these splits to the head of the case. The worst instance is a separation at the case head. This allows high-pressure gas to come rushing back into the action of the gun and into your face, often damaging both. Since eyeballs and ear drums are less robust than a rifle receiver, it is a good idea to wear eye and ear protection when shooting.

Longitudinal Splits

These can be a gun-related problem, namely an oversize chamber. If this is the cause, you will notice swelling of the cases and difficult extraction with normal commercial loads long before you get an actual split. If your gun is bulging cases, *stop shooting!* Have the gun thoroughly checked out by a very competent gunsmith. Rebarreling may be the only solution. If a case suddenly splits with a load you have been using successfully with other brands of cartridge cases, this is likely an instance of poor-quality, brittle brass. If there is visible corrosion inside and/or outside, corrosion may have helped weaken the case. Throw these away.

Circumferential Splits

These may be caused by poor quality, brittle brass, or brass made brittle by mercury contamination. Again, *stop shooting!*

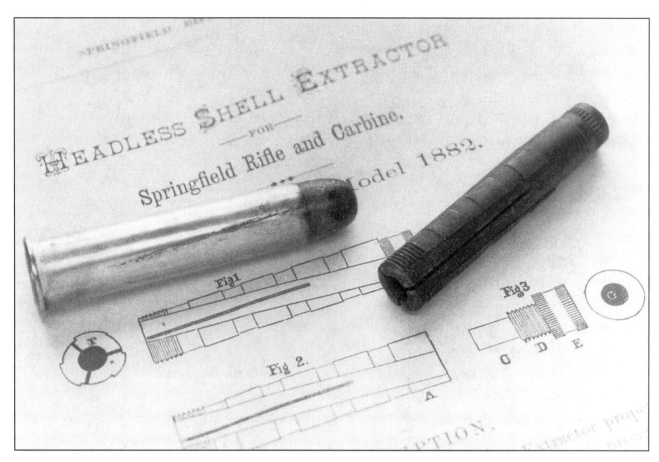

In the last century, the headless shell extractor was a necessary part of the shooter's kit, given the poor quality of the cartridge cases.

If this has not happened before with other makes of case and suddenly happens on a different make or lot, it is likely caused by the above. This situation can also result from excessive headspace which is, in effect, a chamber that is too long. Chambers don't suddenly grow longer. If this is a headspace problem there will be warnings before such a separation occurs, namely stretch marks on the case as it gradually pulls apart over the course of several firings. These will often appear as bright rings and will be found on all the cases you fire in that particular gun. They will be most apparent on higher pressure loads.

Head Separations

These can be more or less disastrous depending on how well your gun is engineered for safety, namely in terms of gas-escape ports. These allow gases flowing from the chamber, back into the action, to be directed sideways and not into your face. Contamination from mercuric primers is a likely cause of this since most of the mercury will contaminate the case area nearest the primer. *Stop shooting!* This batch of cases, from that box or lot, identified by the headstamp markings, is not fit to shoot. Mercury contamination is invisible and the cases look fine until fired. Since mercuric priming was limited to non-military ammunition made from about 1928-1945 there is not that much around any more, but it can still turn up. At times these contaminated cases will pull apart in the resizing die. This is a definite warning.

Stretched Primer Pockets

These occur after many reloadings. They are identified by gas leaks (smoke stains) around primers and by primers seating very easily, sometimes by thumb pressure alone. It's time to junk those cases when these signs appear. Excessively high pressure loadings can also cause these symptoms. This is why maximum loads should only be worked up with new or once-fired cases. With a new case and a heavy load, such leaks tell you to stop shooting!

Primers flattened on firing also indicate high pressure, as do those that are cratered around the firing pin mark, or pierced. If these signs appear with a max load—*stop shooting!* If they appear with a loading that has not produced these signs with other primers, the reason is most likely a soft primer.

Swollen Case Heads

This is nearly always a sign of very high pressure, but can also be caused by a too-soft head that was poorly annealed. If you are working up a max load, excessive pressure is the likely problem. *Stop shooting!* If this occurs with a load that has given no such indications and you have changed to a different make or lot of case it may be a case problem. Excessive pressures are the main culprit, and are additionally identified by cases stretching lengthwise and picking up machining impressions from the chamber walls and breech or bolt face. Such cases will stick tight to the chamber wall and give hard extraction, a definite sign of excess pressure.

Too much of
either of these
could be a
serious problem,
possibly leading
to serious injury
—or worse.

Understanding Pressure and Headspace

GUNS FUNCTION BECAUSE gunpowder burns rapidly to generate tremendous pressure as it is converted from a solid into a gas. This is a process called deflagration. Gunpowder burned in the air burns far more slowly than in the chamber of a gun. Inside the chamber, increasing pressure accelerates burning. As pressure increases the powder forms a churning mass.

The firing sequence begins as the primer ignites the powder. The primer contains a tiny amount of very high explosive that burns with a rapidity that far exceeds that of gunpowder. While gunpowder burned in the open produces a faint whoosh as the gas dissipates into the atmosphere, priming compound burns so quickly it will explode with great violence. This is why explosives such as priming compound, TNT, PETN, etc., are unsuitable for use as propellants. They burn so fast that before a bullet could begin to move down a gun barrel these compounds have burned completely, generating so much gas, so quickly, that for all intents the bullet is simply a plug in a closed container and the gun has become a bomb.

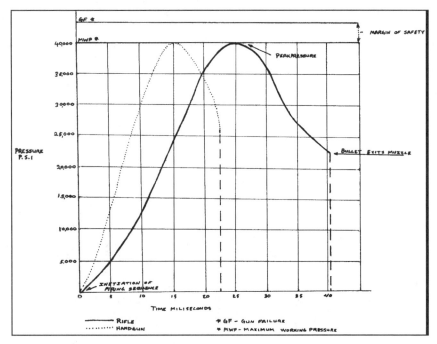

The primer is the sparkplug that starts the powder burning. Magnum primers contain more compounds and additives such as aluminum, which becomes white-hot sparks—blown into the powder to give the charge even ignition. (Photo courtesy of Speer.)

The flash hole on the case at the left was deliberately enlarged to burn a compressed, blackpowder load. If this case were loaded with smokeless powder, dangerously high pressures probably would be generated.

The time-pressure curve starts at the point of ignition. In a few milliseconds, the event is over. The peak pressure is reached as the bullet is an inch or so forward of the chamber. After it has been swaged into the rifling, pressure declines and drops to zero as the bullet exits the barrel. A fast-burning pistol powder in a short barrel develops a sharp curve (broken line), while a slower rifle powder in a long barrel is flatter. The peak of the curve touches the maximum working pressure (MWP) line on a maximum load. Above this is a margin of safety area, and further above that is the point of gun failure.

The priming compound thus serves to get the powder burning. It functions much like burning balls of paper thrown into a pile of dry leaves to get the pile blazing. By throwing a greater number of fire balls into the leaf pile it will be set alight faster and more evenly than if only a few are tossed on. A magnum primer represents a high saturation of fire balls by comparison to a regular primer. By starting the fire in more places at once, the mass of powder is burned more rapidly and completely. More rapid and complete burning will generate more gas and higher pressure.

To continue the bonfire analogy, a fast-burning powder could be likened to dry leaves while a slow burning powder is more like a pile of twigs or wood shavings. The twigs take more/hotter fire balls to get them burning, but they will burn longer than the leaves and generate more hot gas more slowly. The fast-burning powder is ideal for a short-barreled gun. The rapid burn releases gas quickly, generating a high-speed movement of the bullet quickly. This sudden release of gas produces a relatively high pressure in the chamber. Therefore only a limited amount of such a powder can be used without generating dangerously high pressures.

A slow-burning powder can be loaded in greater amount. By virtue of releasing more gas at a slower rate, this works well in long barrels where the burn time is extended by the length of time it takes the bullet to travel to the end of the barrel. The slow-burning powder keeps on generating gas throughout the length of time it takes the bullet to exit. The long burn thus generates lower peak pressure and keeps the average pressure up for a longer time. Once the bullet has passed out the muzzle, further burning is pointless.

This burning process is best illustrated in what is called the time-pressure curve. A fast-burning powder such as Hercules Bullseye is intended for handguns and produces a typically short, sharp curve. A slower-burning rifle powder such as IMR 4320 produces a longer, flatter curve in a rifle-length barrel.

Of most critical interest to the reloader is the *peak pressure* generated by a particular load, for it is this peak pressure that will act as a hammer blow to your gun and wreck it if the peak pressure exceeds the elastic limit of the barrel/action. This will cause it to swell and eventually burst. To keep both guns and shooters from harm, arms and ammunition manufacturers design their products for a maximum working pressure. This is below the failure point by a margin of safety. Loading above this maximum working pressure will drastically shorten the life of a gun and place the shooter at significantly higher risk of a catastrophic failure every time such a load is fired.

Beyond the strength of the barrel and action, working pressure is limited by the strength of the cartridge case. The modern alloy steel in today's rifles make them capable of withstanding peak pressures of well over 100,000 pounds per square inch (psi). Even the strongest brass cartridge cases are not capable of withstanding more than 50,000 to 60,000 psi, and at pressures above that, they will swell, distort or even flow, until an unsupported point gives way and gas escapes, often wrecking the gun. Most cartridge cases are intended for pressures well below these figures.

The most obvious means of raising pressure in a barrel is to put more powder in the cartridge. This also holds true for generating higher velocity. Higher velocity means flatter shooting with less rise and fall in a bullet's trajectory, and thus hitting a target at

The balloon-head case on the 38 Special at left offers more powder capacity, and thus lower pressure. However, this is a weaker design than the solid-head 357 Magnum case on the right.

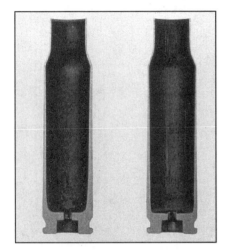

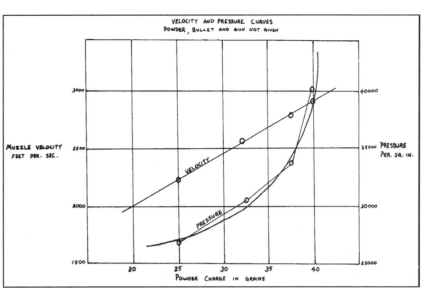

(Above) The pressure-velocity curve illustrates the relationship between velocity and the pressure generated by adding more powder. As powder is added, more of the energy of the expanding gas is worked against the chamber walls and the gas against itself. Additional powder added at the top end of a load generates little additional velocity but considerably more pressure.

The same cartridge with different internal dimensions. The smaller capacity case will generate higher pressures with the same load. Some brands have thicker (or thinner) walls, meaning different capacities. Sort your brass by maker.

an unknown distance is made easier—ask any varmint shooter. The downside to such high velocity loadings is the generation of very high pressures. An interesting phenomenon some shooters may not be familiar with is that as loadings are increased for greater velocity, pressures begin to go up at an increasingly higher rate. This can be most clearly expressed in what is known as the pressure-velocity curve. In conventional smokeless powder firearms, there is a ceiling on the velocity that can be achieved. This is because at a certain point, as the bullet is made smaller and lighter to achieve higher velocity, the base of that bullet has less surface area to be worked upon, and the gas in the chamber is working against the chamber walls and the molecules of gas against one another. This velocity ceiling is in the range of 11,000 feet per second (fps), and has been achieved with a steel ball blown out of a smooth-bore barrel—hardly practical. The pressure and heat generated at velocities of 5000-6000 fps will wash the rifling out of a barrel in a very few shots. A little over 4000 fps is the maximum practical velocity that can be expected to produce a reasonable barrel life—a span of a thousand shots at the very least before accuracy degrades to a marked degree. Thus, the quest for high velocity is at the cost of shortened barrel life and greatly increased pressures as the top end of the maximum working pressure is reached. This is where the last few additions of powder produce far more pressure than they add in velocity.

Other Factors Affecting Pressure

Reduced Loads

Small loads of certain slow-burning powders, well below those recommended in loading manuals, have apparently generated very high pressures. Called detonation, this phenomenon may be caused by what has been termed the log jam effect caused by the position of the powder in the case, wherein the powder charge is forward in the case. Powder ignited in the rear slams the rest of the charge into the base of the bullet and the shoulder of a bottleneck case, resulting in a solid plug. As burning continues, pressures jump and a bomb effect is created.

The problem with this theory is that it has been very difficult to duplicate such events in the laboratory. Undoubtedly, a certain number of supposed detonations were instances of bullets fired from such reduced loadings sticking in rifle, or more likely, revolver barrels. The unwary shooter fires a second shot and this bullet slams into the one stuck in the barrel with unhappy results. Whatever the reason, there have been a significant number of accidents involving reduced loads of slow-burning powders. Thus, it is prudent not to experiment below the starting loads listed in the manuals.

With faster burning powders, it has been noted that the position of the powder charge in the cartridge case in less than full-case loads will affect pressures. If the charge is at the rear near the vent, pressures will be higher since a greater amount of powder will be ignited and is not blown out the barrel. With the charge forward, as when the gun is fired almost straight down, pressures may be lower by more than 50 percent.

Primers

Primers are the fire starters that get powder burning. The more efficient ones, like magnum primers that burn longer and hotter, throw more sparks into the powder charge burning it more completely and more efficiently. This will generate more gas and, naturally, more pressure. It's best to stay with the

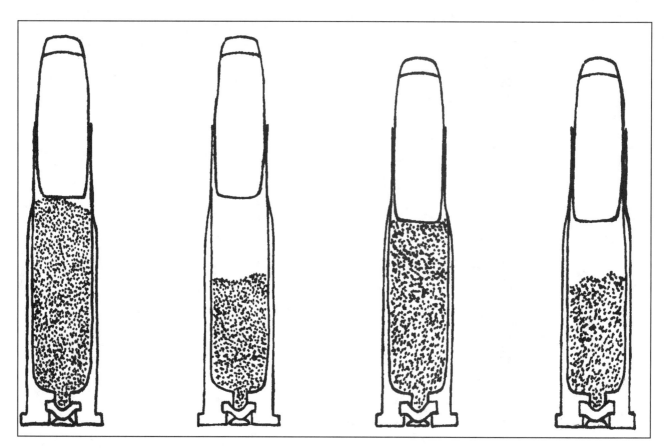

Loading density, the amount of powder and empty space in a cartridge, will affect the pressures therein, all other things being equal. The greater the density of the powder and the less space there is, the higher the pressure will be. On the left is a maximum, high-density load; next is a low-density load with the bullet seated far out. The pressure generated here would not be particularly high. Round number three contains the same load as number one, but it has been compressed by a deep-seated bullet. This would likely generate dangerously higher pressures. Round number four contains the same charge as number two, but will generate higher pressures. Case-wall thickness affects loading density by increasing or decreasing the internal capacity, a very critical point when a maximum load is used.

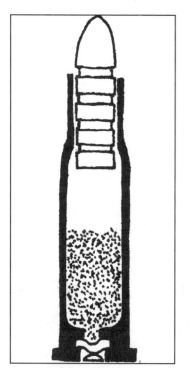

Never seat a cast bullet below the bottom of the neck into the shoulder area of a bottleneck case. The base will be melted and expanded, ruining accuracy and raising pressure.

primer types recommended by the loading manuals because pressure is affected.

Vent Hole Size

The vent hole is at the bottom of the primer pocket. Its size will affect powder burning rate by letting more of the primer flash pass into the case more quickly. A large vent, by increasing the rapidity of the burn, will raise pressures. Don't alter the size of the hole.

Case Capacity

All other things being equal, if the same amount of the same type of powder is loaded into a small capacity case such as a 223 Remington and a large capacity one such as a 45-70, much higher pressures will be generated in the smaller case. This is because there is less volume in the smaller case, thus less surface area for the pressure to work against. According to published data in the *Accurate Smokeless Powder Loading Guide Number One*, a load for the 223 of 23.5 grains of Accurate Arms 2495 BR powder behind an 80-grain jacketed bullet, generates an average of 51,600 psi of chamber pressure, while 66.0 grains of the same powder with a 300-grain jacketed bullet in

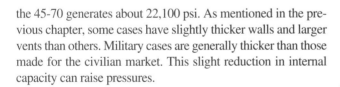

(Above and right) Slugging the bore consists of carefully driving a small, soft pure lead slug down the barrel. If done from both ends, the two slugs can be compared for tight and loose spots in the barrel.

The slug is measured from one land on one side to the land on the opposite side to find the groove diameter of the barrel.

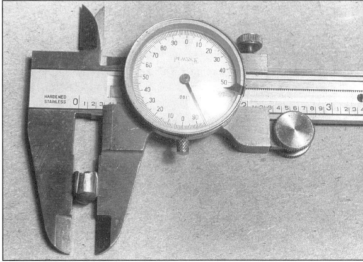

the 45-70 generates about 22,100 psi. As mentioned in the previous chapter, some cases have slightly thicker walls and larger vents than others. Military cases are generally thicker than those made for the civilian market. This slight reduction in internal capacity can raise pressures.

Overall Cartridge Length

By making a finished cartridge longer than it should be, the bullet may rest against or even be forced part way into the rifling. This will raise pressures. If a case is not trimmed to the proper length and the case mouth extends into the rifling, the mouth cannot expand properly and the bullet will be forced through what amounts to an undersize mouth in a swaging action that will jump pressures while degrading accuracy.

Chamber and Bore Size

All American-made guns are standardized according to specifications set forth by the Sporting Arms and Ammunition Manufacturers Institute (SAMMI). Customized, foreign, and obsolete arms, however, may have dimensions different from this standard. Smaller, tight chambers and undersize bores can jump pressures with normal ammunition. When there is a rea-

son for doubt about the size, slug the bore with a piece of soft lead to find the dimension. It's also pretty easy to make a chamber cast with Cerrosafe or sulfur to find the exact dimensions.

Bullets

Bullets affect pressure, with the weight of the bullet having the most influence. The heavier they are the greater the pressure needed to get them moving. Beyond this is the hardness of the bullet.

Hard bronze or copper jacketed bullets require more energy

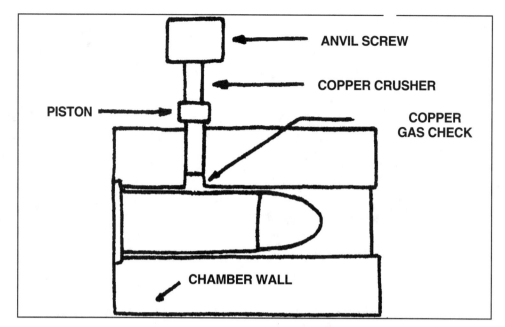

This is a drawing of a simplified crusher-type pressure gun used for measuring pressure. Pure copper and lead slugs are compressed to determine peak pressures on firing.

Diagram labels: ANVIL SCREW, COPPER CRUSHER, PISTON, COPPER GAS CHECK, CHAMBER WALL

to swage them into the rifling than does a soft lead bullet which is more easily engraved. Finally, there is the fit of the bullet in the bore. A tight fit offers more resistance than a loose fit where gas may blow by an undersize bullet which will not obturate the bore properly. A bullet seated too deeply—below the shoulder of a bottlenecked case—particularly a lead-alloy bullet, will often expand in the case and be swaged down as it passes into the neck. This will raise pressures and degrade accuracy.

Instrumental Measurement of Pressure

Until the middle of the 19th century, the only way to test for maximum pressures was to keep increasing powder charges until the test gun blew up. It was thus assumed, at times erroneously, that similar guns would blow up with the same charge. Artillery designer Thomas Rodman developed one of the first pressure testing devices used in the U.S., in 1861. It consisted of boring a hole in a gun chamber and inserting a rod with a chisel point on the other end. A copper plate was affixed to the barrel above the chisel blade. After the gun was fired, the plate was compared to similar plates marked with chisel indentations made by known amounts of force. A year earlier, in England, Sir Andrew Noble developed a more refined device featuring a piston that fit tightly in a hole drilled in a chamber wall. A frame secured to the barrel held an anvil above the opposite end of the piston. Between the piston and the anvil, a small copper cylinder was placed. When the gun was fired, the cylinder was compressed and later compared to similar cylinders compressed by known degrees of force. The accuracy of this system depends on keeping the purity and hardness of the copper cylinders, called crushers, consistent. Calculations are affected by whether the cartridge case is first drilled, or the force needed to blow a hole in the case is factored in. Sharp pressure rises are more easily registered than more gradual ones. For shotgun ammunition, some handgun ammunition and rimfire ammunition that generate relatively low pressures, a lead cylinder is used instead of copper. Measurements taken in this manner are expressed as copper units of

pressure (CUP) or lead units of pressure (LUP). For the handloader, these can be interpreted as pounds per square inch (psi), the LUP, CUP designation simply indicating the means by which the measurement was taken.

More sophisticated systems of pressure measurement developed in this century consist of electronic transducer systems. These are of two types—piezoelectric and strain gage (yes that's how it's spelled). The piezoelectric system, perfected in the mid 1930s, uses a quartz crystal in place of the copper cylinder, which is in a sealed tube with a diaphragm in the interior of the chamber wall. When subjected to pressure, the crystal generates electrical current in direct proportion to the amount of pressure applied. The advantage of such a system is a quick and relatively easy electronic readout and the reusability of the crystal. Disadvantages are calibration of equipment and crystals changing their value or varying in value.

The strain gage system derives pressure readings from implied information rather than direct. The device consists of a thin wire placed on the exterior surface of the chamber or around it. When the gun is fired, the chamber swells to a degree before returning to its original size, thus stretching the wire. The increased resistance in electrical conductivity of the stretched (thinner) wire during the firing sequence indicates pressure through the amount of stretch. Calibration is determined by measurement of inside and outside chamber diameters. Of the three systems, this one is of most interest to handloaders, since it is the only one that is non-destructive, in terms of not having to bore a hole in a gun chamber, and is available for home use. The only such device currently marketed is the Personal Ballistics Laboratory Model 43 available from Oehler Research.

Visible Signs of Pressure

For most handloaders these are the most critical indicators of something being wrong. They are also by far the most unreliable and imprecise. There is no way to estimate pressure from observation or even physical measurement of cartridge cases or primers. Nevertheless, these components can warn of pressures that are in the danger zone.

As indicated in the previous chapter, case failures may have a number of causes, and sorting out the problem is often difficult. The only sensible way to determine whether your reloads may be too hot is to eliminate as many variables as possible, thus leaving only those cartridge anomalies caused by excessive pressure or excessive headspace. These two problems produce similar appearing but different effects. What makes them difficult to differentiate is that any problems of excessive headspace are exacerbated by high pressure! Hard case extraction is a definite sign of high pressure unless you are dealing with an oversize or very rough chamber, which is generally something you can determine by looking into it. If your handload is more difficult to extract than a factory load of the same make, this tells you that you have exceeded the elastic limit of the case and

These three 44 Magnum cartridges were fired under the same conditions with the pressure measured by a copper crusher. Left to right: 31,800 CUP, 39,000 CUP, and 47,700 CUP. As can be seen, there is no discernible difference! (Photo courtesy Speer.)

The cratered primer (center) appears at first glance to be evidence of excessive pressure. The actual cause was an oversize firing pin hole and a soft primer.

Was the flat primer on the left a result of high pressure or being too soft? The answer is likely high pressure since the case head also flowed into the extractor groove (circled).

A pierced or "blown" primer can be caused by excessive pressure or a firing pin that is too long or too sharp. (Photo courtesy Speer.)

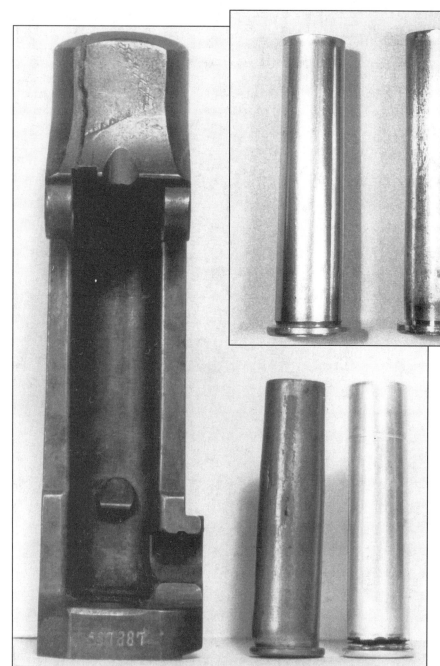

(Above) Definite signs of high pressure are obvious on these 45-70 cases. On the left is an unfired case. The center case was fired with a charge of 68 grains of IMR SR4759 powder—a 174 percent overload of the maximum loading (39 grains) for this powder with a 405-grain bullet. The barrel was bulged by this event, and the case had to be driven out with a rod. The case on the right was fired with 40 grains of Unique behind a 500-grain cast bullet. The maximum load for this bullet is 14.8 grains. This represents more than a 270 percent overload. The barrel of the gun was bulged to the point the receiver cracked. The case required considerable pounding with a hammer and a metal rod to remove it. Note the expansion in front of the solid head and stretching of the case.

A case-head separation is the worst event, with high pressure gas blowing back into the action and often into the face of the shooter. This is why you *always* wear shooting glasses. The old balloon-head case on the left, combined with a double charge, cracked the rifle receiver. The case on the right suffered a nearly complete separation because of mercuric priming.

you are generating significantly higher pressures. A second way to check this is to take a micrometer measurement of the case-body diameter of a factory-loaded case after firing, and a handload using the same make of case after firing it for the first time. A larger diameter will indicate higher pressure than the factory load.

The flattening of primers is a sign of high pressure. However, many high-pressure rifle cartridges will show a good deal of flattening as a matter of course. Again, the critical factor is *the difference* between the flattening of a factory load and a handload using the same components fired for the first time. If the flattening is greater, you are getting higher pressure than the factory round and are in the upper limit of the margin of safety for your particular gun. Most factory loads are near the maximum. This information is based on the "all other things being equal" premise. Whenever you suspect something is wrong, make sure all other things are equal and you are not introducing some factor that will alter your results. Getting oil or other lubricants on cartridge cases is part of the reloading process. This should be removed before firing. Oil in a chamber or on a case will cause the case to slide in the chamber instead of expanding and sticking to the chamber wall during firing. This causes excessive back thrust of the case against the bolt. Back thrust batters the case head, often transferring impressions of machining on the bolt face to the case head. These appear, to the untrained eye, to be caused by high pressure. Battering the bolt face will also—sooner than later—increase the headspace in the gun, which is a serious problem.

The puncturing of primers—a so called "blown primer" where a hole is blown through the primer where the firing pin

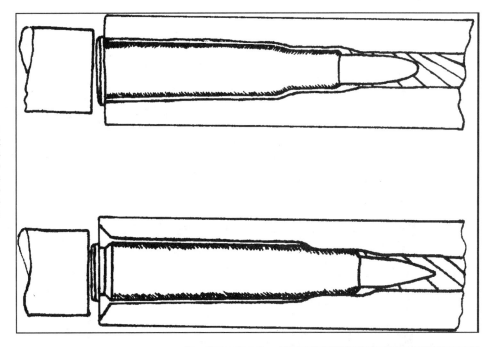

Headspace is measured between the face of the bolt and the front edge of the rim where it touches the breech on any rimmed case (top). Headspace on a rimless case is measured between the bolt face and the point where the case shoulder or the case mouth contacts the chamber.

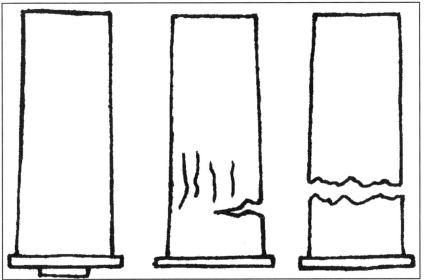

Excessive headspace signs begin as a backed-out primer. Stage two is the appearance of stretching and cracks. Stage three is separation. If excessive headspace is combined with an overload, stage three may be reached on the first loading.

Stretch marks and the crack on this case are indicative of excessive headspace. (Photo courtesy Speer.)

hits it—is a *definite* sign of very high pressure, unless you have a firing pin that is too long. Firing pins do not suddenly grow longer. *Stop shooting!* Before a primer blows, under pressure, there will be evidence of primers "cratering." This is where the metal in the primer flows back around the tip of the firing pin and into the hole where the pin comes through the bolt or breechblock. Cratering can also be caused by a soft primer and an oversize firing pin hole. Here again, a comparison with a fired factory round with the same components is the best way to judge differences.

Gas leaks around primers make a black soot smudge at their edges, and may be a sign of high pressure or an enlarged primer pocket. Primer pocket stretching in a case will occur after a number of loadings, particularly high pressure ones. This tells you the case is finished for reloading. If a leak occurs after long

use this can be assumed to be normal. When such a leak happens the first time with a new case, look for other high pressure signs. Hard extraction, flattened or cratered primers, blown or leaky primers most often occur together.

Soot-streaking of cases when they are fired, particularly staining near the case mouth, is a sign not of high pressure, but of its opposite: low pressure. If a loading is not generating enough pressure to make a complete gas seal between the cartridge case and the chamber wall, a certain amount of gas will leak back into the chamber and smudge the case. Other than being a minor nuisance this causes no danger. It is an indication that combustion is at too low a level, owing to not enough powder or poor ignition of the powder. Such under-powered loads will tend to be inaccurate since the amount of gas that escapes will vary from shot to shot, depending on the elasticity of the individual case.

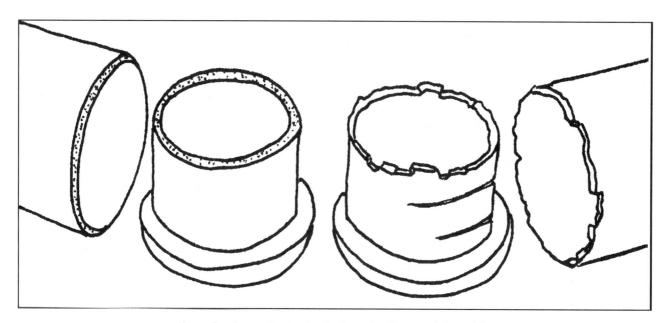

A case head separation has two basic causes. Type one is brass failure, often caused by mercuric priming contamination of brass that is otherwise weak and brittle. Type two is excessive headspace in the gun. These result in different types of fractures. Type one (left) is a clean break with a crystalline surface. Type two is characterized by tearing of the metal and stretch marks on the case.

Understanding Headspace

In order for a cartridge to enter and exit a gun chamber it has to be made a little smaller than the chamber, with enough room for easy extraction after it is fired. To work properly, however the case must be firmly supported by the bolt or breechblock to keep it from rupturing under pressure. The amount of tolerance between the head of the case and the face of the bolt or breechblock is less than .005-inch in a good modern gun. Zero tolerance would be best, but guns and ammunition are mass-produced products and a certain amount of tolerance must be permitted for variations that are part of the manufacturing process. A tolerance of several thousandths of an inch represents the elastic limits of the cartridge case, allowing the fired case to return to close to its original size for extraction. If the tolerance is greater, the elastic limits of the case are exceeded and it will begin to deform or even rupture. This situation is known as excessive headspace.

Tolerances for headspace are set at the factory and remain in place for the life of a gun. That life is shortened by shooting high-pressure loads which batter the bolt or breechblock, gradually increasing the headspace. This problem can be corrected by a skilled gunsmith, depending on the type of gun and how bad the situation has become.

Calculating Headspace

Headspace is measured with gauges to .001-inch. In a rimmed or semi-rimmed case, the headspace measurement is between the surface of the bolt or breechblock and the point where the front of the cartridge rim makes contact with the face of the breech. With rimless cases, the measurement is between the bolt face and the point where the shoulder of the case makes contact with the counterbore in the chamber. For straight rimless cases such as the 45 ACP, the measurement is to the point where the case mouth makes contact with the front of the chamber.

Excessive Headspace

This is when the tolerances are too great. When this situation occurs, the cartridge case is held tightly forward against the chamber walls upon firing. With the case head unsupported by the bolt or breechblock, the case stretches backward under the force of the pressure inside it, until it makes contact with the bolt face and stops. Usually before this happens, the primer is pushed out of its pocket until it meets the bolt face. As pressure drops in the chamber, the case springs back and creeps back over the primer, often jamming the now expanded primer back into the pocket. On examination, the flattened primer will appear for all the world like an example of high pressure. The reloader should make sure he has not loaded a maximum load. If this was a max load, he should try a factory cartridge for comparison. If the problem is excessive headspace the signs should be there with normal loads, and they may appear even with reduced loads although somewhat less obvious. Often, the only sign will be a primer backed out of the case.

After a case is stretched in an overly long chamber, is resized, reloaded and fired, the stretching process is repeated with the next firing. Stretch marks, in the form of shiny rings, begin to appear around the circumference of the case body forward of the head. After a number of reloadings, depending on how much stretching and resizing occurs, the case will become fatigued and rupture, blowing high pressure gas back into the action. This often destroys the gun, and injures the face of the shooter. A combination of poor brass, a heavy load and a lot of extra headspace can bring on this condition in a single shot.

Headspace problems can be created in the reloading process.

Low pressure is evidenced by the soot stains on the case on the right, which failed to make a complete gas seal when fired.

Primer pockets will stretch, as did the one on the left after a number of heavy loads. If the leak or stretch appears suddenly on a new or nearly new case, you are in the *very* high pressure range and should reduce your loads.

A leak around a primer indicates an expanded primer pocket. Time to discard the case.

Soft alloy bullets of lead and tin (the shiny ones on the ends) will yield lower pressures than harder alloy bullets. Jacketed bullets (third from right) create significantly higher pressures, as do heavier bullets.

This occurs with rimless cases such as the 30-06 and 223 where improper use of the sizing die forces the shoulder back on the case body, allowing the case to go further into the chamber than it should. The extractor hook will hold the case in the proper position for firing, but the case has now become too short and has to stretch back to meet the bolt face. If this practice is continued, it is only a matter of time until a rupture occurs with all the grief that goes with it. *Any gun showing signs of excessive headspace should not be fired.* Examination by a skilled gunsmith will tell you if the situation can be corrected.

4

Over the years, ignition of the powder charge has been accomplished in a number of ways. Today, big things come from small packages.

Primers

THE PURPOSE OF the primer is to ignite the main powder charge. This was originally done with a burning splinter or hot wire jammed into a small touchhole at the breech of the gun. Later, a smoldering rope or sparks from iron pyrites and flint striking steel were employed to set off a small charge of powder in a funnel that connected with the main charge in the gun barrel. These systems worked, but they didn't work well, which prompted a search for an ignition system that fulfilled the four criteria of today's modern primers, namely: speed, reliability, uniformity and cleanliness.

Primer Evolution

Early ignition systems failed in all the above criteria. Matchlocks were equipped with a smoldering fuse made of chemically treated rope, called a "match," which would burn out in damp weather and could be blown out by wind. With flintlocks, wind could blow the priming charge out of the pan, and wet, damp weather would saturate it with moisture to the

Modern percussion caps are essentially a primer without an anvil inside it, that part being provided by the nipple on the gun.

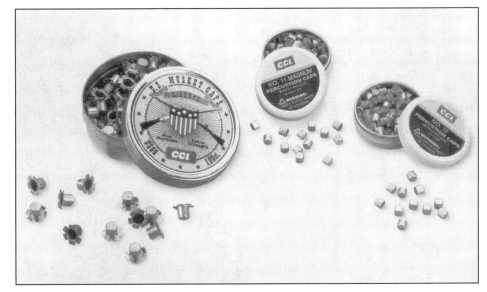

(Below) Berdan (left) and Boxer primer pockets show the differences in the systems. The ease of reloading made the Boxer primer standard in the U.S. (Photo courtesy Speer.)

point where it would not fire. Rust and powder fouling in the touchhole that connected the pan charge to the propelling charge in the barrel often prevented a successful firing, with only the priming charge burning. The expression, "a flash in the pan," is still used to describe a person or enterprise that shows promise, but fails to get past a good beginning. The flintlock system gave only reasonable reliability. A small piece of flint held in the jaws of the "hammer" (called the cock) struck a steel cover on the pan called the frizzen, knocking it open and scraping the inner side to throw sparks into the powder charge in the pan. In terms of speed it was slow. Anyone who has seen a flintlock fired is familiar with the puff-boom! report as the priming charge burns with a one-beat pause before the propelling charge fires. History is filled with untold numbers of targets, animal and human, who have ducked to safety during that beat, which was sometimes two beats if the day was damp and the touchhole a bit clogged.

Explosives such as fulminate of mercury and mixtures including potassium chlorate, that detonated when crushed or struck, were discovered late in the 18th century. After attempts to use them as substitutes for gunpowder failed, they received little attention until the early 19th century.

The breakthrough to improved ignition was made by a Scottish Presbyterian minister, hunter, shooter and gun buff—Reverend Alexander Forsythe. He was the first to come up with the idea of using these detonating explosives to *ignite* propelling charges in firearms. He received a patent in 1807 for a system

that did away with the priming pan on the flintlock. This design filled the tube leading to the barrel with a percussion explosive made of sulphur, potassium chlorate and charcoal. A metal pin was inserted on top of the explosive which caused it to detonate when struck by the gun's hammer. The ignition was far faster and more certain than the flintlock. Forsythe improved his design by attaching a small iron bottle containing a supply of percussion explosive to the side of the lock. The bottle could be tipped or turned to deposit a small pellet of explosive on a touchhole which would be struck by the hammer. The system worked effectively. However, it involved having a small iron bottle filled with high explosive very close to the firing point and to the face of the shooter. I have never seen a report of an accident with a Forsythe lock, but if one happened, it would almost certainly have been fatal.

The superiority of the Forsythe system was soon recognized and dozens of variations were introduced, including percussion wafers, tubes and strips of paper caps, much like those used in toy cap pistols of today. The most successful was the percussion cap, invented in about 1814 by Joshua Shaw, a British subject who emigrated to America. Shaw's system featured a small steel tube, closed at one end, about the size of a modern large pistol primer. The closed end contained the explosive held in place by a tinfoil cover then sealed with a drop of lacquer. This made it waterproof as well as damp proof. The cap was fitted on a short iron nipple, hollow in the center, which allowed the fire to enter the chamber of the gun. Shaw caps were on the market by 1821 and were soon adapted to sporting guns. Improvements were made by changing the cap metal to pewter and later copper. Similar caps were in use about the same time over most of Europe. The percussion cap was not adopted by the U.S. military until after the Mexican War. The military thinking at the time was that the percussion cap was yet another component the soldier had to carry and not reusable in the manner of a gun flint.

Percussion caps made the Colt revolver a practical reality, but the shortcomings of this system became apparent when repeating rifles were made using this system. A cylinder "flash over" from one chamber to the next would occasionally send a

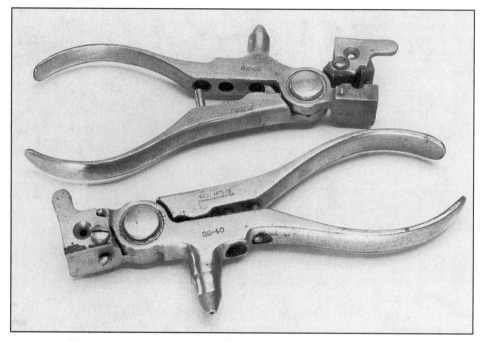

Early tong reloading tools could be carried in the pocket or saddlebag. These in 32-20 (top) and 38-40 WCF from the old Ideal Company cast bullets, decapped, primed and seated bullets in blackpowder calibers.

(Below) The Lee Hand Press Kit is a modern version of the old Ideal tong tool. The kit includes dies, case lube, powder dipper, etc., for a little over $65.

bullet coasting by the side of the gun. With a handgun this was of little consequence since it was a one-hand weapon. With the revolving rifle such an event often amputated the fingers or thumb of the hand supporting the forend of the weapon. Revolving rifles did not gain much popularity.

Not surprisingly, the first really successful breechloaders and successful repeating arms, other than revolvers, required a self-contained, self-primed cartridge. There were a number of important steps between the percussion cap and the rimfire cartridge, but to list them here is not our mission. Suffice it to say there was a fairly logical evolution. In brief, George Morse placed a percussion cap in the head of a metal cartridge using a hairpin-shaped anvil inside the case to fire it. Hiram Berdan shortened the hairpin to a tiny knob, while Edward Boxer placed a tiny anvil inside the cap.

Center Primed

Centerfire ammunition soon eclipsed the rimfire and all the other nonreloadable types because it *was reloadable*. Rimfires were gradually reduced to those types that were so small that the cartridge would not lend itself to reloading. The military had

great influence in ammunition development, stipulating that any ammunition developed for a military small arm had to be reloadable. Spent cases were collected and returned to a government arsenal for reloading during peacetime. Professional hunters in the American west needed cartridges they could reload themselves with simple tools. It was this type of equipment that first appeared in the 1870s.

Early priming mixtures used fulminate of mercury or potassium chlorate, occasionally a combination of both. These fulfilled most of the criteria for good ignition: speed, reliability, uniformity, and cleanliness to some extent. While the chlorate-based primers and caps did not leave an appreciable residue, they did leave a highly corrosive deposit—potassium chloride—that would eat away a percussion nipple or the web of a cartridge. This needed to be neutralized by cleaning the gun with water that removed the salt deposit. The mercury-based compounds were both clean and noncorrosive. Their drawback came when used in combination with brass or copper primer cups and cartridge cases. When fired, the mercury would amalgamate with the copper or brass making it extremely brittle. Reloading and firing such a contaminated cartridge case can lead to a case-head rupture. In a high-pressure loading, this can wreck a gun and possibly your face. Mercuric priming was gone from commercial ammunition by about 1945, but primers made prior to this time were used by commercial reloaders for a number of years later.

Because fulminate of mercury contains free, liquid mercury, this mercury will actually migrate through the priming mixture and into the metal of the primer cup or cartridge head after a certain number of years. Ammunition primed with mercuric mixtures made in the early 1930s will probably not fire today. However, ammunition loaded with chlorate priming made during the Civil War is often still viable, so long as neither the powder or priming compound has been exposed to moisture. Thus a fifth criterion should be added—long life.

From the late '20s through the mid-1930s, American manu-

Pistol and rifle primers come in two sizes, while shotshell primers are of one size.

(Below) Pistol primers should not be used in rifle cases since they will seat too deeply, as in the case on the left. The center case shows proper seating depth, while the high primer on the right will give poor ignition and possibly slam-fire in an autoloader.

facturers worked to perfect a priming mixture akin to one developed in Germany, that was noncorrosive and did not contain mercury. The basis of such priming is in compounds of lead, barium and antimony.

Early noncorrosive, non-mercuric primers did not work very well, giving uneven ignition. Priming material often fell out of the rim in rimfire cartridges as the binding material—a vegetable-based glue—deteriorated.

The Modern Primer

Modern primers of the lead, barium and antimony type fulfill all the necessary criteria for good ignition. The binders are now stable and remain so for long periods under normal "house" storage conditions, where temperatures are under 125 degrees Fahrenheit and moisture is kept at a reasonable level. The newest are the "lead free" primers of tetracene. These, however, are not presently sold as reloading components since the production demand is for use in finished ammunition. The primary use of such primers is in handgun ammunition to be fired in indoor ranges where airborne lead could present a health hazard.

Because of the difficulty of reloading them, cartridges using Berdan primers and the Berdan primers themselves have virtually disappeared from the U.S. Foreign cartridges often still use this type of priming and can only be reloaded with Berdan primers. Any attempt to convert Berdan cases to Boxer priming by drilling them in some manner will not work. Such attempts are very dangerous since they will greatly enlarge the flashhole and may damage the web. At best, such conversions give uneven ignition, at worst they can raise pressures to dangerous levels by causing too rapid a burn of the powder charge. The only current source for Berdan primers and Berdan decapping equipment is The Old Western Scrounger.

A modern Boxer primer differs little in structure from those made over a century ago. It is a brass cup containing the priming compound. A paper seal keeps the compound in the cup and is held in place by the metal anvil made of harder brass. A better understanding of metallurgy and chemistry has resulted in a more uniform primer as well as ones which are specifically tailored to a particular type of cartridge.

Primers for pistols and rifles come in two basic sizes of small (.175-inch) and large (.210-inch). There also is a .317-inch primer made by CCI and used only in the 50 Browning machinegun cartridge. Small pistol primers are used in such rounds as 25- and 32-caliber handgun ammunition, while the large size is used in 41-, 44- and 45-caliber handguns. Large pistol primers are also made in a magnum variant, for use in large capacity cases using hard-to-ignite, slow-burning powders. These require a longer, hotter flame for uniform and complete burning.

Rifle primers are made in the same two diameters as pistol primers, and are designated small and large. They are slightly higher to fit the deeper pocket in the rifle cartridge case. For this reason, pistol primers should not be seated in rifle cases since they will seat too deeply and often give uneven ignition. Rifle primers contain more priming compound than pistol primers since they have to ignite more powder in larger capacity cases.

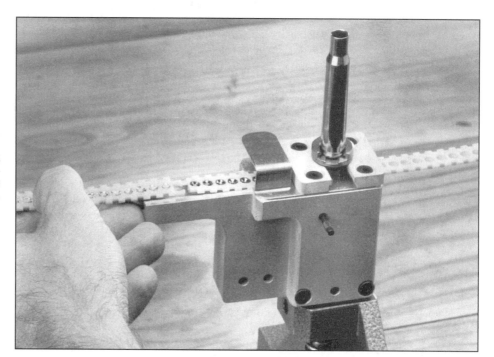

The RCBS APS primer feeder uses plastic strips instead of the conventional stacking tube, reducing the hazard of sympathetic detonation. (Photo courtesy RCBS.)

(Left and above) Primers are sold preloaded in strips, but the strips can be refilled with the RCBS loading tool. You have to buy the system. (Photos courtesy RCBS.)

If you are loading both handgun and rifle ammunition, care must be taken not to mix rifle and handgun primers. If rifle primers are seated in pistol cases they will not fit properly. They can also raise pressures to the danger point. Pistol primers tend to burn cooler, and produce more of a flame type of explosion—good for igniting fast-burning pistol powders. Rifle primers burn longer and hotter. They often contain metallic elements such as aluminum which act as burning sparks that are blown forward into a charge of slower-burning powder. This separates the grains, igniting it in a number of places at once, to achieve an even burning of the charge. This explosive quality is known as brisance. Magnum rifle primers have still more compound, burn longer and hotter and are used in very large-capacity cases such as the 458 Winchester Magnum. Companies such as CCI also market a bench rest rifle primer. This is simply a standard rifle primer, but made to very strict tolerances assuring the reloader that each primer in a given lot will have a very precisely measured amount of compound, and that the diameter and hardness of all components are within very strict tolerances. These premium-quality primers give very even ignition needed for the exacting demands of the expert, competition target shooter.

Shotshell primers have special characteristics needed to work properly in modern plastic shotshells. Early shotshells were

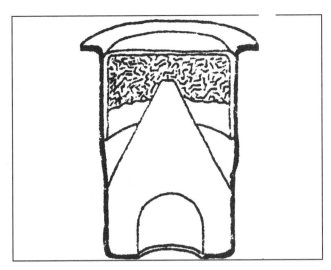

The shotshell battery cup primer comes with the primer pocket and vent as part of the unit, all of which is replaced when the shell is reprimed.

made of brass and were generally of rifle-type of construction. They used rifle-style primers. Modern shells are of a composite construction with a metal head surrounding a paper, now primarily a plastic body. Inside is a base wad made of plastic or compressed paper.

Shotshells have unique ignition problems. As the mouth of the shell becomes worn and softened with repeated firing and reloading, the opening of the crimp becomes progressively easier. Modern shotgun powders require a certain amount of pressure and confinement to function properly. This decreases as the crimp softens. For proper ignition, the powder requires a very high temperature over a longer than usual burn time, but without the brisant quality of the magnum rifle powder which would tend to blow the crimp open before much of the powder was ignited. A shotshell primer produces what is often referred to as a "soft ignition."

Because of the design of modern shotshells, the primer is held in a large, longer than normal housing called a battery cup. This extends well into the base wad so the flame issuing from the primer mouth will not be inhibited by any part of the wad and can direct its full blast into the powder charge.

Handling and Storage

Primers are the most dangerous component in the reloading operation. They are subject to shock and explode with a violence that belies their small size. Children often have a penchant for playing with small shiny objects and primers should definitely be kept out of their hands. Primers are packaged to keep them from shock and from striking one another. Julian Hatcher, in his *Notebook*, tells of a young worker in an ammunition plant carrying a metal bucket of primers, casually bouncing it as he walked. There was a sudden, violent explosion. As I recall, a part of a foot was the largest piece recovered.

Primers should *only* be stored in the original packaging, never in a can or bottle where they can rattle around. Automatic primer feeding devices of a tube design should be loaded with great care, because this brings a considerable number together in way that if one accidentally explodes, the remainder will go

too. The explosive force of a primer is many, many times that of the most powerful smokeless powder.

Properly stored, primers do not present a particularly dangerous hazard. They will pop quite loudly if thrown in a fire, and come flying with enough force to penetrate a cardboard carton a foot or more away. People have lost eyesight from such injuries, so this is *not* the way to dispose of damaged, though unexploded primers. Perhaps the best method is to load them in an empty cartridge case and snap them. If this is not possible, they can be deactivated by soaking in a strong lye solution for a week. The liquid may be flushed away with a large quantity of water. The potassium chlorate in the old corrosive primers is very water soluble and water soaking works well with this type. We are talking here about small numbers of primers, not more than two dozen. If for some reason you should have to dispose of a large number of primers, call your local gun shop to see if they can use them.

Shelf storage should be in a cool dry place, away from containers of gunpowder and away from children's reach. To avoid an explosion hazard in case of fire, primers *should not* be stored in a closed heavy metal container such as a military ammunition can.

The lacquer seals used in modern primers keeps them free of deterioration from dampness, but basement storage is not recommended for any ammunition component unless that basement is kept dry with a dehumidifier. About the only uniquely vulnerable feature about primers is the paper seal which could be attacked by molds under extremely damp conditions.

Three questions are frequently asked by shooters of military, foreign, and obsolete guns: (1) How can you determine if the military ammunition you are planning to shoot and reload is Berdan primed? (2) How can you determine which ammunition is corrosively primed? and (3) How can you tell if a case has been contaminated by mercuric primers?

The answer to the first is fairly simple—usually. The Berdan primers are almost always of a larger diameter than the equivalent Boxer primers, although the CCI primer used in their non-reloadable Blazer ammunition is virtually the same size. Most foreign military primers are the Berdan type and are usually larger. The surest way to know is to examine a fired cartridge case and look into the case for the small twin vents that are the trademark of this system. This is not possible when buying ammunition. About the best you can do is ask the dealer if the stuff is Boxer primed or not, and get a guarantee that if it isn't, he will take the unfired portion back.

Determining which ammunition has corrosive priming is a little more complicated. Corrosive priming was a serious problem in the early days of smokeless powder ammunition, since corrosive salts were deposited in large quantities in the barrels of guns that fired it. Blackpowder fouling, while corrosive to a degree, helped to hold these salts and the fouling was relatively easy to clean with a soap and warm water mixture. After cleaning, the bore was wiped dry and then oiled to protect it. With the introduction of smokeless powder, there was very little powder fouling in the bore. Jacketed bullets moving at high velocities left a hard metallic deposit composed of copper and nickel from the jackets. This was difficult to remove and trapped the corro-

Crystal Cleaner was an ammonia-based metal solvent offered by Winchester in the early days of corrosive priming. The U.S. military bore cleaner in the old dark green can combined ammonia and powder solvent in a brown, evil-smelling liquid. It did/does a good job of removing corrosive primer residue and metal fouling.

sive salt (potassium chloride) in a layer between the barrel surface and the metal fouling. A barrel could appear perfectly clean, but days later even though the bore was saturated with oil or grease, it would rust heavily under this protective coating.

To combat this problem, cleaning solvents were developed that would dissolve this metal fouling and remove the salts from the corrosive priming. Most of these solvents contained ammonia which readily dissolves copper and nickel. A water-based solution of ammonia does a very good job of removing both metal fouling and primer salts. Years ago, after firing a lot of corrosive ammunition, I removed fouling by corking the chamber of my 303 Enfield with a rubber stopper and *carefully* filling the bore with household ammonia, then letting it stand for an hour or so. The dissolved salts and copper fouling were removed when the barrel was tipped. The fouling was obvious in the blue-green tint it gave to the ammonia solution. After dumping the liquid, a couple of wet patches were run through the bore, then a couple of dry patches, and the bore was swabbed with Hoppe's No. 9 solvent until everything came clean. Care had to be taken not to spill ammonia on any blued surface since it will remove the blue. I was also careful not to leave the solution too long, or worse let it dry, on any exposed steel surface since it will readily rust that surface.

Commercial solvents with ammonia, bearing names like "Chlor oil," "Fiend oil" and "Crystal Cleaner" were once marketed for cleaning up corrosive priming. They have been gone from the scene so long that few people remember their names. The U.S. military came up with its own preparation called, sim-

CORROSIVE/NON-CORROSIVE PRIMING: U.S. MILITARY AMMUNITION (U.S.- and Canadian-manufactured ammunition)			
Headstamp	Mfr.	Changeover Date	Non-Corr. Headstamp
FA	Frankford	Oct 1951 (30)	FA 52-
		July 1954 (45)	FA 55-
DEN	Denver	All corrosive during WWII	
DM	Des Moines	All corrosive during WWII	
EC	Eau Claire	All corrosive during WWII	
LC	Lake City	June 1951 (30)	LC 52
		April 1952 (30 AP)	LC 53
SL	St. Louis	May 1952 (30)	SL 53
		July 1952 (30 AP)	SL 53
TW	Twin Cities	Dec 1950 (30)	TW 51
		Feb 1952 (30 AP)	TW 53
U and UT	Utah	All corrosive during WWII	
DAQ	Dominion (Canada)	All noncorrosive	
VC	Verdun (Canada)	All noncorrosive	
FCC	Federal	Nov 1953 (45)	FC 54-
RA	Remington	Nov 1951 (30)	RA 52-
		Sept 1952 (45)	RA 53-
WCC	Western	June 1951 (30)	WCC 52-
		Nov 1952 (45)	WCC 53-
WRA	Winchester	Aug 1951 (30)	WRA 52-
		June 1954 (30 AP)	WRA 53-
		Nov 1951 (45)	WRA 52-

(Above and below) Military ammunition generally has the primer swaged in the case with a primer crimp, which makes first-time removal a little difficult. Once the crimp is removed, however, there is no further problem.

All 223 (5.56mm), 30 Carbine, 308 (7.62mm), 9mm Luger and 38 Special military ammunition is non-corrosive. Exceptions are the 1956 NATO 308 Match ammunition made at the Frankford Arsenal and 30-06 Match ammunition made at the Frankford Arsenal in 1953, 1954 and 1956. All are stamped FA with the two-digit date. (This information was adapted from the NRA *Handloader's Guide*.)

ply, "Bore Cleaner." This was a dark brown concoction with a smell you will never forget (although you wish you could), that combined ammonia with water-soluble oil and powder solvents. Bad as it smelled, it worked quite well.

Corrosive priming was gone from commercial ammunition by the 1930s. In the early 1950s, noncorrosive priming gradually replaced the corrosive type in U.S. military ammunition. A decade or so later, the Army switched to a newer type of bore cleaner which is sold commercially under the name "Break Free." By this time most shooters had forgotten about corrosive-primed ammunition. Today's cleaners do a fine job of removing powder fouling and preventing rust from external causes, but they do not remove corrosive potassium salt. This must be removed with a water-based cleaner since salt does not dissolve in oil.

With the importation of Russian and Chinese Tokarev, Moisin-Nagant, SKS and AKM rifles and ammunition, corrosive priming is back on the American scene. Most of the current powder solvents are ineffective in removing the corrosive salt. Probably the best way to deal with this is to get some of the old Army bore cleaner and clean with that. It is still available at many gun shops, gun shows and military-surplus outlets. Another option is to use one of the solvents that remove copper fouling. After cleaning with that, run several wet patches then dry patches until the bore is clean; then oil with a good protective oil or grease with rust inhibitors.

Identifying corrosive-primed American military ammunition is an easy matter of consulting the nearby list that was compiled by the NRA several years ago. When it comes to foreign ammunition, unless it is in the original box from a commercial manufacturer and clearly marked "Non-corrosive," assume it is corrosive, particularly if it is military ammunition, especially that from any former East Bloc country. If you wish to experiment, collect some fired cases and place them outdoors for a week or two in warm humid weather, or place them on their heads with a drop or two of water in each and let them stand over night. If corrosive salt is present, there will usually be evidence of corrosion inside the case particularly near the vent, especially if that case is made of steel.

The question of mercuric priming is best dealt with on the basis of: If the ammunition or cases are pre-WWII and not corrosive-primed, they are likely mercuric-primed. If the ammunition is in the original box and the box declares it to be "noncorrosive, nonmercuric," and it's in good (appearing) condition, it's probably good to shoot. Keep in mind that if the old nonmercuric primers are no good, the bullets can be pulled and the cartridges can be reloaded, if you think it's worth the effort.

Oftentimes batches of old fired cases turn up and the shooter has no idea whether they are usable. If the caliber is something currently available, don't bother. The knotty problem is when such a batch turns up in some obsolete caliber like 351 or 401 Winchester, and you have one of those rifles and nothing to shoot in it. Converting some other cartridge to these is very difficult. Loaded new ammunition in these calibers is available from The Old Western Scrounger at nearly $40.00 for a box of twenty as of this writing. At that price, a batch of old cases might be a bargain, *if* they are in good condition and all the same make. If there is heavy tarnish and season cracking, forget it. If they have a scaly appearance or are stretched, bulged or otherwise show damage or distortion, forget it. This leaves the possibility of mercury contamination, which leaves no visible evidence. The only test I could find to make the determination of mercury contamination comes from *Handloader's Manual* by Earl Naramore. It was published in 1937. Naramore states that you must sacrifice a case for testing. It must be carefully sectioned with a fine hacksaw. After sectioning, the cut surface it should be filed with a fine metal file to remove the saw marks, then polished on a piece of fine emery paper or crocus cloth. The polished case is then submerged for a few seconds in a 20 percent solution of nitric acid until the polished surface takes on a dull or slightly roughened appearance. Leaving the case in the bath too long will pit the surface.

After the case is properly etched, the walls can be examined with a magnifying glass for flaws in the metal. The case should be removed from the etching bath with a pair of tweezers and washed in clear water. States Naramore: "The action of the nitric acid will clean the fouling from the inside of the case thoroughly and if the surface has a silvery appearance, it is a sure indication that the case has been fired with a mercuric primer. This silver-looking coating, which is really mercury, will disappear into the brass after the specimen has stood a little while, so the condition should be looked for immediately after taking the case out of the etching solution. Unfortunately the failure of the mercury to appear does not offer assurance that the case has never been fired with a mercuric primer, but the mercury will usually show up." Naramore goes on to urge the reloader to examine the etched case for cracks or splits in the head which can usually be seen with the unaided eye or with a magnifying glass.

Primer crimps are easily removed with this handy tool (and others), which also swages the primer pockets to uniform size.

Once you pop
the primer, you
need to fuel
the fire, and
propellants come
in many types,
shapes and sizes.

POWDERS

GUNPOWDER IS THE driving force that makes a gun shoot. It does this by changing from a solid to a large volume of hot gas in a very short time in what is best termed a low-velocity explosion. This works very well for propelling bullets down gun barrels without raising the pressure too suddenly, which would cause the barrel to burst before the bullet gets moving. High velocity or "high" explosives are unsuitable for use in guns for this reason.

Blackpowder and Its Variants

The original "gunpowder" is what is now referred to as "blackpowder," and is actually a dark gray in color. Its origin dates back about a thousand years. All sorts of ingredients have been added at various times, but the basic mixture is composed of potassium nitrate (75 percent), charcoal (15 percent), and sulphur (10 percent). Many people have made blackpowder at home. This practice is *not* recommended simply because it is dangerous. One mistake can prove disastrous. Such a mistake

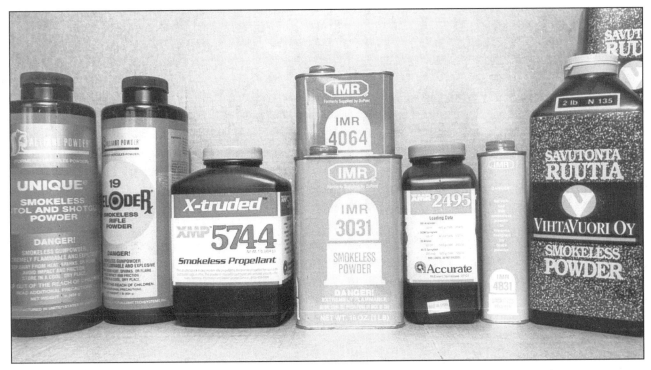

American manufacturers and importers offer a wide variety of smokeless powder for reloaders.

cost me both hands at the age of fifteen. I consider myself lucky I still have everything else intact. For those not impressed by danger, it may be added that homemade powder is never up to the standards of purity and consistency of the manufactured product. The burning rate of blackpowder is determined by the size of the granulation. Very fine powder burns *very* rapidly and can raise pressures into the danger zone if the *improper granulation* is used in an otherwise safe load. Some people say you cannot overload a gun with blackpowder. Not true.

Commercial blackpowder is mixed then ground in a wet state to prevent an explosion. It is pressed into a cake then granulated and sifted through screens to determine grain size. The grains are coated with graphite for ease in pouring. It is sold in four granulations: FFFFg for priming flintlocks; FFFg for handguns and rifles to 40-caliber; FFg for rifles above 40- to 58-caliber; and Fg for rifles over 58-caliber and large bore shotguns.

Blackpowder has many deficiencies. It produces a great deal of smoke and solid fouling when burned. Better than half the residue is in solid form. While most of this is blown out of the barrel, a heavy, often hard-crusted fouling is produced which will soon degrade accuracy and raise pressures unless the bore is cleaned. Blackpowder target shooters often swab their barrels after every shot to maintain top accuracy. The fouling from blackpowder is corrosive mainly because it contains sulfuric acid. The other components are hygroscopic, which means they draw and hold water from the atmosphere—the better to rust your gun.

Because of these and other drawbacks, blackpowder was replaced by smokeless powder about a hundred years ago. With the exception of The Old Western Scrounger, no manufacturer

in this country offers loaded blackpowder ammunition. Interest in shooting both muzzle-loading and blackpowder cartridge guns is increasing. For this reason, there have been efforts to develop a blackpowder substitute that will work well in the old guns and their modern replicas that will give the same performance, without the problems.

Throughout the 19th century, dozens if not hundreds of blackpowder substitutes were made and sold. Their sterling qualities are evident in the fact that none are around today. Two substitutes presently on the market are Pyrodex and Black Canyon Powder.

Pyrodex is an improved version of blackpowder. The burning has been made more complete through the addition of perchlorate. Pyrodex is less dense than blackpowder. With better combustion, there is less fouling and this fouling is softer and easier to remove. Pyrodex, however, is corrosive and the fouling should be removed promptly.

Black Canyon Powder is a mixture of potassium nitrate, charcoal and ascorbic acid (vitamin C). This undoubtedly makes it the most nutritious product of its kind. Black Canyon produces smoke, but little odor and very little fouling. It is non-corrosive. It is less powerful than blackpowder and will only work properly if heavily compressed in the case. I have found this product to give very uneven velocities and pressures and thus poor accuracy. An earlier version of this type of powder was sold under the name of Golden Powder.

The latest variant is ARCO's Black Mag powder, which is ascorbic acid based. It is non-corrosive and cool burning, while generating good velocities at low pressures. Some formulations contain perchlorate. Black Mag is the brain child of Anthony Cioffe, who describes himself as a "seat-of-the-pants chemist." Because the burning characteristics can be varied, the formula

FFg blackpowder is a fairly coarse-grained propellant. The scale above is 1 inch divided into hundredths.

Hodgdon's Pyrodex is an improved form of blackpowder with cleaner burning characteristics.

has found favor with NASA as a rocket propellant. It appears to be the best, according to early testfire reports.

Blackpowder guns were intended for blackpowder, although some of the later, stronger ones will function well with reduced charges of smokeless powder. No muzzleloader, however, should *ever* be loaded with any smokeless powder.

Blackpowder and its variants do not present any unusual problems in storage. They should be kept cool and dry since they are hygroscopic. Never leave powder containers open for any length of time since this will allow moisture to enter. Never shake any can of powder. This tends to break down the granules and alter the burning characteristics. *Never* have any powder near an open flame or burning cigarette, cigar, or pipe. One spark in the can and you have a very sudden very hot fire. Always

keep powder in the original container. Since blackpowder is a mixture of basic elements its life span is indefinite. Unexploded cannon shells filled with blackpowder fired during the siege of Québec in 1759-60, detonated with considerable vigor in the early 1970s after they were discovered during construction.

Reloaders have long made their own "version" of improved blackpowder ammunition by loading a small ignition charge of smokeless powder, and then filling the rest of the case with blackpowder. Known as "duplex loading," this system produces less fouling since the smokeless powder burns up much of the blackpowder fouling. It sounds great, but all of the loading data on duplex loads is anecdotal—not tested in any laboratory and substitutions of one type of smokeless powder for another can have unknown effects. Plenty of blackpowder

The Old Western Scrounger is the only source of new, factory-made blackpowder ammunition. This lets the history buffs replicate original loads in original guns.

Black Canyon Powder is an attempt to make a completely noncorrosive propellant for use in blackpowder guns.

guns have been blown up with duplex loads, or what the shooter thought was a duplex load but perhaps he reversed the proportions of black and smokeless. Or, he forgot to put in any black at all and filled the case with smokeless! Who knows? The list of duplex victims includes some very experienced reloaders. In all good conscience, I cannot and do not recommend this practice.

Smokeless Powder

Development of smokeless powder began in the mid-19th century, with the first really successful type being that developed by Austrian chemist Frederick Volkmann in about 1871. It was made by dissolving wood fiber in nitric acid which was later washed in water to remove the acid, then gelatinized in an ether-alcohol mixture to form a plastic colloid, now known as nitrocellulose. The powder was marketed locally and the Austrian government, in its wisdom, stuck with blackpowder and shut the operation down for not paying proper license fees.

The defining moment in the evolution of smokeless powder came some fifteen years later when the French government switched from a blackpowder single shot rifle to a high-velocity, 8mm repeater called the Lebel. The small-bore cartridge used a smokeless powder similar to that developed by the French chemist Paul Vieille. Within about two years all of Europe had abandoned blackpowder for military rifles, and every government armed its troops with repeaters using jacketed bullets and smokeless powder. The United States was the last major power to switch to a smokeless powder repeater, when it (reluctantly) gave up the 45-70 Springfield in 1892.

Early smokeless powders were hygroscopic and if the acid was not completely washed out would deteriorate. Coatings were later added to make the powder more water resistant and control burning. The power of smokeless powder was further enhanced by the addition of nitroglycerin. These two types of powder—nitrocellulose and nitrocellulose plus nitroglycerin—are the two basic types manufactured today. They are known respectively as single-base and double-base powders. All smokeless powders are coated with graphite to keep them from caking, allowing them to flow smoothly through powder measures, dippers and funnels.

The outstanding characteristic of smokeless powder is that while it is of two basic types, by changing the size and shape of the granulation the burning characteristics can be varied considerably and controlled to a high degree. This gives smokeless

The chore of blackpowder cleanup has been reduced with the introduction of new cleaners and treated patches.

a tremendous advantage over blackpowder, whose burning characteristics could be only roughly controlled.

Smokeless powder varies in granule size from flakes as fine as ground pepper—used in fast-burning pistol powders—to finger-size cylinders nearly two inches long for huge naval guns. The burning can be further altered by extruding powder into macaroni-like tubes, allowing them to burn on both the outside and inside at the same time. Spherical forms can be varied to exact size, while adding various chemical coatings can control the burn rate.

Selecting the Right Powder

Modern powders are divided into three basic types on the basis of their use. These are pistol, shotgun, and rifle powders. Pistol powders are generally of the fast-burning double-base type for use in short-barreled guns. Shotgun powders are also fast burning and double-base, designed to burn completely under low pressures. Rifle powders are generally slower burning to accelerate a rifle bullet down a long barrel with maximum velocity while producing minimum pressures.

In point of fact, many powders for pistol use are quite suitable for shotguns and vice versa. Some slower burning pistol and shotgun powders will also work well for reduced velocity rifle loadings, where a light bullet and light powder charge are used.

Before buying a quantity of powder, it is a good idea to consult one or more reloading guides to see what is offered and what looks to be the best selection for your particular gun or guns. Then, buy a small can to develop your loads. If that powder proves suitable for your uses, it's a good idea to go ahead and buy larger amounts.

Storage and Handling

Modern powders are almost completely gelatinized, making them less affected by dampness. In fact, a sample of Laflin & Rand (later Hercules, now Alliant) Unique powder was placed in storage under water in 1899 to test its viability. It was last tested in 1996. It will be tested again in the next century when it is expected to continue performing as well as when it was made.

As smokeless powders deteriorate, they generate small amounts of nitric acid. Stabilizers are added to these powders to absorb acid byproduct. Most powders have fifty or more years of life before the stabilizers are used up and nitric acid begins to leach out of the nitrocellulose, leaving plain cellulose and reducing the efficiency of the powder. Occasionally powder will deteriorate owing to acid residue that was not properly washed out in the manufacturing process. Such powder will take on an unpleasant acidic smell and a brown dust looking very like rust will appear in the powder. Powder in this condition will not shoot well, giving poor ignition and low power. It should be disposed of. Metal cans containing powder will sometimes rust on the interior, producing a very similar appearing dust, but without the characteristic odor. This does not harm the powder and can be removed by dumping the powder on a flat piece of bed sheet, spreading it evenly, and gently blowing off the dust. The powder should then be placed in another con-

Leaving a powder measure open allows volatiles to escape and dirt to enter. Keep it capped! Never leave powder in a measure after loading or you may find yourself guessing what kind it is.

tainer. An empty plastic powder bottle is good so long as it is *clearly marked* as to what it is. It is a good idea to mark containers of powder with the date of purchase and then use the oldest first. Opened containers of powder should be checked at least every year for signs of rust or deterioration if they are not being used. Sealed containers should be left sealed until they are to be used. Alcohols and occasionally camphor are added to stabilize burning characteristics. Powder containers should be kept tightly closed to keep these volatile additives from evaporating into the air.

Smokeless powder is quite safe to handle because it is not sensitive to shock. The main caution that must be taken is to keep it from open flame or heat. It will ignite above 400 degrees F. Shelf storage is suitable, preferably on a second floor where temperatures remain most stable. Powder should *never* be stored in heavy closed metal containers which could act as bombs in case of a fire. Never have more than one container of powder open at a time. If there is a fire this hopefully limits it to one can.

Smokeless powder is toxic if ingested because the nitroglycerin component causes heart irregularity. British soldiers in WWI chewed smokeless powder from rifle cartridges to cause a brief though severe illness to get off the line, until medical authorities discovered this practice. Children have a tendency to taste things; smokeless powder should not be one of them.

Compressed loads should be approached with extreme caution for obvious reasons.

Loading Density

Various combinations of bullets and powder charges can be assembled to achieve the same velocity. Some are going to be more accurate than others. Various manuals will often indicate loads that gave the best accuracy in particular guns. This is usually the best place to start developing a load, although such a combination will not necessarily be the best performer in *your* gun.

Generally speaking, when selecting a powder there are a few rules of thumb worth following. Larger-capacity rifle cartridges, with heavy bullets, generally perform best with slow-burning powders. For best accuracy, a powder charge that fills the case with little or no air space tends to give better accuracy than a small charge that can shift position in the case. Shooters using reduced loads, particularly in rifles, get better results by tipping the barrel skyward before each shot to position the powder to the rear of the case. This can also be achieved by using wads or wads plus fillers to fill up the space, but the results are usually not as good. A filler wad should *never* be placed over the powder with an air space between it and the bullet. The space must be filled entirely. If there is a space, the wad will come slamming against the base of the bullet with enough force to make a bulged ring in the case and often in the chamber of the gun!

Compressed Loads

Never compress powder in a cartridge case unless such a load is recommended in a reloading manual. Compressed loads should never be more than 10 percent above the case capacity. A compression of more than this often leads to lower than desired velocities. If the compression is excessive it can actually bulge the case or cause the case to stretch in the loading process, resulting in a cartridge that is oversize or too long and will jam the gun.

Available Powders

As of this writing, smokeless powders are available from six manufacturers or importers. These include: IMR Powder Co. (formerly DuPont); Olin/Winchester; Alliant Powder Co. (formerly Hercules); Hodgdon Powder Co.; Accurate Powder Co.; and VihtaVuori Oy.

IMR

IMR makes both single- and double-base powders of the flake type and cylinder type for a wide variety of uses.

Hi-SKOR 700-X— This is a double-base flake powder primarily designed for shotshells, but works well in many target and light handgun loadings.

HI-SKOR 800-X— This is a double-base shotgun powder for heavy shotshell loads. It is also applicable to some handgun loadings.

PB— PB is a porous base, flake powder of the single-base type. It is used for many shotshell loads and in a number of handgun cartridges. PB works well in cast bullet loads.

SR 7625— Although it carries the sporting rifle designation, its main use is for shotshell and handgun cartridges. It works well with a number of cast bullet rifle loadings. It is the fastest burning of the SR series of powders.

SR 4756— A slightly slower burning single-base powder. It works well in some rifle cartridges, with cast bullets. The main use of this powder is in shotshells and a number of handgun loads.

SR 4759— This is the slowest burning powder in this series. It is a cylinder powder rather than a flake type, as are the other SR powders. SR 4759 has a very good reputation with cast-bullet shooters, working well in cases as large as the 45-70. Once withdrawn, it is back by popular demand and will hopefully stay with us.

IMR 4227— IMR stands for Improved Military Rifle. This is the fastest burning in the series. Like all the IMR series, this is a single-base powder of a cylinder type. It works well in small rifle cases such as the 22 Hornet, the 223 Remington, and even in big ones such as the 458 Winchester. It works well in heavy handgun loads and can be used in the 410 shotgun.

IMR 4198— This powder is slightly slower burning, but works very well in small to medium-capacity cases such as the 22 Hornet and 222 and 223, where it is prized for varmint and bench-rest shooting. It works well in large cases including the 444 Marlin and even the 45-70.

IMR 3031— A favorite for the 30-30 and similar medium-capacity cases with jacketed bullets, 3031 is one of the most versatile on the market. It gives good results in cartridges as small as the 17 Remington and as large as the 458 Winchester.

IMR 4064— Very similar to IMR 3031, 4064 has great versatility in the 30-caliber range, performing well in the 30-06 and 308. It also works well in many of the larger rifle calibers.

IMR 4895— This medium-slow burning powder is very similar to the Hodgdon powder of the same number. It is an excellent performer in the 30-06, but works well in slightly reduced loads with cast bullets in rifles such as the 45-70. Excellent accuracy is produced in the 223 with this powder in bolt-action rifles.

IMR 4320— Originally used as a propellent for military match ammunition, it is relatively slow burning and will produce good velocities with less recoil than the faster-burning types. It is applicable to cartridges from 22 to 458.

IMR 4350— This is a slow burning powder intended for large capacity cases. Its bulk fills these cases well. A favorite for the 7x57 Mauser, 30-06, 243 and 270 Winchester, 4350 is an excellent maximum load for long range work.

IMR 4831— Introduced in 1971, this powder carries the same number as the Hodgdon H4831, but it is *not* an equivalent. IMR 4831 is faster burning than the Hodgdon product! IMR 4831 is intended for magnum rifle cartridges, although it works very well in the 270 Winchester.

IMR 7828— This is the slowest burning in the IMR series. It is designed for the 50 Browning, and large magnum rifle cartridges including the 300 and 338 magnums. It will work well in a number of African big game cartridges. IMR 7828 is intended for pushing large, heavy bullets at high velocities, without raising chamber pressures into the danger zone.

Winchester

Winchester makes double-base powders in a spherical configuration. This "ball" powder achieves controlled burning and cooler temperatures by the use of additives. The ball shape makes it flow easily through mechanical powder measures.

231— The fastest burning of the Winchester powders, it is for handguns and is best used for light to medium target loads. It produces excellent accuracy in 9mm, 38 Special and 45 ACP loadings.

296— This is a pistol powder with a fine granulation. It is most useful in large-bore handguns such as the 357 and 44 Magnums. It will also work well in 410-bore shotshell loadings.

Action Pistol—WAP duplicates factory loadings in 38 Super Auto, 9mm and 40 S&W. This powder, new in 1994, offers lower flame temperature and lower recoil for rapid-fire shooting.

Super Lite— WSL is intended for light target loads in handguns. It works well in 9mm and 38 Special cartridges.

Super Target— WST is a shotshell propellent for Skeet and trap shooting. Its burning characteristics make it useful for 38 Special and 45 ACP as well.

Super Field— WSF is a shotshell powder. It works well in 12-gauge and is the powder of choice for 20-gauge. WSF is also applicable for use in 9mm, 40 S&W and 38 Super Auto handloads.

Super Field WAAP— This is the newest powder in the AA+ line. It is the cleanest burning, lowest charge-weight powder in the line. It is designed specifically for loading target shotshells and is used in most factory AA loads.

540— This is a versatile powder for nearly all shotshell loading where long range is desired. Winchester 540 will also work well in 38 Super Auto, 9mm, 10mm, and 40 S&W loadings.

748— Used in military loadings for the 223 (5.56mm) rifle, this powder offers low flame temperature for increased barrel life. It is suitable for a great variety of centerfire rifle loadings in 22- through 30-caliber.

760— This powder duplicates Winchester factory ballistics for the 30-06. It works well in many 30-caliber rifle loadings.

Winchester Magnum Rifle— WMR was introduced in 1994 for high power and magnum rifles. Good results have been achieved in the 243, 257, 270, 280 Remington, and 338 Winchester Magnum.

Alliant

These were formerly made under the Hercules trademark and before that Laflin & Rand. Alliant currently offers fourteen double-base powders.

Winchester has replaced metal powder cans with its new plastic packaging, which keeps volatiles in and moisture out of the powder inside.

Bullseye— A longtime favorite of pistol shooters, this flake powder works well in cases as small as the 25 ACP and as large as the 44 Magnum and 45 Colt. It is a very fast burning powder.

Red Dot— Red Dot is a flake shotshell powder that also will work well in light and medium pressure handgun loads. Some shooters have gotten good results with light cast-bullet rifle loadings as well.

American Select— Alliant's newest powder, American Select is a clean-burning shotshell powder with a burn rate between Red Dot and Green Dot. Its main use is for 12-gauge target loads, but it will work well in a variety of handgun loads.

Green Dot— This flake shotshell powder burns slightly slower than Red Dot and has an equal variety of applications.

Unique— This is a flake powder with a great number of uses. It works well in many handgun loads and is considered one of the most accurate in 44 Magnum and 45 Colt. It is well adapted to cartridges as small as the 25 ACP. It performs equally well in many shotshell loads.

Power Pistol— As the name implies, this powder is for handguns. The primary use is for high performance loads in the 9mm, 10mm and 40 S&W. It will make good medium velocity loads for the 380, 38 Special and the 45 ACP.

Herco— This is a moderately slow burning shotshell powder with application to handgun loads. The granulation is coarse and it is best for magnum loads.

Blue Dot— This is a very slow burning shotshell powder that also works well in magnum handgun cartridges.

2400—A finely granulated powder, 2400 works well in small rifle cases such as the 22 Hornet and similar varmint cartridges. One of the older powders in the line, it is still popular for magnum pistol loads in 357, 41 and 44. It produces good accuracy in reduced cast rifle bullet loadings. Care, however, must be taken not to overload, since this is a powerful powder that takes up very little space in large cases.

Reloder 7— This is the fastest burning of the Reloder series. It works well in medium-capacity rifle cases of the varmint class, on up to the 458 Winchester Magnum, in which it delivers excellent accuracy with heavy bullets. Reloder 7 has been a favorite with benchrest shooters for its accuracy in the 222.

Reloder 12— A cylindrical powder that burns slightly slower than Reloder 7, Reloder 12 has a wide range of applications in medium-size rifle cases.

Reloder 15— Similar to Reloder 12, Reloder 15 is slightly slower burning. It works well in a wide range of rifle cases from the 223 to magnums of the 458 and 416 Rigby size. It is generally used for heavy loadings.

Reloder 19— Reloder 19 is a slow-burning powder that works in heavy varmint cases such as the 22-250 where it yields the highest velocities. It does well in 30-caliber cases, including the magnums.

Reloder 22— This is the slowest powder in the Reloder series. It is intended for large-capacity magnum rifle cases, although some shooters have obtained good results with this powder in the 220 Swift.

Hodgdon

Hodgdon originally packaged surplus military powder and some of this may still be around. If a load is developed with one of the surplus types, and if the newly manufactured type is later substituted, the loading should redeveloped as burning characteristics will be altered. Check the container for identification regarding new and surplus powder. All Hodgdon powders are of the double-base type unless otherwise indicated.

HP-38— This a spherical powder manufactured by Olin for Hodgdon. It is fast burning and is similar to Winchester 231, but loading data should not be substituted. As the name indicates, it was developed as a propellent for the 38 Special. It works well in a variety of medium-size pistol cartridges, producing fine accuracy.

Clays— This is a new shotshell powder that's mainly used for light target loads.

Universal Clays— This is a flake shotshell powder with burning characteristics similar to Unique. The granulation is slightly finer. Universal Clays works very well in a variety of handgun cartridges.

International Clays—This is an improved form of the Clays formula. It yields reduced recoil in 12- and 20-gauge target loads.

HS-6— This spherical powder is good for heavy shotshell loads, and works well in handgun loads in medium and large calibers when high velocities are desired.

HS-7— Faster burning than HS-6, this powder is intended primarily for magnum shotshell loads. It will perform well in large-case magnum handgun cartridges such as the 357, 41 and 44.

H110— This spherical powder was developed for the 30 M-1 Carbine cartridge. It works very well in medium and large handgun cartridges. It is particularly good in magnum handgun cartridges where it will duplicate factory performance in these calibers.

H4227— This is a single-base powder duplicating the performance of the IMR powder of the same name. It gives excellent results in small and medium rifle cases, and does equally well in magnum handgun cartridges.

H4198— Another single-base powder that duplicates the IMR product of the same number. It produces fine accuracy in the 223 and similar small to medium rifle cases.

H322— This single-base powder has found favor with benchrest shooters using the 222 and 6mm Remington BR. It works well in a variety of 30-calibers and even in straight-walled cases as large as the 45-70.

H4895— Hodgdon's version of the IMR powder. The single-base 4895 is one of the most versatile rifle powders around. It produces fine performance in calibers from the 17 Remington to the 458 Winchester Magnum. It works very well in reduced loadings, burning evenly for charges as light as 60 percent of the maximum.

H335— This is a double-base spherical powder that produces good shooting in 22- and 30-caliber cases.

BL-C(2)— This spherical powder known as "ball C lot 2" gives excellent accuracy in the 222 and 223, and was often used for benchrest and competition shooting. It began as a surplus powder but is now newly manufactured.

Varget— A small-grain extruded powder, Varget is known for its insensitivity to heat and cold, which makes it a good choice for year-round hunting. Easy ignition and clean burning help produce excellent accuracy and high velocities. Fine

Alliant's (formerly Hercules) Unique powder is a powerful, fast-burning double-base propellant used in pistol and light rifle loads. It is a fine, flake powder which has been made for nearly a century.

IMR 3031 powder is an extruded single-base propellant made of nitrocellulose. It has a fairly slow burning rate and has long been a standard for military rifle cartridges.

results have been obtained in the 22-250, 308, 30-06 and 375 H&H Magnum.

H380— This is a double-base powder, but slow burning—in the class of IMR 4320. It performs well in 30-caliber cases, but does well in large capacity varmint rounds such as the 22-250.

H414— This works well in the 30-06 and similar 30s, particularly with lighter bullets where higher velocities are desired.

H4350— This single-base powder carries the same designation as the IMR powder, although the Hodgdon version is slightly slower burning. Like the IMR powder, it is intended for large-capacity, magnum-rifle cartridges.

H4831— This was originally a military surplus powder, but is now newly manufactured. It is a single-base, extruded powder and gives the best accuracy with heavy bullets in 30-calibers and larger, though it is excellent in the 270. It carries the same number designation as IMR 4831, but the burning characteristics are *not* the same.

H4831SC— This is the same powder as H4831, but has a shorter grain. The SC stands for "short cut." The finer granulation makes this powder flow more evenly through powder measures.

H1000— This is a very slow burning single-base powder. It is another that works well with heavy-bullet loads in large-capacity cases.

H50BMG—As the name implies, this is for loading the 50 Browning Machine Gun cartridge. The burn rate is very stable in a wide range of temperatures.

H870— This is the slowest burning powder made by Hodgdon. Its use is limited to very large capacity cases such as the 50 BMG and a few of the large magnums for African big game use.

Pyrodex— This is a blackpowder substitute that offers cleaner burning characteristics and slightly less density. (See Blackpowder chapter).

Accurate Arms

Accurate Arms imports powders from abroad, mainly the Czech Republic. It offers a line of powders primarily for rifle and handgun use.

Nitro 100— This is a double-base flake powder for 12-gauge target loads. It works well in the 45 Colt and other medium to large handgun cartridges.

No. 2— This is a fast burning double-base ball powder for use in the 38 Special and similar medium capacity handguns. It does well in light and target loadings. It is similar to Bullseye.

No. 5— This is another double-base ball powder, slightly slower burning and comparable the Unique. It gives good results in a wide variety of medium to large handgun cases.

No. 7— A double-base powder intended for 9mm Luger and similar medium to large capacity pistol rounds. It is clean burning and gives good accuracy at target velocities.

No. 9— No. 9 is a double-base ball powder and considered one of the best for the 44 Magnum. It works very well in the 41 and 357 Magnums as well. Good results have been obtained in the 22 Hornet and the 30 Carbine. It will also work well in the 410 shotgun.

1680— This double-base ball powder was designed specifically for the 7.62x39mm Russian cartridge. It is fast burning and delivers high velocities in the 22 Hornet. Beyond these two, its use is rather limited.

XMR2015BR— A small-grain extruded powder of the single-base type with many uses. It performs very well in small to medium rifle cases producing excellent accuracy in many 22 centerfires. The 6mm PPC and 7mm Remington have produced excellent groups with this powder. It also does well in straight-walled rifle cases.

2230— A double-base ball powder with a fairly rapid burn,

IMR 4320 is a slow-burning single-base rifle powder for use in large-bore and high-powered rifles. The extruded grains are of a "short cut" size.

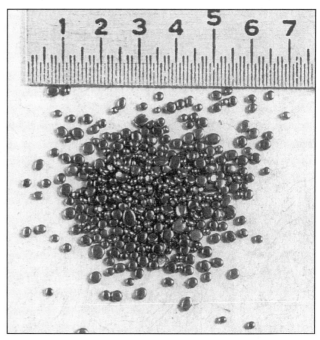

Hodgdon's BL-C(2) is a spherical powder. It's a fast burning double-base powder with a well deserved reputation for flowing very smoothly through powder measures.

2230 does well in the 223 and similar medium-capacity cases.

2460— This double-base ball powder is slower burning than 2230, which extends its use from medium-capacity 22 centerfire calibers to the 308 and 30-06.

XMP5744— Formerly a surplus powder, this double-base powder is again available. It has a burn rate between No. 9 and

1680. It works well in pistol cases such as the 6mm TCU, 357 Magnum, 38-40, 41 Magnum, 44 Special, 44-40, 44 Magnum and 45 Colt. In rifles, it performs well in the 22 Hornet, 222, 25-20, 30 Carbine, 30-30, 308 and 30-06.

Data Powder 2200— This is a surplus powder from Europe. It is a flattened ball powder and is intended primarily for the 7.62x39mm cartridge, but will produce good accuracy in the 223, 22 Hornet, 221 Remington, 30-30 and 35 Remington, even the 458 Magnum.

XMR2495— Formerly known as 2495BR, this has very similar burning characteristics to IMR 4895 and H4895. It is a single-base extruded powder with great flexibility and gives excellent accuracy in 22 centerfires through the 30-caliber class. Accurate's XMR2495 works well with cast bullets and produces the best accuracy in the 45-70 with cast bullets. Reduced loadings as small as 60 percent of maximum produce consistent groups.

2520— A ball powder with a medium-slow burning rate, 2520 gives excellent results in many medium capacity rifle cases. Fine accuracy is obtained in the 308 and 30-06. Its pressure curve makes it suitable for use in autoloaders.

2700— Accurate's latest ball powder, 2700 is designed for use with heavy bullets in the belted magnum class of rifle cartridge. It works well in the 17 Remington, 220 Swift and 22-250—notable exceptions to the rule.

XMR4350— This powder is equivalent to IMR 4350 and H4350. It has the same applications.

XMR3100— This is a single-base extruded powder for use in medium-capacity cases. It delivers fine performance in the 243 and 7mm Remington Magnum. The burning rate is between IMR 4831 and H4831. It works well with heavy-bullet loadings.

8700— This is the slowest burning powder in the Accurate line. It is a double-base ball powder well suited to use in medium- to large-capacity cases. Good results are obtained in the

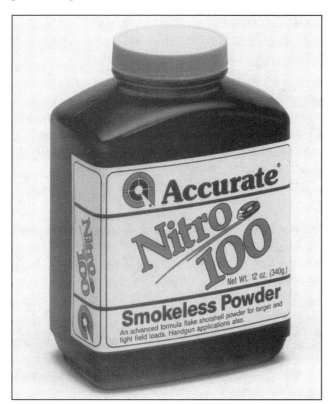

Accurate Arms' Nitro 100 is a double-base flake powder best used in shotgun target shooting. It has pistol applications as well.

264 Winchester Magnum, 270 Winchester, 7mm Remington Magnum, and the Weatherby 257, 270 and 300 Magnums. Good results are obtained with cast bullets, though a magnum primer is needed for consistent burning.

Accurate bought out, and is the source for, the remaining Scot powders, formerly supplied by Scot Powder of McArthur, Ohio.

Solo 1000— This fast-burning, double-base flake powder is for shotgun use. It is similar to Bullseye and has some handgun applications.

Solo 1250— This medium- to fast-burning shotgun powder is primarily for use in 12-gauge hunting loads as well as trap and Skeet loads for the 20- and 28-gauge. It is similar to Unique and has pistol applications for medium-capacity cases such as 9mm and 40 S&W.

4100— This powder is very similar to Accurate No. 9. It is slightly slower burning and is designed especially for the 410-bore 2¹/₂-inch, ¹/₂-ounce Skeet load. It can be used for pistols using No. 9 data with a magnum primer.

Nitro 100— This Accurate Arms powder will be sold under the Scot label.

VihtaVuori

VihtaVuori powder is made in Finland and imported by Kaltron Pettibone. As of this writing, VihtaVuori makes twenty-two powders both single- and double-base for rifle and pistol use.

N110— This is a fast burning powder in the class of Alliant 2400, Winchester 296 and Hodgdon H110. It works well in the 22 Hornet and other small- to medium-case 22 centerfires. It serves well in the 357 and 44 Magnums and 45 Winchester Magnum.

N120— Similar to IMR 4227, N120 is designed to work well in the 22 centerfire class of rifle cartridges. Its application beyond this, however, is limited, though good results have been obtained in the 7.62x39mm Russian.

VihtaVuori Oy's N350 is a slow pistol powder for medium to large calibers. It is also suitable for shotshells.

N130— This powder burns faster than N120. It has applications in 22 centerfires, such as the 223, and medium-capacity cases in the 25- to 27-caliber range.

N133— The burning rate of this powder is close to IMR 4198. It works well in the 222 and 223, and good results have been obtained in the 45-70.

N135— This powder burns with moderate speed, similar to IMR and Hodgdon 4895. It is a versatile powder with applications from the 17 Remington to the 458 Winchester.

N140— A relatively slow burning powder, N140 can be used in place of IMR 4320, Alliant Reloder 15 and Hodgdon H380. Best results are in 30- to 35-caliber rifle cases.

N150— This powder has a slow burn rate similar to IMR 4350. It works well in 30-caliber and up.

N160— This is another slow burning powder designed mainly for magnum rifles. It works well with light-bullet loads and with heavy bullets in the 30-06. Good results have been obtained in the 220 Swift, 243, 25-06, 264 and 7mm Remington Magnum.

N165— Slightly slower than N160, this powder is for heavy-bullet loads in the 30-06 and magnums in the 30-caliber range and up.

N170— The slowest burning powder in this series, N170 is suitable for large-capacity cases only.

24N41— This powder is especially designed for the 50 BMG. This is a single-base powder like the N100 series, but the grain size is larger and burning rate slower.

20N29— Another 50 BMG powder. This one burns slightly slower than 24N41.

N540— This is a double-base powder with a burning rate much like N140. It is designed for the 308 Winchester.

N550— Another double-base powder with a burning rate like N150, but designed especially for the 308 and 30-06.

N560— The burning rate of this powder is like N160, but it is designed for the 270 Winchester and the 6.5x55 Swedish Mauser.

N310— This pistol powder is comparable to Bullseye. Its fast burning rate lends itself to use in the 25 ACP on up to the 44 Magnum, where it proves excellent for light target loads.

N320— Suitable for shotshells and mid-range handgun loads, N320 works well in cartridges in the 38- to 45-caliber class.

N330— The burning rate of this powder is similar to Green Dot. It performs well in pistol cartridges from 38 to 45.

N340— This powder has a slightly slower burning rate and is similar to Winchester 540 or Herco. Good results are obtained in medium to large handgun calibers.

N350— This is the slowest pistol powder in the N300 series, and it lends itself to use in shotshells. In this regard, it is about like Blue Dot. Use in handguns is limited to medium to large calibers like 9mm to 45 ACP.

3N37— This is not really an N300 series powder. It is used in high velocity rimfire loads and shotshells. The burning rate is between N340 and N350. Good results have been obtained in 9mm, 38 Super Auto, 38 Special and the 45 ACP. Similar results have been achieved with the 357 and 44 Magnums.

N105— Super Magnum. This is a special powder with a burning rate between N350 and N110. It was developed for heavy-bullet loads and large capacity cases. Best results have been in magnums in the 357 to 45 class.

Bullets

With so many projectiles available in so many shapes and sizes, how do you find the one that's best? It depends what you're looking for.

BUYING BULLETS FOR reloading is a fairly simple process. Most of today's guns are standardized in terms of bore diameter and rifling characteristics. If you deal with a knowledgeable dealer, a simple request for "some hunting bullets for my 30-30" will probably get you what you want. Unfortunately, there are dealers who are not very knowledgeable and even some who are mainly interested in unloading what they have in stock. Caveat emptor is still the safest position to take.

This section refers to getting the "best" bullet. The first thing you should have in mind when you go to buy bullets is a clear idea of what "best" means for your intended use. For any gun the first consideration should be accuracy. Whether it's for target or game, an inaccurate bullet is worthless. The easiest rule of thumb when it comes to buying bullets is to get what duplicates the factory loading. If you want ammunition for special purposes, which most handloaders eventually will, then you will have to do a little research, such as reading this book. Old guns and those of foreign extraction can often be confusing in

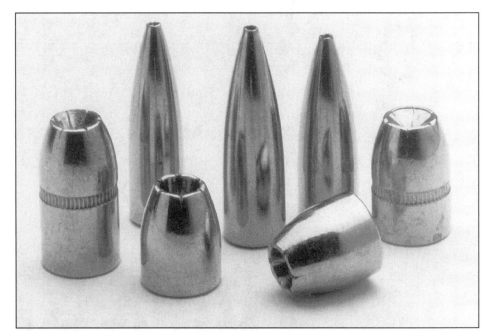

The "best" bullet for your gun is the one that shoots accurately and otherwise does what you want it to do.

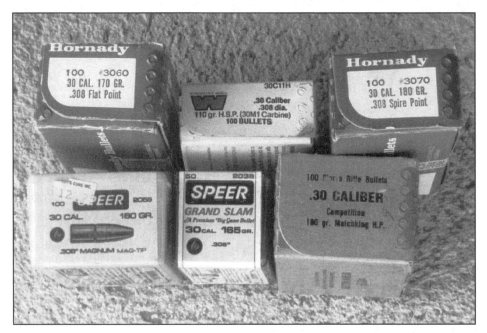

Bullets are packed 100 to a sturdy box, with the diameter, weight and style of bullet—flatpoint, hollowpoint, etc.—marked on the box.

regard to what their bore and groove size actually is. The best information collected over the past century indicates that the most accurate bullet is the one that exactly fits the groove diameter of the barrel. In the final analysis, this is determined by slugging the bore of your gun and measuring the slug with a micrometer or Vernier caliper and getting bullets that fit.

Proper diameter bullets can most easily be determined by reading the information on the box they come in or by measurement, if you are buying bullets in a plastic bag from someone you don't know. This can be a little confusing. For instance, 22-caliber bullets for the early 22 Hornet rifles were properly .223-inch diameter. The modern ones are .224-inch. The 223 Remington (5.56mm) is .224-inch diameter, not .223-inch! Good loading manuals usually give warnings regarding groove diameters for foreign and early rifles, especially if there is a considerable variation in these within a particular type of rifle.

My Lyman manual indicates that groove diameters on the 303 British military rifles vary from .309 to .317-inch. Put too fat a bullet in one of the tight bores along with plenty of powder and you can create a dangerous pressure situation, in addition to inaccurate shooting. The 303 Enfield, if loaded properly, is a fine, accurate rifle, capable of turning in some excellent groups.

Bullet Length, Rifling Characteristics

Beyond the question of bullet diameter, there is the matter of bullet length and the relationship of length to the rifling twist and how this affects accuracy. Bullets aren't identified by length, but by weight when they are sold. All other things being equal, heavier bullets of a given diameter are longer. One way to find out which bullets will work best in your gun is trial and error. Another is to limit yourself to the recommendations in loading manuals. These are only guidelines for performance for the caliber of your gun, and may or may not be satisfactory to you. Beyond this there are also some basic calculations which may save you a lot of time and expense on bullets that don't work. Therefore, a second fact you should know about your gun, beyond its groove diameter, is the rate of the rifling twist. This can be found in loading manuals for a great many standard guns, certainly for the test guns used to prepare the data. This figure will be expressed, for example, as "Twist 1:10"." This indicates that the rifling spiral makes one complete turn in 10 inches. Different lengths of bullets require different rifling twists to shoot to their best advantage. If the match between bullet length and rifling is too far off, bullets may fail to stabilize and tumble in flight. On the other hand, they can be so over-stabilized they will actually break apart in flight.

If there is any doubt about the twist rate of your gun, determining this is simplicity itself, at least with a rifle-length barrel.

(Above) Good shooting *only* comes when you have the correct diameter and weight.

With handguns, you will have to interpolate as best you can. Stand the rifle against a plain vertical surface such as a wall or door. Place a tight cleaning patch on your cleaning rod, but use a rod that does not have a ball bearing in the handle. Once the patch is just started down bore, mark the handle and beside it make a mark on the vertical wall or door. Push the rod down the barrel, allowing the handle to turn freely. Make a second mark at the point where the handle has made one complete rotation. Measure the distance between the top and bottom marks and you know the twist rate to a very close degree. There will always be a slight amount of slippage, but this shouldn't affect your calculations.

As a rule of thumb, longer bullets of a given caliber require a faster twist to stabilize them to the point where they shoot more accurately than shorter bullets. This is true without regard to weight or velocity. The familiar 22 Long Rifle shoots best in a 1:16-inch twist barrel. This holds true for 40-grain target loads as well as 30-grain hyper-velocity hollowpoint hunting bullets. These are always made to be close to the 40-grain LR bullet's length. The stubby, 30-grain 22 Short does best in a 1:20-inch twist barrel. It will stabilize in a 1:16 barrel, but accuracy is not good. Rifles marked "22 Short, Long, or Long Rifle" are actually rifled for the Long Rifle, or occasionally with a compromise twist of 1:17 inches. This may slightly improve the accuracy of the Short, without adversely affecting the accuracy of the Long Rifle.

Once you know the twist of your gun, you can calculate which bullets will likely perform best and save money by not buying those that won't. There are some elaborate computer programs to do this, but there is a very simple method that works with a pocket calculator or even paper and pencil: the Greenhill Formula. The Formula for determining twist rates was the work of Sir Alfred George Greenhill, a mathematics professor at Cambridge University who later served as an instructor at the Woolrich Military Academy from 1876 to 1906. Greenhill discovered that the optimum twist rate for a

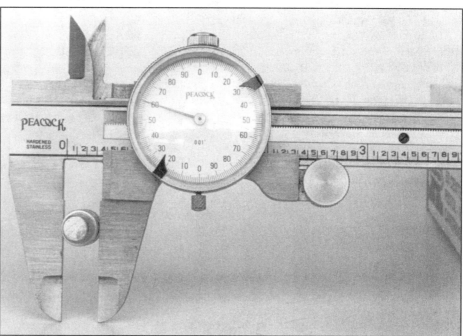

If you have any doubt about the caliber of bullets you are buying, check them with an accurate caliper and/or micrometer.

bullet is determined by dividing 150 by the length of the bullet in calibers (hundredths of an inch) and then dividing again by its diameter. The number 150 is a good choice since it allows a useful margin in the calculations. Most twist rates that are close to the formulated ideal will usually work well. The beauty of this formula is that it works very well for lead or jacketed bullets. Weight does not appear to be that critical a factor. Shape and design do not seem to have that much effect either, up to velocities of 2200 fps and, to a degree, above this. To compensate for increased rotational speed at velocities over 3000 fps, some authorities recommend a slightly reduced twist rate. Although velocity does not appear to be considered within this formula, it is included in the rotation segment in a concealed form. Assume a 1:12-inch barrel firing a bullet at 1000 fps. This equals 1000 rotations per second. At 2000 fps the rotations per second double. Higher velocity yields a faster spin and is thus considered in the calculations, although it is not specifically mentioned. The most recent interpretations of Greenhill opt for a slightly faster twist with the higher velocity cartridges, in the

.224 equals 9.60. Thus a twist of 1:9 or 1:10 inches is required to shoot this bullet accurately. There are other factors involved, such as the amount of bearing surface on the bullet, velocity and barrel length. In some cases bullets that are not well matched to twist rate can be made to function. For example, a short, 40- or 45- grain bullet, in a 223 with a fast twist of 1:9 or 1:10 inches, will perform if the powder charge is cut back. By decreasing the velocity, you can keep the bullet from tearing itself apart. This might be called a limited success, since in the manner of the 22 Short in the Long Rifle barrel, accuracy will likely suffer.

Applying the Greenhill Formula can save time and money. It can serve as a useful guide when it comes to buying a gun or having one custom barreled, if you know in advance what kind of shooting you will be doing and thus what kind of bullets you will use.

Rifle Bullets

Military surplus and military overrun bullets may be a terrific bargain if all you want is some cheap practice ammunition.

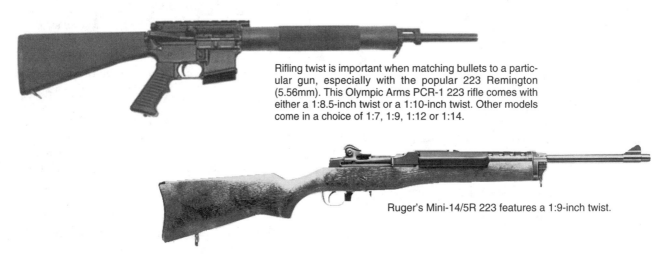

Rifling twist is important when matching bullets to a particular gun, especially with the popular 223 Remington (5.56mm). This Olympic Arms PCR-1 223 rifle comes with either a 1:8.5-inch twist or a 1:10-inch twist. Other models come in a choice of 1:7, 1:9, 1:12 or 1:14.

Ruger's Mini-14/5R 223 features a 1:9-inch twist.

belief that erring on the side of over-stabilization is better than under-stabilization which may result in a tumbling bullet.

The popular 223 Remington is a good candidate for study. Rifles for this cartridge are currently available with the following twist rates: 1:7, 1:8.5, 1:9, 1:10, 1:12 and 1:14 inches. To apply the Greenhill Formula using the original 55-grain bullet yields the following, for one brand of full metal jacket (FMJ) military-type bullet measuring .647-inch in length. The bullet diameter is .224-inch, which, divided into the length of .647-inch, gives 2.89 calibers long. Dividing 2.89 into 150 yields a figure of 51.90, or an ideal twist rate of one turn in 51.90 calibers. Multipling 51.90 by the bullet diameter (.224-inch) equals one turn in 11.63 inches for this particular bullet.

The original twist for the 223-caliber M-16 rifle is 1:12 inches. In its wisdom (?), the Army decided a heavier (longer) bullet was necessary and the M-16A1 is bored with a 1-10-inch twist. The new military bullet will not stabilize in the older barrels. Bullets as heavy as 70 grains are available for the 223 Remington. For a 70-grain bullet measuring .785-inch in length, dividing by .224 equals 3.50. Dividing 150 by 3.50 equals 42.86, or one turn in 42.86 calibers; then 42.86 multipled by

Military bullets suitable for practice are of the full metal jacketed variety. They feature a solid lead alloy core with a copper, bronze or soft steel jacket and are referred to as "ball" ammunition. These bullets are made to military specifications and will produce reasonably good accuracy for preliminary sighting in and practice. The full metal jacket prevents nose expansion and is not good for hunting. Occasionally shooters have tried to make hunting ammunition out of FMJ bullets by filing the points off of the spitzer (pointed) military bullets, exposing the lead cores. This is a dangerous practice since the bullet already has the lead core exposed at the base. Opening the point often results in the core being blown right through the jacket, leaving the jacket stuck in the barrel. When the next shot hits the jacket, the barrel is bulged and ruined. Don't try to modify FMJ bullets! Because of bullet-to-bullet weight variation, military ammunition will never produce fine accuracy.

In a worst-case scenario, a surplus bullet "bargain" could turn out to be a tracer, incendiary, explosive or armor-piercing type. Most military ammunition is identified by the color-coded bullet tips, and in the case of the tracer, by exposed burning material at the base of the bullet. There are various books on military ammunition that will tell you how to interpret these color codes on a country-by-country basis.

Surplus armor-piercing ammunition has been used for years as cheap practice fodder, mainly in military rifles. In his book *The Complete Guide to Handloading*, Philip Sharpe responded to the question of whether AP ammo did any harm to rifle barrels by conducting an experiment. He took a "gilt-edged" match rifle barrel, targeted it with match target ammunition, then fired a few rounds of armor piercing, and targeted it again with the same match ammunition, carefully cleaning between groups. His finding was that after the AP rounds, the match group had opened considerably and in spite of further cleaning did not repeat its former performance. This was with the AP ammunition of WWII, not the so called "light armor" piercing, steel-core ammunition sold today which has a far softer steel center. Would I put this newer kind through the barrel of a fine match rifle I owned? I don't think so, at least not until someone else tests it in *his* match barrel first. Would I use it in a $150 AK or SKS? Sure.

of their frangibility, varmint bullets are not suitable for large game.

Bullets for medium to large game require thicker jackets to keep them together while they penetrate deep into vital areas. They are designed for controlled expansion to allow the bullet to upset or "mushroom" as it goes deeper. This makes a large wound cavity, which renders it far more lethal than a non-expanding type or a frangible one that breaks into fragments shortly after it strikes a body.

In medical terms, "lethality" is the effect of a particular bullet on a body. According to Dr. Martin Fackler—the leading wound ballistics expert in the country—bullet lethality is an easily understood concept. Lethality is determined by answering two questions: How big is the hole it produces? How deep is this hole? Bigger and deeper holes are more likely to intersect with vital organs, cause greater loss of blood, and result in death.

Game bullets are generally of a pointed softpoint design, known as spitzer or semi-spitzer. These hold their velocity

Eagle Arms' M15A2 Post-Ban Heavy Barrel Rifle in 223 has a 1:9-inch twist.

Remington's 40-X target rifle in 223 has a 1:14-inch twist.

Match ammunition is full metal jacketed and of a reduced-base "boattail" design. This type of bullet has good aerodynamic qualities, producing a flat trajectory which is very desirable for hitting targets at long range. Often, these match bullets have a small hollow point to shift the center of gravity slightly back and improve stabilization. Match bullets often have very thin jackets and are "soft swaged" to keep the jackets smooth, flawless and of the exact same thickness. Great care is taken to ensure that these bullets are all of the exact same weight and diameter. Since this type of bullet is used for punching paper targets or knocking down metal silhouettes, expansion is not needed. Even though these bullets have hollow points they are not intended to expand on game and do not. They are very prone to ricochet and are not suitable for hunting.

Bullets for varmint hunting are either of flat base or boattail design and feature a tapered or spire point with the lead core exposed and swaged into a point. The jackets are thin, allowing these bullets to expand rapidly with an explosive force on woodchucks, prairie dogs and similar-size, thin-skinned animals. This design also keeps these bullets from ricocheting when they strike the ground at velocities near 2000 fps. Because

much better than less aerodynamic designs. Also available are hollowpoint, flat-nose or round-nose designs with the lead core exposed. Attempts at improving expansion have been tried by varying the thickness of the jacket, and by making serrations in the jacket at the bullet nose to help it split open and peel back in an even pattern as the core upsets. Other modifications are hollow points filled with hollow copper tubes, metal or nylon plugs which are driven back on impact, expanding the bullet.

Bullets for very large, dangerous game are subject to special requirements, since they often have to penetrate a considerable amount of muscle tissue and heavy bone to reach a vital spot. Bullets for this type of hunting feature very thick jackets. Some, like the old RWS and contemporary Nosler, have two cores with a solid web of bronze alloy running through the center of the bullet so that in section it looks like the letter H. The top half expands, but only to the center web which insures that the base portion will stay together. Barnes Bullets offers what they call a monolithic solid, which is simply a solid bronze-alloy bullet. Speer offers a copper-alloy bullet called African Grand Slam with a tungsten carbide dowel in the center, for use on such extremely dangerous and hard-to-kill game as Cape buffalo.

Bullets for the 22 (from left): 55-, 60-, 63- and 70-grain. They look very alike and can be easily mixed up, which is why unloaded bullets should always be returned to the original container after you are through loading ammunition. The 70-grain bullet will not work well in slow-twist (1:14-inch) barrels.

(Below) Match ammunition usually features a hollowpoint design and often a boattail. While these are very accurate, they are unreliable when it comes to expanding on game or varmint animals and often ricochet rather than break up when they hit the ground.

Handgun Bullets

Handgun bullets for target use are often swaged from lead alloy and deliver good accuracy when properly lubricated. Their design ranges from a simple cylinder, called a "wadcutter" because it punches clean holes in paper targets, to round-nose and truncated-cone styles. Use of such ammunition in indoor ranges has raised fears of lead poisoning, since a certain amount of lead is vaporized from the bullet's surface upon firing. To counter this hazard, the "total metal jacket" or TMJ bullet was developed. The full metal jacket leaves an exposed lead base, while the TMJ covers the entire surface of the bullet. It's applied by electroplating the bullet with copper. After plating, the bullets are forced through a die to bring them into perfect roundness. They don't expand as well as soft lead-alloy bullets and are thus a poor choice for hunting, but they do keep lead levels down in indoor ranges.

Hunting bullets for handguns are modifications of rifle designs, with some major engineering differences. Early attempts to improve handgun bullet lethality led to softpoint and hollowpoint designs based on rifle bullets. Results were unsatisfactory when it was discovered that these generally failed to expand and behaved no differently than FMJ types. In the last few years, new designs have emerged that will expand reliably at handgun velocities of 900 to 1600 fps. The secret to bringing this about was to design bullets with nearly pure lead cores, large hollow points and thin, relatively soft jackets of pure copper, copper alloys or aluminum. Serrations or cuts through the jacket and into the core improve expansion, increasing the lethality of these relative low-velocity bullets. Since most handgun hunting is done at ranges of under 100 yards, expansion is still reliable on most deer size or smaller game animals, assuming that the handgun is a powerful one in the 357 Magnum to 50 magnum class. Handguns of less than this performance level simply cannot be loaded heavily enough to do any serious hunting, and to try to "load them up" for this purpose is a foolish risk to both the gun and its shooter. Shooting any jacketed handgun bullet at low velocities is not recommended, particularly in

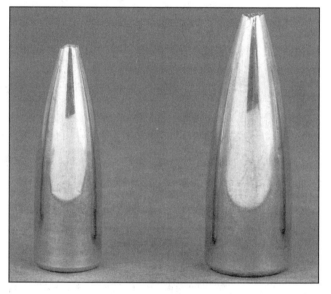

revolvers. The greater resistance of the jacketed bullet to swaging in the barrel requires higher pressures than with lead bullets. Underpowered loads, particularly in revolvers with a generous gap between the cylinder and barrel, may result in a stuck bullet waiting to be slammed by the next one fired.

Handling and Storage

The care and storage of bullets is much the same as for cartridge cases or loaded ammunition. Commercially made bullets are generally packed in boxes of 100, and the boxes they come in are probably the best containers to keep them in. These are generally of plastic or reinforced cardboard and will last a long time. Obviously, bullets should not be dropped or shaken since this will impart nicks and dents which do nothing to improve their accuracy. Lead bullets are the most susceptible to this kind of damage. The early experiments of Franklin Mann, recounted in his book, *The Bullet's Flight From Powder to Target*, demonstrated the frailty of bullets when it comes to having their accuracy severely affected by even

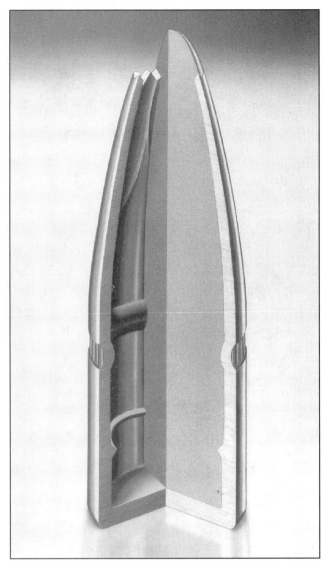

A typical hunting bullet features an exposed lead point and a lead core. The core is held in place by knurled cannelures in the jacket. (Courtesy of Hornady.)

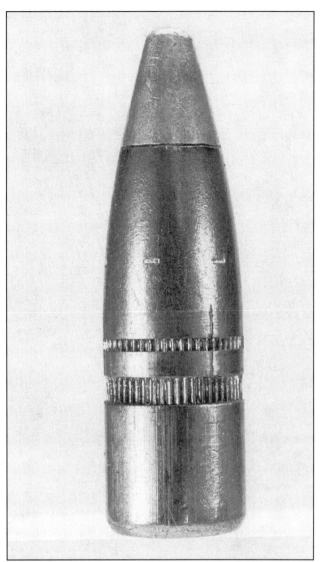

Winchester's Silvertip hunting bullet features a thin aluminum jacket over the lead point. This allows good expansion, but prevents the bullet from getting nicked and dented as the cartridge is fed through the magazine.

minor damage. Bullet bases are the most vulnerable. A lead or soft lead alloy bullet dropped on a wood floor and receiving a ding on the edge of the base has just been converted into scrap. They can be used for warming and fouling shots, but their former accuracy is gone.

Perhaps the most important caution with respect to bullet storage is to be careful that bullets are not mixed up. If you are loading two very similar calibers, there is a possibility of accidentally getting a 10mm bullet in a box of 9mms of the same style and approximate weight. You would likely catch this in the loading process at the time of seating, but there are some people who might persist in attempting to jam such a bullet into a 9mm case. Perhaps more likely is confusing same-caliber bullets but with different weights. These will seat perfectly well, but the heavier ones are going to have a higher trajectory and will land in a different place. A heavier bullet will, of course, raise pressures, and if you are using a maximum load this can have serious consequences. It is a good idea never to have two boxes of similar bullets open on your loading bench at the same time. Using boxes with snap tops or putting a bit of tape on the lid to keep it from opening accidentally is a good idea. I think most people will agree, particularly after spilling a box of the 22-caliber size and picking them all up.

Buying Bullets

Most gun stores carry a good selection of bullets for most needs. The directory in the back of this book lists many suppliers of bullets of every description. As of this writing, bullets can be bought by mail. Most of the large bullet manufacturers such as Sierra, Hornady and Speer offer reloading guides for their products. The smaller companies offer catalogs and sometimes limited amounts of loading data.

Custom bullets are supplied by small manufacturers and are often geared to special types of guns or for special types of shooting such as metallic silhouette competition. At times these makers or their jobbers will sell their bullets at gun shows where they can be bought at a lower cost and without the shipping and handling. I always enjoy attending these affairs and

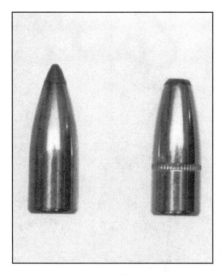

Pointed softpoint and flatpoint bullets are both good hunting bullets. The pointed bullet is more susceptible to damage in feeding; the flatpoint loses velocity slightly faster.

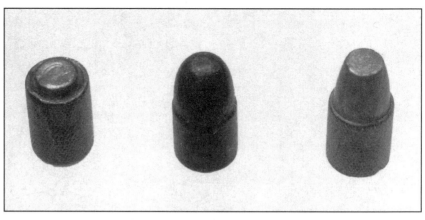

Good handgun bullet designs are the wadcutter (left), so named for the neat holes it makes in paper targets, the round-nose (center) and semi-wadcutter (right).

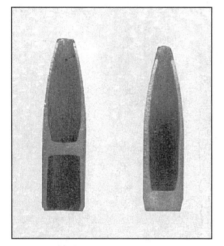

Nosler's Partition bullet (left) is designed so the front half expands in conventional manner, but only to the center. A heavy partition keeps the back half intact, retaining weight and energy, while an ordinary bullet might fragment.

Handgun bullets designed for hunting must offer rapid expansion at relatively low velocities. To this end, they feature large hollow points, serrated jackets and pure lead cores.

chatting with the dealers. It is a good place to pick up information—and misinformation. Buying bullets in a plastic bag is a pig in a poke, but I don't recall getting burned too badly, except for some cast bullets that either had a bad alloy, or too little or a poor quality lubricant, since they deposited generous amounts of lead in one of my rifle barrels.

Bullet Fouling

The subject of cleaning has been touched upon in the powder and primer sections, but the main fouling problem affecting accuracy is caused by bullets. To reiterate, the problem of primer deposits is one of corrosive salts. It is very similar, in effect, to the corrosive deposits left by blackpowder or Pyrodex. A water-based cleaner does a good job of getting these out of your barrel since salt and acid are readily dissolved in water and can be flushed away.

The deposit left by smokeless powder is mainly soot, graphite from the coating on the powder grains, small amounts of unburned powder and bullet lubricant. Often this is a varnish-like layer in the gun bore. It is not corrosive and does not draw water, nor does it tend to build up in thick deposits in the manner of blackpowder fouling. However, after a lot of shooting this fouling will begin to affect accuracy. It is easily removed by the many "nitro" powder solvents on today's market. These are petroleum based and do an excellent job of dissolving lubricant and the sooty deposits of smokeless powder. As mentioned earlier, unless the solvent has a water component it will prove ineffective on corrosive primer and blackpowder deposits.

Metallic fouling is basically of two types, lead and copper. Lead fouling, known as "leading," will ruin accuracy very quickly. A poorly lubricated bullet or an over- or undersize lead bullet can deposit enough lead in a barrel with one or two shots that all those thereafter will fail to stabilize and go tumbling

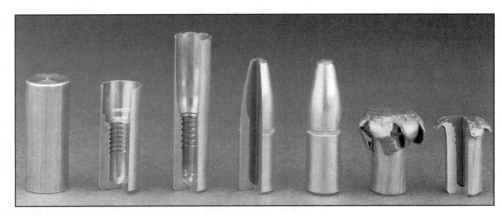

These are the steps in making one version of the Speer Grand Slam hunting bullet. A solid copper slug is punched to form the jacket. The jacket is then drawn and trimmed before the lead core is inserted. The jacket is very thick at the base to keep the bullet from fragmenting. Internal grooves and a thick base ensure the jacket does not shed the core, yet thinning the jacket in the forward portion ensures good expansion. Such bullets are for large dangerous game where deep penetration is needed. (Courtesy of Speer.)

These Speer Gold Dot handgun bullets in 38, 40 and 45 calibers evidence considerable expansion after being fired into ballistic gelatin. (Courtesy of Speer.)

down range to the extreme consternation of the shooter. Exactly what causes leading is not really known and the phenomenon may have more than one cause. The original theory was that lead bullets that were too large—or were inadequately lubricated—stripped as they passed down the barrel, and that the following bullets encountered this lead, plastered it to the bore and in the process stripped off more lead. Gradually, rough clumps of lead piled up in the barrel to the point where the rifling was so clogged that it failed to stabilize the bullets. This certainly seems possible.

This theory, however, fails to explain how undersize bullets with plenty of lubricant on them can do the same thing. The second theory holds that an undersized lead bullet will not obturate the bore fully, especially if made of too hard an alloy. Hot gases rushing by this undersize bullet melt the surface, blowing particles of melted lead down the barrel. These cool and solidify, gradually building up a layer of lead forward of the chamber, which is added to by successive bullets to the point where accuracy is ruined. I tend to be a believer in both since they seem logical. I have had oversize and under-lubricated bullets lead the bore. The surface of the recovered bullet has a scraped, stripped surface with the rifling striae poorly defined.

In the case of undersize bullets, recovered examples show little or no rifling marks whatsoever. The surface has a semi-melted appearance and there is often evidence of gas cutting—melted channels extending forward from the base of the bullet. Furthermore, the leading in each case is of a distinctive type.

Stripping generally happens at about the mid-point of a rifle barrel—or where the bullet runs out of lubricant—and continues out to the muzzle. The deposits are streaks and clumps usually in the corner where the land joins the groove. For some reason the heaviest concentration seems to be about three- quarters of the way down the barrel. Heat soldering, caused by gas blow-by, deposits a smooth coating of lead beginning just forward of the chamber and extending eight to ten inches. Subsequent bullets burnish this coating, making it shine and it is thus difficult to see.

In either case, the problem is to get the lead out. Nitro solvents with good lubricating qualities can flow under the lead and lift it to an extent, but the process takes days. The usual practice is to use a phosphor-bronze bore brush, saturated with solvent, and work it back and forth through the barrel, making sure *not* to change directions until the brush has cleared each end. Failure to do so can damage the bore surface. An overnight soak, heavily coating or filling the barrel with solvent, helps speed things on a badly leaded bore. Outers, among others, sells high powered solvents containing ingredients which actually dissolve metal fouling, but there is still a lot of brush work to do.

Copper fouling is left by copper, brass, bronze and cupronickel bullet jackets, and by steel jackets plated with any of the above. Copper fouling is usually a thin wash that gradually builds into a thicker layer. Occasionally, copper alloy jackets will leave clumps of fouling which will degrade accuracy markedly and suddenly, much like leading. Removal is the

Speer's all-plastic snap-lock boxes keep out moisture and pollutants and prevent corrosion from getting a start on the bullets inside. (Courtesy of Speer.)

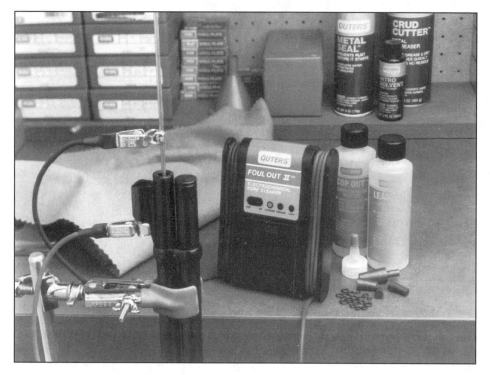

Outer's Foul Out electrochemical system is the easiest method of dealing with serious metal fouling problems.

same as for lead, but the process takes about three times as long. Ammonia-based solvents work well to dissolve copper fouling. The usual thin buildup is barely noticeable, but after it reaches a certain point, groups begin to open up—a timely reminder it's high time for a cleaning.

At present, the Outers "Foul Out" system offers the most advanced cleaning process. Though somewhat complicated and expensive (compared to a rod, brush and solvent combination), this is the best thing since sliced bread or hard ends on shoe laces when it comes to dealing with a really bad case of fouling. Foul Out works on an electroplating system. The gun barrel is plugged at the breech with a rubber stopper, then filled with a solution containing lead or copper, depending on the type of fouling to be removed. A stainless steel rod is inserted in the barrel and held in the center by rubber O-rings. Electrical con-

tacts are attached to the barrel and the rod. A weak current passing through the solution causes the lead or copper fouling to detach itself molecule-by-molecule to be deposited on the rod in the center. Every so often the rod must be removed and the lead or copper scrubbed off. When the solution gets weak it, too, must be replaced. The process takes a couple of hours, but *it works.* All fouling is removed down to the steel of the barrel. Old layers of rust and burned-on powder varnish are loosened as well. Best of all there is no elbow-work—nothing more than a periodic inspection. For barrels that haven't been cleaned in a long time, or those that are a bit on the rough side, it doesn't get much better. When the process is complete, a few damp patches to remove traces of the solution, followed by dry patches and a preservative oil, and your barrel is as clean as the day you bought it.

7

Homemade projectiles have been used for centuries, but recent generations have enjoyed many advancements in the art of...

Casting Bullets

SHOOTERS HAVE BEEN casting bullets out of lead for hundreds of years. In the 19th century, bullet casting came into its own as a craft verging on a science. Experimenters have assembled composite bullets with hard bodies and soft/heavy noses, even going as far as pouring mercury into the mixture. (Horrors!) Those who did that died sooner or later (more likely sooner) from the poisonous vapor. Bullets for blackpowder guns were made of lead and lead alloyed with tin. The latter gave much better results because the tin improved the quality of the cast bullet, causing it to fill the mould more completely. It was found that the velocity of lead bullets could only be raised to a certain point—about 1500 to 1600 fps. At that point lead begins coming off the bullet and gets deposited in the barrel, ruining accuracy until the lead is removed. Higher velocities with conical bullets were obtained by wrapping a slightly undersize lead bullet in a thin, tough, paper jacket (much like banknote paper) which was applied wet and shrunk to a tight fit as the cloth fibers contracted on drying. Paper patch bullets, as

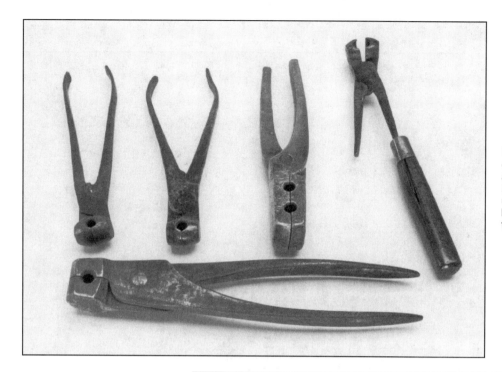

Bullet moulds from the late 18th and early 19th century cast round balls and roughly shaped conical bullets. Most had metal handles that heated up right along with the mould blocks. The finished bullet was trimmed up with a pocketknife.

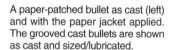

A paper-patched bullet as cast (left) and with the paper jacket applied. The grooved cast bullets are shown as cast and sized/lubricated.

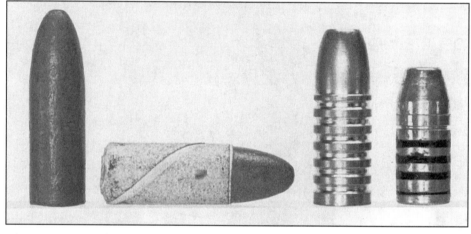

they were known, produced fine accuracy in addition to achieving velocities close to 2000 fps. Expansion was good since the bullet alloy could be kept soft, unlike a grooved, lubricated bullet which had to be hardened to keep it from deforming from the heat, friction and pressure of high-velocity loads. When metal-jacketed bullets supplanted lead bullets for rifle use, about the time smokeless powder appeared on the scene, paper-patched bullets all but vanished, and cast lead bullets were relegated to handguns and blackpowder rifles.

The new jacketed bullets, however, were discovered to have their drawbacks: a considerably shorter barrel life caused by erosion and wear, and a hard copper fouling. This fouling was not only difficult to remove, but often covered up the corrosive salts left by primers which ate up the barrel very quickly.

Shooters began to have second thoughts about abandoning lead alloy bullets. Unfortunately, soft lead bullets and smokeless powder are not always happy together. The higher flame temperature of the smokeless powder had a tendency to melt the bases of lead bullets. Around the turn of the century, John Barlow of the Ideal Manufacturing Company—makers of bullet moulds—came up with the idea of placing a small copper cup known as a "gas check" on the bases of cast bullets to prevent this from happening. Following Barlow's death, the Ideal Company was taken over by the Lyman Gun Sight Company, which began publishing some of the first good manuals on reloading. It was not until the 1930s, however, that the basics of making good cast bullets for smokeless loadings were clearly understood.

Bullet Alloy

Hardening lead bullets with tin improved their casting quality. But tin is expensive and after adding one part to twenty parts lead, by weight, not much additional hardening was achieved. In fact, as the tin content is increased much above this point, it becomes more like solder, since the addition of tin lowers the melting point and metal fouling begins to build up in the barrel. Though antimony does not truly alloy with lead, it will combine in crystalline form and harden it to a great degree. The best hard alloys are composed of lead, tin and antimony. The tin serves to coat the antimony crystals and bond them to the lead. The antimony adds a great deal of hardness in pro-

72

portion to the amount added, by weight. Tin is about twelve times as expensive as lead, while antimony is about three times as much. The addition of both metals to lead increases its fluidity in the molten state which makes it ideal for casting type metal or bullets, both of which require hardness, toughness, and precise dimensions.

When preparing or buying bullet alloy material, it is best to first consider what purpose you wish to use these bullets for, since there is no point in spending the money to produce gold-plated ammunition for plinking. Harder bullets, particularly those hardened with antimony, tend also to become brittle. Hard alloys are a poor choice for making hunting bullets since they will either drill straight through or shatter rather than expand evenly. Hard bullets are a good choice for long-range target use or metallic silhouette shooting where velocity and flat trajectory are important and there is no need for expansion.

Bullets made of lead, tin, antimony alloy will become harder as they age. After two weeks or so, they have reached their maximum hardness. If harder bullets are desired, one way to achieve this without adding additional antimony is to harden them at the time of casting by dropping the bullet (hot out of the mould) into a pan of cold water rather than letting it cool slowly. A bullet of wheelweight metal with a normal hardness of 12.4 BHN can be hardened to better than twice that by the above method. Similar hardening can be done by placing cast bullets in a pan, heating them in an oven to about 500 degrees Fahrenheit, then quenching them in cold water. Hot bullets must be handled *very* carefully since they are soft to the point of being in a near-melted state and are easily damaged.

Bullet alloys can be bought premixed from various sources, or you can buy lead, tin and antimony and mix your own. Since antimony has a melting point almost twice that of lead, it cannot be melted over an ordinary gas stove or electric melting pot. Good bullet alloys can be made from a variety of scrap materials that can be obtained at a lower cost than premixed alloys or pure metals. The main thing is to know what

you are getting, at least as far as possible, and to avoid bad materials that will ruin your metal for further use. Zinc is poison to lead alloys because it will not mix properly and ruins the casting qualities. Bullets have been made of nearly pure zinc under such trade names as Zamak and Kirksite. Zinc alloys are generally too lightweight for shooting at long range. They tend to gas-cut rather badly because they cannot be gas-checked. Battery plates were at one time salvaged for bullet making. That was before they were made of lead and calcium which, like zinc, ruins the casting quality of your alloy. Babbitt, bearing metal with high amounts of tin and antimony, is of use mainly to harden other lead alloys. Babbitt contains slight amounts of copper, but this floats to the surface and generally does not cause serious problems when the metal is melted down.

Bullet alloys can roughly be classed as soft, medium, hard and extra-hard. Soft alloys are lead with about 3 to 4 percent tin or about 1 percent antimony. They are suitable for most handgun loads and low velocity rifle loads to about 1300 fps. Medium alloys need to be about 90 percent lead, 5 percent tin and 5 percent antimony, and are good to about 1700 fps. Hard alloys are about 84 percent lead, 12 percent antimony and 4 percent tin. This is the alloy used in linotype, and it will shoot well at around or above 2000 fps. Extra-hard alloys can be anything up to 72 percent lead, 19 percent antimony and 9 percent tin. Beyond this, bullets begin to become too light in proportion to their size, and efficiency is lowered.

Mixing Alloys

Alloying and bullet casting should be done in a well-ventilated place or, better yet, outdoors. The equipment needed for mixing alloy is an iron melting pot and a lead thermometer or electric melting furnace with a thermostat, a steel spoon or skimmer to stir the metal and skim off dross. A tin can to hold the dross and an ingot mould complete the list of basics. A lead pot costs about $15 to $30, a thermometer about $30. An electric melting pot with a thermostat can cost as little as $80 and go

The cast/lubricated bullet will give equal or better accuracy than the jacketed hunting bullet, while producing less barrel wear, and can be made at a fraction of the cost. At ranges of 100-150 yards, it will kill just as effectively.

Copper gas checks applied to bullets designed for them will allow increased velocities and keep hot gas from melting the bullet bases.

Block lead and tin, as well as pre-mixed alloys, ensure purity in the metal alloy. Many scrap alloys, however, may be used to make good bullets, including wheel-weights, lead plumbing pipe and lead cable sheathing. Scrap 22 rimfire bullets recovered from indoor shooting ranges can also be a viable source, but Federal's new zinc Long Rifle bullet may eventually spoil this.

(Below) This electric melting pot with bottom-pour spigot holds about 10 pounds of alloy. It's an old design that still works well.

to about $265. An ingot mould runs about $15, and a dross and clip skimmer (a spoon with holes) is about $14. It is a good idea to keep the alloying operations and bullet casting separate. Alloy should be made up in 2-pound lots if you are experimenting. Once an alloy is found that suits your needs and shoots well, you can make up as much as you like—the more the better to maintain bullet weight consistency.

Cleaning scrap involves removing dirt, oxides, and such extraneous items as the steel clips on wheelweights by melting it. To keep the metal fluid and separate the unwanted material, it needs to be fluxed with a piece of beeswax or paraffin the size of the first joint of your finger. This creates smoke which can be burned off by holding a lit match in it. The metal should be stirred with a spoon or lead dipper to work the flux into the metal and bring impurities to the top. While this stirring should be fairly rapid, it should not be so vigorous as to flip or spill hot metal on yourself. Impurities will collect on top and should be skimmed after stirring and fluxing. Fluxing will work tin and antimony into the lead which would otherwise float to the top. Do not skim off the tin which forms a silvery gray coating on the surface. When you reach this stage, flux and stir again to blend it all together, then pour the cleaned scrap alloy into moulds for bullet casting, or for blending into a harder (or softer) alloy at another time. This final fluxing and stirring assures a consistent mixture which should be mirror bright with a few brown spots of burned beeswax on it when in the molten state. The alloy can then be poured into a mould for small ingots for bullet making. These should be remelted in a clean pot for bullet casting. Use a scriber or magic marker to mark your finished ingots so you will know what the alloy is, since they all look pretty much alike.

The hardness of lead alloys is determined by the Brinell scale (BHN) and is tested by dropping a known weight a known distance and measuring the impact hole. Lead testers, at about $70, are useful tools when making up precise alloys that

will yield bullets of an exact hardness and weight. Scrap alloys are not always precise in their makeup, so they must be considered "approximate" in their composition. A quick test for pure lead is to see if you can scratch it with your fingernail. Pure lead sources from scrap include plumbing pipe, block lead and cable sheathing, although there are reports some of this may be made of a battery-plate-type alloy. Scrap 22 rimfire bullets contain less than 1 percent antimony and by the

Small ingot moulds are the best way to store bullet alloy. To avoid mixups, ingots should be marked to identify them if different alloys are being used.

(Below) This lead and debris skimmer from Bill Ferguson easily removes clips from tire weights and similar unwanted material from the lead alloy.

(Above) A large plumber's lead pot is best for mixing lead alloys and cleaning scrap alloy, but this one from Ferguson is better suited to the bullet caster's need.

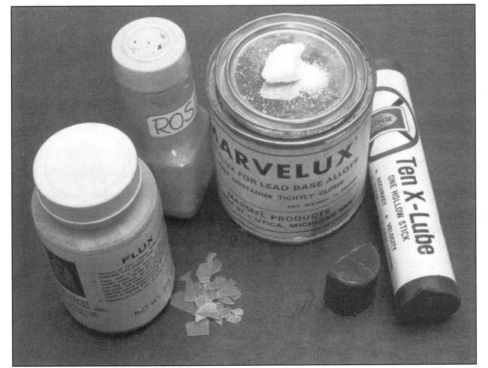

Molten metal needs to be fluxed to remove impurities and to keep tin and antimony mixed evenly throughout the alloy instead of floating on the surface. Commercial fluxes or a piece of bullet lubricant will do the job.

time they are melted, fluxed and skimmed can be considered nearly pure lead. Tin is a component of lead-tin solder and can be bought in ingots, but it is expensive.

BULLET METALS AND THEIR RELATIVE HARDNESS

Alloy	Tin	Lead	Antimony	Copper	BHN
Monotype	9	72	19	—	28
Stereotype	6	80	14	—	23
Linotype	4	84	12	—	22
Electrotype	3	94.5	2.5	—	12
Tin Babbit	83	—	11	6	23
Lead Babbit	—	83	11	6	22
Tire weights	1	96	3	—	12.4
Antimony	—	—	100	—	50
Tin	100	—	—	—	7
Lead	—	100	—	—	5

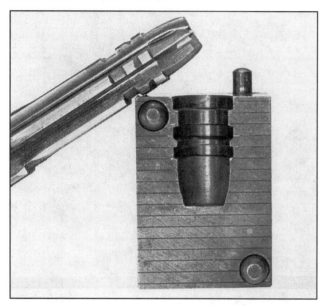

(Above) The mould cavity is given final form with a cherry, a reaming tool in the form of the bullet.

The modern bullet mould is a precision tool and a far cry from the old "nutcracker" moulds of the past. Moulds are damaged by rough treatment, and they should be kept free of rust and *never* battered with a metal tool.

Automobile wheelweights are a good source of alloy and can be used as is for low- to medium-velocity pistol and rifle bullets.

Lead, tin and antimony alloys harden with age. The maximum hardness is reached in about two weeks. Heat-treating and quenching in cold water will harden bullets. If they are worked through a sizer, this will soften the worked surface. Tire or wheelweights, as they are often called, are now being made with slightly more lead and less antimony, and are softer, though the alloy will vary. This alloy should be tested for hardness if hardness is critical.

The Bullet Mould

The bullet mould has two equal metal blocks with a cavity in each where the bullet is cast. The blocks are aligned by pins and held together by handles much like pliers. On top of the blocks is a sprue plate with a funnel-shaped hole, through which molten metal is poured. When the pouring is complete, the sprue plate is given a rap with a wooden mallet to pivot it to one side, cutting off the excess metal or sprue left on top.

Bullet moulds can be made from a variety of materials and each mould maker has his preferences for his own reasons. There is no such thing as the perfect material. Custom mould maker James Andela prefers 11L17, a leaded steel of low carbon content that machines easily to a bright smooth surface. This is the same basic type used in Lyman moulds. The material cost is low, and a cold rolled bar is virtually free of inclusions and holes, and possesses a dense grain-structure. Oil retention is low and thus the break-in time is faster than with iron moulds.

Moulds are generally made by roughing out the cavity with a drill, then cutting the impression for the bullet with a fluted cutting tool called a cherry. The cherry makes an exact negative impression of the bullet as the mould blocks are slowly pushed together on the rotating cherry.

Fine-grain cast iron is a common material with the advantages of low shrinkage and easy machinability. Iron is very stable with

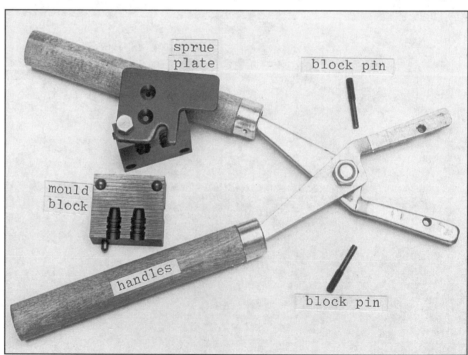

Aluminum moulds do not require as much breaking-in as iron or steel moulds. However, the cavity must often be coated with either carbon smoke or a special compound to get good bullets.

This nose-pour mould from Colorado Shooter's Supply delivers a bullet with a perfect base since the cut-off is at the bullet nose.

less inclination to warp or shrink in manufacture or with heating and cooling. When an iron block is used in conjunction with a steel sprue plate these dissimilar metals work well together to form a polishing action rather than a galling action where alike metals may tend to tear pieces from one another.

Brass and various bronzes (all alloys of copper) have been used for moulds with great success. They generally machine well and take a good finish. Copper alloys of all sorts have the added advantage of being highly corrosion resistant, and they heat quickly and evenly. The main disadvantages of brass and bronze is the cost of the material, which may be three times that of iron or steel. Brass and bronze are softer than steel or iron and such moulds must be handled more carefully to avoid damage. Any copper alloy (both brass and bronze) has an affinity for lead and tin and *must* be kept free of any acidic or similar material that could act as a flux and solder the blocks together in the casting process. Such an event usually finishes the mould. Nickel has been used to a limited extent in mould making and might very well be the perfect material, possessing the qualities of hardness, smooth finish, corrosion resistance and non-solderability, giving it an edge over iron, steel and copper alloys. The main problem is that it is very expensive, and for this reason no one uses nickel any more.

Aluminum and various aluminum alloys are widely used in mould making. Aluminum moulds require no break-in period. Aluminum's resistance to soldering, corrosion and its ability to heat to proper casting temperature quickly when combined with light weight and low cost of material make it nearly ideal. The major problem with aluminum alloy is its proneness to galling. The melting point of aluminum (1200-1600 degrees Fahrenheit) is near enough to that of the lead alloys used in bullet making that the casting process has a tendency to anneal aluminum blocks, and thus soften them to the point where the sprue cutter will gall the blocks. Aluminum blocks are also subject to cutting and denting. Alignment pins, usually of steel, will tend to wear

aluminum blocks, unless the mould is used with greater care than an iron or steel mould. The overall useful life of an aluminum mould will be less than one of iron or steel.

Types of Moulds

The most common mould is a simple, single-cavity type that casts one bullet at a time. These cost from $20 to $50 and run to about $175 for a custom mould. The next size up is the double-cavity at about the same price as a single, for small bullets. Moulds that cast up to ten bullets at a time are known as gang moulds and are used mainly by custom bullet makers because of

This hollowpoint plug fits into the nose end of a base-pour mould.

their speed of production. They are expensive ($200). Moulds are also available with special inserts that will cast hollow-base and hollowpoint bullets in single-cavity blocks for an additional $10 or so. Most moulds are of the base-pour variety with the bullet base at the top of the mould below the sprue plate. A few are nose-pour moulds with the sprue cut made at the nose of the bullet. The theory behind these is that they give a more perfect base, since base regularity is the most important factor in accuracy with cast bullets. Nose-pour moulds are generally custom-made and intended for long-range, heavy target bullets.

While a bullet mould may look like a nutcracker, it is in reality a precision tool that can be easily damaged by rough handling. Dropping a mould can knock the blocks out of alignment, as can whacking it with any kind of tool. Bullets will, at times, tend to stick in one of the mould blocks when they are opened. To get the bullet to drop free, it may be necessary to give the mould a rap with a wooden rod or mallet. This should *only* be done by tapping the joint between the handles. *Never* strike the mould blocks themselves! This will ruin their alignment. By the same token, the sprue cutter plate on top of the mould should never be hit with anything but a wooden rod or mallet. A metal tool will damage the sprue cutter.

Moulds generally require a break-in period before they will cast proper bullets. The first step in preparing a mould for casting is to remove all traces of oil or grease from the blocks, particularly the inner surfaces. A solvent such as Outers' "Crud Cutter" is good for this purpose. Once the blocks are clean and the metal in the melting pot is free-flowing (650-750 degrees Fahrenheit), you can start casting. Remember, with a new mould it may take a couple hundred bullets before the good ones start coming. Patience is required. Aluminum blocks do not require breaking-in, but often need to be coated with carbon (smoke from a candle flame) or a special mould prep before they behave properly.

In a properly made mould, the blocks should make an almost seamless fit, with only a faint line where the blocks join. Operation should be smooth without the alignment pins binding or holding the blocks apart. The setting of these pins is done at the factory so they are usually in proper alignment. Occasionally, it may be necessary to adjust these pins into the blocks if they bind or the blocks do not close completely. Adjustment should never be more than a couple thousandths of an inch at a time. It should be done with the handle and sprue plate removed. Rarely will a mould be manufactured with the two blocks made of steel or iron from different lots that have a different coefficient of expansion. This would result in bullets with a larger side and a smaller side and a seam in the middle. Such a mould along with a sample bullet should be returned to the manufacturer for replacement.

After casting is finished, the iron or steel mould should be coated with a rust inhibiting oil if it will not be used for weeks or months. A rusted mould is ruined if roughened or pitted. A solvent spray removes the oil when you are ready for the next casting session. Aluminum mould blocks don't require any special preservative action since they won't rust.

Bullet Casting

Bullet casting is best done outdoors or in a place where there is cross ventilation or a hood with an exhaust fan to remove

Bullet moulds can be warmed by placing them (carefully) on the edge of the melting pot. A pre-warmed mould will start producing good bullets before a cold one.

The author has had the best casting results by holding the mould about an inch below the spigot rather than having it in hard contact.

lead fumes. Beyond the bullet mould, a lead melting pot capable of holding about 10 pounds of metal is the center of your activity. The best method for keeping the metal the proper temperature is to use an electric melting furnace equipped with a thermostat. A lead thermometer in a plain iron pot with a gas fire under it is less convenient, but it works. The alloy temperature can vary from about 650 to 750 degrees Fahrenheit for the alloy to flow properly. Too much heat will oxidize the tin in the alloy. The metal should be stirred frequently and fluxed every 10 minutes or so to keep the mixture constant. Failure to do this will result in bullets of uneven weight. Most electric pots have a bottom-pour feature with a handle that releases the metal through a spigot in the bottom. This has the advantage of

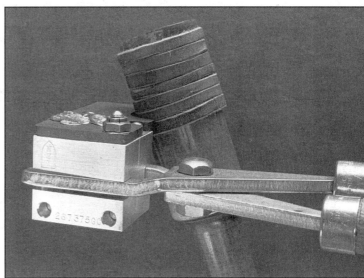

(Above) Never hit the sprue cutter with anything made of metal. A wooden dowel, in this case wrapped with rawhide, makes an effective cut without damage to the mould.

A good puddle of metal on the sprue plate helps force alloy into the mould and keep it hot so all bands in the bullet are filled out.

getting hotter metal into the mould, leaving behind any impurities that may be floating on the top.

Bullet casting, like reloading, is a solitary activity. Children especially should be kept out of the area because of exposure to lead fumes and possible spilled hot metal. A countertop, workbench, or tabletop operation is a good set up. Some prefer to stand while casting, while others like to sit because the activity will usually go on for a couple of hours. The melting pot *must* have a steady base. There is nothing like a lap full of molten lead to drive this point home. The pot is the center of activity and all other components should be laid out in neat order near the pot, all within convenient reach. These include: the bullet mould; a lead dipper with a pouring spout, if you are using an open pot; a supply of alloy ingots to be added when the metal gets low; lumps of beeswax or a container of flux powder and a spoon; matches or lighter to burn off the flux vapor; a spoon or skimmer for stirring the metal and skimming off dross; a can for dross collection; an ingot mould to recover leftover alloy; a wood mallet to rap the sprue cutter and the mould joint; a tray or box lid to catch sprue trimmings; and a folded blanket or soft rug to catch the cast bullets.

A mould should be warmed up for casting. This can be done by placing it on the top edge of the electric pot or by holding it briefly in the gas flame if you are using a stove. Overheating a mould can warp the blocks and ruin it! Never dip an iron, steel or brass mould into the pot of molten metal to warm it. To do so can result in soldering the blocks together and ruining the mould. Aluminum moulds, however, can be dipped to bring them to the proper temperature.

The actual casting process should be done in a smooth rhythmic manner. If you try for quality, speed will follow. Begin by stirring the pot, and continue to do this frequently to keep the alloy from separating and to work the impurities to the top.

Lead from the dipper or from the spigot should be poured smoothly into the mould. Some people advocate placing the spout of the dipper or spigot of the electric pot directly into the sprue funnel. I have found this to trap air in the cast bullet and the resultant bubbles produce bullets of varying weights with different centers of gravity. My best results have been achieved by running a fairly rapid stream into the mould and allowing the metal to puddle out over the sprue plate to about the size of a quarter. This helps keep both the mould and the metal inside hot so the bullets fill out properly. Once the cast is made, I cool the sprue by blowing on it for a couple seconds. The sprue cutter should then be given a sharp rap with the wood mallet to make a clean cut. The sprue plate should turn easily on its pivot, but fit flush to the top of the mould blocks to give an even base to the bullet. If lead begins to smear over the blocks, or if the cutting of the sprue tears a chunk out of the bullet base, the bullet is still too hot for cutting. Slow down and blow a little longer. The sprue plate may tend to come loose with heating and need to be tightened. Do not over-tighten. A drop of melted bullet lubricant or beeswax should occasionally be applied to the hinge on the sprue plate to keep it moving freely. Be sure not to get lubricant into the bullet cavity.

Once the sprue is removed, the handles should be pulled apart quickly. If everything is working properly, the bullet will drop free of the mould. A soft rug or towel should be used to catch the finished bullets. These should be spread apart every so often to keep from dropping one bullet on another and damaging them. Hot bullets are very soft and should be treated gently. If you wish to harden your bullets, drop them from the mould into a pot of cold water.

When the alloy level in the pot gets about two thirds to three-quarters of the way down, it may be a good time for a break to inspect your products and replenish the pot. The first

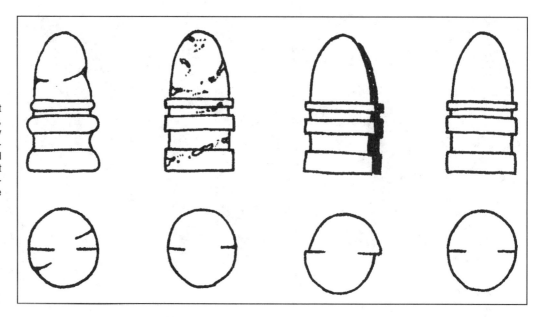

Some examples of bullet casting problems include, left to right: mould or alloy too cool; alloy has impurities; misaligned mould blocks. A good cast bullet will have all bands properly filled out and will be shiny in appearance.

bullets will have seams on the noses and the drive bands between the grooves will not be fully filled out, with clean, square corners on the bands. This is most likely because either the metal or the mould or both were too cold for good casting. A mould that hasn't been broken in will produce similar results, often with one half being better filled out than the other. These bullets, along with the sprues, are returned to the melt pot. Expect quite a few of these in the beginning. A good bullet will be evenly filled out everywhere. Corners on drive bands will be square and the bands will be of even width all round. By rolling a bullet across a flat surface irregularities in band width may be easily seen. Discard all those that are noticeably uneven.

Irregularities, including voids (or holes) in the bullet and drive bands not completely filled out, especially in a limited area, may be caused by oil or grease having not been fully removed from that spot in the mould. Until this is completely clean, you will not get good bullets. The burned-on oil or grease should be removed with a strong solvent and a cleaning brush or wood stick such as an orange stick (available at the nail-care area of your drugstore). Occasionally lead will become stuck on the inside surfaces of the blocks, preventing them from closing properly. Any lead smear of this sort will tend to build up unless completely removed. An orange stick and, in a bad case, solvent will remove this. Never use a metal tool, acid or an abrasive to clean the interior of a bullet mould.

Just as the temperature of the mould or the alloy can be too cool for good results, it can also be too hot. Overheating oxidizes the tin and antimony, thus changing the quality of the alloy. Bullets cast at too high a temperature or from a mould that has become too hot exhibit a dull, frosted appearance rather like the surface of a piece of galvanized sheet metal. Sometimes they will have undersize drive bands as well. When such bullets appear, reduce the alloy temperature and give your mould some time to cool off. A lightly frosted bullet generally causes no problems, but it is an indication you are operating on the hot side.

Since bullet casting is a fairly messy operation, and one that requires a certain amount of preparation and cleanup, it is best

to set aside an afternoon for the project. Once you get into the swing of pouring, sprue cutting and popping the bullets out of the mould, speed will come and production can be expected to rise to 200 or more per hour for plain-base bullets. Casting hollowpoint or hollow-base bullets is more complicated, since an additional pin or post is required to make the cavity. The hollowpoint attachment goes into the bottom of the mould and turns to lock into position. Once in place, the metal is poured. After cooling, the pin is turned for removal and the bullet is then dropped from the mould in the normal manner. The extra step takes a bit more time. The secret of good production is *consistency*. Fluxing and stirring of the metal often is the best way to maintain a consistent alloy mixture throughout the pot. Failure to do this will start yielding bullets of varying weights, depending where you dip from the pot. Dipping serves to stir the mixture. Bottom-pour electric pots have to be stirred or the lighter metals will float to the top.

Like any other task involving hazardous material, casting should be done with a clear head, not when you are tired. At the end of the casting session an inspection of the finished bullets should be made and the obvious duds along with sprue cuttings should be returned to the melt pot. When melted, this should be poured into an ingot mould for storage. If you are using different alloys, mark your ingots with some sort of scriber to identify the alloy so you don't mix them up.

Cast bullets are far more easily damaged than the jacketed variety and must be carefully stored. Never dump or pour a batch of bullets into a bucket or box. This will cut and nick the bases and accuracy will suffer accordingly. Good methods of storage include small boxes where the bullets can be stood on their bases, packed closely together so they don't tip over. Plastic or paper boxes are far less likely to cause damage than metal containers. Proper labeling on the box is necessary to keep things straight. The same bullet cast of different alloys will have different weights and should be kept separate. If they become mixed, it's too bad because they all look alike and the only way to sort them is by weighing each one. I'd rather be shooting!

Now that you've cast a projectile to load, you can't just seat it and shoot it. There's much more to it than that.

Bullet Sizing and Lubricating

AS WITH JACKETED bullets, cast bullets and the moulds for them should be selected with consideration for the twist of the rifling of the gun you plan to shoot them in. Shorter bullets will do best in a relatively slow twist, while longer ones will require a faster twist. Beyond this is the matter of bullet design.

Cast boattail bullets will simply not work well since the unprotected, tapered base will be surrounded by hot gases and melted, with this lead then deposited on the bore of the gun. Cast bullets work best that have a flat or slightly dished base. Hollow-base bullets, in the style of Civil War Minié balls, were designed to be undersize to fit muzzleloaders and expand to bore size when fired at velocities under 1000 fps. Use of this type of bullet in cartridge guns other than handguns is not a good idea. At velocities over 1000 fps, the skirt tends to be blown out too far and may actually separate from the rest of the bullet if loaded too heavily. This can cause serious problems if the skirt remains lodged in the barrel. Accuracy in cartridge rifles is not particularly good.

Excellent accuracy may be obtained from cast bullets. Left and center are plain-base designs; the bullet on the right is designed to take a gas check.

With cast bullets, the best accuracy is generally obtained with bullets that have a relatively short ogive with the greater part of their surface bearing on the rifling. The ogive is that part of the bullet forward of the bearing surface, regardless of its shape. The greatest degree of stability is achieved with a cast bullet that has nearly all of its length in contact with the groove portion of the bore. The downside of this is increased drag and lowered velocities. Cast bullets of this design, however, are sometimes the only ones that will perform well in shallow-groove barrels. The aerodynamic shape of a bullet with a long ogive makes it a good one for long-range shooting, but such bullets are difficult to seat absolutely straight, and accuracy with cast bullets of this design is generally very poor. Much has been said in favor of "bore-riding" bullets which offer the best compromise between the two extremes. Bullets of this design feature a relatively short drive band area with a long nose of smaller diameter which has a short taper to a point. The front portion is designed to coast along the surface of the lands—the bore—without being more than lightly engraved by them if at all. This design provides stability without the drag encountered by a bullet with a long bearing surface, which is engraved by the rifling nearly its entire length.

Proper Bullet Size

The importance of slugging the barrel (as described in Chapter 1) to obtain the correct groove diameter and thus best accuracy cannot be over emphasized. If a barrel is worn or of a type known to have wide variations, this is a must. While undersize jacketed bullets can give good performance in a barrel of larger diameter, undersize cast bullets will often fail to expand or upset properly, filling the grooves, particularly if these bullets are made of hard alloy. The result is considerable lead fouling and terrible accuracy, especially with deep-groove barrels. Cast bullets that are groove size shoot best.

With every rule it seems there is an exception. In this regard there is one that I know of, and possibly others of which I am unaware. This exception is the 45 Allin "Trap-door" Springfield. This rifle was designed for blackpowder ammunition. It features deep-groove (.005-inch) rifling and the groove diameter may be as deep as .463-inch. A .457-inch or even a .460-inch diameter bullet is clearly undersize. If groove-diameter bullets are used in this rifle, the cartridge case will be enlarged to the point the round will not chamber! Some frustrated shooters have gone to the extreme of having their chambers reamed out to accommodate these larger bullets. The bullets worked in the sense they didn't foul the barrels, but they developed fins of lead on the rear and were not very accurate. Springfield 45 barrels were engineered to use a very soft lead-tin alloy bullet of about .549-inch diameter, that would upset *as it left the cartridge case*. The purpose was to design a blackpowder rifle that would shoot accurately with a dirty barrel. Each bullet would thus expand to fill whatever groove space was available. These rifles and carbines will shoot very well using lead-tin bullets of a 20-1 to 30-1 alloy. Bullets with any amount of antimony in them lack the necessary malleability to expand properly and will pile up lead in the bore. If you own an old rifle with a very deep-groove barrel and find that a groove-diameter bullet expands the case to the point where it will not chamber, a soft lead-tin alloy bullet may be the only cast bullet you can shoot in it. As far as I know, this was a unique design, but some of the old Bullard rifles may have also used this type of boring, and there may be others.

Bullet Lubricants

Nobody actually knows how bullet lubricants work since there is no known way to observe a bullet as it is fired through the barrel of a gun. Unlubed lead alloy bullets can be fired at 600 to 800 fps without causing leading, assuming the barrel is a very smooth one. Revolvers, however, are something of an exception to this rule, probably because their bullets tip slightly or some gas blows by the bullets as they jump the gap from cylinder to the forcing cone in the barrel.

Lubricants prevent leading by reducing friction in the barrel,

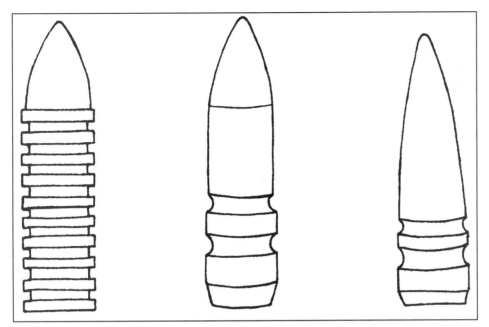

The best rifle accuracy with a cast alloy bullet is with one that has a short ogive. The bullet on the left has many lubricant grooves and will shoot well in multi-groove and shallow-groove barrels owing to good bore contact over most of its length. The center bullet is a "bore-riding" type also with a short ogive. The right bullet is of a long-ogive design. Difficulty in getting such a bullet properly seated in the case makes it a poor shooter.

but they also have a considerable effect on accuracy. There are any number of lubricants that will prevent leading, but their accuracy record is often poor. Through the years any number of lubricant formulas have been tried with success rates ranging from excellent to terrible. Heavy grease of various sorts works well, as can be attested to by anyone who has shot some of the 22 Long Rifle ammunition made in the 1940s and early '50s. The problem, however, was that it would melt in warm weather and, when shot, combined readily with powder fouling to form a black greasy coating that wound up all over your hands. The use of such grease/lubricant in inside-lubricated cartridges ruined them in short order as the grease soaked into the powder and even into the primer, ruining both.

Grease/petroleum jelly in small amounts can be combined with various waxes with reasonable success to make a good bullet lubricant, but under warm conditions it has a tendency to "sweat" out of the mixture and get into the powder. Some greas-es will oxidize and harden over time or evaporate to a degree. These are poor candidates for long term storage if that is desired. Lithium-based grease appears not to sweat out since it has a very high melting point.

Some early formulas for bullet lubricants included resin. Since this is an abrasive and not a lubricant, this is a bad idea. Tests conducted by Philip Sharpe, among others, demonstrated that resin in the mixture actually shortened barrel life.

Japan wax is obtained from an Asian sumac berry and is similar to bayberry wax. It was used in many early lubricant formulas. It has a tendency to dry over time and become brittle, at which point it loses much of its lubricating qualities. It is, to a degree, hygroscopic, which is not good if your bullets may be exposed to moisture. Sharpe found that Japan wax, when combined with copper-plated lead bullets, caused them to corrode to the point they were unshootable in a rather short time. Bullet lubricants which are hygroscopic or evaporate through time,

Bullets must be of the proper size and alloy to shoot well. On the left is a 45-70 rifle bullet cast of 20:1 lead-tin alloy, sized .459-inch—the proper diameter for the original 45 Springfield rifle. Next to it is the same bullet after firing. The bullet became shorter and fatter as it filled the deep-groove bore. Next is a very similar bullet sized .459-inch, but made of an alloy containing a small amount of antimony. On the far right is this bullet after firing. The hard bullet has failed to expand to fill the grooves. The rifling mark is barely visible where hot gas blew by and melted the bullet surface. The results—good accuracy from the left; a leaded bore and terrible accuracy on the right.

allowing bullets to corrode, are for short-term use only. About the only thing that can be done is to keep such ammunition away from heat and moisture.

Carnauba wax is a tree wax from Brazil and is the main ingredient in shoe polish. It is a hard wax that needs softening to make a good bullet lubricant. Paraffin is often included in lubricant mixtures, mainly as a stiffener.

Paraffin has rather poor lubricating qualities unless heated. When subjected to pressure, it crumbles as it forms layers. It can be used in lubricants, but only sparingly.

Beeswax is hard and must be softened for bullet lubricant. In the pure form it can be used for outside-lubricated bullets, like the 22 Long Rifle, since it remains hard and will not pick up dirt and grit in the manner of softer lubricants.

Ozocerite and ceresine waxes are the same, but ceresine is the refined form, often sold as a beeswax substitute. Ozocerite is a mineral wax with many industrial uses since it is cheaper than beeswax. Candles are made of this material, often with coloring added. It is too hard to use as is and must be softened with some form of oil to make it usable for bullet lubricant.

Tallow is animal fat. In refined form it is called lard and was an early lubricant for patched bullets in muzzleloaders. The vegetable equivalent, Crisco, has long been a favorite for muzzleloader fans because it keeps blackpowder fouling soft. Tallow gets rancid and melts in warm temperatures, as does Crisco. These preclude their use in cartridge ammunition except as an additive.

Graphite is a mineral which is neither a wax nor a lubricant, but a very fine abrasive. Colloidal graphite is the finest granulation available and when mixed with waxes and oils remains in suspension. It will not burn off and has a fine polishing action and (so it has been claimed) will improve a barrel by filling pores in the metal. A little goes a long way in a lubricant, but the results have been good.

Commercial and Homemade Lubricants

Commercial lubricants are available in sticks or blocks, with the sticks being molded to fit popular sizing-lubricating machines. The ingredients in commercial lubricants can best be described as some combination of the above in varying amounts. Prices vary, though claims of effectiveness are always high. Most give good results. The formulas are proprietary and the ingredients are sometimes referred to, or at least hinted at, in their various trade names—Bore Butter, Alox, Lithi Bee and so on.

When it comes to getting a good bullet lubricant, there is no magic formula. Most of the commercial products will do the job. They have the advantage of being cast into small cakes or sticks designed to fit into sizer-lubricator machines, and some come in liquid form which can be applied by gently tumbling bullets in it, then setting them on wax paper to dry. They are clean and easy to handle.

The advantage of making up your own lubricant is twofold—economy and versatility. Homemade lubricant is about half as expensive as the commercial product, and less than that if you make it in quantity. Versatility is probably more important since, as is the case with bullet alloys, one formula is not suit-

Liquid Alox is available from Lee and Lyman. It goes on wet and dries to a waxy finish. It works well on handgun bullets, particularly those shot as-cast.

able for all uses. Lubricant for low-velocity handgun bullets does not have to stand up to a lot of heat and pressure and can be fairly soft. A soft, sticky-type of lubricant is an absolute must for use with blackpowder or Pyrodex since the lubricant must keep the fouling soft and easy to remove. A very good lubricant of this type was developed by Spencer Wolf in his research on reproducing original ammunition for the 45 Springfield and Colt SAA revolver. The lubricant consists of beeswax and olive oil mixed in equal parts by volume. Beeswax must be melted in a double boiler to avoid oxidizing it. Overheated beeswax will turn dark brown and lose some of its lubricating properties. When I questioned Wolf if there was something special about olive oil, he replied that it was on sale and was thus the least expensive vegetable oil around at the time. Presumably any vegetable oil would do. These oils blend a little better with beeswax than petroleum-based oils and show no tendency to sweat out even under warm conditions. Interestingly, the beeswax-olive oil mixture does well under fairly high temperatures. The Wolf mixture is very similar in texture to the commercial SPG lubricant and a little softer than Bore Butter. Soft lubricants are the best for cold weather shooting. Hard lubricants become harder when chilled and often fail to work causing bores to lead. Harder formulas, however, are best for shooting high-pressure, high-velocity loads. Harder lubricants generally stand up under warm summer conditions where ammunition may be heated to well over 100 degrees as it sits in a box on a loading block in the sun.

When trying your hand at making bullet lubricant, always remember to keep records of your experiments. It doesn't get much sadder than when you stumble on a perfect formula and can't remember what went into it.

Lyman Orange Magic is a stick lubricant intended for hard-alloy cast bullets to be shot at maximum cast bullet velocities and high temperatures.

LBT Blue Soft Lube is intended for shooting cast bullets at slower velocities and low temperatures.

Lithi Bee is a stick lubricant made of lithium-based grease combined with beeswax. The mixture is an old favorite.

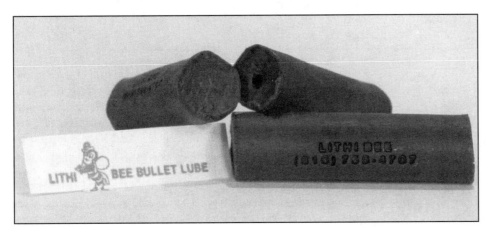

(Below) Taurak bullet lube is a hard grease with a high melting temperature, available in sticks from NECO.

Bullet Lubrication Technique

Some bullets shoot best as cast and should be used that way if they are the proper diameter as they come from the mould. This is often the case with old guns and others that have larger groove diameters. The diameter as well as the roundness of your bullets should be checked by measuring with a Vernier caliper or micrometer.

Lubricating bullets as cast is easily done by placing them base down in a flat, shallow pan of melted lubricant, making sure that the level of the liquid covers all of the lubricating grooves on the bullets. When the lubricant hardens, the bullets are removed using a homemade tool fashioned from a fired cartridge case, of the same caliber, with the head cut off. A short case may have to be soldered or epoxied to a larger diameter case or metal tube to provide a suitable handle. Bullets are removed from the hardened lubricant by simply slipping the case mouth over the bullet and cutting it free. This is known as the cake cutter or cookie cutter method. As the tube handle fills with bullets, they are removed from the top and collected. Finished bullets should have their bases wiped free of lubricant. This is best accomplished by wiping them across a piece of cloth lightly dampened with powder solvent. They should then be placed in clean plastic boxes for storage pending loading. As bullets are run through the mixture, lubricant must be added with each subsequent batch to keep the level at the proper height. It is best to do a full pan load each time.

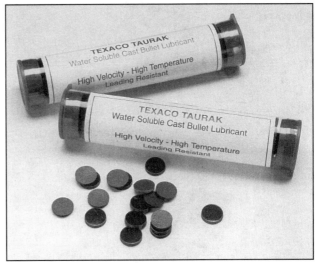

Sizer-Lubricator

Sizer-lubricators are machines that perform three functions. The first is to lightly swage (or size) the cast bullet into perfect roundness; and second to fill the grooves with lubricant. The optional third is to attach a gas check. The tools cost about $125 to $175.

As they come from the mould, bullets are generally larger than required, and it is necessary to bring them to the precise size for best accuracy. This done by forcing the cast bullet through a die, swaging it to exact diameter. When purchasing a

A cake cutter, which is more of a cookie cutter, can be made by drilling out or cutting off the head of a fired cartridge case for the bullets you wish to lubricate. The bullets are placed in a shallow pan of melted lubricant and removed when it has cooled. The pan can be filled to lubricate all or only some of the grooves.

(Below) The Lee Lube and Sizing kit fits on their press. This sizing die and integral container is designed for bullets coated with liquid Alox. The pre-lubed bullets are pushed through the sizer and held in the container.

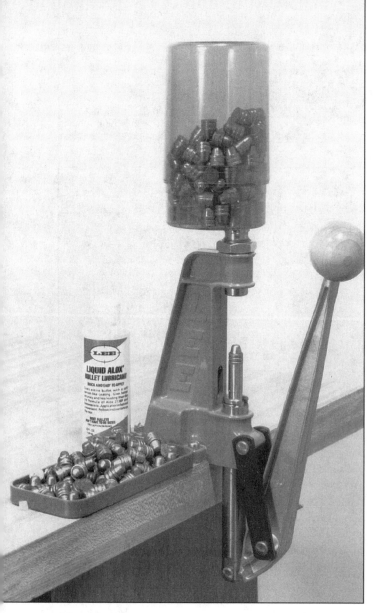

bullet mould and a sizing die, it is a good idea to get a mould that will produce bullets very close to the proper final size. There will always be a certain amount of shrinkage of the bullet as it cools in the mould. If this did not happen, extracting this bullet would be nearly impossible. Moulds are sold with an indication of the cast size, but this will vary depending on the composition of the alloy that is being cast. Bullets should not be sized down much over .003-inch. Excess sizing tends to distort the bullet and adversely affect accuracy. While sizing gives a bullet a shiny mirror-like surface, it also reduces the hardness of the surface by working the metal—another reason to avoid excess sizing.

Sizer-lubricators are made by several manufacturers. They all combine the same basic features: a frame to hold the die, a handle that drives the top punch that forces the bullet through the die, and a lubricating pump that holds a stick of bullet lubricant and forces it through holes in the sizing die and into the grooves of the bullet. One nice feature of the machines made by Lyman and RCBS is that the dies, top punches and lubricating sticks are all interchangeable. Top punches are about $7, dies about $16 to $20.

The sizer-lubricator is a bench-mounted tool for it must have solid support. Otherwise the force delivered to the operating handle would lift it off the bench or take the top off a flimsy table. The tool should be bolted to the loading bench or to a solid plank and held on a sturdy table with C-clamps. Soft alloy bullets size rather easily, while those of linotype metal require far more force. Using these machines takes a bit of skill, much like bullet casting, but mastering it is not very difficult, and speedy production will follow once you master the basics. The first step is to be sure you have the proper top punch. A flat-point top punch will mash the nose on a round-nose bullet, and too large or too small a punch will produce its own distortions, including inaccurate alignment in the sizing die. Top punches should be matched to particular bullets. Loading manuals, particularly those dealing with cast-bullet shooting, include data on the proper top punch for various bullets. Sometimes the exact form of punch is not available. Two solutions are to get the nearest larger size and pack it with varying amounts of aluminum foil or facial tissue coated with a bit of bullet lubricant. Once this is compacted by sizing a few bullets, it will remain in place for a long time and not change shape. The other method, if the top punch is only slightly undersize, is to chuck it in a drill or metal lathe and recontour it with a file, cutting tool or emery cloth. This may be necessary if you are using an obsolete or custom bullet mould.

Once the proper top punch is selected, the reservoir of the lubricator pump should be filled. Most take a solid or hollow stick of lubricant. If you are making your own, you can either cast your own sticks in homemade moulds fabricated from the proper size of pipe or you can try pouring melted lubricant directly into the reservoir itself. This *must* be done with the sizing die in the up (closed) position, otherwise melted lubricant will come welling up through the die to run all over the place. Pouring into the reservoir is difficult, particularly if it is of a type that uses a hollow lubricant stick and has a metal pin in the center. A pouring pot with a long spout is the only kind to use to avoid spilling lubricant all over. Solid lubricant is very difficult to remove—a putty knife will lift it off a flat surface. It is damned near impossible to remove from a rug. I make sticks.

With the reservoir filled and the die in the down position, the lubricator pump handle is pushed two or three times to force lubricant into the die chamber. A bullet is seated in the center of the die and the operating handle is pulled firmly down forcing the bullet into the sizing die. Once sized, the handle is pushed back and the bullet pops up—the proper size and with the grooves filled with lubricant. The die must be adjusted, however, for the length of the bullet you are lubricating. This is done with an adjustment screw on the base of the lug that holds the die. If a short bullet is pushed too far into the die, lubricant will squirt up over the nose. If a long bullet is not seated deep enough it will not get far enough below the level of the lubricating holes in the sizing die, and some of the grooves will not be filled with lubricant.

The up stroke on the operating handle should be faster than the down stroke. This avoids having the bullet in the down position too long. Quick operation avoids lubricant building up on the base of the bullet and the face of the bottom punch where it has to be wiped off. The lubricator pump handle has to be given a couple of turns about every other bullet to keep the pressure high enough to fill all of the grooves completely. Oftentimes the bullet has to be run through the die a second time to fill all the grooves. One advantage of the Redding/ SAECO tool is that the lubricant reservoir has a spring-powered top on it which keeps constant pressure on the lubricant, allowing the operator to lube several bullets before having to run the pump handle. This is essentially all there is to it. The trick to not smearing lube all over the bottom punch and bullet base is not to have too much pressure on the lubricant, and to bring the bullet up out of the die as quickly as possible. Always keep pressure on the handle after completing the down stroke. Failure to do so will allow lubricant to squirt in under the bullet. It is a matter of practice and developing a feel for this operation.

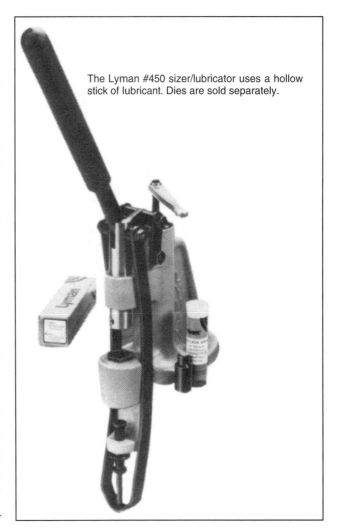

The Lyman #450 sizer/lubricator uses a hollow stick of lubricant. Dies are sold separately.

Lube/sizer dies and top punches are interchageable between Lyman and RCBS.

A bullet pops up after having been lubricated on a SAECO machine. A solid mounting is needed to keep the machine from lifting off the bench top. Proper die adjustment is necessary to keep lubricant from squirting over the bullet nose. The small amount seen here can easily be wiped off.

Seating Gas Checks

Gas checks are intended for use on specially designed bullets. They are of two basic types: the Lyman type that is intended to drop off the base of the bullet shortly after it leaves the muzzle of the gun, and the Hornady crimp-on variety that remains attached until the bullet reaches the target. I prefer the Hornady type since I feel they do a better job of keeping hot gas from getting around the base of the bullet and melting channels in the bearing surface—known as gas cutting. Sometimes the drop-off gas checks do not drop off and remain on the bullet all the way to the target, making that bullet several grains heavier than the others in the series of shots and, particularly at long ranges, causing it to hit low.

Gas checks permit cast bullets to be driven almost as fast as jacketed bullets, about 2200 fps, by acting as a hard gasket at the base of the bullet. High velocities with gas-checked bullets are obtainable only with hard, tough alloys and lubricants that will stand up to high temperatures and pressures. Applying gas checks to hard alloy bullets takes more muscle than for softer ones, but can be done so long as those alloys are no harder than linotype (BHN22).

Seating gas checks is simplicity itself. They are placed on the face of the die punch and the bullet is seated in it. It is then pushed through the sizing die, and the bullet lubricated in the normal manner. Make sure that when the bullet bottoms in the die that it does so firmly in order to get a good fit with the crimp-on type of gas checks. When applying gas checks to soft alloy bullets, care must be taken not to apply too much pressure and flatten the nose of the bullet. The leverage on these machines is very good, allowing you to apply a great deal of pressure with minimal effort.

Bullet Inspection and Storage

Bullets should be inspected after they come out of the sizer to see that the grooves are well filled with lubricant. Sizing will not make out-of-round bullets perfect. If the grooves are wider on one side than they are on the other, this bullet was not completely filled out in the mould. These and ones with irregular drive bands should be scrapped if they are really bad, or separated for use as warming and fouling shots. Finished bullets should be loaded immediately, or stored in closed containers where they will not gather grit, lint and other foreign matter. Bullets that have been dropped on the floor and dented on the base will no longer shoot straight. Those that have rolled on the floor through primer ash, metal filings and the like should be wiped clean with a soft cloth moistened with solvent or light oil and relubricated.

Finished bullets should be weighed on your powder scale. The finest consistent accuracy is from those that are within a tolerance of +/-.05-grain in weight. Changes in alloy and temperature, lack of stirring and fluxing can affect weight by varying the content of the alloy in that particular bullet. By the same token, pouring technique can trap air bubbles in bullets and alter their weight. Bullets should be sorted by weight and stored and marked accordingly for best accuracy. It is best to handle finished, cast and lubricated bullets as little as possible. This keeps them clean, and your fingers won't wipe lubricant out of the grooves.

Wads and Fillers

Distortion of the base of a cast bullet, particularly a rifle bullet, is a constant problem. Smokeless powder of the coarser granula-

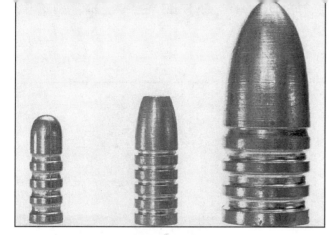

(Above) Bullets should be inspected before sizing and lubricating. Good cast bullets should have square edges and even grooves.

(Left) After lubrication, there should be no evidence of distortion or pieces of lead in the lube grooves. The accurate bullet is one that leaves the barrel evenly rifled with no asymmetrical distortion.

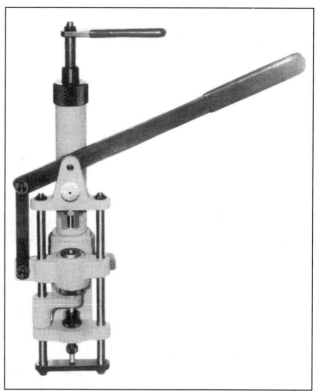

The SAECO Lubri-Sizer is a quality tool that will last a lifetime.

tions will be forced into the base of soft alloy bullets peppering them with small dents and often gas-cutting the sides to a degree.

A number of strategies to overcome this problem have been tried with varying degrees of success. One thing seems absolutely clear, however: *Never* have an airspace between any kind of wad and the base of the bullet! This will cause that wad to come slamming forward to strike the base of the bullet and expand there. This can make a ring in the case and, in many instances, in the chamber of a rifle and ruin the barrel. I have had light tufts of kapok weighing about a grain, used to keep a light charge of powder in the base of a 45-70 case, make a ring in the case. These were propelled by 9 grains of Unique when they hit the base of a 150-grain bullet. Wads of felt, cork and cardboard have been used with success in straight-walled cases. *Never* put any kind of filler wad in a bottleneck case! All wads, however, must *completely* fill the void between the powder and the bullet base. Fillers between wads such as Cream of Wheat have also been tried and the results found unsatisfactory.

From time to time there is a resurgence of interest in various types of lubricating wads for use with both cast and jacketed bullets. Wax wads and grease wads have demonstrated effectiveness in improving accuracy and lengthening barrel life. These consist of a thin disc of bullet lubricant cut to exact case-mouth diameter. The lubricant is generally harder than that used in a lubricating pump. The discs are punched out of a flat sheet about the thickness of the cardboard on the back of a writing tablet. One of the better known formulas was the development of Edward A. Leopold and was sold as "Leopold's Oleo Wads." They consisted of (by weight) 5 ounces each of Japan wax and beeswax, 2 ounces ozocerite, and 3 to 4 teaspoons Acheson Unctious graphite #1340.

According to G.L. Wotkyns and J.B. Sweany, the developers of the 220 Swift, grease wads directly behind the jacketed bullets decreased erosion and improved accuracy.

Lubricated cardboard wads were at one time loaded in rifle ammunition by UMC and Winchester for the 40-70 and 40-90 blackpowder cartridges. Bearing the above warnings in mind, those who wish to experiment with making their own wax wads will find that about the only way to get an even sheet of lubricant is to take a very clean straight-sided glass bottle, fill it with cold water and dip it straight down into a pot of melted lubricant. A deep narrow pan and a bottle that nearly fills it will be most practical. The thickness of the layer is controlled by the number of dips. When the lubricant layer on the bottle is well cooled, a straight cut is made down one side and the sheet is gently peeled off. Wads may be cut by using the mouth of a fired case from which the head has been cut to facilitate removal.

As can be deduced, the easiest and safest kind of loading for use with a wax wad is one in which the case is nearly filled with powder and the wad and bullet base gently compact the charge. Sharpe makes the point that the wad should "stay in the neck of the case." Amen to that. For reduced charge loadings you could try sticking the wad to the bullet base by either warming the bullet base and pressing the wad in place, or wetting the wad surface with a volatile solvent and "gluing" it in place with the melted lubricant. This system is not tried or recommended. Before loading any such ammunition, see how tight the bond is. If the wad drops off or can be easily removed by slipping it or tapping the bullet, don't load it unless it is supported by a charge of powder or a solid wad column of felt, cardboard or cork.

Reloading can be accomplished in any number of ways—from simple inexpensive hand tools to costly progressive equipment. By defining your goals, you'll find which is best for you.

Tooling Up For Reloading

RELOADING BEGAN WITH relatively simple tools that could be carried in the pocket or saddlebag. They were shaped in the manner of pliers and leather punches, and were referred to as "tong tools." Manufacture of this type of equipment more or less ceased about twenty years ago, with Lyman and Lee being the only major manufacturers of this type of tool today. They are portable, cheap and capable of turning out rather good ammunition. The disadvantages are that they are slow and require more muscle power to use than bench tools. As "campfire" ammunition making became more a thing of the past, these tools have all but disappeared. They are, however, useful since you can't take a reloading bench into the woods, and there may be some instances where you might need to produce some quick loads in the field. They qualify nicely as survival equipment, too.

Today's reloader generally does not have all that much spare time and usually prefers speed in production over the option of taking tools to the field. The beginning reloader is

Whether plain or fancy, the reloading bench should have enough space for efficient tool mounting.

(Below) A basic reloading bench should be sturdy and have plenty of storage space. The individual design is up to the maker. (Photo courtesy of Speer.)

faced with some basic issues that must be assessed when it comes time to purchase equipment. These include economy versus speed; speed versus precision; and, finally, precision versus economy. These three issues will be discussed in detail in the hope that you can reach decisions that will match your temperament and shooting habits. The beginning reloader can find himself stunned by information overload while perusing catalogs, absolutely brimming with gadgets and gizmos, all promising more/better/faster.

Basic Equipment: Getting What You Need

One way to enter the water, as it were, is to get acquainted with other reloaders and see what they use and don't use, and quiz them on the whys and wherefores of their equipment. Ask a friend if you can try his equipment. This way you can get a feel for the tools, how they work, and begin to come to some decisions regarding what you might like and what you find difficult or unnecessary.

The reloading bench is the foundation of your work area. There is no standardized design, and it may well serve a dual purpose as a kitchen counter on which reloading tools are temporarily mounted. If you must use a temporary surface of this type, your reloading press and sizer/lubricator should be permanently mounted on a solid 2x6 or heavier plank that can be securely attached to the counter top with C-clamps. The counter must have a solid top since the levering force exerted on the bullet sizer and the loading press can pull the counter top loose. If you have the space, a solid desk or workbench arrangement is best. General requirements are that it have enough weight or be attached to the floor so that it will not rock back and forth in use. It should be solid enough that the top will not pry loose

under the stress of cartridge and bullet sizing. Whether or not it is to be a thing of beauty depends on how much of the public will view it, in a dining room or corner of an apartment, or if it will stay in a garage or basement area. If ammunition and powder are to be stored in the same area, I recommend placement of the bench in a spot that is climate controlled. It should have at least one large drawer and be close to shelving or cabinets where bullets, primers, powder, cases, loading manuals, etc., can be located within easy reach. The top should be smooth and free of cracks, holes and splinters.

The bench I built was assembled entirely from scrap lumber. The top measures 25x47 inches; it stands 33 inches high and features a single 18x20-inch drawer. The legs are made of

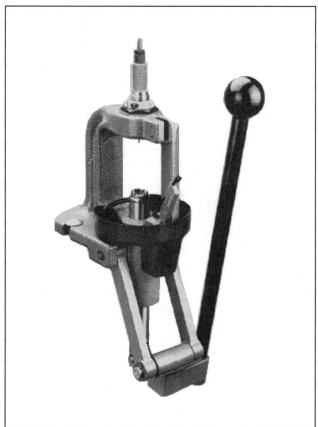

Basic O-frame presses are reliable, rugged and easy to use. The Redding (left) and RCBS are typical examples.

doubled 2x4s blocked so the top sits in them. Single 2x4 support rails connect the sides and back, 4 inches above the floor. These dimensions are not necessarily ideal, but were determined by the most efficient use of a large plywood packing crate and various 2x4s I could scrounge. Everything is held together with wood screws and contact cement. Solidity and weight were achieved by making the top a solid lamination of plywood 5 inches thick. This allowed mounting of the sizer/lubricator and loading press with lag screws. Movers do not like this bench as it must weigh close to 200 pounds—much heavier than is needed. Hey, I had the plywood. If I were to build another, I would have more drawer space and make it lighter. I attached the top so it could be separated from the frame by running screws through heavy prefabricated steel angle pieces, punched with a number of holes. In Canada, where I built the bench, this steel was sold under the name of Dexion. By putting two angled pieces of Dexion inside the top of the drawer and hooking them over two similar pieces mounted on wood 2x4 rails attached to the bottom of the bench top, I made a suspended drawer without having to frame it in the standard manner.

In addition to weight, the biggest mistake I made was failing to consider the location. The dirty, rough wood looked terrible in the corner of the dining room. Thus, I spent an inordinate amount of time sanding, staining and finishing it to make it look (more or less) like furniture. If your bench must look like furniture, start with good quality wood.

Once you have your bench, the next step is to choose the basic reloading tool, the heart of your operation—the press. Before parting with any money, it is best to start with the maximum amount of experience and knowledge. This returns to the above mentioned issues of speed, economy and precision. Your first question should be: Am I going to load for pistol, rifle or both? Shotshell reloading requires its own special loading equipment and will be dealt with later. If the answer is to reload both handgun and rifle cartridges, then you will want to buy a press that is intended for rifle cartridges that will do handgun ammunition as well.

Economy Versus Speed

A bench-mounted loading press of the most basic type costs between $50 and $55 on the low end, but goes up to over $700 for special heavy models. This is the O-frame or C-frame press, so called because the frames are shaped like these letters. Both are rugged and simple. They are also referred to as single-stage presses since they mount a single loading die in the top. Each operation—decapping and sizing, neck expanding and bullet seating—requires that the die be unscrewed and the next die screwed in place for each operation. The manufacturers promise a production rate of about 100 finished rounds per hour.

Similar to these are the arbor presses, which mount a single die in the bottom. Arbor presses require a special straight-line type of die that is not compatible with the top-mounted variety

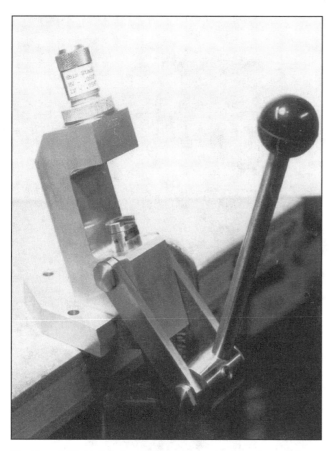

The Ross & Webb Benchrest Press is an extremely strong C-frame design for the serious reloader.

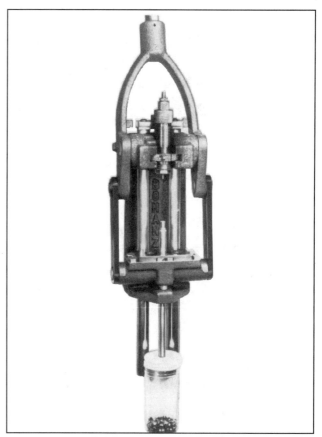

Forster's Co-Ax B-2 Press is a different wrinkle on the C- and O-frame designs. Dual guide rods offer precision alignment; dies snap in and out for quick, easy changing.

used in standard presses. The price range and speed are about the same. Arbor presses are small and compact, and have the advantage of being on a flat base and not requiring permanent bench mounting. This makes them handy to take to the range where ammunition can be fabricated while you shoot. In addition to instant gratification, this portability saves time and material put into long runs of test ammunition.

More expensive and faster are the turret and H-frame machines that allow a full three-die set to be mounted along with a powder measure. All dies are in place and the cartridge is moved from one station to the next, or the turret is rotated to bring the next die into position. Production is estimated at 200 rounds per hour, but the price is up to between $150 to $700.

Near the top end, short of buying an ammunition factory, are the progressive loaders. These are semi-automated machines with feed tubes and hoppers that are filled with cases, bullets, primers and powder. Once the various feeding devices are filled, the operator simply pulls a handle and manually feeds one component, usually bullets or cases, inserting them into a slot on a revolving plate, and the machine does the rest, moving the case from station to station. The finished rounds come popping out at the end of a full plate rotation cycle and are collected in a convenient bin. The cheapest of these machines is about $300, the top of the line $1500. Production rates are from about 500 rounds per hour to 1200. Plan to do a lot of shooting if you invest in one of these. You should also plan to have plenty of space since a progressive stands better than 2 feet high and

The Jones arbor press is typical of the type. Arbor presses are compact and do not need to be bench-mounted, making them convenient to take to the range to assemble ammunition on the spot.

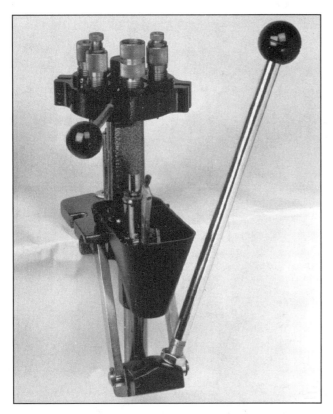

The Lyman T-Mag II is a turret press from a company that has been making this basic design for over forty years. A full set of dies and a powder measure can be screwed into the turret, and each one is then rotated into position for the next step.

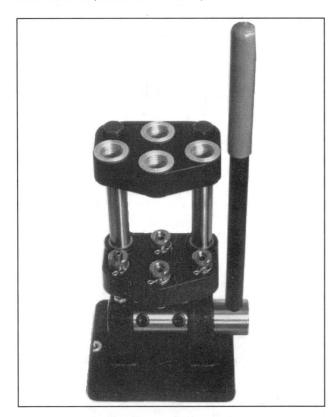

The H-frame press, as typified by the CH/4D No. 444, has many followers since it holds a full set of dies and powder measure. In this system, the "turret" is fixed, thus no rotation between steps is required. The case is simply moved from station to station.

The Dillon RL 1050 will load 1000 to 1200 rounds per hour. A progressive loader of this sort represents an investment of over a thousand dollars. It is definitely not for beginners.

weighs up to 50 pounds. The top end? That would have to be the Ammo Load Mark IV which *is* an ammunition factory. Motor-driven and likely having some computer technology within, this baby will crank out up to 5000 rounds per hour—all for a measly $12,756.

Speed Versus Precision

All of the presses mentioned will produce high quality, precision ammunition, or at least as precise as you make it, since quality control is up to the operator. Careful adjustment, precise measurement, and inspecting every step in production is your job, and if you do it well, the results will show in the finished product. The only real difference between the turret and multi-station machines and the single die units is the price and speed of operation.

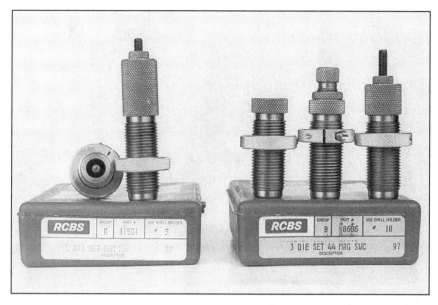

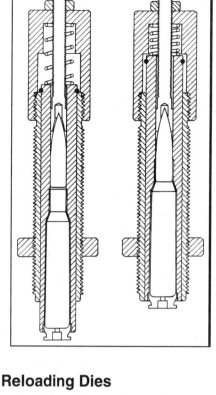

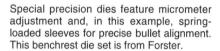

Reloading dies come in two basic formats—a two-die set for rifle cartridges and a three-die set for pistol and cast-bullet rifle loading.

Special precision dies feature micrometer adjustment and, in this example, spring-loaded sleeves for precise bullet alignment. This benchrest die set is from Forster.

Progressive loaders are designed more for speed than precision. In the case of handgun ammunition where benchrest accuracy is not expected, they are the best investment for a shooter who really burns a lot of ammunition. These are generally purchased by clubs, police departments and professional reloaders who sell their ammunition. While progressives churn out tremendous quantities of ammunition, they generally require a fairly complicated set-up period, and if there is a change of caliber of ammunition, this can mean a different set of feed tubes and plates as well as dies. Because they are complicated, progressives require more tinkering and cleaning to keep them running smoothly. Automation of the process means you depend on the machine to do it right every time. That doesn't always happen.

Precision Versus Economy

As I mentioned above, precision and economy lie mainly with the single-die and turret/H-frame (multi-station) machines. Progressives only pay when there is a demand for high-volume production of one caliber at a time. For my money, the price differential between the single-stage and turret/multi-station machines is close enough that it is probably worth the extra money to invest in the latter if you are going to do more than a very modest amount of reloading. They have the advantage of holding a full die set and a powder measure. This means the dies are seated and adjusted once, for the most part, unless you are reloading a number of calibers. The production edge will be noticed as the amount of ammunition you make increases. For a shooter reloading a single caliber, mainly for hunting—someone who does not do a lot of practice and may assemble no more than 200 to 2000 rounds a year—the best buy would be the simple, reliable O-frame machine. It will do the job.

Reloading Dies

Once a press is purchased, it must be equipped with one set of dies for each different cartridge you reload. For handgun ammunition, the first die decaps the cartridge and resizes it to unfired dimensions, the second expands the case mouth, and the third seats the bullet. Rifle dies do not expand the case mouth since this is not necessary for hard, jacketed bullets. Cast bullets, however, require this expansion to keep them from being accidentally cut by a sharp case mouth.

Dies come in grades from plain to fancy. Basic die sets of steel range in price from $40 to about $50. They will last for many years and many thousands of rounds of ammunition. Using tungsten carbide or titanium nitride dies requires little or no lubrication of the cases, which speeds the loading process a bit, and they last longer than steel. Add about $30 for this feature. Forster, Redding and Jones offer micrometer-adjustable bullet seating dies, while Harrell's Precision makes a variable base for reforming benchrest cases to near chamber dimensions. Specialty dies of this sort run from about $55 to $125 each and are worth the price if you are into competition target shooting. There are special neck-sizing dies for use with bottleneck cases that will only be fired in one particular rifle, thus there is no need to put cases through the wear and tear of full-length resizing. There are custom dies for obsolete calibers and loading cartridges as large as 20mm. Nearly anything your heart desires will cheerfully be made up by the 4-D Custom Die Co. of Mount Vernon, Ohio.

Primer Seaters and Shellholders

Primer seaters generally fit in the front bottom of the reloading press, and you will need one for large diameter primers and

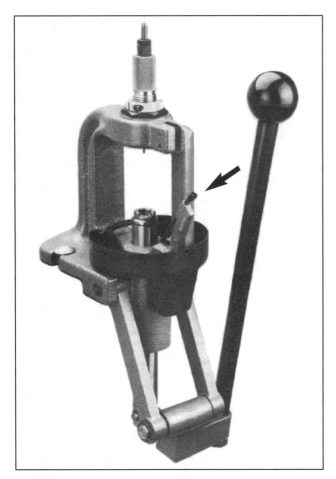

The primer seater (arrow), as shown on this RCBS Rock Chucker, is usually included as part of the press, but if you get used equipment, be sure all parts are there.

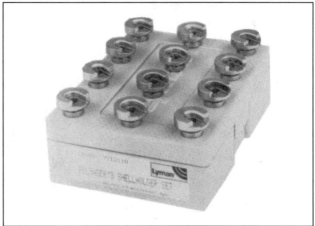

Shellholders must be purchased to fit the cartridge you are reloading. Some accept more than one cartridge, and they can be had in sets.

Problems such as crimped-in primers and stuck cases, like this one with the head torn off, require special tools such as a stuck-case removal kit.

another for small primers. It's probably a good idea to buy both since a pair is generally under $10. Case or shellholders are needed to hold the case as it inserted into the die. One size does *not* fit all, but Lee and Lyman offer sets that cover most popular rifle and pistol cartridges.

A real headache is getting the primer crimp out of a military case. A number of die makers offer a useful die to remove this crimp with a stroke of the loading press handle. There is also a chamfering tool to do this, but I prefer a swager die.

Sizer/Lubricators

The second large bench tool you will need is a sizer/lubricator if you are planning on shooting your own cast bullets. In addition to applying lubricant in the grooves of the bullet, the sizer rounds them out to a dimension determined by the sizing die. By the use of various dies, you can control bullet diameters to .001-inch. These tools cost about $16 for the Lee unit to around $175 for the RCBS and SAECO machines. Sizing dies are around $30 each, while top punches, needed to push the bullet through the die, are about $12. Here again, one size does not fit all.

Small Bench Tools

These are either mounted on the bench or on the press, or are free standing on the bench. The list that follows is a basic list.

Beyond this lies the land of wonderful gadgets that save time and energy, increase production and, in general, do, or at least promise, all those things that helped put men on the moon and otherwise made America great.

Powder scales are absolutely essential when working up loads, as well as for checking those that are measured with a hand dipper or metered by a powder measure. Basic balance scales start at about $50 and top at about $110. Electronic scales with LCD readout start around $160 and go on up to over $300. The speed advantage goes to the electronic models.

Powder measures are not an absolute necessity, but are invaluable when it comes time to get into production loading. They can be mounted on a loading press or a stand. These start at a little over $25 and run on up to well over $200 for models with many bells and whistles. The precision of the adjustment is not all that different. More expensive models adjust faster and a little more precisely, keep their accuracy more consistently, hold more powder and so on. The accuracy of powder-measure metering is mainly dependent on the consistency of the operator as he pulls and returns the handle.

Case trimmers are essential for keeping cartridge length consistent. Cases stretch on firing and in reloading dies, and must be trimmed back every so often. Hand-cranked models start at a little over $80 with a selection of collets and pilots to handle most common calibers. Collets hold the case head, and pilots guide the case mouth straight against the cutter. Motorized models run around $135 and up, as they say.

Hand Tools

Case deburring or chamfering tools come with a bench mount and, in the case of the Forster case trimmer, can be purchased as an add-on feature. They are also made in hand-held versions. These are necessary to take burrs off the outside of a case mouth that has been trimmed and to chamfer (bevel) the inside of the case mouth, removing burrs that will otherwise scratch and gall jacketed bullets. Prices range from $3 to $12.

A primer pocket cleaner can be simply a flat-blade screwdriver, inserted into the primer pocket and turned several times to get the fouling out. However, all the major (and some minor) tool makers have them, and they're not expensive. The two basic types are the scraper and brush styles, and both do good work. Getting the primer ash deposit out of the pocket is necessary or the fresh primer will not seat properly. The ash build-up will either result in a high primer or one that may give poor ignition, as the firing pin blow is cushioned and the vent blocked by ash. A steel straight-edge ruler will check that your primers are seated deeply enough.

Lyman, Redding, RCBS and others offer case-care kits containing primer pocket cleaners and an assortment of case brushes to remove interior fouling, a good investment if you are loading blackpowder or Pyrodex ammunition. About $20 will get you one. If you want to automate things a bit, Lyman and RCBS have a number of options to do so.

Loading blocks are the best way to keep from double-charging your cases. They come in moulded plastic from several

The ultimate in precision and speed is the RCBS PowderMaster electronic powder trickler combined with their PowderPro electronic scale. This the only reliable device of this type the author has seen that allows the loader to program an exact charge and get it *consistently* with accuracy to a $1/10$-grain.

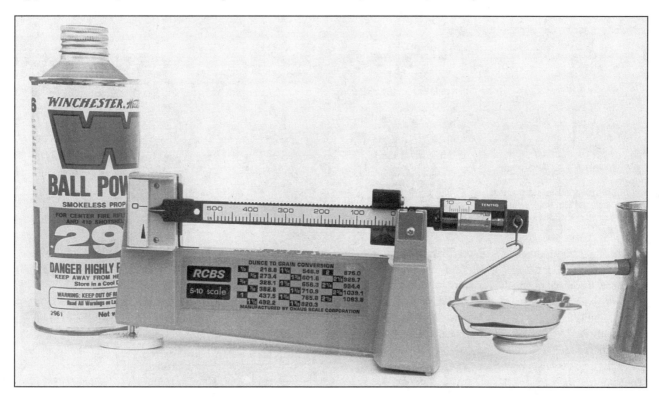

An accurate powder scale is an absolute must for working up loads. The beginner and expert should have and use this valuable piece of equipment.

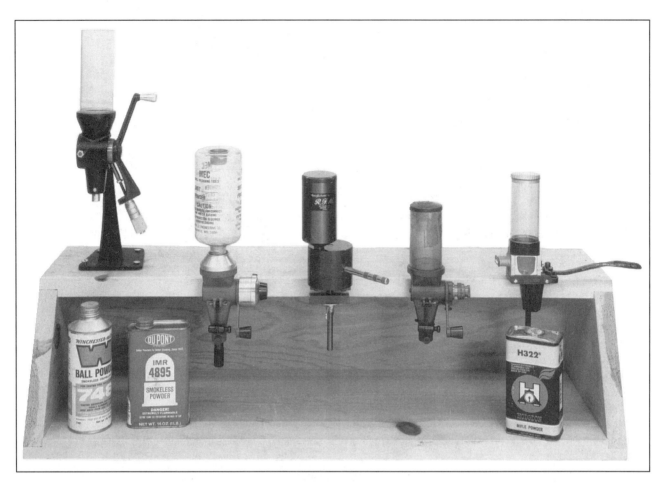

(Above) A powder measure speeds production and can throw accurate loads. Precision, however, depends on the consistency of operation.

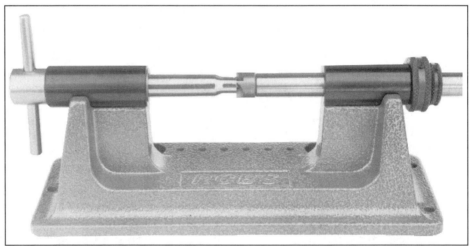

Cases stretch in firing and reloading, and every so often they will need to be trimmed to the proper length. A case trimmer requires various collets and pilots to trim accurately.

manufacturers and cost about $3. You can make your own by drilling holes in a flat piece of 1-inch plank and gluing on a flat bottom. A loading block is the *best* way to inspect your cases after they have been charged with powder, before you seat a bullet. Double-charging is very easy to do, especially when using a powder measure. If you shoot one of these loads, your gun will never forgive you.

Powder funnels cost about $3, and their use is only way to avoid spilling powder when you are working up loads by weighing each one. A charge drawn from a powder measure and dumped into the pan of your scale for checking is the way to maintain accuracy in your measure. If everything is working

as it should, the charge in the pan is then funneled into the case. Forster offers a funnel with a long drop tube for loading nearly compressed charges.

Micrometer/calipers are the best means of making all sorts of precision measurements, like case length, inside and outside diameters, case neck wall thickness, checks for bullet roundness and diameter, case swelling, etc. My favorite version of this tool is the dial caliper with an LCD readout if your eyes have problems with fine lines. B-West has them for about $55. Cheap ones are made of plastic and not to be trusted for fine work. A steel one goes for $30 on up, if you fancy such names as Brown and Sharpe.

Bullet pullers are there for the same reason they put erasers on pencils. Everybody, sooner or later, puts together some loads that won't fly for one reason or another and need to be taken apart. The two basic types are the one that screws into the die hole on your press and the kinetic type which looks like a hammer. The press-mounted type is easy to use, but can mar the bullets, making them unshootable. The kinetic model features a hollow plastic head into which the cartridge is fitted. A wad of cotton or tissue can be used to cushion the bottom of the chamber where the bullet is caught. With this addition, even very soft lead-alloy bullets may be retrieved undamaged. These are very efficient and handy tools.

Case Cleaning Equipment

Do shiny-bright cases shoot bullets straighter than tarnished ones? Case cleaning is something like car washing—you either believe in it or don't. The only real advantage of clean cases is that small cracks and flaws are more easily seen on shiny surfaces. If smokeless powder is used, most cases stay pretty clean, unless they receive a lot of handling with sweaty fingers or fire a number of low-pressure loads that fail to expand the case fully, which coats it with soot. Most cases will shine up in the sizing process, unless you only neck-size. Polishing with a cloth before you put the finished cartridge into the box will generally keep them bright for a long time.

After much use and especially after using Pyrodex or black-powder in them, brass cases will take on the look of an old penny. Since both black and Pyrodex leave corrosive deposits (sulfuric acid), cases should be washed out soon after shooting. There are two basic case cleaning methods, chemical and mechanical. Chemical cleaning involves washing the cases in a bath of an acid-based cleaner. The cleaner is sold as a concentrate to be mixed with water in a plastic, glass or stainless-steel container. The cases are given a wash, then thoroughly rinsed. If the mixture is too strong or the cases are left in too long, these cleaners will begin etching the metal. Tarnish and dirt are removed, but the cases are left a dull yellow color. A polish is achieved by some means of buffing. Liquid cleaners are effective and require no special equipment.

Mechanical polishers are motorized tumblers or vibrators

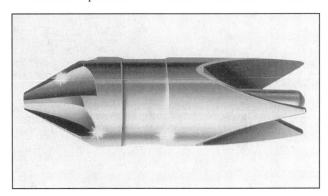

(Above and left) A deburring tool makes bullet seating easier and lessens damage to the bullet base.

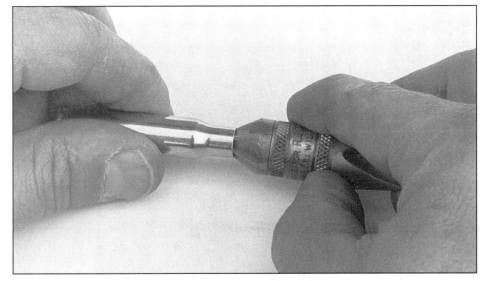

Primer pocket cleaners scour burned residue from the primer pocket. This brush-type tool works quickly.

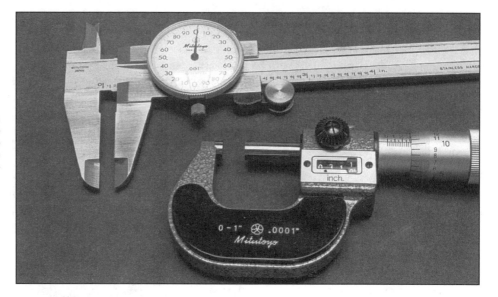

A micrometer and/or precision caliper capable of accurate measurement to .001-inch are necessary tools. Investing in good-quality equipment is worthwhile in the long run.

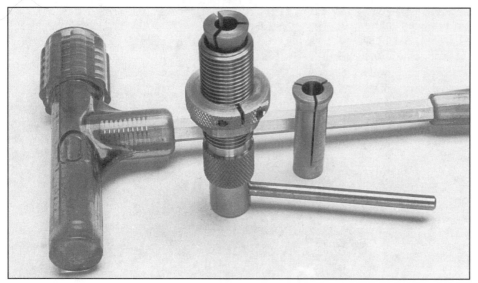

Bullet pullers come in two varieties: those that mount on the reloading press and those of the hammer-type kinetic variety (left). The latter is perhaps gentler on bullets, but requires more energy on the part of the user.

with containers into which the cases are dumped, along with a cleaning media composed of ground walnut shells or ground corn cobs. Liquid polish additives are also available to speed the process. The cases are tumbled or vibrated for an hour or more and come out with a high shine. They must be separated from the cleaning media, and the media must be cleaned and replaced every so often. Prices for tumblers range from about $80 to $130.

Shotshell Reloading

While shotshells can be reloaded with simple hand tools, and RCBS does offer a shotshell reloading die set for use in its O-frame presses, most shotshell reloading is done on press-type machines. They are similar to the turret, multi-station and semi-automated (progressive) loader designs used for metallic cartridges. Shotshells, obviously, do not require the precision alignment of bullet with case that is needed for metallic cartridges. Thus, with a decline in the need for high precision, good speed can be achieved. Precision is, of course, required in sizing, wad column seating and powder charging, although accuracy is a matter of pattern density. This not to say that one can take a cavalier attitude when loading shotshells. A shotgun can be blown up with an overload as easily as any other gun, and with similarly disastrous results.

Basic Equipment

If all you reload are shotshells, your needs for a bench and drawer storage are far less than for metallic cartridges. The stresses involved in sizing and reloading shotshells are less than those in making rifle cartridges. While a bench of some sort is needed, it does not have to be as large or robust. Shotshell presses do have to be firmly mounted. Overhead space is more of a consideration because many of these machines stand 2 feet high—more if you elect to attach hoppers to feed empty shells and/or wads.

Storage space is more of a concern if you are setting up for shotshell reloading, since the components are very bulky and you have more of them. Wads and shot are sold in bulk, which means finding a place to store bread-loaf-size 25-pound bags of shot and grocery-bag-size bags of plastic shot cups. Shotshells, loaded or empty, are bulky, requiring four to five times the space needed for an equivalent amount of handgun ammu-

The Lee Load-All II (left) and MEC 600 Jr. Mark V are excellent machines for the casual shooter. The production rate is fast enough to satisfy most shooters unless they are heavily into competition trap or Skeet shooting.

nition. Shelves or cupboards are a good idea to have close to your bench.

Economy versus Speed

The same rule holds true for shotshell reloading as for rifle and pistol ammunition manufacture: Machines that turn out more ammunition faster cost more money. Because the process is somewhat simpler for loading shotshells, making ammunition goes faster. With most machines, all the necessary dies, the powder charger and the shot charger are contained in the press. With everything close together, and a need to do no more than pull an operating handle and move a shell from one station to the next, even a basic machine like the Lee Load-All II will turn out 100 rounds per hour. At $50 this is a very good investment. Lee offers update kits to convert older presses to the Load-All II for $28 and conversion kits for $20 to load other gauges. Hornady offers a similar single-stage press and a conversion to progressive loader status via a kit. The basic press is about $110. Add on $253 worth of accessories and you have a progressive. The MEC 600 Jr. Mark V, while a single-stage machine, is set up for speed and will double the Lee's output. The price, not surprisingly, is about $160.

Progressive Loaders

Progressive machines are very popular with shotshell reloaders because of their output. Shotgun shooting, unlike rifle or handgun shooting, generally involves a lot of gun handling. Targets are close in the hunting field, but they're there only briefly. Practice for hunting, as well as just plain fun, is on the Skeet or trap range, and this means a *lot* of shooting. Developing the reflexes to become a good scattergunner requires practice, which requires a larger consumption of ammunition than for most rifle or handgun work.

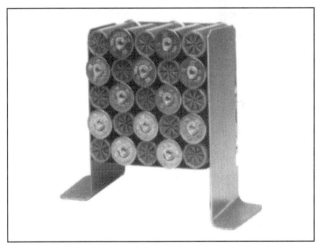

Hornady's Stack 'N' Pack makes boxing shotshells easier and is a good example of an inexpensive accessory that's well worth the money.

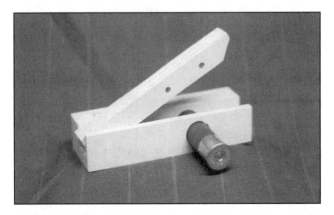

Precision Reloading's D-Loader does for shotshells what a bullet puller does for metallic cartridges. The case, however, cannot be saved, only the contents.

Progressive machines start at around $320, and machines of this general level will turn out between 300 to 400 rounds per hour. Top of the line progressives like the Hollywood Automatic weigh 100 pounds and can crank out an astonishing 1800 rounds per hour, if you have the muscle to keep pulling that long. At $3600, few individuals will invest at this level, when a MEC 8567 Grabber at $460 will turn out 500 finished shells an hour. These numbers are production time, of course, and not counting the time spent loading hoppers, canisters and tubes with wads, primers, shot and powder. Progressive machines, because of their complexity, are more subject to problems than the simpler loaders. They require more cleaning and care as well to keep them running smoothly.

Accessories

Unlike rifle and pistol presses, where you must buy separate die sets, shotshell reloaders come equipped with a set to load the gauge you prefer. Extra sets, of course, may be purchased, but six sets would load everything from 410-bore to 10-gauge. A great many machines come with conversion kits to upgrade performance, handle more gauges or load steel shot, which has its own requirements. There are dies to do six-fold, eight-fold or roll crimps. Most of the accessories for shotshell reloading are, therefore, add-ons to the basic press.

There are, however, several separate items that are necessary and useful. The precision scale for weighing powder and, in this case, shot is a must to work up and check loads. The same dial or digital caliper is also invaluable for checking case lengths and diameters. MEC makes a very handy metal plate gauge, cut with a dozen holes. This ring gauge allows a quick check on the diameters of all the standard U.S.-made shotshells and is essentially a go/no-go gauge for each. Hornady's Stack 'N' Pack and MEC's E-Z Pack are nifty racks for packing shotshells into standard boxes. The answer to the bullet puller is the Precision Reloading D-Loader, which allows the reclamation of shot, powder primers and wads from bad reloads. It also trims 10- and 12-gauge TUFF-type wads to length. It is a cutting tool, however, and will not save the shell itself.

Organization

Getting all your equipment organized is a key to success in reloading. Tools too close together or too far apart for convenient reach slow your work and wear out your temper. Here again, one of the best ways to get started is to see how other reloaders set things up. If possible, try their equipment to get a feel for the process. Smooth operation stems from having the right tools in the right place and components where they can be easily handled and stored. The right way is the one that works best for you.

Generally speaking, sizer/lubricators are mounted on the front of the bench. They do not need to be particularly close to the loading press since bullet sizing and lubricating is generally done as an operation separate from the actual loading process. By the same token, the case trimmer, if bench mounted, need not be near the press since this operation is generally done separately, prior to loading. The press is really the center of your

```
CARTRIDGE_____Overall length_____

Case, make _____Times reloaded_____

Primer, make, type_____

Powder_____ Charge_____

Bullet, make, type , weight_____

For gun_____

Sight setting_____ Range Zero_____

Velocity, Chronographed_____ est_____

Date Loaded_____

Remarks_____

_____
```

A simple reloading data form can be created on a computer and reduced to stick-on labels for cartridge boxes, and/or kept in notebook form for ready reference. Accurate records are essential.

operation and should have clear space around it to place boxes or stacks of primers, bullets, cases and cans of powder. You may want to try mounting tools with C-clamps to start, so a change in position to a final location and bolting down only has to be done once, as you develop a plan for working. A comfortable chair is a real asset since you will be spending many, hopefully happy and productive, hours there.

Record Keeping

The importance of record keeping cannot be overemphasized. Your load-data book of what you load and how it shoots will keep you up on what you have tried, how well it worked and, depending on your analysis and commentary, will serve as a guide to further experimentation. Without accurate records, you have to rely on that poorest of devices—memory. The type of data storage and method you choose is, again, what works best for you. A pocket tape recorder can be carried to the range, and notes and comments transcribed later. Some people prefer data forms because they require the least work. I have gotten along with a vest-pocket notebook for a number of years, but also have a tape machine, since writing takes time away from shooting. The only problem is that tape storage is linear and a page can be scanned at a glance.

Record keeping includes the box in which you keep your finished ammunition. Unmarked boxes equal "mystery" loads. When working up a load, you should mark the box by indicating primer type, primer make, powder type, charge, bullet weight, alloy, lubricant and exact size. You can write on the box or use stick-on notes. Less data may be needed once you have found a load you wish to produce on a regular basis. Here again though, care must be taken to mark *clearly* high-pressure "hot" loads if you have both strong- and weak-action guns of the same caliber.

You've made the decision to reload, so you've collected all the necessary components, set up a safe work space with the proper tools, and done the research, but now what?

Rifle Catridge Reloading

"BEGIN AT THE beginning," the King said, very gravely, "and go on till you come to the end: then stop." This is about the only sensible advice from Lewis Carroll's King in *Alice in Wonderland*. Beginnings are at times a little fuzzy, and there are small, but necessary, side trips to be made along the way. This chapter will try follow the King's directive while getting in the necessary small bits.

The beginner is going to start off with once-fired or, better, new cases to work up a load. Once a load is tested and found to be satisfactory, then quantity production can begin and some of the preliminary steps can be omitted.

Case Inspection

Even new and first-fired cases should be checked over for defects. Any with splits or serious defects in the case mouth that are not ironed out in the resizing die should be discarded. Cases should be segregated by maker as determined by the head-stamp. Even though they are the same caliber, cases of different

Empty cases should go back in the original box after firing so various brands and calibers don't get mixed.

manufacture have slight differences in wall thickness and vent (flash hole) size. Mixing brands can alter velocities and pressures, and open up group size.

Full-Length Resizing

This step is just as necessary for new cases as for fired ones. If these will later be used in only one rifle, further resizing can be limited to neck-sizing only, unless heavy loads are used. Before any operation can take place on the reloading press, the die must first be adjusted to resize the case properly. For full-length resizing, with the shellholder snapped into the ram, lower the press handle completely; screw the sizer die into the press until the bottom of the die hits the shellholder. Now, raise the

press handle enough so you can screw the die down about one-eighth turn more, then set the large lock ring/nut. Make further adjustments so the bottom of the expander ball is $3/16$-inch up inside the die, and the decapping pin should extend $1/8$-inch below the mouth of the die, which is just enough to knock out the spent primer. The best bet is to follow the instructions that come with the die set or take the time to really read a loading manual, which usually will include such instruction.

To resize a case, it must first be given a thin coating of case lubricant to allow it to work easily in the sizing die. Sizing lubricant is a special oil or grease made for this purpose. Regular gun oil will not work. It is best applied by saturating a clean stamp inking pad with lubricant, then rolling the case over it, lightly

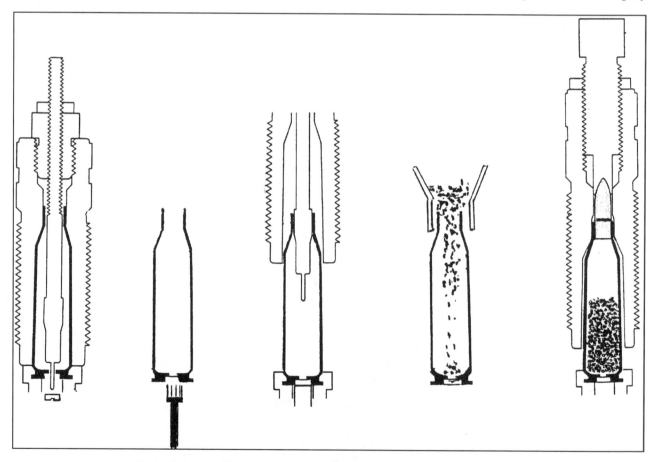

The basic steps in rifle reloading include resizing and decapping, primer pocket cleaning, inside neck expanding (done in the upstroke of the decapping process), powder charging and bullet seating.

coating the outside of the case. Too much lubricant on the outside of the case will cause dents in the walls which will flatten out on firing, but will stress the metal. On bottleneck cases, the inside on the neck should be lubricated with a dry graphite or similar non-oil, case neck lubricant. Oil can run into the powder and ruin it. Neck lubricating keeps the neck from stretching unduly in the die. A light coating of lubricant is all that is needed. My own preference for case lube is Imperial Sizing Die Wax, used primarily for reshaping cases from one caliber to another. It is clean and can be applied easily with the fingers, and only the barest coating is needed. Die wax rarely causes case dents. A minute amount on the case mouth does a good job of inside-neck lubricating.

To begin resizing, the prepared case is inserted in the shellholder, and the press handle is pulled, to run the case completely into the die.

Decapping

The die should be adjusted so the decapping pin just removes the old primer, which will drop out at the end of the up-stroke. The resizing/decapping process should require a medium amount of force. If a lot of force is required to get the case in the die, you have not used enough lubricant. Back it out. If you persist, there's a good chance the case will seize in the die. If that happens, you'll need to send the die back to the maker to remove the case or buy a tool to do the job yourself.

Inside Neck Expanding

The decapping pin is mounted in a rod with an expander ball on it that stretches the case mouth large enough to accept a new bullet. This operation is completed on the up, or removal, stroke of the press operating handle.

Inspection, Gauging and Trimming

The case is now removed from the shellholder for inspection. The case mouth should be smooth and perfectly round. "Trim to length" say the books because a too-long case will enter the throat of the barrel and raise pressures as the bullet is pinched in the case. A quick check with a case length gauge or measurement with your caliper tells you if the case is too long. Sometimes even new ones are. If the case is too long, it goes in the trimmer to cut the case to exact length. After trimming, the burr on the outside of the mouth is removed and the inside is chamfered slightly to give the bullet a smooth start. Do not cut a knife's edge on the case mouth. This trimming/chamfering operation only needs to be done when cases get too long.

Priming

If the case is a fired one, the primer pocket should be scraped free of ash with a screwdriver or cleaning tool. The case is now ready for priming. Place a primer in the priming punch sleeve. This comes up, in most cases, through the center of the shellholder. Place the case in the shellholder and pull the operating handle to lower the case onto the primer punch. This will seat the primer in the case. Enough force should be applied to seat the primer fully, but not crush or flatten it. Difficulty in seating may be experienced if you are using crimped military brass. If so, this crimp must be removed before proceeding.

After priming, the case should be checked to see that the primer is fully in the pocket. This is done by placing a steel straight-edge ruler across the case while holding it to the light to see if the primer sticks up above the case head. It should not. A high primer gives poor ignition or may not fire at all as the firing pin simply drives it into the pocket. The primed, inspected case now goes into the loading block.

Case Mouth Expansion

This step applies only to straight-walled cases loaded with cast, lead-alloy bullets and uses the second die in a three-die rifle set. Three-die sets do not expand the case mouth in the decapping stage. The case is placed in the shellholder and run into this die, which has a stepped or tapered expander plug to open or bell the case mouth for insertion of a soft, cast bullet. This mouth expansion is done before powder charging.

Too much lubricant will make dents in cases. These will flatten out on firing, but this works and weakens the brass.

Case length should be checked *after* sizing and neck expanding.

Powder dippers can be homemade to pick up a fairly accurate charge of a particular type of powder. All dipped loads should be checked regularly on a powder scale.

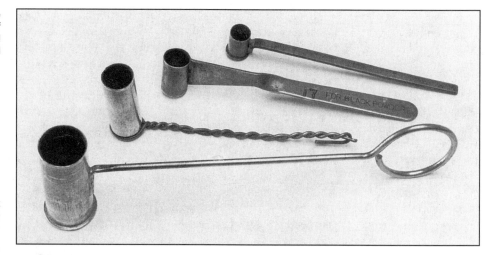

(Below) Powder measures work OK for reduced loads, but should not be used for maximum loads, particularly with fast-burning powders.

Powder Charging

The case is now ready for charging. When working up a load, always start with the beginning load listed in the data manuals. Increases in powder charges should be made by no more than a half-grain (.5) at a time. Load and testfire at least ten test cartridges before going to a heavier charge. Powder charges are weighed precisely on a powder scale for working up loads. The easiest method is to pour a half-cup or so of powder into a small container. I use a glass custard dish and transfer the powder into the scale pan with a small spoon. Plastic spoons are lighter and allow you to tap out the powder in small amounts most easily. This is the slowest part of the operation, and the most critical. The scale should be properly set up and checked for adjustment according to the maker's instructions.

Once the charge is weighed, the powder funnel goes on

The reloader's powder funnel is especially designed to fit over the case mouth and deliver powder without spills. One size fits nearly all commonly reloaded cases.

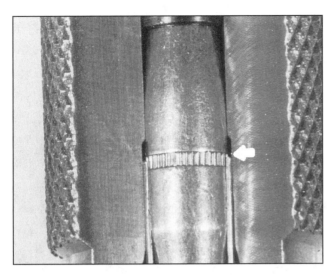

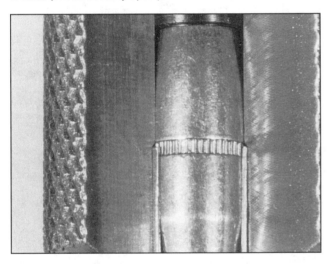

Seating dies have a crimping shoulder in them to crimp some hunting bullets. Never crimp bullets that do not have a crimping cannelure in them. (Photos courtesy Speer)

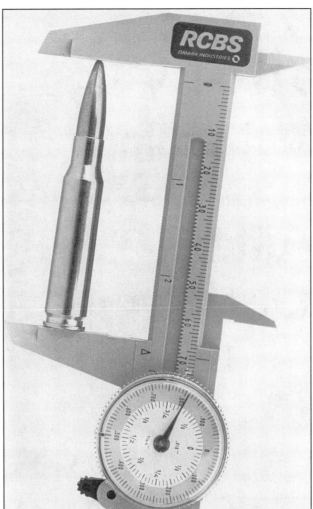

Finished cartridges should be checked to see they do not exceed overall length. If they do, the seater stem in the die can be adjusted to seat the bullets deeper.

the case and the powder is poured in, with no spills, of course. The funnel is moved from case to case until every one in the loading block is charged. Make it a habit to check the powder level in *all* the cases in the loading block, examining them under good light, even though you are sure you did not double-charge any of them. If the powder level in any case looks suspiciously high, weigh it again. The balance may be sticking on your scale or you may have accidentally shifted a weight—you'd be surprised at what can happen.

Using A Powder Measure

Mechanical powder measures should never be used to work up loads, but are useful in making production loads. Precision depends to a great degree on the *consistency* of pulling and returning the operating handle. Use the same motion time after time. After a powder measure is adjusted, check its accuracy, and yours, by dropping every fifth load into the scale pan for weighing. Accurate loads are within a tolerance of +/-$^1/_{10}$-grain (.1). Always visually check cases loaded with a powder measure in the loading block. It is very easy to pull the handle twice on the same case.

Bullet Seating

This is the final step in the loading operation. A case is placed in the shellholder, a bullet is placed in the case mouth as straight as possible, and the case is gently levered up into the bullet seating die. Proper die adjustment is necessary so you don't exceed the maximum overall length of the cartridge as listed in the loading manual. An overly long cartridge will press the bullet into the rifling and raise pressures! The easiest way to avoid this problem is to make up a dummy cartridge. After the die is screwed in to the press, adjust it so the case enters freely its full length. Gradually ease the dummy cartridge into the die and check to see it does not pass the crimping shoulder, which turns over the case mouth. The next adjustment is to the stem of the bullet seater, which gradually drives the bullet deeper into the case. When the correct overall length is reached, tighten the seater adjustment. Keep the dummy for easy readjustment after loading longer or shorter bullets. You may want to make a dummy for every different-length bullet you load to facili-

(Text continued on page 111)

Step-By-Step Reloading

>>>>>>>>>>>>>>>>>>>>>>>

Rifle Cartridges

(Photos courtesy of RCBS Division of Blount)

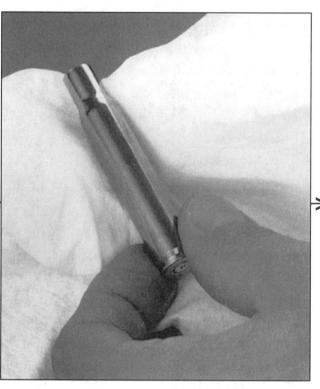

Step 1—Clean and Inspect: It's always a good idea to wipe each case clean to prevent dirt from scratching the case and resizing die. Look for split necks, case cracks and anything else that would compromise safety. Destroy any defective cases by crushing, then throw them away.

Step 4—Adjusting the Sizer Die: With a shellholder installed in the ram, and the ram all the way up, thread the sizer die into the press until it touches the shellholder. Raise the press handle a little and turn the die in another 1/8- to 1/4-turn, then set the die lock ring.

Step 5—Case Resizing: Insert an empty case into the shellholder and gently lower the press handle all the way to the bottom, running the case into the sizing die. Doing so will resize the case to factory dimensions and knock out the fired primer. Raising the press handle will lower the case and expand the case mouth to the proper dimension to hold the new bullet.

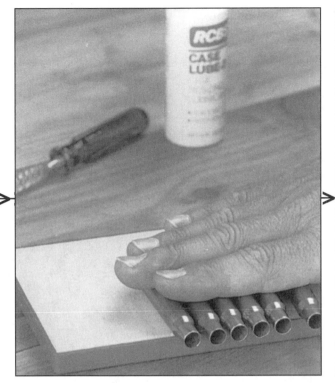

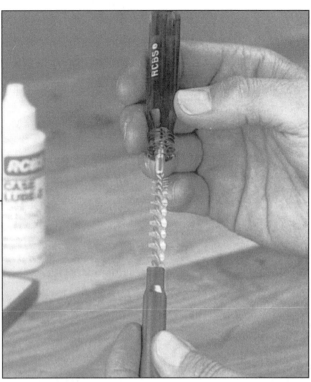

Step 2—Lubricate the Cases: To prevent the case from sticking in the sizing die, it must be lubricated only with sizing die lube. With a bit of lube on the pad, roll a number of cases over it a few times to lightly coat the case body.

Step 3—Case Neck Lubrication: Use a case neck brush to clean and lubricate the inside of the case neck. This will reduce resizing effort and neck stretching. Only a small amount of lube should be applied to the brush.

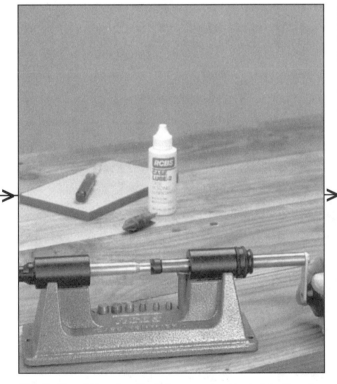

Step 6—Case Trimming: Cartridge cases tend to stretch after a few firings, so they must be trimmed back to allow proper chambering and for safety reasons. Reloading data manuals will give the proper trim and maximum case lengths.

Step 7—Chamfer and Deburr: After trimming, the case mouth will have a slight burr, and the sharp edge of the mouth needs to be smoothed. A twist of a simple hand tool removes the burr with one end and chamfers the case mouth with the other end for easy insertion of the new bullet.

Step 8—Case Mouth Expansion: This step applies only to straight-wall cases and is done in a separate step. Install the expander die in the press, insert a case in the shellholder and run the case up into the die. This die should be adjusted so the case mouth is belled or flared just enough to accept a new bullet.

Step 9—Priming (A): Place a fresh primer, anvil side up, into the cup of the primer arm and insert a case into the shellholder.

Step 12—Powder Charging (A): Look up the load in your loading manual to see exactly how much and what powder you need. It's a good idea to weigh each charge for safety and consistency.

Step 13—Powder Charging (B): After weighing the charge, use a funnel to pour it into the case without spilling.

Step 10—Priming (B): Lower the press handle and push the primer arm all the way into the slot in the ram.

Step 11—Priming (C): Gently and slowly raise the press handle. This lowers the case onto the priming arm, seating the fresh primer. Check each case to be sure the primer is fully seated.

Step 14—Powder Charging (C): Another method of charging is to use the powder measure. It dispenses a precise, uniform charge with each crank of the handle, thereby speeding up the process. Use the reloading scale to adjust the powder measure until it throws several identical charges. Then, weigh about every ten charges to recheck the weight.

Step 15—Bullet Seating (A): Thread the seater die into the press a few turns. With a case in the shellholder, lower the press handle, running the case all the way up into the die. Turn the die further in until it stops. While using the headstamp on top of the die as a reference, back the die out one full turn and lock it in place with the lock ring.

Step 16—Bullet Seating (B): Now, unscrew the seater plug enough to keep the bullet from being seated too deeply.

Step 17—Bullet Seating (C): With the handle up, insert a primed and charged case in the shellholder, and hold a bullet over the case mouth with one hand while you lower the press handle with the other, easing the bullet and case up into the die. This will seat the bullet. Measure the loaded round to see if the bullet is seated deeply enough.

Step 18—Bullet Seating (D): If the bullet needs to be seated deeper into the case, turn the seater plug down a little and run the case back up into the die. Make small adjustments and keep trying and measuring until you get the proper cartridge overall length. Once the proper setting is reached, tighten the seater plug lock ring.

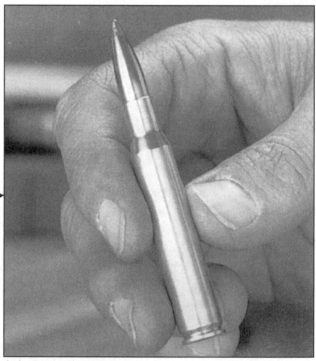

Step 19—The Loaded Round: After wiping off any sizing lube, the first loaded cartridge is ready to be fired.

(Text continued from page 105)

tate easy readjustment. Once the die is adjusted, bullet seating is simply a matter of repetition.

Most dies have a built-in crimping shoulder to turn the case mouth over into a cannelure (groove) in the bullet. This is necessary for high-powered ammunition, particularly if it is jarred by recoil or while being fed through the magazine. Crimping keeps the bullets from being forced back into the case under such circumstances. Military ammunition that will be fed through autoloaders and machineguns is always crimped, as is much commercial ammunition. Crimping degrades accuracy and should never be attempted on bullets that do not have a

should always be returned to the original container, especially from the powder measure. Powder in open containers will lose volatiles and absorb moisture. Primers can absorb moisture, and magnum and standard primers can be confused if not put back in their respective containers. Most of all, there is always the chance of confusion regarding what powder you were using when you start to work the next time.

Selecting A Load

Many people start with factory duplication loads, which, if you have already been shooting them, is a convenient place to start without varying any component. Generally, though, the best accuracy in your rifle will be something you work up on your

Loads should be selected from a loading manual to reflect the type of shooting you want to do. Don't experiment unless you know what you are doing.

crimping cannelure in them. Hunting ammunition used in tubular magazines may have to be crimped.

Easy does it is the rule for all steps. Ramming and jerking leads to damaged cases, mashed bullets, flattened primers and broken decapping pins.

The final, final step is to wipe off any case lubricant that may be on the case and inspect the finished cartridge with a final check for overall length. Oil left on cases will cause excessive backthrust and batter your gun. If all dies are properly adjusted and firmly in place, there should be no difference from one cartridge to the next. Place the loaded rounds in a cartridge box and mark it accordingly.

Cleaning the loading area is always a good idea. Powder

own. This may take some doing, even though many loading manuals list "accuracy loads." If you read the fine print you will see this applies to one particular test rifle. If yours is a different make, this one may not shoot best for you, but it is perhaps the best powder/bullet combination to start with. Loading data is presented as starting loads and maximum loads with a middle ground in between. It is generally in this middle ground where the most accurate loading will be found. Rarely is the hottest, highest pressure load the straightest shooter. Maximum loads, especially with jacketed bullets, shorten both case and barrel life. By working for accuracy, you start to get a clear idea of just how well your rifle will shoot. With this as a starting point, you then have a standard by which other loads can be judged.

The Marlin Camp Carbine in 9mm or 45 ACP is a fairly typical blowback autoloading rifle. There is a growing number of pistol-caliber carbines on the market, intended for home-defense, small game hunting and plinking.

The Ruger Mini-14 is a popular gas-operated autoloader with both civilians and law enforcement agencies.

For the most part, you will probably not have need for more than three or four different loadings, if that many. For 30-caliber rifles and up, about three different loadings will do for most of the shooting you'll be doing. On the bottom end are short-range practice loads. These are usually cast bullets driven at modest velocities of around 1200-1500 fps. These offer good, cheap recreation and training without the expense, wear, noise and recoil of full-bore loads. They can be used for small game and varmint hunting at distances under 100 yards with reasonable accuracy. Varmint loads with light bullets are practical in many 30-caliber rifles that will produce good accuracy and flat trajectory. Hunting loads are the most common for the 30s unless you have a match rifle. For a hunting rifle, used primarily for hunting as opposed to competition, you would do best to work up the most accurate load you can from the selection of hunting bullets available.

Working Up A Load

Working up a load means not merely careful loading of ammunition, but testing it and keeping records of the results. It also involves case inspection, looking for any signs of excessive headspace or pressures. I use a simple notebook for records, listing loads under the name of the rifle and its caliber. Individual loads are listed under the bullet, indicating whether it is cast or jacketed, the weight, diameter and lubrication type. Next, the powder type and charge are shown. Following this is a notation on the make of case and primer type. Finally, there's a section for remarks. This includes a summary of the performance of this particular load, especially its accuracy. Ten-shot groups are the accuracy test standard, although it has been demonstrated that seven-shot groups work just as well. Other remarks include the test range conditions like temperature, wind direction and velocity, and light conditions. Also noted are any indications of pressure problems. These are underlined as a warning for future reference.

Loading for Autoloaders

Since WWII, autoloaders in all calibers and types have become very popular, owing mainly to the change-over by nearly all of the world's governments to this type of rifle for their respective militaries. While all autoloaders rely on the force of the explosion in the cartridge to function the action, there are a number of differences in the ways various actions operate, and these features have a marked effect on how ammunition must be reloaded for them.

There are three basic types of autoloading actions: straight blowback (with a variant known as delayed blowback), recoil-operated and gas-operated.

Blowback actions are the oldest design, and most simple. They function by having the bolt held in contact with the barrel by a spring, thus the two are not locked together. When the gun fires, the bullet is driven down the barrel while the case is driven against the bolt face. The weight of the bolt and force of the recoil springs, and the internal pressure swelling the case against the chamber wall, keep the case from moving backward until the bullet has exited the muzzle. Somewhere around this point, as chamber pressure begins to drop, the case begins to be blown back against the bolt; the inertial force given the bolt causes it to move rearward, cocking the rifle and ejecting the fired case. Tension in the compressed recoil spring sends the bolt forward, stripping a fresh cartridge from the magazine and chambering it. This system works well with low-powered pistol-type cartridges and is used in all 22 Long Rifle and 22 WMR rifles. It was used in only a relatively few centerfire rifles, such as the obsolete Winchester 05, 07 and 10 rifles, and the current Marlin and other carbines in 9mm and 45 ACP. The system is limited to straight-walled cases because a bottleneck case would likely have its neck pulled off or have gas come rushing around it as soon as the pressure seal was broken. Because of the necessity of equalling the forces of the forward-moving bullet with the proper amount of bolt weight and spring pressure, limitations of the system are obvious. To fire a cartridge the equivalent of the 30-06, such a system would need a bolt weighing several pounds and a *very* robust recoil spring. Thus, blowback autoloaders are limited to cartridges developing little better than handgun velocities and pressures.

Not surprisingly, reloads for such guns must be kept very close to factory specifications. Lower-pressure loads will not function the action, and high-pressure loads, even though the barrels can handle them, increase the velocity of the recoiling parts, battering them and causing serious damage to the rifle. Cast-bullet loads, both plain and gas-checked, work well *if* they are heavily crimped to provide proper burning of the powder. Slow-burning powders generally do not perform well in these rifles as they do not generate pressure fast enough to make the action function reliably.

Recoil-operated actions represent an improvement over the blowback in terms of the type and pressure of cartridge they can handle. In this system, the recoil of the rifle drives the operation. Recoil-operated systems keep the bolt and barrel locked together through part of the firing cycle. As the bullet travels forward, the barrel and bolt recoil as a unit. At about the midpoint of the operation, after the bullet has exited the barrel, the bolt unlocks from the barrel and continues traveling backward, ejecting the empty case and cocking the hammer. The bolt then strips a fresh round from the magazine, chambering it as the bolt comes forward. This system was used in the Remington Model 8 in 25, 30, 32 and 35 Remington calibers, and in the Johnson military and sporting autoloaders in 30-06. The downside of this system is the amount of recoil experienced by the shooter, which can be considerable.

Both blowback and recoil-operated autoloaders have fairly generous chambers and require full-length case resizing. Not too surprisingly, they are also rather rough on cases. Here again, the best functioning is with loadings close to factory specifications. The battering of internal parts will result from loads generating high pressures and high velocities. The best way to work up handloads for these two actions is to do so slowly, checking recoiling parts for any evidence of battering. The best loads are ones that will reliably cycle the action and no more.

Gas-operated rifles are by far the best, and most high-powered rifles made today use this system. The gas-operated system features a locked bolt and non-moving barrel, much like the accurate and reliable bolt action. They can thus fire very powerful cartridges. At some point on the barrel, forward of the chamber, there's a small hole in the barrel that taps off a small amount of gas after the bullet passes that point. The gas is trapped in a small cylinder with a piston, much like that in an engine. The piston drives a rod which operates a camming lock on the bolt, that opens it after the bullet has exited the barrel. In some variants, the gas is directed to the surface of the cam lock to unlock the bolt. As the bolt is driven back, the case is ejected and the hammer or striker is cocked, and a spring drives the bolt forward to strip a fresh round from the magazine and chamber it. Today's high-powered autoloaders are gas-operated. The advantages are a minimum of moving parts and an action that is comparatively gentle on cases. Felt recoil is also very manageable.

The placement of the gas port is critical to reliable functioning because the amount and pressure of gas must be enough to operate the rifle, but not enough to cause damage through battering. Needless to say, the amount and type of powder used is also critical to this system's functioning. Gas-operated autoloaders are, therefore, ammunition-sensitive and will work best with loadings duplicating factory or original military specifications. Cast bullets, generally, do not work well in gas-operated guns. Fast burning powders, such as IMR-4227, are about the only ones that will operate these actions reliably with cast bullets. Any cast bullets used in autoloading rifles should be of hard alloy, since soft bullets are often nicked and dented as they pass through the magazine and into the chamber. They are slammed up feed ramps, which will often cause them to catch and stick on something and jam the action. Because of the generous chamber proportions required for reliable functioning, cases fired in autoloaders almost always have to be full-length resized.

Ball powders tend to leave more fouling than some of the

Testing ammunition should be done with a solid rest, firing at a known distance to determine accuracy.

cleaner burning flake powders. The performance of ball powders in terms of reliable functioning is good, *so long as the gas port, piston and/or cam face are kept clean.* For best functioning, the powders used in reloading should be close to those used in factory loadings. Cleaning of the gas system is necessary for reliable functioning.

Reduced loads will not work reliably in any autoloader, with cartridges often getting jammed on the way out and chewed up in the process. Therefore, the range of loading options for autoloaders of any stripe is rather limited. There will usually be only a relatively few loadings that will produce good accuracy and reliable functioning. Ammunition prepared for autoloaders should be given extra care to see that all tolerances are kept close to factory specifications. Exceeding overall length will jam rifles. Cases too short and bullets seated too deeply can have the same effect. In short, ammunition preparation for successful shooting of these guns requires extra care for best results.

Testing Ammunition

Accuracy is, or should be, your first concern. An accuracy test can consist of nothing more than plinking at a few cans at an unknown distance, but this won't tell you very much. The only meaningful test is firing from a solid rest at a known distance. This generally means getting to a target range with permanent bench installations or setting up your own range.

The best kind of shooting bench is a permanent one, with solid legs anchored in concrete.

Portable shooting benches can be homemade or you can buy one of several on the market. The type that has a built-in seat is my recommendation, since with these, the weight of the shooter serves to hold down the bench. The top either has an attached forend rest for the rifle or you can use a sandbag rest on an adjustable base.

Testing should be done on a day with good light, little or no wind and moderate temperatures. Calm conditions are generally found in the early morning or late afternoon. The place to start is with a test of factory ammunition for comparison. Really fine accuracy cannot be obtained without a telescopic sight, since this lets you see exactly where you are aiming. A spotting scope of 20x or more gives you a clear view of a distant target. A distance of 100 yards is good enough to get a fair idea of the long-range performance of your rifle and ammunition, though 200 yards is better. Most shooters use the standard of the "magic inch" at 100 yards as a benchmark by which all rifles are judged. Few hunting rifles will group this well, but will run groups of 2 to 3 inches, which is enough to kill a deer. Shoot seven- or ten-shot groups, taking your time to carefully squeeze off the shots. Be sure to clean the rifle of all copper fouling before shooting lead-alloy bullets, since they will strip lead on the copper fouling.

Shooting into turf will give you an idea of the ricochet potential of your ammunition, if this is critical. You can usually hear the results if the bullets are not ricochet-proof. For testing on game or varmint animals, there is not much in the way of practical substitutes for the real item. Ballistic gelatin is the standard by which determinations are made, but it is dif-

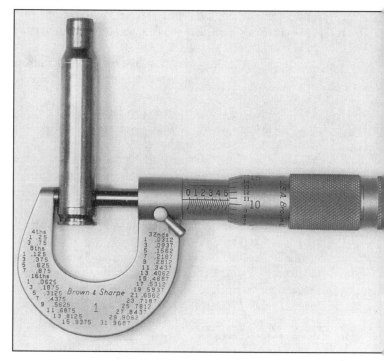

Checking a case for expansion beyond that produced by a factory load (along with stiff extraction) will give you the first indication of excessive pressures. It is a timely warning to tone things down.

ficult to prepare, and it must be calibrated and used at the proper temperature.

One tissue substitute of a cheap and easy sort is newspaper, soaked overnight to get it fully saturated. Stacks of the wet paper are then put in a cardboard carton for shooting into. This is far heavier and more resistant than muscle tissue, but will give you a general idea of bullet behavior.

Packed wet snow is a fairly good tissue simulant, and if there is enough of it, you can find your bullet somewhere along a long snow loaf. High-velocity spitzer bullets are almost impossible to recover, but lower velocity cast bullets can usually be stopped within 20 to 30 feet of packed snow. These will generally be in almost pristine condition. This will give you a good opportunity to study your bullets for evidence of gas cutting and of how well they take the rifling. Large or double sets of rifling marks on the front of a bullet indicate skidding or jumping the rifling—the bullet going straight for a fraction of an inch before taking the rifling and turning, as it should. Rifling marks that are higher on one side than the other indicate the bullet was not straight in the case. Poor alignment of this sort, if there to a marked degree, degrades accuracy. Grease grooves that are heavily compressed and lack of lubricant will explain one cause of leading—not enough groove space and an inefficient lubricant. Bullet recovery is for those who are seriously interested, those wanting answers to questions beginning with the word "Why."

A final warning is to *always check your cases after firing,* particularly when you are testing loads that are on the high side of the pressure curve. Once you are in the field, there is a great temptation to keep shooting. If there are signs of high pressure or excessive headspace, *stop shooting.* Don't risk your eyesight and rifle.

Even though your
favorite handgun
digests all types
of factory ammo,
you can probably
squeeze out a
little more perfor-
mance—and save
money, too.

Handgun Cartridge Reloading

LOADING HANDGUN AMMUNITION is perhaps a little easier than loading rifle cases, but the same level of care and attention must be given the task if good results are to be obtained. The place to begin is with once-fired or, better, new cases to work up a load. Once a load is tested and found to be satisfactory, then quantity production can begin and some of the preliminary steps can be omitted.

Handguns come in three basic classes: revolvers, autoloaders (automatics) and single shot pistols. Each has its own characteristics and will be discussed accordingly. Basic loading procedures apply for all types, but there are special exceptions which will be given separate attention.

Case inspection

Even new and once-fired cases should be checked over for defects. Any with splits or serious defects in the case mouth that are not ironed out in the resizing die should be discarded. Cases should be segregated by maker, as determined by the head-

Good accuracy comes from consistency in the quality of your reloads as much as it does from the gun.

stamp. Even though they are the same caliber, cases of different manufacture have slight differences in wall thickness and flash hole size. Mixing brands will alter velocities and pressures, and will open up group size.

Full-length Resizing

New cases should be sized the same as old ones, just to be sure everything is the same. Before any operation can take place on the reloading press, the die must first be adjusted to resize the case properly. For full-length resizing, with the shellholder snapped into the ram, lower the press handle completely; screw the sizer die into the press until the bottom of the die hits the shellholder. (If you are using a carbide die, as is common with handgun calibers, do not allow the shellholder to contact the bottom of the die.) Now, raise the press handle enough so you can screw the die down about one-eighth turn more, then set the large lock ring/nut. Make further adjustments so the bottom of the expander ball is $3/16$-inch up inside the die, and the decapping pin should extend $1/8$-inch below the mouth of the die, which is just enough to knock out the spent primer. The best bet is to follow the instructions that come with the die set, or take the time to really read a loading manual, which usually will include such instruction.

To resize a case, it must first be given a coating of case lubricant to allow it to work easily in the sizing die. Sizing lubricant is a special oil or grease made for this purpose. Regular gun oil will not work. It is best applied by saturating a clean stamp inking pad with lubricant, then rolling the case over it, lightly coating the outside of the case. Too much lubricant on the outside of the case will cause dents in the walls which will flatten out on

firing, but will stress the metal. On bottleneck cases, the inside of the neck should be lubricated with a dry graphite, or similar non-oil, case neck lubricant. Oil can run into the powder and ruin it. Neck lubricating keeps the neck from stretching unduly in the die.

A light coating of lubricant is all that is needed. My own preference for case lube is Imperial Sizing Die Wax, used primarily for reshaping cases from one caliber to another. It is clean, can be applied easily with the fingers and only the barest coating is needed. Die wax rarely causes case dents. A minute amount on the case mouth does a good job of inside-neck lubricating.

To begin resizing, the prepared case is inserted in the shellholder, and the press handle is pulled to run the case completely into the die.

Decapping

The die should be adjusted so the decapping pin just removes the old primer, which will drop out at the end of the up-stroke. The resizing/decapping process should require a medium amount of force; if a lot of force is required to get the case in the die you have not used enough lubricant, and there's a good chance the case will seize in the die. If that happens, you'll need to send the die back to the manufacturer to remove the case, or buy a tool to do the job yourself.

Inspection, Gauging and Trimming

The case is now removed from the shellholder for inspection. The case mouth should be smooth and perfectly round. "Trim to length" say the books because a too-long case will enter the throat of the barrel and raise pressures as the bullet is pinched in the case. A quick check with a case length gauge or measurement with your caliper tells you if the case is too long. Sometimes even new ones are. If the case is too long, it goes in the trimmer to cut the case to exact length. After trimming, the burr on the outside of the mouth is removed and the inside is chamfered to give the bullet a smooth start. This trimming/chamfering operation only needs to be done when cases get too long. Do not cut a knife edge on the case mouth, but simply remove the burr.

Inside Neck Expansion

For bottleneck cartridges, the decapping pin is mounted in a rod with an expansion ball on it that stretches the case mouth large enough to accept a new bullet. This operation is completed on the up or removal stroke of the operating handle.

Case Mouth Expansion

For straight-walled cases being loaded with cast, lead-alloy bullets, this step uses the second die in a three-die pistol set. Three-die sets do not expand the case mouth in the decapping stage. The case is placed in the shellholder and run into this expansion die which has a stepped or tapered expander plug that opens the case mouth for insertion of a bullet. This mouth expansion is done before powder charging.

Priming

If the case is a fired one, the primer pocket should be scraped

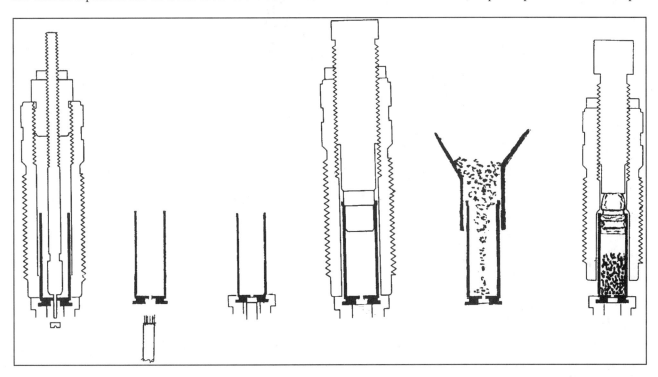

(Above) The basic steps in handgun reloading include: resizing and decapping, primer pocket cleaning, priming, case expanding, powder charging and bullet seating.

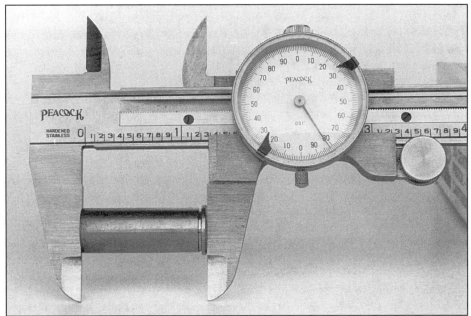

Case length should be checked after sizing and neck expanding, because the case stretches in these operations.

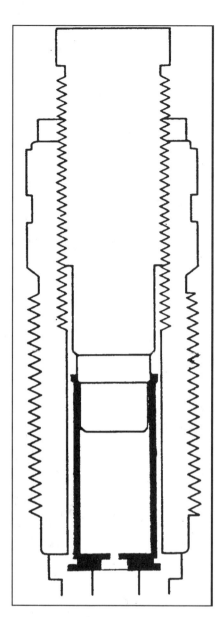

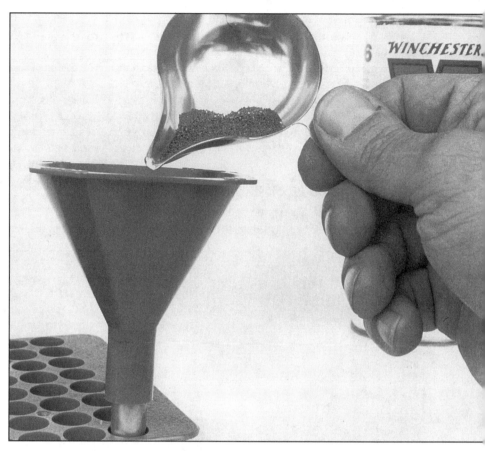

The reloader's powder funnel is especially designed to fit over the case mouth and deliver powder without spills.

Case-mouth expanding, or belling, prepares the case to accept a soft, lead-alloy bullet.

free of ash with a screwdriver or cleaning tool. The case is now ready for priming. Place a primer in the priming punch sleeve. This comes up, in most cases, through the center of the shellholder. Place the case in the shellholder and pull the operating handle to lower the case onto the primer punch. This will seat the primer in the case. Enough force should be applied to seat the primer fully, but not crush or flatten it. Difficulty in seating may be experienced if you are using crimped military brass. If so, this crimp must be removed before proceeding.

After priming, the case should be checked to see that the primer is fully in the pocket. This is done by placing a steel straight-edge ruler across the case while holding it to the light to see if the primer sticks up above the case head. It should not. A high primer gives poor ignition or may not fire at all as the firing pin simply drives it into the pocket. The primed, inspected case now goes into the loading block.

Powder Charging

The case is now ready for charging. When working up a load, always start with the beginning load listed in the data manuals. Increases in powder charges should be made by no more than a half-grain (.5) at a time and less than this for hot, fast burning powders. Load and test fire at least ten test rounds before going to a heavier charge. Powder charges are weighed precisely on a powder scale for working up loads. The easiest method is to pour a half-cup or so of powder into a small container and dip it into the scale pan with a small spoon. Plastic spoons are light and allow you to tap out the powder in small amounts most easily. This is the slowest part of the operation, and the most critical. The scale should be properly set up and checked for adjustment according to the maker's instructions.

Once the charge is weighed, the powder funnel goes on the case and the powder is poured in, with no spills, of course. The funnel is moved from case to case until every one in the loading block is filled. Make it a habit to check the powder level in *all* the cases in the loading block, examining them under good light, even though you are sure you did not double charge any of them. If the powder level in any case looks suspiciously high, weigh it again. The balance may be sticking on your scale or you may have accidentally shifted a weight—you'd be surprised at what can happen. Mistakes with pistol powders are more critical than with slower-burning rifle powders. They are more powerful. A little too much Bullseye can go a long way in wrecking your gun.

Using A Powder Measure

Mechanical powder measures should never be used to work up loads, but are useful in making production loads. Precision depends to a great degree on *consistency* of pulling and returning the operating handle. After a powder measure is adjusted, check its accuracy, and yours, by dropping every fifth load into the scale pan for weighing. Accurate loads are within a tolerance of ±$^1/_{10}$-grain (.1). Always visually check cases loaded with a powder measure in the loading block. It is very easy to pull the handle twice on the same case. Since many loads for handguns are nearly full-case loads, a double charge will run over or fill the case to the point where a bullet can't be seated, but don't bet on it.

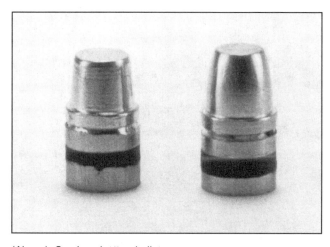

(Above) Semi-wadcutter bullets are among the best cast revolver bullets in terms of both accuracy and killing power, which makes them suitable for both hunting and target shooting.

Bullet Seating

This is the final step in the loading operation. A case is placed in the shellholder, a bullet is placed in the case mouth as straight as possible, and the case is gently levered into the bullet seating die. Proper die adjustment is necessary so you don't exceed the *maximum overall length* of the cartridge as listed in the loading manual. An overly long cartridge can press the bullet into the rifling and raise pressures in autoloaders, or jam them. In revolvers, they will jam the cylinder. The easiest way to avoid this problem is to make up a dummy cartridge to use as a guide. After the die is screwed into the press, adjust it so the case enters freely its full length. Gradually ease the cartridge in the die and check to see it does not pass the crimping shoulder, which turns over the case mouth. The next adjustment is to the stem of the bullet seater, which gradually drives the bullet deeper into the case. When the correct overall length is reached, tighten the seater adjustment. Keep the dummy for easy readjustment after loading longer or shorter bullets. You may want to make a dummy for every different-length bullet you load to facilitate easy readjustment. Once the die is adjusted, bullet seating is simply a matter of repetition.

Most dies have a built-in crimping shoulder to turn the case mouth over into a cannelure (groove) in the bullet. This is necessary for high-powered rifle ammunition, particularly if it is jarred by recoil or while being fed through the magazine. Crimping is necessary on nearly all handgun bullets. Magnum handgun cases require heavy crimping to keep bullets from being jarred loose by recoil. No rimless automatic cartridge such as the 45 ACP should be crimped since it headspaces on

(Text continued on page 126)

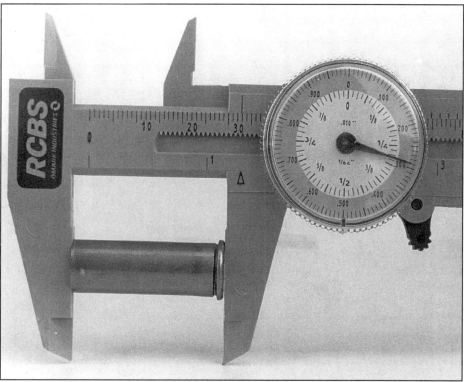

Finished ammunition should be measured to see that the cartridge does not exceed the maximum overall length specified in the loading manual.

Step-By-Step Reloading

›››››››››››››››››››››››››››

Handgun Cartridges

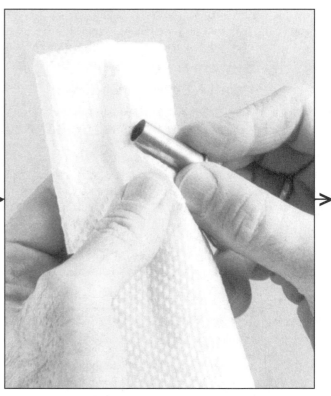

Step 1—Clean and Inspect: It's a good idea to wipe cases clean before beginning to reload them. This also allows you to inspect them for any split necks, cracks, etc. Discard those that are damaged.

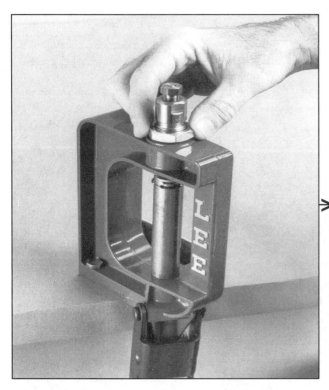

Step 4—Adjusting the Sizer Die: Raise the ram to the top of its travel and screw the sizing die in until it just touches the shellholder. Now, slightly lower the ram and screw in the die an additional ¼-turn. Tighten the lock nut.

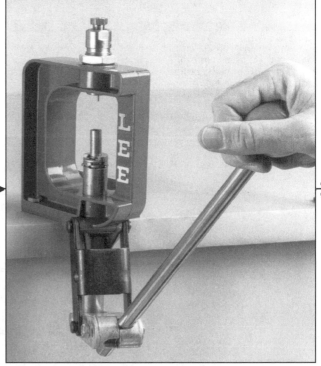

Step 5—Case Resizing: Place a lubed case in the shellholder and raise the ram, guiding the case as it enters the sizing die. This step also knocks out the fired primer. Raise the press handle and remove the case.

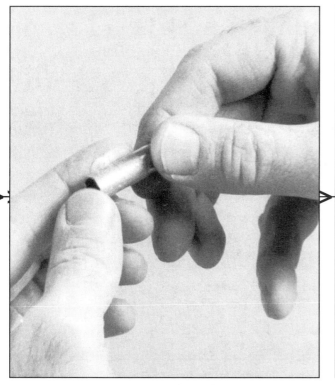

Step 2—Lubricate the Cases: Case lube is needed when not using a carbide resizing die. Lee Precision's lube is a white cream that's not greasy. Spread just a light film on each case with the fingers.

Step 3—Installing the Shellholder: Choose the proper shellholder for the round you are loading. They usually come with the die sets. Raise the ram slightly to snap the shellholder into place with a twisting motion. Position it with the open side out to the left.

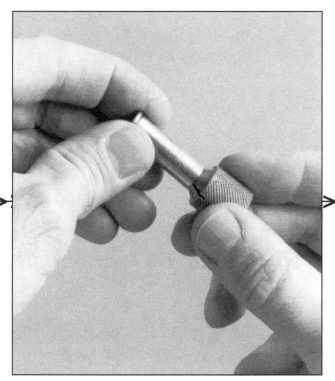

Step 6—Chamfer and Deburr: To ease bullet entry, lightly chamfer the mouth of the case by inserting the pointed end of the chamfering/deburring tool into the case mouth and gently twisting it.

Step 7—Case Mouth Expansion: After installing and properly adjusting the expander die, insert a case and run it into the die to bell the case mouth for easy insertion of a new bullet. Adjust the die just enough to allow easy bullet entry.

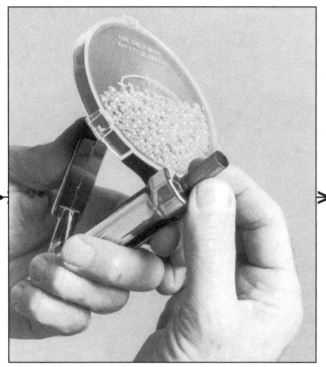

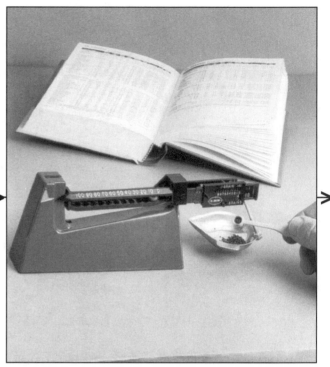

Step 8—Priming: Installing a new primer can be done on the press or with Lee's hand-held Auto Prime tool with CCI or Winchester primers. After filling the primer tray, slip a deprimed case into the shellholder and press the lever to push a primer into the primer pocket. Follow the instructions that come with each tool.

Step 9—Powder Charging (A): Find the proper and safe load for your cartridge in a loading manual or from another reliable source, then weigh each charge on your powder scale. This is the safest method, although a bit slow, and is best for accuracy and maximum loads.

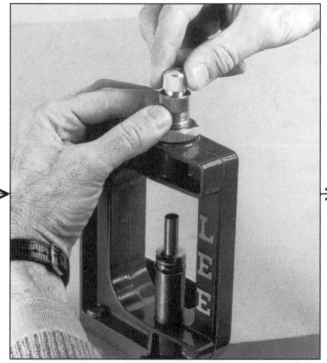

Step 12—Bullet Seating (A): To install the bullet seating die, place a case in the shellholder and raise the ram to the top of the stroke. Screw in the seater die until you feel it touch the case mouth. If no crimp is desired, back the die out a 1/2-turn. If you want a crimp, turn it in a 1/4-turn.

Step 13—Bullet Seating (B): The knurled adjusting screw controls the bullet seating depth. Usually, seating to the same depth as a factory round works well. If you want a crimp, be sure the bullet cannelure is almost completely inside the case mouth. Screw the die in just enough to apply a good crimp. A little trial and error work is needed here.

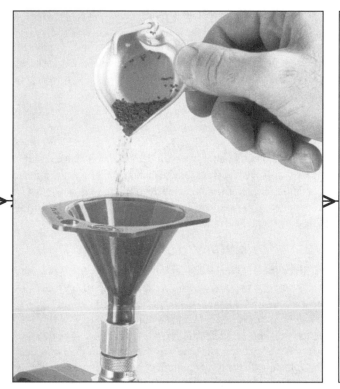

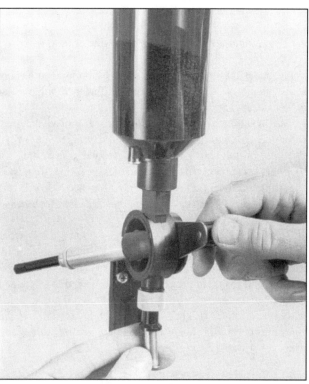

Step 10—Powder Charging (B): Lee's expander die allows the powder charge to be dumped from the scale pan into the primed case through the die. Cases can also be set into a loading block for powder charging.

Step 11—Powder Charging (C): Once the proper load has been found, you can dispense powder directly into the case with the powder measure. It will throw a precise, uniform charge with each turn of the handle. Check-weigh every fifth or tenth charge to be sure it is correct.

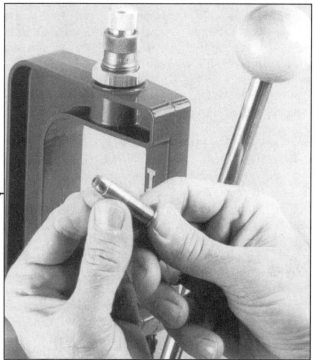

Step 14—Bullet Seating (C): To seat a bullet, place one in the case mouth and guide it into the seating die as straight as possible. If the bullet needs to be deeper, screw in the seater plug a little bit and run the case back into the die. It may take a few tries to get the exact depth required.

Step 15—The Loaded Round: That's all there is to loading a handgun cartridge. A final wipe with a clean cloth and the ammunition is ready to be fired. Don't forget to mark the ammo box with your load data so you can repeat the load.

(Text continued from page 121)

the case mouth and a crimp will allow the case to enter too deeply, giving erratic ignition.

Easy does it is the rule for all steps. Ramming and jerking leads to damaged cases, mashed bullets, flattened primers and broken decapping pins.

The final, final step is to wipe off any case lubricant that may be on the case and inspect the finished cartridge with a final check for overall length. Oil left on cases will cause excessive back-thrust and batter your gun. If all dies are properly adjusted and firmly in place, there should be no difference from one cartridge to the next. Place the loaded rounds in a cartridge box and mark it accordingly.

Cleaning the loading area is always a good idea. Powder should always be returned to the original container, especially from the powder measure. Powder in open containers will lose volatiles and absorb moisture. Primers can absorb moisture and magnum and standard primers can be confused if not put back in their respective containers. Most of all, there is always the chance of confusion regarding what powder you were using when you start the next time.

Selecting A Load

Many people start with factory duplication loads, which, if you have already been shooting them, is a convenient place to start without varying any component. Generally, though, the best accuracy in your handgun will be something you work up on your own. This may take some doing even though many loading manuals list "accuracy loads." If you read the fine print you will see this applies to one particular test gun. If yours is a different make, this one may not shoot best for you, but it is perhaps the best powder/bullet combination to start with. Loading data is presented as starting loads and maximum loads with a middle ground in between. It is generally in this middle ground where the most accurate loading will be found. Rarely is the hottest, highest pressure load the straightest shooter. Maximum loads, especially with jacketed bullets, shorten both case and barrel life. By working for accuracy, you start by getting a clear idea of just how well your handgun will shoot. With this as a starting point, you then have a standard by which other loads can be judged.

For the most part, you will probably not have need for more than three or four different loadings, if that many. On the bottom end are short-range practice loads. These are usually cast bullets driven at modest velocities of around 550-750 fps. These offer good, cheap recreation and training without the expense, wear, noise and recoil of full-bore loads. They can be used for short-range target shooting where noise may be a problem. Hunting loads are really for handguns of the 357 Magnum class and up. These are near maximum pressure and velocity loadings with jacketed expanding bullets. You would do best to work up the most accurate load you can from the selection of hunting bullets available.

Working Up A Load

Working up a load means not merely careful loading of ammunition, but testing it and keeping records of the results. It also involves case inspection, looking for any signs of excessive headspace or pressures. I use a simple notebook for records. I list these under the name of the gun and its caliber. Individual loads are listed under the bullet, indicating whether it is cast or jacketed, the weight, diameter and lubrication type. Next, the powder type and charge are shown. Following this is a notation on the make of case and primer and type. Finally, there's a section for remarks. This includes a summary of the performance of this particular load, especially its accuracy. Ten-shot groups are the accuracy test standard, although it has been demonstrated that seven-shot groups work just as well. Other remarks include the test range conditions like temperature, wind direction and velocity and light conditions. Also noted are any indications of pressure problems. These are underlined as a warning for future reference.

Loading for Autoloaders

Since the 1980s autoloaders in all calibers and types have become very popular, owing mainly to the change-over by nearly all of this country's police departments to this type of handgun for duty carry. While all autoloaders rely on the force of the explosion in the cartridge to function the action, there are a number of differences in the ways various actions operate, and these features have a marked effect on how ammunition must be reloaded for them.

There are three basic types of autoloading actions: straight blowback, with a variant known as delayed blowback, recoil-operated and gas-operated.

Blowback actions are the simplest. They function by having the slide held in contact with the barrel by a spring, thus the two are not locked together. When the gun fires, the bullet is driven down the barrel while the case is driven against the face of the slide. The weight of the slide and force of the recoil spring, and the internal pressure swelling the case against the chamber wall, all keep the case from moving backward until the bullet has exited the muzzle. Somewhere around this point, as chamber pressure begins to drop, the case begins to be blown back against the slide; the inertial force given the slide causes it to move rearward, cocking the pistol and ejecting the fired case. Tension in the compressed recoil spring sends the slide forward, stripping a fresh cartridge from the magazine and chambering it. This system works well with low-powered handgun cartridges and is used in all 22 Long Rifle, 25 ACP, 32 ACP, 380 ACP autoloaders and the 9mm Makarov autoloading pistol. The system is limited to straight-walled, semi-rimmed cases because a bottlenecked case would likely have its neck pulled off or have gas come rushing around it as soon as the pressure seal was broken. Because of the necessity of equalling the forces of the forward-moving bullet with the proper amount of slide weight and spring pressure, limitations of the system are obvious. Thus, blowback autoloaders are limited to cartridges developing low velocities and pressures.

Not surprisingly, reloads for such guns must be kept very close to factory specifications. Lower-pressure loads will not operate the action and high-pressure loads, even though the barrels can handle them, increase the velocity of the recoiling parts, battering them, causing serious damage to the handgun. Cast bullet loads work well if they are crimped to provide proper

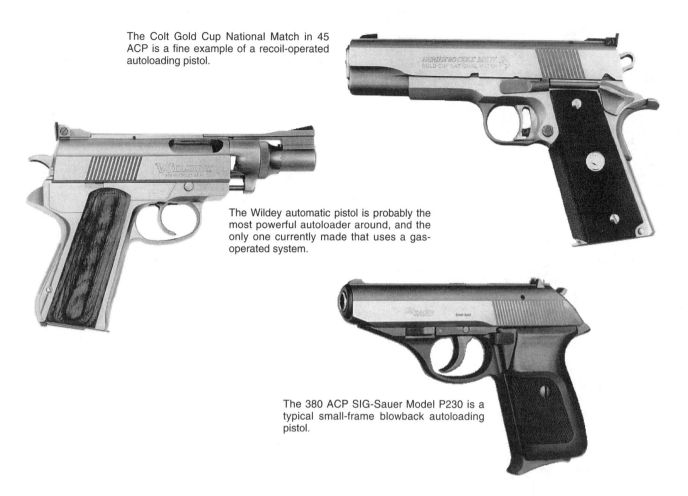

The Colt Gold Cup National Match in 45 ACP is a fine example of a recoil-operated autoloading pistol.

The Wildey automatic pistol is probably the most powerful autoloader around, and the only one currently made that uses a gas-operated system.

The 380 ACP SIG-Sauer Model P230 is a typical small-frame blowback autoloading pistol.

burning of the powder. Slow-burning powders will not generate enough power to operate the action reliably. Taper-crimping, as opposed to roll or "turn over" crimping, is recommended for best functioning.

Recoil-operated actions represent an improvement over the blowback in terms of the type and pressure of cartridge they can handle. In this system, the recoil of the pistol drives the operation. Recoil operated systems are generally designed to keep the slide or bolt and barrel locked together through part of the firing cycle. Some use a toggle-link system, as in the Luger, or a roller-lock, as in the Czech M52, to delay the opening of the breech until the bullet has exited the barrel. As the bullet travels forward, the barrel and slide recoil as a unit. At about the midpoint of the operation, after the bullet has exited the barrel, pressure drops, the action unlocks and the slide continues traveling backward, ejecting the empty case and cocking the hammer. The slide then strips a fresh round from the magazine, chambering it as it comes forward into battery.

This system is used in autoloading pistols using the 9mm Parabellum cartridge, 38 Super Auto, 45 ACP and similar cartridges adopted for military and police use. Battering of internal parts will result from loads generating excessive pressures and velocities.

The best way to work up handloads for autoloaders is to do so slowly, checking recoiling parts for any evidence of battering. The best loads are ones that will reliably cycle the action and no more.

Generally the only cast-bullet loads that do work are those that are near the maximum pressure level. While these may operate the action reliably, they may often not deliver very good accuracy, and the accurate load may not operate the action. Reduced loads will not work reliably in any autoloader, with cartridges often getting jammed on the way out and chewed up in the process. Therefore, the range of loading options for autoloaders of any stripe is rather limited. There will usually be only a relative few loadings that will produce good accuracy and reliable functioning. Ammunition prepared for autoloaders should be given extra care to see that all tolerances are kept close to factory specifications. Exceeding overall length will jam actions. Cases too short and bullets too deep can have the same effect. In short, ammunition preparation for successful shooting of these guns requires extra care for best results.

Full-length resizing is almost always necessary with cartridges used in autoloaders, since the chambers are on the large size to permit reliable feeding even when they are dirty with fouling.

Gas-operated pistols are uncommon and limited to expensive models that fire very powerful magnum cartridges that enter the lower region of rifle velocities. The gas-operated system features a locked bolt and non-moving barrel, much like gas-operated rifles, and is based on a scaled-down rife action. They can thus fire very powerful cartridges. At some point on the barrel, forward of the chamber, there's a small hole that taps off a small amount of gas, after the bullet passes that point. The gas is trapped in a small cylinder with a piston. The piston drives a

Although made of modern steel, this top-break replica of the S&W Schofield revolver by Navy Arms probably should not be fired with maximum-pressure loads.

The Thompson/Center Contender (left) and Magnum Research Lone Eagle (above) represent the ultimate in handgun power, range, recoil and noise in calibers such as 45-70, 30-06 and 444 Marlin.

rod which operates a camming lock on the bolt, that opens it after the bullet has exited the barrel. In some variants the gas is directed to the surface of the cam lock to unlock the bolt. As the bolt is driven back, the case is ejected and the hammer or striker is cocked, and a spring drives the bolt forward to strip a fresh round from the magazine and chamber it.

The placement of the gas port is critical to reliable functioning because the amount and pressure of gas must be enough to operate the pistol, but not enough to cause damage through battering. Needless to say, the amount and type of powder used is also critical to this system's functioning. Gas-operated autoloaders are ammunition sensitive and will work best with loadings that duplicate factory specifications. Cast bullets, generally, do not work well in gas-operated autoloaders. Fast-burning powders such as IMR 4227, Herco, Unique, 2400, H110 and AA1680 are about the only ones that will function gas-operated actions reliably.

Any cast bullets used in autoloading pistols are best cast of hard alloy, since soft bullets are often nicked and dented as they pass through the magazine and into the chamber. Feed ramp polishing may often be necessary when using cast loads with any autoloader to avoid jams. Magazine lips that are bent or sprung are a frequent cause of jamming in autoloading pistols and should be checked for wear or damage if this problem occurs.

Loading for Revolvers

Modern revolvers are all of the solid frame type. The few exceptions are replicas of 19th century top-break guns and those old models that are still around that use this system. The top-break guns are of a weaker design and should be used only with low-pressure "starting loads" listed in the manuals, and then only if they are in good, tight condition.

Unlike the autoloader, with its box magazine, the revolver features a cylinder with multiple chambers. The mechanism in a revolver turns these chambers, via a hand or pawl which aligns each with the barrel. The relationship between this rotation and the firing cycle is referred to as timing. In revolvers where the timing is off because of wear and battering by too many heavy loads, this alignment between the chamber and the barrel is less than perfect, and poor accuracy, even badly shaved bullets, is the result. To an extent this can be corrected by a competent gunsmith.

The revolver has a second problem—the gap between the cylinder and the barrel. The bullet must jump this gap before entering the forcing cone at the rear of the barrel. There has been much written about gas loss in the process, but the final analysis is that it isn't that much in terms of lowering bullet performance. The jump is most detrimental to accuracy because of the aforementioned alignment problems. In addition, by making this jump, the bullet gains a fair amount of speed before it hits the rifling, and may show skid marks as it moves forward for a fraction of an inch before engaging the rifling.

The throat of the revolver cylinder guides but does not really support the bullet, since it is larger than the bore diameter. Sizing revolver bullets is then something of a guessing game. The best course of action is to stick with factory diameters to start with, then experiment with different diameters after slugging the bore. The hardness of cast revolver bullets can have a decided effect on their accuracy. A fairly hard alloy (Lyman #2) generally works best, but softer alloys may be necessary to achieve proper upset and to avoid leading in some revolvers. Leading can be a serious problem in some guns, and these may require a hollow-base bullet to obturate the cylinder throat to avoid hot gas blowing by and melting the surface of the bullet. Before going to a hollow-base mould, it is best to experiment with different lubricants and alloys to see if changes in these will eliminate the problem. Different styles of bullets with larger, deeper lubricant grooves to hold more lubricant may be the answer. Failing that, buy some commercially-made hollow-base bullets or factory loads with hollow-base bullets (if available) before getting another mould. Gas checks and wax wads may come to the rescue in some cases, as will half-jacketed bullets which eliminate leading entirely.

Because they are loaded manually, revolvers work well with cast bullets, both plain and gas-checked. Owing to the recoil a cylinder-full of ammunition receives with each discharge, revolver cartridges should be crimped to keep the bullets from being pushed into the cases. Revolver cases should be full-length resized for ease in loading the gun.

One major advantage of revolvers over autoloaders is their ability to handle low-pressure/low-velocity loadings, because the action is not dependent on cartridge power for operation. These will afford economical practice with minimal wear and tear on the gun. For the same reason, revolvers can take a greater range of bullets in terms of weight and length. Bullets with a long bearing surface generally align better and produce the best accuracy. While revolvers function best with fast-burning pistol powders, the range of loading possibilities surpasses that of the autoloader.

Loading for Single Shots

These handguns are a fairly recent arrival on the shooting scene, and their use is limited to long-range target shooting and hunting. They chamber rifle cartridges and powerfully-loaded handgun cartridges. Because of their solid actions and longer barrels, they generate velocities and pressures in the rifle class. These guns might best be called "hand rifles." Owing to their light weight, most cannot use maximum rifle loadings, and even with more modest pressures and velocities the muzzle blast and recoil are formidable. Most loading manuals contain special loading data for these guns. To use *any* of these loadings in a standard revolver or autoloader would wreck it in short order. Loading procedures for metallic silhouette guns follow rifle instructions. One of the more popular of these guns is the Thompson/Center Contender. This gun allows the use of a number of barrels, each in a different caliber. Contenders can thus shoot anything from the 22 Long Rifle on up to the 45-70, which if you want to get a real "kick" out of handgun shooting will certainly deliver the goods.

Testing Ammunition

Accuracy is, or should be, your first concern. An accuracy test can consist of nothing more than plinking a few cans at an unknown distance, but this won't tell you very much. The only meaningful test is firing from a solid rest at a known distance. With handguns, a test range doesn't really need much more than 50 yards, since this is about the maximum accurate range

of most of them, and 50 to 75 feet to is the standard distance. Accuracy testing requires a solid bench installation with a sand bag or adjustable rest. If you live in a rural area or have access to a range with benches you are set.

Testing should be done on a day with good light, little or no wind and moderate temperatures. Calm conditions are generally found in the early morning or late afternoon. The place to start is to shoot some factory ammunition for comparison. A distance of 50 yards is good enough to get a fair idea of the long-range possibilities of your handgun and ammunition if you plan to use it for hunting. Only the more powerful calibers—357 Magnum and up—have much use in the hunting field.

For most handguns a 2- to 3-inch group at 50 feet is about as good as you will get. Fine target guns will shoot under an inch at this range. Metallic silhouette guns are judged and tested more by rifle standards. Shoot seven- or ten-shot groups, taking your time to squeeze off the shots. If you intend to shoot both cast and jacketed bullets, be sure to clean the barrel of all copper fouling before shooting lead-alloy bullets, since they will strip lead on the copper fouling.

Shooting into turf will give you an idea of the ricochet potential of your ammunition if this is critical. You can usually hear the results if the bullets are not ricochet proof. Most handgun bullets ricochet very readily, even hollowpoints. For testing on game or varmint animals, there is not much in the way of practical substitutes for the real item. Ballistic gelatin is the standard by which such determinations are made, but it is difficult to prepare and must be calibrated and used at the proper temperature.

One tissue substitute of a cheap and easy sort is newspaper, soaked overnight to get it fully saturated. Stocks of the wet paper are then put in a cardboard carton for shooting into. This is far heavier and more resistant than muscle tissue, but will give you an idea of bullet behavior.

Packed wet snow is a fairly good tissue simulant, and if there is enough of it you can find your bullet somewhere along a long snow loaf. High-velocity bullets are more difficult to recover, but lower velocity cast bullets can usually be stopped within 5 to 10 feet of packed snow. These will generally be in almost pristine condition. This will give you a good opportunity to study your cast bullets for evidence of gas-cutting and of how well they take the rifling. Large or double sets of rifling marks on the front of a bullet indicate skidding or jumping the rifling—the bullet going straight for a fraction of an inch before taking the rifling and turning, as it should. Rifling marks that are higher on one side than the other indicate the bullet was not straight in the case or were fired in a revolver with the cylinder slightly out of alignment. Grease grooves that are heavily compressed and lack lubricant will explain one cause of leading—not enough groove space and an inefficient lubricant. Bullet recovery is for those who are seriously interested, and those wanting answers to questions beginning with the word Why.

A final warning is to *always check your cases after firing*, particularly when you are testing loads that are on the high side of the pressure curve. Once you are out in the field, there is a great temptation to keep shooting. If there are signs of high pressure or excessive headspace, stop shooting. Don't risk your eyesight and handgun.

Creating
homemade
scattergun fodder
is not the same
as metallic
cartridge reload-
ing. It requires
different tools,
components and
knowledge.

Shotshell Ammunition Reloading

OF THE THREE basic types of ammunition, shotgun ammunition is perhaps the easiest to load, once you get the hang of it.
Nevertheless, the same level of care and attention must be giv-
en the task if good results are to be obtained. The place to begin
is with once-fired or, better, new cases to work up a load. Once
a load is tested and found to be satisfactory then quantity production can begin.

Shotshell casings are made of plastic for the most part,
although the traditional paper shell is still offered by Federal as
of this writing. Since shotshells operate at far lower pressures
than rifle and most handgun ammunition, they are less robust
in construction. Shotshells come in six sizes or gauges. The
smallest is the 410-bore which is actually .410-inch in diameter
or 410-caliber. The larger sizes are listed by gauge, an old system that determined a "gauge" size by the number of lead balls
of that diameter to weigh a pound. The next size up is 28-gauge,
then 20-gauge, 16-gauge, 12-gauge and, finally, 10-gauge. In
the bad old days of market hunting, the now obsolete 8-gauge,

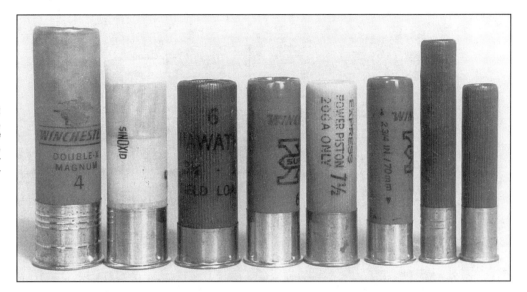

Modern shotshells, from left: 10-gauge 3$\frac{1}{2}$-inch magnum, 12-gauge 3-inch, 12-gauge 2$\frac{3}{4}$-inch, 16-gauge 2$\frac{3}{4}$-inch, 20-gauge 2$\frac{3}{4}$-inch, 28-gauge 2$\frac{3}{4}$-inch, and 410-bore 3- and 2$\frac{1}{2}$-inch.

4-gauge and even 3-gauge guns were used; the latter two were mounted like small cannons on boats for taking waterfowl.

Modern shotshells, in addition to the above six gauges, are available in different lengths. Since 1933, 410 shotguns have been universally available to take the 3-inch shell, which is ballistically superior to the old 2$\frac{1}{2}$-inch shell. The 3-inch shell should *never* be loaded in a gun chambered for the shorter shell. This rule applies to *all* gauges. To do so will result in serious pressure jumps which can wreck your gun and your face. The shorter shell can always be used in the longer chamber, but never the reverse.

The big problem with this potential mismatching of length is that the longer shells will chamber in guns intended for the shorter load. This is because shotgun chambers are made long, allowing space for the opening of the crimp in the case mouth. A 3$\frac{1}{2}$-inch 10-gauge shell measures 3 inches unfired and 3$\frac{1}{2}$ inches fired. If you have an old gun or one of foreign make which is not marked for the length of shell it is chambered for, take it to a competent gunsmith for examination. Foreign shotguns may be chambered for shells of different lengths.

Old guns should be regarded with suspicion unless the length is clearly marked or can otherwise be identified. Old guns should also be regarded as suspect if they cannot be identified as being safe for use with modern smokeless powder. Guns with Damascus barrels, identifiable by the tiger-stripe pattern in the metal, should be examined by a knowledgeable gunsmith to determine if the barrels are sound. If there is any sign of barrel corrosion from blackpowder loads used in the gun, don't try shooting it. Damascus-barreled guns in good condition should be used with blackpowder loads only, just to be on the safe, lower-pressure side. Guns designed for smokeless loads abound on the new and used market, so it's not worth the risk of blowing up Granpap's old double, let alone your hide just to shoot the thing. Again, if there is *any* doubt about the soundness of the gun, don't shoot it at all.

Case Inspection and Storage

As with rifle and handgun cartridges, shotshells should be inspected for defects. Those that are badly worn around the mouth, have splits in the case walls or heads, or leaks around the primers, should be discarded. Paper shotshells are perhaps the most vulnerable of all. The bodies absorb moisture which can also enter the seam around the primer, and moisture-swollen shells will not chamber. Before buying any old ones to shoot, if the shells can't be tested, try chambering the more sus-

Obsolete shotshells, from left: 10-gauge 2$\frac{7}{8}$-inch, 12-gauge brass shell, early 12-gauge roll-crimp all-plastic, original 12-gauge high-brass, 12-gauge roll-crimp paper shell.

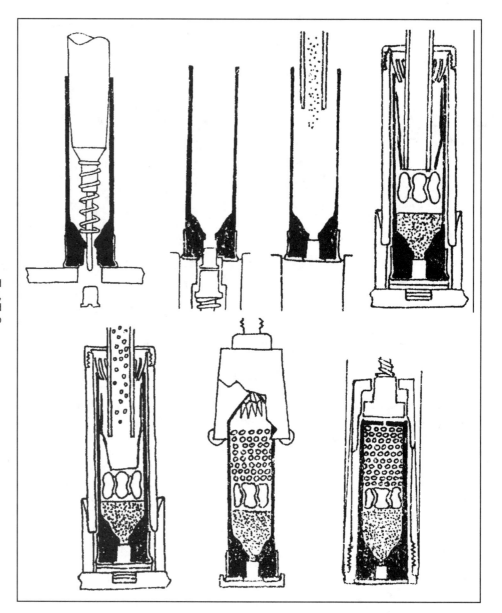

There are seven steps in shotshell reloading: resizing and decapping, priming, powder charging, wad seating, shot metering, crimp starting and crimp finishing.

pect ones or check them with a ring gauge. Study the exteriors for bleaching or water discoloration.

Modern plastic shells don't have this problem, but in an economy move many are no longer made with brass heads. The steel heads are given a thin brass plate which will corrode quickly. The steel beneath will corrode even more quickly if exposed to pollutants. Old plastic shells that have been crimped for a long time tend to hold that crimp and reload poorly unless ironed out with a warming tool made for this purpose. A piece of metal rod or pipe of the proper diameter heated in boiling water will also serve.

Shotshells come in a wide array of colors. There is a good reason for this—so you won't mix them up. Successful reloading depends on fitting all the components together correctly within the shell. There is a considerable difference in the inside capacities of various shells owing to the thickness of the base wad at the head of the shell. Matching loads to the particular brand and type of shell is critical to successful reloading. If the

NORMAL CHOKE PERCENTAGE	
Designation	Percentage of Pellets in 30-inch Circle at 40 Yards
Full	65-75
Improved Modified ($3/4$)	60-65
Modified ($1/2$)	55-65
Improved Cylinder ($1/4$)	45-55
Skeet	40-50
Cylinder	35-40

SHOTSHELL LENGTHS	
Ammo	Shell Length (ins.)
10-Gauge	$2^7/_8$ (obsolete) and $3^1/_2$
12-Gauge	$2^3/_4$, 3 and $3^1/_2$
16-Gauge	$2^9/_{16}$ (obsolete) and $2^3/_4$
20-Gauge	$2^3/_4$ and 3
28-Gauge	$2^3/_4$
410-Bore	$2^1/_2$ and 3

correct shotcup/wad is not used with the matching shell, it may be too long or too short for the shell to crimp properly. Therefore, different companies make their shells of certain colors to identify the make and further color code these shells by gauge so they are not mixed up. A 20-gauge shell accidentally dropped in a 12-gauge gun barrel will stop about where the forcing cone is. If a 12-gauge shell is then fired, the shooter will immediately be reminded of the Big Bang Theory when the gun comes apart in the forend area. The bad part of this is the proximity of fingers and hand to the barrel that just let go. This 12/20 blowup is not uncommon, and that is why all modern American-made 20-gauge shells are some shade of yellow and all 12-gauges are usually red. Winchester uses red for all its shells except 20-gauge; Remington shells are green, 20-gauge excepted; Federal shells, including their paper-tube 12-gauge, are maroon, with the exception of the 10-gauge which is brown; the Activ 12-gauge, which is all plastic and has no brass on it, is red; Fiocchi shells, from Italy, may be purple, blue, red, orange or brown.

Within the various makes you will find shells with different base wads which thus require different shot cups. That is why critical inspection and storage are needed. If you are in doubt, consult a good shotshell reloading manual, such as the one put out by Lyman, which has a great many of these shells pictured

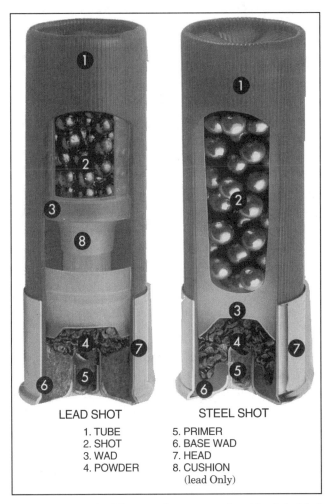

LEAD SHOT   STEEL SHOT

1. TUBE   5. PRIMER
2. SHOT   6. BASE WAD
3. WAD   7. HEAD
4. POWDER   8. CUSHION
                      (lead Only)

There are some big differences between steel and lead shotshell components.

in color, and of actual size. If in doubt about the proper shot cup, sacrifice a loaded one by cutting it down the middle and comparing the sectioned shell with these illustrations. The height of the brass on the outside of the head may or may not indicate a base wad of a different height, but don't count on it. *Never* mix components.

Shotshell Primers

Shotshell primers, while they are all the same size, do have different burning characteristics. This will radically affect pressures. The substitution of one primer for another can raise pressures as much as 2000 psi with all other components being equal. This is why when working up loads, no substitution should be made for *any* component listed in a loading manual. If you have several brands of primers on hand, don't have more than one box open at a time so they don't get mixed up. Primers should be seated flush with the case head. High primers can be detonated accidentally in certain guns with disastrous results. Decapping live primers is not a good idea. Either snap them in the gun or discard the shell.

Shotshell Wads

Old-style brass and paper shotshells used wads of cardboard, felt and similar fibers to serve as spacers between the powder and the charge of shot. This system was used for over a hundred years. It had a serious drawback—the wads did not obturate the shell or the bore of the gun very well, and hot powder gas leaked around their edges and melted and otherwise distorted the pellets in the shot charge. Things improved in the 1940s with the addition of a cup wad over the powder to act as a gas seal. In the early 1960s, a further improvement was made with a plastic wrap being placed around the shot charge to keep it from being distorted by direct contact with the barrel.

Modern shotshells contain a single plastic wad with a cup-shaped base that goes over the powder and expands to obturate the bore. Above this is a cushioning section that compresses on firing to start the shot charge off more gently. At the top is a cup that holds the charge of shot. The sides are cut into several "petals" which open as soon as the wad exits the barrel. Unlike in the old days, when loads were assembled by adding card or fiber wads of varying thickness to get the proper height for good crimping, modern wads with shotcups are designed to hold a certain amount of shot. This way, low-volume wads with shallow shotcups are used for light field and target loads, while high-volume wads are used for heavy loads for waterfowl shooting. Attempting to over or underload these cups gives poor results when you crimp the shell. Components should be properly matched to the shells for which they are intended, and not used in other shells. There are some instances of mixing components, but this area is not for the beginner.

Sizes and Types of Shot

Most shot is made of lead hardened with antimony. So called "premium" shot is made of a harder alloy to keep it from deforming in the firing process. This is a good investment since deformed shot makes for open or irregular patterns, which translates to missed or crippled game. Sometimes hard shot is

Shotcups/wads are designed for particular loads in specific shells. These wads hold $7/8$-ounce of #7, #7$1/2$, #8 or #9 shot. They are intended for use in the compression-formed plastic shells and are for target shooting.

given a copper plating to make it look attractive. Whether this makes it shoot any better or not depends on your powers of imagination.

Steel shot was introduced some twenty years ago after the U.S. Fish and Wildlife Service concluded that bottom-feeding waterfowl were succumbing to lead poisoning. USFWS placed a ban on lead shot for waterfowl hunting, and thus steel shot was born. Steel shot has a number of drawbacks, the least of which is its light weight. Thus, larger shot must be loaded in greater volume to get the same weight equivalent as the old lead loads. While the hardness of the shot makes it less subject to deformation than lead shot, it also means that steel shot will ruin a standard shotgun barrel and should never be fired in it. To do so will likely put a ring in the barrel and finish the choke. Steel shot must be used in barrels marked: "For Steel Shot."

Bismuth shot is more expensive than lead and not as heavy, but is heavier than steel. It has the advantage of being usable in standard shotgun barrels without harming them. As of this writing, the U.S. Fish and Wildlife Service has given its approval for the use of bismuth shot for the 1996-7 waterfowl season. On the horizon is tungsten-iron shot which will offer a density 94 percent that of lead, and have the non-distorting quality of steel. It will have to be used in barrels intended for steel shot. If tungsten shot becomes available as a reloading component, it will likely replace steel. At present, tungsten shot is only available as loaded ammunition from Federal, and has not yet been approved for waterfowl hunting. The cost is in the same price range as bismuth shot.

When it comes to loading shotshells, the machines you will use have different systems from metallic ammunition loaders, and the sequence of steps will vary from one machine to another. As was pointed out in the chapter on loading equipment, shotshell loading is done on a single machine with a lot of attachments, while rifle and handgun ammunition is assembled using two or three bench-mounted tools with a number of attachments and several hand tools. Because of their relative complexity, shotshell reloading machines come with manuals that are (hopefully) clearly written and illustrated. They show you how to load shotshells on *that* machine. If you buy a used machine, be sure that the proper manual is with it and that the tool has *all* the necessary component parts. Failing this, you will have to write the company for a manual, or get someone who knows what he is doing to show you how to operate that particular machine. It is dangerous to attempt to load ammunition on a machine you don't know how to operate on a "I think I can figure this dude out" basis. Obsolete machines that may not have all their parts and manual are no bargain. Manufacturers such as Texan and Herters are out of business and spare parts, manuals and factory support are out of the question.

If you have never done any shotshell reloading it is probably best not to start with a progressive loader. These machines are the most complicated to use, and observing all the steps while determining whether or not they are being done correctly is difficult. Thus the beginner would do best starting with a basic single-stage loader such as the Lee Load-All II or MEC 600 Jr. Mark V. Unlike rifle and handgun loading where the manuals offer suggestions for working up loads to find an accurate one, shotshell loads are pretty much cut and dried. The manual that comes with the loader will instruct you on the use of the powder and shot bushings to be inserted in the charge bar of the machine. These must be matched to the proper type of powder and size of shot. They will dispense preset amounts of powder and shot. *Make sure you match these bushings and powders correctly!* Read the manual.

Case Inspection

Even new and once-fired cases should be checked over for defects. Any with splits or serious defects in the case mouth or body, or splits in the metal head should be discarded. Cases should be segregated by maker as determined not only by the headstamp, but by the base wad configuration. Because they wear out sooner than rifle or handgun cases, and because worn cases give different velocities as the case mouths become softer, shotshells should be carefully identified by their intended loading as well as by maker and the number of times they have been reloaded. This means careful handling when shooting so you don't mix them up, and afterwards boxing or bagging them accordingly.

Materials/Equipment Pre-Check

Make sure that your wads match the shells you are about to load. The loading manual will tell you which to buy. Select the proper primers, powder and proper size shot for your loads. Check that you have the correct bushing and shot bar in place for that combination of powder and shot, or have made the proper adjustments on the bar for those types that are adjustable. Fill the canisters on the machine. Lay out no more than 100 primers on the bench.

Case Resizing and Decapping

With machines such as the Lee, decapping and primer seating are done at the same location. With the MEC, primer seating is a separate step. Place the shell under the sizing die, or slip it into the die body, and pull the handle to the bottom of the stroke. This resizes and decaps the shell.

Priming

A new primer is next placed on the primer seating station and the handle is pulled to bring the shell down on to the primer and seat it. This stroke must be firm, but not overly hard, in order to seat the primer flush with the shell head. Primers should be checked with a straightedge to assure proper seating.

Powder Charging

The case is next moved to the station below the powder container. Depending on the exact configuration of the machine you are using, the handle is pulled to bring the case into contact with the powder/shot tube dispenser. The charge bar is then pushed across the bottom of the powder container (usually to the full left position) and the powder charge will be metered into the case. **Important:** This step should be verified by checking at least ten charges on a powder scale. If you do not use a scale you have no idea whether your charges are close or even in the ball park. If the machine is not delivering the proper amount of powder, within a tolerance of 5 percent of the list-

ed charge, you may have to try another larger or smaller bushing in the charge bar, or the bushing may be clogged if the powder is not dry and free-flowing. This step should be done at the beginning of each loading session and when you change to a different lot of powder. Once it is determined the charge bar is dispensing powder as it should, move on to the next step.

Wad Seating

This step may be done at the same station as powder charging or the shell may have to be moved to a new station. The wad is placed on the wad guide. The handle is pulled fully down and the wad is seated on the powder. Some powders are more sensitive to wad pressure than others, and will yield higher or lower velocities and pressures depending on their degree of compression. Red Dot is one of the more sensitive ones. The better machines have a pressure gauge on them. Note this and the wad seating height to determine that your wads are seated uniformly. If a wad goes far too deep, you have less than a full powder charge or no charge and you will have to recheck your charging operations. Care should be tak-

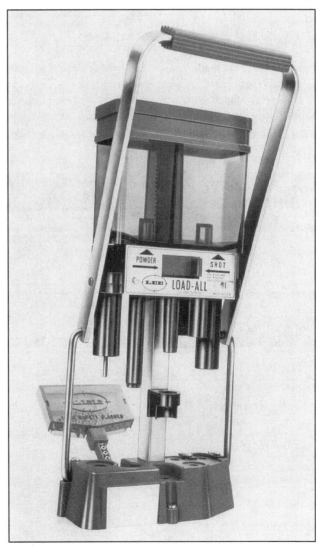

The Lee Load-All II is an excellent entry-level shotshell loader at an affordable price. It can turn out an average of 100 rounds per hour, and loads lead or steel shot.

Each shotshell load is component-specific. Primers, as well as all other components, are not created equal and should not be interchanged.

Various crimp styles, from left: an old-style rolled crimp on a paper shell with top wad; the rolled crimp, still used and necessary for making slug loads; typical six-point and eight-point crimps.

en that the base cup on the wad is not caught and nicked or tipped by folds in the case mouth and descends straight on to the powder. If the seating pressure is too high you may have too much powder or an incorrect wad for that charge, or a wad not properly matched to that case. Wad seating pressure should be at least 20 pounds. Finally, check to see that the petals of the shotcup are in full contact with the case walls so they will not interfere with shot metering.

PELLET COUNT COMPARISON

Shot Size	12-Ga. 1⁷⁄₈ ozs. Lead pellets	Shot Size	12-Ga. 1³⁄₈ ozs. Steel pellets
6	422	4	263
4	253	2	172
2	163	BB	99
BB	94	T	71

SHOT SIZES

Shot Size	Diameter (Ins.)	No. of Pellets/Oz. Lead	No. of Pellets/Oz. Steel
9	.08	585	—
8¹⁄₂	.085	—	—
8	.09	411	—
7¹⁄₂	.095	350	—
6	.11	225	316
5	.12	170	246
4	.13	135	191
3	.14	109	153
2	.15	87	125
1	.16	72	103
B	.17	59	84
BB	.18	50	72
BBB	.19	43	61
T	.20	36	52
F	.22	37	40

Shot Metering

Depending on your machine, the shell may or may not be moved to another station for shot metering. Whatever, the shell is raised to the powder/shot charging tube and the charge bar is generally moved to the right across the bottom of the shot canister dropping the shot into the shell. It is important to have the proper shot bar for the load you are making. MEC tools (at least the older ones) have a different shot charge bar for each weight of shot. Other machines have adjustable shot bars or bars with powder insert bushings. Lee and Hornady machines have bushing inserts for both shot and powder.

As with powder charging, shot charges must be checked on a scale to be sure they are accurate. The same five percent tolerance applies. Run several shot charges on your scale to verify that your machine is behaving properly. Occasionally a shot charge will jam or only partially feed, and a visual inspection of each shell you load should be made. If the shot cup is not full, return the shell to the charging position and give the charging tube a tap or two. This should cause the remainder to drop and you can move to the next step.

The loading of buckshot is a special consideration, since shot this large cannot be metered through the machine. Buckshot is loaded by pellet *count*, not by weight, and the shot have to be counted and hand-fed into the shot cup. More importantly, buckshot must be nested in layers in the cup or they will not fit properly. Some of these loads call for "buffering" with a finely ground plastic material. This should be added with each layer and the case tapped with the finger to settle it into the cup until it is level with the top layer of shot. Needless to say, buckshot loads are best assembled on a single-stage press rather than on a progressive.

Crimp Starting

Shotshells have two forms of fold crimping—six-point and

LEAD VERSUS STEEL PELLET WEIGHT			
—Lead Pellet—		—Steel Pellet—	
Size	Wgt. Grs.	Size	Wgt. Grs.
BBB	10.4	F(TTT)	11.0
BB	8.8	TT	9.6
BB	8.8	T	8.3
B	7.3	BBB	7.1
1	6.1	BB	6.1
2	5.0	B	5.0
3	4.1	1	4.3
4	3.2	2	3.5
5	2.6	3	2.9
5	2.6	4	2.3
6	1.9	5	1.8
7 1/2	1.3	6	1.4

STEEL VERSUS LEAD PELLET COUNT			
—Steel Pellet—		—Lead Pellet—	
Size	No. Per oz.	Size	No. Per oz.
F(TTT)	39	T	34
TT	46	BBB	42
T	52	BB	50
BBB	62	B	60
BB	72	1	72
B	87	2	87
1	103	3	106
2	125	4	135
3	154	5	170
4	192	6	225
5	243	6	225
6	317	7	299

eight-point. The crimp starter should be matched to the fold pattern of the shells you are reloading. Never use a six-point crimp starter on an eight-point shell and vice versa. The crimp starter is adjustable and can be raised and lowered to vary the amount of crimp start. When working with various brands of shells, a certain amount of experimentation is needed to get the proper amount of crimp start. Remington and Federal shells seem to require a little less start than Activ and Winchester shells. If your finished shells show indentations in the crimped end of the shell, the crimp starter is set too deeply and will have to be backed off a bit.

Final Crimp

The shell is now placed on the final crimp station and the handle pulled down until it bottoms. Hold the handle in this position for a second to give the crimp a firm set, then raise the handle. If the crimp is not firmly closed this step may be repeated. Crimp depth should duplicate the original factory load. This die is adjustable and may need some tinkering to get it to accommodate the make of case you are using.

Overall length of the finished shell is critical to feeding through magazines so die adjustment must be kept to a minimum. If the problem is the center of the shell being too high or too low, you can experiment with changing the wad for a longer or shorter one or adding or subtracting shot. Adding shot should be done with caution and not done with a maximum load. A 20-gauge card wad can be added to the bottom of the 12-gauge cup to act as a filler if needed. This should be done before the wad is seated. A supply of 1/8-inch and 1/16-inch card wads is a handy item to stock.

Most shotshell loading machines have a feature to put a slight taper on the case mouth to facilitate feeding in repeating guns. Some of the more expensive loaders such as the Hornady 366 Auto and Apex machines have a third crimping feature. This rounds the front of the shell and locks in the crimp with a slightly raised ring around the edge of the crimped end. This ensures the crimp will not open through jarring as it is fed through an autoloading action.

Final Inspection

Since shotshells are made of plastic or paper and are softer than brass cartridges, it is always good practice to do a final size check before boxing them. Any case with a poor crimp that cannot be repaired in the approved manner should be junked. The same goes for one that has cracked or split in the reloading process. MEC's ring gauge is a handy item for a quick size check with a "go/no go" hole for each standard size shell.

Ammunition Testing

Because shotguns deliver a pattern of shot which is determined primarily by the choke of the barrel, testing mainly depends on duplicating factory performance. Light loads will obviously put fewer shot in the standard 30-inch circle at 40 yards than heavier loads. To check the patterning of your gun, you need a 40-yard range and a large piece of paper at least one square yard in size. Shoot one shot at the center of the target. Draw a 30-inch circle around the most dense area and count the holes. Various loading manuals will give you the number of shot per ounce, so you can figure the percentage or you can make an actual count. Beyond this there are some other observations you can make. One is to see where the greatest area of density lies. It should be in the center of your point of aim and not biased to the side. The shot pattern should be more or less even within the circle. Some guns have a tendency to produce a very dense center with an uneven disbursal of hits at the edge of the circle. This may mean missed clays or crippled game. To check the efficacy of your pattern, cut a clay target-size circle (4 5/16-inch) out of a piece of clear plastic and move it around the pattern. Areas with fewer than three pellets in them are in the doubtful zone in terms of an assured kill on most birds.

Good and Bad Loads

Good loads are the ones that do what you want them to do and often the bad load is one that does not. This may be because it is inappropriate to the situation—too small shot, too light a load, not enough pattern density. These problems are rooted mainly in the ignorance of the shooter and in taking shots that he should not attempt and then blaming the gun or the ammunition. There are, however, a few false notions and a similar number of home truths that should be addressed.

Larger-bore guns kick more than smaller ones with the same loading. Not true. The recoil is mostly determined by the weight of the shot charge and its velocity. The difference in *felt* recoil

Step-By-Step

>>>>>>>>>>>>>>>>>>>>>>>>>>>

Reloading

Shotshell Cartridges

(Photos courtesy Lee Precision, Inc.)

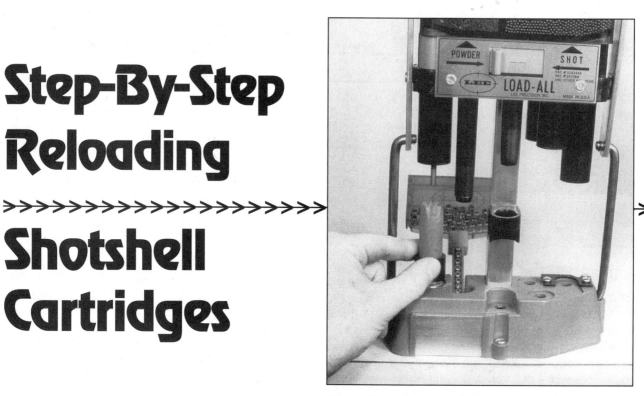

Step 1—Sizing: Sort your hulls by brand and type, and discard the defective ones. Slip the sizing die, *grooved end up,* over the shell. Place the shell in Station 1 and pull down the handle. This full-length resizes and deprimes the shell.

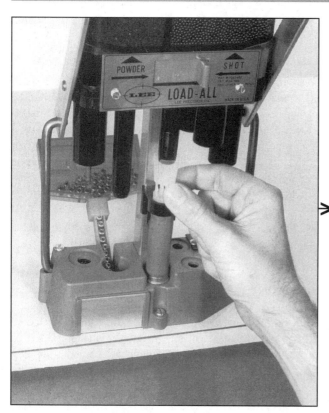

Step 4—Inserting the Wad: Raise the handle, insert the proper wad and lower the press handle until it stops.

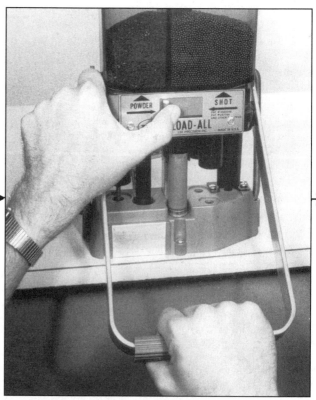

Step 5—Shot Charging: Now slide the charge bar all the way to the left to add the shot. Raise the press handle.

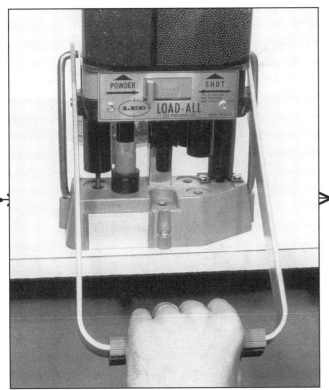

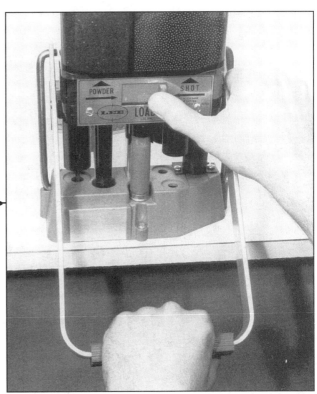

Step 2—Priming: Place a primer in the priming pocket at Station 2. Move the shell onto Station 2 and pull down the handle. The sizing die will automatically be pushed off the shell at this station. Remove it completely.

Step 3—Powder Charging: Slip the shell into the wad guide at Station 3, lower the handle and slide the charge bar to the right to add the powder.

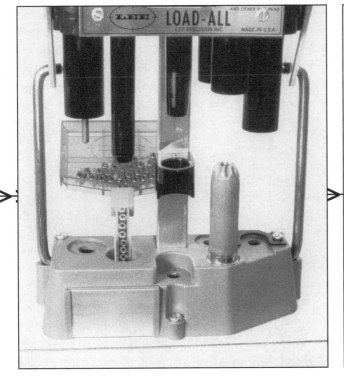

Step 6—Crimp Start: Place the shell under the proper crimp starter, keeping an inward fold of the shell toward the front for proper alignment with the segmented starter. Pull the press handle down all the way, holding it there for about two seconds to set the plastic.

Step 7—Final Crimp: Immediately move the shell into the shell-holder at Station 5, and pull the press handle down to complete the crimp. That completes the loading cycle, giving you a ready-to-shoot shotshell.

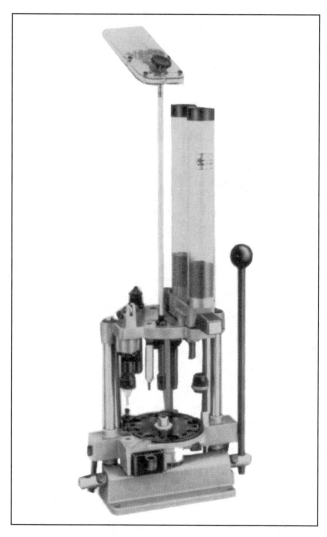

Hornady's 366 Auto machine is for shotgunners who do a lot of shooting. It has a high production rate and is built of high-quality materials.

The MEC 600 Jr. Mark V can turn out an average of 200 rounds per hour. It's available in 10, 12, 16, 20 and 28 gauges.

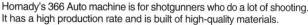

will be affected by the weight of the gun, and a heavy gun will absorb more recoil than a light one.

Larger-bore guns hit harder. Not true. The velocity of all shotgun loads is nearly the same—in the 1200-1500 fps range. A #6 pellet from a 410 is flying as fast and hitting as hard as one moving at the same velocity from a 10-gauge, even though the 410 makes less noise.

The same shot charge from a 20-gauge and a 12-gauge are equally effective. This tends not to be the case. Longer shot columns tend to result in greater compression-distortion of the pellets at the back of the load, and thus produce more fliers, and consequently a less dense pattern. This probably is what led to the notion of larger bore guns "hitting harder."

Harder shot hits harder. Not really, but hard and extra-hard shot deliver more pellets to the central pattern with fewer fliers. Heavy loads, particularly in the 410 and 3-inch 20-gauge shells, and the 3$\frac{1}{2}$-inch 12-gauge magnum, with their longer shot column, are most effective with hard shot.

Certain powders do not perform well at sub-freezing temperatures. This seems to be true, according to the folks at Ballistic Products. They ran tests on powder performance and concluded that Blue Dot gave significantly lower velocities at low temper-

atures, much more so than other powders. However, all velocities will be lower in cold conditions when the air is more dense.

High-velocity shotshell loads have some fans who believe that by pumping the velocity up to 1500 fps there is something to be gained by getting the shot to the target faster. More pressure and more recoil top the list unless the shot charge is reduced. At the velocity top end, patterns get pretty ragged. Around 1400 fps, however, patterns hold well and at ranges of 25 to 30 yards are quite lethal. Unfortunately, this added lethality is at the price of ruining game meat. This is a plus in the varmint-shooting area, not so good for pot hunting. Do these loads really "reach out there and get 'em?" Not really, since pellets are very poor performers in the aerodynamic sense. The initial gain in velocity is soon shed, and at 45-plus yards this hot-rod load is not going to perform much differently than the standard factory loading. If the velocity is achieved at a reduction in the amount of shot, the situation is a little worse because of a lower-density pattern.

The main advantage of such hot loadings would appear to be in trap and Skeet shooting, where the targets are at relatively close range. Hard hitting assures more breakage and higher velocities cut lead calculation in this game of hitting them fast and hard.

Reloading involves a number of processes before the trigger is tripped, but once the powder starts burning, it helps to have...

A Basic Knowledge of Ballistics

"SEND THAT GUN down to ballistics," is a throw-away line from dozens of forgettable TV cop shows. This notion of ballistics, being what police crime labs do, is ingrained in the minds of an astonishing number of people.

James Hamby, now head of the Indianapolis crime lab, tells of a court appearance that illustrates this point quite well. After a lengthy introduction, with explanations of his firearms examiner position, the old judge looked hard at Hamby and said. "Yeah, but what about ballistics?" It took Hamby a while to explain that "ballistics" was only a small part of the criminal investigation process, and that as an examiner he matches crime and test bullets and shell casings with particular guns, which is called "firearms examination" and has *nothing* to do with ballistics.

Calvin Goddard, the father of the field of firearms examination, later admitted that he rued the day he came up with the term "forensic ballistics." This was a hastily conceived name for the emerging science of "firearms examination" which, unfortunately, stuck in the public mind. As of this day, there is only one police organization in the country that still refers to its firearms section as "The Ballistics Lab"—the NYPD. It might be added that this outfit also embraces change with all the enthusiasm of the Vatican.

Ballistics, *real* ballistics, is the scientific investigation of the behavior of projectiles in flight. The name is derived from an ancient Roman siege machine called a *ballista,* a kind of king-size crossbow which launched spears, rocks and whatnot. The field of ballistics, in the modern sense, deals primarily with projectiles fired from guns, and is further divided into three subsections: interior ballistics, exterior ballistics and terminal ballistics. Ballistics spreads over a number of scientific fields, encompassing physics (including Newton's laws of motion), mechanics, dynamic forces, aerodynamics and the forces of air. It links up with chemistry, mathematics (including calculus), meteorology, metallurgy and medicine.

Interior Ballistics

Interior ballistics deals with everything that happens from the beginning of the firing sequence to the point where the projectile exits the barrel of the gun. The first serious use of guns was at the Battle of Crécy, in 1346, in which the English forces employed small cannons against the French. This event initiated the consideration of problems of interior ballistics—questions of pressure and velocity and pressure and gun failure—discussed in Chapter 3. It led to the investigation of propellants and ignition systems and considerations of gun barrel material and manufacture, which eventually led to the creation of the field of metallurgy. The basic questions were: how much pressure can be generated in a gun barrel and have it hold together, and how fast will a projectile be ejected? Rodman in the U.S. and Nobel in Great Britain developed the first reliable systems of pressure measurement.

Beyond the problem of establishing safe means of measuring internal pressures are considerations of increasing velocity without increasing pressure proportionally. There is the assessment of the best materials for making these projectiles, their shape, weight, strength and design, to see that they do not come apart in flight and either expand or penetrate or do some desired combination of both on reaching the target. There is the matter of material for gun barrels, the problems of barrel strength and wear. Suddenly the field of economics raises its dismal head as cost is pitted against longevity and efficiency.

Since a gun is an internal combustion, pressure-driven engine it depends on gases from burning gunpowder to overcome the inertia of the projectile. Considerable pressure builds up (up to 6000 psi in some instances) before the inertial force of the weight of the projectile is overcome and it starts to move. The action of swaging the projectile into the rifling causes pressure to increase to the point where the peak pressure is reached. Once the swaged projectile is in motion, pressure begins to drop as the speed of the projectile picks up and the space behind it increases in volume. When the projectile is out of the barrel, pressure drops rapidly to that of the surrounding atmosphere.

Propellant materials are a major concern under the rubric of interior ballistics. These include priming materials that will burn in such a way as to provide the best possible ignition, propellants that will produce a pressure curve best suited to a particular length of barrel, and both to be of material that will work reliably under a variety of temperature conditions and not change their burning characteristics over time.

These questions and concerns have occupied ballisticians for the past 600-plus years and not all the problems have been solved yet. The 20th century will likely see the end of the evolution of guns (firearms) as we know them, and the 21st will see the practical development of electromagnetic "rail guns" capable of launching projectiles at half-again to twice, to who knows how much, greater velocity than that achieved with conventional firearms. When this comes to pass, it will probably end investigations in interior ballistics, since with rail guns, there is no interior—the projectile is launched by electromagnetic propulsive forces generated by twin rods between which the bullet travels (starting from a flat "launch pad") through the air.

Exterior Ballistics

Exterior ballistics is concerned with hitting the target with accuracy, which means achieving consistency of bullet behavior. It encompasses the study of everything that affects a bullet's flight from the moment it exits the barrel until it reaches the target. The line between interior ballistics and exterior ballistics is blurred since, from the start, the bullet is pushing air within the gun barrel, and for a short distance the muzzle blast continues the acceleration process, often causing the bullet to yaw a bit in flight until rotation stabilizes it. Things happening within the gun barrel have a great deal to do with how a projectile will behave once it has exited that barrel.

Ballistics as a science had its beginning with the publication of Nicholas Tartaglia's treatise on the flight of projectiles, published in 1537. Tartaglia was the first to calculate trajectories and to theorize that maximum range was achieved at an exit angle of 45 degrees. He was wrong in this, but correct in assuming that all trajectories were curved.

The velocity of a projectile was first measured in 1741 by Benjamin Robins, inventor of the ballistic pendulum. He fired projectiles of known weight into the weight of a pendulum, also of known weight, and measured the distance of the swing. Robbins was the first investigator to come up with a system for reasonably accurate velocity measurement to 1700 fps. Using the same pendulum, Hutton in England was the first to note that air resistance had a considerable influence on reducing velocity, and that projectiles lost velocity in direct proportion to their speed—that the higher the initial velocity, the more rapid the decline in velocity.

By the 1840s the ballistic pendulum became obsolete with Wheatstone's proposal to measure bullet flight through time as it passed through screens breaking electrical contacts. The Le Boulengé chronograph using such a system was in use in the 1860s to the 1930s, when the first all-electronic machines using photoelectric screens were perfected.

The trajectory of a bullet is the curved path it takes from the gun muzzle to the target. The basic force affecting this curve (for small arms) is gravity. Temperature, which affects air density, is a second factor. In a vacuum, the trajectory of a bullet would be affected only by gravity, and it would thus describe a flight path that would be parabolic with the angle of descent being the same as the angle of ascent. Air resistance, however, reduces velocity and thus produces a much steeper angle of descent. As the bullet is slowed by this force and its forward velocity declines, the force of gravity predominates and the path of the bullet becomes less horizontal and more vertical.

The ballistic coefficient is a major factor in the calculation of the trajectory of a bullet. This figure is derived from the weight, diameter and form. Form is the degree of streamlining based on an ideal shape of a needle nose tapering back to a rounded body and then to a tapered base. Bullets of this "boattail" design have a high ballistic coefficient and will fly much farther than a flat-nosed wadcutter which is nearly a perfect cylinder.

Air temperature will have a marked effect on bullet trajectory. Hot air is less dense, because the molecules are farther apart, and will offer less resistance than cold air, wherein they are closer together. A rifle zeroed on a summer day at a temperature of 80 degrees Fahrenheit will shoot low on a winter day with a temperature of 10 degrees.

Moving air—wind—serves to accelerate or decelerate the forward motion of the bullet to a degree and will affect where it strikes. Head winds will decelerate velocity and lower the point of impact. Tail winds will accelerate velocity and raise the point of impact, all other things being equal.

Lateral bullet displacement. No one knows who discovered that spin-stabilizing projectiles made a tremendous increase in their accuracy. This permitted the development of highly efficient aerodynamic designs that would fly farther, lose velocity less quickly and retain more energy than a round ball. Arms with barrels containing helical grooves (rifling) first appeared in the late 1500s. While spin-stabilized projectiles fly far straighter than round balls, the rotation is affected by the air, and irregularities on the bullet's surface, caused primarily by the rifling, allow the bullet to work against the air causing it to roll or drift in flight in the direction it is spinning. Lt. Col. A.R. Buffington, U.S.A., developed a sight for the Springfield rifle, in 1883, that contained an automatic compensation feature for this rotational drift.

Crosswinds will have a decided effect on the lateral displacement of a bullet. The greatest displacement is when the wind is blowing at a right angle to the bullet's flight path. Wind velocity affects drift in proportion to the speed of the wind. Bullet velocity also affects the amount of drift, with the greatest degree of drift occurring when the bullet is moving at or slightly above the speed of sound. Above and below this point, wind drift is somewhat less. A bullet traveling above the speed of sound sets up a shock wave which indicates a loss of kinetic energy caused by drag. The degree of drag is dependent on bullet diameter, velocity, air density, and the drag coefficient, which is figured from such factors as projectile shape, air density, yaw and Mach number—the ratio of the projectile velocity to the speed of sound.

Other factors affecting lateral displacement are ricochets and deflections. Ricochets are the result of bullets striking hard ground, ice, pavement or water at a shallow angle. When this occurs the bullet nearly always loses its rotational stability and tumbles in flight. Even when striking water, which most consider an easily penetrated substance, bullets will ricochet if they strike below a critical angle of entry of 5.75 degrees. Bullets striking at angles above 2 degrees will lose their rotational stability.

Deflection might be termed a lateral ricochet. For many years there have been questions raised regarding "brush busting"—the ability of a bullet to hit a small branch and keep going (more or less) straight to the target. Debate over this issue had been fueled by stories of stellar performances by particular bullets which had penetrated small branches, often cutting them off in the process, then felled a game animal some distance away. There were perhaps a greater number of stories of the opposite happening, where a bullet clipped a twig and went spinning out of control, missing a large target entirely. This author's investigation into deflections found support for both claims. The critical factors were the angle of contact of the bullet and the branch, and whether the bullet was damaged by the branch. If the bullet struck the branch dead center and was undamaged, it continued on a relatively straight path. If it was damaged it lost stability. If it struck to one side of dead center it would deflect and usually lose stability and tumble. The greatest degree of deflection was at the point where *half* the bullet was in contact with the branch. The degree of deflection decreased as the point of contact moved closer to dead center or toward the edge resulting in a slight grazing of the branch.

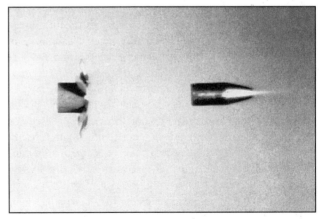

One area of ballistics study is what happens to a bullet after it leaves the gun barrel—exterior ballistics. It involves everything that happens to the bullet from muzzle to target impact. Here's a Remington Accelerator leaving the muzzle at 4080 fps, and (right) the sabot and bullet 18 inches downrange.

Terminal Ballistics

Terminal ballistics involves everything that happens to a bullet from the moment it reaches the target to the point where all motion ceases. The term means different things to different people. For the target shooter, punching paper or knocking over metal silhouettes is all that matters. The big game hunter is concerned with the ability of a bullet to both penetrate into a vital area, and expand, creating a large wound channel and quick incapacitation. The varmint hunter wants quick expansion on relatively thin skinned animals to create a large wound cavity and instant death. The small game hunter needs something between these two extremes—bullets that will expand, killing quickly, but not causing the kind of disruption encountered in the varmint bullet that destroys a great deal of edible meat. For military ends, terminal ballistics includes penetration of concrete, building materials, armor plate and starting fires in fuel tanks.

Wound ballistics is a subset of terminal ballistics and is concerned with the medical aspects of gunshot wounds, including wound trauma incapacitation and treatment of gunshot wounds.

Improvements in terminal ballistics have not been as fast as those in interior and exterior ballistics, and have come about with the development of high speed cinematography and high speed radiography. Development of ballistic gelatin as a tissue substitute has been a particular aid to improved terminal ballistics. In the last ten years, even the past five years, considerable advancements have been made in developing bullets which will produce controlled expansion. This allows them to penetrate while expanding at a rate that will not result in breakup or in overexpansion and inadequate penetration.

A great deal has been written regarding the role of velocity, that is to say high velocity, in the area of terminal and wound ballistics. According to Dr. Martin Fackler, the leading wound ballistics expert in the country, bullet lethality is an easily understood concept. Lethality is determined by answering two questions: How big is the hole it produces? How deep is this hole? Bigger and deeper holes are more likely to intersect with vital organs, cause greater loss of blood, and result in death.

What about high velocity? In the 1960s, reports of horrendous wounds created by the M-16 rifle and, to a lesser degree, the AK-47 rifle used in Vietnam began pouring in. The wounding effects, while genuine, were presented by an ignorant press as being wholly an artifact of high velocity. As often happens, misinformation and half-truths become pillars of public opinion as they receive amplification by politicians and other public figures through the media, without scrutiny from the researcher. In the case of the velocity/lethality controversy, there is *some* truth to the wounding effects of hydrostatic or hydraulic shock of a high velocity bullet *when* it contacts an area of a body such as the liver or cranial vault. Liver tissue has poor elasticity and brain tissue behaves like a semi-fluid in a sealed container. Anyone who has seen the effect of a 3000 fps bullet on a closed container of water has a good idea of the pressure-wave effect it produces. But, this does not apply to other types of tissue with a higher degree of elasticity. While a large, instantaneous cavity is created, the resultant tissue damage of a permanent sort is minimal, not extending far beyond the path of the bullet.

In the case of extreme hyper-velocity impacts—3500-4000+ fps—both the bullet and target behave in the manner of fluids regardless of the material they are made of. This allows a 48-grain copper-jacketed bullet with an exposed lead point to knock a hole through a half-inch of steel armor plate. At less than these velocities, the softer bullet would simply splatter on the surface of the harder material.

Bullet design had more to do with terminal/wound ballistics than other factors. For the first 400 years of their existence, bullets were made of lead. The creation of the jacketed bullet in the late 19th century came as a result of the development of smokeless powder and the quest for flat trajectories, meaning higher velocities. While flatter shooting was achieved, the lethality of the small, round-nose bullets was far less than with large, soft, lead bullets of the 45-70 class. In their efforts to achieve still flatter trajectories, the Germans found that their spitzer (pointed) bullet, in addition to possessing less drag than the round-nose bullet, created a more severe wound. This design, with its long tapering point, had a heavy end and a light end and when the bullet lost stability by striking a body, the heavy rear would flip over the front causing the bullet to make a larger hole—often exiting base first as it tumbled. Soon, nearly everyone was using the spitzer bullet. The flip-over was improved by the British who filled the pointed end with aluminum and the rear with lead. Later, the Russians simply left an air cavity in the front.

The Vietnam era saw the latest improvement in the spitzer bullet that gave it much the same effect as an expanding type. By the simple expedient of increasing velocity, as in the case of the 7.62x39mm AK-47 bullet and the 223 (5.56x45mm) M-16 bullet, greater instability on impact was achieved. The 55-grain M-16 bullet, with a muzzle velocity of over 3000 fps, would often break in half at the cannelure in the middle and the two halves would shred in the body creating a more massive wound. Even more deadly was the 7.62x51mm (308) NATO bullet made by the West German government which featured a very thin steel jacket. It was 50 percent thinner than the U.S. version and would shred in a body, causing an even more massive wound by virtue of its greater size and weight. Velocity was critical to *achieving* these effects, but did not *cause* them. Once velocity dropped below 2500 fps, lethality decreased to handgun level with equivalent-caliber jacketed bullets.

Designs for hunting bullets did not have to work under the constraints placed on nations by the Hague and Geneva conventions, which attempted to create "rules" of warfare. Hunting bullets are intended for killing, as opposed to creating casualties in war, thus they can be made of a more lethal design, i.e. to expand in a controlled manner at predetermined velocities.

Have we gone about as far as we can go along this line of development? In terms of bullet design, we probably have. In terms of making firearms capable of handling more powerful ammunition, making this ammunition more reliable and accurate, and making both more compact, there are still some worlds to be conquered.

14

No single book can supply all of the available knowledge on the subject of reloading, so here's where you can find other...

Sources and Resources

THIS CHAPTER MIGHT be subtitled, "Advanced reloading" or "Where do I go from here?" Anybody who has bought this book and read it must have an interest in learning that goes beyond his own, necessarily limited, experience. Publication in the firearms field must be at an all-time high if one is to judge by the glorious book displays encountered at such gun shows as the one put on by the Ohio Gun Collectors Association. The plethora of new books, beautifully bound and exhaustively illustrated, present a challenge both exhilarating and daunting. Exhilarating because there is getting to be a separate book devoted to nearly every make and model of gun you ever heard of (and plenty you haven't), daunting because these volumes carry price tags that start at about $35 and go over $75 a copy. That's serious money. Unfortunately, few public libraries have any gun book collections to speak of, but interlibrary loan is worth a try. If you want to do in-depth reading you have to build your own library. There are those who ask to borrow gun books, but I refuse to discuss what happened to the last person who failed to return one of mine and have no knowledge regarding the disposition of the body.

The bibliography and source references that follow are a gleaning of some 40 years of study and experience. It is both spotty and idiosyncratic, but contains those books and sources I have found to be worth the money and\or effort.

Ballistics.

The Bullet's Flight From Powder to Target, by Dr. Franklin W. Mann, MD. Originally published in 1909, various reprints.

This is the first *real* book on ballistics. Even today, some 88 years after it was first published, this book contains useful information regarding bullet behavior under an astonishing number of conditions. Mann was more of a tinkerer than a scientist, but was one of those dedicated souls who set out in pursuit of that eternal quest of getting all the bullets in one hole. His experiments were often predicated on the notion of: "I wonder what would happen if...?" The good doctor had enough money to buy a lot of rifles and replacement barrels. His work with cast, lead-alloy bullets is probably second to none. His book probably raises as many questions as it answers. The second volume might have provided these answers had the manuscript not been destroyed.

Understanding Ballistics 2nd Ed., by Robert A. Rinker, Mulberry House, P.O. Box 575, Corydon, IN 47112, 1996. 373 pp. Paper covers. $19.95.

In spite of the occasional sentence that isn't a sentence, this book does an excellent job of explaining the scientific aspects of ballistics. It goes from the basic to the advanced level while keeping the math to a minimum and the explanations clear. A good glossary of ballistic terms is included. If you want to know about ballistics, this is the best single source I have encountered.

Bullet Penetration, by Duncan McPherson, Ballistic Publications, Box 772, El Segundo, CA, 90245, 1994. 303 pp. $39.95.

This book deals exclusively with terminal ballistics with handgun ammunition. Anyone interested in stopping power, shocking power and all that, should forget anything you ever read on the subject except perhaps Julian Hatcher. McPherson, an engineer and one of the charter members of the International Wound Ballistics Association, has analyzed and scrutinized everyone's work in this area before conducting his very thorough research. The result has cleared away a number of cherished myths regarding bullet performance and the measurement of same. Though technical in nature, this work is very accessible to those without a mathematics background.

Wound Ballistics Review, edited by Dr. Martin L. Fackler, MD, Published twice a year by the International Wound Ballistics Association, P.O. Box 701 El Segundo, CA 90245-701. Four issues $40.00.

The IWBA is devoted to the medical and technical study of wound ballistics, including evaluation of literature in the field as well as encouraging and promoting new work. IWBA is an organization of medical, technical and law enforcement professionals devoted to hard research, truth telling and correction of misinformation regarding firearms, bullets, and their effects. Not surprisingly, they are engaged in battles with several popu-

lar gun magazines, the AMA, The Journal of Trauma, the federal medical establishment, and several self-styled stopping power "experts." Quite readable, very informative, not for wimps.

General Reloading

Complete Guide to Handloading, by Philip B. Sharpe. Originally published by Funk & Wagnalls, reprint available from Wolf Publishing Co., Prescott, AZ. 727 pp, illus,. $60.00.

Last updated in 1953, this massive work is dated, but contains a wealth of historical data on powder and cartridge evolution as well as the evolution of handloading. Anybody interested in the hows and whys of ammunition development will find this a treasure. Sharpe's book contains data on experiments of all sorts, many of which have a habit of turning up in contemporary magazine articles as "new" ideas and possibilities. Sharpe was a good experimenter and stands as one of the best known early experts in the field.

Principles and Practice of Loading Ammunition, by Earl

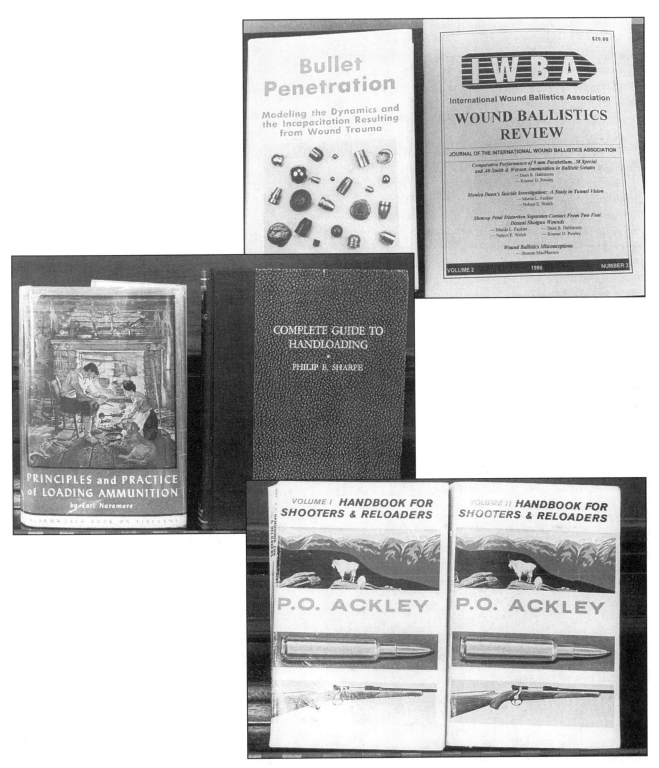

Naramore, Small Arms Technical Publishing Company (Samworth), Georgetown, SC, 1954. 952 pp. One reprint by Stackpole Books.

This last of the Samworth books is now out of print, but hopefully someone will reprint it again. Naramore gets into the "science" of reloading, but does so in layman's terms which makes this book very readable. His emphasis is on what happens to powder, primers, bullets, barrels and actions when guns are fired. His examination of all the forces at work and what they do is expressed in terms of how to deal with them in the reloading process. This is probably the best book when it comes to answering those "Why" and "What If" questions. Naramore and Mann were nearly the only author-experimenters who examined fired bullets, collected in pristine condition, and observed and deduced a good bit of information therefrom. Few writers expend this kind of time and effort on their work these days.

Handbook for Shooters and Reloaders, by P.O. Ackley, Salt Lake City, UT, 1970, (Vol. I), 567 pp., illus. (Vol. II), a new printing with specific new material. 495 pp., illus. $17.95 each.

Ackley was one of the greats in the experimentation and development field of small arms and ammunition. A gun maker and shooter who was also a good writer, Ackley put the better part of a lifetime of experience into these two books, which contain articles answering all sorts of questions regarding gun failures, pressure, headspace, wildcat cartridges, killing power, reduced loads, calculating recoil, bullet energy, loading data, etc.

Hatcher's Notebook, by Julian S. Hatcher, 3rd ed. 2nd printing, Stackpole Books, Harrisburg, PA 1996. 640 pp. $29.95.

Julian Hatcher can be considered one of the fathers of modern firearms writing and co-founder of the field of forensic firearms examination. Hatcher was a technical editor for the *American Rifleman* and held posts as a shooter, coach and military expert that would fill an entire page. This volume is a collection of many of his best articles on military rifles, their development, autoloading and automatic systems, recoil, headspace, triggers, barrel obstructions, military rifle strengths and weaknesses, range, velocity, recoil, etc. This is an excellent companion to the Ackley volumes.

Reloading Data Manuals

Most of the powder, bullet and equipment manufacturers publish loading data for use with their products. If you are looking for that ultimate load, one of these manuals is where you are likely to find it.

Lyman Reloading Handbook 47 Ed., ed. by Edward Matunas, 480 pp. $23.00. *Lyman Shotshell Reloading Handbook, 4th Ed.*, edited by C. Kenneth Ramage, 312 pp. $24.95. *Lyman Pistol and Revolver Reloading Handbook 2nd Ed.*, ed. by C. Kenneth Ramage, 280 pp. $18.95. Lyman Products Corp., Middlefield, CT 1992-1995.

The Lyman manuals are some of the most respected and

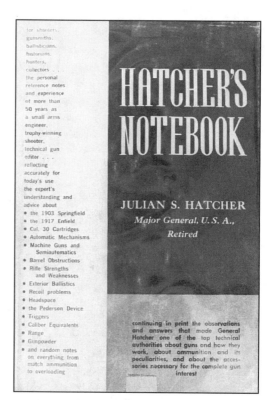

often quoted references, and have a wealth of data and information. These should be a part of every handloader's library.

Accurate Smokeless Powder Loading Guide No. One, Accurate Arms Co., Inc. McEwen, TN, 1994, 346 pp. Paper covers. $10.95.

I like Accurate's big red book for its nice, clear technical drawings of each cartridge listed, and the fact that they give pressure information for nearly all the loads listed. This loading guide cuts right to the chase with no articles—just data. Nice

much ballistic information for the complete line of Hornady bullets.

Sierra Rifle Reloading Manual 50th Anniversary Ed. (4th), 3-ring binder, 1040 pp., and *Sierra Handgun Reloading Manual 50th Anniversary Ed. (4th)*, 848 pp., by Bob Hayden et al, Sierra Bullets, L.P. Sedalia, MO, 1995. $24.95 and $19.95.

Top of the line in data, filled with useful ballistic information on twist rates, barrel wear, articles on long-range shooting, hunting and reloading tools. Three-ring binder format makes using these books about like folding a road map. The reason, I was told, was so the owner could insert his own pages of notes where he wished them.

Nosler Reloading Guide Number Four, edited by Gail Root, Chevalier Advertising, Inc., Lake Oswego, OR, 1996. 722 pp., $24.95.

A solid guide for reloading rifle and pistol ammunition. Articles on hunting and reloading. This is keyed to Nosler bullets and contains useful information on the use of these unique bullets. A must for Nosler bullet shooters.

Speer Reloading Manual Number 12 40th Anniversary Ed., ed. by Allan Jones, Blount, Inc., Lewiston, ID, 1994. 720 pp. $18.95.

One of my personal favorites for its excellent photos (some of which were borrowed for this volume) and clear explanations of the forces and stresses in operation in firearms. Complete loading data for the Speer line of bullets, with a wide variety of powders. The compact size and fine organization of this book make it easy to use.

Metallic Cartridge Reloading 3rd Ed., by M.L. McPherson, DBI Books, Northbrook, IL, 1996. 384 pp. Paper covers. $21.95.

This book contains loading data and more or less begins where the volume you are reading leaves off. It is filled with excellent detailed information for loading a wide variety of cartridges, and includes practical hints and solutions to problems encountered in advanced reloading.

Cartridges of the World, 8th Ed., by Frank C. Barnes, edited by M.L. McPherson, DBI Books, Northbrook, IL, 1997, 480 pp. Paper covers. $24.95.

For the reloader or cartridge collector, this is the first source to reach for when it comes to figuring out what might go in a particular, often peculiar, gun and be fired safely. Filled with load data on foreign, obsolete, military and experimental, and wildcat cartridges, this book is kept up to date as new cartridges come along and others become obsolete. This makes it a bargain compared to those one-edition, collector's-item books that cost $80 to $100 on the rare book shelf.

Handloader's Digest 16th Edition, edited by Bob Bell, DBI Books, Northbrook, IL, 1996. 480 pp. Paper covers. $23.95.

In addition to containing a good selection of articles on loading, this annual contains the best catalog of reloading equipment available—fully illustrated with sources and prices for everything.

Handloader's Guide, edited by Ashley Halsey Jr., Last published as *Handloading* by William C. Davis, NRA Publications, Washington, DC 1992. 400 pp. Paper covers. Originally published at $15.95, but may now be out of print.

features are loadings for some wildcat, scheutzen, obsolete and NRA-approved high-power service rifle loads. Excellent buy for the money.

Hodgdon Data Manual 26th Ed., 795 pp., and *Hodgdon Powder Shotshell Data Manual* by Don Zutz, 208 pp., Hodgdon Powder Co., Shawnee Mission, KS, 1995, 1996. Pub. at $19.95 ea.

The loading data is not limited to Hodgdon powder and you get as many loads as you would find in one of the general reloading books. The new shotshell book is one of the best looking books of its kind, beautifully bound and illustrated.

Hornady Handbook of Cartridge Loading 4th Ed. (2 vols.), Hornady Mfg. Co., Grand Island, NB, 1996. 1200 pp. $28.50.

One of the largest collections of loads between covers with

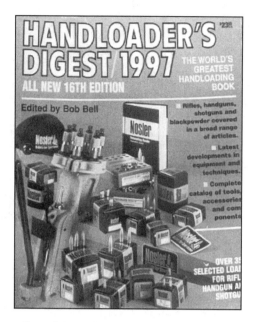

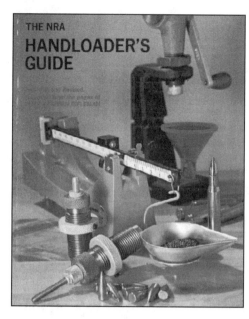

The earlier edition edited by Ashley Halsey Jr. was a grab bag of useful and interesting "How I did it" articles on reloading, and included material never published in the NRA magazines.

Free Material

The IMR Powder Company publishes a pamphlet-size loading guide for use with IMR powders. Similar short guides with basic reloading data are put out by Hodgdon, Alliant, VithaVuori and Accurate. They are *free* and can generally be found at gun shops and sporting goods stores. They can also be obtained by writing the company. These are a good source to start and a collection of them will give you a handful of data to get started with. They are about 30 to 40 pages long and contain data only, no articles or tips.

Special Reloading Topics

Cast Bullets, by E.H. Harrison, NRA Publications, Washington, DC, 1982. 144 pp. Paper covers. Out of print.

Probably one of the best books on bullet casting. It covers

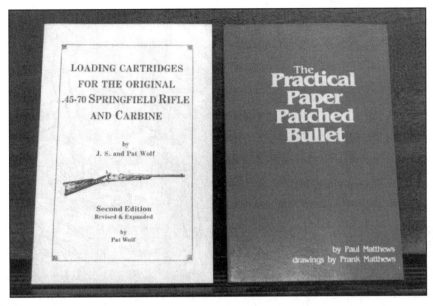

alloys, mould care and handling, and includes a lot of problem-solving pieces of great value when it comes to getting moulds, cast bullets and various alloys to perform the way they should. Hopefully, someone will reprint this fine volume.

Lyman Cast Bullet Handbook 3rd Ed., edited by C. Kenneth Ramage, Lyman Products Corp., Middlefield, CT, 1980. 416 pp. Paper covers. $19.95.

Excellent book on cast bullet making and shooting. Over 5000 cast bullets are covered, with trajectory and wind drift data.

The Paper Jacket (formerly *The Practical Paper Patched Bullet*), by Paul Matthews, Wolfe Publishing Co., Inc. Prescott, AZ, 1991. 75 pp. Paper covers. $13.50.

If you are interested in making and shooting paper-patched bullets this is the book you need.

Loading Cartridges for the Original 45-70 Springfield Rifle and Carbine Second Ed. Revised and Expanded, by J.S. and Pat Wolf. Wolf's Western Traders, Sheridan, WY, 1996. 188 pp. Paper covers. $18.95.

This book is an absolute must if you are going to load for one of these guns, because everyone else's data regarding bullets is wrong. Wolf researched the Frankford Arsenal's records and shot his way through several hundred pounds of lead to discover how to make these old guns shoot. The data is very likely to be valuable in working up loads for similar deep-groove rifles from the 1870-1890 era.

The Home Guide to Cartridge Conversions, by George C. Nonte, Jr., The Gun Room Press Highland Park, NJ, 1976. 404 pp. $24.95.

Detailed instructions on how to make centerfire cartridges for foreign and obsolete rifles and handguns from commonly available cartridges. How to fabricate ammunition for those war souvenirs you never thought you could shoot—chamber casting, fireforming, the works. Not for beginners.

Book Resources

Finding gun books, especially the out-of-print titles, is a difficult job and the costs are often high. There are a few approaches to finding these. The first involves time. This method takes you to used-book stores where you ask where the gun books are. After you get a dumb look in response to this question, you explain utilizing simple words and appropriate gestures to get across what you're looking for. They will direct you to the bottom of the back room where you will paw through a load of junk and occasionally find a treasure for $1.98. The second method is to bite the bullet (a non-lead one, of course) and negotiate with the book dealers at gun shows (who know the price of everything) and pay the going rate. Now and then a bargain can be found. A third variant is the easiest way. Send your want list to Rutgers Book Center. They have about 7000 current titles and 5000 out-of-print books. They also have a publishing adjunct, The Gun Room Press, with about forty current titles.

Another source is Ray Riling Arms Books Co., which is a major source of out-of-print books in the firearms field with more than 6000 titles. They also have a publishing arm with a few titles in print at the present time.

15

Easy Slug Loading

Shotguns shoot more than just shot. In fact, performance in the field can be enhanced by learning the secrets of...

by JOE KRIEGER

THE BUCK STOPPED 50 yards from my stand and stuck his nose into the wind. There was a gale blowing out of the southeast, but I was posted well to the west and safe from detection. Between us, an impenetrable tangle of branches made a shot impossible.

The whitetail had been moving along the well-worn game trail when I first saw him more than an hour ago. That hillside near the village of Humphrey was perfect for a late season wait; it was a good distance from the gravel road and few hunters wasted their time pushing through heavy growth that covered that slope.

At my back, the sun was about to vanish behind Golden Hill and close out the 1990 season. Trying to cut the distance by stalking was not a choice; he was coming right toward me and he'd spot me before I moved a yard. All I could do was sit tight and hope the buck didn't change his direction.

Finally, four hesitant steps put the buck in an opening just large enough for a shot. I checked the safety under my thumb

Choosing between roll-crimp and fold-crimp loads is easy once you've loaded both types. Not only are roll-crimps more difficult to assemble, but the tools needed are tough to find these days. Fold-crimp loads can be put together on any shotshell press.

and brought the Marlin Goose Gun to my shoulder when I was sure the eight-pointer was looking elsewhere. With three minutes of the season left, I pushed the safety forward and touched off the shot. The Vitt/Boos slug hit the buck broadside and didn't stop until it plowed into the frozen hillside behind him.

By the time I reached Miller Road with that heavy load in tow, it was dark as coal, a thick overcast blotting out the cold light of the stars.

The handloads I normally use in the Marlin are roll-crimped and I started out that Thursday afternoon with ten rounds in my shooting box. I also had three boxes of fold-crimped loads using the same Vitt/Boos slugs. I had been experimenting with the fold-crimped loads in March, but hadn't fired them in the cut-down Goose Gun. I had planned on bringing the Marlin/Bushnell combination close to the point

of aim with the fold-crimped loads, then using three or four of the roll-crimped loads to put things just right. Unfortunately, some over zealous torquing on my part had stripped one of the mount-to-base screws; the ten roll-crimped rounds were gone before I found the problem. After replacing the damaged screw, I was back at the range with fold-crimped slug loads. As it turned out, accuracy was fantastic. Velocity was lower by 200 fps than the Blue Dot/roll-crimps I had planned on using, but the buck never noticed the difference.

Fold-crimped slugs? Most of the slug data found in hand-loading manuals is for roll-crimps and *all* factory ammunition is roll-crimped. When I asked why the factories use the roll exclusively, I heard two answers more often than any others. One is for ease of identification—you won't confuse a shot load with a slug load and vice versa. The other is the added resistance a roll-

When handloaded using fold-crimp loads, these slugs perform as well as factory fodder—with the right barrel. From left: Buckbuster, Vitt/Boos, AQ, Brenneke, Lyman Sabot, Lyman Foster.

crimp provides over a fold. That resistance allows the powder charge to burn more completely and produces higher velocities than are possible with a fold.

While the loads I found so successful in 1990 are novel, fold-crimped slug loads have been around for a long time. The very first slug loads I put together were folded.

In the early 1960s, the Brenneke slugs I purchased from Stoeger Arms for reloading were shipped with a data sheet that listed *only* fold-crimped loads. The loads were easily assembled using a $10 dollar Lee Loader and more accurate than factory loads of the time.

In the November, 1964 issue of *The American Rifleman*, E. H. Harrison of the NRA staff provided load information for fold-crimp slug loads. Mr. Harrison's recipes used a Remington Power Piston Wad and Lyman slugs. Mr. Harrison found fold crimping to be a "...promising method of loading...," though he believed further development was needed.

In the '60s, Lyman marketed dies for their Easy Loader for roll-crimping, so there was a choice if you loaded your own slugs. These days, the Easy Loader is just about an antique, and can only occasionally be found used at gun shows.

If you're not fortunate enough to own a Lyman Easy Loader with the roll-crimping dies, you can use one of the roll-crimping heads available from Lyman or Ballistic Products, Inc. In addition to the crimping head, you'll need a regular shotshell press to handle priming, case sizing and slug seating. You'll also need a drill press to spin the crimping head and turn the mouth of the case onto the slug. Or you can load slugs using a fold-crimp!

Originally, I was looking for greater range when I started loading slugs. During the 1967 season, I passed on a shot at the biggest whitetail I'd ever seen—175 yards from where I sat. The Peter's slugs I carried were good out to 75 yards in my Mossberg pump; beyond that distance I had no idea where they were going to hit.

I'd heard and read the horror stories about insufficient energy, and slugs bouncing off target frames and the ribs of deer beyond 100 yards, etc. But the truth is, if you can hit one in the chest cavity, no matter what the distance he's venison when you're using those huge chunks of lead. Slugs, like archery broadheads, seldom kill out-right unless your shot smashes a shoulder or the spine. More often than not, it's blood loss that brings the animal down.

The longest shot I've ever taken on deer was at a measured 210 yards. One of the handloaded Vitt/Boos slugs I was carrying during the 1979 season went right though the animal despite the distance that separated us. That whitetail ran 100 yards before dropping from being hit in the liver.

A shotgun slug that plods its way through the vitals of an animal, whether in the lungs, heart, or liver, is going to help you fill your tag as long as you follow up. That's where a lot of us are found lacking.

In November, 1993, I was posted near the village of Panama in western New York State, overlooking a heavily overgrown ravine. That ravine is a favorite escape route when the woods come alive with first-day hunters. At 2:00 that afternoon, a young hunter posted 100 yards below my stand fired at a small

Because of its bulk and ability to retain energy and velocity far down range, the Vitt slug is one of the best for long-range shotgun shooting. Brenneke uses a similar good design.

whitetail that had gone by me forty minutes earlier. I watched him raise his pump and heard his shot, but he never moved off the stump that had been his seat since noon. Minutes later, a whitetail appeared at the mouth of the ravine. I saw his right front leg dangling. At 70 yards, my Vitt/Boos slug hit the animal in the spine right above the shoulders and put him down for good.

I called the kid over and asked him if he had a permit for an anterless deer, which he did. When I asked why he didn't go after the deer, he acknowledged the shot, but thought he had missed. His shot had hit low, stripped some hair off the yearling buck's chest, and broke one of the animal's front legs.

All the hunters I know are excellent shots with 22 rimfire rifles because they grew up with them. They have shot thousands of rounds through these guns. Rimfire ammunition is cheap compared to shotgun loads and centerfires, recoil is non-existent, and targets are plentiful. The same cannot be said of the shotgun and rifled slugs. Watch a once-a-year hunter at the range the weekend before opening day. He's flinching before he pulls the trigger; he fires three to five slugs and believes he's ready. But that short range session only puts the fear of the gun into his memory. If luck is on his side, that pounding he took at the bench will be forgotten when a buck comes in sight; if not, a miss is almost guaranteed.

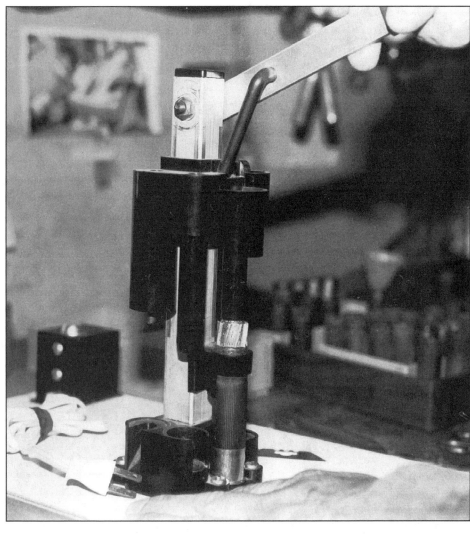

The discontinued Lee Jr. shotshell press has a wad guide large enough to seat the biggest 12-gauge slugs. The ram on this little press will not damage the nose of the slug; the metal ram on other presses will.

In 1964, the first year I hunted whitetails, slugs were packaged like shotshells, 25 to a box. As I remember, they cost $2.99 per box.

During the summer, I bought two boxes and fired one box at cardboard cutouts out to 75 paces. Overall, I was satisfied with the results until that previously mentioned season of '67 and the monster twelve-pointer that got away. I used the two-box system until the late '60s when I began handloading slugs, desperate for added range.

The factory loads of the time were a short range proposition and handloading was the only way to extend that range. Today there are a number of slugs available for home-brewed loads and most can be assembled with a fold-crimp.

On the first Saturday of the 1970 season, I sat shivering in a tangle of polkweed and raspberries near the village of Franklinville, New York. Rain had been falling since midnight and showed no sign of letting up.

At 10:00 o'clock, I spotted deer ears and antler tips moving beyond a gentle rise directly in front of me. A minute or two passed, then the buck climbed onto the rise. At 15 yards, he stopped. A hard-cast Lyman 12-gauge struck after he had turned his head and allowed me to raise my shotgun. The handloaded slug, with a muzzle velocity of 1380 fps, punched through his chest, leaving a 70-caliber hole coming and going.

The four-pointer was off and running without showing any sign of being hit, but I knew there was absolutely no chance of a miss, not at 15 yards. After following the blood trail for 75 yards, I found the buck still as stone on the wet leaves.

That day, I carried a fold-crimped load using a Lyman slug packed into an Alcan Flite-Max #3 wad. The slugs were cast from wheel weights and sized in a .688-inch drill guide. The sizing straightened the bases of the hollow slugs and reduced the slugs' diameter. Measuring .688-inch, the slugs were a perfect fit when matched with the Alcan wads and the smooth-bored barrel I was using. This load proved itself again and again, accounting for a dozen whitetails out to 125 yards.

I've loaded more Lyman slugs than any other since 1970 because they worked, were readily available when other sources dried up, and were cheap to shoot. With wheel weights free for the asking, the fold-crimped Lyman loads cost less than a nickel a shot.

Lyman still makes moulds for the Foster-style 12- and 20-gauge slugs. In 12-gauge, my home-cast slugs weigh 440 to 445 grains, the 20s weigh 310 grains. My slugs weigh less than the weight Lyman lists, probably because I'm casting with wheel weights, not pure lead. These slugs are similar in weight and shape to the Foster slugs in most factory rounds, without the

The Lyman Sabot Slugs shoot well with a number of powders. Blue Dot, Green Dot, Winchester SF (Super-Field) and Universal Clays are top performers.

(Below) The moulds marketed by Lyman allow the price-conscious shooter to put together slug loads for about a dime a shot—less if you can beg used wheelweights away from a neighborhood garage.

rifling. Tests have shown the rifling has no effect on the accuracy of the slugs.

Once proper temperature is reached, the Lyman mould drops slugs without voids or air holes.

Early in 1995, Lyman introduced a new 12-gauge slug mould that casts a lead slug designed exclusively for fold-crimped loads. Weighing 520 to 525 grains, the new slug looks like an over-size air rifle pellet. At 68-caliber, the slug matches up well with a long list of one-piece shotshell wads.

Lyman lists more than forty combinations in the 4th edition of their *Shotshell Reloading Handbook.* To date, I've tried twenty-five of them, and found all to be capable of 5-inch, five-shot groups at 110 yards when fired from rifled barrels.

I've also tried the Lyman Sabot slugs in smoothbore barrels and was pleasantly surprised with the results. At 50 yards, a Marlin Goose Gun with the barrel cut down to 26 inches shoots almost as good as the rifled variety. Beyond that distance, I can't say because my loads ran out at that point.

The sabot slug is easier to cast than the Lyman Foster slugs. A two hour casting session with the Lyman mould leaves me with 250 good slugs, more than enough for a few seasons. Lyman has recently introduced a similar mould for 20-gauge slugs.

I'll admit to a preference for the Vitt/Boos slugs. They'll do things most shooters expect from rifles; they group with sufficient accuracy to make them useful well beyond the normal slug range, and they hit with considerable power. The Vitt/Boos slug is the sure cure for those who believe the shotgun to be an anemic big game gun. This slug is available in 12-gauge only and it is the heaviest slug for handloading in that gauge.

I've been loading Vitt/Boos slugs with fold-crimps for more than 15 years without so much as a stuck shotshell. Lyman published seven fold-crimped loads for these slugs in the 4th edition, several of which are nearly identical to those I've been loading.

Handloads using fold-crimps fall short of maximum roll-

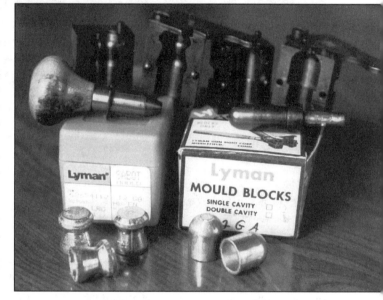

crimped velocities by 100 to 300 fps, depending on the load used and barrel length. They are, however, more than adequate for North American big game. The Vitt/Boos slugs shoot better than most slugs in both rifled and open-bored smooth barrels.

Brenneke slugs for handloading were once available in 12-, 16- and 20-gauge, but Brenneke U.S.A. and Dynamit Nobel import only loaded rounds these days. The Old Western Scrounger may still have component slugs, however. If you can still find the 25-slug packs for handloading, buy them; these slugs will never let you down. Time has proven this slug a capable performer. It has been around in one form or another since 1898, and has been used to take everything from whitetails to Bengal tigers.

The Brennekes I bought recently are an exact match to the ones purchased almost thirty years ago from Stoeger, and they're compatible with the load data shipped with the Stoeger slugs. Lyman also lists a few fold-crimped loads for the 12-

gauge Brennekes in the 3rd and 4th editions of their manuals.

Most of the load data found for the Brenneke slug in 16-gauge is extremely mild, usually below 10,000 LUP. With the Stoeger data and a safe, reliable shotgun, the 16 becomes a magnum deer gun. Velocity is good, though slower than factory ammunition from the big three, but the slug weighs 425 grains. The factory Fosters weigh less than 400 grains.

Initially, I expected the Brennekes to shoot well in both rifled and smooth barrels, this slug being so similar to the Vitt/Boos slug. But in every handload fired from a rifled barrel these slugs were unstable. The holes punched through paper targets were out-of-round, with some worse than others. The worst were hitting the targets sideways. As a result, I use them in smooth-bored barrels only.

Slugmaster of Leavittsburg, Ohio, manufactures Foster slugs in 12-, 16- and 20-gauges. At one time, the company supplied three slug styles in each gauge, differing slightly in weight and design.

At present, Slugmaster is updating their slugs and new products are planned. The information listed in the load tables is for the old slugs, some of which are still available from Slugmaster and Ballistic Products, Inc.

Fold-crimped loads using the Slugmaster slugs are limited to 12- and 20-gauge owing to the lack of data for fold-crimped 16-gauge. These slugs shoot right along with factory ammunition, and handloads using the Lyman-cast Foster slugs. A rifled barrel will produce the smallest groups with these slugs, though they are accurate enough in a smooth barrel once you've found the right load.

The AQ-slug is an unusual 12-gauge slug distributed by Ballistic Products, Inc. The slug is a .740-inch lead ball fitted with a peculiar base that helps stabilize the slug through the barrel and all the way to the target. The base is moulded with ten spiral fins that the maker claims cause the slug to rotate once it leaves the barrel. Average weight for the unit is 455 grains (for forty checked). With the fold-crimp loads provided with the slugs, it's possible to reach 1500 fps, just 80 fps slower than the fastest roll-crimped load using the same slug.

The AQ slugs were extremely accurate in smooth barrels, just so-so in rifled barrels. When fired from a choked barrel, there was a noticeable increase in group size, though not enough to miss a deer within 125 yards.

The Buckbuster Shotgun Bullet was the newest component slug available for handloading. It was made by SG. B. Mfg. and was on the market for only a short time. If you can find them, they're certainly worth trying.

The Buckbuster bullet is a 68-caliber lead slug with a semi-wadcutter profile, weighing about 1 ounce. This slug can be handloaded with either a folded- or rolled-crimp, using one of the fifteen loads prescribed by the maker.

Before loading these slugs, I weighed and miked two boxes of twenty-five. Diameter measured a consistent .681-inch for each of the fifty slugs. Weight, surprisingly, varied by 7.3 grains, from 434.9 grains on the light side, to 442.2. grains for the heaviest of the fifty.

Initially, slugs were segregated by weight and loaded in groups that varied by no more than 2.5 grains. Ten five-shot groups were fired at 50 and 100 yards one bright March afternoon. When I compared the ten targets, there was not enough difference in point of impact to justify the sorting by weight.

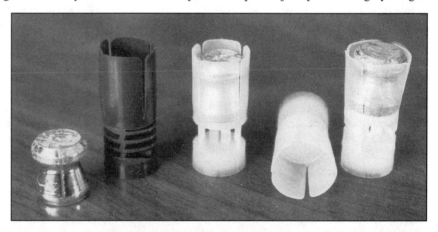

Lyman's Sabot Slug is easy to cast and gives excellent results with the right combination. The Federal 12S4, Winchester WAA12 and WAA12F114 are but three of the shotcups Lyman prescribes.

(Below) Five of the best 12-gauge slugs for handloading, from left: Brenneke, Vitt/Boos, Buckbuster (now discontinued), Lyman Foster and Lyman Sabot.

The author's decades-old Lyman Easy Loader is a capable press for slug and shot loads. With the right collection of dies and accessories, it can load with either a roll- or fold-crimp, in all gauges.

Holding the ten targets up to the light, produced one large ragged hole.

The trajectory table packed with the slugs was right on target: at 1480 fps, my loads are hitting 3 inches high at 50 yards with a 100-yard zero. SG. B. listed the slugs at 2.75 inches high at 50 with the same zero (1500 fps).

I have not used the Buckbuster on targets other than paper woodchucks, but the accuracy potential and relatively low cost per round will have me toting my Mossberg pump and a bag full of Buckbuster handloads for chucks before autumn rolls around.

Using a smoothbore barrel with the Buckbuster slugs produced terrible results. This is another slug that will not work in smooth barrels.

General tips for loading slugs follow here. Hopefully my observations will help the reader have an easy and enjoyable time at the loading bench.

Loading slugs with a fold-crimp is best done on a press that requires manual indexing, rather the a progressive machine. Moving the shotshell from one station to the next takes longer, but you'll seldom run off 200 rounds when loading slugs, anyway.

Powder charges should be weighed rather than metered through a bushing. This extra step improves accuracy and provides a margin of safety when pressures are near maximum, as they are with many slug loads.

Seating slugs can be troublesome on most presses. The wad station on the Lyman Easy Loader is too narrow to accept Brenneke, Vitt/Boos, and the AQ slugs, and the slug/shotcup combinations. The wad guides found on the MEC and Pacific presses are also too narrow.

The wad guide Lee uses on both the 12-gauge Load All and the Load All II is the only one that works with some of the 12-gauge slugs I'm handloading. With the larger 12-gauge slugs and the 16- and 20-gauge, slugs have to be started by hand. A tapered wooden dowel or a powder funnel can be used to open up the mouths of these shells. Rotating a powder funnel rapidly in the mouth of the hull opens them sufficiently so the slug can be started into the shotshell. Once started, the slug can be pressed onto the powder charge with a wooden dowel of appropriate diameter, taking care not to catch the mouth of the hull with the edge of the slug and/or the wad.

Wad pressure should be applied as listed in the load info you're using. If none is listed, use just enough to seat the first wad firmly against the powder charge.

When working with the Brennekes and Vitt/Boos, I drop a flat washer of the proper size over the nose of the slug to keep the wad ram from gouging it. Don't forget to remove the washer before crimping the hull! Lyman and Slugmaster slugs are seated by hand *after* wad pressure has been applied to the last wad in the hull. Using a hollow wad ram on the nose of any slugs will damage the slugs and possibly increase group size.

Once-fired shotshells were used with the initial loads assembled in each gauge here. Hulls that held a good crimp showed only a minor variation in velocity, no matter how many times they were reloaded. When the mouth of a hull was split or the crimp was distorted, velocity was erratic and accuracy suffered. Considering the cost of the slugs and the time it takes to put the loads together, trying to wring too much out of a ten-cent hull seems ridiculous.

Hulls with parallel walls give the best results with the Brenneke, Vitt/Boos, AQ slugs and a number of Lyman sabot combinations. Included in this group are the Federal plastic hunting hull, the Remington SP, Winchester poly-formed, and Fiocchi

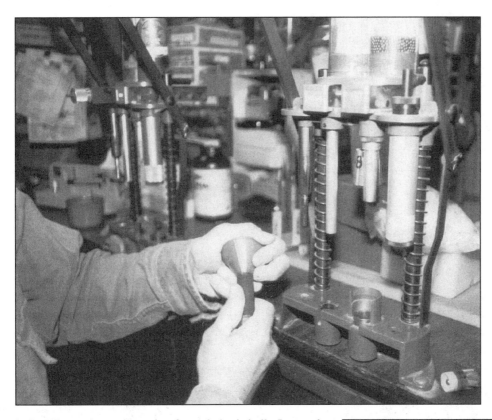

A powder funnel can be used to flare the mouth of the hull. Rotate the funnel rapidly to warm the shell a bit. A tapered wooden dowel also works well.

(Below) When fitted with a roll-crimping kit, the old Lyman Easy shotshell press produces factory-quality loads. Unfortunately, the press is no longer made.

hulls. When using compression-formed plastic hulls, I use only low brass hulls; the high brass types require more than 100 pounds of wad pressured to seat the slugs. Several times, after just a few hours, crimps have opened up when rounds were assembled in high brass, compression-formed hulls. The interior taper of the one-piece hulls combined with the high brass or steel head squeezed the slug/wad units away from the powder charge.

If your loading bench is located in the basement or garage, plastic hulls should be warmed slightly when temperatures are below 60 degrees. Plastic hulls are difficult to crimp below that temperature, and a cold one is more likely to split when a tight fitting slug/wad unit is seated.

In a load using a stacked wad column and any hollow-based slug, a card wad must be placed beneath the slug. The card wad, being less flexible than fiber-filler wads, will not be forced into the base of the slug. Accuracy is always better when a hollow-based slug rests atop a card wad.

Wads designed for compression-formed cases should not be used with straight-walled cases. After a short time, you'll find that more than a few granules of powder have made their way between the wall of the case and the over-the-powder cup. Several years ago, I put together a load using 36.0 grains of WW571. At the end of the season, I had twenty loads left which I set aside until the following summer. When I finally fired these loads, the first gave unusually low velocity. I fired three more, and none came close to the anticipated speed. When I took the remaining loads apart, I found all had more than 10 grains of powder *above* the gas-seal. That powder was not igniting, causing the low pressures and reduced velocities. There should always be a snug fit between the wads and the hull you're using to keep the powder where it belongs.

The Lee Load-All press is a good buy and an excellent shotshell press for loading slugs. Here, the sizing die is being pressed off a fired 16-gauge shotshell.

(Below) The Lee Load-All press is slower than a progressive press, but speed is not wanted or needed when loading slugs. Here, the metal base of a 16-gauge shotshell is being sized before being loaded.

There should also be a tight fit between the bore of the gun and the slug you're using; this is a prerequisite for consistent accuracy. Any bore contact will remove lead from a tight fitting slug, so check the barrel after a few shots. But if the fit is tight, the scuffing will be uniform, around the entire circumference of the slug. When the tight fitting slug exists the muzzle, it's still round and aerodynamically sound.

A loose fitting slug, on the other hand, makes contact with the barrel rather haphazardly. As it travels to the muzzle, it is battered as a result of its imperfect fit and accuracy is poor.

The attached wads on the Vitt/Boos, Brenneke, and the AQ slugs, being equal to or greater than the diameter of the bore, center the slugs in the barrel and provide damage control. The same can be said for the shot cup/slug combinations listed in a number of publications. The plastic petals of the wad absorb the punishment usually reserved for the slug.

Before assembling any slug load, I check the fit between the slug/wad unit and the barrel. This is done by inserting the combination into the muzzle or chamber of the shotgun and forcing it through the barrel. If it slides through easily, I don't expect much in the way of accuracy. I find that a snug fit requiring some force to push through will give the best accuracy.

A number of the load recipes published by Lyman and Ballistic Products prescribe the use of a card wad between the slug or ball and the crimp. I followed their directions in a number of loads, and found it easier to fold-crimp the hulls with that top wad in place. The card wad supports the folds of the crimp and keeps them from caving in on the slug. This practice also improves accuracy because it keeps the powder/wad/slug package neatly compressed. At no time did I have any problem with the slugs over-running the top wad.

Load data for fold-crimped slug loads has been published in Lyman's *Shotshell Handbook,* 3rd and 4th editions, and Ballistic Products, Inc., *Slug and Buckshot Manual.* Other sources include the Stoeger data sheet for Brennekes and a number of load sheets provided by Slugmaster.

Lyman lists a number of unusual loads for the big game shotgun using lead balls and conical bullets meant for muzzle-loading rifles. Many of the 20-gauge loads use a fold-crimp, with the projectiles protected from the bore of the gun by a shot cup.

I've fired a dozen loads in a Mossberg 20-gauge pump fitted with a rifled barrel, and two 20-gauge smoothbores. The rifled barrel shoots well with both the round balls and conical bullets. The smoothbores give acceptable accuracy with the balls, but keyholed more than half the conicals fired.

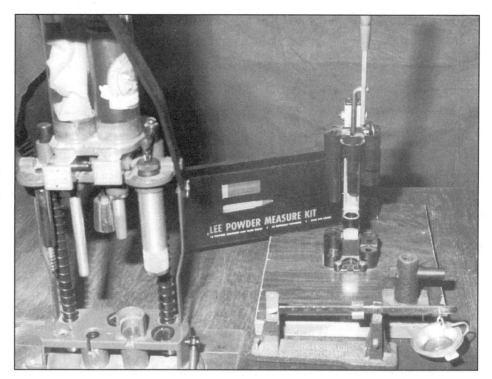

The tools needed for slug loading need not be expensive or complicated. With only a scale and press, all the loads discussed can be assembled.

At the other end of the scale is the 10-gauge. But 10-gauge slug loads are limited by a lack of suitable slugs and tested data. Some time ago, I was sent an ad for a mould to cast 10-gauge slugs. The mould was over $175 as I recall, and I never followed up on the ad.

After checking every source I could put my hands on, I came up with just three fold-crimp slug loads. The three recipes from Ballistic Products use 12-gauge slugs in either the BPD 10 or the BPO-Tuff wads. Velocities are high and accuracy was very good in two 10-gauge slug guns I'm using, but similar results can be had using the same slugs in a 12-gauge gun.

I wanted a projectile in the same class as the Foster slugs Federal Cartridge uses in their 10-gauge Super Slug ammunition. This factory load exits the barrel of a Marlin Super Goose Gun at 1300 fps, and produces 2870 ft-lbs of energy. The Super Slug 10 weighs 765 grains, making it the heaviest shotgun slug available.

Ballistic Products, Inc. catalogs a single projectile for the 10-gauge. The BP Max-10 is a 69-caliber bullet that is an exact copy of the Minie bullets I cast decades ago using a Lyman #68569 mould. This bullet fits snugly in the Ballistic Products BPD-Tuff and the Remington SP-10 Power Piston wads, but accuracy was so poor in the single Ballistic Product's recipe I

Powder charges are best weighed rather than metered. The results are well worth the extra time and effort.

tried, that I simply gave up on the 10-gauge with handloaded slugs.

A rifled 10-gauge barrel might give suitable accuracy with the BP Max-10, but until such a barrel is available I'll use the Federal factory load when I feel a need for a 10-gauge slugger.

I used screw-in rifled choke tubes on two smoothbore shotguns to check their accuracy potential. The first was a Remington 870 fitted with a 28-inch barrel; the second was a Mossberg turkey gun equipped with a 20-inch barrel.

After firing several hundred handloads through the two shotguns, I learned a few things about the add-on rifling tubes. Only the Foster-style slugs, those cast in a Lyman mould, and the Slugmasters, showed any improvement when fired from both the Mossberg turkey gun and the Remington Wingmaster. The Brenneke, Vitt/Boos, AQ, and Buckbuster slugs were less accurate in these two guns, as was the Lyman Sabot slug. Why? I believe the inaccuracy is the result of the slugs hitting the rifled tubes when they are at their near-maximum velocity, that is, at the end of the barrel.

When fired in a fully rifled barrel, the slug has traveled less than an inch before it contacts the lands, and is moving slowly in comparison. The transition is less violent than what occurs in the smoothbore fitted with the rifled tube.

The BRI sabot bullet is the only slug I've worked with that is not compatible with a fold-crimp. Of the forty-plus combinations put together, none produced the desired results. In loads that gave velocity equal to factory loads, pressures were excessive to a point where the case rims were splitting. Accuracy was usually poor. If a particular recipe grouped well at acceptable velocity one day, it had tendency to shoot erratically when fired a second time.

Excellent accuracy was had with a number of loads, but always at speeds below 1150 fps. At that speed, there are more suitable combinations using other slugs.

If you have a supply of BRIs for handloading, use them with a roll-crimp or with no crimp. I put together five loads using Remington SP and Federal HP hulls trimmed to 2⁹/₁₆ inches. Following recommended load information published by Ballistic Research Industries, and by Wallace Labisky in *Handloader's Digest, 5th Edition*, I loaded BRIs as instructed but *without* any crimp. The uncrimped loads gave slightly lower velocities than roll-crimped loads using the same powder recommendation, but accuracy was as good as BRI factory ammo and rolled loads.

George Vitt prescribed uncrimped loads for the slugs he and Ray Boos developed. He noted these were not as fast as roll-crimped loads, but they worked well as long as there was a tight fit between the slug and the shell being used. The extremely

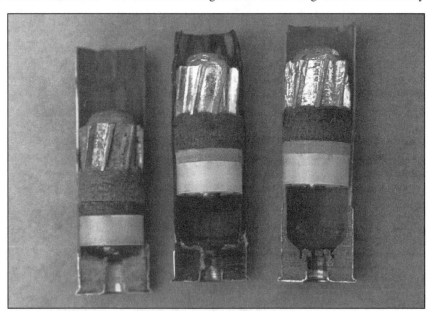

Compression-formed hulls can cause problems, especially with the Vitt/Boos slugs. The Air-Wedge attached to the base of the slug doesn't give as the case wall tapers to the base. Additional wad seating pressure is needed to get the slug into the case, but it will sometimes creep upward and bulge the crimp.

Foster-type slugs from Slugmaster are low in cost yet high in quality. These are the answer for those who shoot often but don't want to cast their own slugs.

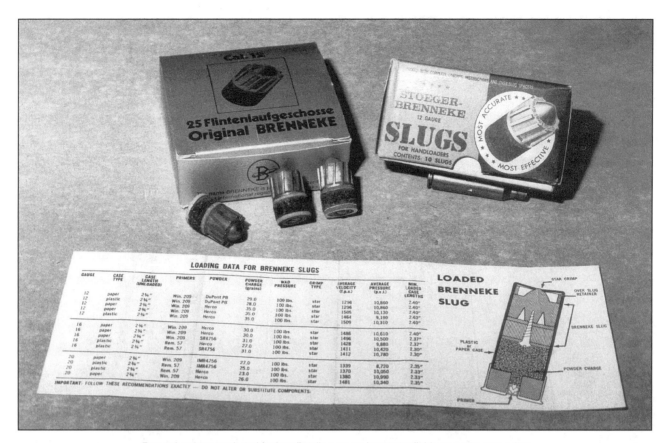

Brenneke slugs marketed for handloading are no longer available as components, but some might still be found on dealer's shelves. Those sold as recently as four years back (left) are an exact match to those sold by Stoeger thirty years ago.

12-GAUGE SLUG LOADS

Slug	Hull	Primer	Load Grs/Powder	Wad	Filler Wad (ins.)	Seating Press. (lbs.)	Barrel (ins.)	Velocity (fps)
Vitt	Fed. HP	Win. 209	43.0/Blue Dot	None	None	20	24	1355
Vitt	Rem. UNI	Win. 209	42.0/Blue Dot	None	None	25	24	1410
Vitt	Win. AA	Win. 209	39.0/WW571	None	None	40	24	1340
Vitt	Win. AA	Won. 209	32.0/SR4756	None	None	35	24	1290
Vitt	Rem. UNI	Win. 209	39.5/SR4756	None	None	25	24	1460
Vitt	Fed. HP	Win. 209	36.0/SR4756	None	None	20	24	1315
Brenneke[1]	Rem. AA	Win. 209	29.0/PB	None	None	85	24	1310
Brenneke	Fed. paper	Fed. 209	37.0/SR4756	BPGS	None	100	28	1470
Brenneke[2]	Fed. HP	Win. 209	33.5/SR4756	BPGS	1/4	20	24	1435
Lyman[2]	Fed. HP	Win. 209	40.0/SR4756	BPGS	1/2 + 1/8	—	26	1530
Lyman[2]	Rem. UNI	Win. 209	27.0/800X	BPGS	1/2 + 1/8	—	26	1415
Slugmaster[4]	Fed. GM	Fed. 209	43.0/W540	BPGS	1/2 + 1/8	—	26	1580
Slugmaster[4]	Win. CF	Fed. 209	38.0/W540	BPGS	1/2 + 1/4 + 1/8	—	26	1465
BRI[5]	Rem. SP	Rem. 57	26.0/Unique	PGS	.200	40	26	1250
BRI[5]	Fed. HP	Fed. 209	28.0/Herco	PGS	.200	40	26	1285
Lyman Sabot	Rem. UNI	Win. 209	45.5/Blue Dot	WAA12F114	None	60	21	1527
Lyman Sabot	Win. AA	Win. 209	35.0/WSF	WAA12	None	—	21	1404
Lyman Sabot	Win. AA	Win. 209	30.0/WSF	WAA12F114	None	20	21	1305
Lyman Sabot	Fed. HP	Win. 209	35.0/Univ. Clay	WAA12F114	None	40	21	1488
Lyman Sabot	Rem. UNI	Win. 209	32.0/WSF	WAA12F114	None	60	21	1384
Lyman Sabot	Win. AA	Win. 209	25.0/Herco	WAA12F114	None	20	21	1166
Buckbuster	Win. AA	Win. 209	30.0/800X	WAA12F114	None	60	24	1428
Buckmaster	Fed. GM	Win. 209	23.0/Green Dot	CB 1118-12	None	40	24	1279
Buckmaster	Rem. UNI	Win. 209	32.5/SR4756	CB 118-12	None	80	21	1250
Buckbuster	Rem. UNI	Win. 209	20.0/Green Dot	CB 1118-12	None	60	21	1240
Buckbuster[3]	Fed. HP	Win. 209	25.0/Unique	WAA12F114	None	40	24	1390
Buckbuster[3]	Fed. HP	Fed. 209A	23.0/Green Dot	WAA12F114	None	40	24	1345
Buckbuster[3]	Win. AA	Win. 209	31.0/WSF	WAA12F114	None	30	21	1480

Notes:[1]Data from Stoeger Arms Data Sheet. [2]Data from Lyman *Shotshell Handbook 3rd. Ed.* [3]Data from Lyman *Shotshell Handbook 4th Ed.* [4]Data from Slugmaster. [5]Indicates no crimp.
Legend: Fed. GM = Gold Medal hull; Rem. UNI = one-piece plastic Express hull; Rem. AA = All American target hull.

16-GAUGE SLUG LOADS

Slug	Hull	Primer	Load Grs./Powder	Wad	Filler Wad (ins.)	Seating Press. (lbs.)	Barrel (ins.)	Velocity (fps)
Brenneke	Fed. HP	Win. 209	28.5/Herco	None	None	80	28	1425
Brenneke	Win. PC	Win. 209	30.0/Herco	None	None	100	28	1478
Brenneke	Rem. SP	Rem. 57	30.0/SR4756	None	None	100	28	1390

Notes: Data from Stoeger Arms Data Sheet.

20-GAUGE SLUG LOADS

Slug	Hull	Primer	Load Grs./Powder	Wad	Filler Wad (ins.)	Seating Press. (lbs.)	Barrel (ins.)	Velocity (fps)
Brenneke[1]	Fed. PC	Win. 209	26.0/Herco	None	1/4	100	26	1475
Brenneke[1]	Rem. SP	Rem. 57	23.5/Herco	None	None	100	26	1400
Brenneke[1]	Win. PF	Win. 209	25.5/Herco	None	None	100	26	1440
Slugmaster[4]	Win. AA	Win. 209	23.0/HS-6	WW	2-.135	20	28	1520
Lyman[2]	Fed. HP	Win. 209	28.5/SR4756	—	3/4 + 2-.135	40	26	1450
Lyman[2]	Rem. SP	Fed. 209	27.0/Blue Dot	—	1/2 + 3-.135	40	26	1420
Lyman[3]	Rem. UNI	Win. 209	28.5/Blue Dot	—	.125 + 1/2 + .125	—	24	1455
Roundball[5]	Fed. HP	Win. 209	25.0/HS800X	Fed. PC#20S1	—	—	26	1580

Notes:[1]Data from Stoeger Arms Data Sheet. [2]Data from Lyman *Shotshell Handbook 3rd Ed.* [3]Data from Lyman *Shotshell Handbook 4th Ed.* [4]Data from Hodgdon; wad is white WW with the petals removed. [5].575-inch round lead ball; 28-gauge wad.

In 20- and 16-gauge, only hulls with straight sides and separate base wads allow the handloader to reach the velocities desired and still use the fold-crimp. All these 20-gauge hulls meet that requirement, as does Remington's SP. Other types reach peak pressure before peak velocity is attained.

tight fit is needed to keep the slug from moving away from the powder charge.

Uncrimped loads using BRI, Brenneke, or Vitt/Boos slugs, should be tapered at the mouth. A smooth crimp starter meant for paper shotshells does the job nicely. The finished rounds will not feed smoothly from the magazine if this step is omitted.

There's really no magic required to handload shotgun slugs. With the machine already bolted to your bench, you can put together a box of slugs, a real box of 25, for about the same price as shot loads if you cast the slugs yourself. With ready-made slugs, the finished product will be every bit as good as the factory variety at about half the price.

The State Of The Progressives

by KENNETH L. WALTERS

Though automated reloading tools date back more than a hundred years, today's handloaders want to know what's available today. So here's a rundown on...

OVER THE COURSE of the last ten or so years, hand-operated progressive reloaders have gone from being virtually unknown to dominating the reloading of metallic cartridge ammunition. Here we're going to examine the various models currently available from the major manufacturers.

There has always been some confusion, I think, as to just what is a progressive. Part of the problem is that several terms are used to describe these machines, and the terms have never been all that clearly defined. We'll look at this first. Where I've included a definition, the word is in **bold** type so you can easily find it.

A **progressive** at minimum does all the various reloading functions simultaneously, minimizes case handling and incorporates both automatic priming and powder charging.

Some progressive-like reloaders haven't quite lived up to this minimum list of functions. Usually, such machines require manual effort to seat the primer or throw the powder charge. For lack of a better name, I call these machines **pseudo-progressives**.

Pseudo, of course, means false. Some of the early Dillon, Hornady and RCBS machines were pseudo-progressives. They were nice machines, mind you, but they weren't true progressives.

Another term you'll occasionally run into is **semi-progressive**. In this design, all the reloading steps were done simultaneously, but each and every case had to be manually advanced between the reloading stations. Semi-progressives were usually just an automated variation of the old H-press idea.

Historically, there have also been several progressive designs, but one, in particular, the circular, has dominated. **Circular progressives** have all their reloading stations laid out in a circular pattern. All the machines discussed here are circular progressives.

On many circular progressives, the dies and powder system can be removed as a unit by removing a **tool head**. Caliber conversion by tool head removal considerably speeds up the conversion process.

Circular progressives have another unique feature. All the cases are held in a **shellplate**. The shellplate is the circular progressive's equivalent to the single station's shellholder. This plate may be either manually or automatically advanced, but advancing one case advances them all.

Finally, the progressive design that competed against the circulars from the mid-1930s until just recently was the **straightline**. In these, the dies are laid out in a straight line across the front of the machine.

The departure of the straightline shouldn't be grieved. Though for awhile they were a price-attractive alternative to some of the earlier circulars, they all were rather mechanically complex.

Why did the circular progressives eventually dominate? Because they are easier to use and because they were very aggressively marketed.

The appeal of a progressive is its high reloading rate. This is possible because all reloading functions are done simultaneously and because many of these functions are automated.

Though we tend to think of progressives as a rather recent invention, that's not true. Patent literature clearly indicates that such machines were in use as early as the mid-1880s. Obviously, progressives have been around for a very long time.

Star Machine Works

Star Machine Works introduced their first progressive in the late 1920s. Though there are design differences between the Star and most of the other models available today, in many ways the Star design set the layout of the reloading stations for the machines that followed. Thus, we'll look at the Star's reloading station layout in order to see how most progressives work.

The Star has six reloading stations that perform all of the tasks indicated below. Most other progressives are at least similar.

Reloading Station: Task Performed
1: Case insertion.
2: Full-length resizing and spent primer removal.
3: Case-mouth flaring and priming.
4: Powder charging.
5: Bullet seating and crimping.
6: Cartridge removal and double-charge prevention.

Currently, Star offers three models. The Universal is available in a fairly large selection of popular pistol cartridges and 30 Carbine. The pistol/rifle tool loads most popular pistol cartridges and several short rifle rounds. The rifle machine loads most of the popular large rifle cartridges.

The Star design has an interesting mix of manual and automatic processes. Case insertion, **case advancement** (advancing the cases between the various reloading stations) and **bullet placement** (the placing of the bullet on top of the case before seating) all require manual effort. In the Star Universal, rimmed cartridges must be manually removed, but rimless rounds and, for that matter, spent primers fall through a hole in the base of the machine. Priming and powder charging are automatic. Caliber conversion by pulling the tool head is trivial.

Though Star has never made accessories to automate their manual operations, others have. No other progressive, in fact, has received so much after-market attention. Using these accessories, a Star can be virtually automated to death.

The Star has another interesting historic distinction. It was extensively copied. Star-like copies have loaded everything

A semi-progressive press.

from 25 ACP to 50 Browning. I always wanted to see one of the 50 Browning clones because it must have been one *big* press. Unfortunately, it also had one *big* price tag—$6000+, if memory serves.

On the Star Universal, two types of dies are available. Because this Star was introduced long before the industry standardized on $7/8x14$s, it has its own unique size. You can, however, special order a Universal with $7/8x14$ dies. Some machining of the dies may be necessary, however, to make them fit into the tool head. Star will do this for you. The other two Star models use only $7/8x14$ dies.

The Star comes completely assembled and adjusted. On virtually all other progressives, some assembly is required. This assembly can range from truly trivial to quite a bit of work.

The Star has one final distinction. Because they have been made for more than sixty years, if given anything approaching proper care, it is a documentable fact that a Star will last a lifetime. Certainly there are other excellent progressives, but only Star can point to decades of long-term survivability for their quality product.

Dillon Precision

Star Machine Works essentially introduced the progressive, but Dillon Precision popularized it. More than any other company, Dillon understood the power of advertising. There can be no doubt that Dillon's aggressive advertising not only made them the leading progressive manufacturer, but also established the progressive as the dominant metallic cartridge reloader.

Dillon also excels at customer support. Many firms do a fine job here, but Dillon pushes this hard. All Dillon progressives have a lifetime guarantee, and whether your unit is in current production or not, if you need support, you'll get it.

Dillon also aggressively upgrades, improves or replaces their models almost continuously. Many of the improvements Dillon has made over the years were easily retrofitted to their earlier, similar units. Some competitors have suggested that this continuous product refinement is somehow bad. Not true!

The current Dillon line consists of four machines: the RL1050, the RL550, the XL650 and the Square Deal. This isn't quite the right way to refer to them, as some have a B suffix, meaning the second version of, but I've ignored that distinction.

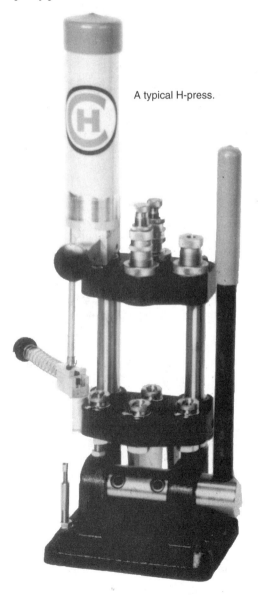

A typical H-press.

A typical straightline press.

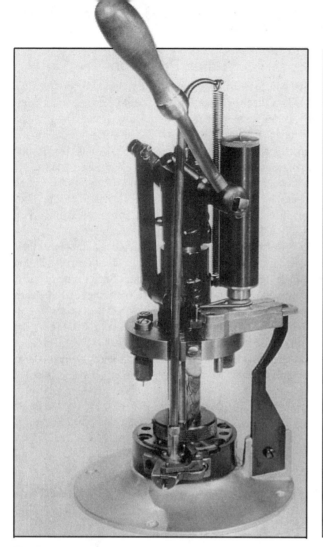

The Star Universal

A totally automated Star

All these machines, incidentally, have removable tool heads.

The RL1050 is the current top of the Dillon line. The RL1050 can load pistol rounds and a few short rifle cartridges, as well as incorporate automatic case insertion and advancement, automatic priming and powder charging, and primer pocket swaging.

As good as the RL1050 is, it's the RL550, and its predecessors, that made Dillon what it is today. This design, a Dillon original, is based on a modified single-station O-press. This approach, which many other firms have now adopted, is, I think, the force behind low-cost, reliable progressives. As was true of the Stars, there is an interesting mix of manual and automatic operations in the RL550. Case insertion, case advancement and bullet placement require manual effort. Priming and powder charging are automatic.

Tool head change is particularly easy on the RL550 because the tool head is held in place by only two small pins. Though it may appear that this arrangement isn't all that stout, when the dies come into contact with the shellplate, this pressure forces proper tool head alignment.

The RL550 can handle a very wide variety of both pistol and rifle cartridges, is very reliable and easy to use, and makes caliber conversion trivial.

The newest member of the Dillon lineup is the XL650. Apparently, it is a cross between the RL1050 and the RL550. With the exception of primer pocket swaging, which the XL650 cannot do, the XL650 is an RL1050-like unit set in an RL550-like frame. In addition, there is a double-charge prevention mechanism. This and the case feeding system are options that can be purchased separately. Finally, the XL650 loads a wide selection of both pistol and rifle cartridges.

The final Dillon unit is the Square Deal, the only Dillon progressive that loads only pistol cartridges. Cases are automatically advanced, priming and powder charging are automatic, and, as is true on all current Dillon models, the completed round is automatically ejected. About all you have to manually do is case insertion and bullet placement. Unlike Dillon's other current units, however, this one does not use $^7/_8$x14 dies.

Two machines discussed here don't use $^7/_8$x14 dies—one version of the Star Universal and the Dillon Square Deal. Some potential buyers seem concerned about that. Don't be.

Lee Precision

Lee Precision is the unquestioned master of inexpensive reloading equipment. Thus, you can start out by using Lee gear

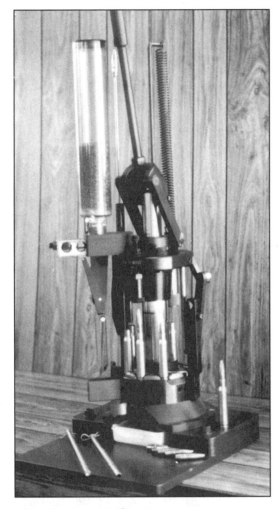

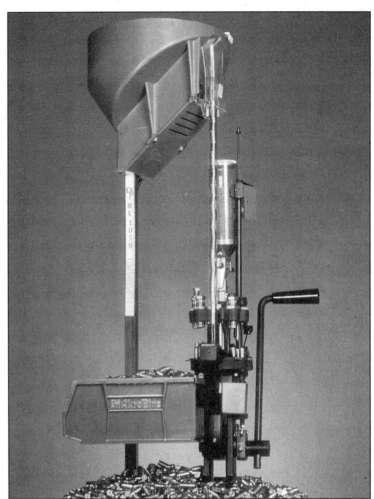

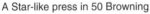
A Star-like press in 50 Browning

The Dillon RL1050

and find out if you're really interested without investing much money. The Lee Pro 1000 progressive is an excellent case in point.

Derived from their earlier turret press, the Lee Pro 1000 loads most popular pistol cartridges and a few short rifle rounds. It also has just about every automated feature—either built-in or available as an option—that you could possibly want. Case advancement, priming, powder charging, and loaded-round ejection are all automated. Automatic case-inserting gear can be bought as an option.

The more advanced Lee progressive is the Lee Load-Master. The Load-Master can load both rifle and pistol rounds, and has automatic case insertion and advancement, automatic priming and powder charging, automatic cartridge ejection and automatic bullet placement.

The novel feature in the Load-Master is the automatic bullet placement. This is done by an automatic bullet feeder. Automatic bullet feeders have been made before, but, well, they just didn't work. If Lee has a reliable design, and I would certainly assume that they do, this is a real achievement.

RCBS

The current RCBS progressives consist of the Auto 4x4, the Piggyback and the new AmmoMaster.

The Auto 4x4 is the automatic version of an earlier machine called, naturally enough, the 4x4. That unit required manual effort to seat the primers and throw the powder charge. Thus, the 4x4 was a pseudo-progressive.

The Auto 4x4 is a true progressive. It incorporates automatic case advancement, priming, powder charging and loaded-round ejection. Both pistol and rifle cartridges can be loaded. It does not, however, have removable tool heads.

Why would a progressive not have a removable tool head? Because this is an older design introduced before removable tool heads were commonly employed. Since the Auto 4x4 still sells well, it's still available.

The RCBS Piggyback is more of a conversion kit than a progressive. Basically, this is a set of parts that, when installed on a single-station press, converts that press into a progressive. The automatic features are the same as those found in the Auto 4x4. Tool head change isn't possible here for the simple reason that the kit is, essentially, a tool head. The unit can load most pistol and a few small rifle rounds.

The Piggyback idea, I think, is a fascinating one because it lets almost anyone who has a single-station O-press convert it, essentially upon demand, to a progressive. Thus, you have got a single-station press when you need one and a progressive when you like. Since the Piggyback is relatively inex-

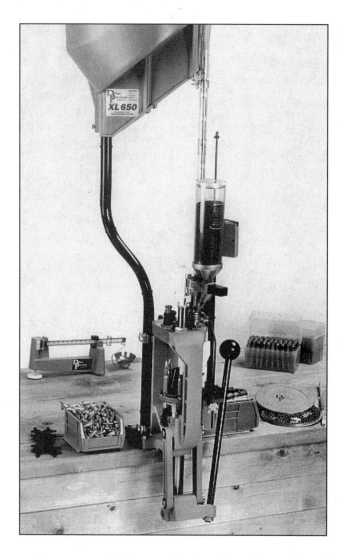

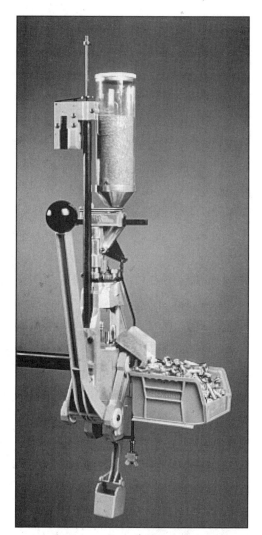

(Left) The
Dillon XL650

(Right)
The Dillon
Square Deal

pensive, you probably can afford one in each cartridge of interest.

The RCBS AmmoMaster is, essentially, a single-station H-press that can be upgraded to a progressive. Obviously, there is a logical link between the Piggyback and the AmmoMaster concepts. The idea here was that a buyer could start out with an RCBS single-station press and upgrade this machine if desired. Clever.

The AmmoMaster has the usual list of circular progressive features. It can do either manual or automatic case advancement, and has automatic priming, powder charging and loaded-round ejection. Though not obvious, caliber conversion by tool head change is possible because the top plate in the Ammo-Master can be unbolted and removed. That's the tool head.

RCBS also offers two dies that are of interest, no matter what progressive you might have. One lubricates cases; the other checks powder levels. Not every progressive has enough stations to use these two dies, but if your machine has an unused station or two at the right places, I'd certainly recommend installing these.

A couple of final points about RCBS. All their equipment comes with a lifetime guarantee, and they excel at customer support. Oddly enough, however, they don't make a big deal out of this. I've never understood that.

170

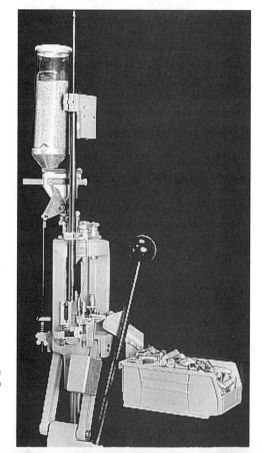

(Right) The
Dillon RL550

Hornady

Hornady, of course, makes excellent reloading equipment. Their progressive, the Pro-Jector, has the normal list of features. It can load rifle and pistol cartridges, and does automatic case advancement, priming, powder charging and loaded-round ejection. Like the RCBS Auto 4x4, however, the Pro-Jector does not employ a removable tool head. Why not? Because it's an older design introduced before this feature became commonly available.

Final Comments

I've come to believe that some facets of progressive design aren't all that important. One is the number of reloading stations. Whether a machine has four or eight doesn't really matter because it will get the job done with the number it has.

Another aspect of progressive design that I don't think is highly important is the degree of automation. Automatic case insertion, for instance, might be nice, but I don't think it's really necessary. I recommend sticking to the basics and skipping the options, at least initially. You can always add the optional features later if you think they'll help.

If you're seriously considering purchasing a progressive, find a friend who has the model you want and have him show you how to use it. As common as progressives are these days, this really shouldn't be all that hard. Actually, I'd try, before purchase, as many different progressives as I could find.

Also, at least for the first-time progressive buyer, I strongly suggest that you buy a new one. You're going to have to learn how your machine works. You don't need the additional potential hassle of trying to figure out what's wrong with the used machine that you have. Then, too, with a new one, you have a warranty and the manufacturer is there to help you if you need support.

Where can you get these machines? In the back of this book is a directory listing the addresses of these firms. I'd contact Dillon and Star directly. The rest sell through distributors who advertise in *Shotgun News* or *Gun List*. If you are unfamiliar with these publications, you should be able to buy copies at any large gun store.

One last point: The two greatest safety features inherent in any progressive are the intelligence and the attention of the person using it. Sooner or later, any progressive will develop a problem. Most will be due to operator error.

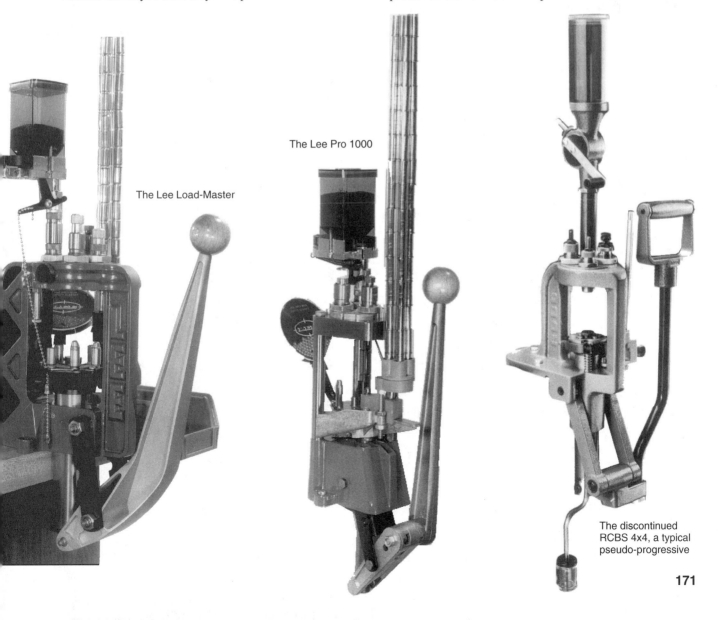

The Lee Load-Master

The Lee Pro 1000

The discontinued RCBS 4x4, a typical pseudo-progressive

171

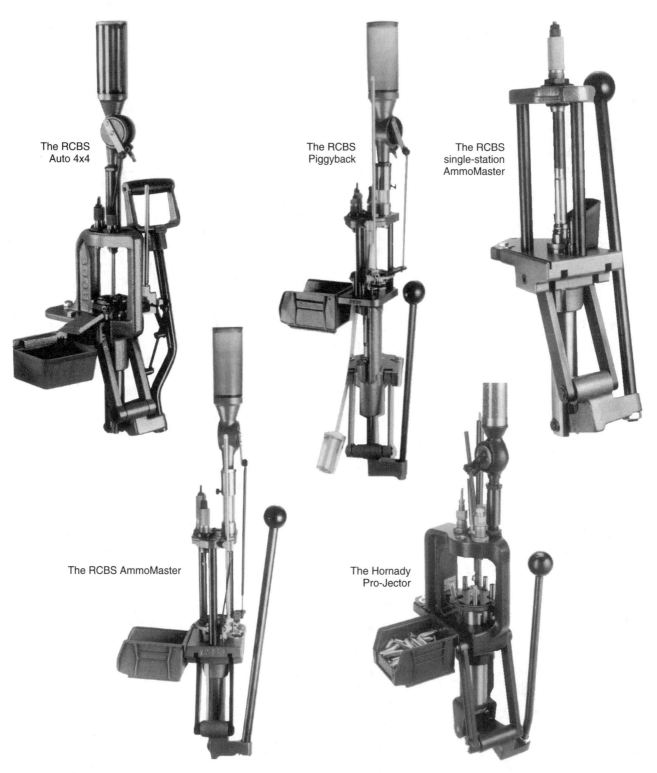

The RCBS
Auto 4x4

The RCBS
Piggyback

The RCBS
single-station
AmmoMaster

The RCBS AmmoMaster

The Hornady
Pro-Jector

When you get your machine, learn how to use it. Study the manual. Prove to yourself that you know what's going on. When something goes wrong, and this will happen, stop and figure out what's up. Never just try to force one.

Pay particular attention to the primer and powder systems. Some primer systems don't like some brands of primers. Personally, I think that Winchester primers and, for that matter, Winchester brass work best. Also, be sure that your powder system is set up correctly. If it is not, the machine will occasionally throw a partial charge or not throw a charge at all.

Check the weight of your powder charge every time you get a new can of powder. Weights thrown volumetrically can vary between lots by as much as 12 percent. I know that may be hard to believe, but it's true.

No one is a greater fan of progressives than I. However, I want to make one point very clear. Progressives work well, but only if you pay attention and know what you're doing. If you cannot give them your undivided, skilled attention, don't buy one. There isn't a progressive out there, new or used, that can compensate for an operator who doesn't know what he's doing.

17

All dedicated
riflemen—big
game hunters,
varmint shooters,
whoever—should
know what their
guns and loads
are really capap-
ble of. Here's
how to go
about...

Evaluating Accuracy

by EDWARD A. MATUNAS

ACCURACY CAN MEAN different things to different shoot-ers. For a deep woods deer hunter, a 3-inch five-shot group at 100 yards might be just dandy. For a serious general big game hunter, groups half that size might be deemed essential. Long-range varmint hunters are seldom impressed with groups con-taining ten shots of more than $3/4$-inch. And benchrest competitors need less than $1/4$-inch groups to prevent being thor-oughly overwhelmed with embarrassment.

But regardless of the degree of accuracy required for specif-ic purposes, not all shooters become aware of the true accuracy capability of any firearm/ammo combination. This is because accuracy evaluations are often made on the basis of just one or, perhaps, a few groups. The truth is, a few groups simply do not tell a great deal about overall accuracy potential. Having fired countless tens of thousands of groups during more than forty-five years of extensive shooting has proven that a few groups can, in fact, be very misleading. And the larger the group, the less it reflects actual potential accuracy. I have often heard

Accuracy demands vary greatly with the type of hunting and shooter skill. Obviously, this long-range varmint shooter will need sub-MOA accuracy capability. Without such capability, long-range hits will not be possible.

Those who pursue deer in dense forest can settle for a lot less accuracy than many other hunters. Nonetheless, even these shooters need a full understanding of total accuracy capability. George Emmanuel has proven his understanding, as shown by this nice Anticosti Island buck.

about, read of, and been shown groups that included one or more of what the shooter called "fliers." These are the shots not hitting in the main portion of the group and which the shooter often conveniently excludes from the accuracy appraisal of the combination being tested. However, let me clearly state that I believe there is no such thing as a flier when using today's superb components.

In decades past, flier was a justified term. At that time, accuracy, being dependent upon the uniformity of the components used, was somewhat iffy. One might unknowingly load an out-of-specification bullet or primer with a degree of frequency that was disconcerting. Even if the reloader carefully inspected each and every component, sooner or later something would go wrong and produce one or more shots that substantially enlarged a group. These errant shots were generally ignored when evaluating accuracy because they were "beyond the shooter's control."

Today, however, the quality of most components far surpasses

the average rifle and shooter's accuracy capability. There are few individual components that, if properly used with a firearm so capable, will not go into less than a minute-of-angle group. The few components that will not perform are simply eliminated by the reloader as part of the normal load development procedure.

That many components are actually capable of a much greater degree of accuracy is easily proven. For example: Most of my hunting rifles average about 1-inch five-shot groups at 100 yards when using specific Nosler Partition bullets. But when these same bullets with identical powder charges are loaded using typical benchrest techniques, and then fired in heavy target-grade rifles, groups shrink to $1/2$- to $1/4$-inch.

It does little good to argue with match scorers that a certain bullet hole is the result of a flier. The shot will be scored as it hit the target. This is only fair as it is indeed a reflection of the accuracy of the shooter/firearm/ammunition combination. Calling any poorly placed shot a flier will console no one except a

(Above) Remote hunting areas are not the place to learn about the accuracy of your favorite rifle and load. A critter at the top of this path would be a challenging, but possible, shot for the shooter who has fully evaluated his load's accuracy capability.

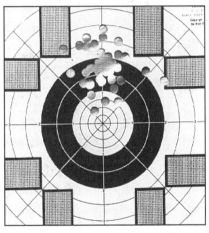

(Above) Here are eight individual targets fired over the course of a month. Note that some groups contain shots that some shooters would refer to as fliers.

(Left) This is the backing target used in the firing of the eight groups. Notice how the fliers disappear in the overall conglomerate target. It is this target that suggests true potential accuracy.

less than informed shooter. Additionally, in game fields, every shot fired also counts. You can't justify a miss (or worse, a badly hit and crippled animal) by calling that offending shot a flier.

Placing well in matches and proper hunting sportsmanship demand that the shooter know the true accuracy capability of the equipment and components being used. To find the true potential of any load is certainly not difficult, but it requires a number of trips to the range and the firing of at least twenty-five, and perhaps as many as fifty, rounds of ammo.

Testing For Accuracy

Just how many rounds are needed will be determined by the overall worth of the shooter/firearm/ammo combination. High degrees of accuracy (less than 1½ MOA) can be practically evaluated with twenty-five rounds. But in combinations that produce only ho-hum accuracy, it will be best to fire more shots to make sure the full range of shot dispersion has been included in your evaluation.

Accuracy evaluation is begun by using a double target. Start by carefully aligning two targets, one on top of the other. Make sure there is no slippage as you hang them at a range of at least 100 yards. Now fire a group. Don't allow the barrel to cool between shots; simply shoot at a pace necessary for carefully controlled

shots, just as would be done in the field or at a match. Next, remove the top target and put it aside for future reference. Place another target over the bottom one (which now has a five-shot group on it), carefully align it and fire the second group. But before doing so, allow ample time for the barrel to completely cool.

The number of shots in each group should be based on the type of shooting that will be done in the field or during competition. If you typically shoot ten-shot groups, or rapidly fire a lot of shots during a prairie dog shoot, then ten-shot groups should be fired. However, for most situations, five-shot strings will be satisfactory. My experience shows that firing three-shot groups will seldom reflect a firearms' true precision. Is there ever a time when a three-shot group would be acceptable? Not for me; but for your needs, you are the best judge.

When the second group has been fired, remove the top target, preserve it for later reference, and carefully store the bottom (now the master) target for use on another day. The shooting for this portion of the test program is now over for the day.

The point in firing two groups during the first shooting session is to eliminate a lot of loads that have poor accuracy. These two groups may quickly show the shooter less accuracy than he deems acceptable. However, regardless of the precision of these two groups, do not yet form an opinion in regard to accuracy.

(Above) Small critters like this 35-pound duiker demand a great deal of accuracy if shots are to result in bagged trophies. It takes at least five groups and four trips to the range to fully evaluate a load's potential.

(Right) Rick's long-range prowess comes in part from understanding the real accuracy potential of his favorite load. This chuck was taken at a range most folks simply would not believe—a full quarter of a mile.

(Left) The author busted this record-book kudu at a very long range. Total familiarity with his load's potential let him realize the shot was a sporting one. A single bullet at more than 300 yards did exactly what was expected.

day for each shooting session so you have one group fired in early morning light, another in midday light, and still another in the late evening. Also try to have at least one group fired under bright sunshine and another in heavy overcast or rainy conditions. Mark each top target with the time of day and light conditions. Put as many days or weeks between group firings as practical. The greater the time between targets, the better the chance for seeing any effects of stock warpage due to humidity.

When the shooting is done, you will have five (minimum) targets, each with a single group on it. The master target will, of course, contain a conglomerate group of all the test shots. It is this target that will tell you about your true accuracy capabilities.

Evaluating The Tests

Examination of the single-group targets generally will reveal a comparatively small group, a rather large group, and maybe a target or two with a so-called flier on it. Actual group sizes will,

Return to the range on another day to fire another group. This will be done with a fresh target carefully placed over the master, which already includes the first two groups. Only one group should be fired on this day.

Repeat the process on different days, firing only a single group each time, until you have one bottom target with at least twenty-five rounds (five five-shot groups) on it. Try to select the time of

Chronographing can show ammunition velocity variations that can be the cause of bullet stringing on the target.

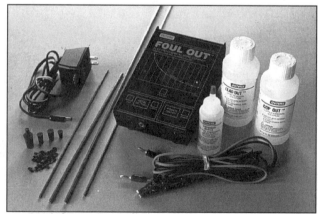

A quick, no-hassle means to an extremely clean bore (required for proper accuracy evaluation) is Outers' electric Foul Out system.

of course, be dependent on the potential capability of the specific shooter/rifle/load combination. These targets may also reveal any point of impact change that occurs with your rifle over the passage of time due to stock moisture content, temperature changes, etc. They should also reveal any tendency to see the sights differently under varying light conditions. This can cause point-of-impact variations, which will be most pronounced with open iron sights and least noticeable with telescopic sights.

The master target will indicate the overall potential of the firearm/load combination as it will occur at matches, or in the field, over a period of time and under differing light conditions. Even when each individual group is relatively small, the conglomerate group containing all shots will normally be considerably larger. You will, in all likelihood, note that any "fliers" appearing on individual targets will disappear into the overall group on the master target. This is because they were not flukes (read fliers), but part of the overall grouping ability of the gun and ammo combination.

Finally, to fully evaluate the accuracy potential of the shooter/firearm/ammo combination, set up a target at a range that shooter skill and gun/ammo efficiency suggest as a practical maximum for shooting in the field, or that equals your longest match shooting range. Fire at least three groups into a single target, allowing for complete cooling of your barrel between groups.

You will now have a real understanding of your load's capability, rather than a misconception based on one or two 100-yard groups.

Bore Cleaning And Other Test Aspects

How about barrel cleaning during the test program? Knowledgeable folks generally recognize that accuracy is best from a clean barrel. But when evaluating accuracy, the bore's condition should reflect circumstances as they will occur during matches or as they are anticipated in the field. A benchrest shooter is able to clean his barrel after every group, and therefore doing the same during testing makes sense. But if you are testing a safari rifle, you may well want to shoot the entire test string of five groups without barrel cleaning. (I have had a few rifles that would shoot well for twelve to eighteen rounds and then accuracy would go sour. These rifles were deemed unsuitable for my safari purposes.)

The ammo evaluation process should also include a look at how the gun functions. This means cycling the ammo through the firearm as if it were being used under field conditions, rather than loading in single shot fashion.

You will need to consider a few more points. The first is, will the first shot from a cold, clean barrel have a point of impact similar to succeeding shots fired from a warm and fouled barrel? Your conglomerate target will usually answer this question. Most often, shots fired from a cold barrel will evenly disperse themselves throughout the conglomerate group. More rarely, they will favor a closer impact point, but still within the group. In cases where the cold shots hit outside of the conglomerate group (this is extremely rare), there is little to do but to try rebedding the rifle in hopes of correcting the problem. If the gun places shots from a clean bore outside of the conglomerate group, it is a simple matter to fire one or two fouling shots before a match or going afield to hunt.

It helps in the evaluation of first-shot point of impact to circle the first shot fired on each of the single-group targets. This means using a spotting scope at the range sessions.

Ammo evaluation is slow and nettlesome work, requiring frequent trips to the range and the consumption of expensive

(Above) Uniform (generally showing no undue vertical or horizontal stringing) groups suggest a rifle that is properly tuned and a load well suited to it.

(Right) These groups were fired with the same rifle and load, but months apart. The slightly enlarged groups that struck considerably higher (bottom two targets) were the result of the stock's forend warping and placing upward pressure against the bottom of the barrel, which previously had no stock contact.

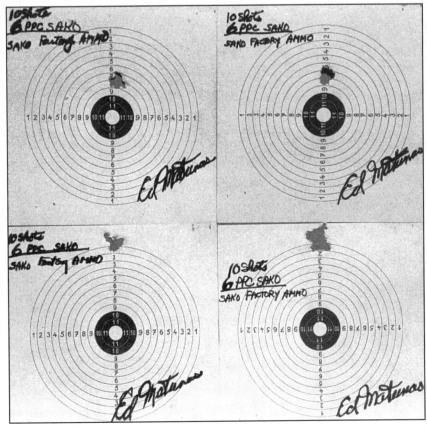

components. But if it results in winning matches or prevents one lost animal, it will all prove worthwhile and rewarding. Only two things will replace this kind of testing. The first is luck, and I cannot imagine what the other is.

Hints On Accuracy Problems

The very best possible accuracy demands that some basic conditions exist. With respect to the firearm, internal barrel condition and the muzzle crown are very important. The bedding of the rifle must also be nearly perfect. The groove diameter of the barrel must be exactly the same as bullet diameter. A barrel that is under- or oversize by 0.0005-inch may provide suitable accuracy for some shooters, but larger variations place serious limitations on potential precision.

The muzzle crown must be precise. No nicks or unevenness can be tolerated. The bullet base must be released at precisely the same instant around its entire circumference.

The bedding of barrel and action must be without compromise, meaning the action must fit the stock exceedingly well. It must be held firmly in place without any possible movement during firing

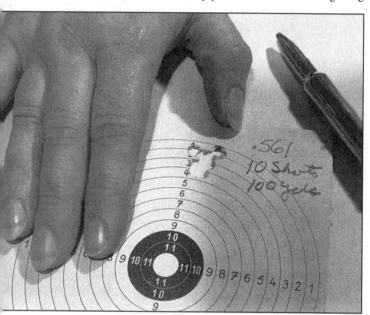

When retesting, after beginning new lot numbers or altering loading dimensions, groups like this would suggest that extensive firing is not essential.

and recoil. Even a minute amount of movement is self-defeating. Glass and pillar bedding is the best way to eliminate action bedding as a potential source of poor accuracy. The barrel should be free-floating (no contact with the stock) for the most uniform results. However, some barrels which have certain internal stresses will perform best with some degree of upward forend pressure against them. In these instances, the pressure is best applied on the extreme leading edge of the forend. The correct amount of pressure can vary from rifle to rifle, but will invariably be 5 to 15 pounds.

Group Shapes Can Tell Problems

Groups that are consistently at least 2½ times as high as they are wide may be indications of either large shot-to-shot velocity variation or poor barrel bedding. This type of shot placement is called stringing. In extreme cases, shots can string up and down as much as 7 inches (at 100 yards), while horizontal dispersion may be as little as an inch, even less.

The problem of velocity variation can, of course, be investigated with a chronograph. If a ten-shot string shows an extreme velocity spread no greater than 2 percent of the average muzzle velocity, there is little likelihood that stringing is due to velocity variation.

Bedding that allows the barrel to receive varying degrees of upward pressure from the forend will invariably result in shot stringing. Sometimes a pressure-bedded barrel will see additional pressure with each successive shot. This is caused by the barrel diameter increasing as it gets hotter. Depending upon the individual barrel, each shot may go higher than the last. However, some barrels will string shots vertically without specific progression. If the barreled action can shift in the stock under recoil,

(Above) The Tonoloway Bullsbag and portable benchrest are extremely effective for accuracy evaluation shooting. This bench assembles and disassembles in minutes, making it practical to tote anywhere. The built-in seat adds the shooter's weight to the entire rig and thus a substantial amount of "solidness" to the unit.

(Left) A Harris bipod will offer a high degree of steadiness for accuracy testing when no form of benchrest is available.

A hunter needs to be cognizant of true accuracy capability. Crippling animals simply is not acceptable. Thus, the hunter should compare basic load evaluations to results used when shooting from field positions.

stringing may also occur. Make sure all screws are evenly tight.

Groups that are consistently at least $2\frac{1}{2}$ times as wide as they are tall also suggest a bedding problem, caused by the barrel coming in contact with the sides of the barrel channel. Or, there simply may be greater pressure from one side of the channel than the other.

The best approach with most rifles is a free-floating barrel and a glass-bedded action to prevent the action from shifting under recoil.

Groups that are simply poor but have random dispersion may be caused by a number of gun conditions too numerous to get into at this time. Or, such groups may be the result of a less than ideal load.

Group Position Shifting

If groups are uniformly small but shift in point of impact as time passes, one suspect condition is stock warpage. A free-floating barrel or synthetic stock will eliminate this problem. Another cause could be the inadvertent change in bullet seating depth, or a change in the lot number of one or more of the components being used.

Careful attention to detail can be all that is required to prevent group shifting of a noticeable degree, perhaps as much as an inch or more. It is important to remember that not every group will be centered exactly as any preceding group. Therefore, ignore shifts that are comparatively small with respect to the overall composite group. Also, if only one group shifts, this can simply be the effect of random shot placement and can equally be ignored.

Shooting Conditions

The conditions under which the test targets are fired must be carefully controlled if results are to be considered meaningful. Generally, this means shooting from a solid and comfortable position—sandbags placed on a suitable benchrest table. Tar-

gets must be mounted carefully on a solid backstop, because windblown targets will give windblown results.

Not every shooter has access to a range with good benchrests, but most serious shooters can justify the purchase of a portable benchrest table, a good set of sandbags and a portable target frame. A good portable benchrest is made by Tonoloway Tack Drivers. Sandbags are also available from these same folks, as well as from Hoppe's and other sources. A great portable target frame is available from Targ-A-Tote. This target frame has a built-in level that helps eliminate precision discrepancies caused by canting the target or gun.

If shooting from a benchrest is impossible for you, then at least use *some* sort of rest for your testing. A Harris bipod mounted to the front swivel stud is a major improvement over any hand-held shooting position.

Retesting

Whenever any component lot number changes, retesting is necessary. Though accuracy seldom changes with lot numbers, it is possible for a good load to go sour. I recall when a bullet lot change caused accuracy to go from MOA to totally unsatisfactory. Assume nothing and retest with each change in lot number, loading specifications, or procedures.

With but a bit of shooting, you can gain a great deal of insight into actual load performance. Also, you will learn enough to realize that opinions based on limited results are best left unsaid, as they can be far from a realistic evaluation of accuracy. If you are a target shooter, the foregoing approach will tell you all you need to know about a load's performance. If you are a hunter, you will also need to evaluate bullet performance after striking game. That, however, is a topic for another time. In addition, hunters should test accuracy capability as it occurs when firing from field positions. Benchrest testing sometimes leaves a hunter overconfident of his capabilities; shooting some groups from field positions will bring everything back to a realistic level.

Electronics are replacing mechanics in testing, so here are some helpful suggestions for...

Understanding The "New" Shotshell Terminologies

by DON ZUTZ

ANY SHOTSHELL RELOADER who peruses handloading manuals and data sheets invariably sees a lot of terminology which reports the interior and exterior ballistics of his loads. Especially important are such things as chamber pressure and velocity, both of which are normally listed in shotshell reloading publications.

There is nothing absolutely new about chamber pressures and velocities, of course. Shotgunners have bandied about those terms forever. "My trap loads are doing 1187 fps," one clay target shooter will say, while a goose hunter may claim that, "These steel-shot magnums I reloaded have a chamber pressure of 10,600 LUP." And all of that is just fine, of course, because it means that handloaders are giving some attention to ballistics rather than just cobbling up any ol' combinations of shot, wad and primer.

But what do those numbers *really* mean? Do we fully understand how they are taken? Do we know how they are used to judge the load's potential effectiveness and safety? In other

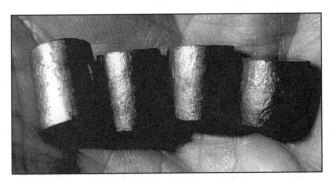

Lead crusher units shown in various degrees of compression after test firings.

At one time, shotshell pressures were mainly checked by the lead unit method, meaning cylindrical lead "crushers" were measured after firing to detect the amount of compression, which was then reported by the LUP method.

words, what are we reading and saying when we use such terms as feet per second (fps), lead unit pressures (LUP), and pounds per square inch (psi) when they're applied to shotshells? For although 1187 fps and 10,600 LUP are nice numbers, we've got to know more. This is a good time to define them, since some new thinking has come into this field of shotshell ballistics terminology relative to velocities, as has the piezo-electric equipment been taking over from the former lead crusher method of gauging pressures. Let's begin by updating the pressure-reading method...

Pressure Terms In Transition

Anyone who carefully reads shotshell reloading manuals will notice that chamber pressure values are being given in two different manners. One is the "lead unit pressure" method, which is listed as LUP. We've all seen those initials. Another method of stating chamber pressure values is done with the abbreviation psi, which is coming more and more into vogue these days as the industry switches from the old lead crusher test gun to the newer electronic gear. But the major point to be made here is that LUP and psi values *are not* the same. The abbreviations LUP and psi do *not* interchange. A shotshell with a chamber pressure of 10,600 LUP *cannot* also be described as having a pressure of 10,600 psi. The equipment employed to take chamber pressures via the LUP method doesn't track pressures in the

same manner as does the electronic gadgetry used to check the same pressures as stated in terms of psi. Thus, handloaders must learn to differentiate between LUP and psi pressure values. Now let's back up and take an historical approach to this terminology.

After shotshell powders had been employed for a few centuries, gunmakers wondered what kind of pressures built up in the chambers. This wasn't just a matter of scientific curiosity, but rather a very practical necessity in learning how to build guns stout enough for safety. Both gunmakers and ammo manufacturers wanted to know their parameters. When both gunmakers and ammo suppliers get together, they can set industry standards. The problem, of course, was twofold: (1) How do you measure pressure; and (2) How do you calibrate it?

The first successful system for obtaining a pressure measurement came from the lead unit pressure method. It was based on finding how far a fired shotshell's chamber pressure would compress a small, cylindrical lead unit set between an anvil and a piston for a crusher-type pressure gun. On firing, the shotshell's hull ruptures and drives the piston upward. In turn, the lead crusher unit is compressed against the anvil. The operator removes the lead crusher unit and measures it with a micrometer; then he applies his results against a conversion table which states the amount of compression in terms of LUP. All that would have been simple enough, but something went awry.

Some of the results weren't only reported as LUP. Instead, some sources began reporting chamber pressures in terms of psi, which to the public means pounds per square inch. Other early experimenters went so far as to call their results "psi, LUP," which is translated as "psi as taken by the lead unit pressure method." This has confounded the scene, as it lumped the psi and LUP designations, causing many people to consider them to be the same—which, as I said previously, they aren't. Nevertheless, until well into the aftermath of WWII, these sets of initials were thought by most reloaders to be the same.

After WWII, however, we began applying new technologies to chamber pressure measurements. Labs began taking small arms pressures with strain gauges and electronic transducer equipment rather than with the older lead crusher method. This was excellent, of course, but how were pressures taken with piezo-electric gear to be reported? As things evolved, the psi designation came to be applied. Thus, today "psi" indicates pressures read by electronic gear while "LUP" still reports those pressures taken by the old crusher gun. (For riflemen, it must be stated that the "CUP" pressure designation came from a pressure gun using a copper crusher unit rather than a lead unit; copper was needed at the higher rifle cartridge pressures because lead was too soft once pressures reached beyond 13,000-14,000 units.)

Now we come to the complicated part. Although the LUP (and CUP) method is calculated according to one scale, it became impossible to equate that with the psi readings which come from the piezo-electric equipment. The twain are calibrated differently, and they "read" pressures differently. The fact is that it takes more time for the LUP system

Handloader-type chronographs are a help to amateurs, but one must always remember that they, such as this PACT unit, clock only the leading pellet(s), while the industry uses coils to report the average speed of the entire shot string.

to begin registering pressure when a shotshell is fired, whereas the more sensitive piezo-electric equipment requires almost no time to begin registering the rising gas pressures. With piezo-electric gear, for instance, the gases apply their energy directly to a piston gauge which transmits it to a quartz disc or crystal, which in turn produces an electric charge that is collected by an electrode and sent into the condenser to generate a proportional voltage. The voltage is then shown on a cathode-ray tube. All this happens quickly before the chamber pressure can start to fade. Likewise, electronic gear will give more uniform results, because it is possible to have lead crusher units of varying quality that give irregular results.

The point is, then, that we have two systems which measure the same pressure differently. As a rule of thumb, the piezo-electronic equipment will give higher values, generally by *about* 1000 units. Let's say, for example, that a given shotshell registers an average chamber pressure of 10,000 units on the old LUP scale. When tested in piezo-electric settings, it will tend to average around 11,000 psi. (Note: This comparison is *only* for shotshell pressures; rifle and handgun pressures, being higher, will have greater distance between them and the old CUP pressure values, and there is no likelihood of calculating the differential between CUP and piezo-electronic psi results as each cartridge has its own "flow factor" to influence final results. This crude method of adding 1000 units to an LUP value to obtain the psi value is only for shotshells.)

The U.S. sporting arms industry has established a table of equivalencies for shotshells. These have been provided by Mr. John C. Delaney, who has served as the chief ballistician of Alliant Techsystems (Hercules) and is now also handling customer relations and information. The following figures show the industry's maximum working averages for the respective gauges in both lead unit pressures and the current psi values as taken on piezo-electric equipment:

SHOTSHELL EQUIVALENCIES

Gauge	LUP	PSI
10	10,000	11,000
12	10,500	11,500
16	10,500	11,500
20	11,000	12,000
28	11,500	12,500
410-bore (2¹/₂″)	11,500	12,500
410-bore (3″)	12,500	13,500

The important thing for me to get across is that these numbers represent the same *actual* pressure for their respective gauges. The sole difference is the way in which the equipment reads and reports that pressure due to its calibrations and sensitivities.

Some handloaders have been told blandly that 10,000 LUP is the highest pressure they should use, thus when they see the 13,500 psi max listed for piezo-electric equipment, they may react in surprise. No need to. The smaller the bore, the more pressure that is needed to move a payload forward; hence, the industry heightens the allowable chamber pressures for the smaller gauges and bores.

The sporting arms industry will soon be shifting completely to the piezo-electric gear, and in the future most, if not all, reloading data will be reported in terms of psi. Keep your eyes

When chronographing with the shotgun, as this shooter is doing using the Oehler rigging with printer, he'll get the velocity of the leading edge of the shot charge.

peeled for those little initials to know which pressure system was used in developing certain reloading data. By no means are LUP and psi identical.

Understanding Shotshell Velocities

The term "fps" is quite common in reloading literature. It means "feet per second" and thus tells how fast a shot charge is going.

But therein lies the crux of the problem. No shot charge retains its velocity; therefore, we must ask two questions about shot-string velocity figures: (1) At what point is the load doing the published velocity; and (2) What happens beyond the point at which the speed is measured?

Many shotgunners have long believed that the published velocity figures for shotshells are muzzle values—but they aren't. Practically all published shotshell velocities, including those printed in handloading manuals and on data sheets, are taken 3 feet from the muzzle. This may seem like no big deal to casual reloaders, but, scientifically speaking, it is a major point in understanding shot-charge dynamics as there is a considerable loss of velocity during a shot load's first 3 to 4 feet of free flight. The culprit is air drag, alias air resistance. This point was emphasized in an article by E.D. Lowry, former ballistician with Winchester, which appeared in the December, 1989, issue of *American Rifleman* magazine. Titled "Shotgun Ballistics Reconsidered," the article shows that there can be a differential of 75 to 100 fps between a load's actual muzzle velocity and its 3-foot instrumental readings.

In accompanying data made available through the editorial office of the National Rifle Association, Lowry presented figures indicating that a lead shot charge with a published (3-foot) velocity of 1200 fps, which is a common figure for 3 drams equivalent trap loads, comes from the muzzle with an actual velocity of 1302 fps (#7$^1/_2$ shot). A steel shot load of BBs with a published velocity of 1350 fps really needs a true muzzle velocity of 1459 fps to retain 1350 fps at a 3-foot instrumental reading, according to Lowry. Thus, it is wrong to assume that published shotshell velocities are indeed muzzle data.

If shot charges lose so much speed in the first 3 to 4 feet of free flight, how do they manage to retain effective energies farther downrange? It is a fact of physics that air resistance works harder against fast-moving objects than it does against slower ones; hence, as the pellets slow down, they are less affected by air resistance and thus manage to retain more of their velocity/energy values. But in that first collision with air, the shot charge is slowed abruptly.

There is also a problem in interpreting chronograph data when shotshells are tested over handloader-type screens, namely, the popular skyscreens. Published shotshell data isn't taken with such screens, which trigger on the leading pellet(s). Instead, industry chronographing of shotshells is mainly done with a coil screen. The shot string is fired through the coils, and the resulting velocity figure is an average for the entire shot string. The combination of a coil and an industry chronograph, then, triggers on mass rather than the leading edge of the shot charge. The difference can be meaningful.

Although many reloaders think that a shot string doesn't lengthen much in its first 3 to 4 feet of free flight—it does. It especially stretches out from a Full-choke barrel, which is the commonly employed test choke. From data this writer has seen, there can be a 25 to 40 fps differential between readings of the same loads, depending upon whether they are clocked by the industry's coil equipment or an amateur's skyscreens. The sky-screens report the higher velocities, of course, since they pick up only the front pellet(s) and don't have to wait for the center of mass.

The LUP pressure designation is based on lead crusher compression and, although still around, is gradually being replaced by...

The point is that reloaders using handloader-type chronographs can't expect to get the same velocities as printed in manuals for their reloads. The triggering of the respective chronographs is different. As an example, let's take a 12-gauge trap reload with a published velocity of 1200 fps. It was probably tested in a modern lab with coil equipment, and the velocity figure is an average for the entire shot string at 3 feet. Now, you buzz it over the skyscreens of an Oehler or a PACT chronograph and get 1225 fps or, perhaps, as high as 1240 fps. What's wrong? Is your reload too hot? In general, nothing's wrong and your reload is easily within acceptable parameters, for your skyscreens are timing just the leading shot, whereas the coil equipment timed the center of mass. In an elongating Full-choke shot string, as mentioned, the skyscreen can show 25 to 40 fps higher velocities than will a coil screen. Thus, reloaders checking their home brew over amateur equipment can expect to find somewhat higher velocities than they read in manuals for any shotshell.

Retained Ballistics

The work of E.D. Lowry has also pinpointed some other interesting information about shot-charge velocities relative to retained values. Since air resistance is the main cause of deteri-

oration in velocity/energy values, it only stands to reason that: (1) pellet form (aerodynamics) and (2) pellet weight are important qualities. Deformed pellets are quickly slowed by air resistance, as are the lighter ones.

According to Lowry, the most efficient loads are those in which the lead pellets are bedded in a granulated polyethylene buffer. This buffer helps to minimize pellet deformation and, given the density of lead, provides an optimum shape plus weight to combat air drag. (Of course, a sphere is acknowledged to be a relatively poor aerodynamic shape, but even that is better than a mashed, out-of-round lead lump!) As an example, Lowry's data indicate that an unbuffered #4 lead pellet with a published (3-foot, coil) velocity of 1330 fps retains 648 fps and 3.02 foot-pounds of energy (fpe) at 50 yards, while an identical, albeit buffered, #4 lead shot retains 694 fps and 3.46 fpe at 50 yards. That's an advantage of near-ly 50 fps and about one-half foot-pound of energy for the

...the piezo-electric equipment which lists its pressures under the psi designation. Look carefully in reloading manuals for these specific terms, as they are *not* the same!

buffered pellet. When we're dealing with the exterior ballistics of shotshells over 40 to 60 yards, those can be meaningful figures.

Steel shot can be somewhat of a Catch-22 situation. Although steel pellets retain their shapes, they are lighter than lead and, consequently, can be slowed, anyway. In general, steel loads need more actual muzzle velocity to reach their published (3-foot) velocities. Lowry has presented data which show that a load of steel #2s with a published velocity of 1365 fps really needs a muzzle velocity of 1500 fps to reach the 3-foot instrumental range at roughly 1365 fps! This is one reason waterfowl hunters must think in terms of the bulkier shot sizes (#1s and BBs for ducks; BBs, BBBs and Ts for geese), as they are better able than the smaller diameters to overcome air drag and provide adequate penetrating power for clean kills.

The terminologies of modern shotshell ballistics, then, must be understood if they are to be of any benefit to handloaders. The fanciest, most expensive reloading press is of little value unless the loads produced on it are effective. By knowing the terms that describe a shotshell's interior and exterior performances, one can improve his assessment of each round during load development work.

19

Why swaging is safe, fast, precise and cheap— compared to casting your own bullets.

Modern Bullet Swaging

by DAVID R. CORBIN

IN THE 1890s, certain precision rifle shooters and gunmakers discovered how to make bullets without using hot lead. By pressing room-temperature slugs of lead into a polished steel die under tons of pressure, they made bullets which took on the exact shape of the die every time. No air pockets, bubbles or voids remained. The die, being a solid steel cylinder with a perfectly round hole, didn't have to snap open and clang shut with every bullet, like a mould, wearing the hinges and letting the hole become oblong. The finished bullet was pushed out by its nose, through the same hole it entered. Since the swage die operated at room temperature, there was no thermal expansion and contraction with every pour, no variation caused by heating and cooling of the mould, no warpage or shrinkage of either the bullet or the tool.

Bullet swaging in those days was a slow process. The original dies were operated with brass mallets. The bullet maker would pound on a tough steel punch, fitted more accurately than today's high performance car engines, into the matching cylinder. The hammer blows would develop the tons of pressure required to cold-flow the lead and form a precise bullet shape. Not surprisingly, this kind of die became known as a "pound die." The people who appreciated them most were the slug-gun shooters, who fired big-bore rifles at ranges up to 1000 yards and were the forerunners of today's benchrest competitors.

As experience was gathered by the following generations of bullet makers, the process became faster, easier and more accurate. One of the more famous of the short-lived swaging firms of the 1950s was Biehler and Astles, a couple of fellows who actually used the tools belonging to a technical school shop class to make a vastly better kind of bullet swage system. Instead of using one die that came apart, they designed the operation to be done in three dies. Each die was solid and had a punch through both ends. The final die had a small spring-steel ejection pin that pushed the bullet out by its nose. First the lead core was swaged to shape and weight by itself. Then the core and jacket were put together and expanded upward in diameter by pressure applied to the core in a second, larger die. Finally, the precise cylinder with its balloon-tight jacket, expanded by internal lead pressure, was put into the ogive or point-forming die and shaped into a bullet.

The advantage of this system was versatility, speed and precision: the ogive and shank were always in perfect alignment with nothing to cause this to change. The B&A company didn't last very long, and prices were high even with the use of virtually free tooling from a school shop to make the dies, but it established without a doubt that the handloader, working with simple equipment, could create bullets of greater accuracy than any punched out by high-speed machinery. The era of benchrest bullet swaging had begun.

Over the years, a handful of die makers have built bullet swaging equipment, but most handloaders still know little about swaging. There are three reasons for that. First, there has been a lack of widespread information about the process, tools and techniques. Most handloaders have misconceptions about swaging based on very old ideas which are perpetuated by people who don't keep up with the latest developments. Second, there are different marketing concepts among the swaging toolmakers which can keep handloaders from seeing the whole picture and where they might benefit from the process. And third, the most vocal and published bullet swagers who sell their precision bullets are not anxious for anyone else to know how easy it can be to make good bullets at home. The commercial mass-production bullet firms certainly are not interested in promoting the idea either!

These are some of the misconceptions: swaging is too expensive and only for benchrest shooters or "experts"; swaging is too involved, meticulous and slow for practical handloading; swaged bullets have to be made of soft lead and therefore are of limited design; and swaging is too hard to learn (except, of course, for those who make good money selling you their swaged bullets).

All these things were true long ago. Before there were books, articles and the resources of people willing to share information, swaging was very hard to learn. The people who learned it gen-

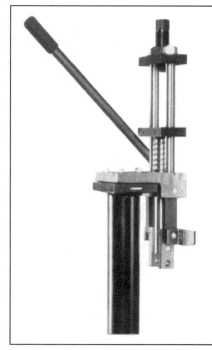

Corbin CSP-1 Series II   Corbin CSP-2 Mega Mite

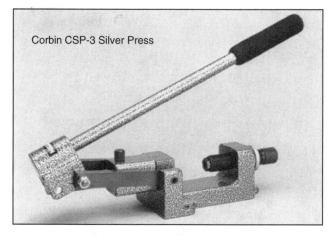

Corbin CSP-3 Silver Press

erally kept their secrets to improve their own shooting or to sell bullets. The people who made swaging dies generally didn't care to tell how they did it, which in turn meant swaging was a business full of dark secrets. When Charlie Heckman (C-H Tool and Die Co. founder) and Ted Smith (S.A.S. Dies) began marketing low-cost, simple swage dies for basic pistol-bullet designs in the half-jacket style, many shooters got the impression this was the only thing swaging could do. Indeed, unless one spent the equivalent of a few thousand of today's dollars for better equipment, that *was* all swaging could do! But times and products have changed.

Today, there are still firms that market simple swage dies which are inexpensive and make the soft lead half-jacket style bullets. The dies are good tools that can make a limited number of bullet styles.

A person who sees only these products advertised, however, quickly assumes that swaging is a low-cost way to make soft lead bullets—period. If it were suggested that a handloader might make a better quality multi-jacketed big game bullet for a

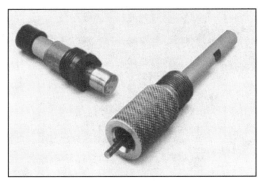

Corbin Swage Die

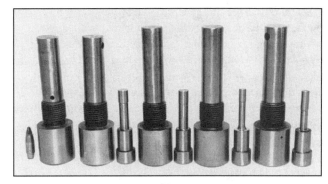

Corbin 5-Die Boattail Rifle Set

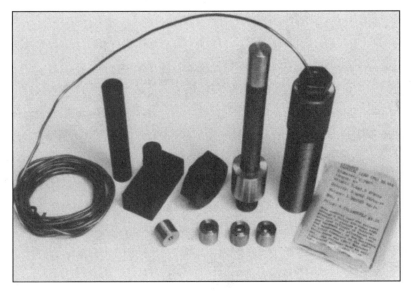

Corbin LED-1 Lead Wire Extruder Kit

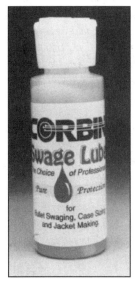

Corbin Swage Lube

475 Nitro Express with home swaging tools, using a press designed for swaging rather than reloading, or that it might be possible to build a fully jacketed expanding pistol bullet or a hard lead slug for practical pistol matches that had just the right weight to make major caliber with minimum recoil, or make bullets superior to the usual factory offerings, the idea would probably be shrugged off as a fantasy.

On the other end of the spectrum, some die makers are building extremely expensive, high-quality tools to make precision benchrest bullets in 224, 243 and 308 calibers. With these tools, you get a strong dose of ritual and an introduction to the "dark side" of swaging: the black art, so to speak, where you do things just because someone said it tightened the group by .001-inch and there is no other logical reason. This is the slow, ritualized aspect of bullet swaging, and it has evolved its own myths and legends. It would spoil some of the fun to debunk them. But a newcomer introduced to this extreme fringe of swaging then believes that swaging is too costly, slow and difficult for the average shooter. This is just as tunnel-visioned as the first example. Swaging has much more to offer the modern handloader.

The truth is that swaging encompasses far more territory than either of these extremes. Between the low cost, limited capability bullets and the super-precision, voodoo rituals is the entire "rest of the story," as Paul Harvey would say. The marketing philosophy of the firms which build for mass retail sales, and that of the people which build only for the benchrest sport, are just two out of three ways to market swaging tools. The third way is to make them available to everyone on a semi-custom basis, where the presses and dies are standardized so they will interchange within broad groups of calibers (from 14 to 458, for example), yet the shapes and caliber can be tailored to individual shooters' needs. This method makes high-precision equipment available in a price range that is closer to the low end of the scale. The volume then helps reduce the cost of making precision equipment even further, so that benchrest-quality equipment can be offered at closer to the half-jacket handgun-die prices.

You can get jackets, jacket-maker kits, lead extruders, lead wire, core cutters, lubricants, core-bonding chemicals, presses, computer software for bullet design, and a wealth of information from the same source as the swage dies. Today, you can make any caliber of bullet, from the tiny 0.145-inch rifle bullets to the 10-gauge shotgun slug, in equipment that fits into a corner of the garage or den. Several specialized presses, including both hand-operated and hydraulic-powered, are built for bullet making. Swaging presses are made to accept the dies in a different manner than reloading presses: The dies screw into the ram, where the design of the ram can be used to take the force applied to the internal punch and to move the punch forward on the downstroke, resulting in automatic ejection of the bullet.

Swaging presses are generally much more powerful and tougher, and have shorter strokes (on hand-operated models) than reloading presses. Some swaging presses are now designed to convert into a longer stroke with lower leverage for use with reloading dies, which may be like using a 460 Weatherby to shoot field mice, but it gets the job done. You can, of course, use a reloading press for some kinds of swaging, with the more limited design of die that fits into it. But since swaging presses are generally from 200 to 300 percent faster than reloading presses at forming and ejecting the bullet, it makes sense to have the right tool for the job.

Swaging presses accept the die in the ram, instead of in the press head. This means the bullet components simply drop into the die mouth, instead of having to be pushed up into the bottom of an open hole and held there while you try to get the punch into the die and your finger out of the way. Swaging presses eject the bullet on the backstroke and do not require any special ejection tools, mallets, or other ways to work around the lack of an ejection mechanism built into a reloading press. Finally, swaging presses can be made to accept much larger, tougher dies and punches, capable of forming hard lead, solid copper or aluminum, or pressing powdered metals and plastics together to make non-lead bullets.

Most handloaders have not yet heard that they can manufacture bullet jackets at home, since this is something that has not been widely available until recent years. There are three ways to make bullet jackets at home. The oldest is a wartime expedient: using empty cartridge cases. During periods of ammunition shortages, empty military cartridge cases have been filled with lead and swaged into larger-caliber bullets.

The 30 Carbine case can be used to make a 375-caliber bullet, for instance. Just about any straight-walled pistol case can be made into some caliber of rifle-bullet jacket. Fired 22 rimfire cases make very good jackets for 224 rifle bullets and can also be used for 243 and even 25 ACP jackets. It is even possible to make 257-, 264-, and 270-caliber bullets using fired 22 Magnum cases, but it isn't easy enough to recommend on a daily basis. The brass will expand under internal pressure if you use several short lengths of lead and expand each one separately, so the brass takes on the larger diameter in short steps, like a rattlesnake digesting a rabbit.

The second way to make jackets is to use copper tubing. Barnes Bullets originally popularized this concept; a number of other firms made specialty bullets (such as Cor-Bon and Grizzly). Copper tubing can be partially rolled over and closed at one end using a hand press, or it can be completely swaged into a closed cup with the right tools in a hydraulic swaging press.

It's well proven by now, with hundreds of thousands of bullets fired, that a "pure" copper jacket, using the same kind of material as ordinary plumbing, air conditioner and boiler tubing, won't cause any more fouling than a typical factory bullet provided that the surface finish is as good. When you hear someone complain about fouling from pure copper jackets, the odds are extremely high that the bullet was not polished or burnished by the tooling to remove the loose oxide layer which always forms when the tube is heat-treated (as it must be, to form the base without cracking the edges). It is this loose, pow-

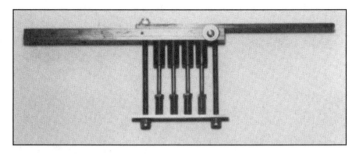

Bullet Swaging Supply Core Mould

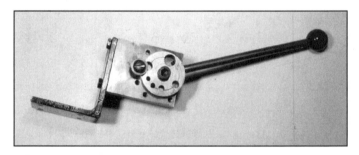

Bullet Swaging Supply Core Cutter

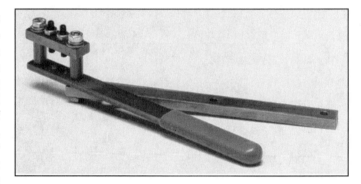

Sport Flite Wire Core Cutter

dery surface that comes off in the bore and contributes heavily to fouling. A well-finished, reasonably work-hardened tubing jacket is as clean-shooting as anyone would want.

A third way to manufacture your own bullet jackets is to use flat strips of copper, or gilding metal, commercial bronze, aluminum, or even mild steel, but not necessarily with the same set of tooling designed for another material. Tools for these materials have taken a long time to evolve, since a number of technical problems had to be solved to produce as good a jacket at home as can be made on $350,000 transfer presses. But now, the only differences between factory jackets and those you can make at home are the speed with which they are produced, and the fact that you can control the jacket taper, thickness and length to make jackets not available from any factory.

Using .030-inch-thick roofing copper in a 1-inch wide strip, you can punch out a disk and turn the disk into a shallow cup like a gas check or half-jacket. Then, redraw this cup in one or more stages to make it longer, smaller in diameter, and to adjust the taper and wall thickness, depending on the design of the punches and dies. Each set of jacket-drawing tooling works as a closely matched package, designed for a given kind of material. You can't throw just any old sheet of metal into the process and expect it to produce a good jacket, but

Berger J-4 Jackets

Bullet Swaging Supply Tubing Die

Bullet Swaging Supply
Jacket Draw Die

Sport Flite 22 Denim Jacket Form Die

Corbin Copper Tubing

Lyman Gas Checks

Corbin Copper, Steel and Brass Jackets

you can buy modest quantities of the right material at a reasonable price (even as little as 5 pounds, which in the above dimensions would give you 42.5 feet of strip and make about 550 jackets for around $35).

The advantage of home jacket making is that you can have virtually any caliber, length and wall thickness you desire. This helps you control the performance of the bullet in ways that were previously available only to the research departments of the military and ammunition companies. The jacket design is the single most critical element in the terminal performance of your handloaded round other than the velocity you give to the bullet. By handing control to you, swaging breaks down the last barrier between true ballistic engineering and the home construction of handloads by recipe. In fact, the power over performance is so vast that, without some written guidelines, some handloaders would be in over their heads. Fortunately, the information available today is as complete as the swaging field is wide.

There are more articles appearing in gun magazines each year, explaining new techniques and designs made possible by bullet swaging. There are also many books in print, about bullet swaging, how to design bullets, how to make them, and even how to start your own bullet business on the side. This can provide a good income, if the 350 or more custom bullet firms who are full-time specialty bullet suppliers are any indication.

If you have been casting bullets, you know about the time it takes to melt a pot of lead, prepare the moulds, and get the first few bullets to come out right. Then, after being exposed to the lead vapors and the potential for a drop of sweat to land in the pot and blow it all out in a huge explosion, you know about the time it takes to put it all away, cool down the pot, and start the long process of sizing and lubricating, all the while being careful not to burn yourself or any small children that might reach curiously toward a shiny drop of molten metal. When you buy equipment, you know that it takes a lead pot, a ladle, a sizer-lubricator, lubricant sticks, mould handles, and a separate mould for every weight and shape you want in every caliber.

With swaging, a single die or set of dies is required for each diameter of bullet, but within that diameter, you can produce nearly infinite weights and styles. Using a spool of lead wire removes any need for hot lead, so you and your family are not exposed to burns, explosions or toxic fumes. Since you won't have to wait for a pot to melt, you can come home, put the die in the swaging press, and make a dozen bullets in any desired weight or style in just a few minutes time. In fact, you can probably swage a box of bullets and reload them before a lead pot would have time to liquefy its contents.

If you have casting equipment, you can use the pot and a special top-ejecting core mould to produce lead cores instead of using lead wire. It has the same drawbacks as casting bullets except that you don't have to worry so much about perfect casts, and the piston- and cylinder-type of mould is considerably faster than a butterfly-type bullet mould. And, of course,

Corbin Power Cannelure

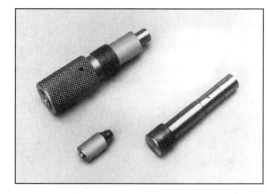

Corbin Base Guard Bullet Swage Die Kit

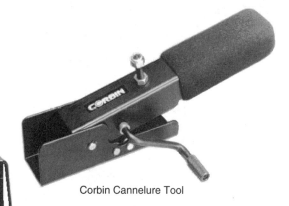

Corbin Cannelure Tool

Corbin Base Guard Kit

once the cores are formed you can turn them into any number of different styles of bullets later on. Most bullet swagers use both lead wire and casting. The wire is used for making experimental weight bullets, or when time is short and the range beckons. Cast cores are made in the summer, outdoors, on those few weekends when there is time, and used the rest of the year.

Swaging is so much more precise than casting that there is no need for resizing. You eliminate not only the lead pot, ladle, moulds and handles, but also the sizer-lubricator and lubricant. You exchange those tools for a swaging press, dies and a lead wire cutter, and either jackets, a jacket-maker kit, a base-guard kit (similar to gas checks but far more effective at removing fouling and eliminating the need for lubricant), or a liquid dip-lube. The net cost for one exact caliber, weight and style favors casting, but if you want to experiment with various weights and styles, the cost for swaging equipment is far less. How much would it cost for moulds to make every weight of 38-caliber semi-wadcutter bullet from 80 to 250 grains? One swage die does that. Changing the nose or base shape only requires a different punch, typically $20. You can make a hollow base and a hollow point at the same time with a swage die, something that is difficult with most moulds. And you can make splined, hexagon, or other unusual-shaped hollow cavities just by changing the nose-forming punch.

Some of the other advantages swaging gives you are 1) the ability to turn commonly available materials into bullets without the need for components that would be considered "reloading supplies," which could mean that taxes and restrictions on your future handloading would be reduced or eliminated; 2) the

power to design and build bullets that perform as well as or better than those currently in the news, even exotic designs made of solid copper or with extreme serrations or hollowpoint features, so you can shoot bullets that may be "banned" by adverse sentiment simply because they work too well; 3) technical advantages so great (including tolerances that average 100 times closer than cast bullets) that there is really no comparison to a cast lead bullet; and 4) the ability to quickly use the same investment in tooling to make other designs and other weights, and to use other materials if the need arises. For instance, if a high "environmental protection" tax on lead is imposed, the right swage tools let you make high quality bullets of solid copper, brass or aluminum—the anti-handloading politicians can't ban or tax *every* metal!

Bullet swaging has progressed to the point where handloaders will find an array of tools, supplies and information covering everything from the making of precision airgun pellets to production of superior 50 BMG bullets. Partitioned or multiple-jacketed bullets; bonded cores (where the jacket and the lead core are fused into a unit that cannot separate on impact); fouling-scraper "base guards" that make it possible to shoot soft lead slugs at jacketed bullet velocity without any lubrication; lightweight plastic balls that compress within the jackets to shift the balance and produce stable, lightweight bullets within the airframe of a heavy, slow projectile—all these are just a glimpse of what people are doing with swaging today. Some of them have found that swaging turns the shooting hobby into a source of income, as the demand for custom bullets continues to skyrocket. It might be worth your while to take a look at modern swaging.

Here's a movable, carefully designed loading bench that is easy to build and yet decorative in most areas. Complete plans, detailed instructions and a bill of materials are included for a...

Compact Loading Bench

by WM. F. GREIF

THE LOT OF the reloader is a happy one these days. An almost limitless variety of presses, dies, gadgets and components are available to the cartridge stuffer, excepting only one basic necessity, the reloading bench itself!

Most handloaders would, I think, agree that something in modern monolithic, about 12 feet long, would just manage to fill their needs. Unfortunately, apartment dwellers like myself are apt to have unreasonable objections raised to our erecting a functionally attractive creation of 2x12s in the living room.

Having had to face this sad situation, I was told that, if I built my little reloading center, it had damned well better be little *and* good looking, if I expected to keep it in any visible area of our home.

In laying out my plans, then, an attractive exterior, compact design and storage space were vital needs. The apartment-dwelling handloader has trouble right from the start finding enough storage space, and certainly esthetic reasons require concealment of equipment between working sessions. Weight and sturdiness were my next consideration. Weight that would keep the bench from jumping around could be attained in part by the storage of lead, bullets, cases, etc., and the use of fairly heavy structural components would also give me the sturdiness needed.

I decided on a basic closed box design, with interior shelving and a pegboard for the inside face of the door to give me maximum storage space. I also included a small cupboard on top, both for storage and to allow eye-level placement of my powder scale. The work top was drilled with various holes so that all my presses, powder measures, etc., could be securely mounted on the top. While the counter as designed is more than strong enough, a Masonite covering was added since the top is bound to become somewhat battered with the passage of time, and a detachable one is easy to replace or to refinish.

Since I am not a journeyman cabinet maker by any means, my design was planned with emphasis on the simplest forms of construction, using basic hand tools and a minimum of power equipment. The average guy, given only a bit of skill and a few tools, can attack this project with confidence. Make no mistake, though, for my construction technique, while simple, is strong. Though I used butt or lap joints, with no mortising, everything is securely glued and screwed together. The heavy shelving also contributes mightily to the strength of the bench. The work top, made of two thicknesses of ply, totals a rigid 1^1/$_2$ inches thick, not counting the Masonite.

Few Tools Needed

The plywood panel was cut on a table saw, but it could have been cut, as everything else was, with my sabre saw. I used an electric sander, which can be rented or, even better, borrowed from a friend. The only other power tool used was a ^{1}/$_4$-inch electric drill.

Of course, if you have your lumber and Masonite pre-cut and are willing to depend on elbow grease and a sanding block, the only power tool needed is the electric drill—all those screw holes make it a necessity. Incidentally, a great time and sweat saver is a little contoured spade bit made by Stanley. This marvelous gadget simultaneously cuts screwhole, shank relief hole and countersink! A bonus benefit is that each countersink is exactly the right depth. I did find that in tough ply, operations were greatly speeded by drilling a small pilot hole first.

As for finishes, I felt that a good stain varnish would be best for the interior, but the outside of the cabinet was something else. There would be so many screw heads pocking the bench surfaces that some sort of opaque finish would have to be used. Paint or lacquer wouldn't have suited our furnishings, so I used a self-adhesive, wood-grained vinyl. The one I chose, "Contact," is well known and nationally distributed. It comes in two widths, 18 inches and 27 inches. Get the wider type to avoid seams. Con-tact comes in two or three different wood grains. I chose a dark walnut. The 5^1/$_2$ yards needed cost about $6.50.

Basic material is ^{3}/$_4$-inch interior, A-D plywood. Flaws and knotholes on the D side can easily be handled with a little plastic wood. I chose plywood because of its superior strength and stiffness compared to plain lumber of like thickness. Elmer's glue was used on every joining surface, and the basic box was tied together with 8x1^1/$_2$-inch flat-head screws on 2-inch centers. (The cupboard top and the Masonite work top were fas-

Here's the pre-assembled loading bench, ready for the application of the Con-tact vinyl covering material.

tened with 8x1 inch screws; door construction and hinge used 6x^5/$_8$ inch wood screws.)

In the interest of economy, the bench was planned so that, with careful layout, all of the required pieces could be cut from one 4x10-foot sheet of plywood. Since I planned on using a pegboard door interior, hollow door construction had to be used. For the door exterior, ^{1}/$_4$-inch tempered Masonite was used with ^{1}/$_8$-inch pegboard for the inside. The two panels were spaced ^{1}/$_2$-inch apart, using ^{1}/$_2$x^3/$_4$-inch stock for framing.

A door lock was added to discourage little noses from poking around where they shouldn't. For the top cabinet, I used aluminum channels as sliding door guides, with ^{1}/$_8$-inch Masonite doors. Be sure that you get the correct door height. The measurement I give is correct for the channel used, but yours may have different dimensions. Normally, the bottom channel will be ^{1}/$_4$-inch deep and the top ^{1}/$_2$-inch, to allow for door removal. Make sure your doors are ^{5}/$_{16}$-inch shorter than the maximum groove-to-groove measurement.

I wanted my unit to be movable, so casters were indicated. I had some Fairbanks heavy-duty 3-inch rubber wheel casters on hand, so I used them. Locking casters would be better, but those

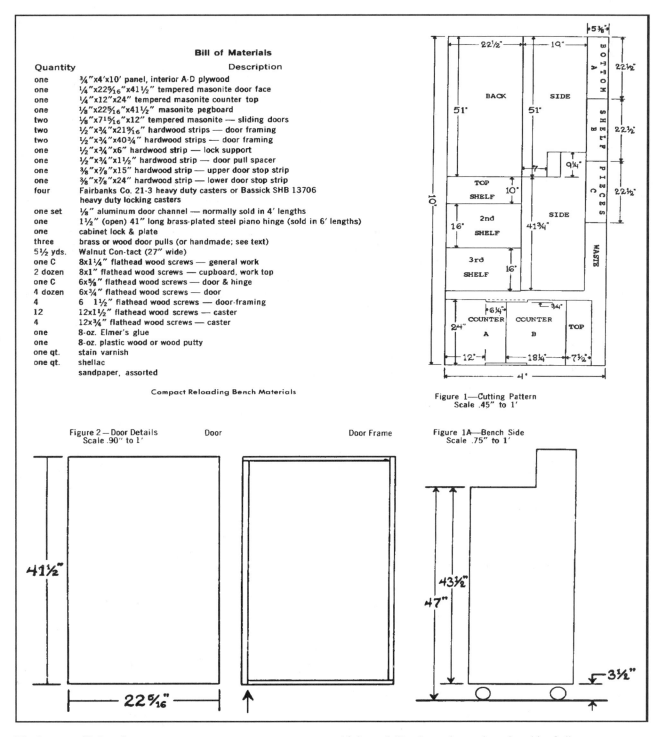

Bill of Materials

Quantity	Description
one	¾"x4'x10' panel, interior A-D plywood
one	¼"x22⁵⁄₁₆"x41½" tempered masonite door face
one	¼"x12"x24" tempered masonite counter top
one	⅛"x22⁵⁄₁₆"x41½" masonite pegboard
two	⅛"x7¹⁵⁄₁₆"x12" tempered masonite — sliding doors
two	½"x¾"x21⁹⁄₁₆" hardwood strips — door framing
two	½"x¾"x40¾" hardwood strips — door framing
one	½"x¾"x6" hardwood strip — lock support
one	½"x¾"x1½" hardwood strip — door pull spacer
one	⅜"x⅞"x15" hardwood strip — upper door stop strip
one	⅜"x⅞"x24" hardwood strip — lower door stop strip
four	Fairbanks Co. 21-3 heavy duty casters or Bassick SHB 13706 heavy duty locking casters
one set	⅛" aluminum door channel — normally sold in 4' lengths
one	1½" (open) 41' long brass-plated steel piano hinge (sold in 6' lengths)
one	cabinet lock & plate
three	brass or wood door pulls (or handmade; see text)
5½ yds.	Walnut Con-tact (27" wide)
one C	8x1¼" flathead wood screws — general work
2 dozen	8x1" flathead wood screws — cupboard, work top
one C	6x⅝" flathead wood screws — door & hinge
4 dozen	6x¾" flathead wood screws — door
4	6 1½" flathead wood screws — door-framing
12	12x1½" flathead wood screws — caster
4	12x¾" flathead wood screws — caster
one	8-oz. Elmer's glue
one	8-oz. plastic wood or wood putty
one qt.	stain varnish
one qt.	shellac
	sandpaper, assorted

Compact Reloading Bench Materials

Figure 1—Cutting Pattern
Scale .45" to 1'

Figure 2 — Door Details
Scale .90" to 1'

Door

Door Frame

Figure 1A—Bench Side
Scale .75" to 1'

I had were sufficient for my purpose.

Because of the weight of the door when loaded with tools and other bric-a-brac, a piano hinge was used. Brass-plated steel is preferred to solid brass, both for its superior strength and much lower price. Piano hinge is only sold in 6-foot lengths, so you'll have to cut it to size and think up another project.

Standard cabinet knobs can be used for the doors, but for a distinctive touch I used 38 Special cases for the sliding cupboard doors and a 30-06 for the large door. Shotshell bases could also be used, say 12-gauge and 410, but no knobs are required, really. The door-lock key could serve well.

I designed the bench to be used while standing or seated on a high stool. For those chores that take a bit of elbow grease, you can't beat getting off your butt and on to your feet.

Please note that I am 6 feet 2 inches tall and that you might want to make some adjustment in bench height to suit your dimensions. Just leaving off the casters lowers the bench 3¾ inches. I suggest setting up a mock work surface, at various heights, and decide for yourself.

Construction Notes

Now for the actual construction. Be extremely careful when laying out your cuts on the sheet of ply. There is little room for error, so check and recheck your layout before putting a saw to the panel, and don't forget to allow for the saw cuts (kerfs) by adding the width of the teeth of your saw in figuring your layout. First, cut off the counter and top pieces, then cut the rest into the component pieces.

It's a good idea to pre-sand the bench parts, otherwise you'll find yourself scrunching into some pretty weird positions trying to finish those awkward spots.

Cut the rest of your material: Masonite, door framing, etc. In some cases, we'll cut and fit certain parts, but we won't install them permanently until we get to the final stage of applying the Con-tact. More on that later.

Assemble the sides and back with glue and screws, remembering that the back goes *between* the sides. Continue by putting in the shelves. The short (10-inch) shelf was made shallower than the others to allow storage of my RCBS A2 press, which is held to the shelf with a "C" clamp. Spacing of the shelves is not critical. I spaced mine about 10 inches apart. Just remember to align the underside of the bottom shelf flush with the bottom of the bench as it will form part of the support for the casters.

To provide sufficient strength, the 8x1¼-inch screws should be spaced no more than 3 inches apart through the sides and back. Next, glue and screw the counter pieces together and attach to the bench proper. Lightly tack the cupboard top in place with a few brads, drill the attaching screw holes, then remove the cupboard top. Cut the door tracks to fit, but do not attach. Clamp the Masonite top to the counter and drill for the attaching screws. This is also the time to drill the top for the tool mounting holes. Plan carefully and use as few holes as possible.

Cut the Masonite-pegboard doors and check for fit. Next, build the main door frame, with lock reinforcement. If it seems rather flimsy, don't worry. The door will get its rigidity from the Masonite facings. Now fit the front and permanently attach it to the framing with the usual glue and screws. Next, carefully position the wooden block that will act as the door knob spacer and reinforcement, and nail and glue it to the inside of the door face. Now, temporarily attach the inside face and drill it and the frame for the mounting screws. Next, drill through the door sandwich for the door knob screw and for the lock cylinder, then remove the inner face. I placed the lock 16 inches from the top of the door to the center of the lock. The length of the door stop pieces in the bill of materials reflects this positioning, so if you decide to reposition the lock, be sure to alter the length of the two door stop pieces to match. Cut the piano hinge and fit it to the inside of the left wall so that the door can be opened to a full 180 degrees. Mark the bench and door, and drill both for the hinge screws. With this done, fill all the screw holes, cracks, etc., with plastic wood or wood putty. Let it dry thoroughly, at least for 24 hours, before sanding. Then sand the entire bench. Be sure that all spots you filled are level, and slightly chamfer all the outside edges.

With the construction and sanding completed, we have only to apply our finish.

Con-tact Vinyl Finish

Con-tact won't adhere to raw wood, so all surfaces to be covered must receive a coat of shellac to seal them. For those surfaces not to be covered by Con-tact, brush on one (preferably two) coats of stain varnish. Let dry for several days so that the varnish and shellac are good and hard.

Before applying the Con-tact, read the directions printed on the backing material, and keep these hints in mind when you start using the stuff.

When cutting the material, allow enough extra for folding over the edges, and when actually laying the Con-tact, be sure that the surfaces to be covered are scrupulously clean. I found that tiny pieces of grit will stick out like a sore thumb. Work in a clean area and, when you are about to apply a piece of Con-tact, wipe the surface with a clean, lint-free cloth. If despite your precautions you should miss some debris, the Con-tact can be carefully pulled up and relaid. Pull off the backing little by little, as you apply the covering, and press it down with a soft cloth to eliminate bubbles and avoid stretching.

Now we come to the reason for not completely assembling the bench during construction. By covering the various portions of the bench and *then* doing our final assembly, we hide and firmly fasten the edges of the Con-tact under the joints, hinges and so on.

First cover the cupboard top. Screw the upper aluminum track to it and set it aside. Now cover the front edge of the countertop. After that, cover the sides, working from the bottom up. On the side where the hinge will fasten, be sure that the Con-tact laps around a hair less than the width of the hinge. On the opposing side, carry the vinyl around on the inside so that its edge will be covered and secured by the door stop strips.

Cover the door, attach the pegboard backing (which will seal down the edges of the Con-tact) and attach the hinge. An easy way to find the screw-holes covered by the Con-tact is to press along the area with your fingers, making a depression at each hole and then pierce the spots with a pointed tool. Cover the small sliding doors, attach the knobs and you're ready to finish our assembly.

Attach the Masonite work top and the lower sliding door track. Hang the main door and then attach the cupboard top. Use a razor blade to trim away the excess material over the screw holes. If you drilled your screw holes carefully, the screws will pull up flush, or very slightly below the surface. I used a ½-inch wadcutter to cut pieces of Con-tact to cover the screw heads, which gives a doweled effect.

Now coat the lock bolt edge with a marking medium such as chalk. Close and align the door so that it is flush with the front edge of the right wall, and turn the lock so that the bolt will make a clear impression on the inside wall. Use your razor and cut away enough Con-tact to clear the bolt, then cut a recess in the side wall for it. With that done, attach the lock-plate.

The last items are the stop strips. Cover them with Con-tact, carefully measure the thickness of the door, then lightly tack the upper strip in place, the thickness of the door from the edge. Check the accuracy of the placement, then nail permanently in place. Follow the same procedure with the lower strip.

All that's left to do is to reattach the casters, which I hope you removed when you were applying the covering to the sides.

As a finishing touch, I bought an unfinished bar stool and finished it to match, complete with a foam rubber, Naugahyde-covered seat.

The completed project has been a great success. It gives me a lot of bench in a very small space (3 square feet to be exact), yet it isn't an eyesore to the rest of the family.

So, if you've stuck with me this far, put your tool hooks on the door, load the cabinet with your reloading equipment and get to it!

If you need
a handgun that
will handle widely
differing loads
and doesn't
depend on
perfect ammo for
functioning, as an
autoloader does,
remember that...

Revolvers Are Omniverous

by JOHN HAVILAND

WITH ANY HALFWAY suitable powder, bullet and reloading technique, revolvers produce fine performance for a variety of uses from plinking to target shooting to hunting. That statement can be made about few, if any, autoloaders.

When I bought my 41 Magnum Ruger Blackhawk, I loaded 220-grain bullets for it right up to the maximum with Alliant (Hercules) 2400 powder. The load worked fine for hunting deer and an occasional coyote. After a couple of years, though, the thought dawned that all that power was unnecessary for most of my shooting, which was punching paper targets and cans. So for target loads, I switched to a light amount of Unique powder. Velocity of the bullets dropped to a more manageable 1000 feet per second. The minor change of powder created a much more useful handgun.

The Unique load took up almost the same amount of space in the 41 cases as the maximum charge of 2400, even though the Unique weighed less than half of the 2400. My rather incomplete records show that loading bulky powders like Unique,

Fast or slow, revolvers shoot a variety of bullet weights and powders.

Red Dot and others produce more uniform velocities with min-imum-speed loads than using reduced amounts of the "magnum pistol" powders like 2400, Winchester 296 and Hodgdon 110. With a fairly full case, the powder is positioned about the same for every shot.

Some of my favorite powders for maximum loads for revolver cartridges from the 32 H&R Magnum up through the 44 Remington Magnum include H-4227, 296, H-110 and 2400. For reduced-velocity loads, Unique, Red Dot, 231, HS6 and even Winchester Action Pistol (WAP) powder, intended for autoloading handguns, are excellent.

The variety of bullet designs that revolvers readily shoot is what makes wheelguns truly versatile. Bullet shapes are insignificant. Once a loaded cartridge is placed in the chamber of the cylinder, it is ready to fire, unlike autoloading handguns that may require a specific point shape to smoothly feed a car-tridge from the magazine to chamber.

My 357 Magnum revolver shoots every style and weight of bullet from 110- to 160-grain jacketed bullets to swaged lead wadcutters and bullets cast from lead alloys. The heavier bullets for a given caliber, though, produce somewhat more consistent velocities and accuracy.

Much fuss has been made about bullet diameters exactly matching the bore diameters for the best accuracy. But when I first started to reload for my 32 H&R Magnum I didn't have any .312-inch bullets. However, I did have a box of Speer .308-inch 110-grain hollowpoints. A friend of mine said Speer .308-inch 100-grain bullets shot accurately through his Smith & Wesson 32 S&W Long, so I decided to give them a try.

The first problem to overcome was loading the smaller diam-eter bullets because they dropped right through the case mouths with the cases properly sized to accept .312-inch bullets. I could have gone to the expense of buying a smaller diameter expander plug to accommodate the .308-inch bullets, but I didn't. Instead, I turned the expanding plug out of the die so it only slightly opened the case mouth. That allowed the bullets to enter the cases, although rather loosely. With the correct amount of pow-der in the cases, I seated the bullets and crimped the case mouths in the bullet cannelures. The undersize bullets rotated freely in the cases, which concerned me about their accuracy.

But the .308-inch bullets surprised me. At the range, my Ruger SP101 in 32 H&R shot five-shot groups of 2.25, 1.56 and 1.85 inches at 25 yards, loaded with WAP powder, and 2.9 inches with Unique.

A month later I got my hands on a box of Speer .312-inch 100-grain bullets. I used them with five different powders. Five-shot groups at 25 yards went like this—2.73 inches with HS-6, 4.14 with Red Dot, 3.0 with Unique, 2.17 with 296 and 1.56 with WAP. That was no better, and with some powders worse, than the supposedly undersize .308-inch bullets.

The advice has generally been that a bullet will probably be inaccurate if it's smaller in diameter than the cylinder mouth of the revolver. The .308-inch bullets dropped right through the cylinder mouths of the Ruger, but the .312s bullets didn't. Yet both sizes shot roughly the same.

That made me wonder about the diameters of the chamber mouths and bore of the Ruger revolver. I drove a lead slug through one of the chambers and another down the bore. The chamber mouth measured .311, and the grooves of the barrel, 312-inch.

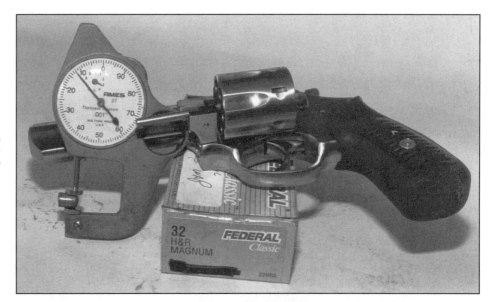

The grooves of the barrel of this S&W 44 Magnum measured .429-inch, and bullets from .429- to .431-inch shot fine.

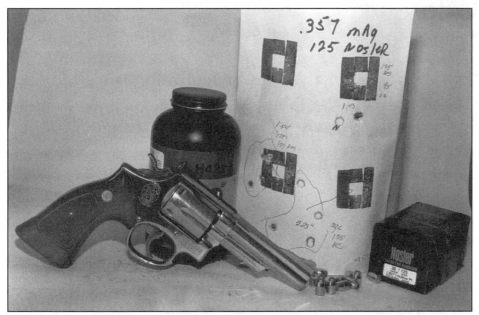

Trying different powders in a revolver shows which one groups best for a particular bullet, in this case the 357 Magnum and 125-grain Nosler bullets.

A cast bullet from the RCBS 41-210-SWC mould for the 41 Magnum can be loaded on the mild side with Unique for target practice or to the max with 296 for hunting.

The Nosler .429-inch 200-grain HP dropped right through the chamber mouths of the Model 29 S&W 44 Magnum, yet shot great.

A revolver can tame the mighty 44 Magnum by loading and shooting round balls (left) for short range plinking, or you can load it with a heavy charge of powder and let it rip with 200-grain Noslers (center) or 250-grain cast bullets (right).

That caused me to consider the dimensions of my 44 Magnum Smith & Wesson Model 29. A lead slug pushed through one cylinder chamber measured .431; another pushed through the bore showed the grooves measured .429.

A Nosler .429-inch 200-grain hollowpoint bullet dropped right through the chamber mouths of the 44. Yet just the front band of a .431-inch cast bullet fit into them. Still, both bullets shot very well. Five Noslers went into 1.1 inches at 25 yards with a load of Unique, 2.0 inches with H-4227 and 2.2 with 296. The cast bullets grouped into 1.1 with H-4227, 2.36 (four in 1.53) with HS-6, 2.15 with 296, and 2.95 (four in 1.5) with Unique.

The 32 Ruger had smaller chamber mouths than its bore grooves, while the Smith & Wesson was the other way around. Yet both shot fine. The conclusion is that everyone should shoot a variety of bullets with an assortment of powders to develop an accurate load for a revolver.

Jacketed handgun bullets have been widely used only in the last twenty-five years or so. They are very accurate because of their uniform diameters and weights. They are also clean to shoot because their copper jackets require no messy lubrication as lead bullets do. However, the velocity of jacketed bullets must be kept above 800 fps to overcome the friction of the bul-

let in the bore. A load with insufficient pressure may cause the bullet to lodge in the bore.

The current trend in jacketed handgun bullets is toward expanding bullets. That's the wrong direction for hunting big game with the 357, 41 and 44 Magnums. These revolver cartridges lack the energy much past fifty yards to expand a bullet and at the same time penetrate deeply through game.

The whitetail, mule deer and one black bear I have shot with the 41 and 44 Magnums all quickly died when shot with semi-wadcutter (SWC) jacketed bullets. As near as I could see, the bullets retained their original shape and punched a clean hole in one side of the ribs, through the lungs, and out the far ribs.

That's no surprise. Handgun hunters have killed big game for decades with hard cast SWC or "Keith shaped" bullets.

Ultimately, bullets cast of lead alloy are what make revolvers so flexible.

I shoot a 213-grain SWC bullet cast of wheelweights in my Ruger 41 Magnum when I go to the range for an afternoon of stopping determined charges from a row of cans. Five grains of WAP gives the bullets a velocity of a mere 629 fps. Recoil is negligible, and the cans give up long before I do.

During October and November, I strap the 41 on my belt when I hunt a river bottom thicket for whitetails. The 41 is

The chamber mouths of the S&W 44 Magnum measured .431-inch and the grooves of the bore .429-inch, but the gun accurately shot a variety of bullets. The old advice has always been that a bullet that was narrower in diameter than the chamber mouths of a revolver would give poor accuracy, which is not the case here.

The 44 Magnum loaded with 250-grain cast bullets and a mild charge of powder is great for targets; loaded with a maximum charge of H-4227, it's great for deer and bear.

loaded with the same cast bullets, but with 21 grains of 296 powder for a velocity of 1382 fps.

One season I had both buck and doe licenses, so I planned on shooting the first deer that ran my way. The first morning I waited along the edge of an opening for my friends to push deer out of a jungle of willows. A doe jumped from cover and ran toward me. As she ran past at about 25 yards, I swung the sights of the 41 past her chest and fired. The bullet hit too far back, but slowed her. My second shot dropped the doe in the tall grass.

I gave a friend a box of 38 Specials loaded with 151-grain SWC bullets cast of wheelweights. So far he has killed three mule deer. One took two shots, while the other two required only one shot each. He thinks the loads are great for deer. In spite of his success, I think 38 Special loads are borderline at best.

If maximum velocity is wanted, cast bullets can be driven faster than jacketed bullets of the same weight with the same amount of powder. Lead alloy bullets being driven down the bore offer less resistance than the harder copper jacketed ones. As a result, more of the pressure from the burning powder is put into velocity instead of overcoming friction in the bore. A 213-grain cast bullet in my 41 Magnum produces an average veloc-

ity of 1379 fps. Yet a Sierra 210-grain jacketed bullet with the same charge of H-4227 produces 1309 fps.

Many shooters turn up their nose at cast bullets. They think the bullets will clog up the barrel of their handguns with lead that is impossible to remove without some sort of nuclear reaction. They may be confusing soft swaged lead bullets, which do leave streaks of lead if they are driven much over 800 fps, with hard cast bullets.

I have cast bullets with a variety of alloys from as soft as 1 part tin to 15 parts lead to as hard as linotype with excellent results. I usually cast with plain wheelweights because the metal is inexpensive and easy to obtain, and it makes good bullets. After shooting 150 wheelweight bullets through my 357 Magnum, a smidgen of lead shows at the start of the rifling where the bullets first slam into the bore. A brush wipes it right out.

My Lyman #429244 mould casts bullets to accept gas checks. When I first used these bullets for my 44 Magnum, I left the gas checks off. I thought that if the bullets left any lead in the bore I could always add gas checks to the next batch and never have to worry about leading. So far, the gas checks have gone unused.

Work is the only drawback to using cast bullets. Mixing alloys, casting, sizing and lubricating the bullets takes time. I like the work for the satisfaction of making my own bullets, sort

A cast bullet, like these from an RCBS 32-098-SWC mould for the 32 H&R, can be driven fast or slow to make a good target or hunting load.

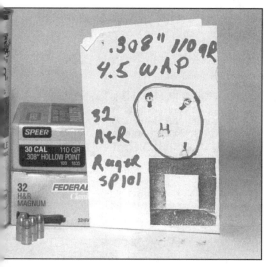

The distance across the grooves in the barrel of this Ruger SP101 in 32 H&R measured .312-inch. Bullets from .308- to .314-inch shot well through the gun.

REVOLVER LOADS

—Bullet—		Load	Primer	Case	Velocity
Wgt. Grs.	Type	(Grs./Powder)			(fps)
32 H&R Magnum, Ruger Single-Six, 5½" barrel					
115/Lyman #311316[1]		7.3/W-630	CCI-500	Fed.	1012
		9.2/296	CCI-500	Fed.	1022
32 H&R Magnum, Ruger SP101, 4" barrel					
118/Lyman #311316[1] (sized .313")		9.2/296	Rem. 1½	Fed	1071
		4.0/HS6	Rem. 1½	Fed.	764
		3.5/Unique	Rem. 1½	Fed.	857
		4.0/Unique	Rem. 1½	Fed.	952
110/Speer .308" JHP		4.5/WAP	Rem. 1½	Fed.	757
		4.4/Unique	Rem 1½	Fed.	886
100/Speer .312" JHP		6.0/HS6	Rem. 1½	Fed.	1019
		3.5/Red Dot	Rem. 1½	Fed.	907
		4.4/Unique	Rem. 1½	Fed.	993
		9.5/296	Rem. 1½	Fed.	929
		5.0/WAP	Rem. 1½	Fed.	993
100/RCBS #32-098-SWC (sized .313")		4.5/HS6	Rem. 1½	Fed.	854
		4.0/Unique	Rem. 1½	Fed.	966
		2.5/Unique	Rem. 1½	Fed.	660
		9.0/H-4227	Rem. 1½	Fed.	1039
		4.5/WAP	Rem. 1½	Fed.	950
98/Speer .314" lead HBWC[2]		2.8/Unique	Rem. 1½	Fed.	653
98/Speer .314" lead HBWC[3]		2.8/Unique	Rem. 1½	Fed.	846
		2.0/Red Dot	Rem. 1½	Fed.	742
		6.0/HS6	Rem. 1½	Fed.	1128
		3.5/WAP	Rem. 1½	Fed.	884
38 Special, S&W Model 19, 4" barrel					
125/Nosler JHP		14.0/H-4227	Rem. 1½	Win.	1014
		6.0/Unique	Rem. 1½	Win.	904
151/RCBS #38-150-SWC (sized .357")		3.5/WAP	Rem. 1½	Win.	480
		4.0/WAP	Rem. 1½	Win.	519
		4.5/WAP	Rem. 1½	Win.	658
		5.0/WAP	Rem. 1½	Win.	753
		5.5/WAP	Rem. 1½	Win.	825
		6.0/WAP	Rem. 1½	Win.	917
		4.0/Unique	CCI-500	Rem.	578
		3.7/W-231	CCI-500	Win.	699
		4.0/W-231	CCI-500	Win.	752
		4.2/W-231	CCI-500	Win.	806
		5.0/HS6	Rem. 1½	Win.	1030
		13.0/H-4227	Rem. 1½	Win.	1030
158/Nosler JHP		5.4/Unique	Rem. 1½	Win.	838
		12.5/H-4227	Rem. 1½	Win.	973

of like catching a trout on a fly tied by your own hand. But for those who would rather spend their time shooting, small shops that cast and sell bullets have sprung up all over the country. When sloth overcomes me, I buy mine from Cast King, of Alberton, Montana. Their bullets are as good as any I could ever hope to cast.

The reloader is free to experiment somewhat with the final dimensions and length of his loaded cartridges.

Cases usually wear out with splits on the mouth from repeated flaring to accept the bullet and crimping to securely hold it. Crimping supposedly keeps the bullet from pulling out of the case from recoil of a fired shot. Crimps also presumably provide resistance so heavy weights of relatively slow-burning powders, like 2400 and 296, burn completely for consistent velocities.

With light loads such as Red Dot in my 41 Magnum, I leave the case mouths uncrimped. A crimp is also unnecessary with some magnum loads here. After firing five magnum rounds of 17.5 grains of 2400 powder and 213-grain cast bullets, the sixth bullet always remains tight in its case. Uncrimped loads average 1294 fps with a standard deviation of 18. The same load with a heavy crimp clocks 1282 fps and also has a standard deviation of 18.

However, my 44 Magnum requires a heavy crimp to keep its bullets in place, despite the fact that the expander plug of the reloading die sizes the inside of the case walls .005-inch under bullet diameter. Giving each load a road test is the only way to find out if it works in your revolver.

When I first loaded Speer 98-grain wadcutters in my 32 Magnum, I seated the cylinder-shaped bullets flush with the case mouth, as recommended. Still, I worried that the bullets might enter the forcing cone at a slight angle and ruin their accuracy if they had so far to jump. To find out, I loaded forty cases with Unique and seated twenty wadcutters flush with the case mouths for an overall length of 1.075. The remaining twenty were loaded to a length of 1.24-inch, just short enough so the front edge of the bullets fit against the taper at the entrance of the cylinder mouths.

REVOLVER LOADS

—Bullet—		Load	Primer	Case	Velocity
Wgt. Grs.	Type	(Grs./Powder)			(fps)
357 Magnum, S&W Model 19, 4″ barrel					
125/Nosler JHP		19.0/296	Rem. 1½	Fed.	1275
		17.5/H-4227	Rem. 1½	Fed.	1219
		8.0/Unique	Rem. 1½	Fed.	1248
151/RCBS #38-150-SWC (sized .357″)		5.0/WAP	Rem. 1½	Win.	624
		5.5/WAP	Rem. 1½	Win.	748
		6.0/WAP	Rem. 1½	Win.	789
		6.5/WAP	Rem. 1½	Win.	913
		7.0/WAP	Rem. 1½	Win.	960
		7.5/WAP	Rem. 1½	Win.	1024
		14.0/296	Rem. 1½	Fed.	1273
		15.0/H-4227	Rem. 1½	Fed.	1125
		4.0/Unique	Rem. 1½	Fed.	610
		6.0/HS6	Rem. 1½	Fed.	753
158/Nosler JHP		14.5/296	Rem. 1½	Fed.	1022
		14.5/H-4227	Rem. 1½	Fed.	1063
		7.5/Unique	Rem. 1½	Fed.	1067
41 Remington Magnum, Ruger Blackhawk, 6½″ barrel					
170/Sierra JHC		23.0/296	CCI-300	Rem.	1302
210/Sierra JHC		21.0/296	CCI-300	Rem.	1225
		21.0/H-4227	CCI-300	Rem.	1309
213/RCBS #41-210-SWC (sized .410″)		5.0/WAP	WLP	Win.	629
		6.0/WAP	WLP	Win.	750
		7.0/WAP	WLP	Win.	863
		8.0/WAP	WLP	Win.	987
		7.0/Red Dot	CCI-300	Rem.	1066
		7.0/Red Dot	CCI-350	Rem.	1069
		8.0/Red Dot	CCI-300	Rem.	1142
		21.0/296	CCI-300	Win.	1257
		21.0/296	CCI-350	Win.	1382
		15.0/2400	CCI-300	Win.	1089
		18.0/2400[4]	CCI-300	Win.	1294
		18.0/2400[5]	CCI-300	Win.	1282
		7.0/Unique	CCI-300	Rem.	930
		8.0/Unique	CCI-300	Rem.	1051
		8.0/HS6	CCI-300	Rem.	883
		21.0/H-4227	CCI-300	Rem.	1379
210/Win. Factory JSP		21.0/H-4227	CCI-300	Rem.	1322
44 Remington Magnum, S&W Model 29, 6″ barrel					
200/Nosler JHP		10.5/Unique	CCI-300	Win.	1067
		27.0/H-4227	CCI-300	Win.	1348
		26.5/296	CCI-300	Win.	1302
240/Speer JHP		10.3/Unique	CCI-300	Win.	1204
250/Lyman #429244 (sized .431″)		8.0/Unique	CCI-300	Win.	711
		10.0/HS6	CCI-300	Win.	892
		22.0/296	CCI-300	Win.	1205
		23.0/H-4227	CCI-300	Win.	1266

Fed. = Federal, Rem. = Remington, Win. = Winchester, WAP = Winchester Action Pistol, WLP = Winchester Large Pistol.
[1] Gas check bullet.   [2] 1.24″ O.A.L.   [3] 1.075″ O.A.L.   [4] No crimp.   [5] Heavy crimp.

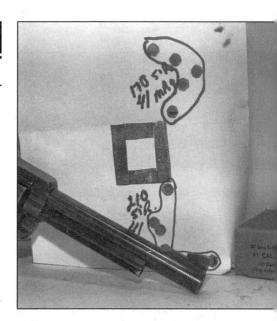

Different weight bullets may have a different trajectory, so adjustable sights are a plus on a versatile revolver. The 41 Magnum 170-grain Sierra bullets are the top group; Sierra 210-grain bullets the bottom.

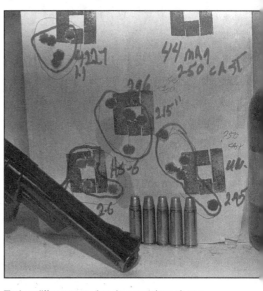

Trying different powders in a revolver shows which one groups bullets the best. In this case, the S&W 44 Magnum preferred H-4227 with 250-grain cast bullets.

There wasn't a dime's worth of difference in accuracy between the different seating depths. Yet the flush-seated wadcutters had a velocity of 846 fps, while the longer cartridges shrank to 653 fps.

Primers can also affect velocity. Usually, though, the gains are limited to magnum cartridges with heavy charges of slow powders.

With 21 grains of 296 powder under a 213-grain cast bullet in my 41 Magnum, CCI magnum primers gain 125 fps over standard CCI primers. On the other hand, magnum primers showed an average increase of only 3 fps over standard primers when fired with 7 grains of Red Dot and the 213-grain bullet.

When I bought my Ruger 32 H&R, I thought of it as sort of a centerfire 22 Long Rifle, good for blue grouse along the trail. The first spring I had the gun, I loaded a few hundred rounds with 100-grain cast bullets. At 1000 fps, they drilled right through ground squirrels. Then I remembered a colony of marmots living in a rockslide face in the mountains. I loaded up a batch of 118-grain cast bullets. They stopped even the most determined rockchuck. During the heat of summer I shot targets with 98-grain wadcutters in the Ruger to sharpen my eye.

Before I realized it, the various bullets and powders had made the Ruger into a very versatile handgun. Then again, it was a revolver, so what do you expect?

The blackpowder cartridge was a link between the muzzleloader and the modern smokeless round. Today, a large number of marksmen are once again shooting these old designs with blackpowder.

Loading the Blackpowder Cartridge

by SAM FADALA

THE BLACKPOWDER CARTRIDGE has gained considerable ground over the past several years. There are at least three major reasons. The first is extended availability of blackpowder cartridge rifles. Importation of Sharps replicas, for example, has increased recently with several companies, such as Armsport, offering various models of the Italian-made Sharps rifle. McMillan Gunworks, well-known for its 1/2-inch-at-100-yard guarantee with modern rifles, extends a similar promise for its Antietam Sharps, which is chambered for the 40-65 Winchester or 45-70 Government cartridge. Naturally, McMillan's claim is for the rifle, not the shooter. Half-inch groups mean the rifle is fired from a solid bench, by a good marksman, and with a scope sight, which is only fair. McMillan is not shy about its Sharps rifle, saying, "Know the thrill of taking plains game at long range or knocking down the rams at 500 yards [meters] with a single shot, blackpowder cartridge, iron sights and a lead alloy cast bullet."

A second reason for the rise in blackpowder cartridge interest is the silhouette target game. There is a special match for the

Today, shooting the blackpowder cartridge rifle means handloading. Of course, in the 19th and early 20th century, blackpowder cartridges were factory-made.

blackpowder cartridge, exclusively. This Mexican-born shooting contest has been popular for many years in the United States, with several offshoots from the original game, including pistol and rimfire rifle *metalica* matches. The fact that the blackpowder cartridge has its own silhouette theme is not surprising since long-range blackpowder cartridge rifles of the past were entirely capable of high performance. The breech-loading blackpowder rifle brings a lot of interest to this already interesting shooting sport, where metallic silhouettes are fired at, the object being to knock them over at ranges up to 500 meters.

Third, big game hunting with single shot blackpowder cartridge rifles has gained a larger following.

The Basics

No single chapter in any book can do justice to the subject of loading the blackpowder cartridge. This chapter is presented to give the blackpowder fan some background, as well as a get-started posture. As with muzzleloaders, blackpowder cartridge shooting entails considerable hands-on application. Muzzleloaders are often thought of as simple, and perhaps they are, in design. But it is the modern cartridge firearm that offers simplicity—put ammo in the gun and shoot. The muzzleloader requires specific "handloading" of every round. The blackpowder cartridge also demands personal attention. You definitely do not pour black-

powder, Pyrodex or Black Canyon powder into a case; seat a bullet; and fire away. There's a lot more to it than that. We're still learning how to get the most from the blackpowder cartridge.

The Cartridge Case

Special attention to the cartridge case is imperative for safe and successful blackpowder cartridge loading and shooting. New brass is available once again for a number of older rounds. In many instances, old-time cartridges never went away. For example, 44-40 Winchester brass is readily available, brand new. So is 38-55 Winchester brass, and 32-40 Winchester, another good blackpowder cartridge from yesteryear. Cartridge cases for the 45-70 are easily found, also in brand-new manufacture. Meanwhile, Mast Technology in Las Vegas, Nevada, offers new brass cases which can be formed into a number of old-time cartridge configurations.

Old brass, however, can be a problem. In the first place, old cartridge cases may be weakened from corrosion or normal metal fatigue. In the second place, some older brass has the balloon-type head with less metal in the head area than the modern-style case. Remember, the head of the case is the end where the primer goes, so the balloon case, though it held more powder, was weaker in design. Because the balloon-head case could hold more powder than the modern, stronger case, load designations from

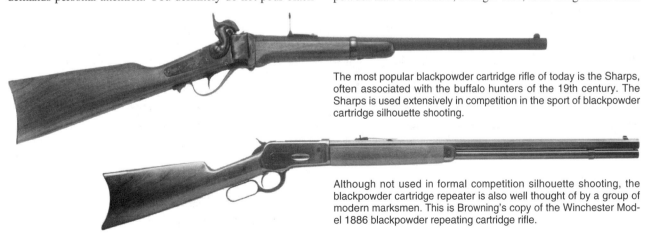

The most popular blackpowder cartridge rifle of today is the Sharps, often associated with the buffalo hunters of the 19th century. The Sharps is used extensively in competition in the sport of blackpowder cartridge silhouette shooting.

Although not used in formal competition silhouette shooting, the blackpowder cartridge repeater is also well thought of by a group of modern marksmen. This is Browning's copy of the Winchester Model 1886 blackpowder repeating cartridge rifle.

A first step in reloading the blackpowder cartridge is finding the correct shellholder. This one is for the 45-70 Government cartridge.

First, the fired cartridge must be resized, either full-length (the entire length of the case) or partially, which is sometimes called neck resizing only. The appropriate sizing die is used in the reloading press to accomplish this job.

the past don't always pan out exactly today. For example, old-time 44-40 brass did hold 40 grains of blackpowder. Remember the nomenclature. A 44-40 meant 44-caliber with 40 grains of blackpowder. Never mind that the 44-40 was not 44-caliber; that's still how rounds were named. The 45-70—another popular example—meant caliber 45, which it was, and 70 grains of blackpowder, which the old balloon-head case readily held.

Most modern 44-40 brass won't take much over 35 grains of FFFg, however, and I can't seem to get more than about 67 grains of FFg in some 45-70 Government cases. The 5-grain difference in the 44-40 is meaningful, but nothing to be concerned about. The 3-grain difference in the 45-70 is also not very meaningful, and I have been able to get 70 grains of powder in certain 45-70 cases on occasion. The only reason I mention the differences in old-time brass capacity over new is the fact that shooters may be frustrated trying to stuff in more powder than the newer case design is capable of holding. Furthermore, I see no reason to compact powder into the case. It simply is not worth the bother. Don't do it. One more thing: You'll need room for some sort of lubrication disc. So don't worry about getting that last grain of powder in the case just because the old-time designation suggests a certain powder capacity. Also, see "100-Percent Load Density" below for an explanation of case capacity and good loads.

Because of the problems just described concerning balloon-head cases, it is easy to see that old-time loading data may not work precisely for us today. Simply stated, powder charges rec-ommended in the past may not fit into modern cartridge cases. This is not a problem because the differences are slight, and if there is a loss in velocity, it is of no practical importance. As for balloon-head cases, do not use them. They have been known to split upon firing. Keep them as interesting items of your cartridge collection, but nothing more.

Powder and Granulations for the Blackpowder Cartridge

The powders found useful in blackpowder cartridge cases for this study were blackpowder, both GOEX and Elephant Brand, Pyrodex, and Black Canyon powder. All granulations were used with success. For example, smaller calibers did well with FFFg and Pyrodex P. Larger cases did well with FFg and RS. However, CTG and Fg were decided upon as the best of all granulations for calibers 40 and larger. Absolute proof remains lacking on this factor, however, and other shooters much prefer smaller granulation powder, even in big bores, due to their penchant to burn a bit cleaner. As far as my shooting is concerned, there was evidence of best accuracy with CTG and Fg powder granulations over smaller granulations. Evidence, I said. Not proof. Incidentally, Black Canyon has only one granulation, so granulation factors do not apply to that powder. Personally speaking, if I were limited to only one Pyrodex granulation, it would be CTG for the cartridge. If I were limited to only one blackpowder granulation, it would be Fg for the cartridge. Other shooters would, and do, disagree strongly with that assessment.

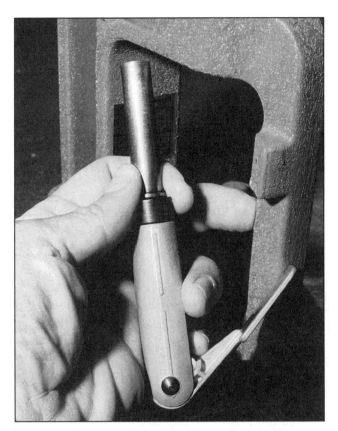

Normally, the cartridge case is deprimed (old primer expelled) during the sizing operation. Now, the case must receive a new primer. One way of priming is with a hand tool. These allow a "feel" for the correct seating of the primer to just the right depth in the primer pocket.

100-Percent Load Density

Benchrest shooters who are out to set world records with astonishingly small groups consider 100-percent load density important to accuracy. This is not to say that air space within a cartridge case precludes accuracy. For example, a particularly accurate 30-06 load I like happens to be 50.0 grains of IMR-4350 powder behind a 190-grain bullet. That is not a case full of powder. However, for uniformity and safety, plus accuracy considerations, I have gone to 100-percent load density with all blackpowder cartridges. This simply means that the case is full of powder, with no space left over. Once again, proof is difficult to come by, but some dedicated blackpowder cartridge shooters feel that air space in the case can cause erratic powder combustion.

Benchrest shooters also talk about the *shape* of the powder charge with regard to accuracy. They believe that a shorter, "fatter" powder charge is more conducive to accuracy than a long, narrow powder charge. A look at the 6mm PPC cartridge, which has cleaned house in benchrest competition over the past several years, shows a rather squat cartridge case. When this case is filled with powder, which it is for competitive shooting, the shape of the powder charge is also short and squat, not long and narrow. Most blackpowder cartridges are of the long and narrow configuration, because they need the powder capacity to gain anything like reasonable muzzle velocity. However, with 100-percent load density, uniformity in powder charge shape is assured. The powder charge maintains the same configuration at all times.

(Above) Of extreme importance to the sizing operation is case sizing lubricant. This RCBS lube is well-recognized as one of the best on the market. Without lube, a cartridge case can become stuck in the sizing die, severely stuck, requiring case removal steps and special tools to free it. The author prefers to lightly apply by rubbing the case in the palm of the hand with a small amount of lube.

A drop tube, like this Shiloh Creek model, will help settle powder in the case.

When there is air space within the case, the powder can lie in a trough, or more powder can be up against the bullet than against the primer, or more powder may be back against the primer instead of against the base of the bullet. It all depends upon whether the rifle is pointed muzzle up or muzzle down. The attitude of the cartridge can also dictate where the powder goes. If the shooter lifts the case up, head down, powder flows back toward the primer. If he loads the cartridge by pointing the bullet downward, powder flows toward the base of the bullet. To make the point abundantly clear, 100-percent load density means that the shape of the powder charge remains the same at all times, including the important instant of ignition.

It follows then that no fillers were used in blackpowder cartridges for this work. Of course, the lubrication disc used in the case acts to take up case capacity, but the function of the disc is lubrication, not case filler.

Primers

Evidence is often difficult to come by in shooting, while proof in many shooting issues never seems to surface. For example, I

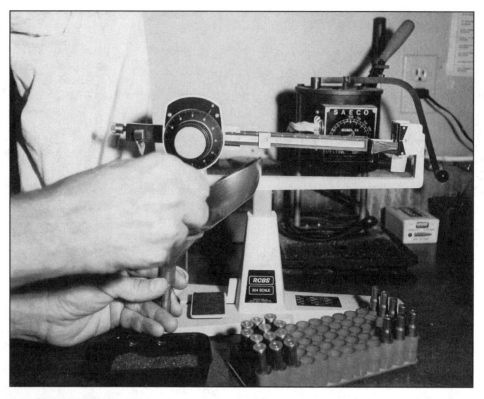

No matter the blackpowder cartridge, from 32-40 to 50-140, charges can be scale-weighed. Many shooters prefer to scale-weigh charges in an effort to leave an exact amount of room in the case for both the bullet and a lubricating disk.

(Below) There are various ways to recharge the fired cartridge case after the case is resized and reprimed. One way is with a powder measure, by volume.

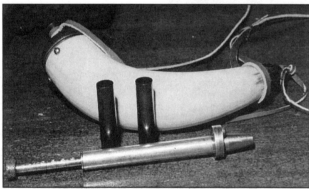

mention the fact that several test barrels have ruptured or bulged with separated bullet/powder loads, and yet proof—true proof—showing that separated bullet/powder loads bulge or break barrels has never been brought forth. Likewise on primers in blackpowder cartridges. The literature has certainly suggested use of standard primers. I still find standard large rifle and small rifle primers entirely acceptable; however, with cases like the 32-40 Winchester, I used benchrest primers satisfactorily. Unfortunately, I found no evidence to support an increase in accuracy. To muddy the waters even more, I turned to magnum primers. I cannot prove, but I tend to believe, that magnum primers did a better job in terms of cleaning up the inside of the cartridge case with muzzleloader propellants. While I cannot prove this, I have turned to magnum primers with my own loads, including a particulary accurate 40-65 Winchester.

Bullets

The "real" experts in blackpowder cartridge shooting are the lads, and a few ladies, who shoot the single shot blackpowder cartridge rifle as a way of life. They perforate target paper with their rifles, knock down metallic silhouettes, shoot long-range matches, and put big game in the freezer regularly with these old-style guns. Wouldn't these shooters have all the answers concerning bullets for blackpowder cartridge rifles? I'm afraid not. One blackpowder cartridge hunter told me that he has turned to cast alloy bullets for big game, finding that softer bullets did not penetrate well enough. Another said that he used pure lead bullets on big game, never having trouble with penetration. A third shooter said he preferred hard bullets for silhouette shooting, claiming that soft bullets did not always knock over the targets.

Yet another marksman said that, when a bullet reaches 40-caliber, it doesn't matter whether it is soft or hard; silhouettes topple over either way. But yet another held that soft bullets were best because they "mushed up" against the metal plate, smashing against the silhouette, thereby gaining more contact with the plate, while harder bullets sort of glanced off the metal. Why should I be surprised at so many different opinions? Isn't that the way it goes in shooting? So let's think it over. Bullets for blackpowder cartridges must meet several criteria, aside from the obvious factors of accuracy potential, such as concentricity. Two of these factors are good bearing surface and ability to hold onto lube somehow. Good bearing surface seems important to accuracy, possibly in part due to rifling guidance (good contact between bullet and bore). I cannot prove any of this, by the way, so if you have another opinion you are welcome to it. One thing is certain, however; bullets with long shanks usually have good sectional density, and good sectional density means better carry-up and penetration.

I contend that since high velocity is out of the question anyway, give me bullet weight. I mean, if a 45-caliber blackpowder cartridge gains 1250 fps MV with a long, heavy bullet, compared with 1375 fps MV with a squat bullet, I'll take the former every time. At long range, the advantages of high sectional density really show up. Silhouette shooters know this. Furthermore, that 100 to even 200 fps advantage at the muzzle with a bullet of lower sectional density is not maintained, even at 100 yards, let alone silhouette distances. As to how the bullet holds lube, I cannot say which design is best. I only know that the bullet darn well better hang on to its lube, because lubrication is important.

Casting Lead Bullets for The Blackpowder Cartridge

Since we discuss casting lead bullets elsewhere in this book, I'll not walk over the same ground here. However, it is my opinion that an alloy bullet is probably better, overall, than one of pure lead for the blackpowder cartridge. The bullet must remain soft enough to upset in the bore to some degree, but it need not be "pure" lead to do that, and should not be pure lead for best results. An alloy somewhere between 1:20 and 1:30, tin to lead, is probably best. I cannot say with total certainty, because there are many factors at work here, including how a bullet works in a certain rifle. Nobody has proved that one specific alloy is ideal, but the 1:20 to 1:30 range seems at least workable for starters. This means 1 part tin to 20 or 30 parts lead. In casting these bullets, kick the heat up to around 850 to 950 degrees Fahrenheit to ensure the alloy runs freely into the mould cavity for perfect formation.

Lubrication, Lubrications Discs and Grease Grooves

Of course, the bullet must be precise in order to achieve accuracy. Naturally, the rifle must also be accurate to begin with, because no matter how perfect a bullet is, it won't perform well from an inaccurate rifle. But unless the shooter is willing to clean the bore after every shot, lubrication is vital. I never realized how important lube was to the blackpowder cartridge until recently, and that was with a single shot blackpowder rifle of high accuracy potential. I ran a small test, cleaning between every shot and cleaning only after five-shot groups. Cleaning between shots brought good groups. Not cleaning between shots ruined groups. I suspected a lube problem.

What exactly does the lube do? Several things. It reduces friction between the bullet and the bore, although that benefit can go too far, reversing itself in value. Lube can deter leading of the bore. Lube can also keep fouling soft so that one or two passes with a cleaning patch from the breech end of the breech-loading blackpowder cartridge rifle takes the bulk of fouling away. Lubrication can also help maintain a uniform bore condition. Instead of the bore being almost dry for one shot, or overly greasy for the next, lubrication on the bullet and in the lubrication disc help maintain a uniform bore condition.

Here's what Sharps Rifle Company had to say about reloading cartridges and providing bore lubrication for their rifles over a century ago. This may not confirm current thinking on lubrication in the blackpowder cartridge, but the information is interesting all the same.

Instructions for Re-Loading Metallic Shells (issued with Sharps Rifles and Carbines)

The cartridge issued with the Sharps Company's Arms are made up of shells that are susceptible of being re-loaded and fired many times.

After the cartridge has been fired, the following process must be strictly observed in re-loading:

Bore a hole in a piece of hard wood, the size of the body of the cartridge, leaving the rim of the cartridge even with the surface of the board, in which place the empty shell.

Perforate the exploded cap on one side of its centre with the awl, and pry out the exploded cap; clean out the debris in the small end of the shell perfectly, and insert a new cap in the head of the shell, setting it home snugly by pressure.

Charge with 70 grains of powder, with a pasteboard wad upon the powder, forcing the wad down the full length of the follower.

Insert upon the wad a lubricant disk composed of 1 part of pure beeswax to 2 parts sperm oil in weight, to occupy 3/16 of an inch in length of the shell.

Dip the base of the ball [bullet] up to the forward ring [grease groove] in the melted lubricating compound, taking care to fill the grooves.

Insert the point of the ball in the chamber of the Ball Seater, and introduce the shell through the circular orifice at the opposite end of the Ball Seater, and press the shell home with the hand or a soft piece of wood.

Wipe the cartridge clean and it is ready for use.

That's how Sharps rifle owners were to reload the cartridge in this particular instruction booklet. The instructions conclude with a note on seating what Sharps called a "patched ball." This is not to be confused with the patched round ball of a muzzle-loading rifle. This was a conical bullet with a paper patch. Sharps suggested seating such a bullet by hand. Remember, the Sharps rifle was/is a single shot and the bullet did not have to be retained that firmly in the neck of the cartridge, because the cartridge was not loaded into a magazine. However, modern shooters who are

Seating the bullet means installing the bullet seater die and adjusting so that a perfect overall cartridge length results.

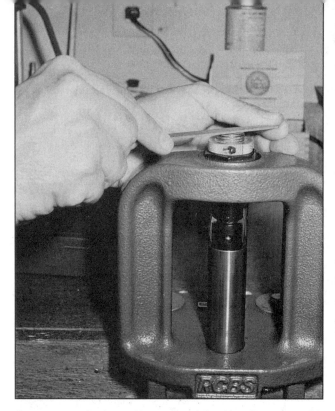

One way to maintain proper case length is with a die, such as this RCBS unit. Screw the die in place so that full contact is made with the head of the ram. Then run the case fully into the die. That portion of the case neck which protrudes above the level of the die is smoothly filed away, and then the mouth of the case is chamfered.

Chamfering the mouth of the case is very simple, and one tool serves a multitude of cartridge cases from small to big bores. A simple deburring tool is used.

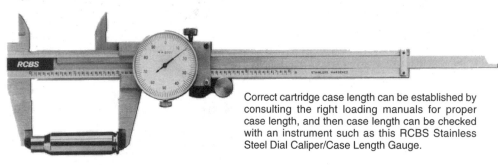

Correct cartridge case length can be established by consulting the right loading manuals for proper case length, and then case length can be checked with an instrument such as this RCBS Stainless Steel Dial Caliper/Case Length Gauge.

interested in ultimate accuracy will want to seat bullets with a fairly uniform grip in the mouth of the case. Neck friction must be uniform, in other words, from one round to the next.

Lubricating Discs

For our purposes here, the part about the "lubricant disc" is most important. Think about the major difference in lube behavior between the muzzleloader and the cartridge rifle. With the muzzleloader, lube is essentially applied to the bore when the projectile is seated. After all, the patch is lubed, and the lubrication rubs off, as it were, as the projectile is pushed downbore. Now think about the cartridge rifle. Lube goes the other way, from the breech to the muzzle. Lubrication "rubs off" the bullet as it flies down the bore. But look at what's happening. Powder gases are blasting behind the projectile, as well as some gas heading down the grooves of the rifling. The bullet itself is tearing downbore at terrific speed, even at blackpowder velocities. How in the world can we expect lube to hang on to the bullet from breech to muzzle? First of all, it has to be a darn special lube, correctly applied to the bullet. That is why proper blackpowder bullets

have grease grooves—to retain the lube so it can be transferred to the bore. Second, the lube disk helps protect the lubed bullet from hot gases and plays a role in the transfer of lube to the bore.

How that transfer takes place is not a subject for this work. We are most interested in seeing that the bore is lubed upon every shot—hence the lubrication disc. I use commercial lubricant for my lubrication discs. Though I have tried many formulas, it is difficult to say that one was absolutely better than the others. Commercial lubes that seem to work well include Rooster Laboratories BP-7 and SPG from Montana Armory. My method of making the lube disc is so simple that it could easily be impeached by a dedicated blackpowder cartridge fan. Anyone with a better idea should stick with it, but my discs do work. We'll take a 45-70 cartridge as an example. I drill out the primer pocket of the case, making the opening large enough to accept a metal rod. Then I chamfer the mouth of the case to make it sharp. This is now my punch and disc storage area, crude that it may be. I now apply lube to the center of a large piece of wax paper and cover it with another equally large piece of wax paper. Then, gently, I roll the wax paper with a rolling

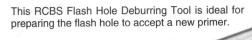
This RCBS Flash Hole Deburring Tool is ideal for preparing the flash hole to accept a new primer.

Here is Lyman's "Power Pack" to convert Lyman's Universal Trimmer to a power trimmer. Cases of various dimensions can be trimmed to length with this tool.

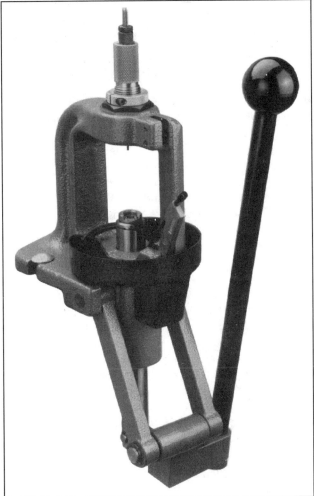
A reloading press like this one is perfect for reloading blackpowder cartridges.

pin until a thin layer of lube exists between the two pieces. The lube is not perfectly uniform, but it is uniform enough. Next, I place the wax paper sheets, with lube in between, in the refrigerator or freezer, depending on the lube.

Some lubes won't harden up at all in the refrigerator, and very little in the freezer. After a couple hours, I remove the wax paper sheets and punch out the lubricant discs with the mouth of the case. As noted, it is important to bevel the mouth of the case to sharpen its edges. Little discs of wax paper with lube in between them are collected in the body of the cartridge case. These can be pushed out one by one using the metal rod mentioned earlier by inserting the rod through the enlarged primer pocket and pushing to force the lubrication discs out of the mouth of the case. I load them, one disc per case, on top of the powder charge, then I seat the bullet. The end result is 100-percent load density, plus a thin lubrication disc in between the powder and the bullet.

Loading the Blackpowder Cartridge

Three-piece die sets are useful in loading the blackpowder cartridge. Three-piece die sets are available with the capability of expanding the case mouth, which flares (bells) the mouth to prevent the bullet from being shaved as it is seated.

Step 1: Deprime/Reprime/Resize

The case must be deprimed, expelling the spent primer, and then reprimed with a new primer. First, the case is lightly lubed so that it does not gall (stick) inside the die. The sizing die has a small metal rod (decapping pin) that forces the spent primer from its pocket. As the decapping pin knocks the fired primer free, the case is forced up into the die and is resized at the same time. Most reloading tools have a priming arm, which, when activated, allows the seating of a new primer during this initial step. Many shooters prefer priming with a hand tool, however.

The shooter will have to decide whether he wants to full-length resize or neck-size only. I want my loaded cartridge to enter easily into the chamber. If that requires full-length resizing of the fired case, then I full-length resize that case. If neck-sizing alone will do the job, I neck-size only. Neck-sizing has some benefits. One is case life. Anything that prevents working the brass helps the case last longer. Working the brass, as in full-length resizing, can fatigue the metal case sooner. I have no data to prove how significant this factor is, nor any information on how many more times a case can be reloaded with neck-sizing only versus full-length resizing. Regardless, metal fatigue is a proven factor. Another possible value of neck-sizing only is "custom fit" to the chamber. The fired case formed itself somewhat to the chamber, and by neck-sizing only, that shape remains mainly intact. Brass

An old original blackpowder cartridge rifle like this one can be fired, quite often and safely, with blackpowder loads. Every old rifle should be checked by a gunsmith before shooting it, however.

Cases should be polished, as in a vibrating unit like this one. The polished case not only looks nice, it is also easier to check for cracks or other problems.

is a bit "springy," so the case does not conform 100 percent to chamber dimensions because, after firing, a case tries to return to its fired dimensions. Neck-sizing also allows for a minor increase in powder capacity, since the slightly expanded case remains somewhat larger. But all of these benefits are for nothing if cartridges won't fit readily into the rifle chamber, or if they get stuck in the chamber after the rifle is fired.

Step 2: Priming

The new primer may be installed when the case is worked back down out of the sizing die. Some tools have separate priming arms or priming stations built in, however, I prefer a hand priming tool such as the RCBS model because I can feel the primer bottom out in the primer pocket. Perfect seating sensitizes the primer, but does not crush the anvil deeply into the priming mixture within the primer cup. The primer should not be forced too deeply into the primer pocket, only to where the edge of the cup rests firmly in the primer pocket seat. **Tip:** Before seating the primer, clean the primer pocket. There are special tools for this operation.

Step 3: Belling/Chamfering

The three-piece die set offers an expander plug that forces the mouth of the case open. Ideally, the mouth of the case is belled only enough to accept the lead bullet without shaving part of that bullet away when it is seated in the cartridge case. It is also helpful to chamfer the mouth of the case with a deburring tool, which forms a slight bevel on the mouth, as well as removing irregularities.

Step 4: Charging the Case

At this point, the fired cartridge case has been either neck-sized or full-length resized; the old primer is expelled and a new primer installed in the primer pocket; and the case mouth is belled out a little, in preparation to accept a bullet. Now the case is charged. Without doubt, the factors expressed earlier about blackpowder efficiency remain in force. Weighing muzzle-loader powders to .1-grain does nothing whatsoever for accuracy, and there's no doubt that if the shooter does a very careful job with a powder measure, a specific powder charge can be

produced time and again with ample precision. But, because we want to leave an exact amount of room for the bullet to be seated in the case, and because a lubrication disc may also be used, it is permissible to use a powder scale in preparing charges for the blackpowder cartridge. This will give a very exact powder charge volume in the case, with just the right room left for bullet seating and for the lubricating disc. While modest pressure on the powder charge is all right, there is no need to smash the bullet down upon the charge. I prefer 100-percent load density, where an exact powder charge is used, plus lubricating disc, so that the bullet firms the powder charge under pressue, but does not smash it. It is perfectly acceptable, and even recommended, to use a drop tube in pouring the powder charge into the case. A drop tube is just what it sounds like: a long tube through which powder flows. The drop tube helps evenly settle the kernels of powder down into the case.

Warning: *Do not use a modern powder measure to prepare blackpowder loads. The friction created could conceivably cause the powder to detonate.*

Step 5: Seating the Lubrication Disc

My lubrication disc is admittedly primitive in nature. My method of installing the disc is likewise simple. I take one disc in my fingers and rest it on top of the powder charge in the case. That's it.

Step 6: Seating the Bullet

Recall that the mouth of the case was belled out so that the bullet, when seated, would not be shaved by the sharp edges of the unbelled case mouth. Now bullets are friction-seated only. They are not crimped in place, as such. But the mouth of the neck is returned to previous dimensions within the bullet seater die. A taper crimp, which is a gentle crimping of the neck area, can be accomplished with the full-length die by removing the "guts" of the die. With the expander plug and decapping pin removed, the cartridge is very gently nudged up into the die, which puts force on the neck area to help hold the bullet in place. If the correct powder charge is in the case, with room for the lubricating disc taken into account, the bullet will seat perfectly, squashing the powder charge down into the case, but not crushing it.

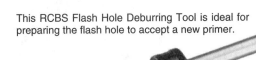

A three-die set may include an expander die, which is ideal for very light expansion of the case neck area to accept the lead conical bullet without shaving part of the bullet away when it is seated upon the sharp edges of the case mouth.

Polishing media comes in many forms. This is corn cob dry media. It works well in the vibratory case cleaner.

Here is a fine reloading die, one of high precision and excellent manufacture. A die like this will last a lifetime. RCBS has die sets for hundreds of different cartridges, including many old-time blackpowder rounds.

Since the major thrust of this chapter is the single shot blackpowder cartridge rifle, nothing has been said about the blackpowder cartridge revolver, or the blackpowder cartridge repeating rifle. Seating bullets into a cannelure and crimping them in place is often ideal for these guns for the following reasons: In the revolver, a bullet may jump forward out of the case when the gun is fired. A crimped bullet won't do that. In the repeating rifle, recoil may slam the cartridge's bullet against the case head in a tubular magazine, which can force the bullet back into the case.

I let the seating of the bullet compact the powder, but do not use heavy force. I see no purpose in it, though others do. And they could be right in their compaction of the powder charge. However, I think there is a sensible middle ground here, where the powder charge is *definitely compacted, but not crushed.* However, in breaking down original blackpowder cartridge ammunition, the powder charge often seems compacted into a veritable cake. I've had to tease the charge out of the case using a dental probe.

Cleaning the Breechloader

Cleaning the breechloader is really no different than the muzzleloader. After shooting, be certain to swab out the bore completely, using a bristle brush, from the breech end. Water can be used; so can solvent. I like solvent. Be certain to clean the action of the gun as well. Blackpowder residue can eventually blemish metal parts in the action. Incidentally, some shooters like to pour water down the bore with a funnel in order to flush away powder residue. I have not found this necessary.

Cleaning Cartridge Cases

There are no doubt several methods for doing this job. Ordinary water, with a few drops of dish detergent, works well. The cases are soaked, then scrubbed with a small brush (like a tiny bottle brush). The primer pocket can also be cleaned out. There are several sources of small brushes, including hardware stores. Sometimes brushes used in cosmetics also fit cases. It is important to clean out the inside of the cartridge case, as well as the primer pocket. Rinse well afterward. Then dry the cases in the oven on low heat. Now put the cases into a tumbler- or vibrator-type machine for case cleaning. This is a more important step than I realized in the past. The vibrator or tumbler polishes the exterior of the case nicely, but that's not as important as what the cleaning medium in the vibrator or tumbler can do

for the inside of the case, helping to polish away that last little bit of fouling.

Special Safety Instructions

1. If a shooter wishes to fire an original breechloader, revolver or repeating rifle with blackpowder cartridges, the firearm should be professionally checked out by a gunsmith who can vouch for its safe condition. In many instances, these old guns are "shot out," meaning not only that the bore is ruined, but that internal parts may also be worn and/or damaged.

2. Be certain to check for overall case length. Before reloading any cartridge case, be certain that it is not too long for the chamber. If it is too long, the neck of the case might poke into the leade of the chamber, crimping there, and possibly causing a rise in breech pressure. There are tables that show proper case lengths, e.g., Lyman's reloading manual. Looking at a Lyman manual, we find the 32-20 Winchester, an old blackpowder round, listed. A figure of 1.315 inches is given for overall length. But the shooter is admonished by Lyman to trim this case to 1.305-inch length. If in doubt about the correct case length of a given cartridge in your specific rifle, especially a firearm with a custom chamber, have a gunsmith check for you.

3. Bore diameters in the old guns, as well as some not-so-old guns, do not always hold to rigid specifications. A rifle can be "slugged" by a gunsmith. The resulting lead slug gives an impression of the bore. (A cast can also be made of the chamber.) Knowing the exact groove to groove dimension of the bore is useful in selecting and sizing bullets. Hard cast bullets should be no more than about .001-inch oversize for reasons of pressure.

This is a glance at the fascinating world of blackpowder cartridge reloading. The field is far too expansive to cover here. However, the shooter interested in furthering his knowledge will find a number of useful sources to help him do just that, including detailed data on paper-patched bullets and bullet lubing.

Thinking about a
new choke or
choke tubes?
Forget it. You can
open up your
patterns by
using...

12-Gauge Paper X Spreaders

by C.A. WOOD

FOR THOSE WHO sometimes need a more open choke but have a fixed Full-choke shotgun, here's an old solution. It's easy, inexpensive and very effective as well. All that's required is a quantity of tough, thin paper. I've used manila folders with good results, because they're universally available and easy to cut up. For the standard $1^1/_8$-ounce 12-gauge load, the measurements for the "X" spreader wad should be just under $^5/_8$ by $^3/_4$-inch. For your particular plastic wads, a little variation may be necessary. Cut strips just under $^5/_8$-inch from the manila stock in the longest lengths possible, then cut them into the $^3/_4$-inch lengths. Now match two of these together and scissor them down the middle (lengthwise) to just over half of their length. Fit them together by this slice and you now have an X spreader for 12-gauge. For other gauges, just change dimensions to suit the plastic wads to be used. The principle stays the same. All that remains now is to insert this X into the plastic shotcup before the shot is added. The star crimp may then be applied as with any other shot load. You now have a shotshell which will

In an effort to open up patterns, the author rolled his own, complete with paper spreaders. Some were star-crimped; others were roll-crimped with clear plastic over-shot wads.

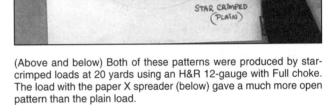

(Above and below) Both of these patterns were produced by star-crimped loads at 20 yards using an H&R 12-gauge with Full choke. The load with the paper X spreader (below) gave a much more open pattern than the plain load.

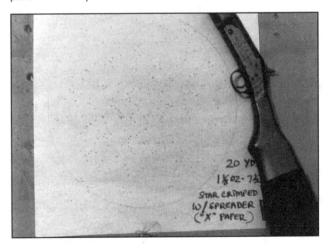

give Modified (or less) patterns when fired from a Full-choked gun, which is quite an accomplishment for such a little piece of paper!

There are excellent plastic spreader wads on the market, but for those who only need a few, this X paper insert is a good alternative. Should you choose to explore this area further, there's another option. In keeping with the paper aspect of this subject, try loading "old time" paper cases and roll-crimp them as well! Initially, that's what I did because I believed that the over-shot wad coupled with the X spreader in the shot charge would really open up the patterns. Surprisingly, however, I could see little difference between the roll-crimped shells with X spreaders and the star-crimped X spreaders on the 20-yard pattern paper.

I also tried modifying the shotcup, attempting to weaken it by cutting an additional four slits in the petal walls making a total of eight slits. It seemed to have little effect on the pattern, so I felt the additional effort not worthwhile. As the photos show, there is no evidence of any doughnut patterns sometimes erroniously (in this case, at any rate) attributed to use of over-shot wads.

I patterned these loads at 20 yards, and then a 15-inch diameter circle was drawn around the center of each pattern. Since these loads will be best used at close range, this closer patterning distance gives a much better perspective. I used once-fired Federal 2³/₄-inch paper cases for my tests. After sizing/depriming, I rewaxed the case mouths to renew and stiffen them a bit. I primed them after the paraffin had hardened into a nice thin coat, thus avoiding any chance of waxy vapor being deposited on the open primers. The cases were charged with 18.5 grains of 452 AA propellant, and a Winchester WAA 12 plastic wad was inserted. The X wad is then placed into the shotcup, and 1¹/₈ ounces of #7¹/₂ shot is dropped in. The over-shot wad is then placed on top of the shot, and a roll-crimp is applied. Moderate drill press speed is usually best. My crimper is an old Lyman unit they no longer make, but Ballistic Products sells one.

The top wad itself is plastic and is made from a discarded clear, large, plastic soda bottle. The center parallel section is cut out and split into a sheet. I used a penny as a template, drawing

around it, and cut the little discs out with scissors. This produces a very tough see-through plastic top wad. I prefer to seat them convex side down upon the shot charge.

Once finished, you'll have a rather handsome cartridge, and there is a satisfaction in resurrecting the roll-crimped paper case. And these once fired paper cases can be used a number of times, as well.

The X spreader wad can be used in any shot loading and has no real drawbacks that I'm aware of. So should you want to open your patterns by about one choke, this method is worth considering. Especially if you enjoy being a bit creative and aren't needing big volume production.

A comparative
look at ballistic
software from
Barnes Bullets,
Speer/RCBS
(ADC, Inc.),
Corbin, Lee,
Oehler and
Sierra.

The Great PC Shootout

by DAVE EPPERSON

SHOOTERS WHO ARE addicted to firearms sports as well as to personal computers may not know there exist, at this writing, more than twenty-five personal computer (PC) ballistics software suppliers worldwide. Together these programs reflect the ancient sexist adage about women and whiskey: They're all good; some are just better than others.

Though the software packages are out there, they're not very widely advertised. Often the programs appear listed as small adjunct items in reloading equipment and chronograph suppliers' catalogs, or among items shown in general firearms merchandise catalogs. Ballistics software advertising never appears in popular computer journals, not often in shooting and reloading publications, and then usually only in the classified ad section.

To review all twenty-five-plus software programs in the scope of one article would be impossible. So here's a look at six of what I consider to be the best from Barnes Bullets, Speer/RCBS (ADC, Inc.), Corbin, Lee Precision, Oehler Research and Sierra Bullets.

The interested shooter can choose from an array of PC programs.

(Below) One of the most recent offerings is Barnes Ballistics for Windows. It is one of the more user-friendly programs.

A check of PC ballistics software publishers shows available programs require use of an IBM-compatible PC. Only recently, programs have been produced to operate in the Microsoft Windows environment. Apple devotees will find there's nothing ballistic out there to fly on older Macs.

Because ballistics requires some complex mathematical calculations, math coprocessor chips installed in a CPU will prove the quick, efficient ticket for rapid computations and graphing. Most of the ballistics software reviewed for this article was written for MS-DOS.

Ballistics software has value for all who enjoy hunting, precision reloading, competitive bullseye or silhouette shooting, and for those who simply wish to know the truth about firearms and the ammunition the guns shoot. These programs can help reloaders work through several potential loads without unlimbering the press and wasting expensive powder, primers and bullets, not to mention time and effort. Software can tell a pistol shooter just how much energy a particular load can deliver with respect to barrel length, for example. Some software can be linked to an owner's ballistic chronograph to record test firings for later computer analysis.

During preparation of this review, I consulted printed source material to cross-check and validate computer results. This article assumes readers know how to travel about PC keyboards among functions, pull-down menus, icons, bells and whistles.

Here's a quick look at the ballistics software produced by some of the best-known names in the shooting industry. Prices were current at time of writing; they might have changed by now.

Barnes Bullets

New for 1997, Barnes Bullets has introduced a ballistics software program for use with Windows. It replaces their old MS-DOS software package, which was really four distinct programs with a three-ring loose-leaf manual. No such manual is needed for the new, redesigned single program because of its user-friendly nature.

For $49.95, Barnes Ballistics for Windows 1.0 offers advantages never before available. After entering the specifics for your gun and load, trajectories are shown in table and graph form. Then, as you change the specifics, the table and graph are automatically updated. Also, the progam allows the table, graph, gun information, sighting calculations and note sections to be displayed and printed all on one page. There is no flipping back and forth between different programs or notebook pages. This is extremely helpful.

The package contains a current listing of all of Barnes' bullets, along with the sectional density and ballistic coefficient for each. Moreover, the program will create a table for any manufacturer's bullet; just enter the required information about the bullet and let the computer do the rest.

There are numerous other features that may be explored, including calculations for velocity and energy at the muzzle and upon impact. BB for Windows also allows the shooter to anticipate the various factors that influence a bullet's flight. The effects of altitude, temperature, uphill/downhill angles and wind deflection can be calculated and displayed. Finally, a load's recoil forces can be determined, as well as the optimum zero for a particular gun and load.

The program comes with a full help directory right at the shooter's fingertips. All information can be easily graphed and printed for quick interpretation. The user can create a library of bullets, loads and/or firearms, depending on what best serves his purposes. As an added advantage, files can be copied or pasted into all popular word-processing programs. For some people, this might prove to be a better alternative to notebooks and files.

Barnes Ballistics for Windows 1.0 will run on any 486 PC with 8 Mb of RAM that is Windows 3.1 or Windows '95 compatible.

Speer/RCBS (ADC, Inc.)

Developed by ADC, Inc., the Speer/RCBS program from Blount, Inc., **PC Bullet**, appears to be a precision reloader's dream. This software operates with either a mouse or use of key letters of the alphabet.

Enter data for a chosen cartridge, i.e., 30-06 Springfield, and the cartridge length, 3.25 inches. Next enter bullet diameter, manufacturer, bullet weight in grains, type of bullet, sectional density and BC. Now enter cartridge case data, including length, manufacturer and lot number.

This particular program, in sequence, calls for data entry in regard to a specific firearm, primer and powder. With all the data for a load entered, simply punch up the choice of velocity tables or trajectory graphs.

Data entry can be completed quickly and easily on a single screen, augmented by pull-down lists of fifty-five bullet calibers, seventy-seven powder choices and twenty-eight primer choices.

The software provides for record keeping, chronograph inputs, ballistic coefficient calculations, selection of a printer port and printout of text, tables and graphic displays.

Graphs available depict a bullet-path curve, a bullet's declining velocity over distance, time of bullet flight, a bullet's departure from the line-of-sight over distance, and a target-view graph. The latter shows point of impact appropriate to a selected range.

PC Bullet documentation, presented in a paperback user's manual, appears aggressively clear and thorough. In addition to explanations of basic computer operation, the manual contains a section on ballistics math and an in-depth glossary of ballistic scientific terminology.

The Speer/RCBS 1996 catalog listed the PC Bullet software package at $49.95, but the program has been discontinued for 1997. ADC, Inc. now offers this software package. Meanwhile, Speer/RCBS is developing a new program scheduled for release late 1997.

Corbin

Corbin, the Oregon bullet swaging machinery manufacturer, supplies sophisticated, specialized software. The firm's bullet engineering bundle, listed as **DC-1015**, and selling for under $75, guides the user step-by-step through the design of a bullet.

The software calculates BC, form factor, bullet length, ogive and shank lengths and volumes, average density, sectional density, and stable twist rate required, among other mathematical functions.

Corbin offers parts of the bundle separately. These programs include DC-1001, Spitzer Design, $25; DC-1002, Handbook on a Disk, two floppies, $12; DC-1003, Ppatch (Paper Patch), $10; DC-1004, Tplot/WD Chart, $25; DC-CUPS, $49.95; DC-

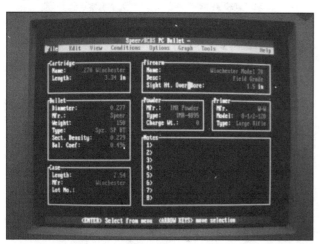

Speer/RCBS (ADC, Inc.) provides the PC Bullet program, which accepts data and then graphs the results.

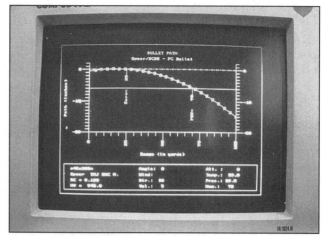

The Speer/RCBS (ADC, Inc.) PC Bullet program shows a trajectory for a spitzer bullet.

ENTER BULLET DESIGN DATA...

Enter data or press return key for default values.

CALIBER (in.) ? .308
TIP DIAM. ? .02
WEIGHT (grains) ? 185
OGIVE (cals.) ? 6   (DEFAULT VALUE)
JACKET WT.(gr.) ? 50   (DEFAULT VALUE)
CORE Lb/cu-in ? .4097   (DEFAULT VALUE)
JACKET Lb/cu-in ? .32   (DEFAULT VALUE)
AIR DENS. (Gm/l)? 1.2034   (DEFAULT VALUE)

WEIGHT (lb)   =   .0264   BALLISTIC COEFFICIENT =   .4579
SECTIONAL DENSITY   =   .2786   FORM FACTOR (i)   =   .6004
SHANK LENGTH (in)   =   .521   O.A.L. (in)   = 1.237
CORE WEIGHT (gr)   =   135   AVG. DENSITY   =   .3855
OGIVE LENGTH (in)   =   .715   OGIVE RADIUS (in)   = 1.848
OGIVE VOLUME (cu-in) =   .0297   BULLET VOLUME (cu-in) = .0686
SHANK VOLUME (cu-in) =   .0389   MIN. TWIST (in/turn) = 11.451
CORE VOLUME (cu-in)   =   .0471   JACKET VOLUME (cu-in) = .0223
               CHANGE THIS DATA? (Y/N)_

Corbin's Bullet Design program calls for data input on the first screen (left), then displays the design on the succeeding screen.

LEAD, $10; and DC-DIES, $10. Documentation may be printed from the Corbin floppies.

DC-1001 takes the user's input for a specific caliber, bullet tip diameter, weight in grains, ogive, jacket weight, core (pounds per cubic inch), jacket (pounds per cubic inch), and air density. Then the program calculates everything the operator needs to know about the bullet—and then some. Press a couple of keys, and the software puts an engineering drawing of the bullet on the screen. The next routine fires the computer bullet and presents various energy, pressure and velocity results. When the user can't come up with a certain number, the program supplies a default value.

DC-1004 requires input for a specific bullet, then calculates a bullet's vertical flight to zero and its return to earth, tracking

Lee's Shooter software comprises a Personal Firearms Log database, handy in the event of a burglary or probate.

diminishing upward and increasing downward velocities along the bullet's path. If such is the case, Tplot reports, "Safe for fire over friendly troops."

DC-CUPS, largely for custom bullet makers, asks for bullet size and weight data, then arrives at an appropriate jacket design configuration. This routine tracks materials use and costs.

DC-LEAD provides calculations for lead extrusions of solid and hollow lead wire. **DC-DIES**, for use with hydraulic swaging presses, calculates the failure point of a swaging die and critical internal hydraulic pressures.

Corbin also offers mailing and billing systems software for custom bullet manufacturers.

Lee Precision

Lee Precision, the Wisconsin manufacturer of a vast array of reloading tools, markets a solid ballistics bundle that contains some unusual features.

The **Lee Shooter** program offers a reloading log function in which a user can record various loads by date and by caliber. Entries can be displayed by date, caliber and the users' names.

Another program, titled **Ballistics Generator**, requires input of muzzle velocity, bullet weight, BC, zero range, yardage increments, number of desired increments and sight height. The Generator then calculates a table from the input data that shows range, drop, velocity, energy and time of flight of the selected bullet. Press Control-P on the keyboard at this point to obtain a printout of the table.

Unique among software reviewed is the **Personal Firearms Log** routine. With this function, the user can create a database comprising every firearm in a personal arsenal. List the guns by

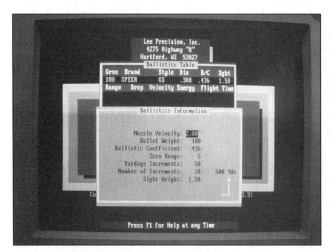

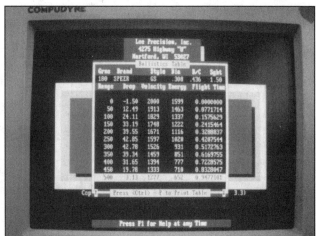

Lee Precision's Shooter calls for ballistics info on an initial screen (left), then generates a table that shows a load's critical factors.

caliber, manufacturer, name and serial number, then choose whether to display the entries by caliber or by make. The log shows the firearms' purchase value and estimated current value. This routine also will supply a printout—essential for insurance purposes in event of a burglary or other problem.

Shooter includes a **Bullet Energy Calculator** segment. Enter a selected bullet weight in grains and approximate muzzle velocity, and the calculator supplies a figure for foot-pounds of energy at the muzzle. Press F-10 at this point and up comes a small table that shows the energy usually required to bring down deer, elk, moose and bear.

The program also includes a cost calculator of reloads for handguns, rifles and shotguns. The handgun and rifle routines tally up the costs of bullets, powder and primers, then deliver the cost of fifty rounds of reloaded handgun ammo or twenty homemade rifle cartridges. The shotgun routine accounts for costs of shot, powder, wads and primers to result in the cost of reloading twenty-five shells.

Last in the bundle, the **Lee Perfect Powder Measure** calculates micrometer settings for users of the Lee device. Input data required includes powder brand and volume measure density.

The Lee Shooter may represent the best bargain among software offerings reviewed here. The Shooter, in buyer's

choice of 5 1/4- or 3 1/2-inch disks, sells for but $15, with $1.75 for shipping.

Oehler Research

Oehler Research, Inc., the Texas chronograph firm, offers **The Ballistic Explorer 5.0** program for $70. Users of older software may upgrade for $35.

Documentation, in an eighty-page saddle-stitched user's manual, thorough and fully indexed, starts the reloader with "Condensed Instructions." Explorer software employs a command-line/key-letter/arrow-key/function-key selection system for moving about various screens and dialog boxes. For mouse users, this practice may seem cumbersome and outdated.

The Ballistic Explorer deals with exterior ballistics on six different screen displays. The user enters bullet, atmospheric and range data on Explorer's Main screen. Three loads may be entered simultaneously.

The user then presses D for the Graph Display screen, and a dialog box provides selection of ammo and bullet libraries, graphs of entered cartridge and atmospheric data, printouts and screen viewing options.

First up in the Graph Display routine come graph controls for titles and setting graph parameters. Then the user can punch up

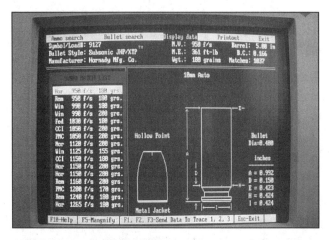

Oehler's Ballistic Explorer features ammo and bullet libraries. Here the software displays 10mm cartridge data.

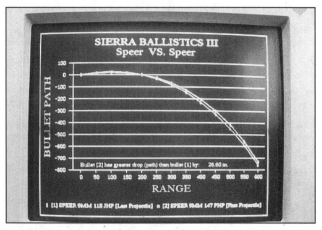

The Sierra Ballistics III program compares two 9mm loads.

ENTER BULLET DESIGN DATA...

Enter data or press return key for default values.

```
CALIBER (in.)      ? .308
TIP DIAM.          ? .02
WEIGHT (grains)    ? 185
OGIVE (cals.)      ? 6              (DEFAULT VALUE)
JACKET WT. (gr.)   ? 50             (DEFAULT VALUE)
CORE Lb/cu-in      ? .4097          (DEFAULT VALUE)
JACKET Lb/cu-in    ? .32            (DEFAULT VALUE)
AIR DENS. (Gm/l)?  1.2034           (DEFAULT VALUE)

WEIGHT (lb)          = .0264    BALLISTIC COEFFICIENT =  .4579
SECTIONAL DENSITY    = .2786    FORM FACTOR (i)       =  .6084
SHANK LENGTH (in)    = .521     O.A.L. (in)           = 1.237
CORE WEIGHT (gr)     = 135      AVG. DENSITY          =  .3855
OGIVE LENGTH (in)    = .715     OGIVE RADIUS (in)     = 1.848
OGIVE VOLUME (cu-in) = .0297    BULLET VOLUME (cu-in) =  .0686
SHANK VOLUME (cu-in) = .0389    MIN. TWIST (in/turn)  = 11.451
CORE VOLUME (cu-in)  = .0471    JACKET VOLUME (cu-in) =  .0223
            CHANGE THIS DATA? (Y/N)_
```

Corbin's Bullet Design program calls for data input on the first screen (left), then displays the design on the succeeding screen.

LEAD, $10; and DC-DIES, $10. Documentation may be printed from the Corbin floppies.

DC-1001 takes the user's input for a specific caliber, bullet tip diameter, weight in grains, ogive, jacket weight, core (pounds per cubic inch), jacket (pounds per cubic inch), and air density. Then the program calculates everything the operator needs to know about the bullet—and then some. Press a couple of keys, and the software puts an engineering drawing of the bullet on the screen. The next routine fires the computer bullet and presents various energy, pressure and velocity results. When the user can't come up with a certain number, the program supplies a default value.

DC-1004 requires input for a specific bullet, then calculates a bullet's vertical flight to zero and its return to earth, tracking diminishing upward and increasing downward velocities along the bullet's path. If such is the case, Tplot reports, "Safe for fire over friendly troops."

DC-CUPS, largely for custom bullet makers, asks for bullet size and weight data, then arrives at an appropriate jacket design configuration. This routine tracks materials use and costs.

DC-LEAD provides calculations for lead extrusions of solid and hollow lead wire. **DC-DIES**, for use with hydraulic swaging presses, calculates the failure point of a swaging die and critical internal hydraulic pressures.

Corbin also offers mailing and billing systems software for custom bullet manufacturers.

Lee Precision

Lee Precision, the Wisconsin manufacturer of a vast array of reloading tools, markets a solid ballistics bundle that contains some unusual features.

The **Lee Shooter** program offers a reloading log function in which a user can record various loads by date and by caliber. Entries can be displayed by date, caliber and the users' names.

Another program, titled **Ballistics Generator**, requires input of muzzle velocity, bullet weight, BC, zero range, yardage increments, number of desired increments and sight height. The Generator then calculates a table from the input data that shows range, drop, velocity, energy and time of flight of the selected bullet. Press Control-P on the keyboard at this point to obtain a printout of the table.

Unique among software reviewed is the **Personal Firearms Log** routine. With this function, the user can create a database comprising every firearm in a personal arsenal. List the guns by

```
═══ Display Firearms by Gauge or Caliber ═══
LOCATE: _

 [INS] to Add      [DEL] to Delete      [ENTER] to View or Change

.22 LR             RUGER          GOVT. TARGET     217-20692
.22 LR             RUGER          MK. II STD.      19-61494
.22 LR             TAURUS         PT-22            AML20620
.22 LR             TAURUS         PT-22            AMA24527
.22 PELLET/DART PUMP  BENJAMIN    132              B224671
.223 (5.5 MM NATO) RUGER          MINI-14          185-50914
.30-30             WINCHESTER     94AE TRAPPER     5585247
.36                CANE GUN       ??               NONE
.36                COLT           1851 NAVY        5373
.410               CBC            SB               C1009473
.44                COLT           1860 ARMY        208489
.44 SPECIAL        AM. DERRINGER  MODEL 1          92290
.45                JUKAR          KENTUCKY PISTOL  140072
.45                THOMPSON CENTER PERCUSSION      19939
.50                DIXIE GUN WORKS KENTUCKY RIFLE  ?
.50                LYMAN          HAWKEN RIFLE     72136
9 MM LUGER         SIG SAUER      P-226            U134910
9 MM LUGER         SIG SAUER      P-226            U172150
?                  MANLICHER      BOLT-ACTION      14499
```

Lee's Shooter software comprises a Personal Firearms Log database, handy in the event of a burglary or probate.

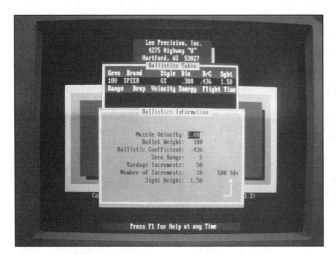

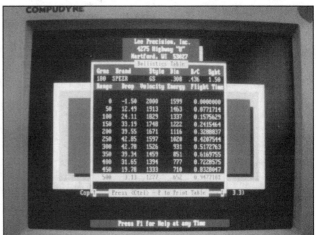

Lee Precision's Shooter calls for ballistics info on an initial screen
(left), then generates a table that shows a load's critical factors.

caliber, manufacturer, name and serial number, then choose whether to display the entries by caliber or by make. The log shows the firearms' purchase value and estimated current value. This routine also will supply a printout—essential for insurance purposes in event of a burglary or other problem.

Shooter includes a **Bullet Energy Calculator** segment. Enter a selected bullet weight in grains and approximate muzzle velocity, and the calculator supplies a figure for foot-pounds of energy at the muzzle. Press F-10 at this point and up comes a small table that shows the energy usually required to bring down deer, elk, moose and bear.

The program also includes a cost calculator of reloads for handguns, rifles and shotguns. The handgun and rifle routines tally up the costs of bullets, powder and primers, then deliver the cost of fifty rounds of reloaded handgun ammo or twenty homemade rifle cartridges. The shotgun routine accounts for costs of shot, powder, wads and primers to result in the cost of reloading twenty-five shells.

Last in the bundle, the **Lee Perfect Powder Measure** calculates micrometer settings for users of the Lee device. Input data required includes powder brand and volume measure density.

The Lee Shooter may represent the best bargain among software offerings reviewed here. The Shooter, in buyer's

choice of 5¼- or 3½-inch disks, sells for but $15, with $1.75 for shipping.

Oehler Research

Oehler Research, Inc., the Texas chronograph firm, offers **The Ballistic Explorer 5.0** program for $70. Users of older software may upgrade for $35.

Documentation, in an eighty-page saddle-stitched user's manual, thorough and fully indexed, starts the reloader with "Condensed Instructions." Explorer software employs a command-line/key-letter/arrow-key/function-key selection system for moving about various screens and dialog boxes. For mouse users, this practice may seem cumbersome and outdated.

The Ballistic Explorer deals with exterior ballistics on six different screen displays. The user enters bullet, atmospheric and range data on Explorer's Main screen. Three loads may be entered simultaneously.

The user then presses D for the Graph Display screen, and a dialog box provides selection of ammo and bullet libraries, graphs of entered cartridge and atmospheric data, printouts and screen viewing options.

First up in the Graph Display routine come graph controls for titles and setting graph parameters. Then the user can punch up

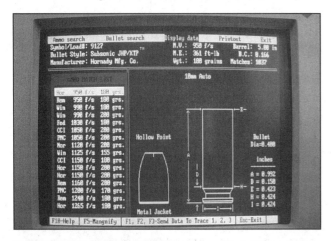

Oehler's Ballistic Explorer features ammo and bullet libraries. Here the software displays 10mm cartridge data.

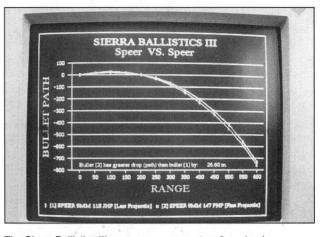

The Sierra Ballistics III program compares two 9mm loads.

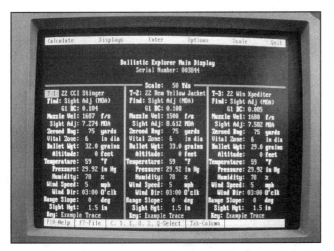

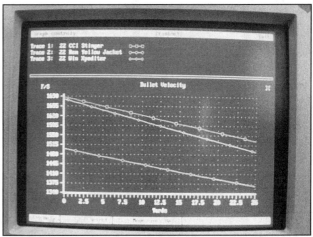

Oehler's Ballistic Explorer demonstration screen shows three 22 LR cartridges (left), then calculates and displays specific graphic traces that record velocity decay.

Here, Ballistic Explorer charts the decreasing velocities of three 22 LR bullets and features a crosshair cursor that can track a velocity anywhere along a trace curve.

graphed traces for chosen loads. Each curve provides a visually distinct curve line. Next the user can display graph curve data results in tabular numeric form.

The Explorer also offers an **Ammo Library Display** screen on which the user may see drawings of custom bullets or one of 1200 commercial loads produced by ten major manufacturers. Likewise, the user can choose the **Bullet Library Display**, which facilitates scanning BC and weight data for 900 cast and jacketed bullets from major bullet and mould manufacturers.

Ballistic Explorer permits the user to transfer data collected with an Oehler Model 43 chronograph system directly into the software's trace library.

The Oehler program operates with velocities up to 6000 feet per second and ranges up to 2500 meters. A metric version of Explorer is programmed into the software.

This program seems to be the most thorough software going among entries reviewed here—no gimmicks, no foolin'.

Sierra Bullets

Sierra of Sedalia, Missouri, markets Version III of **Exterior Ballistics Software** at $49.95. With this program, the user must print twenty-eight pages of documentation from the program disk. Though not written expressly for Windows, this software can run in the Windows environment and supports VGA color and laser printers.

The documentation explains program default values (i.e. maximum range, zero range, increment range, sight height and atmospheric conditions) and provides a glossary of ballistic terms, plus a list of abbreviations used in the Sierra software databases. Next, the documentation explains record names, range tables and anomalies created by various low-BC lightweight bullets. There follows an overview of the software's graphing capabilities and printouts.

Following a "hello" screen, Version III puts up a file retrieval menu screen, from which the user can select databases and records on file. This array also allows the user to navigate among editing, deletion, copy and print functions.

Here the user, with arrow keys, selects a database from a list that includes Speer, Sierra, RWS, Remington-Peters, Olin-Winchester,

Nosler, Hornady, Federal and Barnes. The program allows the user to browse through these database entries. In addition, one can create a personal custom load database and add it to the list.

Should the user select the on-board Speer database, the next step is to choose a caliber, say, 355, for 9mm loads. Press *Enter* and choose among eleven combinations, from 88-grain jacketed hollowpoint to 147-grain thin metal jacket. Arrow keys guide selection of, say, a 115-grain JHP load. Now press *Enter* again, and the Speer database supplies pertinent data on the load: BC, BC high and low breakpoints, and muzzle velocity.

Once the user selects a specific load or loads, the software can calculate range tables and/or draw graphs of one load, or compare two loads graphically. The range table tracks a bullet's velocity, energy, altitude, drop, drift and time of flight, and provides lead figures for running antelope, deer and elk. The graph depicts the bullet's flight curve over a selected range.

This software also offers point-blank range, zero range and maximum range calculations for loads listed in the several commercial and the user's personal databases.

Once a shooter gets the hang of this Sierra software, data retrieval and creation of ballistics tables and graphs become a piece of cake.

Summary

PC reloading and shooting activities can be conducted off-season, in the dead of winter or when it's too hot to leave the air-conditioned computer room. Software can show shooters what's what in exterior ballistics. Moreover, at $80 or less, one of these programs can save the reloader considerable money before setting up to produce a run of cartridges.

What's more, ballistics on a home computer is utterly fascinating.

Bibliography

Hatcher, Maj. Gen. Julian S., *Hatcher's Notebook.* Harrisburg: The Stackpole Co., 1962.

Matthews, Charles W., *Shoot Better.* Boulder: Johnson Publishing Co., 1984.

Sierra Bullets Reloading Manual, 2nd Ed. Santa Fe Springs: Sierra Bullets, 1978.

When it comes to target shooting, two calibers have repeatedly proven them- selves over time. This is why the 38 Special and 45 ACP are...

All-Time Competitive Favorites

by STAN TRZONIEC

IN THE DAYS before the development of today's popular target games like PPC, IPSC and newer space-age competitive sports that help the shooter with trick guns fitted with laser sights, gentlemen participated in what most termed "bullseye" shooting. Standing in an offhand position with one arm forward and out, you brought the gun to bear on a paper target up to 50 yards distant. There were, in most matches, three classifications in which to shoot—the 22 rimfire, 38 Special and 45 ACP.

Some may say, "Heck, I can shoot at a stationary paper target 50 yards away, but it takes a real man to run, jump and even enter into the more popular competitive games." To this all the author says is, give it a try. Back when bullseye was really in vogue, to compete took a certain breed of man with the right mental attitude, excellent physical self-control, a very specialized handgun and top-flight ammunition. Favored pistols in the 22 matches included Smith & Wesson, High Standard and Hammerli. All were tuned to perfection and all were very accu-

To the serious target shooter's delight, there are still two guns equally well suited to the game. On the left is the Smith & Wesson Model 52 chambered in 38 Special; on the right, Colt's famed Gold Cup in 45 ACP. Optional weights on the bottom left are for the Model 52; they add stability to the muzzle of the gun.

(Left) For target shooting, the author demonstrates the correct position for shooting. The gun is held out front, the sights lined up, then fired. A light trigger pull is an asset here.

For small charges in target loads, you want a fast-burning propellant. Any of those shown here is equally suited to the task.

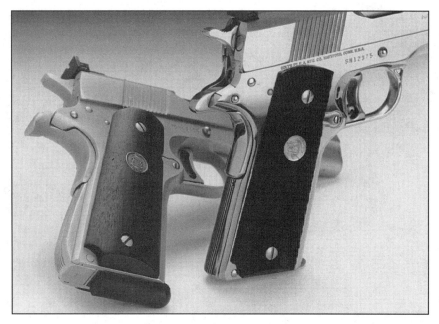

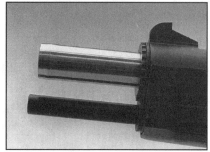

(Above) On the Model 52, that bulge on the barrel helps to lock up the gun for consistent shot-after-shot accuracy within the slide itself. The sights are plain and visible.

(Left) One nice feature of the Colt is the ability to change the mainspring housing for target shooting. On the right is how the gun comes from the factory. Left, Trzoniec added an arched housing to fit his hand better.

rate, considering the rimfire shooter had only factory ammunition with which to work.

In 38 Special, most dedicated shooters relied on Smith & Wesson's finely crafted (albeit expensive) Model 52 autoloader. An extremely accurate gun in the right hands with good ammunition, the Model 52 could easily turn in downright respectable groups at the terminal end. Even today, the Model 52 is a hand-built gun with tolerances held tight enough to make the gun group very well while functioning perfectly with 38 Special wadcutter ammunition.

When I accepted this assignment, I was reminded that handloads are the primary focus. Fair enough, but since the guns used in bullseye shooting are very different from your standard, run-of-the-mill production guns, I hope you'll allow me a few paragraphs to better describe them and their role in this old but hallowed sport of precision shooting.

The Model 52 was built on the original Model 39 frame with a factory lockout to prevent the use of the double-action trigger. It has the best of everything, including an upper and lower trigger stop screw, over-travel adjustment and a trigger pull that always puts a smile on your face. Set at 2³⁄4 pounds, just about ¹⁄4-inch of slack precedes sear release. And like its predecessor, today's Model 52 has top-notch sights ready for tough competition. Target sights, no matter the gun, have to be rugged and reliable, especially on a semi-automatic where the constant battering of the slide is a major consideration. A change of even ¹⁄1000th-inch can move your group almost 2¹⁄2 inches at 50 yards. Combine that with a gun that has a very unusual barrel bushing and lockup, and shoots a blunt-nose bullet traveling at "target" velocities, and you have your work cut out for you.

In the 45 ACP class, most bullseye competitors shot modified Colts tuned up by experts like Jimmy Clark or Richard Shocky. With low-slung BoMar ribs, extendable sight packages and long slides, they were state-of-the-art guns of the day. Today, countless target shooters have come to rely on the semi-production Gold Cup for their shooting duties. Orig-

inally called the National Match, this autoloader has been upgraded to modern times and demands. Though not quite as detailed as the Model 52 for target use, the Colt Gold Cup will do fine for paper punchin' or, better yet, for our testing program. It has better than adequate sights, is made of stainless steel (polished bright) and has a target trigger set at 4¹⁄2 pounds with only a barely detectable amount of slack before engagement.

Factory ammunition is fine for the casual target shooter, but in the end, handloads are the saving grace for those serious enough to practice, practice, practice. Remington, Federal and Winchester all make "target" or "classic" loads for both the 38 Special and 45 ACP, and most are available in either lead or jacketed designs.

Handloading serves many purposes, and in dedicated target shooting it seems to become even more evident. First and foremost is the ability to literally custom blend a load that shoots in your particular gun to near-perfection. With all the bullets, primers and propellants out there, combinations could number into the zillions, but with a bit of work on your part, the selection process starts to narrow. Economy is yet another very important consideration. With factory 38 Special wadcutters going for about $18 a box (that's 36 cents every time you pull the trigger), its not hard to see that, after you have the brass, those same 38s can be had for just 6 cents per shot when handloaded in lots of 500. Even less if you cast your own bullets, but that's another story.

Bullets used in target loads are usually lead, either swaged or home-cast. Since the "game" is only a paper target, it hardly makes sense to waste your weekly stipend on higher-priced jacketed bullets in larger calibers like the 45 ACP. Keeping in mind that velocities are within the 700-800 fps range, powder charges are light, which translates into less shooter fatigue and barrel wear—and economy.

Exotic bullets are not needed or desired in target shooting. Distances are close, so projectiles that make a well-defined opening on the paper rather than a ragged hole are used.

They are called "wadcutters," and when shot into heavy-gauge target stock they produce a hole reminiscent of a hand paper punch. For scoring in close matches, they are necessary as their clean holes allow the judge to properly score each contestant, especially in higher scoring areas like center bull.

If you use the 38 Special semi-automatic Model 52, your choices are narrowed quite a bit. This gun fires the common 38 Special cartridge, but only with the bullet seated flush with the case mouth. Period. While revolvers can tolerate some leeway with regard to bullet seating, the Model 52 tolerates nothing. It's flush with the case mouth or nothing at all. The 45, on the other hand, can use a "semi-wadcutter" which has a bit of a nose or point similar to a typical round-nose bullet. For the purpose of our testing program, the traditional 148-grain 38 Special wadcutter was our choice in the Smith & Wesson, the 200-grain semi-wadcutter in the Colt Gold Cup. Bullet moulds are available for shooters who enjoy casting their own; however, I have found factory swaged bullets much more uniform in weight and consistency than most home-cast slugs of the same caliber and nominal weight. The choice is yours.

Reloading target loads for optimum accuracy is not hard to do, but it does take a certain amount of patience to get things exactly right. Over years of testing and shooting, I've found that powder charge variations as little as .2- to .5-grain can make a marked difference in downrange performance.

Probably the best place to start our quest is with a good set of reloading dies. These days, quality is easy to find in die sets from Hornady, Lyman, RCBS or Redding, to name a few. Since you will be shooting and shooting to hone your skills, a carbide sizing die is a must. Pick a die set that includes a variety of seating stems. These will be listed on the end label with initials like RN (round-nose), WC (wadcutter) and SWC (semi-wadcutter). They may be somewhat different from one maker to another, but in the end will accomplish the same task.

When assembling target loads, the sequence that works the best usually goes like this: The first die should contain both the resizer (with carbide insert) and decapper, so one run through this die takes care of two operations at once. The second die is called the expander, and it does just that. A graduated plug inside the expander will open up the case to accept the bullet, a good asset especially when using lead bullets. This die should be set to not only expand (or bell) the case mouth for easy bullet entry, but to allow the bullet to enter without shaving lead. This shaving effect can be a nuisance when it comes time to seat bullets, as lead shavings around the case mouth can actually plug up the inside of the seating die with the end result of uneven seating depths. Not too much belling is wanted—just enough to hand-seat a flat-based bullet straight up in the case for final seating.

Brass can be purchased by the case (500), which assures you of one lot number. Nickel cases take a bit more effort and don't seem to last as long as traditional brass—this is an observation on my part, not an opinion tallied up after years of shooting for the gold. Ditto on the 45. Stay away from bargain prices and especially the steel cases (military surplus) used many years ago. Standard primers are good; magnum primers are not needed or desired in small cases stoked with fast-burning propellants. When the shooting session is complete and the cases are resized, always check case length on both the 38 and 45, and trim to proper length. Long cases will hamper the operation of your precision pistol.

Powders, no matter the cartridge, always seem to be an emotional issue. The choices are wide open, but after a short time you can almost "feel" what type is best for your gun or situation. In this case, fast burners were in force, including Accurate Arms 2, Bullseye, Olin 231, Unique and others within this burning range. Most are easy to drop from convention-

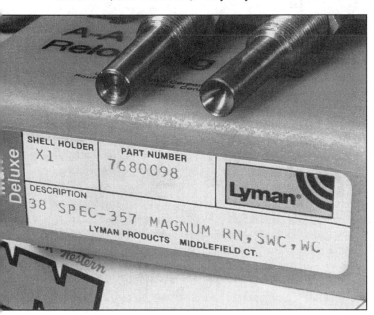

When purchasing a die set, make sure a seater is included for wadcutter bullets. This would be the seater on the left. WC on the box stands for "wadcutter."

This is .2 of a grain. You can almost count the granules. This small amount can alter a target load.

(Right) With all the components that are out there, you will never run out of combinations to try for that near-perfect, one-hole accuracy load.

(Below) Differences, ever so slight, are evident here in bullets made by Hornady, Remington and Speer. Try them all until you are satisfied with the end results.

148-Grain Hollow-Base Wadcutters

Hornady   **Remington**   **Speer**

al measures, but a check on a good scale every tenth charge is always a good idea. You'll also note that, in these powder-puff loads, charges are small. It often seems they hardly fill half the case. This should start another bell ringing: *beware of double charges.* I visually check each batch of fifty cases with a penlight before any bullet is seated. A double charge of Bullseye, for instance, will certainly ruin your day, not to mention the gun in hand.

When actual loading starts, and more so in the assembly of fine target loads, you'll find it better to complete each step— sizing, belling and priming, charging, seating, then crimping— as you move along within each cartridge. In that way, the concentration is more exact, especially in such stages as priming and charging each case with propellant. The final step, that of crimping, needs your full attention, because here is where you are going to make or break both the accuracy and full functioning of your weapon. Here are a few more pointers.

After resizing and checking the cases for overall length, let's get back to the science of expanding that case, as this part of the operation is critical to both accuracy and operation of the pistol. A brand-new, out-of-the-box Winchester 38 Special case reads .373-inch about one-third of the way down from the mouth. If you size that same case before loading (a good idea), it should

FACTORY TARGET LOADS 38 SPECIAL/45 ACP				
Cartridge		**Wgt.** (grs.)	**MV** (fps)	**Grp.** (ins.)
Mfg.	**Type**			
Hornady	38 Special HBWC	148	795	3/4
Rem.	38 Special LWC	148	734	7/8
CCI/Blazer	45 ACP TMJ	200	882	1¼
Rem.	45 ACP MCWC	185	772	1½

read about .371- to .372-inch on your micrometer, depending on the die set, brass, etc. The amount of flare (or bell) at the mouth should never exceed .005- to .007-inch, so the total would now read about .376- to .379-inch at the case mouth. Any more is overkill and will only work the brass to no advantage, shortening case life.

On the setting of small powder charges, I find it best to load the measure as full as possible. Tap the side of the reservoir to pack the propellant within this cylinder. The end result will be a much more uniform disbursement of powder, even with minute charges like that famous—and very accurate—2.7 grains of Bullseye. And don't forget to tighten the adjustment screw before making a charge run. This fine adjustment, if not secured, can move and drastically alter your small charges as you work the handle up and down.

Shaved bullets caused by improper case flaring can lead to case denting. This comes from a buildup of lead in the seating die.

Some pitfalls to avoid when loading target loads (from left): not enough flare on the case (bullet is being shaved); improper start to seating the bullet; finally, too much lube on the bullet as it comes from the factory box. Remove this excessive lubricant before proceeding to the seating die.

Only a bit of case mouth flare is needed to permit starting a bullet straight into the case. Too much only works the brass; too little shaves the bullet. That can lead to loss of accuracy downrange.

We've seen 38 Special bullets, now look at some on the 45 ACP side. From left to right we see examples from Hornady, American and Speer.

After powder charging, carefully start each bullet to allow a straight run into the case. This eliminates shaving, as previously discussed. Even minor shaving can affect accuracy, perhaps by the reduction of bullet mass or more likely due to imbalance. Finish up by seating to the proper length. These guns require different approaches. The Smith & Wesson Model 52 requires that you seat the bullet flush with the mouth of the case for proper feeding and functioning. A roll crimp is preferred here. On the other hand, Colt's Gold Cup uses bullets of either round-nose or semi-wadcutter design to help in feeding as the cartridge goes from magazine to chamber. Because the 45 ACP headspaces on the case mouth, be absolutely sure the leading bullet band is flush with or a bit below the case mouth. Finish the 45 ACP with a taper- rather than roll-crimp for flawless feeding.

After all this work, embark on a formal testing program complete with all the bells and whistles. Gather your guns, handloads and factory ammunition to compare with your reloads, and a rest of one kind or another. Keep in mind you are testing the gun and loads, not the shooter. You can use a hand-held rest like the Outers Pistol Perch where the barrel is placed in a V-like affair, or go more elaborate and use a Ransom Rest as I do. The Ransom is often called a machine rest, as it is secured to a platform and the gun is locked into various grip inserts, then fired for accuracy. After the gun recoils up and back, it is manually rotated downward to a predetermined position for subsequent firing. This Ransom Rest is very precise. It is expensive, but if you do a lot of testing, as I do, it is the only way to go. Used in conjunction with the rest, a chronograph records velocities. Currently, I use Oehler's fine Model 33 for my readings. A camera is an option for recording targets, and a notebook and steel ruler complete the equipment needed for a serious and productive outing.

The day for testing these target loads was almost too good to be true. Temperature was in the mid-60s, wind was very light from the my back, and the sun was shining bright for good chronograph readings. I allowed myself plenty of time to do the job right. The 22 loads listed nearby took the better part of the morning. Distance for these loads was 50 feet, groups were five rounds, and the Oehler Chronotach was positioned 8 feet from the muzzle of each gun.

(Above) Even though case loads are on the light side, the best way to get consistency is to settle the propellant within the powder measure by tapping the side of the measure.

(Left) The author is placing the trigger transfer bar within the trigger guard of the Colt. When the gun is in the down position, it is ready to fire. With target loads, recoil will never send the gun to this position—it is only for loading or adjusting.

Two prime examples of some of the targets shot that day.

HANDLOADED TARGET LOADS 38 SPECIAL/45 ACP

Bullet	Load (Wgt.Grs./Powder)	MV (fps)	Group (ins.)
S&W Model 52—Wadcutter, 148-grain			
Hornady	2.7/Bullseye	703	1 1/4
	3.3/231	759	1 1/4
	3.4/Unique	745	1 5/8
Remington	2.7/Bullseye	688	5/8
	3.0/HP-38	748	7/8
	3.0/AA-2	764	5/8
Speer	2.7/Bullseye	689	5/8
	2.8/700-X	671	5/8
	3.0/Hodgdon Clays	767	2
Colt Gold Cup—Semi-Wadcutter, 200-grain			
Hornady	4.4/Bullseye	711	1
	5.4/Unique	742	1 1/4
	6.4/Herco	822	1 1/2
American	4.4/HP-38	684	1
	5.0/Unique	714	1
	7.0/AA-5	691	1
Speer	4.2/700-X	693	1 1/4
	4.5/AA-2	824	1 1/8
	5.0/231	805	1

A nearby chart shows much was accomplished in the one session. Naturally, once you do a reasonable amount of experimenting, it is a good idea to go back and reshoot the best of the best two or even three times to establish a good baseline for accuracy. One group can be an impressive fluke or a complete disaster depending upon weather, wind or perhaps an error in loading. Most of the loads listed here are repeats, culled from years of experimenting with target loads for bullseye use or for small game hunting. (Yes, wadcutters do make excellent squirrel loads. My personal Model 52, a handful of handloads, a few sandwiches and a thermos of cider make for a super outing in the hardwoods of New England on a crisp fall day.)

Except for a few of the loads which they didn't like, you have to say both guns were really consistent. With the Model 52, the Hornady sample came in with groups over an inch, but they were all within 1/4-inch of each other. Using the Remington bullet, the famous load of 2.7 grains of Bullseye proved that it remains a good performer. Accurate Arms 2, a relative newcomer, did quite well, as did HP-38. The Speer bullet loaded with Bullseye proved its worth again and tied 700-X with groups approaching 5/8-inch. Hodgdon's newest powder, Clays, did not fare as well, as you can see. Coming in with 2-inch groups, this powder is still a mystery to me; all bullets hitting the target impacted almost broadside! For some reason, and this is a good example, handloading can bring out the best or worst in a gun, powder or bullet.

With my Colt Gold Cup, again consistency was the watchword. Of the nine groups fired, over 50 percent were in the 1-inch category. I think that's terrific considering the wide range and variety of powders I used. Bullseye was a winner again, as well as trusted Unique, Olin 231 and HP-38. Sometimes you just can't beat success, as this chart shows. The older brands seem to get better.

With reference to velocities, slower seemed more accurate. Contrary to that last statement is a group which registered an average of 805 fps on my Oehler and still turned in groups within that 1-inch circle. As a sidenote, it was very interesting that with the 45 ACP, after the last target was pulled down, the hole under it measured only 1 3/4 inches across for a total of fifty-five shots, of which ten were factory loads! Quite a feat...

As a reference, I shot some factory target loads in addition to the handloads. Overall, the handloads did better than the commercial loadings, but given the mass-production techniques used with these loads, they are a force with which to be reckoned. Velocities were within target standards, and the resulting accuracy in some cases was better than my handloads. We must give credit where credit is due.

Assembling mild loads for either target, competitive use, plinking or small game hunting is a labor of love, but when you see the results, it's well worth it. With this world going around at top speed, it's nice to sit down occasionally, take your time and relax. I can't think of any better way to do it than handloading. Can you?

Sometimes this is one of the most important considerations in handloading.

Shooting For Cheap

by JOHN HAVILAND

TALK ABOUT STICKER shock. After driving to a "sale" at the local sporting goods store, I found factory-loaded ammunition costs at least 50 cents a shot, and the price of reloading supplies has gone the way of my blood pressure. I drove home with a few paltry items. To keep my firearms in forage, I had to come up with a number of ways to get more discharges for the dollar.

I am sure someone has found a way to recharge primers, but for the rest of us, the only way to save money on primers is to buy a lot of them on sale. I use one brand and type for as many firearms as possible. Rifles from 22-250 to 35 Whelen are all loaded with standard large rifle primers. For the 41 and 44 Magnums, standard primers work just as well as magnum primers. Buying standard instead of magnum primers saves 10 cents per hundred.

Because of the variety of powders, money can be saved several ways. Instead of filling the case with a maximum of pow-

Revolvers like this Model 57 S&W 41 Magnum easily fire light loads. Only half the weight of Unique or Red Dot is needed to achieve the approximate velocities of slower powders such as 2400. When developing a load for self-loading firearms, make sure the powder charge develops enough pressure to cycle the action.

der, a minimum charge saves around a penny per shot. My 41 Magnum revolver shoots, as a maximum load with a 210-grain bullet, 18 grains of Hercules 2400 powder. My 30-06 shoots 59 grains of IMR-4350 powder every time the sear trips to eject a 150-grain bullet. For the sake of argument, say powder costs $12 a pound. That works out to 3.09 cents for powder per shot in the 41 and 10.1 cents in the 30-06.

By substituting a minimum load for the 41, a penny per shot is saved. Shooting a minimum, instead of a maximum, charge of IMR-4350 in my 30-06 saves only about half a penny.

But changing to a faster-burning powder can cut powder expense by half in a handgun. Switching from 18 grains of 2400 to 8 grains of Red Dot powder saves me 10 grains of powder per shot while only losing 99 fps. By using a faster-burning powder in my 30-06, like IMR-4895, I can save 2.3 cents a shot. (See Table 1.)

Allan Jones, of Blount, Inc., which manufactures Speer bullets and RCBS reloading equipment, said when he first started reloading he never considered the cost of powder. "Now that powder is up around $12 to $15 a pound, I think about it a lot," he told me.

Jones said by shooting IMR-4895 in his 30-06 instead of IMR-4831, he saves 10 grains of powder per shot. "If I am not looking for top velocity, but just a load for practice and enjoyment of my gun, I'll even go to a minimum charge of these faster powders to get even more loads per pound," he said.

But performance can suffer when a cartridge case is only

TABLE 1: POWDER COMPARISON AND SAVINGS

Load (Grs./Powder)	MV (fps)
41 Magnum, 210-Grain Bullet	
18.0/2400	1258
8.0/Red Dot	1159
30-06, 150-Grain Bullet	
59.0/IMR-4831	2861
49.5/IMR-4895	2865
45.5/IMR-4895	2621

partly filled with powder. Douglas Engh, of Hornady Mfg., pointed out that with reduced loads powder shifts to different positions in the case when the gun is raised and lowered. "This often leads to a wide deviation in velocity," he said. "In a handgun, the cost of powder is cheap, so shooting for cheap and shooting well are not necessarily the same."

Engh said he loads his handgun cartridges with a powder that almost fills the case. He shoots the same loads in practice as in competition. "I don't like surprises on the firing line," he said.

An example of what Engh is talking about is my 25-06.

Cast bullet loads in rifles save not only on bullet cost but powder as well. The 7mm Magnum can be shot for pennies a round with a cast bullet and Unique powder.

Gas checks on cast bullets permit using less desirable alloys, like wheelweights.

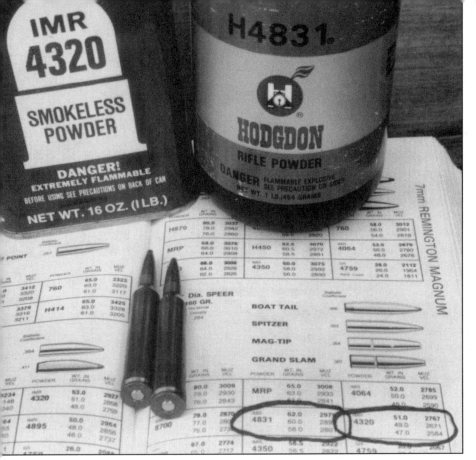

Powder selection in rifle cartridges can save a couple of pennies a shot. Eleven grains of powder can be saved by using IMR-4320 instead of 4831 in a 7mm Magnum.

The jacketed bullet load with H-4831 powder in a 6mm Remington costs almost 20 cents a shot. In contrast, a 100-grain cast bullet with 9 grains of Unique costs only 4 cents.

Loaded with 75-grain bullets and a light charge of IMR-4320, and then increasing the charge a grain at a time, the velocity variation noticeably shrinks. Loads that essentially fill the case also tend to shoot tighter groups, although I have shot a few 2-inch groups at 300 yards with the light loads. (See Table 2.)

A chronograph test with a 38 Special and a 41 Magnum showed consistent results with light charges of powder. (See Table 2.)

Jones said a friend of his developed an accurate load for a target handgun and shot it for years. One day, the friend happened to test the load over a chronograph. The load had a wide velocity deviation, but still shot well. "At the short range of a pistol, this high velocity deviation in relation to accuracy is more theory than reality," Jones said.

Self-loading firearms are very particular about powders. Take a 30 Carbine of mine: By loading Unique instead of 2400 in a batch of reloads, I saved enough money to buy a candy bar. What I didn't consider was the Unique load did not build enough pressure to cycle the action. So now I have 300 30 Carbine shells, which I am slowly shooting one at a time.

One thing about lower pressure, though, is cases last much longer. I assembled a batch of mild 6mm Remington practice loads with 70-grain jacketed and 100-grain cast bullets. These cases are still going strong after twelve years and many, many loadings. On the other hand, maximum hunting loads for this rifle with 100-grain jacketed bullets last about eight firings.

Engh owns a 32 H&R Magnum which is hard to find cases

for, and they're expensive when he does. "When I reload them, I treat them like gold," he said.

Engh leaves the cases uncrimped to prolong their life. Constant belling of the mouth to accept the bullet, then crimping the edge to the bullet, chews the case mouths and causes them to split. "You don't need a crimp to hold the bullet tightly if you are just going to put the loaded rounds in a plastic box, then take them out and shoot them," Engh said.

At least one reloading manual states a heavy crimp is needed on handgun cartridges to hold bullets in place during recoil and on firing to retard the start of the bullet and give the powder time to fully burn. Again I took my chronograph and 41 Magnum revolver to the range. I measured the length of one uncrimped cartridge and left it in the cylinder while I shot ten others. The loaded round measured the same 1.63 inches when it came out as when I put it in.

I also recorded the velocity of the heavy and light loads with and without crimps. As Table 3 shows, for some reason, the crimp worked better with the light load, but not as well with the heavy load—which is the opposite of what the theory states.

Because cases are used over and again, their cost per shot is small. A bullet, though, is used only once. Engh said bullet selection is the best way to save money. He shoots swaged lead bullets in his handguns because they are so much cheaper than jacketed bullets. "Lead bullets are shot slower than jacketed bullets," he said, "so I don't have to worry about leading the bore."

Jones said while Blount sells swaged lead bullets, they cannot compete with local one-man operations who make and sell cast bullets with little overhead. "Before you make the initial investment for the equipment to cast your own bullets, you had better ask yourself if the money wouldn't be better spent on someone else's cast bullets or jacketed bullets," Jones told me. "You can buy a lot of jacketed bullets for what the equipment costs."

A look in the back of *Handloader's Digest,* 12th Ed., showed a retail price of $427 for all the RCBS equipment needed to cast pistol bullets. Half of that cost is for a Pro-Melt furnace. For years, I took a cheaper, yet satisfactory, route and melted my lead in a pot on a Coleman stove. I ladled the molten lead from the pot into the mould with a dipper. The pot and dipper cost only $20. The Pro-Melt furnace is easier and faster to use, of course.

After the equipment has been amortized, Jones said that cast bullet handgun loads cost about the same as 22 rimfire ammo.

For handgun velocities, the copper cup swaged onto the base of a cast bullet is an unneeded expense. "About the only reason to use a gas check on pistol bullets is so you can use softer alloys," Jones said. With linotype becoming scare, a person can add a gas check to bullets cast from softer wheelweights and still keep the bore from leading.

Before Jones went to work for Blount, he worked in a crime lab in Texas. In his work, he recovered and studied bullets shot into a water tank. The water stopped the bullets without distorting them.

"I noticed the base of lead bullets did not melt," Jones said. "If anything, the gas cut around the sides of the bullets." He noticed bullets with square bases swelled slightly to fill the bore and kept powder gas from forcing past the bullet.

A square base is essential for cast bullets shot at higher velocity from rifles. "A gas check at the higher velocities keeps the bullet base square. The powder gas hits the gas check and flattens it to seal the bore," Jones said.

Some of the more affluent authorities recommend buying several mould designs to see which bullet design shoots the best in a particular firearm. With the price of a double-cavity mould from $40 to $100, I will take my chances that one mould will produce accurate bullets. Jones recommends trying several different powders instead as a cheaper alternative. "There's one powder out there that is going to work better with a particular bullet design than any of the others," he said.

In my 6mm Remington, Unique shoots 100-grain cast bullets very well. The bullets poke along at 1453 fps, but have an extreme velocity spread of only 8 fps and group well at 50 yards. My son, who has just started shooting big game rifles, shoots these 6mm loads as fast as I can seat the bullets.

Practicing is where I save the money on rifle bullets. When my son wants to take the 6mm or his 7mm-08 to the range to rehearse for the morning when a buck will step out of the forest, I supply him with plenty of cast bullet loads for only pennies apiece. The recoil of these loads is slight. That lets him concentrate on aiming and squeezing.

However, cast bullets have not replaced jacketed bullets for hunting. Jacketed bullets allow much higher velocities and

All the equipment you need to cast bullets: an RCBS mould, Pro-Melt furnace and Lub-A-Matic lubricator-sizer.

expand better than cast. When opening morning comes and a buck is standing at the far side of a park, a jacketed bullet is worth the dime and a nickel it costs.

Going to a plumbing supply house or junkyard to buy alloys for casting takes some of the fun out of shooting for cheap. I prefer to scrounge my materials.

One of my ancestors must have rubbed the picture off every coin he owned before it passed from his hand. Whoever it was, I have a hunch he is from my maternal side of the family. My mother always finds a deal. Every Saturday, she cruises the garage sales. I usually go along, because the best bargains for shooting components are from people cleaning their attics and basements.

This past spring I read a classified ad for an estate sale at the edge of town. The ad read "50 years of good stuff."

The sale was at an old farmhouse and barn that, over the years, the expanding town had overtaken. Rusted tractor parts and tools for non-existent machinery lined the yard. But in the middle of it all stood tables of bullets, lead shot, powders, car-

TABLE 2: POWDER WEIGHT AND UNIFORM VELOCITY

Bullet		Load	MV	Stan. Dev.
(Wgt. Grs.)	(Type)	(Grs./Powder)	(fps)	(fps)
25-06 Remington				
Ruger M77, 24-inch barrel. L.C. military cases necked down.				
75	Hornady	46/IMR-4320	3406	83
75	Hornady	47/IMR-4320	3450	61
75	Hornady	48/IMR-4320	3455	50
75	Hornady	49/IMR-4320	3484	30
38 Special				
Model 19 S&W, 4-inch barrel.				
150	Cast	4.0/Unique	638	16
150	Cast	3.7/W-231	699	22
41 Magnum				
Ruger Blackhawk, 6.5-inch barrel.				
210	Cast	18.0/2400	1258	62
210	Cast	7.0/Red Dot	1032	10

Middle of skyscreens of Oehler Model 33 Chronotach is 15 feet from muzzle.

Old loading manuals often found at garage sales contain a wealth of cast bullet and obsolete cartridge loading data.

Factory 6mm jacketed bullets cost at least a dime apiece, while cast bullets cost, at most, three pennies.

tridge cases, shotgun shells, wads, and factory and reloaded rifle and shotgun shells.

I prefer to leave reloaded cartridges alone, because of the possibility of blowing up my gun with someone else's reloading mistake. Unless cartridge cases are new or once fired, I also avoid them. The first time you reload them, they might all separate at the head. About the only way to tell if they have been fired once is if the factory primer is still in place, such as the brass-colored

primer in Remington cartridges. Shotgun shells are a different matter. As long as the shell mouths are not ragged, they are fine.

I bought one box of 12-gauge reloads for $1. I bought them primarily for the Herter's plastic box they came in. I also bought wads and bullets at give-away prices. The best buy of the day was a dollar for a box, missing four shells, of 3-inch magnum Federal 12-gauge shells.

At other yard and estate sales, I have bought linotype bullet metal in 20-pound ingots, factory-loaded 38 Specials, rifle shells in plastic Case-Gard boxes, and old shooting and hunting books and reloading manuals. These old manuals, such as the old Lyman Ideal handbooks numbers 39, 40 and 41, have a wealth of loading information for cast bullets and obsolete cartridges, such as the 348 Winchester, 35 Winchester and 38-40 WCF, and loads for a variety of cast bullet weights.

Yet for all the sweating over the casting pot and penny pinching at the garage sales, I haven't really saved a dime. I have just ended up buying more components and shooting more. But that's what shooting for cheap is all about.

TABLE 3: CRIMP OR NO CRIMP		
Crimp	MV (fps)	SD (fps)
41 Magnum		
18.5/2400, 210-grain cast bullet		
Crimp	1282	18
No Crimp	1294	18
7.0/Red Dot, 210-grain cast bullet		
Crimp	1032	12
No Crimp	1015	20

Handloading can be simple... basic...if that's all you need. But when ultimate accuracy is demanded, things are much more complex. Here's....

How the Benchresters Do It

by FRED SINCLAIR

IN THE RIGHT hands, today's state of-the-art benchrest rifle is capable of shooting much less than .200-MOA. For example, at the 1992 International Benchrest Shooters National Championship Matches, the winning shooter, Tony Boyer, fired a total of fifteen five-shot groups at 100 yards and another fifteen five-shot groups at 200 yards, and the total of the 150 rounds fired averaged only .1942-MOA. In doing so, Tony won the prestigious Heavy Varmint Class with an average of .1587-MOA (twenty-five shots at 100 yards and twenty-five more at 200 yards).

Benchrest rifles are built using only the best components and assembled to exacting tolerances. Normally, chambers on these rifles are reamed to "close tolerances." This is to say, headspace is set at the minimum, case body diameters are minimum SAA-MI specs, and neck diameters are well below standard chambers. Chambers, reamed to close tolerances, will not accept a standard loaded cartridge. Such chambers will, when the case is properly prepared, limit the expansion of a fired case. Once the case is fireformed, body and headspace dimensions are limited

A ball micrometer will be a must when working with a benchrest rifle with a close tolerance chamber.

The Wilson neck reamer is being used to chamfer a case mouth with an 8-degree angle. It produces a smoother entry than the standard case mouth chamfering tool.

The Sinclair neck wall thickness gauge speeds the case sorting operation. A ball micrometer can be used for the same purpose.

to zero expansion and neck expansion is limited to .002-inch maximum.

Loading for such capable firearms involves much more than working the handle of a reloading press. It requires that the handloader become a cross between a quality-control engineer and a proficient mechanic. If the benchrest shooter expects to shoot well, he must prepare and load each cartridge case to the most exacting standards that his ability will allow.

Precise case preparation is a must. It is tedious and time-consuming, especially in large numbers. Performed separately, you will be hard pressed to see accuracy improvements from some of the prep operations. But as you multiply the steps, the uniformity and efficiency of the cartridge case will be improved, and you will find that each operation enhances the previous one.

Because of the close tolerance chamber specs used for modern B/R rifles, cartridge case life can be extended so that twenty cases will normally outlast the usable life of the rifle barrel. For this reason, plus the fact that most benchrest shooters reload on site, case preparation is normally confined to ten to twenty cases at a time.

Preparation is started with new commercial cases; anything less will be a waste of time and effort. Trying to save a few bucks on cases for a first-rate B/R rifle is foolish, not frugal. Brass that has been fired and reloaded a number of times

becomes work-hardened and brittle. This condition will not allow the case to properly respond to some prep operations. Military brass, even the match type, is of a harder alloy and not manufactured with reloading in mind. The life of this brass will be short, and the end result will be frequent replacement.

Now that Federal and Norma are no longer offering unprimed brass, our choices are narrowed to Remington, Winchester and PMC. With the availability of bulk Remington and Winchester brass at reasonable prices, there is little reason not to use these brands. I have heard some reloaders comment that bulk brass is inferior to factory-boxed brass, but let me assure you it all comes from the same place.

Quality measuring tools are required for precision reloading. A good pair of stainless steel dial calipers is a must, a 1-inch micrometer comes in quite handy, and, when working with a close tolerance chamber, some type of .0001-inch reading ball-end micrometer is mandatory. For case sorting, a neck wall thickness gauge will add speed to the operation. Just remember that dial-type calipers are not the last word in measuring tools and are normally capable of only plus or minus .001-inch accuracy. Your needs will require measuring in the tenths of thousands, so use a standard-style micrometer made for such tolerances.

If I wish to end up with twenty prepared cases, I normally

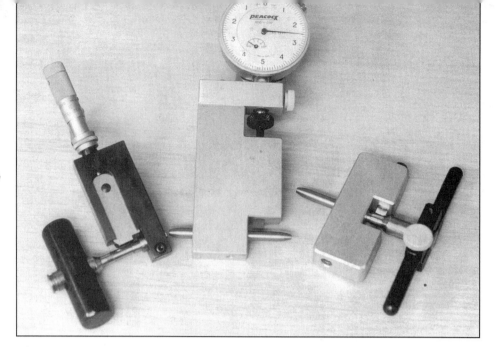

R.W. Hart and Sinclair outside neck turning tools.

start with twice that number. I know from experience that a few will be discarded and I may ruin a couple during the neck-turning operation.

Most prep operations are influenced by the case neck. More likely than not, the neck and/or mouth are distorted during manufacturing, so the first operation is to resize the neck in some fashion. Use either an expanding mandrel or resizing die that will straighten the full length of the neck.

While resizing, check for any small creases in the case shoulder and neck, and for off-center flash holes. Cases having these imperfections should be discarded.

Most new brass, sized or unsized, has a noticeable burr just inside of the case mouth. Most of us use a standard 60-degree deburring tool to remove this burr. But close inspection will likely reveal that such removal has not been complete. I use a Wilson case trimmer and neck reamer of the correct caliber for inside chamfering. The reamers have about an 8-degree taper for the first .060- to .085-inch. I run the reamer into the case just to where the major diameter of the reamer contacts the mouth. This produces a nice gradual taper that results in a couple of benefits. It eliminates the "bump" as the bullet is being seated, plus it allows the cartridge case to start over a neck-turning tool mandrel with greater ease. It is a slower method of case mouth chamfering, but it will produce benefits.

I weigh each case when preparing B/R cases. Normally, the weight does not vary much within each lot. I feel that a variance here of 1.5 percent of case weight is a maximum acceptable limit.

Gauging flash hole diameters is an operation I do on a random basis. Most commercial manufacturers aim for an .082-inch diameter flash hole. There are exceptions, such as PPC. A wire size #45 drill bit (.082) can be used to check hole size, if desired. I do not worry about undersized flash holes, as most flash hole deburring tools, except RCBS, will open the hole to .082.

The next step is to sort the cases by neck wall thickness. The theory is that if neck wall thickness varies, body thickness will vary even more. Extreme body wall variance will create a powder chamber that is off-center with the rifle bore. Knowledgeable B/R reloaders feel this is an undesirable condition.

Using a tool designed for the purpose, check neck wall thickness. You will find it does vary around the circumference. The amount of variance will determine if a case is a "keeper." Discard any with a variance exceeding .0015-inch.

The use of an outside neck-turning tool is mandatory for close-tolerance B/R rifle chambers. Not only is it required to uniform the case neck walls, but it is also needed so the shooter can match the neck diameter of his loaded round to that of the rifle's chamber. Inside neck reamers will not work for neck wall uniforming. The neck reamer is designed to remove excess material. The reamer will only follow the existing hole, unless it is supported—such as in a $^7/_8$-14 ream die. Neck ream dies can be valuable in case-forming operations, but not neck wall uniforming. The major problem with ream dies is that the user has no control over the amount of material being removed. The preferred practice is to outside neck turn.

A number of neck-turning tools are available, but the best for B/R use are the hand-held type. This kind of tool produces the most accurate results. Some are available with micrometers or dial indicators, so the adjustment can be fine tuned to .0001-inch when desired.

Fit of the cartridge case on the neck-turning tool mandrel/pilot is the most important part of the turning operation. A case neck too loose on the mandrel/pilot will sure make for easy turning, but is a waste of time. Any clearance between the mandrel/pilot will be transferred to the finished product. The result will be a neck wall thickness variance equal to the amount of the clearance, the very thing you were trying to correct.

If the resizing performed prior to initial case inspection does not produce the desired fit, you may have to alter or replace the die's expander ball. The expander ball's diameter must be compatible with the neck-turning tool mandrel. An expander ball .001-inch larger than the mandrel will normally obtain an ideal fit.

Unfortunately, resizing dies and neck-turning tool mandrels often have incompatible diameters. To correct the problem, the handloader may have to polish either the expander ball or the mandrel to obtain the most desirable fit. This is a fairly simple task that can be done using nothing more than a drill motor and 320-grit emery.

Turn the case neck so that the base of the bullet, when seated, is in the turned portion of the neck. Better yet turn the full length of the neck.

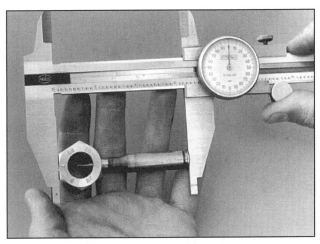

Tools such as this Bullet Comparator will be quite beneficial when working with bullet seating depths.

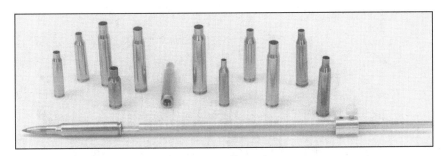

Stoney Point Chamber-All seating depth tool. There are a number of tools available for finding correct seating depth, but this tool takes out all the guesswork.

Adjustment of most neck-turning tools can be a little tricky for the beginner. Until you get acquainted with the procedure, use some of those culled cartridge cases when adjusting your tool.

It is best to turn the full length of the neck, but don't go too far into the shoulder. Doing so would cause a weak area at the neck and shoulder junction.

If you are a beginner at turning cases for benchrest-type tight chambers, I suggest turning the case neck so your finished *loaded* round will measure .002-inch smaller than the neck diameter of your rifle's chamber. Once you become acquainted with the tool and the neck-turning operation, you may want to work to a closer neck tolerance, but not the first time around.

At this point, it is time to prime (more on priming will be discussed later) and charge the cases in preparation for fireforming. When selecting a powder charge for fireforming, check one of the current loading manuals. Select a powder that has a mid-range burning rate for the cartridge you are working with, and use a charge that is on the low end of the reloading manual's suggestions.

If you are working with some sort of wildcat that will be blown out considerably during the fireforming operation, use caution not to "over do." If the wildcat has a fairly large case capacity, do not fireform with a slow-burning powder.

Do not use powder XYZ just because you have a lot of it or because it was cheap. And for gosh sakes, *do not* start with somebody's pet load without reducing it first.

Remember that case capacity is at a minimum on new cases. Also keep in mind that when you start with new cases, you may encounter a variation in case volume from manufacturer to manufacturer, and even from lot to lot of the same manufacturer. The load that was right for your last batch of brass may not work as well for the new cases you have just purchased.

I prefer to fireform new cases with the bullets firmly touching the rifling—not jammed against it, but firm. I do so using a reduced load.

Seating against the rifling has several benefits. It forces the case head flush against the bolt face, which helps keep the primer from backing out, and it helps to center the round in the chamber. Results will be an evenly fireformed case, eliminating most of the off-center firing pin indentation and much of the one-sided bulge which can be created by a maximum-size chamber.

Without the proper tools, finding the overall length (OAL) that has the bullet just touching the rifling will be trial and error. Smoking a bullet or drawing lines on a cleaning rod shoved down the barrel went out with the hula hoop. Use one of the accurate seating depth tools that are available today. The new Stoney Point Chamber-All gauge is the most versatile tool I have used.

Once you establish that initial seating depth, assemble an unprimed sample round. Assemble samples with other weights and brands of bullets that you might be using. Be sure to mark them accordingly. Such samples should be used as references. They will be used later when you begin fine tuning the seating depth for that ultimate load. They will serve as a gauge for tracking throat wear and initial bullet seater adjustment.

The OAL, when measuring across the bullet's point, is going to vary a little from round to round. Bullets out of the same box will vary as much as .015-inch in length due to the way the bullet swage die works. The use of a Bullet Comparator, Davidson Seating Depth Checker, or the RCBS Precision Mic will allow the handloader to arrive at correct seating depths and eliminate these variations. These tools contact the bullet at the major diameter and, by doing so, offset individual bullet length differences.

Another benefit of using a seating depth tool is that you can, from time to time, remeasure the barrel to analyze the amount of throat wear. As the throat erodes, you must adjust cartridge OAL an equal amount to compensate for the wear, if you expect to maintain peak accuracy.

Once you have arrived at the correct OAL, so the bullet touches the rifling, you are ready to adjust your bullet seater to that measurement. Here is where you can use that sample round. Back off the seater adjustment enough that you are sure it will not contact the sample round. Insert the sample and gently screw the seater stem down until it contacts the bullet of the sample. At this point, seat another bullet in another case and measure it, using a Bullet Comparator or similar tool. The measurement at this stage will likely be a bit longer than your sample round, and the seater will have to be adjusted until the correct OAL is obtained.

For benchrest loading, use hand-type reloading dies. Reasons

tion is some sort of shortened wildcat, it may be necessary. If the case is a standard, there is no need to trim until the case has been fireformed, but it should be done before the case is resized.

If you review standard SAAMI chamber and cartridge drawings, you will note that between minimum chamber specs and maximum cartridge specs there is a minimum case-to-chamber average of .024-inch. Unless new brass exceeds this allowance, there is no need to trim prior to initial fireforming. Trimming prior to resizing enhances alignment as the case enters the sizing die.

I suggest that cases not be trimmed to published trim lengths without knowing the actual chamber length of the firearm in which they will be used. Published trim-to dimensions will result in a safe case length, but experience has shown that the actual length of a chamber does not always fall within SAAMI specs. If you have access to a lathe, a simple gauge can be made that will allow you to measure actual chamber length. (See July/August, 1989, *Handloader*.)

Once a case is trimmed, chamfer the mouth in the previously

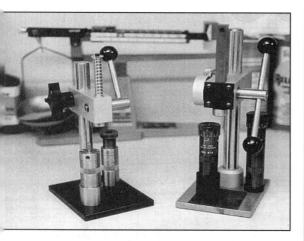

Hand dies put the handloader in control of the sizing and seating operations. Most are used with small arbor presses. Shown are (left) Sinclair press with Wilson dies and R.W Hart & Son press with Custom Products dies.

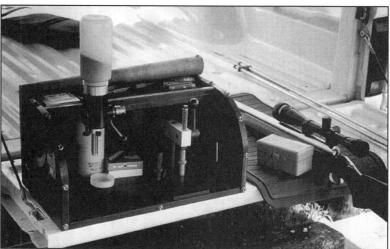

Benchrest shooting requires on-site reloading. Pictured is the author's loading box set up to load off the tailgate.

are simple. Due to the close tolerance chambers, resizing is at a minimum. Neck reduction from a fired case to a resized case should not exceed .002-inch. Such minimum resizing reduces seating effort as well as sizing effort, and either operation can be done by hand if so desired. Normally, a small arbor press is used. The major advantage of hand-type neck dies is that they do not require an expander ball. Actual resizing is done by interchangeable sizing inserts. The handloader is in complete control of the amount of neck reduction and the resultant neck-to-bullet tension. Bullet seaters are designed so that the cartridge case is fully supported in the die body prior to seating the bullet. Portability is another advantage as most benchrest shooters load at the range during practice and when attending a match.

Once the cases are fireformed, clean any powder residue from the outside and inside of the case neck. Use 000 steel wool or a treated brass polishing cloth on the outside and a nylon brush on the inside. At this point, I remove the spent primers, without doing any resizing, and then trim the cases to proper length.

Trimming a case to length is normally one of the first steps a novice handloader will perform. If the cartridge case in ques-

described manner. Case mouth chamfering is crucial and must be performed so that the bullet's base and bearing surface do not become damaged during the seating operation. From an accuracy standpoint, the bearing surface of a bullet—the surface that has actual contact with the barrel—plus the bullet's base are the important areas of the bullet.

Chamber pressures are sealed by the base of the bullet. If the base is deformed, the seal will not be evenly distributed around the circumference of the base as it exits the barrel. This condition can cause a tipping effect on the bullet. If the bullet's bearing surface is damaged, it will more than likely create abnormal jacket wear, or fouling, as the bullet travels through the barrel.

When cases have been trimmed to equal length, their heads are ready to be squared. Case head squaring creates excessive headspace until the case is once again fireformed. This operation should never be performed on unfired cases or full-length resized cases. Due to the manufacturing process, an unfired case is not likely to have its head surface at right angles with the body centerline. Squaring at the unfired state results in removing excessive amounts of material.

Whitetail Design makes a special carbide cutter for the Wilson case trimmer specifically for squaring case heads. This cutter has a .56-inch diameter cutting face, so it will handle case diameters up to and including the standard belted mags.

If the head face does not clean up at .002- to .003-inch after it has been fireformed, you have more problems than just a cartridge case. More than likely there is an alignment problem between the barrel and action that may require major attention.

Once the head squaring is completed, it is time to rework flash holes and primer pockets.

Cartridge cases are manufactured by a series of drawing and punching operations. Primer pockets and flash holes are formed by swaging, punching or both. This is done from the outside of the case, leaving internal problems for the handloader.

As the flash hole is punched, exit burrs are formed on the inside of the case. This is a major problem. Such burrs cause an uneven dispersion of the primer flash, which, in turn, creates ignition problems.

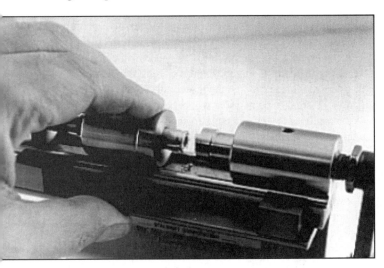

Case head squaring can be done using the Whitetail Engineering cutter in a Wilson case trimmer.

Removal of this burr and normalizing the length of the flash hole will allow the primer flash to ignite the powder more uniformly. I firmly believe that flash hole deburring is an important operation in any case preparation, perhaps the most important.

Prior to the deburring of any case, *be sure* that the primers are removed. I have never experienced it, but I suspect a live primer could be detonated during this operation. Deburring with a spent primer still in the case will restrict the cutting depth of the tool and defeat the purpose. Fortunately, this is a one-time operation for each case.

Inspection of a new case will also reveal that primer pockets have a radius where the wall meets at the bottom of the pocket. Also note that the bottom is somewhat dished. On the other hand, if you take a good look at a primer, you will see it is constructed so the anvil protrudes from the bottom of the cup. This is necessary so the anvil will rest on the bottom of the primer pocket. When the firing pin strikes the primer, the explosive pellet inside the primer cup is crushed between the anvil and cup, causing the material to detonate. Variations in the depth and configuration of the pocket, not to mention the primer seat-

ing operation, can and will alter the effect of the firing pin blow.

If the blow of the firing pin is varied, it will in turn vary the primer ignition and thus result in erratic pressures and velocities. This can create vertical shot dispersion; that is to say, shots will string up and down on the target.

Depending upon the action manufacturer, firing pin protrusion will range from .045- to .060-inch. With this in mind, it is easy to see that a primer seating variance of only .010-inch could alter firing pin influence as much as 20 percent.

Primer pocket uniformers are designed to cut the pockets to uniform depths and, at the same time, square the primer seating surface in relation to the case head. The tools do not alter the primer pocket diameter as the cutters are ground to cut depth only. Alignment is controlled by the pocket walls.

Do not panic if a primer pocket uniformer does not clean up a new case. After a couple of firings, it should. *I do not suggest cutting the pockets deeper just to get them to clean up. If pockets are that far off specifications, discard the cases.*

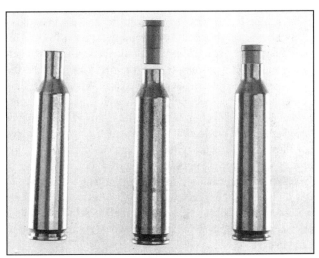

Chamber lengths are not always what they should be. A simple gauge can be made to check the actual length.

It must be remembered that not only do cases grow longer with repeated firing, but primer pockets also become shallower, so will require an occasional recutting. For this reason, it is wise to use a carbide tool for the uniforming operation and continue to use the same tool as a primer pocket cleaner. Once the radius has been removed from the bottom of the pocket, some primer pocket cleaners will not clean the pocket completely.

Primer pocket uniforming completes the case preparation operations. It is now time to neck size the finished cases and prepare for load development operations.

Primers are the one component in the reloading process over which we have no control. Their overall height may vary considerably...by as much as .012-inch.

Some years ago, I did a good deal of experimenting with primer variations. I spent hours sorting by overall height, seating by feel, and seating to a predetermined depth. After seating, I lathe-turned the case head so I could reclaim the seated primer for measuring. Hundreds of rounds were also fired using a return to battery rifle. Doing so, I came to the conclusion that the only way to get around the problem inherent with primers is to seat them by feel.

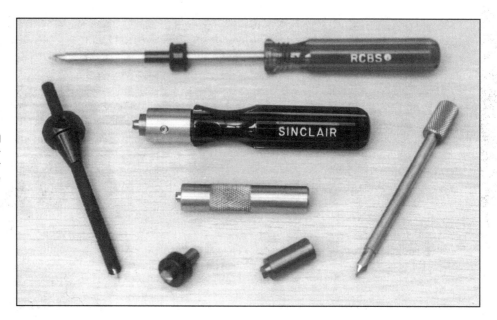

Flash hole deburring tools and primer pocket uniformers are available from a number of sources. Pictured are tools by R.W. Hart & Son, RCBS and Sinclair.

Even with primer pockets of uniform depth and primers sorted by height, I found that most priming tools on the market would not evenly seat primers. For uniform seating, the handloader must use a priming tool that allows him to "feel" the primer as it travels down the primer pocket. When you feel the primer bottom ever so slightly, you have already given it a preload of about .005-inch, which, in testing, proved to be the preferred amount of pre-load. If your present seating method does not allow you to feel the primer as it contacts the bottom of the primer pocket, you are not using the correct tool.

You can spend from $15 to $120 for priming tools. You can buy tools with "bells and whistles." Whatever your preference may be, a good tool can be judged by the way it "feels" and the ease in which it seats the primer. The two do not necessarily go hand in hand.

Regardless of what type of priming tool you use, keep in mind that most tools hold the cartridge case on the upper side of the rim. Case rims can and do vary in thickness and become worn by the rifle's extractor, reloading tool shellholders, and so on.

When priming, give all your cases a visual inspection and discard any that show major damage to the rim. Such damage could result in a "poor feel" and misalignment during primer seating.

Many handloaders, not acquainted with B/R shooting, are a bit shocked when they find out that B/R shooters charge cases right out of the measure. Some mistrust measures for one reason or another and prefer weighing each charge. I have no problem with that. I do feel, however, that measures get shortchanged due to the manufacturer's lack of usage instructions or the user's failure to read instructions.

Granted, most B/R cartridges require charges of 30 grains or less. Most prefer powders which are fine-grained, but the secret to making most measures perform consistently is in the operation technique.

I hasten to point out that every reloader should use a good scale to verify original charge weights. It is *not* a good practice to accept any powder measure setting on faith, even if the information comes from someone with a measure identical to yours.

The operation of a measure is not just a matter of pulling a crank or lever. The reloader must develop a consistent rhythm when using any measure if he desires to throw uniform charges. The name of the game is uniformity, so "play" with your measure, using different techniques and weighing the charges as you go to see which produces the most uniform results.

I find the crank-type measure works best when the operator taps the handle at the top and bottom of the handle's stroke. The tapping helps equally settle the powder in the charge drum and reservoir each time. This procedure produces very uniform charges on most measures of this design.

When filling the reservoir of your measure, do not just dump the powder in and start throwing charges. To do so could create problems. Just after filling the measure, it will normally throw heavier charges for the first few charges. This is caused by the powder being compacted as it is poured into the reservoir. Generally, you will want to cycle about a dozen charges before actually charging your cases. Measures with long reservoirs are bad about this, while those with some type of baffle may not be affected. Regardless, check out this potential problem while you acquaint yourself with the measure.

When using *any* powder measure, be sure it is *always* mounted *solidly*. Make sure your mounting bracket does not flex in any manner. You would be surprised how poorly some measures operate when the mounting is allowed to flex, even to a minor degree. Here again some manufacturers insist on a mount that is nothing more than sheet metal. A cheap mount just will not work.

If you encounter static electricity problems when using a measure, try wiping out the reservoir and affected parts with one of the anti-static sheets your wife uses in the clothes dryer. Works on powder funnels also.

Although it may sound trivial, a measure that has interchangeable drop tubes, of different lengths, is highly desirable. The longer tubes allow the reloader to use "full-density" charges without the fear of compressing the charge.

With a capable benchrest rifle and properly prepared cases, finding a good load combination is normally an easy task. Finding the ultimate load is a matter of fine tuning that good load.

A benchrest shooter is going to know what loads the winning

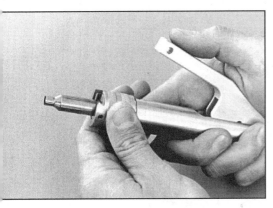

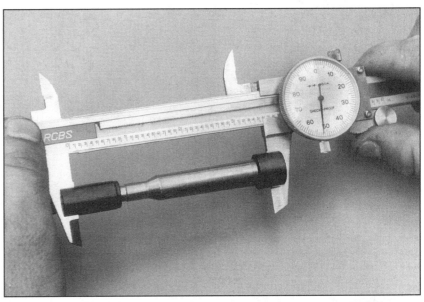

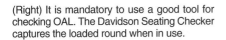

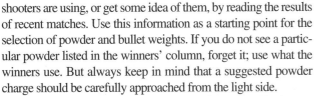

(Above) A good priming tool can be judged by the way it "feels" the primer as it is being pressed home. Pictured is the stainless steel Sinclair tool.

(Right) It is mandatory to use a good tool for checking OAL. The Davidson Seating Checker captures the loaded round when in use.

shooters are using, or get some idea of them, by reading the results of recent matches. Use this information as a starting point for the selection of powder and bullet weights. If you do not see a particular powder listed in the winners' column, forget it; use what the winners use. But always keep in mind that a suggested powder charge should be carefully approached from the light side.

Bullets used will most always be custom-made. Obtain two or three different brands. Your rifle will probably have a preference in bullet weights and brands.

Published match results will show you that two or, maybe, three powders are preferred. This simplifies load development. Start with the two most popular powders for your cartridge. Charge only three cases per powder. Using the same brand and weight bullet, seat them to touch the rifling, as described for fireforming.

My experience has been that most 22-caliber rifles perform best with the bullet .010- to .020-inch off the rifling; most 25 and 6mm rifles from just touching to .010-inch off; and larger calibers just touching. This is not a "carved-in-stone" rule, as each rifle is individual, but generally speaking it has been a reliable guide for my loading. Normally I seat bullets to these beginning settings.

You will note the only variation in my load is the different powders I am going to try. Everything else is the same: bullet, seating depth, primer, etc. Do not try several different things at one time; it will only confuse the process.

Shooting three-shot groups, I fire the different powders and record the results. Usually one of these groups will look better than the others. For example, let's say I used H-4895 and H-322, and the group size ranked in just that order. The next step would be to reload using the H-4895 load. Try it again to just be sure it was not a fluke. If it works well the second time, you are ready to try some load adjustments. If it did not, try the other powder.

Once I settle upon which of the two powders worked best, I inspect the fired primers to see that the load is not too hot. I do not want to see primers all mashed flat around the edges. I prefer a very slight crater around the firing pin dent with the corners of the primer still showing a radius. Look for burnished areas on the case head. Such signs indicate that the load is too

hot, a condition normally accompanied by increased resistance when opening and closing the bolt.

If you encounter these high pressure signs, then back your charge down a little bit. If not, continue to increase the charge to the next step shown in the reloading manual you are using, but *always* proceed with caution.

Load another three cartridges and fire them. If the group improves, make another powder charge change in that direction. If it does not, go the other direction with your charge. Continue this procedure until you have settled on the charge that performs best.

Always bear in mind that changes in brands of powder, and even lots of the same powder, require adjustments in powder charges.

Powders are graded by burning rates that are on a scale. For example, let's say powder #1234 is on a scale from 1 to 10, powder #5678 is on a scale from 10 to 21, etc.

You may have worked up a load with powder #1234 that shoots well for you. When that powder was graded by the manufacturer, it fell in their 1 to 10 scale at 2. You just purchased another can of #1234, but it was from a different manufactured lot, and maybe it was graded at 10 on their scale. You may find, especially if your load is near maximum, that this new can of #1234 may be too hot with your earlier load. You may have to back down on the powder charge. Always use caution when changing lots of powders. Also remember that the super accurate load you worked up in the hot weather of July just might be too mild on a cool October day, or vice versa.

Once you have established a powder preference, it is time to make seating depth changes. Let's say we started with the bullet touching the rifling. Now, load three rounds at this setting and three more at .005-inch off the rifling. Fire both of the groups and then look for an improvement.

If the .005-inch group looks the most promising, load three more at that setting, another three at .010-inch, and try them again. Work the seating depth toward the optimum group. Once you find what looks best, try changes of .002-inch. A good shooting rifle will know the difference. Seating depth is one of the most important factors in obtaining peak accuracy.

Besides being an excellent toolmaker and machinist, Sinclair is a top shooter. Here he's testing a counter-sniper rifle he built for a federal law enforcement agency. Carefully tested handloads bring out the best accuracy in such rifles.

It may, at this point, be a good idea to try another bullet. You have already found a working range for the powder charge and a seating depth measurement that performs well. When changing bullets, use a Bullet Comparator to get a correct seating depth measurement of your "pet." Once you have found the correct seating depth for one bullet, these tools will allow you to reset your seating die for different bullets.

Let's say you have worked up a pet load using Smith 65-grain bullets that works well in your custom-built 6mm PPC B/R rifle. Measure this round with the Comparator and also measure the original dummy for the 65-grain Smith bullet.

For example, assume that the pet measured .005-inch shorter than the original dummy. This tells us that the pet load prefers the bullet to be .005-inch off the rifling. Remember, the dummy was assembled from seating depth gauge measurements that had the bullet just touching the rifling.

Now, let us say you are going to try a Jones bullet of a different ogive. Measure your dummy, the one with the Jones bullet, and adjust your seater so that assembled rounds are .005-inch shorter than the dummy. For correct evaluation of the Jones bullet, it must be seated so that the major diameter of the bullet is the same distance from the rifling as the bullet in the "pet" load. Keep in mind that just trying different bullets at the same bullet seater setting will not give you a correct evaluation of each bullet. The ogives would have to be identical to get the same measurement, and that rarely happens.

It is mandatory that the handloader use some type of bullet comparator when making seating depth changes. In the first place, bullets, especially the hollowpoint bullets that generally give best accuracy, will vary by as much as .025-inch in their length. Variations in bullet length may not affect the accuracy of the rifle. They do make it impossible to deal accurately with seating depth in terms of overall cartridge length when mea-

suring across the bullet's point. Secondly, bullets of the same weight from different makers are quite often of different lengths due to variations in the shape of the bullets' ogives. They also will have varying lengths of bearing surfaces (the major diameter).

Since bullets often vary in length, it is important that OAL measurements be made from a fixed reference point, such as that provided by the Bullet Comparator or the Davidson SDC. Based on my experience, I feel that bullet seating depth, when it is measured in terms of the amount of free bullet travel prior to land contact, is a constant for a given rifle.

In other words, while overall cartridge length will vary with bullets of different weights and shapes, for best accuracy, the relationship of the bearing surface of the bullet and the origin of the bore's lands must remain the same regardless of bullet shape or weight.

The OAL figures published in loading manuals are only reference figures to use for correct magazine length. Other than determining whether or not a loaded round will function through a rifle's magazine, published OAL measurements, when measured across the bullet's point, are useless for B/R use.

Remember, however, OAL eventually must be increased to compensate for throat wear in the bore. The frequency with which these changes must be made will depend on the intensity of the cartridge being used and on the number of rounds fired. If you notice that accuracy begins to deteriorate after several hundred rounds, check the seating depth and increase as required.

Summarization of benchrest reloading can be stated by a single sentence: "Nothing is so important as a trifle." Maybe the late L.E. "Sam" Wilson made it even more direct and simple: "Garbage in, garbage out." Either way, if you are not willing to spend the time and effort to become a novice machinist and pay attention to all the details, forget it.

240

Sometimes—as when a copperhead is curled up in the chicken coop—a lot of little projectiles is better than one big one.

Shot Loads For Handguns

by C.E. HARRIS

SHOT LOADS HAVE been used as defensive expedients or to kill small game for the pot as long as there have been handguns. Single shot muzzle-loading pistols were often loaded with multiple shot or "buck and ball." The Civil War-era LeMat 44-caliber revolver featured a 20-gauge shotgun barrel in the middle of the cylinder and was favored by foraging Confederates. In frontier days, shot loads were common for large-bore revolvers. The 44-40 enjoyed a particular variety of factory loads up until about WWII. Specialized smoothbore "shot revolvers" or break-open guns like the H&R Handy-Gun and Marble's Game Getter were popular among outdoorsmen until they became subject to federal tax stamp requirements in the 1930s.

While technically possible, handgun shot loads in small calibers are virtually useless because they can't hold enough shot to throw a useful pattern. The 22 LR and 22 WMR shot loads are, at most, effective for about as far as you can spit. The 38 Special is the smallest handgun cartridge for which a shot load makes any sense. Shot loads for this round can be improvised with 3.5 grains of Bullseye, simply by placing a gas check over the powder, filling the case with #9 shot and crimping another gas check in the mouth of the case. These are effective on snakes and small rodents within about 10 feet. In 357 Magnum brass, you can add a pinch more shot with about 4 grains of a fast-burning, dense pistol powder such as W-231 or Bullseye.

These loads spread about 1 inch per foot of range, so the patterns are ineffective beyond about 10 feet until you get to the larger calibers. Cases over 40-caliber hold enough shot to add about 5 feet of effective range. You can load 5 grains of Bullseye or W-231 in the 41 Magnum with a case full of fine shot, and 6 grains in the 44 Magnum or 45 Colt.

The disadvantages of improvised shot loads are that unprotected shot tend to lead the bore and are scattered into a patchy pattern by the rifling. Gas checks aren't very effective as over-powder or over-shot wads, but cardboard or felt doesn't give much improvement either.

Far better are shot capsules, because patterns are more even and bore leading is no longer a problem. The first handgun shot capsules I remember were Remco Shot Caps, which could be had in a variety of calibers during the 1960s. These are no longer available, but Speer Shot Caps, introduced in the early 1970s, are still being made for the 38/357 and 44 calibers. Speer provides complete instructions for loading these, and nothing I could say can improve much on the data provided by the manufacturer.

The 38/357 Speer shot loads were introduced in 1972 and have changed little. They hold 105 grains or about 147 pellets of #9 shot. Like most handgun shot loads, they spread about 1 inch per foot of range, but their patterns are even, and 85 percent of the shot hit within a 15-inch circle at 15 feet. Their velocity is about 1140 fps from a 6-inch revolver and 960 fps from a 2-inch. From my S&W Chief's Special, the shot penetrate about 1/2-inch into soft pine. From a 6-inch revolver, a dozen or so shot will exit a 3/4-inch pine board at 10 feet. While these loads are certainly dangerous at short range, I do not recommend them as defense loads, because they are not a sure incapacitant on anything bigger than a rabbit. I keep Speer 38 shot loads in my kit and "never leave home without them." A shot load is always the first round up in the cylinder when in snake country. I've also put rabbits and birds in the pot with them, but you have to be *close*.

Speer also makes a 9mm shotshell which is a nice item for owners of pistols in that caliber; it offers performance similar to the 38 load, but with a slightly smaller payload. Loaded Speer shotshells are also available as loaded ammunition in the 22 LR, 22 WMR, 9mm Luger, 44 Magnum and 45 ACP.

The 44 Magnum shot loads carry enough pellets to have real potential as small game loads. The regular Speer 44 shot loads intended for revolvers will positively kill rabbits at 25 feet. Better choices for the serious handgun hunter are the specialized 44 Hot Shot or 45/410 rifled shot barrels for the T/C Contender pistol. The 45 Colt is not very accurate from the 45/410 shot barrel. Regular 44 Magnums give normal accuracy in the 44 Hot Shot barrels. If you will use mostly the shotgun, buy the 45/410 so you can use regular 410 loads, which are cheap and plentiful. If you intend to use the thing mostly with standard bulleted cartridges, and use shot only occasionally, the 44 Hot Shot is a better deal. Just remember to remove the choke tube

The exact powder charge is gun-specific, but will almost always be within the range of 6.2+/-0.3 grains of W-231. Both heavy and light charges cause stovepipes, but for different reasons.

The 45 ACP shotshell cases are made from cut-down 308 Winchester or 7.62 NATO military brass using the RCBS trim die and loaded using the RCBS die set.

with either of these before firing a solid ball! These barrels have a detachable choke tube and give patterns better than many 410-bore Skeet guns. Their wide, even patterns are easy to hit with. Like any 410, their 7/16-ounce payload limits them to about 20-25 yards, but within those limits they are quite effective.

Shot loads for the Model 1911 45 service pistol were developed for aircrew survival use during WWII. The military M-12 and M-15 shot loads were too long to fit into the magazine and had to be single loaded. They would not eject from the pistol nor operate the action. Although they were said to be adequate for small game within about 20 feet, the larger #7 1/2 shot produced thin patterns and weren't very effective at the 720 fps velocity obtained. I have used these afield (yes, I can hear the cartridge collectors moaning) and can say from experience they were less effective than the modern Speer 38 Special shot loads.

In the early 1970s, I developed a handloaded 45 ACP shot cartridge that could be mixed interchangeably in a magazine with Ball ammunition. It would feed and operate the pistol in the normal fashion. This was described in *American Rifleman*, April, 1976, p. 20. The article is also reprinted in the NRA booklet, *The 45 Automatic*.

These 45 shotshell cases are made from 308 Winchester brass by using an extended shellholder to push lubricated cases into the forming die. They are cut off with a fine-toothed hacksaw, filed flush, and inside deburred while in the die. Use of 30-06 cases or others with a narrow extraction groove may cause extractor breakage. Cases should *not* be annealed because the extractor may tear through the rim, due to the mouth obturating into the rifling upon firing.

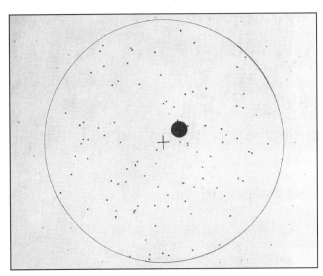

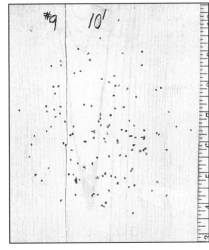

WWII-era GI M-15 45-caliber shot cartridges and instruction sheet are collector's items today. Cartridges in foreground are (from left) author's handloaded 45 ACP semi-auto shotshell, M1911 "hardball," and RA44 M-15.

At 5 feet, the 45 ACP shot load throws a 3-inch pattern which makes snake burgers of rattlers! At 10 feet, the pattern is about 8 inches and most shot penetrate a 3/4-inch pine board

To prepare cases for loading, they are outside deburred, full-length sized, primed, and flared slightly. The recommended starting powder charge is 6.2 grains of W-231. No powder substitutions or changes other than minor adjustments to obtain reliable functioning are recommended. This exact powder charge is gun specific as not all 45s will function reliably with the same charge. This load functions most reliably in slightly worn bores which do not have a sharp origin of the rifling. Start with the suggested charge and load just a magazine full to try. If they cycle, great. If they don't, examine the fired cases.

A too heavy charge causes the case to obturate into the rifling, causing stovepipes from hard extraction. This is the hardest thing to convince reloaders—everyone thinks the more powder, the better the extraction, but that ain't always so! If you can see distinct rifling marks on the case, particularly if accompanied by rim distortion, reduce the charge 0.3-grain and things will work better. If you get jams from short recoil (most jams with this load will be stovepipes, regardless of whether there is too little or too much powder), there will be *no* marks on the mouth of the case. That means the charge is too light, so increase it 0.3-grain. If the powder load is *just right*, you should have very light rifling marks on the case mouth with no obvious rim distortion, and the gun will cycle with near perfection.

The only correct wad to use is the Remington SP410 shot cup used for 1/2-ounce 410-bore Skeet loads. Others do not fit properly in the cut-off rifle brass. Seat the wad firmly over the powder charge using a 3/8-inch dowel and a few light blows with a plastic mallet. Then trim the protruding wad tabs off flush with the case mouth using a sharp knife. The case holds about 105 (+/-5) grains of #8 or #9 shot.

Good results can be had using 35-caliber gas checks for the top wad. Just fill the case and shot cup full to 1/16-inch below the case mouth and place the gas check cup down on top of the load. The gas check will find its way to the right place, and the case will crimp onto it giving a finished shell with a nice appearance.

Typical velocity is 1200 fps in the Model 1911A1 pistol, and patterns average 70 percent in a 15-inch circle at 25 feet. This produces ten pellet hits in a 5-inch-diameter target, simulating a small game animal, and defines the maximum effective range for this load on snakes or small game. A good handgun shot can break

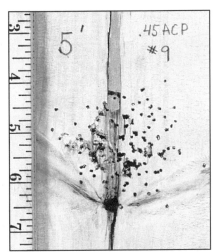

Author's 45 ACP shot load exceeds the performance of factory loads. This 25-foot pattern in a 15-inch circle shows fine coverage for small game, with 93 pellet hits and 77 percent of the charge in the circle. Penetration of #9 shot in soft pine at 25 feet is 1/2-inch. No rabbit would escape this pattern. Twenty years' field use has proven the reliability of this load.

claybirds from stations one, seven or eight on a Skeet field fairly easily. I have found they are sure killers on cottontails to 10 yards with #8 shot. I don't recommend shot larger than #8 as the patterns are too thin. The 45s pattern about as well as ordinary 44 Magnum shotshells (not the longer Hot Shot) in a Thompson Contender with choke tube, but you have a seven-shot semi-auto!

Dies for forming cases and reloading this 45 ACP shotshell are available from RCBS, but are a bit pricey. Remington and CCI both offer factory-loaded 45 ACP shotshells for occasional users who can't justify the expenditure of time and money to make their own.

To sum up, any outdoorsman who carries a handgun afield on a routine basis occasionally needs a few shot loads. Whether you handload them or buy them, get a few. I don't use all that many—maybe a half-dozen a year—but when I get surprised by a copperhead or rattler in the woodpile or chicken house, they are sure comforting! And then, there's always a chance that a grouse may appear under my treestand during deer season...

New and Novel Shotshell Concepts

by DON ZUTZ

With the options for gauges/chamberings and components constantly changing and expanding, the careful handloader more than ever needs to keep updated on...

DON'T LOOK NOW, but American waterfowl and upland game hunting have gone through a lot of changes in the last decade. Take goose hunting, for example. Twenty seasons ago, the 10-gauge was practically obsolete, thanks to the potency of the $1^{7}/_{8}$-ounce lead-shot load in the 3-inch 12. But then along came steel shot, and the 10-bore was suddenly the "in" thing. Its huge plastic shot bucket held more of the heavy steel BBBs, Ts and Fs that we found were necessary for positive penetration on geese at the longer ranges, so we reversed gears and went back to the old slugger.

One problem that has cropped up, however, is that the 10-gauge magnum is too much gun for most typical hunters. At 10 pounds or thereabouts, it handles differently than does a $7^{1}/_{2}$-pound 12-gauge. And that, of course, upsets one's trigger timing. The question is: How does one get meaningful practice with a 10-gauge? As one hunter put it, "I'd like to use my 10-gauge on practice clays, but who can afford it with steel loads? And who wants to try it with 2- or $2^{1}/_{4}$-ounce lead ones kicking off your shoulder?" He does have a point. The 10-gauge loads are tough on your wallet and anatomy.

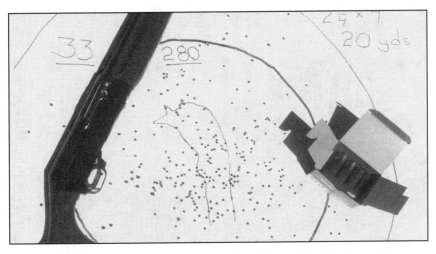

The 3¹/₂-inch 12-gauge magnum, in this case a Benelli Super Black Eagle, can hammer a turkey target with its 2¹/₄-ounce reload of lead #4s or #5s.

For a tight-shooting dove reload in the 12-gauge, try the writer's recommendation for 1¹/₈ ounces of hard lead shot over Green Dot. Patterns like this with #7¹/₂s are dynamite on long-range shots.

Unless you reload, that is, because light 10-gauge fodder can indeed be assembled on any press-type equipment. These will not be the cheapest reloads because they require a stack of filler wads to take up space. However, such reloads are still less costly than commercial stuff, and they kick a whole lot less. A couple can be rolled like this:

LOADS

HULL: Rem. plastic SP (3¹/₂″)
PRIMER: CCI 209 Magnum
POWDER: 28.5 grs. Green Dot
WAD: Rem. SP-10; six 20-ga. .135″ cards
SHOT: 1¹/₄ oz. lead
PRESSURE: 8800 psi
VELOCITY: 1265 fps
NOTE: Same basic loading can be used in Winchester Polyformed 10-ga. case for nearly identical ballistics.

HULL: Fed. plastic 10-ga. (3¹/₂″) (paper base wad)
PRIMER: CCI 209 Magnum
POWDER: 36.0 grs. Herco
WAD: Rem. SP-10; four 20-ga. .135″ cards
SHOT: 1⁵/₈ oz. lead
PRESSURE: 10,300 psi
VELOCITY: 1285 fps

These will let you swing the 10-bore on hand-trapped clays out behind Uncle Jake's barn without busting either your budget or your collarbone.

Another new use for the 10-gauge magnum is as a duck gun. With husky loads of steel BBs, it can be devastating on high mallards or low divers on the far fringe of the decoys. A snappy performer is:

LOAD

HULL: Fed. plastic 10-ga. (3¹/₂″) (paper base wad)
PRIMER: Fed. 209
POWDER: 39.5 grs. Blue Dot
WAD: MEC 105; ¹/₂″ MEC filler; 25.0 grs. MEC plastic buffer
SHOT: 1¹/₂ oz. steel BBs
PRESSURE: 10,400 LUP
VELOCITY: 1301 fps

A relatively new concept is the 3¹/₂-inch 12-gauge magnum,

(Above) A 16-gauge such as this Bill Hanus Bird Gun is an ideal upland gun, and new components give the handloading hunter a chance to work up effective rounds for hunting specialties.

(Right) The 10-gauge is making a brilliant comeback because it can deliver the heaviest loads of large steel shot for long-range wing-gunning. Loads of steel BBs took these formerly high mallards.

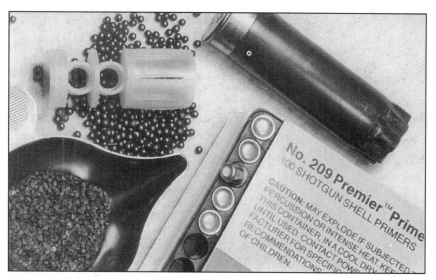

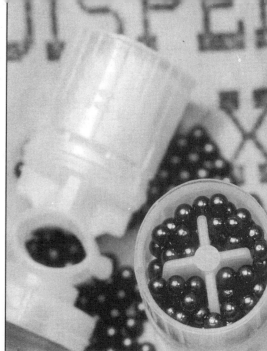

(Above) The makings of a tight-patterning dove reload include Green Dot and the Remington 209P primer plus the TGT-12 wad.

(Right) Close-range, scatter-load performance can be had by using the Dispersor-X wad from Ballistic Products, Inc.

which was developed to give hunters a shot charge similar to the 10-bore in an easier-to-handle 12-gauge package. With steel shot loads, the 3¹/₂-inch 12 falls just short of the 10-gauge, but it can equal the 10's husky 2¹/₄-ounce lead load. Unfortunately, that 2¹/₄-ouncer hits as hard on the butt end as it does at the muzzle. Great turkey load though it may be, it's simply uncomfortable to shoot. For those who enjoy the versatility of the 3¹/₂-inch 12, but don't like getting smashed around, reloading is the answer. In fact, by reducing the shot charge, one can use a wad with a cushioning section for potentially less pellet deformation. Here are a couple that I ran through a Benelli Super Black Eagle with excellent tight-patterning results and a more tolerable recoil level.

LOADS

HULL: Fed. plastic 12-ga. (3¹/₂")
PRIMER: Win. 209
POWDER: 40.0 grs. Blue Dot
WAD: Fed. 12S0; one 20-ga. .135" card
SHOT: 1⁷/₈ oz. lead
PRESSURE: 9000 psi
VELOCITY: 1200 fps

HULL: Rem. SP 12-ga. (3¹/₂")
PRIMER: CCI 209 Magnum
POWDER: 39.5 grs. Blue Dot
WAD: Rem. R12L
SHOT: 2 oz. lead
PRESSURE: 11,100 psi
VELOCITY: 1220 fps

For anyone who simply *must* stuff a full 10-gauge magnum shot charge into his new 3¹/₂-inch 12-gauge, however, here is a recipe that'll provide any gobbler with Excedrin headache No. 1:

LOAD

HULL: Fed. plastic 12-ga. (3¹/₂")
PRIMER: CCI 209 Magnum
POWDER: 38.5 grs. Blue Dot
WAD: Fed. 12S4; Winchester WAA12F114
SHOT: 2¹/₄ oz. lead
PRESSURE: 11,100 psi
VELOCITY: 1150

All these reloads pattern best when given hard, high-antimony lead shot or copper- or nickel-plated pellets. These resist deformation during firing setback and bore travel far better than ordinary chilled shot does. Despite its name, chilled shot isn't very hard, and it normally deforms to such an extent that it patterns 10-25 percent lower than hard, high-antimony or plated shot. Thus, if you're going to use a big-bore for optimum pattern density, be sure to use shot that will deliver rather than deform.

There are already some areas where steel shot must be used in the uplands. One new reload that I've tried seems especially good for this on close-flushing birds with #5 steel. It will also be a good steel-shot clay-target reload, in my opinion, especially for Sporting Clays. It's assembled like this, according to Hodgdon Powder Co. data:

LOAD

HULL: Win. AA
PRIMER: Win. 209
POWDER: 31.0 grs. Hodgdon HS-7
WAD: MEC 12-TW steel shot
SHOT: 1¹/₈ oz. steel
PRESSURE: 10,700 LUP
VELOCITY: 1264 fps

A lot of hunters are turning to commercial preserves these days, a place where pheasants and chuckars can be almost as challenging as they are on the wing in the wild. An excellent game-preserve 12-gauge load is the old live pigeon round which uses a 3¹/₄ drams equivalent powder charge under a 1¹/₄-ounce lead shot load for about 1220 fps. This one patterns nicely from Skeet, Improved Cylinder and Modified chokes for target coverage at hunt club ranges, and with hard #6 lead shot, it'll account for many positive retrieves. One of the best such reloads that I've found is:

LOAD

HULL: Fed. Gold Medal
PRIMER: Fed. 209
POWDER: 24.0 grs. Unique
WAD: Fed. 12S4
SHOT: 1¹/₄ oz. lead

PRESSURE: 10,500 psi
VELOCITY: 1220 fps
NOTE: The Winchester WAA12F114 wad can interchange for the same ballistics.

Accurate Arms Co. makes a powder that should interest hunters because of the way it excels in cold conditions. This is Nitro 100, a flake-type propellant made of nitro-cotton for uniformity. Tests have shown that Nitro 100 loses very little in low temperatures. For example, the following reload was tested in temperatures of 10, 70 and 125 degrees F to determine stability and consistency:

LOAD

HULL: Win. AA
PRIMER: Win. 209
POWDER: 18.0 grs. Nitro 100
WAD: Win. WAA12
SHOT: 1 1/8 oz. lead
PRESSURE: +10F—9400 psi; +70F—9600 psi; +125F—9700 psi
VELOCITY: +10F—1185 fps; +70F— 1200; +125F—1208

All of this makes Nitro 100 look pretty good for those who hunt hard regardless of the weather. And while the above reload is a solid one for much uplanding, this is another with a bit more velocity in it. Accurate Arms has not published the pressure for it, although the velocity is in their manual, but I'm assured that it is indeed within SAAMI parameters:

LOAD

HULL: Win. AA
PRIMER: Win. 209
POWDER: 19.0 grs. Nitro 100
WAD: Rem. RXP-12
SHOT: 1 1/8 oz. lead
VELOCITY: 1255 fps

This is a snappy upland load that patterns nicely and is best stuffed with hard, high-antimony shot or copper-plated pellets.

Bird or cottontail hunters who use open-choked guns do so because they want to take advantage of a wide pattern's effective hitting area on close- or moderate-range targets. However, not all reloads give truly wide, evenly distributed patterns from an open-choked barrel. Many still throw tight center densities

with weak outer rims. But a pair of powders with which I've been experimenting have shown a tendency to fill out the fringes of a 30-inch-diameter pattern better than most other powders. These are Solo 1250 from Scot Powder Co. and Super-Lite from Winchester. A pair of exact reloads are:

LOADS

HULL: Win. AA
PRIMER: Win. 209
POWDER: 24.5 grs. Solo 1250
WAD: Windjammer
SHOT: 1 1/8 oz. lead
PRESSURE: 7400 LUP
VELOCITY: 1200 fps
NOTE: Can be taken to 1255 fps with 26.0 grs. Solo 1250 with a pressure of 8400 LUP

HULL: Rem. Premier
PRIMER: Fed. 209
POWDER: 20.5 grs. Super-Lite Ball
WAD: Win. WAA12
SHOT: 1 1/8 oz. lead
PRESSURE: 9900 psi
VELOCITY: 1255 fps

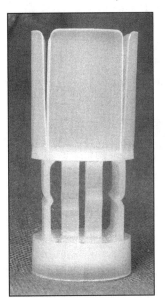

Using the 3-inch 20-gauge hull for 1 1/8-ounce loads makes it possible for the handloader to employ wads with longer cushioning sections, such as the Winchester WAA20.

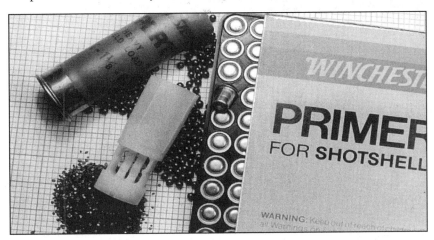

(Above) Winchester's relatively new Super-Field Ball powder and WAA16 wad make up into some excellent upland game and Sporting Clays reloads.

(Right) A novel 20-gauge "plinker" reload with just 3/4-ounce of lead shot is both economical and light on a beginner's shoulder.

247

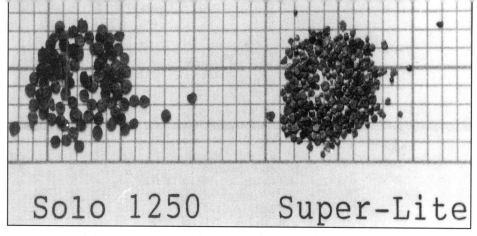

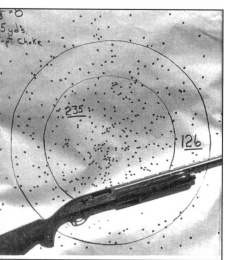

A pair of modern powders that tend to give more even pellet distributions than other propellants which hammer tight center densities are Scot Powder Co.'s Solo 1250 and Winchester's Super-Lite.

(Left) A 12-gauge reload with 22.5 grains of Unique printed this pattern at 25 yards with a light Improved Cylinder choke and hard #8s. Not a bad upland cluster.

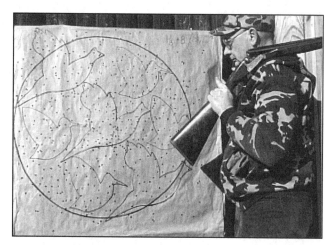

(Right) Shotguns are individuals, and the only way to learn how a given reload will perform is to shoot it through a specific bird gun and evaluate it.

Fans of the 16-gauge have long been frustrated by the lack of specialized factory loads and the paucity of reloading components. However, there are now some new and interesting 16-gauge reloading possibilites about. Winchester's Super-Field Ball Powder is a fine match to the 16, especially with Winchester's WAA16 wad. And there are now Gualandi (Italian) wads around for use in the spacious ACTIV all-plastic cases as well as for 1-ounce reloads in some other hulls. Scot's Solo 1250 and 1500 are also good in the 16-gauge case. When using Solo 1500 in the 16—as well as in any other gauge—always follow the company's instructions for wad seating pressures. A couple of hard-hitting 16-gauge field reloads are:

LOADS
HULL: ACTIV all-plastic 16-ga.
PRIMER: Win. 209
POWDER: 28.0 grs. Solo 1500
WAD: Rem. SP-16 seated with 40 lbs. pressure
SHOT: 1¼ oz. lead
PRESSURE: 10,800 LUP
VELOCITY: 1220 fps

HULL: Win. AA 16-ga.
PRIMER: CCI 209
POWDER: 20.5 grs. Winchester Super-Field
WAD: Win. WAA16
SHOT: 1⅛ oz. lead
PRESSURE: 10,800 psi
VELOCITY: 1185 fps
NOTE: A solid Sporting Clays or Skeet reload for the 16 as well as a light field load

A concept that is quite novel in 16-gauge is the Dispersor-X wad being distributed stateside by Ballistic Products, Inc. A basic one-piece plastic wad, the Dispersor-X has an X-divider moulded into its shotcup to produce a quick-opening pattern from Full-choked guns. (The same is obtainable for the 12-gauge.) The supplier offers some published data for this one, and a good-looking recipe is:

LOAD
HULL: Fiocchi plastic 16-ga.
PRIMER: Fiocchi 616
POWDER: 23.0 grs. Herco
WAD: Dispersor-X
SHOT: ⅞-oz. lead
PRESSURE: 9800 psi
VELOCITY: 1230 fps

The ⅞-ounce load may seem light, but it is needed to keep chamber pressure in line. Also, the ⅞-ouncer is adequate for close-in birds like woodcock.

Through the seasons, we have noted that the 20-gauge is very effective with its heavier charges, but it is often difficult to cram a full 1⅛-ounce baby magnum load into the 2¾-inch case. Hunters complain of bulged or opened crimps, and in general velocities aren't impressive. So why try? Most 20-gauge guns today have 3-inch chambers, and the 1⅛-ounce loading can be assembled much easier in the magnum-length case. In the 3-inch hull, there is room left for a longer wad with the 1⅛-ounce shot charge; this not only provides somewhat more cushioning, but the added expansion room for early powder gases helps create a more favorable pressure/velocity ratio for higher speeds than the standard-length 20 could cook up with the 1⅛-ounce load. For example...

Additional Special Concept Reloads

Extra-Heavy 10-ga.
Magnum Turkey Load
HULL: Fed. plastic (3½″)
PRIMER: Fed. 209
POWDER: 38.0 grs. SR-4756
WAD: Rem. SP-10
SHOT: 2³/₈ oz. lead
PRESSURE: 10,000 LUP
VELOCITY: 1125 fps

High-Velocity 12-ga. 3″ Magnum
HULL: Win. C/F 12-ga. (3″)
PRIMER: Fed. 209
POWDER: 36.0 grs. SR-4756
WAD: Win. WAA12F114
SHOT: 1³/₈ oz. lead
PRESSURE: 10,800 LUP
VELOCITY: 1380 fps

Tight-Shooting 12-ga. Dove Load
HULL: Rem. Premier
PRIMER: Rem. 209P
POWDER: 19.0 grs. Green Dot
WAD: Rem. TGT-12
SHOT: 1¹/₈ oz. lead
PRESSURE: 7300 psi
VELOCITY: 1145 fps
NOTE: Can be taken to 21.0 grs. Green Dot for 1200 fps and 8800 psi.

Mild-Recoil 12-ga. "Plinker" Load
HULL: Rem. Premier
PRIMER: Rem. 209P
POWDER: 17.6 grs. Clays
WAD: Rem. TGT-12
SHOT: ⁷/₈-oz. lead
PRESSURE: 6600 LUP
VELOCITY: 1200 fps
NOTE: Can be reduced to 16.5 grs. Clays for about 1150 fps and lower recoil.

Light 16-ga. Reload
HULL: Win. C/F 16-ga.
PRIMER: Win. 209
POWDER: 20.0 grs. Super-Field Ball
WAD: Win. WAA16
SHOT: 1-oz. lead
PRESSURE: 8400 psi
VELOCITY: 1165 fps

Buffered 20-ga. Magnum
HULL: Win. C/F 20-ga. (3″)
PRIMER: Win. 209
POWDER: 23.0 grs. 571 Ball Powder
WAD: Win. WAA20F1
SHOT: 1³/₁₆ oz. lead
BUFFER: 12.0 grs. Win. "Grex" buffer
PRESSURE: 10,900 LUP
VELOCITY: 1115 fps
NOTE: Tight-patterning, close-range load for turkey hunting with 20-ga. gun.

Beginner's 20-ga. Light Load
HULL: Win. AA 20-ga.
PRIMER: Win. 209
POWDER: 15.5 grs. Unique
WAD: Fed. 20S1
SHOT: ³/₄-oz. lead
PRESSURE: 9700 psi
VELOCITY: 1200 fps

NOTE: May not function in autoloaders; can be reduced to 15.0 grs. of Unique for even lighter recoil in single shots.

Solid 28-ga. Field Reload
HULL: Win. AA 28-ga.
PRIMER: Win. 209
POWDER: 20.5 grs. Hodgdon HS-7 Spherical
WAD: Win. WAA28
SHOT: ³/₄-oz. lead
PRESSURE: 11,200 LUP
VELOCITY: 1260 fps

Beginner's Light-Recoil 28-ga. Load
HULL: Win. AA 28-ga.
PRIMER: Fed. 209
POWDER: 12.0 grs. SR-7625
WAD: Win. WAA28
SHOT: ³/₄-oz. lead
PRESSURE: 10,600 LUP
VELOCITY: 1100 fps
NOTE: Not a hunting load; adequate for hand-trap clay shooting and Skeet.

Ultra-High Velocity 410 Reload
HULL: Win. C/F 410 (3″)
PRIMER: Win. 209
POWDER: 26.5 grs. IMR-4198
WAD: Fed. 410SC
SHOT: ¹/₂-oz. lead
PRESSURE: 10,490 LUP
VELOCITY: 1435 fps
NOTE: May not pattern well; can be reduced to 25.0 grs. of IMR-4198 for 1350 fps and about 8500 LUP.

LOADS

HULL: Win. C/F 20-ga. (3″)
PRIMER: Win. 209
POWDER: 27.0 grs. Win. 571 Ball
WAD: Win. WAA20
SHOT: 1¹/₈ oz. lead
PRESSURE: 11,000 LUP
VELOCITY: 1220 fps

HULL: Fed. plastic 20-ga. (3″) case (paper base wad)
PRIMER: Win. 209
POWDER: 26.0 grs. SR-4756
WAD: Win. WAA20F1
SHOT: 1¹/₈ oz. lead
PRESSURE: 10,600 LUP
VELOCITY: 1265 fps

Another interesting use of a 3-inch case is with the 410. This pee-wee bore can use all the pellets it can get into its patterns, but the basic 3-inch 410 load is rather pedestrian and plagued by a long in-flight shot string. A novel approach to 410 field reloads is using the 3-inch hull with an unconventional ⁵/₈-ounce (273 grains) shot charge. This puts the shot charge near maximum for the 410, while also providing a bit more room in the case for a slightly heavier charge of slow-rate powder for a higher velocity with a shorter shot string.

Solo 1250 is a powder that tends to give a more even distribution of pellets rather than bunching them in the center of a Full-choke pattern. Winchester Super-Lite Ball powder has a similar quality.

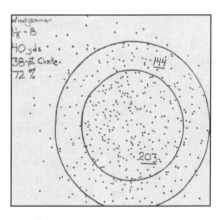

LOAD

HULL: Win. C/F 410 (3″)
PRIMER: Rem. 209P
POWDER: 20.0 grs. IMR-4227
WAD: Trico No. 4
SHOT: ⁵/₈-oz. lead
PRESSURE: 11,900 LUP
VELOCITY: 1230 fps

An important point here is sticking with the Remington 209P primer, which is a mild cap. Hotter primers will send chamber pressures beyond industry parameters. Do not substitute!

Many handload-
ers take pride in
rolling their own
ammo, but for
the ultimate in
homegrown
fodder, why not
try some...

Simple Homemade Bullet Lubes

by C.E. HARRIS

THE SHEAR COST of commercial bullet lubricants can be a deterrent if you shoot a great deal, which some of us do. I found myself going through literally "pounds" of lubricant while shooting revolver loads, ram bashing with blackpowder cartridge rifles and stuffing Maxi-Balls in my muzzleloaders, as well as shooting cast bullets for high-power competition in my vintage military rifles.

Eventually, I got tired of spending several dollars per "stick" of commercial lube and went back to making my own. It is true that homemade lubricants are not as effective as the "store-bought" variety for high-velocity rifle loads or in magnum revolvers. However, they work fine for standard-velocity handgun loads in the 38 Special, 45 ACP, in blackpowder cartridge rifles and in centerfire cast bullet rifle loads below 1800 fps, which comprise the bulk of my shooting.

It is easy to make effective bullet lubricants from common ingredients. I don't purport to know all there is to know about this subject, but I'm happy to share what I have learned picking

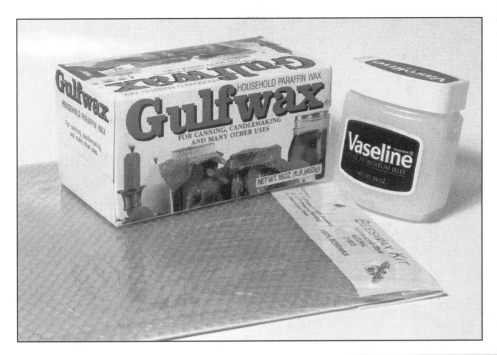

These common ingredients—beeswax, paraffin and Vaseline—can be melted in a double boiler to make your own homemade bullet lube.

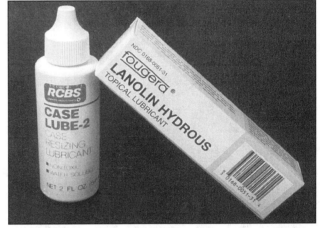

(Below) To improve the basic formula's lubrication, a small amount of Case Lube-2 or lanolin may be added to the mix.

the brains of those who are more knowledgeable than I am, as refined by over twenty-five years of trial and error.

The smoke generated by lead-bullet handgun rounds on indoor ranges is as much a function of the volume of lubricant as the type. Most people try to use the least amount possible of the most effective lube for gallery loads. This approach was advocated by the late Col. E.H. Harrison. He wrote in *American Rifleman* that, in making accurate ammunition with the H&G No. 50 wadcutter bullet, it was only necessary to lube the bottom cannelure when using Alox Beeswax and 2.7 grains of Bullseye. Today, many people use a light tumbled coat of Lee Liquid Alox for the same purpose. However, if minimum smoke for use on indoor ranges is important to you, try to avoid Alox altogether. This is because the additives in complex hydrocarbon fractions produce more smoke in combustion.

The effectiveness of conventional wax- or grease-type bullet lubricants is determined by their ability to flow smoothly under pressure and to "wet" or coat the bore surface. This "boundary layer lubrication" prevents the adhesion of lead particles washed away from the bullet surface by the hot powder gases. The "wetting" of powder fouling and primer residues reduces fouling buildup because fouling is swept out by succeeding shots, producing a steady state of condition once the bore is properly "seasoned."

To effectively coat the bore of a long barrel requires a larger volume of lubricant, depending on the specific caliber, bullet alloy, chamber pressure and powder type. Some pistol powders tend to produce less smoke than others, so it is worthwhile to experiment.

In my opinion, the best powders to reduce smoke for light indoor gallery loads in the 38 Special and 45 ACP are SR-7625, Green Dot, PB and W231. These all flow nicely through progressive loading machines and produce less smoke than the "traditional" Unique or Bullseye.

If you want to make your own non-Alox lubricant using readily available materials, start with equal parts of beeswax,

paraffin and petrolatum, or Vaseline. A heavy petrolatum like Cosmolene, available from Brownells, is best. Ordinary drugstore Vaseline works quite well, but results in a less stiff mixture. The materials should be melted in a double boiler taking precautions against fire. To improve lubrication, a tablespoon per quarter-pound of RCBS Case Lube-2 or lanolin (topical lubricant) from the drugstore may be added.

RCBS Case Lube-2 has some interesting properties in that it mixes readily with and will actually dissolve other lubricants. Dennis Marshall put me on to Case Lube-2 when I was at the NRA and highly recommends its use as an additive. Never add petroleum-based oils because they weep from the lubricant and will attack the powder over time.

Paraffin has a coarse grain structure which impairs its flow, so it must be used in combination with a plasticizer. Vaseline or lanolin serve this purpose. If using equal parts of paraffin, beeswax and Vaseline results in too soft a lubricant in hot weather, cut the Vaseline in half, but don't use less than 6 ounces of Vaseline (or lanolin) to a pound of paraffin. I prefer to use Vaseline in lubricants intended for smokeless powder loads, because it's cheaper. The affinity of lanolin to absorb water

A popular homemade blackpowder lube can be concocted from Criso, paraffin and Vaseline.

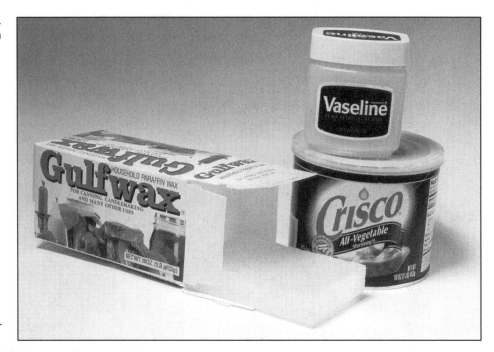

(Below) Lanolin can be substituted for Vaseline, but for a cost.

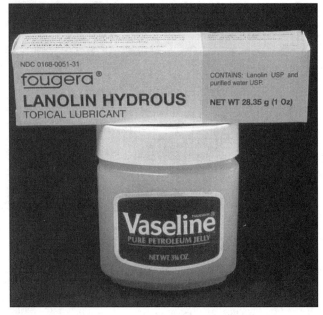

makes it preferable to use in blackpowder lubricants. This is because it goes into solution with other waxes, aiding easy cleanup with plain water or water-based blackpowder cleaners.

The standard U.S. Army bullet lubricant during the blackpowder era was one part mutton tallow to three parts of beeswax. This soft lubricant is well suited for blackpowder arms and cap 'n' ball revolvers, but it gets runny in hot weather. It will also spoil and turn rancid, so you should use up a batch within a year. If tallow-based lubricants are used in guns which are not immediately water cleaned, there is always risk of bore after-rusting from residual salts in the tallow. Usually, this is a problem when light smokeless loads are fired in blackpowder single shot rifles, because conventional nitro solvents don't remove the salts. Rusting is not a problem when using blackpowder or Pyrodex loads, which will prompt a thorough water cleaning anyway.

Modern blackpowder shooters generally substitute Crisco vegetable shortening for tallow, and it works very well. My favorite blackpowder grease is two parts of Crisco, one part paraffin and one part Vaseline or lanolin. In hot weather, you can mix equal parts of Crisco, paraffin, and Vaseline or lanolin to produce a stiffer mixture, or simply substitute beeswax for the paraffin and it will be less "runny." Some blackpowder shooters prefer to substitute anhydrous lanolin for the Vaseline. My Yankee heritage reminds me that lanolin costs about $10 per pound while Vaseline is about $2. It is true that the lube with the lanolin reduces caking if you fire long strings without wiping, but I generally clean after every five-shot group. When so used, both lubricants provide about equal accuracy with Minie bullets and Maxi-Balls in blackpowder muzzleloaders; with grooved bullets for blackpowder cartridge rifles such as the Trapdoor Springfield; or as a cylinder top grease in cap 'n' ball revolvers.

Another blackpowder lube formula favored by the Washington Blue Rifles of the North-South Skirmish Association is made from one part beeswax, two parts Crisco, $1/2$-part paraffin and $1/2$-part Vaseline. I find it is good, but no more better or accurate than the other "recipes" previously mentioned. Which one you should use is mostly a matter of personal preference.

I don't recommend incorporating any solid additives, such as graphite or molybdenum disulfide. This is because they increase smoke and do nothing to improve effectiveness of the lube in controlling leading or powder fouling. You must remember that bullet lubes work by the principle of boundary-layer lubrication, so their coating and wetting action is not enhanced by the addition of particulates. It is actually impaired by doing so.

To arrive at an exact mixture that works best for all climatic conditions requires a little experimentation. If you find an especially "good" mix, please write to me in care of the editor, so we can all learn from your experiences.

Good luck and safe shooting.

It is often associ-
ated with black-
powder and
frontstuffers, but
this author says
for centerfire cast
bullet hunting...

Try the Paper Patch

by PAUL A. MATTHEWS

MENTION PAPER-PATCHED bullets today and most shooters conjure up an image of Sharps rifles, blackpowder and endless prairie dotted with vast herds of buffalo. And while such an image is always pleasing to the nostalgic mind, it is far from accurate. The paper-patched bullet is not some archaic form of projectile best relegated to the dim past, but one of the best, if not *the* best, homegrown projectiles within the grasp of today's hunter. In the larger calibers at velocities up to 2200 fps, the paper-patched bullet is far superior to any other bullet you can get for hunting purposes, cast or jacketed.

I say this for two reasons. First, in many of the larger calibers, the paper-patched bullet can be driven as fast as any jacketed bullet of comparable weight and with equal or better accuracy. And second, expansion of the paper-patched bullet is easily controlled by the alloy used—anything from pure lead to linotype.

Not only is this true for many of the larger calibers, but also for some of the smaller ones like the 30-30 and 32 Special. I have a friend whose favorite 30-30 load is a maximum charge

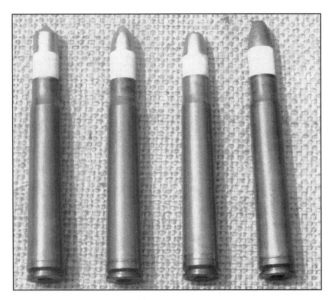

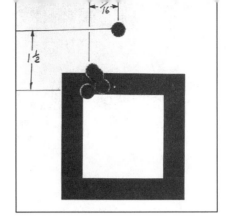

(Left) Four 375 H&H cartridges loaded with different paper-patched bullets. The three cartridges on the left are loaded with grooved paper patched bullets—Lyman 375110, 375118 and 375449—while the one on the right is loaded with the conventional smooth-sided cupped-base paper-patched bullet.

Ordinary grooved bullets designed for grease lubrication can give superb accuracy when paper-patched. This group was fired from a Ruger No. 1 375 H&H using a 302-grain bullet backed by 47 grains of IMR-3031 for a velocity of 1980 fps. This load is only slightly less powerful than the old 405 Winchester and is certainly more than enough for any deer or black bear on the North American continent.

of IMR-4320 behind a 176-grain paper-patched bullet for a chronographed velocity of 2198 fps in his Remington 788. This equals or surpasses any factory loading for the 30-30, and has no metal corset to restrict expansion.

Over the past ten years, my son, my brother and myself have taken several deer and wild boar with paper-patched bullets. And I have successfully used them in everything from a 54-caliber flintlock to a 30-30, 30-40, 375 Winchester, 375 H&H, 45-70 and 458 Winchester. I have fired them in front of blackpowder, Pyrodex and smokeless at velocities ranging from 1200 to 2300, and I've cast them of everything from pure lead to lead-tin alloy, scrap metal and type metal.

Of all the various cast bullets I've used in the past forty-five years, the paper-patched bullet is by far the most versatile. It might be a bit more time-consuming to produce, and it might require a little more care in loading and handling, but its terminal performance on game is so far superior to anything else that the extra time and effort are well worth it.

Perhaps the biggest psychological hangup against the use of paper-patched bullets is the term "patched," a holdover from the late 1800s. If the word "jacketed" is substituted for "patched," then we have a different mental image of the projectile. When we use the term "jacketed," we lose the blackpowder image and think in terms of smokeless. Indeed, when metal-jacketed bullets were introduced during the blackpowder era, they were marketed as "metal-patched" to differentiate from the paper-patched.

Basically, the paper patch does exactly the same thing as the metal jacket. It seals the bore against escaping gases, prevents gas cutting of the bullet and, most important, prevents leading. With properly prepared paper-patched bullets, there is no metal fouling of any kind left in the barrel. One can shoot with smokeless powder all day long and clean the barrel at night with a single pass of a snug-fitting cloth patch.

Because the active life span of the paper-patched bullet was so short—from about 1870 to 1900—there are many old wives' tales and myths that scare the interested shooter away. The three foremost myths:

1. Paper-patched bullets require a barrel with shallow grooves.

Terminal performance of the paper-patched bullet! The bullet on the left weighs 385 grains and is cast of pure lead with 3 percent tin. The expanded bullet was cast from the same mould of the same melt and lost only 9 grains weight after penetrating 15 to 18 inches through muscle and bone. The load was 53 grains of IMR-3031.

The author's brother Allan with a wild hog taken in North Carolina with a Ruger No. 3 45-70 using a 389-grain paper-patched bullet backed by 51 grains of IMR-3031. The boar dropped in its tracks with one shot.

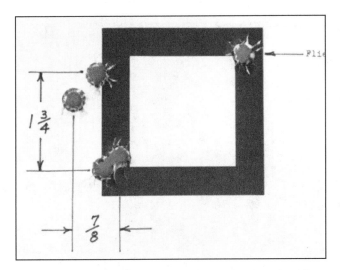

Paper-patched bullets can be used in lever-action rifles with Micro-Grooved barrels, too. This group was fired from a Marlin 1895SS 45-70 using a 400-grain paper-patched bullet and 50 grains of IMR-3031.

A 200-pound boar taken by the author with one shot using a 405-grain paper-patched bullet backed by 53 grains of IMR-3031.

2. The paper patch must remain intact as it leaves the bullet.

3. The patch must be of special, very strong paper, preferably with linen fiber.

All three myths are a bunch of horseradish! As for shallow-groove barrels, this came about when Sharps and Remington realized that because a paper-patched bullet had twice the gripping surface of a grooved bullet—grooves don't grip anything—they could produce barrels with shallow rifling and still get good accuracy, saving money in the process.

The second myth is self-exploding. When the paper patch remains intact, as it does from a shallow-groove barrel, it sometimes clings to the bullet causing a flyer. Target shooters of the late 1800s got around this by using the cross-patch and the Chase patch, neither of which were intact with the bullet and thus always left the bullet at the muzzle of the rifle. Our deeper grooved barrels of today—.003-inch and over—slice the patch into shreds, thus accomplishing the same thing as the target patches of a hundred years ago.

Finally, in order to promote shredding of the patch, if there is anything we *don't* want for a patch, it is strong linen-fiber paper. The best paper I've ever used for patching is a 9-pound, 25-percent cotton-fiber onionskin paper cut *across* the grain to further weaken it.

Now, most rifle shooters are a pretty sensible lot. They are not too excited about spending hard-earned dollars for special equipment just to try something to see if they like it. However, most shooters who develop an interest in paper-patched bullets are involved with cast lubricated bullets and already have on hand one or more moulds for such bullets. There is no reason bullets from these moulds can not be paper-patched instead of lubricated. I've done it many times.

Patching grooved bullets works best in the larger calibers for reasons that will become apparent later. However, before I had a 30-caliber paper-patched bullet mould, my practice for the 30-40 was to cast a bunch of bullets from my RCBS 30-180-FN mould, wipe them lightly with a thin case lubricant and then run them through a .309-inch sizing die. After this, they were wiped free of lube and patched with 9-pound onionskin, bringing their diameter up to .316- or .317-inch.

After the patches had dried and shrunk tightly to the bullets, each patch was coated with a thin film of lube consisting of 45 percent beeswax and 55 percent Vaseline by weight, and then again put through the .309-inch sizing die. Here is where we encounter problems with the smaller calibers. Because of their small diameter, these bullets have to be fairly hard—about 12 Bhn—to prevent distortion on their second trip through the die. With large diameter—.375-inch and over—distortion is not a problem even with soft alloys.

After the patched bullet has been run through the sizing die, it is ready to be loaded. And, again, just before seating the bullet, the patch should be wiped with a thin film of the aforementioned lubricant.

These paper-patched grooved bullets will give superb accuracy, as evidenced by the photo of a group fired from a Ruger No. 1 375 H&H Magnum. Here, four shots went into about $1/2$-inch with the fifth shot bringing the group out to $1\,1/2$-inches. This is no piker load! Average velocity over the Oehler 33D is 1980 fps and muzzle energy is 2442 fpe. More than that, the heavy bullet was cast of a soft alloy that would readily expand on deer.

Once the decision is made to go to the paper-patched bullet, my suggestion is to purchase a custom nose-pour, adjustable, cup-based, paper-patched bullet mould from one of the many custom mould makers listed in this book. Or one can purchase swaged paper-patched bullets—though these are usually limited to the larger calibers—from a number of producers. I personally have used many 45-caliber bullets produced by Idaho Bullets and Montana Precision Swaging. Both make an excellent bullet.

What is the correct diameter for the paper-patched bullet? Although there are exceptions to every rule, almost always the diameter of the unpatched bullet should be equal to or slightly larger than the bore diameter—across the tops of the lands—of the rifle. For the 45-70, I use bullets having an *unpatched* diameter of .452-inch. For the 375 H&H, it's .368-inch, and for the 30-caliber it's .302-inch.

There is a very good reason for these diameters. First, you have to realize the paper patch in itself can not grip the rifling firmly enough to rotate the bullet as does the metal jacket. And second, you have to realize smokeless powders will *not* slug up the bullet enough in the bore to grip the rifling if the bullet is undersize, not even if the bullet is made of pure lead.

With a bullet whose *unpatched* diameter is slightly over the bore size of the rifle, one can use any alloy desired from pure lead to linotype, patch it with 9-pound onionskin and drive it up to 2200 fps—and sometimes faster—with good accuracy.

Since I use paper-patched bullets for hunting purposes and want immediate expansion, I use a soft alloy comprised of pure lead with 3-5 percent of tin added. Almost without excepion, the lead-tin alloy has always given me a shade better accuracy than the same bullet cast of pure lead. Whether this is due to increased strength or better casting from that alloy, I'm not certain, though I strongly suspect the latter has a lot to do with it. Most commercial paper-patched bullets, including those from Idaho Bullets and Montana Precision Swaging, are swaged from pure lead and give good accuracy.

Regardless of whether you use pure lead or lead-tin alloy for a hunting bullet, you can be assured of reliable expansion and very little weight loss, providing the bullet is of solid-nose configuration. Only once have I ever retrieved a solid-nose bullet from game. This was a 385-grain lead-tin alloy bullet pushed by 53/IMR-3031 for an average velocity of about 1850 fps. It struck the buck low on the left side of the neck and ranged upward and back through lungs and spine for 15 to 18 inches before coming to rest under the hide. This bullet expanded from 45-caliber out to .94-inch—more than double its original size—and lost only 9 grains of its original weight, a paltry 2 percent.

By contrast, my son and I both shot bucks during the 1990 season using 419-grain hollowpoint paper-patched bullets cast of pure lead and driven at 1450 fps by 29/SR-4759. Of three shots fired, only one bullet penetrated completely through the deer. The other two bullets broke into pieces and shed considerable weight, even though their velocity was only a little higher than that of a normal blackpowder load.

I did not expect this kind of performance from a pure lead bullet. With the cohesive characteristic of lead and the low velocity involved, I fully expected the nose to peel back to the bottom of the cavity as I'd seen years ago when using the famous 330-grain Gould hollowpoint bullet. The only reason I can give for the breakup and weight loss is the fact the hollowpoint was .375-inch deep and the nose of the bullet was swaged into a long, gentle ogive, resulting in fairly thin wall structure. However, the incident has cured me of any further inclination toward hollowpoint bullets on game.

The big Ruger No. 1 single shot 458 Winchester is a natural for paper-patched bullets, regardless of whether you are using blackpowder, Pyrodex or heavy smokeless loads. Its SAAMI chamber includes a long tapered throat extending 1.115 inches ahead of the chamber proper, allowing the use of long, heavy bullets seated well out of the case.

To duplicate some of the old 45-caliber buffalo cartridges such as the 45-100-550 Sharps, I used a 550-grain paper-patched bullet backed by a priming charge of 12/SR-4759 and a main charge of 72/Goex FFg black. This gives an accurate clean-burn-

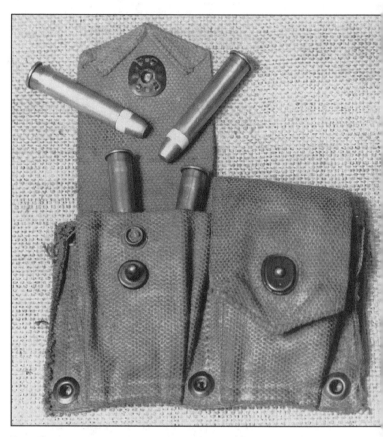

One of the best ways to carry cartridges loaded with paper-patched bullets is to use a pair of belt pouches cut from an old bandoleer. These pouches have wax worked into the fabric for waterproofing to protect the patch. They are carried on the belt underneath the hunting coat.

ing load with an average velocity of 1342 fps and 2739 fpe.

For a steamier smokeless load, I used the same bullet ahead of 78/H-4831 for an average velocity of 1686 fps. And for a still heavier load, I used a 562-grain swaged paper-patched bullet ahead of 76/IMR-4350 for an average velocity of 1860 fps and an energy figure of 4316 fpe.

All of these loads give good accuracy, always staying within 2 inches at 100 yards and sometimes much less. And all of them are more powerful than the old 450 Express blackpowder cartridge that Frederick Courteney Selous and John "Pondoro" Taylor spoke so highly of for elephant hunting. That cartridge, too, used paper-patched bullets.

Whatever your previous thoughts about the paper-patched bullet, rest assured this is probably the best homemade hunting bullet available to the present-day shooter. While I believe it is at its best in the larger calibers—from 35 on up—the paper-patched bullet was at one time used in such diminutive cartridges as the little Maynard 22-10 centerfire using a 45-grain paper-patched bullet.

While most of us today place the paper-patched bullet in an age of antiquity, we seldom consider the fact that this age was also the age of the greatest herds of game the world has ever seen. From our Western plains teeming with buffalo to the vast plains and bush of Africa, to the steaming tiger-haunted jungles of India, the paper-patched bullet killed more heavy and dangerous game in thirty years than has been killed with jacketed bullets since.

It is still a good bullet.

Why Not Try Heavy Bullets?

Do you want your rifle to perform bigger than it is? Do you want higher energy figures and deeper penetration in the field?

by JOHN HAVILAND

LOADING HEAVIER-THAN-standard bullets can step up the performance of your rifle a whole caliber and make it more versatile for hunting big game. Heavy bullets make a 270 into a 30-06, an '06 into a 35 Whelen, a 338 Winchester into a 375 H&H, and a 375 into a stump puller. But not without compromise.

You give up some velocity to gain bullet weight. The extra length of heavy bullets means they must be seated deep in cartridge case to clear the rifling and to fit in the rifle's magazine. The bullets thus intrude on powder space. Extra long bullets may also require faster rifling twists to stabilize them in flight. On the plus side, bullet weight remains constant while velocity is lost, so heavy bullets give deep penetration and make your rifle better for bigger game and those iffy angling shots in the timber.

The special beauty of big bullets is the extra penetration they give on big targets like elk, according to Randy Brooks of Barnes Bullets. Barnes Bullets is synonymous with heavy bullets.

"You can shoot game going away from you and be sure a heavy bullet is going to penetrate up into the lungs," Brooks

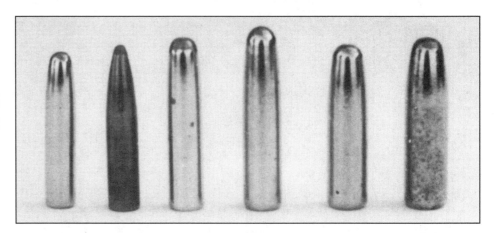

Left to right: 180-grain 277 Barnes, 190-grain 284 Woodland, 250-grain 308 Barnes, 300-grain 338 Barnes, 300-grain 358 Barnes and 350-grain 375.

said. "You can kill an antelope or deer with just about any bullet because of the shock it gives them," Brooks said. "But game heavier than deer, like elk, hasn't read the book on shock. You need the penetration of a heavy bullet for big animals."

Brooks said heavy bullets, such as the 180-grain round-nose loaded in the 270, are not made for shooting long range, but that you do not handicap yourself with such a round-nose bullet.

"Hunters like to think they make 700-yard shots," Brooks

CARTRIDGE OVERALL LENGTHS WITH HEAVY BULLETS

Cartridge/Rifle	Bullet Weight/Type	Length (ins.)
270 Win. FN Mauser	180-grain round-nose Barnes	3.25
7mm Rem. Magnum Remington 700	190-grain spitzer point Woodland	3.24
30-06 Mark X Mauser	250-grain round-nose Barnes	3.31
338 Win. Magnum Ruger 77	300-grain round-nose Barnes	3.30
35 Whelen Remington 700	300-grain round-nose Barnes	3.33
375 H&H Model 70 Winchester	350-grain round-nose Barnes	3.59

said, "but most of the shots we take are at 100 or 150 yards."

Ideally, heavy bullets should shoot close to the same point of impact as lighter bullets so a hunter does not have to twist the adjustment dials on his rifle scope like a TV dial every time he shoots a different weight bullet. Say a hunter, carrying a 270, hunts in the morning for mule deer on the open south face of a mountain. For the mule deer, he had his 270 loaded with 130-grain bullets. Around noon the hunter decides to hunt elk on the cool north side of the mountain in the thick trees and downfall where elk bed down in the heat of the day. His shots will be at 50 yards on elk standing at something other than broadside or at an elk jumping out of its bed and running through the trees. Before he slips into the dark of the forest, he replaces the 130-grain bullets with 180-grain bullets because he knows the 180s will hold together better and penetrate deeper than the shorter 130s.

My 270 is an FN Mauser with a 24-inch barrel. The 180-grain bullets have a round-nose and are made by Barnes. I loaded a good size pile of 270 cartridges with IMR-4350, -4831 and -7828, and 760 with the 180-grain bullets and shot them over a chronograph at targets at 100 yards.

As the load chart shows, the relatively slower powders gave the highest velocities in the 270 with the 180-grain bullet. IMR-4831 gave the bullet 2652 fps, which is the velocity most 30-

Good powders for reloading heavy bullets in the 270 Winchester. The slower the powder, the higher the velocity in my 270.

Good powders for reloading heavy bullets in the 7mm Magnum.

A couple of powders I tried in the 35 Whelen.

Slow powders like 4350 and 4831 worked fine in the 375 H&H. However, I found that a couple of loads of 4831 would not fit in the 375 case.

06s shoot with the same weight bullet. The 270 was sighted-in to put 130-grain bullets 3 inches high at 100 yards. With the same scope setting, the 180-grain printed right on the mark at the same distance. At 200 yards, the 180-grain bullets had dropped 5.5 inches and grouped into 2 inches, a smaller cluster than the shot at 100 yards.

In *Handloader #6*, Bob Hagel states in the article, "Quest for Accuracy," he has seen many hunters become disappointed after shooting long heavy bullets out of their rifles at 100 yards. "What they did not realize is that very often those same loads would shoot just as tight at 200 yards as they did at 100," Hagel stated.

"What's the reason?" Hagel asked. "The long bullet has not gone completely 'to sleep' at 100 yards. It has not settled down into a true smooth spin around its axis, so it's showing a slight yaw at the shorter ranges and less accuracy," he stated.

The rate of rifling twist in a barrel has an affect on the accuracy of long heavy bullets. Everything else being equal, long

bullets need a faster rate of twist than short bullets.

Jim Carmichel stated in his work, *The Book of the Rifle*, that "the need for a specific rate of spin to best stabilize a bullet of a given weight and diameter helps explain the relatively narrow range of bullet weights in a given caliber." However, one turn of rifling for each 10 inches of barrel, which is standard for

100- AND 200-YARD GROUPS

Cartridge	Bullet Weight/Type	100 yds. (ins.)	200 yds. (ins.)
270 Winchester	180 RN	1.25	2.0
7mm Rem. Mag.	190 SPT	2.5	3.7
30-06	250 RN	6.0	worse yet
338 Win. Mag.	300 RN	1.5	1.35
35 Whelen	300 RN	1.6	5.0
375 H&H	350 RN	2.8	5.0

RN = Round-Nose; SPT = Spitzpoint.

I could not find a powder that would make my 30-06 shoot 250-grain bullets with a darn. Groups looked like buckshot patterns from a shotgun.

Good powders for reloading the 338 Winchester.

Cartridge	Bullet Wt. Grs./Type	Powder Grs. Wgt./Type	Vel. (fps)	Group† (ins.)	Cartridge	Bullet Wt. Grs./Type	Powder Grs. Wgt./Type	Vel. (fps)	Group† (ins.)
270 Mauser	180 RN	47/IMR-4350	2514	1.75	338 Win. Mag.	300 RN	71/IMR-4831	2574	1.5
FN Mauser	180 RN	52/IMR-4831	2652	2.75	Ruger 77	300 RN	72/IMR-4831	2642	2.25
24″ barrel	180 RN	44/W-760	2400	3.0	24″ barrel	300 RN	65/IMR-4350	2498	2.0
	180 RN	54/IMR-7828	2644	1.5		300 RN	59/W-760	2192	3.0
	*180 RN	51/H-4831	2434	—		*300 RN	70/H-4831	2508	—
	*180 RN	54/H-4831	2581	—		*300 RN	76/H-4831	2724	—
	*180 RN	46/H-4350	2269	—		*300 RN	60/IMR-4350	2167	—
	*180 RN	48/H-4250	2387	—		*300 RN	66/IMR-4350	2375	—
7mm Rem. Mag.	190 SPT	75/H-870	2632	1.75	35 Whelen	300 RN	54/IMR-4350	2207	1.6
Remington 700	190 SPT	75.5/H-870	2663	—	Remington 700	300 RN	53/IMR-4320	2349	1.75
24″ barrel	190 SPT	62.5/IMR-7828	2640	1.5	22″ barrel	300 RN	54/W-760	2069	2.1
	190 SPT	63/IMR-7828	2645	2.2		*300 RN	38/IMR-3031	—	—
	190 SPT	59/IMR-4831	2593	2.5		*300 RN	42/IMR-3031	2031	—
30-06	250 RN	51/IMR-4831	2232	5.0	375 H&H	350 RN	71/IMR-4350	2386	.8
Interarms Mark X	250 RN	46/W-760	2089	6.0+	Winchester 70	350 RN	72/IMR-4831	2244	2.8
24″ barrel	250 RN	43.5/W-748	2072	6.0	26″ barrel	*350 RN	71/H-4350	—	—
	*250 RN	48/H-4350	2049	—		*350 RN	72/H-4350	2100	—
	*250 RN	50/H-4350	2131	—					
	*250 RN	54/H-4831	2450	—					

*Untested loads; †Groups shot at 100 yards.
RN = Round-Nose; SPT = Spitzerpoint.

270s, seemed to work well for the short 130-grain and long 180-grain bullet in my FN Mauser.

Rifling is a mystery. Still, I do not lose any sleep over rifling pitch. Correct powder, good bullet selection and good reloading techniques have just as much to do with accuracy as the rate of twist—within reason, of course.

Randy Brooks said the heavy bullets Barnes makes will all stabilize in rifles with a standard twist. Some of the real heavies, he says, like the 195-grain in 7mm with a 1:9 twist, are borderline stable. Brooks said a barrel can also have too fast a twist and overstabilize a bullet, and ruin accuracy that way.

Kevin Thomas, a ballistic technician with Sierra Bullets, said the average hunter fails to realize that an off-the-shelf 30-06 is incapable of stabilizing a heavy bullet, such as a 250-grain. Sierra makes a 250-grain, .308-inch bullet. "Our 250-grain, 30-caliber, for example, takes a 1:8-inch twist in a 30-06 or a 1:9-inch in a magnum to stabilize properly," Thomas said.

Tom Bricker, of Manheim, Pennsylvania, makes his 7mm Woodland bullets at 190 grains. He said with the pointed flat-base bullets in that weight the standard 1:9 rifling in a 7mm Remington Magnum will stabilize the bullet. Bricker makes a 190-grain pointed boattail in 7mm which he said needs a faster twist to shoot accurately. He also said Ruger 7mm Magnum rifles are made with this faster rate of twist.

"Ruger is definitely on the right track with the faster twist," Bricker says, "because it handles a wider range of bullet weights."

Bricker said shooting heavy bullets requires a trajectory tradeoff. The higher ballistic coefficient of a heavy bullet makes up for its slower velocity. A heavy bullet's advantage is deeper penetration than lighter bullets. "There's more bullet there for the bigger game like moose and elk," Bricker said.

Bricker makes his 190-grain bullets by swaging down 30-caliber jackets for the extra metal to make the long 7mm jack-

ets. He inserts a flux along with the lead core. Then he heats the bullets until lead melts. The flux bonds the lead to the jacket.

I shot a half-dozen 190-grain Woodland bullets at 2600 fps out of my 7mm Remington Magnum into a line of hardcover books at 100 yards. The bullets all weighed around 100 grains with cores and jackets intact after penetrating 16 inches. A 210-grain Nosler Partition out of a 338 Winchester did not go any deeper.

On a paper target, the 190s hit right on the point of aim at 100 yards when the rifle is sighted-in to put 162-grain bullets 2 inches high at the same distance. At 200 yards, the 190s only drop off 3 inches.

On the other hand, my 30-06 grouped 250-grain bullets over 10 inches higher than 150-grain bullets at 100 yards, if you consider a 6-inch spread of group. I loaded four different powders behind the Barnes 250-grain round-nose bullets in my Interarms Mark X 30-06. None of the loads grouped better than a shotgun pattern. Even when they did group well, they shot so high when sighted-in with 150-grain bullets I had to do some serious resighting to get them to shoot anywhere close to where the crosshair pointed. The heavier the bullet fired in my 30-06, the higher it prints. The other calibers I fired shot heavier bullets lower at 100 yards than light bullets.

My 338 took to heavy bullets like a drug dealer to dirty money. With one load of 4831, the 300-grain round-nose Barnes Bullet grouped into 1.5 inches at 100 yards and averaged 2642 fps. I settled on a grain less powder and an average bullet speed of 2574 fps. That load printed 2 inches high at 100 yards, the same as the 225-grain Hornady the rifle was sighted-in for. However, at 200 yards the 225 is still a smidgen high and the 300-grain is 3.5 inches low. Still, that's a very usable bullet combination.

Randy Brooks said he has noticed more hunters every year switching to the bigger magnum rifles, such as the 338, for elk and bigger game.

However, hunters have passed over Remington's newly intro-

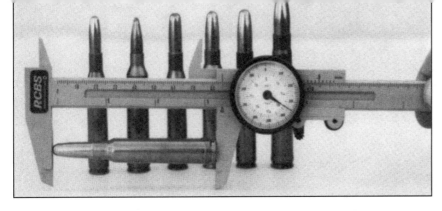

Loading long and heavy bullets means the handloader must keep loaded cartridge overall length short enough to fit in a rifle's magazine and also keep the bullet from engaging the rifling.

(Below) Here are the loaded cartridges (from left): 270 Winchester, 7mm Remington Magnum, 30-06, 338 Winchester Magnum, 35 Whelen and 375 H&H.

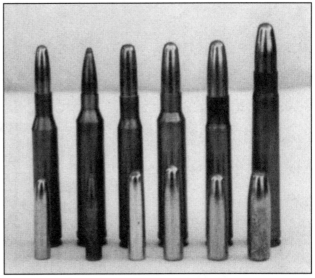

duced old cartridge, the 35 Whelen. I do not know why, either. The Whelen shoots the same range of bullet weights as the 338. All the Whelen gives up is 200 feet of velocity to the 338 with the same bullet weights. For this slight loss of velocity, the Whelen comes in a rifle that is 3/4-pound lighter, and has a 2-inch shorter barrel than the 338 and a noticeable reduction in recoil.

For a heavy bullet in the Whelen, I loaded a Barnes 300-grain round-nose. The medium-rate burning powder, IMR-4320, left enough space in the Whelen case for that big chunk of a bullet. With a velocity of 2349 fps, the 300-grain bullets hit 2 inches high at 100 yards, but then 6 inches high at 200 yards.

Other weight bullets shot out of that Whelen fly the same curve. Remington factory-loaded 250-grain pointed bullets and my reloads with 250-grain pointed Hornady and Speer bullets land 4 inches high at 200 when sighted 2 inches high at 100. The rather high scope mounts on the Whelen are probably responsible for this looping trajectory.

One thing is for sure: The Whelen is a pleasure to shoot after shooting a box of 338s.

After shooting the nice 35 Whelen, I picked up a 375 H&H Magnum. The rifle started life as a pre-'64 Model 70 300 H&H Magnum and was rebarreled with a 26-inch 375 barrel. Corey Huebner, of Missoula, Montana, stocked the rifle in a piece of New Zealand walnut.

The rifle was pretty to look at, but had a vicious backhand. I am not used to shooting rifles with such heavy recoil. The recoil from the 350-grain bullets torqued the rifle to the right and off the shooting stand. A sandbag between my shoulder and the butt of the rifle along with a tight hold on the forearm helped tame the kick.

Loaded with 71 grains of IMR-4350, the Barnes 350-grain round-nose cut a three-shot group of .8-inch at 100 yards. The bullet speed was just short of 2400 fps. Why anyone would need one of the various 416s when you can get that speed and accuracy with that heavy a bullet out of a 375 is beyond my limited thinking.

A little quirk this rifle had was that the 350-grain bullets shot 1.5 inches to the left of its zero with Speer 285-grain Grand Slams.

Corey Huebner used this rifle with the Grand Slams to take a Canadian bull moose with one shot. On an angling shot from the rear, the bullet went clear through the moose. With penetration like that, Huebner does not see any need for a heavier bullet.

A few of the loads I found in old reloading manuals for the 375 and H-4831 powder with a 350-grain bullet were very optimistic. Not about the velocity, but about pouring that much powder into the case and expecting to seat a bullet on top if it.

Little reloading data for heavy bullets is available. Randy Brooks will quote you a few loads; Vol. 1 of P.O. Ackley's has a few loads;

so does the 25th edition of the Hodgdon's reloading manual. After developing and shooting heavy bullet loads for six different cartridges, I still have all my fingers, although my shoulder remembers every shot.

Of the rounds I tested, the 35 Whelen and 375 were the only two that were short on case capacity with heavy bullets. Both still gave excellent velocity and accuracy with the loads developed.

The only extraordinary reloading step I took when loading heavy bullets was to make sure the inside of the case mouths had a good bevel chamfered on them so the long bullets seated easily. Only the 375 gave any problems when seating these long bullets on a RCBS Jr. standard-size press. I had to slip a bullet up into the seating die and hold it there, while with my other hand I placed the charged case in the shellholder, then pulled on the handle to run the case into the die and seat the bullet.

Round-nose bullets must also be seated deeper in the case than pointed bullets to keep the bullet from engaging the rifling when a round is chambered. The tapered point of a spitzerpoint can get up into the barrel without touching the rifling, while a round-nose at the same overall length has little taper at the tip and will catch the rifling. No problems came up as long as the recommended overall lengths were not exceeded.

So, is there a need for these heavyweights? As sure as TV evangelists ask for money. A heavy bullet makes a big game rifle more versatile for game bigger than deer and gives more penetration on less-than-perfect broadside shots. If your rifle will shoot a heavy bullet to near the same point at 100 and 200 yards, you are in business for any halfway decent shot under the open sky or forest canopy.

One-hole accuracy is fascinating as an abstract goal for a cartridge-stuffer, but most back-pasture chuck shooters can go with...

Practical Handloading For Varmints

by LONNY WEAVER

VARMINT SHOOTERS RELOAD for accuracy, but can a varminter get carried away with accuracy reloading?

Let me give you a relatively recent practical example of what I am getting at.

My all-time favorite varmint cartridge is the sizzling 220 Swift. Well, a couple of years back, Remington's Custom Shop began putting together a varmint hunting version of their famed 40X target series of bolt actions chambered for the Swift. The rifle, as you may know, wears a Kevlar stock, sports a 27¼-inch heavy stainless steel barrel, and has about the sweetest trigger you'll ever come across on a factory rifle.

Anyway, as soon as I could scrape together the cash (Remington does not give these babies away), I dashed off my order and settled back for a not very patient year-long wait.

As luck would have it, the rifle came the first week of May. I was so excited I took a day's vacation, mounted a Redfield 6-18x Golden Five-Star scope, grabbed a couple of boxes of reloads consisting of 38.0 grains of IMR-4064 behind a Sierra

Varmint rounds the writer is currently loading (from left): 17 Remington, 22 Hornet, 224 Weatherby, 220 Swift, 223 Remington and 240 Weatherby Magnum.

52-grain hollowpoint boattail bullet and ignited by a CCI 200 primer in a full-length sized Winchester case, and headed for the range for a morning sight-in session to be followed the rest of the day by chuck busting on a previously scouted farm.

I used the first twenty rounds to gently break in the barrel, settle the action and scope mounts, and to get the scope adjusted to print 1½ inches high at 100 yards. The second box was used for serious paper punching. Four five-shot groups averaged .588, the smallest going into a tight .340-inch.

I used this load all summer to ring up eighty-three chucks out of eighty-six shots.

The following winter I decided to see just what this Reming-ton Swift would do with "proper" handloads.

Starting with new brass sharing the same case lot number, I spent nearly a week's worth of evenings turning necks, weighing cases, and performing an endless list of nit-pickings guaranteed to put me in the one-hole class of paper punchers.

It just did not happen.

My best "super" load beat my everyday load by a mere .004-inch.

A case of overkill, in my humble opinion.

The trick to developing a top-notch load for your favorite varmint rifle is to complete the task without burning out the barrel, breaking the family budget, and wearing yourself out.

These two chucks won't be eating more soybeans, thanks to a practical handload in this sporter-weight Remington 700 BDL chambered for the 223.

This RCBS Posi-Prime tool uses a standard shellholder and allows the handloader to "feel" the primer into place during the seperate priming operation.

I've loaded for all of the current commercial varmint rounds, a couple of obsoletes, and a small handful of wildcats over the last quarter-century, and can't recall a single instance when a good, practical handload couldn't be put together with a minimum of fuss.

This is not to imply that all benchrest loading techniques are a waste of the varmint shooter's time, money and effort. Quite the contrary, in fact. But, the bitter truth of the matter is that few, if any, production-grade hunting (and that includes varminting) rifles are capable of significantly benefitting from super loads. For sure, darn few shooters, myself included, are capable of profiting from such loads in a practical hunting sense.

What's a "good practical handload?"

For my purposes, it's the one that produces the best combination of speed and accuracy.

One of my favorite rifles is a beautiful little Kimber Model 82 Custom Classic chambered for the mild-mannered 22 Hornet. Mine wears a 24-inch semi-target barrel. Topped with a 3-9x Leupold Compact scope in Kimber mounts and rings, this little honey weighs a scant 8 3/4 pounds.

For some reason, the Hornet cartridge's famed accuracy had always evaded my efforts. When I got this Kimber, I was also using an old Savage 219 break-action single shot that usually could be counted upon to put five rounds of Winchester Super-X ammo (both the 45-grain softpoint and the 46-grain hollowpoint) into a shade under 2 inches at 100 yards. The Kimber routinely shaded that average by a little more than a quarter-inch. I tried every 45-grain bullet I could lay my hands on and still had a tough time beating the Winchester-made stuff in both rifles.

And talk about problems! For some reason I still haven't figured out, I began getting stuck cases in both rifles with mild charges of IMR-4227. That's when I threw out the book on conventional wisdom relating to loading the Hornet.

Realizing the Hornet is a 150-yard cartridge, I asked myself why I should confine bullet choice to the single selection everyone in the know recommended—the 45-grain slug. The fact was, at the time, the only load I had come up with capable of marginally beating the factory offering barely exceeded the velocity of the rimfire 22 WMR!

I began using 40-grain softpoints from Speer and Sierra and immediately cut group size dramatically, while boosting velocities to between 2700 and 2800 fps with W-680 powder teamed with the Winchester 6 1/2 primer. And guess what—no more stuck cases. So what if the 40-grain pill loses velocity faster than the usually recommended 45-grainer? Started out much faster, the lighter bullet has more than enough punch left to level any 150- to 175-yard chuck in my neighborhood.

About the time I traded away the Model 219 to a buddy, I stumbled upon another unconventional Hornet tip when an acquaintance of my father mentioned that he always used pistol primers when loading the round back in the late '40s. About a year later, Ross Seyfried passed on the same tip received from a *Guns & Ammo* reader.

By substituting a CCI 500 pistol primer for the usual Winchester 6 1/2 I had been using to ignite my load of W-680, I cut average group size from a hair over an inch to a neat .824. This got my attention, and I subsequently settled on 13.0 grains of W-680 teamed with the CCI pistol primer. The load generates 40 fps less velocity than with the small rifle primer, but shrinks average group size to a startling .626.

Speed and accuracy.

One other thing before we get down to actual mechanics: I believe in loading my varmint rifles to their potential. Not overloading, of course, but to the level that will give me the highest practical velocities with trouble-free loads. A lot of emphasis is placed by some of the accuracy clan on the importance of loading below maximum in order to obtain top accuracy. Sorry, but I don't buy this line of wisdom. If I wanted a lesser cartridge than say, a 22-250, I would buy a Hornet, 222 or 223. It has been my experience that 1/2- to 3/4-inch groups (and often less)

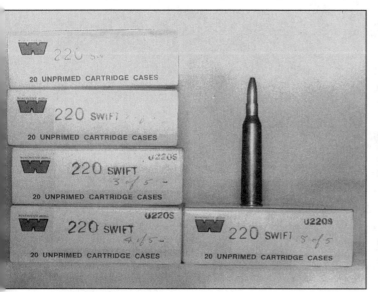

When buying new brass, always order from the same lot number and keep cases separated by lot, as done with these 220 Swift cases.

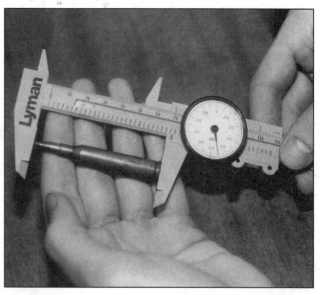

Correct bullet seating depth is a prerequisite to superb accuracy. Once that overall cartridge length is determined, record the information for future loads.

Always test your handloads from a solid shooting position. The writer is trying a batch of loads in a 220 Swift Ruger No. 1V from a benchrest. Note the sandbags under the forearm (never the barrel) and the rest under the buttstock.

are just as easy to get when loading a given centerfire varmint cartridge to full throttle as it is to underload. Remember, you are loading for practical hunting—to humanely dispatch varmints—not just for shooting the tiniest possible groups off a rock solid rest at known distances with the help of wind flags and other aids.

At the very least, you should begin load development by separating your brass into brands. Naturally, I use only Remington brass for my 17 Remington reloads simply because that's the only source. I began using only Winchester brass for all of my 220 Swift reloads when it became apparent that was more readily available locally than offerings from Norma and Frontier. Likewise, Weatherby is still the only source of 224 WM and 240 WM brass for the varmint hunter. In the instance of the more popular rounds such as the 222, 223, 22-250, 243 and 6mm, which are available from many sources as either factory loaded ammo or new unprimed brass, my advice is to confine yourself to the one that is most available or, perhaps, the most accurate factory offering in your particular rifle.

When the opportunity arises, it's a good idea to latch on to five or six boxes of new, unprimed brass sharing the same lot number. That number is usually found on the inside flap of the box. If your local gun shop doesn't stock an extensive line of reloading supplies, simply ask that they order you "six boxes of _____ (fill in the blank)." More than likely it will be of the same lot.

By the way, I always start with six boxes. I load the first 100 rounds and save the remaining 20 for replacements due to wear, reloading slips, losses in the field, etc.

The idea behind sorting by brand is uniformity. Not all brands of brass are of uniform wall thickness. Chances are, though, that each Federal 22-250 case, for instance, is very close dimensionally to the one before and after it. By buying new brass from the same lot, you are improving your chances in regard to case dimensions as well as chemical properties, annealing, etc.

Some handloaders weigh their cases to ensure even better uniformity. I've done that, but if my purpose is to slay wood-

chucks in farmer Hale's pasture, consider the task a waste of time. Case weighing doesn't tell you all that much anyway. A better indication of case uniformity, if you simply have to do this in order to sleep, is to check water capacity. Then, separate the cases by capacity.

Unless you have put a few thousand dollars into a super-duper pasture-poodle plasterer, you will also find case head squaring a royal waste of time. I make mention of it only for the record.

In the instance of new brass, I always run the cases through a full-length sizing die to square them up (you will be surprised how "unsquare" new brass can be), trim to an even overall case length and do a couple of things to the primer pocket.

Until a few years back, I didn't do much to primer pockets except make sure they had a flash hole and to clean them up after every couple of loadings. Don't laugh about that "flash hole" business. I've got a 224-caliber Weatherby case that slipped by without one.

After reading about reaming flash holes to the same diameter and squaring primer pocket bases, I gave both a try over an extended period of time and do believe they encourage uniform powder ignition and thus improve accuracy in a practical sense. Both jobs are easy and quick, which, in my opinion, adds to their appeal.

American cases have their flash holes punched. Usually left behind on the inside of the case head is a burr of varying degrees; this tends to hinder uniform ignition of the powder charge. I use a K&M Flash Hole Uniformer that, at the twist of the wrist, deburrs the hole and turns it to a uniform diameter. Then I grab a Match Prep from Whitetail Design and Engineering and, with another twist of the wrist, recut the primer pocket to a uniform depth.

Before each reloading of a fired case, I clean the primer pocket. Some experts doubt the usefulness of this, but I figure that if I'm going to the trouble of uniforming flash holes and primer pockets, it would be folly not to clean up the area after each firing.

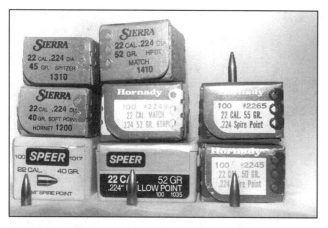
In working up a handload, first pick the weight and style of bullet you wish to use and go from there.

By the way, you can get away with using a drill bit for flash hole reaming, if you wish. Supposedly, American cases have a hole measuring .080. But if you have a new 22 or 6mm PPC, don't let someone sell you a reamer. These cases have drilled holes that should not require deburring/uniforming.

Oᴋ, now for neck turning. I believe Neal Knox was the first to write about neck turning and, my goodness, it seemed like overnight every shooter in America was shopping for the tool. Admittedly, many cases have lopsided necks due to manufacturing processes that leave the case thicker on one side than on the other. Outside neck turning helps this, as does, to a lesser degree, inside neck reaming. There are a number of outside neck turners to choose from, and most are hand held. All are difficult to adjust and no fun to operate. I don't use them and doubt that you should either, unless you have a rifle that requires it to get the round chambered.

I currently own varmint rifles from Kimber, Ruger, Remington and Weatherby, and can honestly say that neck turning did nothing to dramatically enhance the accuracy of these fine rifles. No difference was apparent in my 17 Remington Kimber 84 Super Varmint, 22-250 Ruger No. 1V, or 224 Weatherby Varmintmaster. As noted at the beginning of this piece, there was a very slight improvement in my 220 Swift Remington 40X KS Varmint Special. The reason, of course, lies in the chamber dimensions of my production rifles. I believe that if you are not already shooting half-inch or better average groups with your varmint rig, neck turning will not show an apparent improvement.

The last step to perform before actually loading the new brass is case mouth chamfering. This is an important step that prevents base deformation when seating the bullet in the case. The trick is not to put a knife-like edge on the case, but rather a smooth, gentle bevel on both the inside and outside of the case mouth. Done properly, this bevel will also encourage square seating of the bullet. I've used a chamfering tool from Lyman for at least twenty years. Just give the tool a gentle twist. That's all.

Since you are only going to load "new" brass once, now is the time to touch on the arguments of full-length sizing versus neck sizing only of fired cases.

When you gently stroke the trigger on your Remington 700 Varmint Special or maybe your tack-driving Winchester 70 Varmint, tremendous gas pressure caused by the burning powder charge expands the flexible walls of the brass cartridge case

against the rifle's chamber wall and bolt face. When the bullet rushes out of the case mouth, the elasticity of the brass case makes it instantaneously retract, though it doesn't completely go back to its original dimensions. You now have a "custom fitted" case, so to speak, that very closely matches the dimensions of your rifle's chamber.

If this case is to be used again in only this particular varmint rifle, you do not need to resize the case back to its pre-fired dimensions. All you need to do is resize the neck portion of the case so that it will once again tightly hold the bullet in place. This is known as neck sizing.

Full-length sizing, then, is done by forcing the entire case fully into the resizing die. This essentially returns the entire case to its original unfired dimensions.

Most benchrest shooters neck size only. Reloading experts generally recommend neck sizing only for maximum accuracy and minimum wear and tear on the expensive brass case.

I full-length size all of my cases and have found no loss of practical accuracy or brass longevity compared to neck sizing. Almost without exception, neck-sized cases are harder to chamber smoothly and quickly, and in my opinion will, over a number of reloads, likely cause a flexing of the action upon chambering of the round due to uneven bearing on the locking lugs.

This recalls the first real problem I encountered when I began reloading in earnest many years ago. My first true varmint rifle was a Winchester M70 220 Swift. Until I bought it, I had never loaded in quantity and found the superb, hand-held, neck-sizing Lee Loader at under $10 fit my needs perfectly.

All went well until the fourth loading of my Winchester brass. The stuff would not chamber except with great effort. Guessing that the brass was "worn-out," some new was purchased, and on about the third reload, the same chambering problem was encountered.

Having read of the strength of 220 Swift brass from the popular writers at the time, I wrote to the National Rifle Association for a solution to my problem. I still have the letter that stated, "the 220 Swift is a difficult cartridge to reload and cannot be safely reloaded by the neck sizing method."

I stumbled on the real cure myself when a case length gauge was bought. Case trimming cured the problem. On reflection, I have no idea why that Model 70 did not blow to pieces.

Neck stretching is unpredictable. I remember a particular lot of 223 Remington brass that required trimming every other firing. Later, using the same load but with a different lot of brass from the same source, my records show I got six firings before having to trim. Actually, those cases still hadn't reached maximum length, but they were trimmed for uniformity. Be safe and use a case length gauge or calipers and check for safe length every time following resizing.

I've always made case priming a separate operation. At first, this was done because that was the procedure required by my Lee Loaders. Later, when my budget allowed the purchase of a benchmounted press—an RCBS Jr. that I'm still using with perfect satisfaction—I had the option of priming in conjunction with case resizing, but just couldn't get used to the idea or feel. "Feel" is what primer seating is all about.

The hand-held tool allows me to actually feel the primer bottoming in the primer pocket, and firm contact is another element of accuracy loading that is essential as well as practical.

Some years back, I began using the beautifully made RCBS Posi-Prime tool when I discovered that a Lee or MRC tool could not be readily had to accommodate the odd-size case head of my 224 Weatherby. The RCBS tool uses the same shellholder employed in the reloading press.

When handling primers, be extra careful not to contaminate them with oil or resizing lube. That's another reason I make priming a separate operation. After lubing and sizing the cases and cleaning the primer pockets, I wipe the excess lube from the resized cases, clean up the loading area, wash my hands and only then begin handling my primers.

For the most part, I use standard primers. Despite some rather lengthy testing on the subject, I can't really detect much difference between them in terms of practical accuracy. The only exception concerns my loading of the 17 Remington. Here, I normally use only the rather thick Remington $7^1/_2$ to protect against pierced primers. The CCI BR4 match-grade primer has also given me excellent service in this 17-caliber.

Of course, brands and types of primers often differ in "hotness." If you change primer brands or types (magnum for standard rifle, for example), always cut the powder charge in your established load by 10 percent and work back up in order to avoid any potential pressure problems.

When I sit down to load a batch of 100 cases for one of my rifles, I fill the powder measure, adjust it to give the desired charge, throw and check-weigh a couple of charges, and then proceed to rhythmically get the job done. I do not weigh individual charges for my varmint rifles.

Done correctly, with a bump of the charging handle at the top and bottom of each stroke, charge weight is, for all practical purposes, as accurate as individual weighing. The only time, in fact, that I individually weigh charges for my varmint rifles is when I get involved with a load development project.

Developing a load can be a bewildering task unless you absorb a little ballistic fact, sit back and look at things logically.

The first step in developing a good, practical varmint load without burning out the barrel in the process is to decide on the bullet weight and type you wish to use. The second step is to go through several handloading manuals and pick out the powders giving the highest velocities for that particular bullet weight. More times than not, these powders and the heaviest listed charges will come very close to filling the case to the base of the neck. Such loads are "balanced" and likely to produce the best accuracy.

For example, let's say you just became the proud owner of a spanking new 22-250 Ruger No. 1V single shot and want to come up with a crackerjack load using the explosive Speer 52-grain hollowpoint bullet.

Grabbing *Nosler Reloading Manual Number Three*, you will find three loads producing the highest velocities with the 52-grain bullet: 34.0 grains of IMR-4895 or 40.0 grains of IMR-4350 will give you an even 3800 fps, while 36.0 grains of IMR-4320 generates 3780 fps.

I'd go for the two heavier loads employing IMR-4350 and IMR-4320, cut the charges by 10 percent and load three rounds each in increasing half-grain increments until reaching the top listed charges. This little task is done to make sure I don't get into excessive pressures and to quickly determine the most potentially accurate load boasting the highest practical velocity (remember: "speed and accuracy").

Next I'd select the two most accurate of these loads, put together twenty rounds of each, return to my benchrest and squeeze off four five-shot 100-yard groups, allowing a full minute between shots to avoid overheating the barrel. That can destroy accuracy in no time flat. The barrel is then given a thorough cleaning, a fouling shot is sent up the barrel, and the next string of five-shot groups is carefully fired.

This done, I'd measure each group, come up with an average, and pick the most accurate as the winner.

Some time should be put into the selection of bullets, but expensive match or custom-grade bullets are not always needed for top-notch accuracy in off-the-shelf varmint rigs. And, some bullets in my experience always seem to turn in superb accuracy and terminal performance. Several that immediately come to mind are the 25-grain Hornady 17-caliber hollowpoint; the Sierra 40-grain softpoint, Nosler 45-grain softpoint and Speer's 52-grain hollowpoint in the 224 calibers; and the 75-grain 243/6mm Hornady hollowpoint. Of course, some rifles simply will not shoot a particular bullet worth a darn for no apparent reason.

At present, my "contrary rifle" is a beautiful Kimber Model 84 Super Varmint chambered for the 17 Remington. For example, it simply will not shoot any Remington bullet (factory load or handload) worth a darn. I tried some custom pills in 20-, 22- and 25-grain weights, and still came up short in the accuracy department. Yet, when fed the little Hornady driven to 4018 fps,

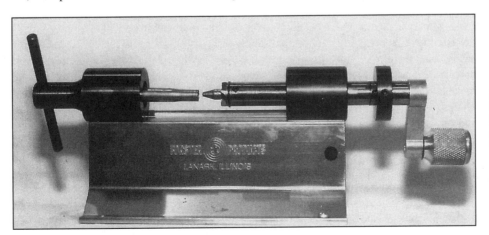

Excessive case length is an invitation to trouble. Trim cases when they approach maximum length. Also, "true up" new unfired cases, such as this 22 Hornet.

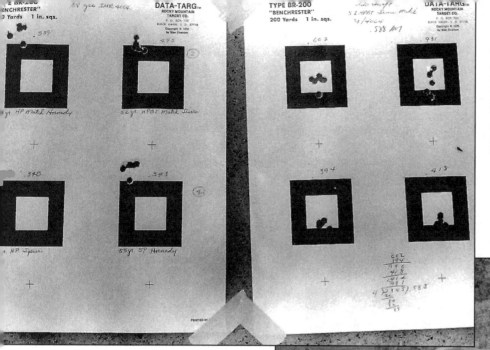

The four groups on the left represent the same charge (38 grains IMR-4064) behind four different bullets—53-grain HP Match Hornady, 52-grain HPBT Match Sierra, 52-grain HP Speer and 55-grain SP Hornady. The four groups on the right, fired from the same 220 Swift Remington 40XB with the same load, used only the 52-grain HPBT Sierra Match bullet.

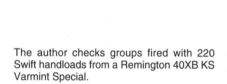

The author checks groups fired with 220 Swift handloads from a Remington 40XB KS Varmint Special.

this rifle will stay well under minute-of-angle all day, every day, so long as I clean the barrel regularly.

Occasionally, I hear or read of match-grade bullets that fail to expand on chuck-size varmints at the longer ranges when driven at moderate velocities. I have never experienced this problem, but confess to confining the more expensive match bullets to the bigger cased 22 centerfires like the 224 WM, 22-250, 220 Swift and a 22-243 wildcat that I played with awhile back.

Once I settle on a specific varmint load, the only refining you will find me doing to it will concern bullet seating depth. Most of my varminters shoot best with the bullet barely "kissing" the rifling. However, not all of my chuck rigs (if they have a magazine that I wish to utilize) will allow me to seat my bullet to that magic overall length. It has been my experience that one of the biggest contributions to accuracy is finding and using the correct bullet seating depth.

By the way, if your varminter has some age on it or an unusual amount of barrel wear, you might be able to restore its formerly superb accuracy by simply going to a heavier, and thus

longer, bullet. I did this very thing a few years back with a Ruger 77V 22-250 that was bought new back in the early '70s. My standard load utilized a 52-grain Speer hollowpoint pushed to almost 3800 fps. After nearly 4500 rounds of this load, the throat area was showing wear, which in turn was showing up on targets. I did some experimenting with 55-, 60- and 70-grain bullets, and finally settled on the Speer 70-grain pushed along with 38.0 grains of IMR-4350 to a snappy 3376 fps. In my Ruger, this load keeps on drilling neat little five-shot groupings measuring a hair or so beyond a half-inch.

Lastly, always keep good records. I have most of my handloading data on computer disc dating all the way back to that first Winchester Model 70 220 Swift. My loading records are broken down by rifle and contain not only load development and experimentation data, but information on the rifle (serial number, date of purchase, rifle cost, etc.) as well. Just as important, I can account for practically every round sent down a particular rifle's barrel, whether fired at varmint or target, thus allowing me to keep tabs on barrel wear.

Not everyone needs or is totally infatuated with magnum shotshells. If light-recoiling loads will handle things, try...

Soft Pushers In the 12 And 20

by HOLT BODINSON

TIRED OF FEELING physically abused after a session with your shotgun? Would you like to magically convert your 12-gauge pet into a 20 or even a 28? Or your 20 into a 410? Would you like to encourage your children, spouse or significant other to share your love of shooting without their having to fight that old devil, recoil?

You can achieve all these ends with a little bit of handloading ingenuity. Reduced target and field loads are a wonderfully useful extension of handloading. Loading reduced powder charges and possibly lighter bullets or shot charges, shooters can enjoy all the benefits of target accuracy without the concomitant boom, recoil, and simple wear and tear inherent in firing full-powered munition. It is a concept as old as handloading itself, as evidenced by the reduced "gallery" loads published in the distant past for such classic cartridges as the 45-70, 30-40 and 30-06.

While handloading literature is full of information and data on reduced loads for rifle and handgun cartridges, very little has been written about stepping down the common shotshell. Indeed, most shotshell loading data, and particularly that issued

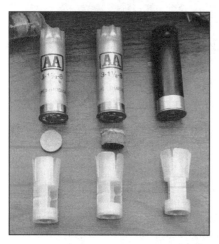

Three bags of Butler wads and a can of IMR-7625: These are the ingredients that make soft pushing shotshell loads possible.

Combining card and Butler wads with Winchester plastic wads, the handloader can transform his 12-gauge into a 20-gauge or, better yet, even a 28-gauge.

by the component manufacturers, approaches maximum allowable industry standards. Their emphasis is on the highest possible performance, and rightfully so. They don't want any "bloopers" to occur with their components.

One does find reference today to "light" loads. Winchester, for example, offers "SuperLite" wads and propellants. Federal listings also contain data for "Extra-Lite" loads. I tried them, but they still pushed back pretty hard. I was looking for something lighter still.

Why? Two reasons. First and foremost is the reduction of recoil to a truly enjoyable level. Second, with the high cost of components today, particularly for good hard shot, it simply doesn't make much sense to blow away $1\frac{1}{8}$ ounces of shot when $\frac{3}{4}$-ounce, possibly, or even a $\frac{1}{2}$-ounce would accomplish the same ends.

The 12- and 20-gauge "soft pushing" loads I finally ended up with are remarkable. With the proper components, one can transform a 12-gauge into a 20-gauge or, even better yet, a 28-gauge. Similarly, a 20 can be transformed into a 28-gauge or 410. The two critical components that make this possible are relatively slow-burning powders and filler wads.

The most outstanding powder I've used to date in both the 12- and 20-gauge has been IMR-7625. This sporting rifle powder has been around a long time and is slightly dirty, but for me nothing has come close to equaling its ability to produce a slow-pushing, progressive burn at low pressures in shotshells. Used today almost exclusively in handgun and shotshell loads, IMR-7625 is one of the unsung heroes of the handloading game.

Before the days of one-piece plastic wads, any gauge or reasonable thickness of card and felt shotgun wads could be bought over the counter at the nearest gun store. No longer. Now one has to search for these other secret ingredients of soft pushing shotgun loads. The unique quality that makes filler wads possi-

ble is that a 20-gauge fiber or card wad will fit perfectly in the bottom of a 12-gauge one-piece plastic wad/shotcup. Similarly, a 28-gauge card or fiber wad will snuggle down perfectly in a 20-gauge plastic shotcup. Fortunately, we have, available by mail through Butler Enterprises, the most incredible assortment of fiber and card wads imaginable, and they are inexpensive.

Combining light charges of IMR-7625, reduced shot charges, and filler wads placed inside of one-piece plastic wad shotcups to take up the space, reduced shotshell loads are easy to assemble using standard procedures and tools. The only real difference is the preparation of the one-piece plastic wad.

The easiest procedure is to line up whatever number of plastic wads will fit on a clear area of your loading bench and to insert the filler wads before loading the plastic wad. Then, seat the combined plastic/filler wad with a single pull of your press handle.

Here are some of the best reduced loads I've developed so far. They probably won't cycle your semi-automatic, but regardless of what gun you fire them in, I think you and your family will experience a whole new level of shotgun shooting enjoyment.

12-GAUGE

HULL: Winchester AA
PRIMER: Winchester 209
POWDER: 20.0 grs. IMR-7625
WAD: AA12SL + .125 (Butler 20-ga. card wad in shotcup)
SHOT: $\frac{7}{8}$-ounce #8 or #9

HULL: Winchester AA
PRIMER: Winchester 209
POWDER: 20.0 grs. IMR-7625
WAD: AA12SL + .5 (20-ga. card wad in shotcup)
SHOT: $\frac{3}{4}$-ounce #8 or #9

HULL: Winchester AA
PRIMER: Winchester 209
POWDER: 20.0 grs. IMR-7625
WAD: AA12SL + .5 (20-ga. fiber wad in shotcup)
SHOT: $\frac{1}{2}$-ounce #8 or #9

HULL: Remington Black Plastic
PRIMER: CCI 209
POWDER: 20.0 grs. IMR-7625
WAD: AA12SL
SHOT: $\frac{7}{8}$-ounce #8 or #9

20-GAUGE

HULL: Winchester AA
PRIMER: Federal 209 or CCI Magnum
POWDER: 14.5 grs. IMR-7625
WAD: WAA20 + Butler .5 (28-ga. fiber wad in shotcup)
SHOT: $\frac{1}{2}$-ounce #8 or #9

Why only one 20-gauge recommendation? It simply works so well I've never seen the need to experiment any further. Fellow shotgunner Merrill Brown put me onto this one. It has proved to be a dandy. Try it. You're in for a real treat.

In terms of shot sizes, I've recommended #8s and #9s only because I assume most of these loads will be used for informal clay pigeon shooting. But don't let that stop you from using them for dove and quail. These loads do perform in the field, and shot sizes can always be adjusted accordingly.

So get a can of IMR-7625, some Butler wads, and go to it.

35

After fifty-plus
seasons of deer
hunting, this
Pennsylvania
guncrank has
some definite
opinions about...

Handloads for Whitetails & Mulies

by DON LEWIS

"PUT SIERRA 60-GRAIN hollowpoints in these 243s, and shove the velocity up as high as possible," a constant critic of my reloads stated. "I'm sure you're aware that a lot of speed with the 60-grain hollowpoint bullet makes a top 243 deer load."

"No, I'm not, and I'm not putting 60-grain bullets in your deer loads," I answered. "Your idea of a top 6mm deer load goes against all ballistic common sense."

"I've been using 60-grain slugs on chucks all summer, and the results I've seen have proved to me this bullet weight would be perfect for deer, especially at long ranges."

"There's a heck of a difference between the bone structure of a woodchuck and a deer," I tossed back. "A 60-grain bullet sure does a lot of damage on a 7-pound chuck, but it could literally blow to pieces on the shoulder of a 140-pound buck. The chances would be high that it wouldn't penetrate the heavier bones and muscles of a deer. If you want me to load your deer shells, you'll have to settle for bullet weights in the 100-grain class. Keep in mind the 243 is not my idea of a top deer car-

Lewis is dubious about the 7mm Magnum as a true large game load, but has found it to be excellent for deer at the longer ranges. He dropped this whitetail at about 300 yards with a 140-grain Sierra spitzer and 63 grains of IMR-4350. In his No. 1 Ruger, this load gives about 3000 fps MV and is extremely accurate.

tridge even with its heaviest bullet."

The last remark brought an outburst of expletives that nicely seasoned a complete analysis of my total ignorance of ballistics, handloading and deer cartridges. The man claimed that more knowledgeable handloaders had advised him to use lightweight bullets for deer, and he fully intended to take their advice. When the two-minute tirade ended, he left with his empty brass.

That wasn't the first time I had encountered the low-weight/high velocity argument from deer hunters. Most of these hunters had very successfully used lightweight bullets during summer chuck hunts and felt they would get the same results in the deer woods.

There's no question that any cartridge from the 6mm to the 338 Winchester is usable for deer under certain conditions, assuming the proper load is chosen. But after a half-century of deer hunting in a number of states under all conditions, plus fifteen years of operating a handloading shop, I think a whitetail or mule deer hunter should not only pick the best cartridge for the terrain hunted, but also choose the right primer/powder/bullet combination. What is a good caliber and load for one type of terrain may not be the best for another.

Since deer hunting is done in various types of cover, it's reasonable to assume one caliber or cartridge can't be the complete answer. For instance, in very thick cover or dense stands of timber, I feel deer hunters are better off with slower velocities and heavier bullets. Under these conditions, my pick would be cartridges such as the 348 Winchester, 35 Remington and 30-30 Winchester.

The 348 Winchester and 35 Remington have few peers where brush is thick and shots are close, and the 30-30 Winchester is still the most popular short-range deer cartridge on the market.

I'm sure not too many 348s are still being used in the deer woods. Model 71s have become collector's items. However, since this famous lever action is the epitome of Depression Era craftsmanship and the 348 cartridge is one of the most powerful rimmed cartridges—suitable for elk and moose as well as deer—it deserves mention. My choice whitetail load is 64.5 grains of H-4831 behind a 200-grain Hornady flat-nose bullet. Muzzle velocity is about 2350 fps. It is a deadly woods outfit. Velocity with this bullet can easily be pushed to 2500 fps if bigger critters are the objective.

The 35 Remington cartridge appeared in 1906 in the Model 8 autoloading rifle and was later chambered in the Remington 14, 141 and 760 slide actions, as well as several bolt and lever guns. It has some inherent drawbacks for the handloader, especially in regard to selecting the right powder.

To start with, the 35 Remington case doesn't have a lot of powder capacity and has a very short shoulder. Optimum results usually come from powders such as H-414 and BL-C2. Since the 35 Remington does its best at ranges well under 150 yards, the deer hunter will get excellent results from 38 grains of BL-C2 behind a 200-grain round-nose bullet. Muzzle velocity is a smart 2000 fps, and energy touches 1800 foot pounds. This load is basically for brush, but that's what the old 35 is all about.

The 30-30 Winchester has been a popular deer cartridge for almost a century. Unfortunately, the 30-30 doesn't offer the reloader a wide assortment of bullet weights. The 150- or 170-grain should be used for deer. Only flat-nose bullets can safely be used in tubular magazine rifles. Bolt-action fans may opt for pointed bullets, but the 30-30 cartridge does not generate enough velocity to properly benefit from a spitzer design, so its absence

Ray Claypool (left) took this wide-spreading whitetail with an all-time favorite outfit, an M70 Winchester 30-06 carrying a Weaver K4. The load was the 150-grain Sierra spitzer and 48 grains of IMR-4895. Nick Sisley (right) needed only one shot from his 280 for this Alabama trophy. His load was the 150-grain Nosler and 56 grains of AA-3100, which chronographs at almost 2800 fps MV.

isn't important. My favorite deer load in the 30-30 is 35 grains of H-4350 behind a 150-grain flat-nose bullet. My Oehler 35P gives this load instrumental velocity readings of 2130 fps 15 feet from the muzzle. True muzzle velocity would be slightly higher.

In post-World War I days, deer hunting in the East was almost exclusively a brush and heavy timber sport. That's not the case today. Large electric power and gasline rights-of-way, timber harvesting, and clear cutting have opened up the once darkened woods. Cartridges designed for medium ranges such as the old 300 Savage and the newer 308 Winchester and 7mm-08 Remington are ideally suited for this kind of shooting.

The 300 Savage came to life in the Savage 99 lever-action rifle in 1921. Some enthusiastic supporters claimed it was equal to the 30-06, but that isn't true. Its smaller case capacity and the strength limitations of the lever action just won't permit the 300 to be loaded equal to the 30-06. But it is a much more efficient cartridge for deer than the 30-30, and many elk and deer have been taken with it, though it really isn't suited for large North American big game. If it were, it wouldn't have lost much of its popularity when the Winchester 308 came along.

Either 150- or 180-grain bullets work well in the 300 Savage for ranges up to 200 yards on deer. Bullets in the 200- to 220-grain category can't be given enough velocity for long shots. I prefer 44 grains of H-414 behind a 180-grain Speer Mag-Tip or round-nose for wooded areas. Velocity in my gun is a snappy 2275 fps.

In open country, the 300 Savage will easily reach the 250-

yard mark with 41.2 grains of IMR-4320 behind the 150-grain Sierra spitzer. Chronograph readings of this powder charge/bullet weight combination average just under 2600 fps. I have to point out that 39.9 grains of IMR-4064 driving a 165-grain Sierra hollowpoint boattail shot my tightest three-shot groups in this caliber at 100 yards. Its muzzle velocity of 2500 fps is not far below the 150-grain spitzer load. It might be worth considering.

The 308 Winchester began life as the military 7.62 NATO. When introduced as a sporting cartridge, some rather impressive claims were made for the 308, but like so many fantastic accolades from early enthusiasts, they lack ballistic support. The most common myth, which some riflemen still quote, is that the 308 Win-

The 348 Winchester, besides being an excellent choice for most American game at woods ranges, has the added advantage of being convenient for southpaws.

chester stands shoulder to shoulder with the 30-06. This can't be. The 308 can no more equal the '06 than the '06 can equal the 300 Magnum. There's just too much difference in case capacity.

Due to the 308's reduced powder capacity, bullets heavier than 180 grains are not recommended. I prefer somewhat lighter weights. My tests revealed I could easily stay in the 2700 fps velocity range with either 150-grain or 165-grain bullets, so I concentrated on these. Over the years, I have used the 308 to drop eight deer with these weights. My favorite woods load is 47 grains of W-748 behind the Speer 150-grain spitzer. This load leaves the muzzle at over 2700 fps and is extremely accurate. In open terrain, I switched to a 165-grain Hornady spirepoint in front of a near-max load of 45.5 grains of Winchester 748 powder. Velocity with this powder charge is just under 2700 fps.

You may wonder why a boattail was not selected for long range. Maybe it's because the 308 is not my idea of a true long-range cartridge. The way I see it, the 308 falls into the 250-yard category. That's not a short shot by any means, but a boattail adds little efficiency here. Distances beyond 250 yards or so require bullets with top aerodynamics, and that means a boattail every time.

For comparison's sake, maximum loads of several powders will drive a 190-grain bullet out of an '06 muzzle at 2800 fps. In the 308, maximum powder charges will give a 165-grain spitzer a muzzle velocity just topping 2700 fps. The moral of this is that the '06 can shove a 190-grain bullet out of the muzzle faster than can the 308 with a bullet weighing 25 grains less. The 308 just doesn't give the velocity needed to offer flat trajectory with the heavier bullets over extreme ranges. I think this points out rather emphatically that the 308 is not equal to the 30-06.

The 7mm-08 Remington is an extraordinary deer cartridge. It took Americans a long time to recognize the potential of the 7mm (284) caliber bullet. *Speer Reloading Manual* No. 11 says, "It [the 7mm caliber bullet] has good sectional density in all weights and an excellent ballistic coefficient in any given weight compared to

other bullets of the same weight." With bullets from 100 to 175 grains readily available, the Remington 7mm-08 is a much better deer cartridge than the 30-30 or any of the 6mms.

Varmint hunters may reload the 100- or 115-grain HP 284 bullets, but deer hunters should stick with the 139- to 154-grain category, I believe. Some years ago, I drove a 175-grain Speer Grand Slam through an antlerless deer's ribcage at about 90 yards. It was a standing shot, and I had a solid rest. When the Model 788 Remington 7mm-08 cracked, the deer bounded away. I found it hard to believe I had missed, but the doe showed no signs of being hit. I found her 122 steps from where she had been standing. The 175-grain Grand Slam had simply driven through her light-boned ribcage without expanding. In all fairness, I must point out that the 175 Grand Slam is designed for elk and other large animals, and the heavily constructed bullet didn't meet enough resistance to properly expand. I would have been far better off with the 145-grain Speer spitzer, say, leaving the a muzzle at around 2850 fps.

In the 7mm-08, I also stick with the medium-weight bullets, because the heavier ones must be seated so deep to function in the short-action rifles commonly used for this cartridge that powder capacity is greatly reduced.

It might not be fair to put cartridges in classes such as short range, medium range and long range, since it's possible to make a 300-yard shot with almost any centerfire big game cartridge. Yet, that's the most practical approach for a deer hunter. The 300 Savage, 308 Winchester, 7mm-08 Remington and others obviously have long-range potential, but when distances stretch way out, they can't really compete with the 270 Winchester, 280 Remington, 30-06 or 7mm Remington Magnum. At the same time, it's worth pointing out that these four cartridges can't compete with some of the super magnums, either. But from a logical point of view, there are few cases where super magnums are needed for whitetails or mule deer.

Lewis feels the 338 Magnum has more power than is needed for deer, and he's right. But sometimes—as on an Idaho elk hunt— that's what you're carrying, and with the 275-grain Speer and a compressed charge of H-4831, it gets the job done.

Nowadays, the 30-30 Winchester gets criticized by many high-velocity, bolt-action fans, but Lewis thinks it's a fine woods load—and so does old-timer Hurley Mensinger, who has good reason to feel that way. Five or six million M94 Winchester users can't all be wrong.

Tim Lewis stoked his fast-working M760 Remington 308 with 150-grain Speer spitzers, 46/4064 and 9½ Remington primers for his '92 hunt. One shot through the shoulders dropped this 153-pound (field dressed) 6-point.

(Above) The M77 Ruger chambered for the high-performance 284 Winchester cartridge was Helen Lewis's choice for anterless season in Pennsylvania. The 150-grain Remington SPCL pushed to 2800 fps by a heavy charge of IMR-4350 penetrated both shoulders for an instant kill.

(Right) Mary Ann Workosky with proof that the little 7mm-08 Remington does all that's necessary at conventional ranges. The rifle is Mel Forbes' Ultra Light M20.

It's strange to me that the 277-caliber attracted only two factory entries—the 270 Winchester and the 270 Weatherby Magnum. But .277-diameter bullets have been featured in a fair share of wildcats. Several that come to mind are the 270 Savage, 270-308 and 277 Brooks Short Magnum. The 270 Winchester's popularity stems largely from the fact that it gained a reputation as being a better long-range cartridge than the 30-06. Time has shown this is debatable. The 30-06 can be loaded to achieve superb downrange ballistics. I have to concede that the Hornady 130-grain 270 spitzer, say, has a much higher BC (.409) than their 130-grain 308-caliber spirepoint bullet (.295). This gives the 270 a flatter trajectory in this bullet weight than the '06 can produce, when both are max-loaded to about 3100 fps. Zeroed at 200 yards, the 270/130 load is about 38 inches low at 500, while the '06/130 combination is some 46 inches low. But if, instead of matching bullet weights in the two calibers, which isn't too logical, we try to match ballistic coefficients, the 30-caliber Hornady that's closest to the 130-grain 270 is the 165 grain 308, which has a BC of .435. In a heavily loaded '06, this bullet can be given 2900 fps, which with a 200-yard zero is 43 inches low at 500 yards. That's just a few inches more drop than the 270's, but the '06 load has more remaining energy at this range, 1359 fpe vs. 1186, according to the latest *Hornady Handbook, Vol. 2.*

My best results with the 270, both on the range and in the woods, came from 57.5 grains of IMR-4831 behind a 130-grain boattail or spitzer bullet. My other favorite powders for this weight are W-760 and IMR-4064.

Since the 130-grain 277 slug often damages a lot of meat, many deer hunters prefer a 150-grain spitzer in front of either IMR-7828, -4831 or Norma MRP if it can be found. Tighter groups often will be fired with powder charges several grains below maximum. Another excellent choice would be the Hornady 140-grain spirepoint pushed by 57 grains of H-450. Velocity is just under 2900 fps, and that's moving a 140-grain 277 bullet.

Maybe I'm old-fashioned, but I still see the 130-grain bullet as the top choice for the 270 Winchester. The Nosler Partition bullet in front of 54 grains of Accurate Arms 3100 ignited by a Federal 210 primer is my pick for a top woods primer/powder/bullet combination. Velocity is around 2800 fps, and that's sufficient velocity to make the Partition bullet very effective.

Ranges beyond 250 yards benefit from bullets with high BCs. For example, a Speer 130-grain boattail with a .411 BC really reaches out when muzzle velocity is in the neighborhood of 3000 fps.

Since I've taken only two deer with Remington's 280 cartridge, my association with it stems mostly from range tests. Remington introduced the 280 in 1957 and eventually chambered several of their models for it, including the M740 autoloader and M760 slide action. In 1979, they changed the name to 7mm Express. It was the same cartridge, but there were suggestions that the newly named load was more powerful than the original factory 280. But having two names for the same cartridge caused an inordinate amount of confusion and Remington went back to the 280 listing about a year later.

The 280 Remington is a little more powerful than the 270 Winchester. Also, with new slow-burning powders, another hundred feet per second or so of velocity can be obtained when used in strong bolt-action rifles. Loads which are maximum for bolt actions should be avoided when loading the 280 for slide actions and autoloaders.

My first serious range tests with the 280 were fired shortly after Remington changed the name to 7mm Express. I was torn between the 139-grain Hornady spirepoint and the 160-grain Speer spitzer. With 55 grains of IMR-4831, the chronograph reading with the 139-grain Hornady averaged 2875 fps at 15 feet from the muzzle, which meant at least 2900 fps at the muzzle. Sandbox tests showed good expansion with this bullet. With 55.5 grains of N-205 behind the Speer 160-grain spitzer, instrumental velocity was 2785 fps. Muzzle velocity would be over 2800 fps. You can see why I was confused, with less than a 100 fps velocity difference between the two bullet weights.

I used the 139-grain load to drop a walking deer at 117 steps. Apparently, this Hornady reacted in the deer's chest cavity pretty much the same as it had in the sandbox. It wasn't an instant kill, but the deer collapsed only moments after the shot.

Later, I received a test model Remington 700 Mountain Rifle chambered for the 280. I expected to be hunting in heavy brush, so chose the 162-grain Hornady bullet rather than the 139-grain. The manual indicated that 51 grains of IMR-4350 would give about 2800 fps, so I assembled a box of cases with that load and zeroed-in.

At 4:30 p.m. on the last day of Pennsylvania's antlerless season, a large deer trotted through an opening about 80 yards from me. I got a quick flash of deer in the scope before it melted into the dark heavy brush. There wasn't enough time to make certain it was a legal target. I felt all was lost, but a dozen or so yards farther out, it passed through a spot where the brush had thinned enough for me to see it was a legal doe and to get the crosswires on to her body. An angling shot through the ribcage dropped the deer instantly. The bullet exited in front of the far shoulder. No heavy bones were struck, but the size of the exit hole showed good expansion. It was only one shot, but I'm convinced this is a top brush load.

The venerable 30-06 needs no introduction. Born in the early 1900s as a military cartridge, it derived its common name from its caliber, 30, and the year it came out, 1906. It was a military success for years, and it is still probably the most versatile big game cartridge ever developed. The 30-06 is quite capable of taking all North American big game when the proper bullet is used. Since all bullet weights from a 125-grain spitzer to the 220-grain round-nose can handle deer, the handloader can have his cake and eat it, too.

I've probably tested more 30-06 rifles than any other cartridge, and I've fired hundreds of their slugs into sand, woodpiles and through heavy piles of small limbs into life-size deer targets a few feet beyond. I finally settled on two bullet weights for deer, the 150-grain spitzer and the 165-grain boattail.

When I was developing '06 loads in the early days, I didn't have a chronograph. My 150-grain loads came from the 1950 edition of Lyman's *Handloading—an NRA Manual*. That book's max load of 52 grains of IMR-4895 behind a 150-grain Speer bullet showed a muzzle velocity of 2943 fps at 20 feet, but warned it was "excessive." I dropped down a full grain and loaded thousands of 30-06 empties with 51 grains of 4895 behind a 150-grain bullet.

Interestingly, a somewhat later manual by another publisher gives 55 grains of 4895 as the maximum load and 51 grains as the lowest suggested charge, with a muzzle velocity for the latter of 2816 fps. Why the significant disparity between the two manuals is still a mystery to me, but I never went above 51 grains of the early 4895 ex-military powder.

A word of caution is needed here. Current IMR-4895 apparently is somewhat different than the old military stuff. Suggested maximum loadings with 4895 in the Speer No. 11 manual tops off at 49 grains behind a 150-grain bullet, while the 4th Edition of the *Hornady Handbook* lists 48.7 grains with H-4895. Velocity readings are in the 2900 fps realm from 22-inch barrels.

I believe the 165-grain boattail bullet is unequaled for long-range 30-06 shooting at whitetails and mulies. Many will not agree, claiming the 180-grain boattail is superior, but I tend to think of the 180-grain weight as an elk or grizzly bullet. The 165-grain is more apt to expand better on the light skeletal makeup of a deer. The thick, tough skins and heavy bones of truly big game animals need heavier bullets such as the 180- and 200-grain slugs. The 30-06 will drive a 200-grain spitzer out of the muzzle at 2600 fps, but the same weight slug in the 300 Winchester Magnum can easily top the 2900 fps mark. From many years of shooting, I'm convinced the 150- to 165-grain bullets are the best in the 30-06 for deer.

The last deer I shot with an '06 was a small "Y" buck. I dropped it at 134 steps with a 150-grain Speer spitzer and 51 grains of 4895. Because the trotting buck never lifted its head while it was in view, I felt it was hot on a doe's track. I didn't have much time, but my hastily fired shot hit just behind the near shoulder and angled into the left one. The buck hit the ground with the crack of the 30-06.

I don't believe magnum big game cartridges are necessary for deer, but doubt that the Remington 7mm Magnum should be classed as a true large game magnum. Bullet weights run to only 175 grains, and that seems light for dangerous animals such as Cape buffalo and Kodiak bears.

While it may not be a true big game magnum, Remington's Big 7 is a heck of a long-range whitetail and mulie cartridge. My favorite all-around whitetail load is the 140-grain Sierra spitzer with 63 grains of IMR-4350. Chronograph tests averaged 2975 fps at 15 feet from the muzzle. The 140-grain Sierra has a high BC of .490. I usually sight-in about 3 inches high at 100 yards. This gives a trajectory arc with a 250-yard zero, falling a couple inches low at 300 and about six inches low at 350. In other words, with this sight-in picture, I have a point-blank range of 350 yards. You might call it a dead-on hold to that distance.

For mule deer hunters, the 160-grain boattail might be a wiser choice, as mulies usually are heavier than whitetails. In my M700, 79 grains of H-870 behind a Speer boattail will produce a muzzle velocity touching the 3000 fps mark. I have also found that Accurate Arms 8700 with the 160-grain Sierra boattail gives superb accuracy. My best groups came from 78 grains of AA-8700 behind the Sierra 160-grain boattail. Muzzle velocity is down a little, to about 2850, but getting tight groups from any magnum cartridge is always impressive.

There's no end to what the handloading deer hunter can have. To me, bullet design is more important than getting the last foot second of velocity. Bullets are designed for specific purposes. I feel a hunting bullet should enlarge its frontal diameter to at least twice the bullet's original caliber. This is only a rule of thumb, but it's important. From my experiences, bullet expansion and killing power go hand in hand. Maybe it's like love and marriage. To get a high degree of expansion in whitetails and mulies without fragmentation, the handloader must choose his bullets carefully. Testing by firing into wet telephone books, sand or even ballistic gelatin isn't conclusive, but does give some idea of how a bullet will perform when it hits.

There's one more factor to consider. Each rifle, regardless of its brand or caliber, handles certain weights, types and makes of bullets better than others. To get optimum results, the handloader must use the process of elimination to find the best load. While that sounds like a lot of work and expense, and to some degree it is, the end results are too significant to overlook. That's one thing I think you can write in stone.

Directory of The Reloading Trade

A

AAL Optics, Inc., 2316 NE 8th Rd., Ocala, FL 33470/904-629-3211; FAX: 904-629-1433
A.B.S. III, 9238 St. Morritz Dr., Fern Creek, KY 40291
AC Dyna-tite Corp., 155 Kelly St., P.O. Box 0984, Elk Grove Village, IL 60007/847-593-5566; FAX: 847-593-1304
Acadian Ballistic Specialties, P.O. Box 61, Covington, LA 70434
Acculube II, Inc., 4366 Shackleford Rd., Norcross, GA 30093-2912
Accupro Gun Care, 15512-109 Ave., Surrey, BC U3R 7E8, CANADA/604-583-7807
Accura-Site (See All's, The Jim Tembellis Co., Inc.)
Accuracy Den, The, 25 Bitterbrush Rd., Reno, NV 89523/702-345-0225
Accuracy Innovations, Inc., P.O. Box 376, New Paris, PA 15554/814-839-4517; FAX: 814-839-2601
Accuracy Unlimited, 7479 S. DePew St., Littleton, CO 80123
Accuracy Unlimited, 16036 N. 49 Ave., Glendale, AZ 85306/602-978-9089; FAX: 602-978-9089
Accurate Arms Co., Inc., 5891 Hwy. 230 West, McEwen, TN 37101/615-729-4207, 800-416-3006; FAX 615-729-4211
Accuright, RR 2 Box 397, Sebeka, MN 56477/218-472-3383
Ackerman, Bill (See Optical Services Co.)
Ackerman & Co., 16 Cortez St., Westfield, MA 01085/413-568-8008
Action Bullets, Inc., 1811 W. 13th Ave., Denver, CO 80204/303-595-9636; FAX: 303-595-4413
Action Target, Inc., P.O. Box 636, Provo, UT 84603/801-377-8033; FAX: 801-377-8096
Actions by "T", Teddy Jacobson, 16315 Redwood Forest Ct., Sugar Land, TX 77478/713-277-4008
ACTIV Industries, Inc., 1000 Zigor Rd., P.O. Box 339, Kearneysville, WV 25430/304-725-0451; FAX: 304-725-2080
Ad Hominem, RR 3, Orillia, Ont. L3V 6H3, CANADA/705-689-5303
Adair Custom Shop, Bill, 2886 Westridge, Carrollton, TX 75006
Adaptive Technology, 939 Barnum Ave, Bridgeport, CT 06609/800-643-6735; FAX: 800-643-6735
ADC, Inc., 33470 Chinook Plaza, Scappoose, OR 97056/503-543-5088
ADCO International, 10 Cedar St., Unit 17, Woburn, MA 01801/617-935-1799; FAX: 617-935-1011
Advance Car Mover Co., Rowell Div., P.O. Box 1, 240 N. Depot St., Juneau, WI 53039/414-386-4464; FAX 414-386-4416
Adventure 16, Inc., 4620 Alvarado Canyon Rd., San Diego, CA 92120/619-283-6314
Adventurer's Outpost, P.O. Box 70, Cottonwood, AZ 86326/800-762-7471; FAX: 602-634-8781
AFSCO Ammunition, 731 W. Third St., P.O. Box L, Owen, WI 54460/715-229-2516
Ahlman Guns, Rt. 1, Box 20, Morristown, MN 55052/507-685-4243; FAX: 507-685-4247
Aimpoint, Inc., 580 Herndon Parkway, Suite 500, Herndon, VA 22070/703-471-6828; FAX: 703-689-0575
Aimtech Mount Systems, P.O. Box 223, 101 Inwood Acres, Thomasville, GA 31799/912-226-4313; FAX: 912-227-0222
Air Venture, 9752 E. Flower St., Bellflower, CA 90706/310-867-6355
Airrow (See Swivel Machine Works, Inc.)
Alaska Bullet Works, P.O. Box 54, Douglas, AK 99824/907-789-3834
Alex, Inc., Box 3034, Bozeman, MT 59772/406-282-7396; FAX: 406-282-7396
All's, The Jim J. Tembellis Co., Inc., 280 E. Fernau Ave., Oshkosh, WI 54901/414-426-1080; FAX: 414-426-1080
All American Lead Shot Corp., P.O. Box 224566, Dallas, TX 75062
Alley Supply Co., P.O. Box 848, Gardnerville, NV 89410/702-782-3800
Alliant Techsystems, Smokeless Powder Group, 200 Valley Rd., Suite 305, Mt. Arlington, NJ 07856/800-276-9337; FAX: 201-770-2528
Allred Bullet Co., 932 Evergreen Drive, Logan, UT 84321/801-752-6983
Alpec Team, Inc., 201 Ricken Backer Dr., Livermore, CA 94550/510-606-8245; FAX: 510-606-4279
Alpha 1 Drop Zone, 2121 N. Tyler, Wichita, KS 67212/316-729-0800
Alpha LaFranck Enterprises, P.O. Box 81072, Lincoln, NE 68501/402-466-3193
AmBr Software Group Ltd., P.O. Box 301, Reistertown, MD 21136-0301/410-526-4106; FAX: 410-526-7212
American Ammunition, 3545 NW 71st St., Miami, FL 33147/305-835-7400; FAX: 305-694-0037
American Derringer Corp., 127 N. Lacy Dr., Waco, TX 76705/800-642-7817, 817-799-9111; FAX: 817-799-7935
American Gas & Chemical Co., Ltd., 220 Pegasus Ave., Northvale, NJ 07647/201-767-7300
American Handgunner Magazine, 591 Camino de la Reina, Suite 200, San Diego, CA 92108/619-297-5350; FAX: 619-297-5353
American Products Co., 14729 Spring Valley Road, Morrison, IL 61270/815-772-3336; FAX: 815-772-7921
American Sales & Kirkpatrick, P.O. Box 677, Laredo, TX 78042/210-723-6893; FAX: 210-725-0672
American Safe Arms, Inc., 1240 Riverview Dr., Garland, UT 84312/801-257-7472; FAX: 801-785-8156
American Target, 1328 S. Jason St., Denver, CO 80223/303-733-0433; FAX: 303-777-0311
American Whitetail Target Systems, P.O. Box 41, 106 S. Church St., Tennyson, IN 47637/812-567-4527
Ames Metal Products, 4324 S. Western Blvd., Chicago, IL 60609/312-523-3230; FAX: 312-523-3854
Ammo Load, Inc., 1560 E. Edinger, Suite G, Santa Ana, CA 92705/714-558-8858; FAX: 714-569-0319
Amrine's Gun Shop, 937 La Luna, Ojai, CA 93023/805-646-2376
Analog Devices, Box 9106, Norwood, MA 02062
Andela Tool & Machine, Inc., RD3, Box 246, Richfield Springs, NY 13439
Anderson Manufacturing Co., Inc., 22602 53rd Ave. SE, Bothell, WA 98021/206-481-1858; FAX: 206-481-7839
Anschutz GmbH, Postfach 1128, D-89001 Ulm, Donau, GERMANY
Answer Products Co., 1519 Westbury Drive, Davison, MI 48423/810-653-2911
Apel GmbH, Ernst, Am Kirschberg 3, D-97218 Gerbrunn, GERMANY/0 (931) 707192
Arco Powder, HC-Rt. 1, P.O. Box 102, County Rd. 357, Mayo, FL 32066/904-294-3882; FAX: 904-294-1498
Arms, Peripheral Data Systems (See Arms Software)
Armfield Custom Bullets, 4775 Caroline Drive, San Diego, CA 92115/619-582-7188; FAX: 619-287-3238
Armor Metal Products, P.O. Box 4609, Helena, MT 59604/406-442-5560
Armory Publications, P.O. Box 4206, Oceanside, CA 92052-4206/619-757-3930; FAX: 619-722-4108

A.R.M.S., Inc., 230 W. Center St., West Bridgewater, MA 02379-1620/508-584-7816; FAX: 508-588-8045
Arms & Armour Press, Wellington House, 125 Strand, London WC2R 0BB ENGLAND/0171-420-5555; FAX: 0171-240-7265
Arms Corporation of the Philippines, Bo. Parang Marikina, Metro Manila, PHILIPPINES/632-941-6243, 632-941-6244; FAX: 632-942-0682
Arms Ingenuity Co., P.O. Box 1, 51 Canal St., Weatogue, CT 06089/203-658-5624
Arms Software, P.O. Box 1526, Lake Oswego, OR 97035/800-366-5559, 503-697-0533; FAX: 503-697-3337
Armscorp USA, Inc., 4424 John Ave., Baltimore, MD 21227/410-247-6200; FAX: 410-247-6205
Armsport, Inc., 3950 NW 49th St., Miami, FL 33142/305-635-7850; FAX: 305-633-2877
Aro-Tek, Ltd., 206 Frontage Rd. North, Suite C, Pacific, WA 98047/206-351-2984; FAX: 206-833-4483
Artistry in Wood, 134 Zimmerman Rd., Kalispell, MT 59901/406-257-9003
Aspen Outdoors, Inc., 1059 W. Market St., York, PA 17404/717-846-0255, 800-677-4780; FAX: 717-845-7447
A-Square Co., Inc., One Industrial Park, Bedford, KY 40006-9667/502-255-7456; FAX: 502-255-7657
A-Tech Corp., P.O. Box 1281, Cottage Grove, OR 97424
Atlantic Mills, Inc., 1325 Washington Ave., Asbury Park, NJ 07712/800-242-7374
Atlantic Research Marketing Systems (See A.R.M.S., Inc.)
Atlantic Rose, Inc., P.O. Box 1305, Union, NJ 07083
Atsko/Sno-Seal, Inc., 2530 Russell SE, Orangeburg, SC 29115/803-531-1820; FAX: 803-531-2139
Audette, Creighton, 19 Highland Circle, Springfield, VT 05156/802-885-2331
Autauga Arms, Inc., 817 S. Memorial Dr., Prattville, AL 36067-5734/800-262-9563; FAX: 334-361-2961
Automatic Equipment Sales, 627 E. Railroad Ave., Salesburg, MD 21801
A Zone Bullets, 2039 Walter Rd., Billings, MT 59105/800-252-3111; 406-248-1961

B

B&D Trading Co., Inc., 3935 Fair Hill Rd., Fair Oaks, CA 95628/800-334-3790, 916-967-9366; FAX: 916-967-4873
B&G Bullets (See Northside Gun Shop)
Baer Custom, Inc., Les, 29601 34th Ave., Hillsdale, IL 61257/309-658-2716; FAX: 309-658-2610
Bain & Davis, Inc., 307 E. Valley Blvd., San Gabriel, CA 91776-3522/818-573-4241, 213-283-7449
Balaance Co., 340-39 Ave. S.E. Box 505, Calgary, AB, T2G 1X6 CANADA
Bald Eagle Precision Machine Co., 101 Allison St., Lock Haven, PA 17745/717-748-6772; FAX: 717-748-4443
Balickie, Joe, 408 Trelawney Lane, Apex, NC 27502/919-362-5185
Ballard Bullet, P.O. Box 1443, Kingsville, TX 78364/512-592-0853
Ballard Industries, 10271 Lockwood Dr., Suite B, Cupertino, CA 95014/408-996-0957; FAX: 408-257-6828
Ballistic Engineering & Software, Inc., 185 N. Park Blvd., Suite 330, Lake Orion, MI 48362/313-391-1074
Ballistic Products, Inc., 20015 75th Ave. North, Corcoran, MN 55340-9456/612-494-9237; FAX: 612-494-9236
Ballistic Program Co., Inc., The, 2417 N. Patterson St., Thomasville, GA 31792/912-228-5739, 800-368-0835
Ballistic Research, 1108 W. May Ave., McHenry, IL 60050/815-385-0037
Ballistica Maximus North, 107 College Park Plaza, Johnstown, PA 15904/814-266-8380
Ballisti-Cast, Inc., Box 383, Parshall, ND 58770/701-862-3324; FAX: 701-862-3331
Bansner's Gunsmithing Specialties, 261 East Main St. Box VH, Adamstown, PA 19501/800-368-2379; FAX: 717-484-0523
Barnes Bullets, Inc., P.O. Box 215, American Fork, UT 84003/801-756-4222, 800-574-9200; FAX: 801-756-2465; WEB: http://www.itsnet.com/home/bbullets
Barrett Firearms Manufacturer, Inc., P.O. Box 1077, Murfreesboro, TN 37133/615-896-2938; FAX: 615-896-7313
Barska Optics Int'l., 1765 E. Colorado Blvd., Pasadena, CA 91106/818-568-0618; FAX: 818-568-9681
Barsotti, Bruce (See River Road Sporting Clays)
Bartlett, Don, P.O. Box 55, Colbert, WA 99005/509-467-5009
Bartlett Engineering, 40 South 200 East, Smithfield, UT 84335-1645/801-563-5910; FAX: 801-563-8416
Baumgartner Bullets, 3011 S. Alane St., W. Valley City, UT 84120
Bauska Barrels, 105 9th Ave. W., Kalispell, MT 59901/406-752-7706
Bear Reloaders, P.O. Box 1613, Akron, OH 44309-1613/216-920-1811
Beartooth Bullets, P.O. Box 491, Dept. HLD, Dover, ID 83825-0491/208-448-1865
Beaver Park Products, Inc., 840 J St., Penrose, CO 81240/719-372-6744
Beeline Custom Bullets Limited, P.O. Box 85, Yarmouth, Nova Scotia CANADA B5A 4B1/902-648-3494; FAX: 902-648-0253
BEC, Inc., 1227 W. Valley Blvd., Suite 204, Alhambra, CA 91803-2438/818-281-5751; FAX: 818-293-7073
Behlert Precision, Inc., P.O. Box 288, 7067 Easton Rd., Pipersville, PA 18947/215-766-8681, 215-766-7301; FAX: 215-766-8681
Beitzinger, George, 116-20 Atlantic Ave., Richmond Hill, NY 11419/718-847-7661
Belding's Custom Gun Shop, 10691 Sayers Rd., Munith, MI 49259/517-596-2388
Bell & Carlson, Inc., Dodge City Industrial Park/101 Allen Rd., Dodge City, KS 67801/800-634-8586, 316-225-6688; FAX: 316-225-9095
Bell Reloading, Inc., 1725 Harlin Lane Rd., Villa Rica, GA 30180
Bell's Gun & Sport Shop, 3309-19 Mannheim Rd, Franklin Park, IL 60131
Belltown, Ltd., 11 Camps Rd., Kent, CT 06757/860-354-5750
Belt MTN Arms, 107 10th Ave. SW, White Sulphur Springs, MT 59645/406-586-4495
Ben's Machines, 1151 S. Cedar Ridge, Duncanville, TX 75137/214-780-1807; FAX: 214-780-0316
Benchmark Guns, 12593 S. Ave. 5 East, Yuma, AZ 85365
Beomat of America Inc., 300 Railway Ave., Campbell, CA 95008/408-379-4829
Beretta S.p.A., Pietro, Via Beretta, 18-25063 Gardone V.T. (BS) ITALY/XX39/30-8341.1; FAX: XX39/30-8341.421
Berger Bullets, Ltd., 5342 W. Camelback Rd., Suite 200, Glendale, AZ 85301/602-842-4001; FAX: 602-934-9083
Bergman & Williams, 2450 Losee Rd., Suite F, Las Vegas, NV 89030/702-642-1901; FAX: 702-642-1540

Berry's Bullets, Div. of Berry's Mfg., Inc., 401 N. 3050 E., St. George, UT 84770-9004
Berry's Mfg., Inc., 401 North 3050 East St., St. George, UT 84770/801-634-1682; FAX: 801-634-1683
Bertram Bullet Co., P.O. Box 313, Seymour, Victoria 3660, AUSTRALIA/61-57-922912; FAX: 61-57-991650
Bestload, Inc., Carl Vancini, P.O. Box 4354, Stamford, CT 06907/203-978-0796; FAX: 203-978-0796
Biesen, Al, 5021 Rosewood, Spokane, WA 99208/509-328-9340
Biesen, Roger, 5021 W. Rosewood, Spokane, WA 99208/509-328-9340
Big Bore Bullets of Alaska, P.O. Box 872785, Wasilla, AK 99687/907-373-2673; FAX: 907-373-2673
Birchwood Casey, 7900 Fuller Rd., Eden Prairie, MN 55344/800-328-6156, 612-937-7933; FAX: 612-937-7979
Bismuth Cartridge Co., 3500 Maple Ave., Suite 1650, Dallas, TX 75219/800-759-3333, 214-521-5880; FAX: 214-521-9035
Bitterroot Bullet Co., Box 412, Lewiston, ID 83501-0412/208-743-5635
Black Belt Bullets, Big Bore Express Ltd., 7154 W. State St., Suite 200, Boise, ID 83703
Black Hills Ammunition, Inc., P.O. Box 3090, Rapid City, SD 57709-3090/605-348-5150; FAX: 605-348-9827
Black Hills Shooters Supply, P.O. Box 4220, Rapid City, SD 57709/800-289-2506
Blackhawk East, Box 2274, Loves Park, IL 61131
Blackhawk West, Box 285, Hiawatha, KS 66434
Blacksmith Corp., 830 N. Road No. 1 E., P.O. Box 1752, Chino Valley, AZ 86323/520-636-4456; FAX: 520-636-4457
BlackStar AccuMax Barrels, 11501 Brittmoore Park Drive, Houston, TX 77041/713-849-9999; FAX: 713-448-7298
BlackStar Barrel Accurizing (See BlackStar AccuMax Barrels)
Blacktail Mountain Books, 42 First Ave. W., Kalispell, MT 59901/406-257-5573
Blackwell, W. (See Load From a Disk)
Blair Engraving, J.R., P.O. Box 64, Glenrock, WY 82637/307-436-8115
Blammo Ammo, P.O. Box 1677, Seneca, SC 29679/803-882-1768
Blount, Inc., Sporting Equipment Div., 2299 Snake River Ave., P.O. Box 856, Lewiston, ID 83501/800-627-3640, 208-746-2351; FAX: 208-799-3904
Blue and Gray Products, Inc. (See Ox-Yoke Originals, Inc.)
Blue Book Publications, Inc., One Appletree Square, Minneapolis, MN 55425/800-877-4867, 612-854-5229; FAX: 612-853-1486
Blue Mountain Bullets, HCR 77, P.O. Box 231, John Day, OR 97845/503-820-4594
Blue Ridge Machinery & Tools, Inc., P.O. Box 536-GD, Hurricane, WV 25526/800-872-6500; FAX: 304-562-5311
BMC Supply, Inc., 26051 - 179th Ave. S.E., Kent, WA 98042
Bob's Gun Shop, P.O. Box 200, Royal, AR 71968/501-767-1970
Bohemia Arms Co., 17101 Los Modelos, Fountain Valley, CA 92708/619-442-7005; FAX: 619-442-7005
Boltin, John M., P.O. Box 644, Estill, SC 29918/803-625-2185
Bo-Mar Tool & Mfg. Co., Rt. 12, Box 405, Longview, TX 75605/903-759-4784; FAX: 903-759-9141
Bonanza (See Forster Products)
Bond Custom Firearms, 8954 N. Lewis Ln., Bloomington, IN 47408/812-332-4519
Boonie Packer Products, P.O. Box 12204, Salem, OR 97309/800-477-3244, 503-581-3244; FAX: 503-581-3191
Border Barrels Ltd., Riccarton Farm, Newcastleton SCOTLAND U.K. TD9 0SN
Bowen Classic Arms Corp., P.O. Box 67, Louisville, TN 37777/615-984-3583
Bowerly, Kent, HCR Box 1903, Camp Sherman, OR 97730/541-595-6028
Bowlin, Gene, Rt. 1, Box 890, Snyder, TX 79549
Boyds' Gunstock Industries, Inc., 3rd & Main, P.O. Box 305, Geddes, SD 57342/605-337-2125; FAX: 605-337-3363
Brace, Larry D., 771 Blackfoot Ave., Eugene, OR 97404/503-688-1278
Bradley Gunsight Co., P.O. Box 340, Plymouth, VT 05056/860-589-0531; FAX: 860-582-6294
Brass and Bullet Alloys, P.O. Box 1238, Sierra Vista, AZ 85636/602-458-5321; FAX: 602-458-9125
Brass-Tech Industries, P.O. Box 521-v, Wharton, NJ 07885/201-366-8540
Break-Free, Inc., P.O. Box 25020, Santa Ana, CA 92799/714-953-1900; FAX: 714-953-0402
Brenneke KG, Wilhelm, Ilmenauweg 2, 30851 Langenhagen, GERMANY/0511/97262-0; FAX: 0511/97262-62
Bridgers Best, P.O. Box 1410, Berthoud, CO 80513
Briese Bullet Co., Inc., RR1, Box 108, Tappen, ND 58487/701-327-4578; FAX: 701-327-4579
Briganti & Co., A., 475 Rt. 32, Highland Mills, NY 10930/914-928-9573
Broad Creek Rifle Works, 120 Horsey Ave., Laurel, DE 19956/302-875-5446
Brown Co., E. Arthur, 3404 Pawnee Dr., Alexandria, MN 56308/612-762-8847
Brown Precision, Inc., 7786 Molinos Ave., Los Molinos, CA 96055/916-384-2506; FAX: 916-384-1638
Brown Products, Inc., Ed, Rt. 2, Box 492, Perry, MO 63462/573-565-3261; FAX: 573-565-2791
Brownell Checkering Tools, W.E., 9390 Twin Mountain Circle, San Diego, CA 92126/619-695-2479; FAX: 619-695-2479
Brownells, Inc., 200 S. Front St., Montezuma, IA 50171/515-623-5401; FAX: 515-623-3896
Browning Arms Co. (Gen. Offices), One Browning Place, Morgan, UT 84050/801-876-2711; FAX: 801-876-3331
BRP, Inc. High Performance Cast Bullets, 1210 Alexander Rd., Colorado Springs, CO 80909/719-633-0658
Bruno Shooters Supply, 111 N. Wyoming St., Hazleton, PA 18201/717-455-2281; FAX: 717-455-2211
Brunton U.S.A., 620 E. Monroe Ave., Riverton, WY 82501/307-856-6559; FAX: 307-856-1840
Brynin, Milton, P.O. Box 383, Yonkers, NY 10710/914-779-4333
B-Square Company, Inc., P.O. Box 11281, 2708 St. Louis Ave., Ft. Worth, TX 76110/817-923-0964, 800-433-2909; FAX: 817-926-7012
Buck Stix—SOS Products Co., Box 3, Neenah, WI 54956
Buckeye Custom Bullets, 6490 Stewart Rd., Elida, OH 45807/419-641-4463
Buckhorn Gun Works, 8109 Woodland Dr., Black Hawk, SD 57718/605-787-6472
Buckskin Bullet Co., P.O. Box 1893, Cedar City, UT 84721/801-586-3286
Buffalo Arms, 123 S. Third, Suite 6, Sandpoint, ID 83864/208-263-6953; FAX: 208-265-2096
Buffalo Bullet Co., Inc., 12637 Los Nietos Rd., Unit A, Santa Fe Springs, CA 90670/310-944-0322; FAX: 310-944-5054
Buffalo Rock Shooters Supply, R.R. 1, Ottawa, IL 61350/815-433-2471
Bull Mountain Rifle Co., 6327 Golden West Terrace, Billings, MT 59106/406-656-0778
Bullberry Barrel Works, Ltd., 2430 W. Bullberry Ln. 67-5, Hurricane, UT 84737/801-635-9866
Bullet, Inc., 3745 Hiram Alworth Rd., Dallas, GA 30132
Bullet Swaging Supply, Inc., P.O. Box 1056, 303 McMillan Rd, West Monroe, LA 71291/318-387-7257; FAX: 318-387-7779
BulletMakers Workshop, The, RFD 1 Box 1755, Brooks, ME 04921
Bullseye Bullets, 1610 State Road 60, No. 12, Valrico, FL 33594/813-654-6563
Bull-X, Inc., 520 N. Main, Farmer City, IL 61842/309-928-2574, 800-248-3845 orders only; FAX: 309-928-2130
Bushnell Sports Optics Worldwide, 9200 Cody, Overland Park, KS 66214/913-752-3443, 800-423-3537; FAX: 913-752-3489
Burgess & Son Gunsmiths, R.W., P.O. Box 3364, Warner Robins, GA 31099/912-328-7487
Burkhart Gunsmithing, Don, P.O. Box 852, Rawlins, WY 82301/307-324-6007
Burres, Jack, 10333 San Fernando Rd., Pacoima, CA 91331/818-899-8000
Burris Co., Inc., P.O. Box 1747, 331 E. 8th St., Greeley, CO 80631/970-356-1670; FAX: 970-356-8702
Bushmann Hunters & Safaris, P.O. Box 293088, Lewisville, TX 75029/214-317-0768
Bustani, Leo, P.O. Box 8125, W. Palm Beach, FL 33407/305-622-2710
Butler Creek Corp., 290 Arden Dr., Belgrade, MT 59714/800-423-8327, 406-388-1356; FAX: 406-388-7204
Butler Enterprises, 834 Oberting Rd., Lawrenceburg, IN 47025/812-537-3584
Buzztail Brass (See Grayback Wildcats)
B-West Imports, Inc., 2425 N. Huachuca Dr., Tucson, AZ 85745-1201/602-628-1990; FAX: 602-628-3602

C

C&D Special Products (See Claybuster Wads & Harvester Bullets)
Calhoon Varmint Bullets, James, Shambo Rt., Box 304, Havre, MT 59501/406-395-4079
Calibre Press, Inc., 666 Dundee Rd., Suite 1607, Northbrook, IL 60062-2760/800-323-0037; FAX: 708-498-6869
Cali'co Hardwoods, Inc., 3580 Westwind Blvd., Santa Rosa, CA 95403/707-546-4045; FAX: 707-546-4027
California Magnum, 20746 Dearborn St., Chatsworth, CA 91313/818-341-7302; FAX: 818-341-7304
California Sights (See Fautheree, Andy)
Camdex, Inc., 2330 Alger, Troy, MI 48083/810-528-2300; FAX: 810-528-0989
Cameron's, 16690 W. 11th Ave., Golden, CO 80401/303-279-7365; FAX: 303-628-5413
Camilli, Lou, 4700 Oahu Dr. NE, Albuquerque, NM 87111/505-293-5259
Campbell, Dick, 20,000 Silver Ranch Rd., Conifer, CO 80433/303-697-0150
Camp-Cap Products, P.O. Box 173, Chesterfield, MO 63006/314-532-4340; FAX: 314-532-4340
Canjar Co., M.H., 500 E. 45th Ave., Denver, CO 80216/303-295-2638
Canons Delcour, Rue J.B. Cools, B-4040 Herstal, BELGIUM/+32.(0)41.40.61.40; FAX: +32(0)412.40.22.88
Canyon Cartridge Corp., P.O. Box 152, Albertson, NY 11507/FAX: 516-294-8946
Cape Outfitters, 599 County Rd. 206, Cape Girardeau, MO 63701/314-335-4103; FAX: 314-335-1555
Carbide Die & Mfg. Co., Inc., 15615 E. Arrow Hwy., Irwindale, CA 91706/818-337-2518
Carnahan Bullets, 17645 110th Ave. SE, Renton, WA 98055
Carroll Bullets (See Precision Reloading, Inc.)
Carter's Gun Shop, 225 G St., Penrose, CO 81240/719-372-6240
Cartridge Transfer Group, Pete de Coux, 235 Oak St., Butler, PA 16001/412-282-3426
Cascade Arms, Inc., P.O. Box 268, Colton, Oregon 97017
Cascade Bullet Co., Inc., 2355 South 6th St., Klamath Falls, OR 97601/503-884-9316
Cascade Shooters, 2155 N.W. 12th St., Redwood, OR 97756
Case Sorting System, 12695 Cobblestone Creek Rd., Poway, CA 92064/619-486-9340
Catco-Ambush, Inc., P.O.Box 300, Corte Madera, CA 94926
Caywood, Shane J., P.O. Box 321, Minocqua, WI 54548/715-277-3866 evenings
CBC, Avenida Humberto de Campos, 3220, 09400-000 Ribeirao Pires-SP-BRAZIL/55-11-742-7500; FAX: 55-11-459-7385
C.C.G. Enterprises, 5217 E. Belknap St., Halton City, TX 76117/817-834-9554
CCI, Div. of Blount, Inc., Sporting Equipment Div., 2299 Snake River Ave.,, P.O. Box 856/Lewiston, ID 83501
800-627-3640, 208-746-2351; FAX: 208-746-2915
Celestron International, P.O. Box 3578, 2835 Columbia St., Torrance, CA 90503/310-328-9560; FAX: 310-212-5835
Center Lock Scope Rings, 9901 France Ct., Lakeville, MN 55044/612-461-2114
Century International Arms, Inc., P.O. Box 714, St. Albans, VT 05478-0714/802-527-1252; FAX: 802-527-0470; WEB: http://www.generation.net/~century
CFVentures, 509 Harvey Dr., Bloomington, IN 47403-1715
C-H Tool & Die Corp. (See 4-D Custom Die Co.)
CHAA, Ltd., P.O. Box 565, Howell, MI 48844/800-677-8737; FAX: 313-894-6930
Chambers Flintlocks Ltd., Jim, Rt. 1, Box 513-A, Candler, NC 28715/704-667-8361
Champion Target Co., 232 Industrial Parkway, Richmond, IN 47374/800-441-4971
Champion's Choice, Inc., 201 International Blvd., LaVergne, TN 37086/615-793-4066; FAX: 615-793-4070
Champlin Firearms, Inc., P.O. Box 3191, Woodring Airport, Enid, OK 73701/405-237-7388; FAX: 405-242-6922
Cheddite France, S.A., 99, Route de Lyon, F-26500 Bourg-les-Valence, FRANCE/33-75-56-4545; FAX: 33-75-56-3587
Chem-Pak, Inc., 11 Oates Ave., P.O. Box 1685, Winchester, VA 22604/800-336-9828, 703-667-1341; FAX: 703-722-3993
CheVron Bullets, RR1, Ottawa, IL 61350/815-433-2471
CheVron Case Master (See CheVron Bullets)
Chicasaw Gun Works (See Cochran, Oliver)
Chopie Mfg., Inc., 700 Copeland Ave., LaCrosse, WI 54603/608-784-0926
Christensen Arms, 192 East 100 North, Fayette, UT 84630/801-528-7999; FAX: 801-528-7494
Christman Jr., David, 937 Lee Hedrick Rd., Colville, WA 99114/509-684-5686 days; 509-684-3314 evenings
Chronotech, 1655 Siamet Rd. Unit 6, Mississauga, Ont. L4W 1Z4 CANADA/905-625-5200; FAX: 905-625-5190
Chu Tani Ind., Inc., P.O. Box 2064, Cody, WY 82414-2064
Chuck's Gun Shop, P.O. Box 597, Waldo, FL 32694/904-468-2264
Churchill, Winston, Twenty Mile Stream Rd., RFD P.O. Box 29B, Proctorsville, VT 05153/802-226-7772
Cincinnati Swaging, 2605 Marlington Ave., Cincinnati, OH 45208
C.J. Ballistics, Inc., P.O. Box 132, Acme, WA 98220/206-595-5001
Clark Co., Inc., David, P.O. Box 15054, Worcester, MA 01615-0054/508-756-6216; FAX: 508-753-5827
Clark Custom Guns, Inc., 336 Shootout Lane, Princeton, LA 71067/318-949-9884; FAX: 318-949-9829
Claro Walnut Gunstock Co., 1235 Stanley Ave., Chico, CA 95928/916-342-5188
Classic Brass, 14 Grove St., Plympton, MA 02367/FAX: 617-585-5673
Claybuster Wads & Harvester Bullets, 309 Sequoya Dr., Hopkinsville, KY 42240/800-922-6287, 800-284-1746, 502-885-8088; FAX: 502-885-1951
Clearview Mfg. Co., Inc., 413 S. Oakley St., Fordyce, AR 71742/501-352-8557; FAX: 501-352-8557
Clenzoil Corp., P.O. Box 80226, Sta. C, Canton, OH 44708-0226/330-833-9758; FAX: 330-833-4724
Clerke Co., J.A., P.O. Box 627, Pearblossom, CA 93553-0627/805-945-0713
Clift Mfg., L.R., 3821 Hammonton Rd., Marysville, CA 95901/916-755-3390; FAX: 916-755-3393
Clift Welding Supply & Cases, 1332-A Colusa Hwy., Yuba City, CA 95993/916-755-3390; FAX: 916-755-3393
Cloward's Gun Shop, 4023 Aurora Ave. N, Seattle, WA 98103/206-632-2072
Clymer Manufacturing Co., Inc., 1645 W. Hamlin Rd., Rochester Hills, MI 48309-1530/810-853-5555, 810-853-5627; FAX: 810-853-1530
C-More Systems, P.O. Box 1750, 7553 Gary Rd., Manassas, VA 22110/703-361-2663; FAX: 703-361-5881
Coats, Mrs. Lester, 300 Luman Rd., Space 125, Phoenix, OR 97535/503-535-1611
Cobra Gunskin, 133-30 32nd Ave., Flushing, NY 11354/718-762-8181; FAX: 718-762-0890
Cochran, Oliver, Box 868, Shady Spring, WV 25918/304-763-3838
Coffin, Charles H., 3719 Scarlet Ave., Odessa, TX 79762/915-366-4729
Coffin, Jim, 250 Country Club Lane, Albany, OR 97321/541-928-4391
Cole's Gun Works, Old Bank Building, Rt. 4, Box 250, Moyock, NC 27958/919-435-2345
Coleman's Custom Repair, 4035 N. 20th Rd., Arlington, VA 22207/703-528-4486
Colonial Arms, Inc., P.O. Box 636, Selma, AL 36702-0636/334-872-9455; FAX: 334-872-9540
Colonial Repair, P.O. Box 372, Hyde Park, MA 02136-9998/617-469-4951
Colorado Gunsmithing Academy Lamar, 27533 Highway 287 South, Lamar, CO 81052/719-336-4099
Colorado Shooter's Supply, 1163 W. Paradise Way, Fruita, CO 81521/303-858-9191
Colorado Sutlers Arsenal (See Cumberland States Arsenal)

Combat Military Ordnance Ltd., 3900 Hopkins St., Savannah, GA 31405/912-238-1900; FAX: 912-236-7570
Companhia Brasileira de Cartuchos (See CBC)
Compass Industries, Inc., 104 East 25th St., New York, NY 10010/212-473-2614, 800-221-9904; FAX: 212-353-0826
Competition Electronics, Inc., 3469 Precision Dr., Rockford, IL 61109/815-874-8001; FAX: 815-874-8181
Competitor Corp., Inc., Appleton Business Center, 30 Tricnit Road, Unit 16, New Ipswich, NH 03071-0508/603-878-3891; FAX: 603-878-3950
Concept Development Corp., 14715 N. 78th Way, Suite 300, Scottsdale, AZ 85260/800-472-4405; FAX: 602-948-7560
Conetrol Scope Mounts, 10225 Hwy. 123 S., Seguin, TX 78155/210-379-3030, 800-CONETROL; FAX: 210-379-3030
CONKKO, P.O. Box 40, Broomall, PA 19008/215-356-0711
Conrad, C.A., 3964 Ebert St., Winston-Salem, NC 27127/919-788-5469
Cook Engineering Service, 891 Highbury Rd., Vermont VICT 3133 AUSTRALIA
Cooper Arms, P.O. Box 114, Stevensville, MT 59870/406-777-5534; FAX: 406-777-5228
Cooper-Woodward, 3800 Pelican Rd., Helena, MT 59601/406-458-3800
Corbin, Inc., 600 Industrial Circle, P.O. Box 2659, White City, OR 97503/541-826-5211; FAX: 541-826-8669
Cor-Bon Bullet & Ammo Co., 1311 Industry Rd., Sturgis, SD 57785/800-626-7266; FAX: 800-923-2666
Costa, David, Island Pond Gun Shop, P.O. Box 428, Cross St., Island Pond, VT 05846/802-723-4546
Country Armourer, The, P.O. Box .308, Ashby, MA 01431-0308/508-827-6797; FAX: 508-827-4845
CP Bullets, 340-1 Constance Dr., Warminster, PA 18974
Crane & Crane Ltd., 105 N. Edison Way 6, Reno, NV 89502-2355/702-856-1516; FAX: 702-856-1616
Crane Sales Co., George S., P.O. Box 385, Van Nuys, CA 91408/818-505-8337
Crawford Co., Inc., R.M., P.O. Box 277, Everett, PA 15537/814-652-6536; FAX: 814-652-9526
CRDC Laser Systems Group, 3972 Barranca Parkway, Ste. J-484, Irvine, CA 92714/714-586-1295; FAX: 714-831-4823
Creative Cartridge Co., 56 Morgan Rd., Canton, CT 06019/203-693-2529
Creedmoor Sports, Inc., P.O. Box 1040, Oceanside, CA 92051/619-757-5529
Crit'R Call, Box 999G, La Porte, CO 80535/970-484-2768; FAX: 970-484-0807
Crouse's Country Cover, P.O. Box 160, Storrs, CT 06268/860-423-8736
CRR, Inc./Marble's Inc., 420 Industrial Park, P.O. Box 111, Gladstone, MI 49837/906-428-3710; FAX: 906-428-3711
Cryo-Accurizing, 1160 South Monroe, Decatur, IL 62521/217-423-3070; FAX: 217-423-2756
Cubic Shot Shell Co., Inc., 98 Fatima Dr., Campbell, OH 44405/216-755-0349; FAX: 216-755-0349
Cumberland States Arsenal, 1124 Palmyra Road, Clarksville, TN 37040
Cummings Bullets, 1417 Esperanza Way, Escondido, CA 92027
Cunningham Co., Eaton, 607 Superior St., Kansas City, MO 64106/816-842-2600
Curly Maple Stock Blanks (See Tiger-Hunt)
Curtis Gun Shop, Dept. ST, 119 W. College, Bozeman, MT 59715/406-587-4934
Custom Barreling & Stocks, 937 Lee Hedrick Rd., Colville, WA 99114/509-684-5686 (days), 509-684-3314 (evenings)
Custom Bullets by Hoffman, 2604 Peconic Ave., Seaford, NY 11783
Custom Checkering Service, Kathy Forster, 2124 SE Yamhill St., Portland, OR 97214/503-236-5874
Custom Chronograph, Inc., 5305 Reese Hill Rd., Sumas, WA 98295/360-988-7801
Custom Gun Products, 5021 W. Rosewood, Spokane, WA 99208/509-328-9340
Custom Gun Stocks, Rt. 6, P.O. Box 177, McMinnville, TN 37110/615-668-3912
Custom Hunting Ammo & Arms (See CHAA, Ltd.)
Custom Products (See Jones Custom Products, Neil A.)
Custom Quality Products, Inc., 345 W. Girard Ave., P.O. Box 71129, Madison Heights, MI 48071/810-585-1616; FAX: 810-585-0644
Custom Riflestocks, Inc., Michael M. Kokolus, 7005 Herber Rd., New Tripoli, PA 18066/610-298-3013
Custom Tackle and Ammo, P.O. Box 1886, Farmington, NM 87499/505-632-3539
Cutsinger Bench Rest Bullets, RR 8, Box 161-A, Shelbyville, IN 46176/317-729-5360
C.W. Cartridge Co., 242 Highland Ave., Kearney, NJ 07032/201-998-1030
C.W. Cartridge Co., 71 Hackensack St., Wood Ridge, NJ 07075

D

D&D Gunsmiths, Ltd., 363 E. Elmwood, Troy, MI 48083/810-583-1512; FAX: 810-583-1524
D&G Precision Duplicators (See Greene Precision Duplicators)
D&H Precision Tooling, 7522 Barnard Mill Rd., Ringwood, IL 60072/815-653-4011
D&H Prods. Co., Inc., 465 Denny Rd., Valencia, PA 16059/412-898-2840, 800-776-0281; FAX: 412-898-2013
D&J Bullet Co. & Custom Gun Shop, Inc., 426 Ferry St., Russell, KY 41169/606-836-2663; FAX: 606-836-2663
D&R Distributing, 308 S.E. Valley St., Myrtle Creek, OR 97457/503-863-6850
Dahl's Custom Stocks, N2863 Schofield Rd., Lake Geneva, WI 53147/414-248-2464
Daisy Mfg. Co., P.O. Box 220, Rogers, AR 72757/501-636-1200; FAX: 501-636-1601
Dakota Arms, Inc., HC 55, Box 326, Sturgis, SD 57785/605-347-4686; FAX: 605-347-4459
Dangler, Homer L., Box 254, Addison, MI 49220/517-547-6745
Dapkus Co., Inc., J.G., Commerce Circle, P.O. Box 293, Durham, CT 06422
Dara-Nes, Inc. (See Nesci Enterprises, Inc.)
Data Tech Software Systems, 19312 East Eldorado Drive, Aurora, CO 80013
Datumtech Corp., 2275 Wehrle Dr., Buffalo, NY 14221
Davis, Don, 1619 Heights, Katy, TX 77493/713-391-3090
Davis Products, Mike, 643 Loop Dr., Moses Lake, WA 98837/509-765-6178, 509-766-7281 orders only
Dayson Arms Ltd., P.O. Box 532, Vincennes, IN 47591/812-882-8680; FAX: 812-882-8446
Dayton Traister, 4778 N. Monkey Hill Rd., P.O. Box 593, Oak Harbor, WA 98277/206-679-4657; FAX:206-675-1114
DBI Books, Division of Krause Publications, 4092 Commercial Ave., Northbrook, IL 60062/847-272-6310; FAX: 847-272-2051; For consumer orders, see Krause Publications
D.C.C. Enterprises, 259 Wynburn Ave., Athens, GA 30601
D.D. Custom Stocks, R.H. "Dick" Devereaux, 5240 Mule Deer Dr., Colorado Springs, CO 80919/719-548-8468
de Coux, Pete (See Cartridge Transfer Group)
de Treville & Co., Stan, 4129 Normal St., San Diego, CA 92103/619-298-3393
Dead Eye's Sport Center, RD 1, Box 147B, Shickshinny, PA 18655/717-256-7432
Decker Shooting Products, 1729 Laguna Ave., Schofield, WI 54476/715-359-5873
Deepeeka Exports Pvt. Ltd., D-78, Saket, Meerut-250-006, INDIA/011-91-121-512889, 011-91-121-545363; FAX: 011-91-121-542988, 011-91-121-511599
Defense Training International, Inc., 749 S. Lemay, Ste. A3-337, Ft. Collins, CO 80524/303-482-2520; FAX: 303-482-0548
deHaas Barrels, RR 3, Box 77, Ridgeway, MO 64481/816-872-6308
Del Rey Products, P.O. Box 91561, Los Angeles, CA 90009/213-823-0494
Delhi Gun House, 1374 Kashmere Gate, Delhi, INDIA 110 006/(011)237375+239116; FAX: 91-11-2917344
Del-Sports, Inc., Box 685, Main St., Margaretville, NY 12455/914-586-4103; FAX: 914-586-4105
Delta Co. Ammo Bunker, 1209 16th Place, Yuma, AZ 85364/602-783-4563
Delta Enterprises, 284 Hagemann Drive, Livermore, CA 94550
Delta Frangible Ammunition, LLC, 1111 Jefferson Davis Hwy., Suite 508, Arlington, VA 22202/703-416-4928; FAX: 703-416-4934
Denver Bullets, Inc., 1811 W. 13th Ave., Denver, CO 80204/303-893-3146; FAX: 303-893-9161
Denver Instrument Co., 6542 Fig St., Arvada, CO 80004/800-321-1135, 303-431-7255; FAX: 303-423-4831
DeSantis Holster & Leather Goods, Inc., P.O. Box 2039, 149 Denton Ave., New Hyde Park, NY 11040-0701/516-354-8000; FAX: 516-354-7501
Desert Industries, Inc., P.O. Box 93443, Las Vegas, NV 89193-3443/702-597-1066; FAX: 702-871-9452
Desert Mountain Mfg., P.O. Box 2767, Columbia Falls, MT 59912/800-477-0762, 406-892-7772
Detroit-Armor Corp., 720 Industrial Dr. No. 112, Cary, IL 60013/708-639-7666; FAX: 708-639-7694
Dever Co., Jack, 8590 NW 90, Oklahoma City, OK 73132/405-721-6393
Devereaux, R.H. "Dick" (See D.D. Custom Stocks)
Dewey Mfg. Co., Inc., J., P.O. Box 2014, Southbury, CT 06488/203-264-3064; FAX: 203-262-6907
DGR Custom Rifles, RR1, Box 8A, Tappen, ND 58487/701-327-8135
DGS, Inc., Dale A. Storey, 1117 E. 12th, Casper, WY 82601/307-237-2414
DHB Products, P.O. Box 3092, Alexandria, VA 22302/703-836-2648
Diamond Mfg. Co., P.O. Box 174, Wyoming, PA 18644/800-233-9601
Diamondback Supply, 2431 Juan Tabo, Suite 163, Albuquerque, NM 87112/505-237-0068
Dilliott Gunsmithing, Inc., 657 Scarlett Rd., Dandridge, TN 37725/615-397-9204
Dillon, Ed, 1035 War Eagle Dr. N., Colorado Springs, CO 80919/719-598-4929; FAX: 719-598-4929
Dillon Precision Products, Inc., 8009 East Dillon's Way, Scottsdale, AZ 85260/602-948-8009, 800-762-3845; FAX: 602-998-2786
Division Lead Co., 7742 W. 61st Pl., Summit, IL 60502
DKT, Inc., 14623 Vera Drive, Union, MI 49130-9744/616-641-7120; FAX: 616-641-2015
Doctor Optic Technologies, Inc., 4685 Boulder Highway, Suite A, Las Vegas, NV 89121/800-290-3634, 702-898-7161; FAX: 702-898-3737
Dohring Bullets, 100 W. 8 Mile Rd., Ferndale, MI 48220
Donnelly, C.P., 405 Kubli Rd., Grants Pass, OR 97527/541-846-6604
Double A Ltd., Dept. ST, Box 11306, Minneapolis, MN 55411
Douglas Barrels, Inc., 5504 Big Tyler Rd., Charleston, WV 25313-1398/304-776-1341; FAX: 304-776-8560
Dowtin Gunworks, Rt. 4, Box 930A, Flagstaff, AZ 86001/602-779-1898
Dressel Jr., Paul G., 209 N. 92nd Ave., Yakima, WA 98908/509-966-9233; FAX: 509-966-3365
Dri-Slide, Inc., 411 N. Darling, Fremont, MI 49412/616-924-3950
Dropkick, 1460 Washington Blvd., Williamsport, PA 17701/717-326-6561; FAX: 717-326-4950
Duane Custom Stocks, Randy, 110 W. North Ave., Winchester, VA 22601/703-667-9461; FAX: 703-722-3993
Duane's Gun Repair (See DGR Custom Rifles)
Du-Lite Corp., 171 River Rd., Middletown, CT 06457/203-347-2505; FAX: 203-347-9404
Duncan's Gun Works, Inc., 1619 Grand Ave., San Marcos, CA 92069/619-727-0515
Dunphy, Ted, W. 5100 Winch Rd., Rathdrum, ID 83858/208-687-1399; FAX: 208-687-1399
DuPont (See IMR Powder Co.)
Dutchman's Firearms, Inc., The, 4143 Taylor Blvd., Louisville, KY 40215/502-366-0555
Dybala Gun Shop, P.O. Box 1024, FM 3156, Bay City, TX 77414/409-245-0866
Dykstra, Doug, 411 N. Darling, Fremont, MI 49412/616-924-3950
Dynamit Nobel-RWS, Inc., 81 Ruckman Rd., Closter, NJ 07624/201-767-7971; FAX: 201-767-1589

E

E&L Mfg., Inc., 4177 Riddle by Pass Rd., Riddle, OR 97469/541-874-2137; FAX: 541-874-3107
Eagan, Donald V., P.O. Box 196, Benton, PA 17814/717-925-6134
Eagle International, Inc., 5195 W. 58th Ave., Suite 300, Arvada, CO 80002/303-426-8100; FAX: 303-426-5475
Eagle Mfg. & Engineering, 2648 Keen Dr., San Diego, CA 92139/619-479-4402; FAX: 619-472-5585
E-A-R, Inc., Div. of Cabot Safety Corp., 5457 W. 79th St., Indianapolis, IN 46268/800-327-3431; FAX: 800-488-8007
Echols & Co., D'Arcy, 164 W. 580 S., Providence, UT 84332/801-753-2367
Edmisten Co., P.O. Box 1293, Boone, NC 28607
Edmund Scientific Co., 101 E. Gloucester Pike, Barrington, NJ 08033/609-543-6250
Ednar, Inc., 2-4-8 Kayabacho, Nihonbashi, Chuo-ku, Tokyo, JAPAN 103/81(Japan)-3-3667-1651; FAX: 81-3-3661-8113
Eezox, Inc., P.O. Box 772, Waterford, CT 06385-0772/860-447-8282, 800-462-3331; FAX: 860-447-3484
Beretta, Effebi SNC-Dr. Franco, via Rossa, 4, 25062 Concesio, Italy/030-2751955; FAX: 030-2180414
Eggleston, Jere D., 400 Saluda Ave., Columbia, SC 29205/803-799-3402
Eichelberger Bullets, Wm., 158 Crossfield Rd., King of Prussia, PA 19406
Eldorado Cartridge Corp. (See PMC/Eldorado Cartridge Corp.)
Electronic Shooters Protection, Inc., 11997 West 85th Place, Arvada, CO 80005/303-456-8964; 800-797-7791
Electronic Trigger Systems, Inc., P.O. Box 13, 230 Main St. S., Hector, MN 55342/612-848-2760
Eley Ltd., P.O. Box 705, Witton, Birmingham, B6 7UT, ENGLAND/021-356-8899; FAX: 021-331-4173
Elite Ammunition, P.O. Box 3251, Oakbrook, IL 60522/708-366-9006
Elkhorn Bullets, P.O. Box 5293, Central Point, OR 97502/541-826-7440
Elko Arms, Dr. L. Kortz, 28 rue Ecole Moderne, B-7060 Soignies, BELGIUM/(32)67-33-29-34
Emerging Technologies, Inc. (See Laseraim Technologies, Inc.)
Engineered Accessories, 1307 W. Wabash Ave., Effingham, IL 62401/217-347-7700; FAX: 217-347-7737
Enguix Import-Export, Alpujarras 58, Alzira, Valencia, SPAIN 46600/(96) 241 43 95; FAX: (96) (241 43 95) 240 21 53
Ensign-Bickford Co., The, 660 Hopmeadow St., Simsbury, CT 06070
EPC, 1441 Manatt St., Lincoln, NE 68521/402-476-3946
Epps, Ellwood (See "Gramps" Antique Cartridges)
Erhardt, Dennis, 3280 Green Meadow Dr., Helena, MT 59601/406-442-4533
Erickson's Mfg., Inc., C.W., 530 Garrison Ave. N.E., P.O. Box 522, Buffalo, MN 55313/612-682-3665; FAX: 612-682-4328
Essex Metals, 1000 Brighton St., Union, NJ 07083/800-282-8369
Estate Cartridge, Inc., 12161 FM 830, Willis, TX 77378/409-856-7277; FAX: 409-856-5486
Euber Bullets, No. Orwell Rd., Orwell, VT 05760/802-948-2621
Europtik Ltd., P.O. Box 319, Dunmore, PA 18512/717-347-6049; FAX: 717-969-4330
Evans, Andrew, 2325 NW Squire St., Albany, OR 97321/541-928-3190; FAX: 541-928-4128
Evans Gunsmithing (See Evans, Andrew)
Eversull Co., Inc., K., 1 Tracemont, Boyce, LA 71409/318-793-8728; FAX: 318-793-5483
Excalibur Enterprises, P.O. Box 400, Fogelsville, PA 18051-0400/610-391-9105; FAX: 610-391-9223
Exe, Inc., 18830 Partridge Circle, Eden Prairie, MN 55346/612-944-7662
E-Z-Way Systems, P.O. Box 4310, Newark, OH 43058-4310/614-345-6645, 800-848-2072; FAX: 614-345-6600

F

F&A Inc., 50 Elm St., Richfield Springs, NY 13439/315-858-1470; FAX: 315-858-2969
Faith Associates, Inc., 1139 S. Greenville Hwy., Hendersonville, NC 28792/704-692-1916; FAX: 704-697-6827
Fajen, Reinhart, Inc., Route 1, P.O. Box 214-A, Lincoln, MO 65338/816-547-3030; FAX: 816-547-2215
Far North Outfitters, Box 1252, Bethel, AK 99559

Farmer-Dressel, Sharon, 209 N. 92nd Ave., Yakima, WA 98908/509-966-9233; FAX: 509-966-3365
Farr Studio, Inc., 1231 Robinhood Rd., Greeneville, TN 37743/615-638-8825
Fautheree, Andy, P.O. Box 4607, Pagosa Springs, CO 81157/303-731-5003
Feather Industries, Inc., 37600 Liberty Dr., Trinidad, CO 81082/719-846-2699; FAX: 719-846-2644
Federal Cartridge Co., 900 Ehlen Dr., Anoka, MN 55303/612-323-2300; FAX: 612-323-2506
Federal Champion Target Co., 232 Industrial Parkway, Richmond, IN 47374/800-441-4971; FAX: 317-966-7747
Federated-Fry (See Fry Metals)
Feken, Dennis, Rt. 2 Box 124, Perry, OK 73077/405-336-5611
Ferguson, Bill, P.O. Box 1238, Sierra Vista, AZ 85636/520-458-5321; FAX: 520-458-9125
Fibron Products, Inc., P.O. Box 430, Buffalo, NY 14209-0430/716-886-2378; FAX: 716-886-2394
Finch Custom Bullets, 40204 La Rochelle, Prairieville, LA 70769
Fiocchi of America, Inc., 5030 Fremont Rd., Ozark, MO 65721/417-725-4118, 800-721-2666; FAX: 417-725-1039
Fisher, R. Kermit (See Fisher Enterprises, Inc.)
First, Inc., Jack, 1201 Turbine Dr., Rapid City, SD 57701/605-343-9544; FAX: 605-343-9420
Fisher, Jerry A., 553 Crane Mt. Rd., Big Fork, MT 59911/406-837-2722
Fisher Enterprises, Inc., 1071 4th Ave. S., Suite 303, Edmonds, WA 98020-4143/206-771-5382
Fitz Pistol Grip Co., P.O. Box 610, Douglas City, CA 96024/916-778-0240
Flaig's, 2200 Evergreen Rd., Millvale, PA 15209/412-821-1717
Flambeau Products Corp., 15981 Valplast Rd., Middlefield, OH 44062/216-632-1631; FAX: 216-632-1581
Flents Products Co., Inc., P.O. Box 2109, Norwalk, CT 06852/203-866-2581; FAX: 203-854-9322
Flitz International Ltd., 821 Mohr Ave., Waterford, WI 53185/414-534-5898; FAX: 414-534-2991
Flores Publications, Inc., J., P.O. Box 830131, Miami, FL 33283/305-559-4652
Fluoramics, Inc., 18 Industrial Ave., Mahwah, NJ 07430/800-922-0075, 201-825-7035
FN Herstal, Voie de Liege 33, Herstal 4040, BELGIUM/(32)41.40.82.83; FAX: (32)41.40.86.79
Folks, Donald E., 205 W. Lincoln St., Pontiac, IL 61764/815-844-7901
Ford, Jack, 1430 Elkwood, Missouri City, TX 77489/713-499-9984
Forgett Jr., Valmore J., 689 Bergen Blvd., Ridgefield, NJ 07657/201-945-2500; FAX: 201-945-6859
Forgreens Tool Mfg., Inc., P.O. Box 990, 723 Austin St., Robert Lee, TX 76945/915-453-2800
Forkin, Ben (See Belt MTN Arms)
Forster, Kathy (See Custom Checkering Service)
Forster, Larry L., P.O. Box 212, 220 First St. NE, Gwinner, ND 58040-0212/701-678-2475
Forster Products, 82 E. Lanark Ave., Lanark, IL 61046/815-493-6360; FAX: 815-493-2371
Forty Five Ranch Enterprises, Box 1080, Miami, OK 74355-1080/918-542-5875
Fouling Shot, The, 6465 Parfet St., Arvada, CO 80004
4-D Custom Die Co., 711 N. Sandusky St., P.O. Box 889, Mt. Vernon, OH 43050-0889/614-397-7214; FAX: 614-397-6600
4W Ammunition, Rt. 1, P.O. Box 313, Tioga, TX 76271/817-437-2458; FAX: 817-437-2228
Fowler Bullets, 806 Dogwood Dr., Gastonia, NC 28054/704-867-3259
Foy Custom Bullets, 104 Wells Ave., Daleville, AL 36322
Frank Custom Classic Arms, Ron, 7131 Richland Rd., Ft. Worth, TX 76118/817-284-9300; FAX: 817-284-9300
Freedom Arms, Inc., P.O. Box 1776, Freedom, WY 83120/307-883-2468, 800-833-4432 (orders only); FAX: 307-883-2005
Freeman Animal Targets, 5519 East County Road, 100 South, Plainsfield, IN 46168/317-487-9482; FAX: 317-487-9671
Fremont Tool Works, 1214 Prairie, Ford, KS 67842/316-369-2327
From Jena (See Europtik Ltd.)
Frontier Products Co., 164 E. Longview Ave., Columbus, OH 43202/614-262-9357
Fry Metals, 4100 6th Ave., Altoona, PA 16602/814-946-1611
Fujinon, Inc., 10 High Point Dr., Wayne, NJ 07470/201-633-5600; FAX: 201-633-5216
Fusilier Bullets, 10010 N. 6000 W., Highland, UT 84003/801-756-6813

G

G96 Products Co., Inc., River St. Station, P.O. Box 1684, Paterson, NJ 07544/201-684-4050; FAX: 201-684-3848
G&C Bullet Co., Inc., 8835 Thornton Rd., Stockton, CA 95209/209-477-6479; FAX: 209-477-2813
Gaillard Barrels, P.O. Box 21, Pathlow, Sask., S0K 3B0 CANADA/306-752-3769; FAX: 306-752-5969
Galati International, P.O. Box 326, Catawissa, MO 63015/314-257-4837; FAX: 314-257-2268
Game Haven Gunstocks, 13750 Shire Rd., Wolverine, MI 49799/616-525-8257
Gammog, Gregory B. Gally, 14608 Old Gunpowder Rd., Laurel, MD 20707-3131/301-725-3838
Gander Mountain, Inc., P.O. Box 128, Hwy. "W," Wilmot, WI 53192/414-862-2331,Ext. 6425
GAR, 590 McBride Avenue, West Paterson, NJ 07424/201-754-1114; FAX: 201-742-2897
Garrett Cartridges, Inc., P.O. Box 178, Chehalis, WA 98532/360-736-0702
G.B.C. Industries, Inc., P.O. Box 1602, Spring, TX 77373/713-350-9690; FAX: 713-350-0601
GDL Enterprises, 409 Le Gardeur, Slidell, LA 70460/504-649-0693
Genco, P.O. Box 5704, Asheville, NC 28803
Gene's Custom Guns, P.O. Box 10534, White Bear Lake, MN 55110/612-429-5105
Gentex Corp., 5 Tinkham Ave., Derry, NH 03038/603-434-0311; FAX: 603-434-3002
Gentner Bullets, 109 Woodlawn Ave., Upper Darby, PA 19082/610-352-9396
Gentry Custom Gunmaker, David, 314 N. Hoffman, Belgrade, MT 59714/406-388-GUNS
George & Roy's, 2950 NW 29th, Portland, OR 97210/503-228-5424, 800-553-3022; FAX: 503-225-9409
Gervais, Mike, 3804 S. Cruise Dr., Salt Lake City, UT 84109/801-277-7729
Getz Barrel Co., P.O. Box 88, Beavertown, PA 17813/717-658-7263
G.G. & G., 3602 E. 42nd Stravenue, Tucson, AZ 85713/520-748-7167; FAX: 520-748-7583
G.H. Enterprises Ltd., Bag 10, Okotoks, Alberta T0L 1T0 CANADA/403-938-6070
Gibbs Rifle Co., Inc., Cannon Hill Industrial Park, Rt. 2, Box 214 Hoffman, Rd./Martinsburg, WV 25401
304-274-0458; FAX: 304-274-0078
Gilman-Mayfield, Inc., 3279 E. Shields, Fresno, CA 93703/209-221-9415; FAX: 209-221-9419
Gilmore Sports Concepts, 5949 S. Garnett, Tulsa, OK 74146/918-250-4867; FAX: 918-250-3845
Giron, Robert E., 1328 Pocono St., Pittsburgh, PA 15218/412-731-6041
Glaser Safety Slug, Inc., P.O. Box 8223, Foster City, CA 94404/800-221-3489, 415-345-7677; FAX: 415-345-8217
Gner's Hard Cast Bullets, 1107 11th St., LaGrande, OR 97850/503-963-8796
Goddard, Allen, 716 Medford Ave., Hayward, CA 94541/510-276-6830
Goens, Dale W., P.O. Box 224, Cedar Crest, NM 87008/505-281-5419
Goergen's Gun Shop, Inc., Rt. 2, Box 182BB, Austin, MN 55912/507-433-9280
GOEX, Inc., 1002 Springbrook Ave., Moosic, PA 18507/717-457-6724; FAX: 717-457-1130
Goldcoast Reloaders, Inc., 2421 NE 4th Ave., Pompano Beach, FL 33064/305-783-4849
Golden Age Arms Co., 115 E. High St., Ashley, OH 43003/614-747-2488
Golden Bear Bullets, 3065 Fairfax Ave., San Jose, CA 95148/408-238-9515
Gonic Bullet Works, P.O. Box 7365, Gonic, NH 03839
Gonzalez Guns, Ramon B., P.O. Box 370, Monticello, NY 12701/914-794-4515
Gordie's Gun Shop, 1401 Fulton St., Streator, IL 61364/815-672-7202
Gotz Bullets, 7313 Rogers St., Rockford, IL 61111
Goudy Classic Stocks, Gary, 263 Hedge Rd., Menlo Park, CA 94025-1711/415-322-1338
Gozon Corp., U.S.A., P.O. Box 6278, Folson, CA 95763/916-983-2026; FAX: 916-983-9500
Grace, Charles E., 6943 85.5 Rd., Trinchera, CO 81081/719-846-9435
"Gramps" Antique Cartridges, Box 341, Washago, Ont. L0K 2B0 CANADA/705-689-5348
Grand Falls Bullets, Inc., P.O. Box 720, 803 Arnold Wallen Way, Stockton, MO 65785/816-229-0112
Granite Custom Bullets, Box 190, Philipsburg, MT 59858/406-859-3245
Graphics Direct, P.O. Box 372421, Reseda, CA 91337-2421/818-344-9002
Graves Co., 1800 Andrews Ave., Pompano Beach, FL 33069/800-327-9103; FAX: 305-960-0301
Grayback Wildcats, 5306 Bryant Ave., Klamath Falls, OR 97603/541-884-1072
Great American Gun Co., 3420 Industrial Drive, Yuba City, CA 95993/916-671-4570
Great Lakes Airguns, 6175 S. Park Ave., Hamburg, NY 14075/716-648-6666; FAX: 716-648-5279
Green, Arthur S., 485 S. Robertson Blvd., Beverly Hills, CA 90211/310-274-1283
Green Bay Bullets, 1638 Hazelwood Dr., Sobieski, WI 54171/414-826-7760
Green Genie, Box 114, Cusseta, GA 31805
Green Mountain Rifle Barrel Co., Inc., P.O. Box 2670, 153 West Main St., Conway, NH 03818/603-447-1095; FAX: 603-447-1099
Green, Roger M., P.O. Box 984, 435 E. Birch, Glenrock, WY 82637/307-436-9804
Greene Precision Duplicators, M.L. Greene Engineering Services, P.O. Box, 1150/Golden, CO 80402-1150
303-279-2383
Greenwood Precision, P.O. Box 468, Nixa, MO 65714-0468/417-725-2330
Greg's Superior Products, P.O. Box 46219, Seattle, WA 98146
Grier's Hard Cast Bullets, 1107 11th St., LaGrande, OR 97850/503-963-8796
Griffin & Howe, Inc., 33 Claremont Rd., Bernardsville, NJ 07924/908-766-2287; FAX: 908-766-1068
Grizzly Bullets, 322 Green Mountain Rd., Trout Creek, MT 59874/406-847-2627
Group Tight Bullets, 482 Comerwood Court, San Francisco, CA 94080/415-583-1550
GSI, Inc., 108 Morrow Ave., P.O. Box 129, Trussville, AL 35173/205-655-8299; FAX: 205-655-7078
GTM, 15915B E. Main St., La Puente, CA 91744
Guardsman Products, 411 N. Darling, Fremont, MI 49412/616-924-3950
Gun Accessories (See Glaser Safety Slug, Inc.)
Gun City, 212 W. Main Ave., Bismarck, ND 58501/701-223-2304
Gun Doctor, The, 435 East Maple, Roselle, IL 60172/708-894-0668
Gun Doctor, The, P.O. Box 39242, Downey, CA 90242/310-862-3158
Gun Hunter Books, Div. of Gun Hunter Trading Co., 5075 Heisig St., Beaumont, TX 77705/409-835-3006
Gun List (See Krause Publications, Inc.)
Gun Parts Corp., The, 226 Williams Lane, West Hurley, NY 12491/914-679-2417; FAX: 914-679-5849
Gun Room Press, The, 127 Raritan Ave., Highland Park, NJ 08904/908-545-4344; FAX: 908-545-6686
Gun Shop, The, 5550 S. 900 East, Salt Lake City, UT 84117/801-263-3633
Gun Shop, The, 62778 Spring Creek Rd., Montrose, CO 81401
Gun South, Inc. (See GSI, Inc.)
Gun Works, The, 247 S. 2nd, Springfield, OR 97477/541-741-4118; FAX: 541-988-1097
Guncraft Books (See Guncraft Sports, Inc.)
Guncraft Sports, Inc., 10737 Dutchtown Rd., Knoxville, TN 37932/423-966-4545; FAX: 423-966-4500
Gunnerman Books, P.O. Box 214292, Auburn Hills, MI 48321/810-879-2779
Guns, 81 E. Streetsboro St., Hudson, OH 44236/216-650-4563
Guns, Div. of D.C. Engineering, Inc., 8633 Southfield Fwy., Detroit, MI 48228/313-271-7111, 800-886-7623 (orders only); FAX: 313-271-7112
GUNS Magazine, 591 Camino de la Reina, Suite 200, San Diego, CA 92108/619-297-5350; FAX: 619-297-5353
Gunsmith in Elk River, The, 14021 Victoria Lane, Elk River, MN 55330/612-441-7761
Gunsmithing Ltd., 57 Unquowa Rd., Fairfield, CT 06430/203-254-0436; FAX: 203-254-1535

H

H&P Publishing, 7174 Hoffman Rd., San Angelo, TX 76905/915-655-5953
H&S Liner Service, 515 E. 8th, Odessa, TX 79761/915-332-1021
Hakko Co. Ltd., Daini-Tsunemi Bldg., 1-13-12, Narimasu, Itabashiku Tokyo 175, JAPAN/03-5997-7870/2; FAX: 81-3-5997-7840
Half Moon Rifle Shop, 490 Halfmoon Rd., Columbia Falls, MT 59912/406-892-4409
Hallberg Gunsmith, Fritz, 33 S. Main, Payette, ID 83661/208-642-7157; FAX: 208-642-9643
Halstead, Rick, RR4, Box 272, Miami, OK 74354/918-540-0933
Hammerli USA, 19296 Oak Grove Circle, Groveland, CA 95321/209-962-5311; FAX: 209-962-5931
Hammets VLD Bullets, P.O. Box 479, Rayville, LA 71269/318-728-2019
Hammonds Rifles, RD 4, Box 504, Red Lion, PA 17356/717-244-7879
Handgun Press, P.O. Box 406, Glenview, IL 60025/847-657-6500; FAX: 847-724-8831
Hank's Gun Shop, Box 370, 50 West 100 South, Monroe, UT 84754/801-527-4456
Hanned Line, The, P.O. Box 2387, Cupertino, CA 95015-2387
Hanned Precision (See Hanned Line, The)
Hansen & Co. (See Hansen Cartridge Co.)
Hansen Cartridge Co., 244-246 Old Post Rd., Southport, CT 06490/203-259-6222, 203-259-7337; FAX: 203-254-3832
Hanson's Gun Center, Dick, 233 Everett Dr., Colorado Springs, CO 80911
Hardin Specialty Dist., P.O. Box 338, Radcliff, KY 40159-0338/502-351-6649
Harold's Custom Gun Shop, Inc., Broughton Rifle Barrels, Rt. 1, Box 447, Big Spring, TX 79720/915-394-4430
Harper's Custom Stocks, 928 Lombrano St., San Antonio, TX 78207/512-732-5780
Harrell's Precision, 5756 Hickory Dr., Salem, VA 24133/703-380-2683
Harris Engineering, Inc., Rt. 1, Barlow, KY 42024/502-334-3633; FAX: 502-334-3000
Harris Enterprises, P.O. Box 105, Bly, OR 97622/503-353-2625
Harris Gunworks, 3840 N. 28th Ave., Phoenix, AZ 85017-4733/602-230-1414; FAX: 602-230-1422
Harrison Bullets, 6437 E. Hobart St., Mesa, AZ 85205
Hart & Son, Robert W., Inc., 401 Montgomery St., Nescopeck, PA 18635/717-752-3655, 800-368-3656; FAX: 717-752-1088
Hart Rifle Barrels, Inc., P.O. Box 182, 1690 Apulia Rd., Lafayette, NY 13084/315-677-9841; FAX: 315-677-9610
Haselbauer Products, Jerry, P.O. Box 27629, Tucson, AZ 85726/602-792-1075
Hastings Barrels, 320 Court St., Clay Center, KS 67432/913-632-3169; FAX: 913-632-6554
Hawk, Inc., 849 Hawks Bridge Rd., Salem, NJ 08079/609-299-2700; FAX: 609-299-2800
Hawk Laboratories, Inc. (See Hawk, Inc.)
Hawken Shop, The (See Dayton Traister)
Haydon Shooters' Supply, Russ, 15018 Goodrich Dr. NW, Gig Harbor, WA 98329/206-857-7557
Heatbath Corp., P.O. Box 2978, Springfield, MA 01101/413-543-3381
HEBB Resources, P.O. Box 999, Mead, WA 99021-09996/509-466-1292
Hecht, Hubert J., Waffen-Hecht, P.O. Box 2635, Fair Oaks, CA 95628/916-966-1020
Heidenstrom Bullets, Urds GT 1 Heroya, 3900 Porsgrunn, NORWAY
Heilmann, Stephen, P.O. Box 657, Grass Valley, CA 95945/916-272-8758
Heinie Specialty Products, 301 Oak St., Quincy, IL 62301-2500/309-543-4535; FAX: 309-543-2521
Hensler, Jerry, 6614 Country Field, San Antonio, TX 78240/210-690-7491
Hensley & Gibbs, Box 10, Murphy, OR 97533/541-862-2341
Hensley, Darwin, P.O. Box 329, Brightwood, OR 97011/503-622-5411
Heppler, Keith M., Keith's Custom Gunstocks, 540 Banyan Circle, Walnut Creek, CA 94598/510-934-3509; FAX: 510-934-3143
Hercules, Inc. (See Alliant Techsystems, Smokeless Powder Group)

Heritage/VSP Gun Books, P.O. Box 887, McCall, ID 83638/208-634-4104; FAX: 208-634-3101
Hermann Leather Co., H.J., Rt. 1, P.O. Box 525, Skiatook, OK 74070/918-396-1226
Hertel & Reuss, Werk für Optik und Feinmechanik GmbH, Quellhofstrabe, 67/34 127 Kassel, GERMANY
0561-83006; FAX: 0561-893308
Hesco-Meprolight, 2139 Greenville Rd., LaGrange, GA 30240/706-884-7967; FAX: 706-882-4683
Heydenberk, Warren R., 1059 W. Sawmill Rd., Quakertown, PA 18951/215-538-2682
Hickman, Jaclyn, Box 1900, Glenrock, WY 82637
Hidalgo, Tony, 12701 SW 9th Pl., Davie, FL 33325/305-476-7645
High Tech Specialties, Inc., P.O. Box 387R, Adamstown, PA 19501/215-484-0405, 800-231-9385
Hillmer Custom Gunstocks, Paul D., 7251 Hudson Heights, Hudson, IA 50643/319-988-3941
Hiptmayer, Armurier, RR 112 750, P.O. Box 136, Eastman, Quebec JOE 1P0, CANADA/514-297-2492
Hiptmayer, Klaus, RR 112 750, P.O. Box 136, Eastman, Quebec J0E 1P0, CANADA/514-297-2492
Hirtenberger Aktiengesellschaft, Leobersdorferstrasse 31, A-2552 Hirtenberg, AUSTRIA/43(0)2256 81184; FAX: 43(0)2256 81807
Hiti-Schuch, Atelier Wilma, A-8863 Predlitz, Pirming Y1 AUSTRIA/0353418278
Hobson Precision Mfg. Co., Rt. 1, Box 220-C, Brent, AL 35034/205-926-4662
Hoch Custom Bullet Moulds (See Colorado Shooter's Supply)
Hodgdon Powder Co., Inc., P.O. Box 2932, 6231 Robinson, Shawnee Mission, KS 66202/913-362-9455; FAX: 913-362-1307; WEB: http://www.unicom.net/hpc
Hoehn Sales, Inc., 75 Greensburg Ct., St. Charles, MO 63304/314-441-4231
Hoelscher, Virgil, 11047 Pope Ave., Lynwood, CA 90262/310-631-8545
Hoenig & Rodman, 6521 Morton Dr., Boise, ID 83704/208-375-1116
Hoffman New Ideas, 821 Northmoor Rd., Lake Forest, IL 60045/312-234-4075
Holland's, Box 69, Powers, OR 97466/503-439-5155; FAX: 503-439-5155
Hollywood Engineering, 10642 Arminta St., Sun Valley, CA 91352/818-842-8376
Home Shop Machinist, The, Village Press Publications, P.O. Box 1810, Traverse City, MI 49685/800-447-7367; FAX: 616-946-3289
Hondo Ind., 510 S. 52nd St.,I04, Tempe, AZ 85281
Hoppe's Div., Penguin Industries, Inc., Airport Industrial Mall, Coatesville, PA 19320/610-384-6000
Horizons Unlimited, P.O. Box 426, Warm Springs, GA 31830/706-655-3603; FAX: 706-655-3603
Hornady Mfg. Co., P.O. Box 1848, Grand Island, NE 68802/800-338-3220, 308-382-1390; FAX: 308-382-5761
Howell Machine, 815½ D St., Lewiston, ID 83501/208-743-7418
H-S Precision, Inc., 1301 Turbine Dr., Rapid City, SD 57701/605-341-3006; FAX: 605-342-8964
HT Bullets, 244 Belleville Rd., New Bedford, MA 02745/508-999-3338
Huebner, Corey O., P.O. Box 2074, Missoula, MT 59806-2074/406-721-7168
Hughes, Steven Dodd, P.O. Box 545, Livingston, MT 59047/406-222-9377
Hungry Horse Books, 4605 Hwy. 93 South, Whitefish, MT 59937/406-862-7997
Hunterjohn, P.O. Box 477, St. Louis, MO 63166/314-531-7250
Huntington Die Specialties, 601 Oro Dam Blvd., Oroville, CA 95965/916-534-1210; FAX: 916-534-1212
Hydrosorbent Products, P.O. Box 437, Ashley Falls, MA 01222/413-229-2967; FAX: 413-229-8743

I

ICI-America, P.O. Box 751, Wilmington, DE 19897/302-575-3000
Idaho Ammunition Service, 2816 Mayfair Dr., Lewiston, ID 83501/208-743-0270; FAX: 208-743-4930
Illinois Lead Shop, 7742 W. 61st Place, Summit, IL 60501
IMI, P.O. Box 1044, Ramat Hasharon 47100, ISRAEL/972-3-5485222
IMI Services USA, Inc., 2 Wisconsin Circle, Suite 420, Chevy Chase, MD 20815/301-215-4800; FAX: 301-657-1446
Imperial (See E-Z-Way Systems)
Imperial Magnum Corp., P.O. Box 249, Oroville, WA 98844/604-495-3131; FAX: 604-495-2816
IMR Powder Co., 1080 Military Turnpike, Suite 2, Plattsburgh, NY 12901/518-563-2253; FAX: 518-563-6916
Independent Machine & Gun Shop, 1416 N. Hayes, Pocatello, ID 83201
Info-Arm, P.O. Box 1262, Champlain, NY 12919
Innovative Weaponry, Inc., 337 Eubank NE, Albuquerque, NM 87123/800-334-3573, 505-296-4645; FAX: 505-271-2633
Innovision Enterprises, 728 Skinner Dr., Kalamazoo, MI 49001/616-382-1681; FAX: 616-382-1830
INTEC International, Inc., P.O. Box 5708, Scottsdale, AZ 85261/602-483-1708
Intermountain Arms & Tackle, Inc., 1375 E. Fairview Ave., Meridian, ID 83642-1816/208-888-4911; FAX: 208-888-4381
International Shooters Service (See I.S.S.)
Iosso Products, 1485 Lively Blvd., Elk Grove Village, IL 60007/708-437-8400; FAX: 708-437-8478
Iron Bench, 12619 Bailey Rd., Redding, CA 96003/916-241-4623
Ironside International Publishers, Inc., P.O. Box 55, 800 Slaters Lane, Alexandria, VA 22313/703-684-6111; FAX: 703-683-5486
Ironsighter Co., P.O. Box 85070, Westland, MI 48185/313-326-8731; FAX: 313-326-3378
Israel Military Industries Ltd. (See IMI)
I.S.S., P.O. Box 185234, Ft. Worth, TX 76181/817-595-2090
I.S.W., 106 E. Cairo Dr., Tempe, AZ 85282
Ivanoff, Thomas G. (See Tom's Gun Repair)

J

J-4, Inc., 1700 Via Burton, Anaheim, CA 92806/714-254-8315; FAX: 714-956-4421
J&D Components, 75 East 350 North, Orem, UT 84057-4719/801-225-7007
J&J Products, Inc., 9240 Whitmore, El Monte, CA 91731/818-571-5228, 800-927-8361; FAX: 818-571-8704
J&L Superior Bullets (See Huntington Die Specialties)
J&R Enterprises, 4550 Scotts Valley Rd., Lakeport, CA 95453
Jackalope Gun Shop, 1048 S. 5th St., Douglas, WY 82633/307-358-3441
Jaeger, Inc./Dunn's, Paul, P.O. Box 449, 1 Madison Ave., Grand Junction, TN 38039/901-764-6909; FAX: 901-764-6503
JagerSport, Ltd., One Wholesale Way, Cranston, RI 02920/800-962-4867, 401-944-9682; FAX: 401-946-2587
Jamison's Forge Works, 4527 Rd. 6.5 NE, Moses Lake, WA 98837/509-762-2659
Jarrett Rifles, Inc., 383 Brown Rd., Jackson, SC 29831/803-471-3616
Javelina Lube Products, P.O. Box 337, San Bernardino, CA 92402/714-882-5847; FAX: 714-434-6937
J-B Bore Cleaner, 299 Poplar St., Hamburg, PA 19526/610-562-2103
JBM, P.O. Box 3648, University Park, NM 88003
Jeffredo Gunsight, P.O. Box 669, San Marcos, CA 92079/619-728-2695
Jensen Bullets, 86 North, 400 West, Blackfoot, ID 83221/208-785-5590
Jensen's Custom Ammunition, 5146 E. Pima, Tucson, AZ 85712/602-325-3346; FAX: 602-322-5704
Jensen's Firearms Academy, 1280 W. Prince, Tucson, AZ 85705/602-293-8516
Jester Bullets, Rt. 1 Box 27, Orienta, OK 73737
Jewell, Arnold W., 1490 Whitewater Rd., New Braunfels, TX 78132/210-620-0971
J-Gar Co., 183 Turnpike Rd., Dept. 3, Petersham, MA 01366-9604
JGS Precision Tool Mfg., 1141 S. Summer Rd., Coos Bay, OR 97420/503-267-4331; FAX:503-267-5996
J.I.T., Ltd., P.O. Box 230, Freedom, WY 83120/708-494-0937
JLK Bullets, 414 Turner Rd., Dover, AR 72837/501-331-4194
Johnson Wood Products, RR 1, Strawberry Point, IA 52076/319-933-4930
Johnson's Lage Uniwad, P.O. Box 2302, Davenport, IA 52809/319-388-LAGE
Johnston Bros., 1889 Rt. 9, Unit 22, Toms River, NJ 08755/800-257-2595; FAX: 800-257-2534
Jonad Corp., 2091 Lakeland Ave., Lakewood, OH 44107/216-226-3161
Jones, J.D. (See SSK Industries)
Jones Custom Products, Neil A., 17217 Brookhouser Road, Saegertown, PA 16433/814-763-2769; FAX: 814-763-4228
Jones Moulds, Paul, 4901 Telegraph Rd., Los Angeles, CA 90022/213-262-1510
J.P. Enterprises, Inc., P.O. Box 26324, Shoreview, MN 55126/612-486-9064; FAX: 612-482-0970
J.P. Gunstocks, Inc., 4508 San Miguel Ave., North Las Vegas, NV 89030/702-645-0718
JP Sales, Box 307, Anderson, TX 77830
JRW, 2425 Taffy Ct., Nampa, ID 83687
Jurras, L.E., P.O. Box 680, Washington, IN 47501/812-254-7698
JWH: Software, 6947 Haggerty Rd., Hillsboro, OH 45133/513-393-2402

K

K&M Services, 5430 Salmon Run Rd., Dover, PA 17315/717-764-1461
K&P Gun Co., 1024 Central Ave., New Rockford, ND 58356/701-947-2248
K&S Mfg., 2611 Hwy. 40 East, Inglis, FL 34449/904-447-3571
K&T Co., Div. of T&S Industries, Inc., 1027 Skyview Dr., W. Carrollton, OH 45449/513-859-8414
Kahles, A Swarovski Company, 1 Wholesale Way, Cranston, RI 02920-5540/800-426-3089; FAX: 401-946-2587
Kandel, P.O. Box 4529, Portland, OR 97208
Kapro Mfg. Co., Inc. (See R.E.I.)
Ka Pu Kapili, P.O. Box 745, Honokaa, HI 96727/808-776-1644; FAX: 808-776-1731
Kasmarsik Bullets, 152 Crstler Rd., Chehalis, WA 98532
Kaswer Custom, Inc., 13 Surrey Drive, Brookfield, CT 06804/203-775-0564; FAX: 203-775-6872
K.B.I., Inc., P.O. Box 5440, Harrisburg, PA 17110-0440/717-540-8518; FAX: 717-540-8567
K-D, Inc., Box 459, 585 N. Hwy. 155, Cleveland, UT 84518/801-653-2530
KDF, Inc., 2485 Hwy. 46 N., Seguin, TX 78155/210-379-8141; FAX: 210-379-5420
Keeler, R.H., 817 "N" St., Port Angeles, WA 98362/206-457-4702
Keith's Bullets, 942 Twisted Oak, Algonquin, IL 60102/708-658-3520
Keith's Custom Gunstocks (See Heppler, Keith M.)
Kelbly, Inc., 7222 Dalton Fox Lake Rd., North Lawrence, OH 44666/216-683-4674; FAX: 216-683-7349
Kellogg's Professional Products, 325 Pearl St., Sandusky, OH 44870/419-625-6551; FAX: 419-625-6167
Ken's Kustom Kartridges, 331 Jacobs Rd., Hubbard, OH 44425/216-534-4595
Ken's Rifle Blanks, Ken McCullough, Rt. 2, P.O. Box 85B, Weston, OR 97886/503-566-3879
Keng's Firearms Specialty, Inc., 875 Wharton Dr. SW, Atlanta, GA 30336/404-691-7611; FAX: 404-505-8445
Kennebec Journal, 274 Western Ave., Augusta, ME 04330/207-622-6288
KenPatable Ent., Inc., P.O. Box 19422, Louisville, KY 40259/502-239-5447
Kent Cartridge Mfg. Co. Ltd., Unit 16, Branbridges Industrial Estate, East, Peckham/Tonbridge, Kent, TN12 5HF ENGLAND
622-872255; FAX: 622-872645
Kesselring Gun Shop, 400 Hwy. 99 North, Burlington, WA 98233/206-724-3113; FAX: 206-724-7003
Kilham & Co., Main St., P.O. Box 37, Lyme, NH 03768/603-795-4112
King & Co., P.O. Box 1242, Bloomington, IL 61702/309-473-3964
KJM Fabritek, Inc., P.O. Box 162, Marietta, GA 30061/404-426-8251
KLA Enterprises, P.O. Box 2028, Eaton Park, FL 33840/941-682-2829; FAX: 941-682-2829
Kleen-Bore, Inc., 16 Industrial Pkwy., Easthampton, MA 01027/413-527-0300; FAX: 413-527-2522
Klein Custom Guns, Don, 433 Murray Park Dr., Ripon, WI 54971/414-748-2931
Klingler Woodcarving, P.O. Box 141, Thistle Hill, Cabot, VT 05647/802-426-3811
Kmount, P.O. Box 19422, Louisville, KY 40259/502-239-5447
Knippel, Richard, 500 Gayle Ave, Apt. 213, Modesto, CA 95350-4241/209-869-1469
noell, Doug , 9737 McCardle Way, Santee, CA 92071
Kodiak Custom Bullets, 8261 Henry Circle, Anchorage, AK 99507/907-349-2282
KOGOT, 410 College, Trinidad, CO 81082/719-846-9406
Kokolus, Michael M. (See Custom Riflestocks, Inc.)
Kolpin Mfg., Inc., P.O. Box 107, 205 Depot St., Fox Lake, WI 53933/414-928-3118; FAX: 414-928-3687
Kopp, Terry K., Route 1, Box 224F, Lexington, MO 64067/816-259-2636
Kowa Optimed, Inc., 20001 S. Vermont Ave., Torrance, CA 90502/310-327-1913; FAX: 310-327-4177
Kramer Designs, 36 Chokecherry Ln., Clancy, MT 59634/406-933-8658; FAX: 406-933-8658
Krause Publications, Inc., 700 E. State St., Iola, WI 54990/715-445-2214; FAX: 715-445-4087; Consumer orders only 800-258-0929
Krieger Barrels, Inc., N114 W18697 Clinton Dr., Germantown, WI 53022/414-255-9593; FAX: 414-255-9586
Kris Mounts, 108 Lehigh St., Johnstown, PA 15905/814-539-9751
KVH Industries, Inc., 110 Enterprise Center, Middletown, RI 02842/401-847-3327; FAX: 401-849-0045
Kwik Mount Corp., P.O. Box 19422, Louisville, KY 40259/502-239-5447
Kwik-Site Co., 5555 Treadwell, Wayne, MI 48184/313-326-1500; FAX: 313-326-4120

L

L&S Technologies, Inc. (See Aimtech Mount Systems)
Labanu, Inc., 2201-F Fifth Ave., Ronkonkoma, NY 11779/516-467-6197; FAX: 516-981-4112
LaBounty Precision Reboring, P.O. Box 186, 7968 Silver Lk. Rd., Maple Falls, WA 98266/360-599-2047
Lake Center, P.O. Box 38, St. Charles, MO 63302/314-946-7500
Lakewood Products, Inc., 275 June St., P.O. Box 230, Berlin, WI 54923/800-US-BUILT; FAX: 414-361-5058
Lane Bullets, Inc., 1011 S. 10th St., Kansas City, KS 66105/913-621-6113, 800-444-7468
Lane Publishing, P.O. Box 459, Lake Hamilton, AR 71951/501-525-7514; FAX: 501-525-7519
Lanphert, Paul, P.O. Box 1985, Wenatchee, WA 98807
Lapua Ltd., P.O. Box 5, Lapua, FINLAND SF-62101/64-310111; FAX: 64-4388991
L.A.R. Mfg., Inc., 4133 W. Farm Rd., West Jordan, UT 84088/801-280-3505; FAX: 801-280-1972
Laseraim Arms, Inc., P.O. Box 3548, Little Rock, AR 72203/501-375-2227; FAX: 501-372-1445
Laseraim Technologies, Inc., P.O. Box 3548, Little Rock, AR 72203/501-375-2227; FAX: 501-372-1445
Laser Devices, Inc., 2 Harris Ct. A-4, Monterey, CA 93940/408-373-0701; FAX: 408-373-0903
LaserMax, 3495 Winton Place, Bldg. B, Rochester, NY 14623/716-272-5420; FAX: 716-272-5427
Laurel Mountain Forge, P.O. Box 224C, Romeo, MI 48065/810-749-5742
Lawrence Brand Shot (See Precision Reloading, Inc.)
Lawson Co., Harry, 3328 N. Richey Blvd., Tucson, AZ 85716/520-326-1117
LBT, HCR 62, Box 145, Moyie Springs, ID 83845/208-267-3588
Lead Bullets Technology (See LBT)
Le Clear Industries (See E-Z-Way Systems)
Lectro Science, Inc., 6410 W. Ridge Rd., Erie, PA 16506/814-833-6487; FAX: 814-833-0447

Lee Precision, Inc., 4275 Hwy. U, Hartford, WI 53027/414-673-3075
Lee's Red Ramps, 4 Kristine Ln., Silver City, NM 88061/505-538-8529
Lee Co., T.K., One Independence Plaza, Suite 520, Birmingham, AL 35209/205-913-5222
Legend Products Corp., 1555 E. Flamingo Rd., Suite 404, Las Vegas, NV 89119/702-228-1808, 702-796-5778; FAX: 702-228-7484
Leica USA, Inc., 156 Ludlow Ave., Northvale, NJ 07647/201-767-7500; FAX: 201-767-8666
LEM Gun Specialties, Inc., The Lewis Lead Remover, P.O. Box 2855, Peachtree City, GA 30269-2024
Lenahan Family Enterprise, P.O. Box 46, Manitou Springs, CO 80829
Lethal Force Institute (See Police Bookshelf)
Leupold & Stevens, Inc., P.O. Box 688, Beaverton, OR 97075/503-646-9171; FAX: 503-526-1455
Lewis Lead Remover, The (See LEM Gun Specialties, Inc.)
Liberty Metals, 2233 East 16th St., Los Angeles, CA 90021/213-581-9171; FAX: 213-581-9351
Liberty Shooting Supplies, P.O. Box 357, Hillsboro, OR 97123/503-640-5518
Lightfield Ammunition Corp., The Slug Group, P.O. Box 376, New Paris, PA 15554/814-839-4517; FAX: 814-839-2601
Lightning Performance Innovations, Inc., RD1 Box 555, Mohawk, NY 13407/315-866-8819, 800-242-5873; FAX: 315-866-8819
Lilja Precision Rifle Barrels, P.O. Box 372, Plains, MT 59859/406-826-3084; FAX: 406-826-3083
Lincoln, Dean, Box 1886, Farmington, NM 87401
Lindsley Arms Cartridge Co., P.O. Box 757, 20 College Hill Rd., Henniker, NH 03242/603-428-3127
List Precision Engineering, Unit 1, Ingley Works, 13 River Road, Barking, Essex 1G11 0HE ENGLAND/011-081-594-1686
Lithi Bee Bullet Lube, 1885 Dyson St., Muskegon, MI 49442/616-726-3400
Littler Sales Co., 20815 W. Chicago, Detroit, MI 48228/313-273-6889; FAX: 313-273-1099
Littleton, J.F., 275 Pinedale Ave., Oroville, CA 95966/916-533-6084
Load From A Disk, 9826 Sagedale, Houston, TX 77089/713-484-0935
Loadmaster, P.O. Box 1209, Warminster, Wilts. BA12 9XJ ENGLAND/01044 1985 218544; FAX: 01044 1985 214111
Lock's Philadelphia Gun Exchange, 6700 Rowland Ave., Philadelphia, PA 19149/215-332-6225; FAX: 215-332-4800
Lofland, James W., 2275 Larkin Rd., Boothwyn, PA 19061/610-485-0391
Lohman Mfg. Co., Inc., 4500 Doniphan Dr., P.O. Box 220, Neosho, MO 64850/417-451-4438; FAX: 417-451-2576
Lomont Precision Bullets, RR 1, P.O. Box 34, Salmon, ID 83467/208-756-6819; FAX: 208-756-6824
London Guns Ltd., Box 3750, Santa Barbara, CA 93130/805-683-4141; FAX: 805-683-1712
Lortone, Inc., 2856 NW Market St., Seattle, WA 98107/206-789-3100
Lothar Walther Precision Tool, Inc., 2190 Coffee Rd., Lithonia, GA 30058/770-482-4253; Fax: 770-482-9344
Loweth, Richard, 29 Hedgegrow Lane, Kirby Muxloe, Leics. LE9 9BN ENGLAND
L.P.A. Snc, Via Alfieri 26, Gardone V.T., Brescia, ITALY 25063/30-891-14-81; FAX: 30-891-09-51
LPS Laboratories, Inc., 4647 Hugh Howell Rd., P.O. Box 3050, Tucker, GA 30084/404-934-7800
Lucas, Mike, 1631 Jessamine Rd., Lexington, SC 29073/803-356-0282
Luch Metal Merchants, Barbara, 48861 West Rd., Wixon, MI 48393/800-876-5337
Lyman Instant Targets, Inc. (See Lyman Products Corp.)
Lyman Products Corp., 475 Smith Street, Middletown, CT 06457-1541/860-632-2020, 800-22-LYMAN; FAX: 860-632-1699
Lynn's Custom Gunstocks, RR 1, Brandon, IA 52210/319-474-2453

M

M&D Munitions Ltd., 127 Verdi St., Farmingdale, NY 11735/800-878-2788, 516-752-1038; FAX: 516-752-1905
M&M Engineering (See Hollywood Engineering)
M&N Bullet Lube, P.O. Box 495, 151 NE Jefferson St., Madras, OR 97741/503-255-3750
MA Systems, P.O. Box 1143, Chouteau, OK 74337/918-479-6378
Mac-1 Distributors, 13974 Van Ness Ave., Gardena, CA 90249/310-327-3582
Mac's .45 Shop, P.O. Box 2028, Seal Beach, CA 90740/310-438-5046
Madis, David, 2453 West Five Mile Pkwy., Dallas, TX 75233/214-330-7168
Magma Engineering Co., P.O. Box 161, 20955 E. Ocotillo Rd., Queen Creek, AZ 85242/602-987-9008; FAX: 602-987-0148
Magnum Grips, Box 801G, Payson, AZ 85547
Magnum Power Products, Inc., P.O. Box 17768, Fountain Hills, AZ 85268
Magnum Research, Inc., 7110 University Ave. NE, Minneapolis, MN 55432/800-772-6168, 612-574-1868; FAX: 612-574-0109
Magnus Bullets, P.O. Box 239, Toney, AL 35773/205-828-5089; FAX: 205-828-7756
MagSafe Ammo Co., 2725 Friendly Grove Rd NE, Olympia, WA 98506/360-357-6383; FAX: 360-705-4715
MAGTECH Recreational Products, Inc., 5030 Paradise Rd., Suite A104, Las Vegas, NV 89119/702-736-2043; FAX: 702-736-2140
Maine Custom Bullets, RFD 1, Box 1755, Brooks, ME 04921
Maionchi-L.M.I., Via Di Coselli-Zona Industriale Di Guamo, Lucca, ITALY 55060/011 39-583 94291
Malcolm Enterprises, 1023 E. Prien Lake Rd., Lake Charles, LA 70601
Mandall Shooting Supplies, Inc., 3616 N. Scottsdale Rd., Scottsdale, AZ 85252/602-945-2553; FAX: 602-949-0734
Marchmon Bullets, 8191 Woodland Shore Dr., Brighton, MI 48116
Markell, Inc., 422 Larkfield Center 235, Santa Rosa, CA 95403/707-573-0792; FAX: 707-573-9867
Marmik Inc., 2116 S. Woodland Ave., Michigan City, IN 46361-7508/219-872-7231
Marple & Associates, Dick, 21 Dartmouth St., Hooksett, NH 03106/603-627-1837; FAX: 603-627-1837
Marquart Precision Co., Inc., Rear 136 Grove Ave., Box 1740, Prescott, AZ 86302/602-445-5646
Marshall Enterprises, 792 Canyon Rd., Redwood City, CA 94062
Martin Bookseller, J., P.O. Drawer AP, Beckley, WV 25802/304-255-4073; FAX: 304-255-4077
Masen Co., Inc., John, 1305 Jelmak, Grand Prairie, TX 75050/817-430-8732; FAX: 817-430-1715
MAST Technology, 4350 S. Arville, Suite 3, Las Vegas, NV 89103/702-362-5043; FAX: 702-362-9554
Master Class Bullets, 4209-D West 6th, Eugene, OR 97402/503-687-1263, 800-883-1263
Master Lock Co., 2600 N. 32nd St., Milwaukee, WI 53245/414-444-2800
Match Prep, P.O. Box 155, Tehachapi, CA 93581/805-822-5383
Matco, Inc., 1003-2nd St., N. Manchester, IN 46962/219-982-8282
Mathews & Son, Inc., George E., 10224 S. Paramount Blvd., Downey, CA 90241/310-862-6719; FAX: 310-862-6719
Maxi-Mount, P.O. Box 291, Willoughby Hills, OH 44094-0291/216-944-9456; FAX: 216-944-9456
Mayville Engineering Co. (See MEC, Inc.)
Mazur Restoration, Pete, 13083 Drummer Way, Grass Valley, CA 95949/916-268-2412
McCament, Jay, 1730-134th St. Ct. S., Tacoma, WA 98444/206-531-8832
McCann's Machine & Gun Shop, P.O. Box 641, Spanaway, WA 98387/206-537-6919; FAX: 206-537-6993
McCullough, Ken (See Ken's Rifle Blanks)
McDonald, Dennis, 8359 Brady St., Peosta, IA 52068/319-556-7940
McFarland, Stan, 2221 Idella Ct., Grand Junction, CO 81505/303-243-4704
McGowen Rifle Barrels, 5961 Spruce Lane, St. Anne, IL 60964/815-937-9816; FAX: 815-937-4024
McGuire, Bill, 1600 N. Eastmont Ave., East Wenatchee, WA 98802/509-884-6021
McKee Publications, 121 Eatons Neck Rd., Northport, NY 11768/516-575-8850
McKillen & Heyer, Inc., 35535 Euclid Ave. Suite 11, Willoughby, OH 44094/216-942-2044
McKinney, R.P. (See Schuetzen Gun Co.)
McMillan Fiberglass Stocks, Inc., 21421 N. 14th Ave., Phoenix, AZ 85027/602-582-9635; FAX: 602-581-3825
McMillan Optical Gunsight Co., 28638 N. 42nd St., Cave Creek, AZ 85331/602-585-7868; FAX: 602-585-7872
McMillan Rifle Barrels, P.O. Box 3427, Bryan, TX 77805/409-690-3456; FAX: 409-690-0156
McMurdo, Lynn (See Specialty Gunsmithing)
MCRW Associates Shooting Supplies, R.R. 1 Box 1425, Sweet Valley, PA 18656/717-864-3967; FAX: 717-864-2669
MDS, P.O. Box 1441, Brandon, FL 33509-1441/813-653-1180; FAX: 813-684-5953
Measurement Group, Inc., Box 27777, Raleigh, NC 27611
MEC, Inc., 715 South St., Mayville, WI 53050/414-387-4500; FAX: 414-387-5802
Meier Works, P.O. Box 423, Tijeras, NM 87059/505-281-3783
Meister Bullets (See Gander Mountain)
Men-Metallwerk Elisenhuette, GmbH, P.O. Box 1263, D-56372 Nassau/Lahn, GERMANY/2604-7819
Meprolight (See Hesco-Meprolight)
Mercer Custom Stocks, R.M., 216 S. Whitewater Ave., Jefferson, WI 53549/414-674-5130
Merit Corp., Box 9044, Schenectady, NY 12309/518-346-1420
Merkuria Ltd., Argentinska 38, 17005 Praha 7, CZECH REPUBLIC/422-875117; FAX: 422-809152
Michael's Antiques, Box 591, Waldoboro, ME 04572
Michaels of Oregon Co., P.O. Box 13010, Portland, OR 97213/503-255-6890; FAX: 503-255-0746
Micro Sight Co., 242 Harbor Blvd., Belmont, CA 94002/415-591-0769; FAX: 415-591-7531
Mid-America Recreation, Inc., 1328 5th Ave., Moline, IL 61265/309-764-5089; FAX: 309-764-2722
Midway Arms, Inc., 5875 W. Van Horn Tavern Rd., Columbia, MO 65203/800-243-3220, 314-445-6363; FAX: 314-446-1018
Military Armament Corp., P.O. Box 120, Mt. Zion Rd., Lingleville, TX 76461/817-965-3253
Miller Arms, Inc., P.O. Box 260 Purl St., St. Onge, SD 57779/605-642-5160; FAX: 605-642-5160
Miller Enterprises, Inc., R.P., 1557 E. Main St., P.O. Box 234, Brownsburg, IN 46112/317-852-8187
Miller Single Trigger Mfg. Co., Rt. 209 Box 1275, Millersburg, PA 17061/717-692-3704
Millett Sights, 16131 Gothard St., Huntington Beach, CA 92647/714-842-5575, 800-645-5388; FAX: 714-843-5707
Milstor Corp., 80-975 E. Valley Pkwy. C-7, Indio, CA 92201/619-775-9998; FAX: 619-772-4990
Miniature Machine Co. (See MMC)
Minute Man High Tech Industries, 10611 Canyon Rd. E., Suite 151, Puyallup, WA 98373/800-233-2734
Mirador Optical Corp., P.O. Box 11614, Marina Del Rey, CA 90295-7614/310-821-5587; FAX: 310-305-0386
Mitchell Arms, Inc., 3433-B. W. Harvard St., Santa Ana, CA 92704/714-957-5711; FAX: 714-957-5732
Mitchell Bullets, R.F., 430 Walnut St., Westernport, MD 21562
MI-TE Bullets, R.R. 1 Box 230, Ellsworth, KS 67439/913-472-4575
MJM Mfg., 3283 Rocky Water Ln. Suite B, San Jose, CA 95148/408-270-4207
MKL Service Co., 610 S. Troy St., P.O. Box D, Royal Oak, MI 48068/810-548-5453
MMC, 2513 East Loop 820 North, Ft. Worth, TX 76118/817-595-0404; FAX: 817-595-3074
MMP, Rt. 6, Box 384, Harrison, AR 72601/501-741-5019; FAX: 501-741-3104
MoLoc Bullets, P.O. Box 2810, Turlock, CA 95381-2810/209-632-1644
Montana Outfitters, Lewis E. Yearout, 308 Riverview Dr. E., Great Falls, MT 59404/406-761-0859
Montana Precision Swaging, P.O. Box 4746, Butte, MT 59702/406-782-7502
Montana Vintage Arms, 2354 Bear Canyon Rd., Bozeman, MT 59715
Moreton/Fordyce Enterprises, P.O. Box 940, Saylorsburg, PA 18353/717-992-5742; FAX: 717-992-8775
Morrison Custom Rifles, J.W., 4015 W. Sharon, Phoenix, AZ 85029/602-978-3754
Morrow, Bud, 11 Hillside Lane, Sheridan, WY 82801-9729/307-674-8360
Mountain Bear Rifle Works, Inc., 100 B Ruritan Rd., Sterling, VA 20164/703-430-0420; FAX: 703-430-7068
Mountain South, P.O. Box 381, Barnwell, SC 29812/FAX: 803-259-3227
Mountain View Sports, Inc., Box 188, Troy, NH 03465/603-357-9690; FAX: 603-357-9691
MPI Fiberglass Stocks, 5655 NW St. Helens Rd., Portland, OR 97210/503-226-1215; FAX: 503-226-2661
MSR Targets, P.O. Box 1042, West Covina, CA 91793/818-331-7840
Mt. Baldy Bullet Co., 12981 Old Hill City Rd., Keystone, SD 57751-6623/605-666-4725
MTM Molded Products Co., Inc., 3370 Obco Ct., Dayton, OH 45414/513-890-7461; FAX: 513-890-1747
Mulhern, Rick, Rt. 5, Box 152, Rayville, LA 71269/318-728-2688
Mullins Ammo, Rt. 2, Box 304K, Clintwood, VA 24228/703-926-6772
Multipax, 8086 S. Yale, Suite 286, Tulsa, OK 74136/918-496-1999; FAX: 918-492-7465
Multiplex International, 26 S. Main St., Concord, NH 03301/FAX: 603-796-2223
Multi-Scale Charge Ltd., 3269 Niagara Falls Blvd., N. Tonawanda, NY 14120/905-566-1255; FAX: 905-276-6295
Mundy, Thomas A., 69 Robbins Road, Somerville, NJ 08876/201-722-2199
Murmur Corp., 2823 N. Westmoreland Ave., Dallas, TX 75222/214-630-5400
Muscle Products Corp., 112 Fennell Dr., Butler, PA 16001/800-227-7049, 412-283-0567; FAX: 412-283-8310
Mushroom Express Bullet Co., 601 W. 6th St., Greenfield, IN 46140-1728/317-462-6332
Muzzleload Magnum Products (See MMP)
MWG Co., P.O. Box 971202, Miami, FL 33197/800-428-9394, 305-253-8393; FAX: 305-232-1247

N

Nagel's Bullets, 9 Wilburn, Baytown, TX 77520
National Bullet Co., 1585 E. 361 St., Eastlake, OH 44095/216-951-1854; FAX: 216-951-7761
National Target Co., 4690 Wyaconda Rd., Rockville, MD 20852/800-827-7060, 301-770-7060; FAX: 301-770-7892
Naval Ordnance Works, Rt. 2, Box 919, Sheperdstown, WV 25443/304-876-0998
N.B.B., Inc., 24 Elliot Rd., Sterling, MA 01564/508-422-7538, 800-942-9444
NECO, 1316-67th St., Emeryville, CA 94608/510-450-0420
Necromancer Industries, Inc., 14 Communications Way, West Newton, PA 15089/412-872-8722
NEI Handtools, Inc., 51583 Columbia River Hwy., Scappoose, OR 97056/503-543-6776; FAX: 503-543-6799; E-MAIL: neiht@mcimail.com
Nelson, Stephen, 7365 NW Spring Creek Dr., Corvallis, OR 97330/541-745-5232
Nesci Enterprises, Inc., P.O. Box 119, Summit St., East Hampton, CT 06424/203-267-2588
Nettestad Gun Works, RR 1, Box 160, Pelican Rapids, MN 56572/218-863-4301
New Democracy, Inc., 751 W. Lamar Blvd., Suite 102, Arlington, TX 76012-2010
New England Ammunition Co., 1771 Post Rd. East, Suite 223, Westport, CT 06880/203-254-8048
New England Arms Co., Box 278, Lawrence Lane, Kittery Point, ME 03905/207-439-0593; FAX: 207-439-6726
New England Custom Gun Service, 438 Willow Brook Rd., RR2, Box 122W, W. Lebanon, NH 03784/603-469-3450; FAX: 603-469-3471
New Win Publishing, Inc., Box 5159, Clinton, NJ 08809/201-735-9701; FAX: 201-735-9703
Newark Electronics, 4801 N. Ravenswood Ave., Chicago, IL 60640
Newman Gunshop, 119 Miller Rd., Agency, IA 52530/515-937-5775

NgraveR Co., The, 67 Wawecus Hill Rd., Bozrah, CT 06334/203-823-1533
Nic Max, Inc., 535 Midland Ave., Garfield, NJ 07026/201-546-7191; FAX: 201-546-7419
Nickels, Paul R., 4789 Summerhill Rd., Las Vegas, NV 89121/702-435-5318
Niemi Engineering, W.B., Box 126 Center Road, Greensboro, VT 05841/802-533-7180 days, 802-533-7141 evenings
Nikon, Inc., 1300 Walt Whitman Rd., Melville, NY 11747/516-547-8623; FAX: 516-547-0309
Norma Precision AB (See U.S. importers—Dynamit Nobel-RWS Inc.; Paul Co. Inc., The)
Norman Custom Gunstocks, Jim, 14281 Cane Rd., Valley Center, CA 92082/619-749-6252
North American Shooting Systems, P.O. Box 306, Osoyoos, B.C. V0H 1V0 CANADA/604-495-3131; FAX: 604-495-2816
North American Specialties, P.O. Box 189, Baker City, OR 97814/503-523-6954
North Devon Firearms Services, 3 North St., Braunton, EX33 1AJ ENGLAND/01271 813624; FAX: 01271 813624
North Specialty Products, 2664-B Saturn St., Brea, CA 92621/714-524-1665
Northern Precision Custom Swaged Bullets, 329 S. James St., Carthage, NY 13619/315-493-1711
Northside Gun Shop, 2725 NW 109th, Oklahoma City, OK 73120/405-840-2353
Nosler, Inc., P.O. Box 671, Bend, OR 97709/800-285-3701, 503-382-3921; FAX: 503-388-4667
Novak's, Inc., 1206½ 30th St., P.O. Box 4045, Parkersburg, WV 26101/304-485-9295; FAX: 304-428-6722
Nowlin Custom Mfg., Rt. 1, Box 308, Claremore, OK 74017/918-342-0689; FAX: 918-342-0624
Numrich Arms Corp., 203 Broadway, W. Hurley, NY 12491
Nu-Teck, 30 Industrial Park Rd., Box 37, Centerbrook, CT 06409/203-767-3573; FAX: 203-767-9137
NW Sinker and Tackle, 380 Valley Dr., Myrtle Creek, OR 97457-9717

O

Oakland Custom Arms, Inc., 4690 W. Walton Blvd., Waterford, MI 48329/810-674-8261
Oakshore Electronic Sights, Inc., P.O. Box 4470, Ocala, FL 32678-4470/904-629-7112; FAX: 904-629-1433
Obermeyer Rifled Barrels, 23122 60th St., Bristol, WI 53104/414-843-3537; FAX: 414-843-2129
Oehler Research, Inc., P.O. Box 9135, Austin, TX 78766/512-327-6900, 800-531-5125; FAX: 512-327-6903
Oil Rod and Gun Shop, 69 Oak St., East Douglas, MA 01516/508-476-3687
Oklahoma Ammunition Co., 4310 W. Rogers Blvd., Skiatook, OK 74070/918-396-3187; FAX: 918-396-4270
OK Weber, Inc., P.O. Box 7485, Eugene, OR 97401/541-747-0458; FAX: 541-747-5927
Old Wagon Bullets, 32 Old Wagon Rd., Wilton, CT 06897
Old West Bullet Moulds, P.O. Box 519, Flora Vista, NM 87415/505-334-6970
Old Western Scrounger, Inc., 12924 Hwy. A-l2, Montague, CA 96064/916-459-5445; FAX: 916-459-3944
Old World Gunsmithing, 2901 SE 122nd St., Portland, OR 97236/503-760-7681
Old World Oil Products, 3827 Queen Ave. N., Minneapolis, MN 55412/612-522-5037
Olsen Development Lab, 111 Lakeview Ave., Blackwood, NJ 08012
Olympic Optical Co., P.O. Box 752377, Memphis, TN 38175-2377/901-794-3890, 800-238-7120; FAX: 901-794-0676, 800-748-1669
Omark Industries, Div. of Blount, Inc., 2299 Snake River Ave., P.O. Box 856, Lewiston, ID 83501/800-627-3640, 208-746-2351
One Of A Kind, 15610 Purple Sage, San Antonio, TX 78255/512-695-3364
Op-Tec, P.O. Box L632, Langhorn, PA 19047/215-757-5037
Optical Services Co., P.O. Box 1174, Santa Teresa, NM 88008-1174/505-589-3833
Orchard Park Enterprise, P.O. Box 563, Orchard Park, NY 14227/616-656-0356
Ordnance Works, The, 2969 Pidgeon Point Road, Eureka, CA 95501/707-443-3252
Or-Un, Tahtakale Menekse Han 18, Istanbul, TURKEY 34460/90212-522-5912; FAX: 90212-522-7973
Orvis Co., The, Rt. 7, Manchester, VT 05254/802-362-3622 ext. 283; FAX: 802-362-3525
Ottmar, Maurice, Box 657, 113 E. Fir, Coulee City, WA 99115/509-632-5717
Outdoor Connection, Inc., The, 201 Cotton Dr., P.O. Box 7751, Waco, TX 76714-7751/800-533-6076; 817-772-5575; FAX: 817-776-3553
Outdoorsman's Bookstore, The, Llangorse, Brecon, Powys LD3 7UE, U.K./44-1874-658-660; FAX: 44-1874-658-650
Outers Laboratories, Div. of Blount, Inc., Sporting Equipment Div., Route 2,, P.O. Box 39, Onalaska, WI 54650/608-781-5800; FAX: 608-781-0368
Ox-Yoke Originals, Inc., 34 Main St., Milo, ME 04463/800-231-8313, 207-943-7351; FAX: 207-943-2416
Ozark Gun Works, 11830 Cemetery Rd., Rogers, AR 72756/501-631-6944; FAX: 501-631-6944

P

P&M Sales and Service, 5724 Gainsborough Pl., Oak Forest, IL 60452/708-687-7149
P&S Gun Service, 2138 Old Shepardsville Rd., Louisville, KY 40218/502-456-9346
Pac-Nor Barreling, 99299 Overlook Rd., P.O. Box 6188, Brookings, OR 97415/503-469-7330; FAX: 503-469-7331
Pachmayr, Ltd., 1875 S. Mountain Ave., Monrovia, CA 91016/818-357-7771, 800-423-9704; FAX: 818-358-7251
Pacific Precision, 755 Antelope Rd., P.O. Box 2549, White City, OR 97503/503-826-5808; FAX: 503-826-5304
Pacific Research Laboratories, Inc., 10221 S.W. 188th St., Vashon Island, WA 98070/206-463-5551; FAX: 206-463-2526
Pacific Rifle Co., 1040-D Industrial Parkway, Newberg, OR 97132/503-538-7437
Pacific Tool Co., P.O. Box 2048, Ordnance Plant Rd., Grand Island, NE 68801
Paco's (See Small Custom Mould & Bullet Co.)
P.A.C.T., Inc., P.O. Box 531525, Grand Prairie, TX 75053/214-641-0049
Page Custom Bullets, P.O. Box 25, Port Moresby Papua, NEW GUINEA
Pagel Gun Works, Inc., 1407 4th St. NW, Grand Rapids, MN 55744/218-326-3003
Palmer Manufacturing Co., Inc., C., P.O. Box 220, West Newton, PA 15089/412-872-8200; FAX: 412-872-8302
Paragon Sales & Services, Inc., P.O. Box 2022, Joliet, IL 60434/815-725-9212; FAX: 815-725-8974
Parker Div. Reageant Chemical (See Parker Reproductions)
Parker Gun Finishes, 9337 Smokey Row Rd., Strawberry Plains, TN 37871/423-933-3286
Parker Reproductions, 124 River Rd., Middlesex, NJ 08846/908-469-0100; FAX: 908-469-9692
Parsons Optical Mfg. Co., P.O. Box 192, Ross, OH 45061/513-867-0820; FAX: 513-867-8380
Parts & Surplus, P.O. Box 22074, Memphis, TN 38122/901-683-4007
Pasadena Gun Center, 206 E. Shaw, Pasadena, TX 77506/713-472-0417; FAX: 713-472-1322
Passive Bullet Traps, Inc. (See Savage Range Systems, Inc.)
PAST Sporting Goods, Inc., P.O. Box 1035, Columbia, MO 65205/314-445-9200; FAX: 314-446-6606
Paterson Gunsmithing, 438 Main St., Paterson, NJ 07502/201-345-4100
Patrick Bullets, P.O. Box 172, Warwick QSLD 4370 AUSTRALIA
Pattern Control, 114 N. Third St., P.O. Box 462105, Garland, TX 75046/214-494-3551; FAX: 214-272-8447
Paul Co., The, 27385 Pressonville Rd., Wellsville, KS 66092/913-883-4444; FAX: 913-883-2525
Paulsen Gunstocks, Rt. 71, Box 11, Chinook, MT 59523/406-357-3403
PC Bullet/ADC, Inc., 52700 NE First, Scappoose, OR 97056-3212/503-543-5088; FAX: 503-543-5990
Pease Accuracy, Bob, P.O. Box 310787, New Braunfels, TX 78131/210-625-1342
Peasley, David, P.O. Box 604, 2067 S. Hiway 17, Alamosa, CO 81101
PECAR Herbert Schwarz, GmbH, Kreuzbergstrasse 6, 10965 Berlin, GERMANY/004930-785-7383; FAX: 004930-785-1934
Pecatonica River Longrifle, 5205 Noddingham Dr., Rockford, IL 61111/815-968-1995; FAX: 815-968-1996
Pedersoli Davide & C., Via Artigiani 57, Gardone V.T., Brescia, ITALY 25063/030-8912402; FAX: 030-8911019
Peerless Alloy, Inc., 1445 Osage St., Denver, CO 80204-2439/303-825-6394, 800-253-1278
Pejsa Ballistics, 2120 Kenwood Pkwy., Minneapolis, MN 55405/612-374-3337; FAX: 612-374-3337
Pell, John T. (See KOGOT)
Peltor, Inc., 41 Commercial Way, E. Providence, RI 02914/401-438-4800; FAX: 401-434-1708
PEM's Mfg. Co., 5063 Waterloo Rd., Atwater, OH 44201/216-947-3721
Pence Precision Barrels, 7567 E. 900 S., S. Whitley, IN 46787/219-839-4745
Pend Oreille Sport Shop, 3100 Hwy. 200 East, Sandpoint, ID 83864/208-263-2412
Pendleton Royal, c/o Swingler Buckland Ltd., 4/7 Highgate St., Birmingham, ENGLAND B12 0XS/44 121 440 3060, 44 121 446 5898; FAX: 44 121 446 4165
Penn Bullets, P.O. Box 756, Indianola, PA 15051
Penrod Precision, 312 College Ave., P.O. Box 307, N. Manchester, IN 46962/219-982-8385
Pentax Corp., 35 Inverness Dr. E., Englewood, CO 80112/303-799-8000; FAX: 303-790-1131
Pentheny de Pentheny, 2352 Baggett Ct., Santa Rosa, CA 95401/707-573-1390; FAX: 707-573-1390
Perazone-Gunsmith, Brian, Cold Spring Rd., Roxbury, NY 12474/607-326-4088; FAX: 607-326-3140
Perazzi USA, Inc., 1207 S. Shamrock Ave., Monrovia, CA 91016/818-303-0068; FAX: 818-303-2081
Personal Protection Systems, RD 5, Box 5027-A, Moscow, PA 18444/717-842-1766
Petersen Publishing Co., 6420 Wilshire Blvd., Los Angeles, CA 90048/213-782-2000; FAX: 213-782-2867
Petro-Explo, Inc., 7650 U.S. Hwy. 287, Suite 100, Arlington, TX 76017/817-478-8888
Pettinger Books, Gerald, Rt. 2, Box 125, Russell, IA 50238/515-535-2239
Phil-Chem, Inc. (See George & Roy's)
Phillippi Custom Bullets, Justin, P.O. Box 773, Ligonier, PA 15658/412-238-9671
Phillips, Jerry, P.O. Box L632, Langhorne, PA 19047/215-757-5037
Pinetree Bullets, 133 Skeena St., Kitimat BC, CANADA V8C 1Z1/604-632-3768; FAX: 604-632-3768
Pioneer Arms Co., 355 Lawrence Rd., Broomall, PA 19008/215-356-5203
Pioneer Research, Inc., 216 Haddon Ave., Suite 102, Westmont, NJ 08108/800-257-7742; FAX: 609-858-8695
Plum City Ballistic Range, N2162 80th St., Plum City, WI 54761-8622/715-647-2539
PlumFire Press, Inc., 30-A Grove Ave., Patchogue, NY 11772-4112/800-695-7246; FAX:516-758-4071
PMC/Eldorado Cartridge Corp., P.O. Box 62508, 12801 U.S. Hwy. 95 S., Boulder City, NV 89005/702-294-0025; FAX: 702-294-0121
P.M. Enterprises, Inc., 146 Curtis Hill Rd., Chehalis, WA 98532/206-748-3743; FAX: 206-748-1802
Pohl, Henry A. (See Great American Gun Co.)
Pointing Dog Journal, Village Press Publications, P.O. Box 968, Dept. PGD, Traverse City, MI 49685/800-272-3246; FAX: 616-946-3289
Police Bookshelf, P.O. Box 122, Concord, NH 03301/603-224-6814; FAX: 603-226-3554
Policlips North America, 59 Douglas Crescent, Toronto, Ont. CANADA M4W 2E6/800-229-5089, 416-924-0383; FAX: 416-924-4375
Polywad, Inc., P.O. Box 7916, Macon, GA 31209/912-477-0669
Pomeroy, Robert, RR1, Box 50, E. Corinth, ME 04427/207-285-7721
Ponsness/Warren, P.O. Box 8, Rathdrum, ID 83858/208-687-2231; FAX: 208-687-2233
Pony Express Reloaders, 608 E. Co. Rd. D, Suite 3, St. Paul, MN 55117/612-483-9406; FAX: 612-483-9884
Portus, Robert, 130 Ferry Rd., Grants Pass, OR 97526/503-476-4919
Powder Horn, Inc., The, P.O. Box 114 Patty Drive, Cusseta, GA 31805/404-989-3257
Powder Valley Services, Rt. 1, Box 100, Dexter, KS 67038/316-876-5418
Powell Agency, William, The, 22 Circle Dr., Bellmore, NY 11710/516-679-1158
Prairie River Arms, 1220 N. Sixth St., Princeton, IL 61356/815-875-1616, 800-445-1541; FAX: 815-875-1402
Precise Metalsmithing Enterprises, 146 Curtis Hill Rd., Chehalis, WA 98532/206-748-3743; FAX: 206-748-8102
Precision, Jim, 1725 Moclip's Dr., Petaluma, CA 94952/707-762-3014
Precision Cartridge, 176 Eastside Rd., Deer Lodge, MT 59722/800-397-3901, 406-846-3900
Precision Cast Bullets, 101 Mud Creek Lane, Ronan, MT 59864/406-676-5135
Precision Castings & Equipment, Inc., P.O. Box 326, Jasper, IN 47547-0135/812-634-9167
Precision Components, 3177 Sunrise Lake, Milford, PA 18337/717-686-4414
Precision Components and Guns, Rt. 55, P.O. Box 337, Pawling, NY 12564/914-855-3040
Precision Delta Corp., P.O. Box 128, Ruleville, MS 38771/601-756-2810; FAX: 601-756-2590
Precision Munitions, Inc., P.O. Box 326, Jasper, IN 47547
Precision Ordnance, 1316 E. North St., Jackson, MI 49202
Precision Reloading, Inc., P.O. Box 122, Stafford Springs, CT 06076/860-684-7979; FAX: 860-684-6788
Precision Shooting, Inc., 222 McKee St., Manchester, CT 06040/860-645-8776; FAX: 860-643-8215
Precision Sport Optics, 15571 Producer Lane, Unit G, Huntington Beach, CA 92649/714-891-1309; FAX: 714-892-6920
Premier Reticles, 920 Breckinridge Lane, Winchester, VA 22601-6707/540-722-0601; FAX: 540-722-3522
Prescott Projectile Co., 1808 Meadowbrook Road, Prescott, AZ 86303
Price Bullets, Patrick W., 16520 Worthley Drive, San Lorenzo, CA 94580/510-278-1547
Preslik's Gunstocks, 4245 Keith Ln., Chico, CA 95926/916-891-8236
Prime Reloading, 30 Chiswick End, Meldreth, Royston SG8 6LZ UK/0763-260636
Primos, Inc., P.O. Box 12785, Jackson, MS 39236-2785/601-366-1288; FAX: 601-362-3274
Pro Load Ammunition, Inc., 5180 E. Seltice Way, Post Falls, ID 83854/208-773-9444; FAX: 208-773-9441
Pro-Shot Products, Inc., P.O. Box 763, Taylorville, IL 62568/217-824-9133; FAX: 217-824-8861
Professional Hunter Supplies (See Star Custom Bullets)
Prolix® Lubricants, P.O. Box 1348, Victorville, CA 92393/800-248-LUBE, 619-243-3129; FAX: 619-241-0148
Protector Mfg. Co., Inc., The, 443 Ashwood Place, Boca Raton, FL 33431/407-394-6011
Protektor Model, 1-11 Bridge St., Galeton, PA 16922/814-435-2442
ProWare,Inc., 15847 NE Hancock St., Portland, OR 97230/503-239-0159

Q

Quack Decoy & Sporting Clays, 4 Ann & Hope Way, P.O. Box 98, Cumberland, RI 02864/401-723-8202; FAX: 401-722-5910
Quarton USA, Ltd. Co., 7042 Alamo Downs Pkwy., Suite 370, San Antonio, TX 78238-4518/800-520-8435, 210-520-8430; FAX: 210-520-8433
Quartz-Lok, 13137 N. 21st Lane, Phoenix, AZ 85029

R

R&J Gun Shop, 133 W. Main St., John Day, OR 97845/503-575-2130
R&S Industries Corp., 8255 Brentwood Industrial Dr., St. Louis, MO 63144/314-781-5400
Radiator Specialty Co., 1900 Wilkinson Blvd., P.O. Box 34689, Charlotte, NC 28234/800-438-6947; FAX: 800-421-9525
Radical Concepts, P.O. Box 1473, Lake Grove, OR 97035/503-538-7437
Rainier Ballistics Corp., 4500 15th St. East, Tacoma, WA 98424/800-638-8722, 206-922-7589; FAX: 206-922-7854

Ram-Line, Inc., 545 Thirty-One Rd., Grand Junction, CO 81504/303-434-4500; FAX: 303-434-4004
Ranch Products, P.O. Box 145, Malinta, OH 43535/313-277-3118; FAX: 313-565-8536
Randolph Engineering, Inc., 26 Thomas Patten Dr., Randolph, MA 02368/800-541-1405; FAX: 800-875-4200
Range Brass Products Company, P.O. Box 218, Rockport, TX 78381
Ranger Products, 2623 Grand Blvd., Suite 209, Holiday, FL 34609/813-942-4652, 800-407-7007; FAX: 813-942-6221
Ranging, Inc., Routes 5 & 20, East Bloomfield, NY 14443/716-657-6161; FAX: 716-657-5405
Ransom International Corp., P.O. Box 3845, 1040-A Sandretto Dr., Prescott, AZ 86302/520-778-7899; FAX: 520-778-7993; E-MAIL: ransom@primenet.com; WEB: http://www.primenet.com/~ransom
Rapine Bullet Mould Mfg. Co., 9503 Landis Lane, East Greenville, PA 18041/215-679-5413; FAX: 215-679-9795
Raytech, Div. of Lyman Products Corp., 475 Smith Street, Middletown, CT 06457-1541/860-632-2020; FAX: 860-632-1699
RCBS, Div. of Blount, Inc., Sporting Equipment Div., 605 Oro Dam Blvd., Oroville, CA 95965/800-533-5000, 916-533-5191; FAX: 916-533-1647
Reagent Chemical & Research, Inc. (See Calico Hardwoods, Inc.)
Reardon Products, P.O. Box 126, Morrison, IL 61270/815-772-3155
Red Cedar Precision Mfg., W. 485 Spruce Dr., Brodhead, WI 53520/608-897-8416
Red Diamond Dist. Co., 1304 Snowdon Dr., Knoxville, TN 37912
Red Star Target Co., P.O. Box 275, Babb, MT 59411-0275/800-679-2917; FAX: 800-679-2918
Redding Reloading Equipment, 1089 Starr Rd., Cortland, NY 13045/607-753-3331; FAX: 607-756-8445
Redfield, Inc., 5800 E. Jewell Ave., Denver, CO 80224-2303/303-757-6411; FAX: 303-756-2338
Redman's Rifling & Reboring, 189 Nichols Rd., Omak, WA 98841/509-826-5512
Redwood Bullet Works, 3559 Bay Rd., Redwood City, CA 94063/415-367-6741
R.E.I., P.O. Box 88, Tallevast, FL 34270/813-755-0085
Reiswig, Wallace E. (See Claro Walnut Gunstock Co.)
Reloaders Equipment Co., 4680 High St., Ecorse, MI 48229
Reloading Specialties, Inc., Box 1130, Pine Island, MN 55463/507-356-8500; FAX: 507-356-8800
Remington Arms Co., Inc., P.O. Box 700, 870 Remington Drive, Madison, NC 27025-0700/800-243-9700
R.E.T. Enterprises, 2608 S. Chestnut, Broken Arrow, OK 74012/918-251-GUNS; FAX: 918-251-0587
R.G.-G., Inc., P.O. Box 1261, Conifer, CO 80433-1261/303-697-4154; FAX: 303-697-4154
Rice, Keith (See White Rock Tool & Die)
Richards Micro-Fit Stocks, 8331 N. San Fernando Ave., Sun Valley, CA 91352/818-767-6097; FAX: 818-767-7121
Rickard, Pete, Inc., RD 1, Box 292, Cobleskill, NY 12043/800-282-5663; FAX: 518-234-2454
Ridgetop Sporting Goods, P.O. Box 306, 42907 Hilligoss Ln. East, Eatonville, WA 98328/360-832-6422; FAX: 360-832-6422
Riebe Co., W.J., 3434 Tucker Rd., Boise, ID 83703
Rifle Works & Armory, 707 N 12 St., Cody, WY 82414/307-587-4914
RIG Products, 87 Coney Island Dr., Sparks, NV 89431-6334/702-331-5666; FAX: 702-331-5669
Riling Arms Books Co., Ray, 6844 Gorsten St., P.O. Box 18925, Philadelphia, PA 19119/215-438-2456; FAX: 215-438-5395
Rimrock Rifle Stocks, P.O. Box 589, Vashon Island, WA 98070/206-463-5551; FAX: 206-463-2526
R.I.S. Co., Inc., 718 Timberlake Circle, Richardson, TX 75080/214-235-0933
River Road Sporting Clays, Bruce Barsotti, P.O. Box 3016, Gonzales, CA 93926/408-675-2473
RLCM Enterprises, 110 Hill Crest Drive, Burleson, TX 76028
R.M. Precision, Inc., Attn. Greg F. Smith Marketing, P.O. Box 210, LaVerkin, UT 84745/801-635-4656; FAX: 801-635-4430
RMS Custom Gunsmithing, 4120 N. Bitterwell, Prescott Valley, AZ 86314/520-772-7626
Robar Co.'s, Inc., The, 21438 N. 7th Ave., Suite B, Phoenix, AZ 85027/602-581-2648; FAX: 602-582-0059
Roberts Products, 25328 SE Iss. Beaver Lk. Rd., Issaquah, WA 98029/206-392-8172
Robinett, R.G., P.O. Box 72, Madrid, IA 50156/515-795-2906
Robinson, Don, Pennsylvania Hse., 36 Fairfax Crescent, Southowram, Halifax, W. Yorkshire HX3 9SQ, ENGLAND/0422-364458
Robinson Firearms Mfg. Ltd., 1699 Blondeaux Crescent, Kelowna, B.C. CANADA V1Y 4J8/604-868-9596
Robinson H.V. Bullets, 3145 Church St., Zachary, LA 70791/504-654-4029
Rochester Lead Works, 76 Anderson Ave., Rochester, NY 14607/716-442-8500; FAX: 716-442-4712
Rockwood Corp., Speedwell Division, 136 Lincoln Blvd., Middlesex, NJ 08846/908-560-7171, 800-243-8274; FAX: 980-560-7475
Rocky Fork Enterprises, P.O. Box 427, 878 Battle Rd., Nolensville, TN 37135/615-941-1307
Rocky Mountain Arms, Inc., 600 S. Sunset, Unit C, Longmont, CO 80501/303-768-8522; FAX: 303-678-8766
Rocky Mountain High Sports Glasses, 8121 N. Central Park Ave., Skokie, IL 60076/708-679-1012; FAX: 708-679-0184
Rocky Mountain Rifle Works Ltd., 1707 14th St., Boulder, CO 80302/303-443-9189
Rocky Mountain Target Co., 3 Aloe Way, Leesburg, FL 34788/904-365-9598
Rod Guide Co., Box 1149, Forsyth, MO 65653/800-952-2774
Rolston, Inc., Fred W., 210 E. Cummins St., Tecumseh, MI 49286/517-423-6002, 800-314-9061 (orders only); FAX: 517-423-6002
Rooster Laboratories, P.O. Box 412514, Kansas City, MO 64141/816-474-1622; FAX: 816-474-1307
Rorschach Precision Products, P.O. Box 151613, Irving, TX 75015/214-790-3487
Rosenthal, Brad and Sallie, 19303 Ossenfort Ct., St. Louis, MO 63038/314-273-5159; FAX: 314-273-5149
Ross, Don, 12813 West 83 Terrace, Lenexa, KS 66215/913-492-6982
Ross & Webb (See Ross, Don)
Roto Carve, 2754 Garden Ave., Janesville, IA 50647
Rowe Engineering, Inc. (See R.E.I.)
Royal Arms Gunstocks, 919 8th Ave. NW, Great Falls, MT 59404/406-453-1149
RPM, 15481 N. Twin Lakes Dr., Tucson, AZ 85737/602-825-1233; FAX: 602-825-3333
Rubright Bullets, 1008 S. Quince Rd., Walnutport, PA 18088/215-767-1339
Rucker Dist. Inc., P.O. Box 479, Terrell, TX 75160/214-563-2094
Rupert's Gun Shop, 2202 Dick Rd., Suite B, Fenwick, MI 48834/517-248-3252
Rusteprufe Laboratories, 1319 Jefferson Ave., Sparta, WI 54656/608-269-4144
Rusty Duck Premium Gun Care Products, 7785 Foundation Dr., Suite 6, Florence, KY 41042/606-342-5553; FAX: 606-342-5556
Rutgers Book Center, 127 Raritan Ave., Highland Park, NJ 08904/908-545-4344; FAX: 908-545-6686
Ryan, Chad L., RR 3, Box 72, Cresco, IA 52136/319-547-4384

S

S&B Industries, 11238 McKinley Rd., Montrose, MI 48457/810-639-5491
S&K Mfg. Co., P.O. Box 247, Pittsfield, PA 16340/814-563-7808; FAX: 814-563-7808
S&S Firearms, 74-11 Myrtle Ave., Glendale, NY 11385/718-497-1100; FAX: 718-497-1105
Sabatti S.R.L., via Alessandro Volta 90, 25063 Gardone V.T., Brescia, ITALY/030-8912207-831312; FAX: 030-8912059
SAECO (See Redding Reloading Equipment)
Safari Press, Inc., 15621 Chemical Lane B, Huntington Beach, CA 92649/714-894-9080; FAX: 714-894-4949
Sako Ltd., P.O. Box 149, SF-11101, Riihimaki, FINLAND
Samco Global Arms, Inc., 6995 NW 43rd St., Miami, FL 33166/305-593-9782
San Francisco Gun Exchange, 124 Second St., San Francisco, CA 94105/415-982-6097
Sanders Custom Gun Service, 2358 Tyler Lane, Louisville, KY 40205/502-454-3338
Sanders Gun and Machine Shop, 145 Delhi Road, Manchester, IA 52057
Sandia Die & Cartridge Co., 37 Atancacio Rd. NE, Albuquerque, NM 87123/505-298-5729
Saunders Gun & Machine Shop, R.R. 2, Delhi Road, Manchester, IA 52057
Savage Range Systems, Inc., 100 Springdale RD., Westfield, MA 01085/413-568-7001; FAX: 413-562-1152
Saville Iron Co. (See Greenwood Precision)
Savino, Barbara J., P.O. Box 1104, Hardwick, VT 05843-1104
Scattergun Technologies, Inc., 620 8th Ave. S., Nashville, TN 37203/615-254-1441; FAX: 615-254-1449
Schaefer Shooting Sports, 1923 Grand Ave., Baldwin, NY 11510/516-379-4900; FAX: 516-379-6701
Scharch Mfg., Inc., 10325 Co. Rd. 120, Unit C, Salida, CO 81201/719-539-7242, 800-836-4683; FAX: 719-539-3021
Schiffman, Curt, 3017 Kevin Cr., Idaho Falls, ID 83402/208-524-4684
Schiffman, Mike, 8233 S. Crystal Springs, McCammon, ID 83250/208-254-9114
Schmidtke Group, 17050 W. Salentine Dr., New Berlin, WI 53151-7349
Schmidt & Bender, Inc., Brook Rd., P.O. Box 134, Meriden, NH 03770/603-469-3565, 800-468-3450; FAX: 603-469-3471
Schmidtman Custom Ammunition, 6 Gilbert Court, Cotati, CA 94931
Schneider Bullets, 3655 West 214th St., Fairview Park, OH 44126
Schneider Rifle Barrels, Inc., Gary, 12202 N. 62nd Pl., Scottsdale, AZ 85254/602-948-2525
Schroeder Bullets, 1421 Thermal Ave., San Diego, CA 92154/619-423-3523
Schuetzen Gun Co., P.O. Box 272113, Fort Collins, CO 80527/970-223-3678
Schuetzen Pistol Works, 620-626 Old Pacific Hwy. SE, Olympia, WA 98513/360-459-3471; FAX: 360-491-3447
Schumakers Gun Shop, William, 512 Prouty Corner Lp. A, Colville, WA 99114/509-684-4848
Schwartz Custom Guns, David W., 2505 Waller St., Eau Claire, WI 54703/715-832-1735
Schwartz Custom Guns, Wayne E., 970 E. Britton Rd., Morrice, MI 48857/517-625-4079
Scope Control, Inc., 5775 Co. Rd. 23 SE, Alexandria, MN 56308/612-762-7295
ScopLevel, 151 Lindbergh Ave., Suite C, Livermore, CA 94550/510-449-5052; FAX: 510-373-0861
Scot Powder, Rt.1 Box 167, McEwen, TN 37101/800-416-3006; FAX: 615-729-4211
Scot Powder Co. of Ohio, Inc., Box GD96, Only, TN 37140/615-729-4207, 800-416-3006; FAX: 615-729-4217
Scott, Dwight, 23089 Englehardt St., Clair Shores, MI 48080/313-779-4735
Seattle Binocular & Scope Repair Co., P.O. Box 46094, Seattle, WA 98146/206-932-3733
Seebeck Assoc., R.E., P.O. Box 59752, Dallas, TX 75229
Seligman Shooting Products, Box 133, Seligman, AZ 86337/602-422-3607
Selsi Co., Inc., P.O. Box 10, Midland Park, NJ 07432-0010/201-935-0388; FAX: 201-935-5851
Sentinel Arms, P.O. Box 57, Detroit, MI 48231/313-331-1951; FAX: 313-331-1456
Service Armament, 689 Bergen Blvd., Ridgefield, NJ 07657
Shappy Bullets, 76 Milldale Ave., Plantsville, CT 06479/203-621-3704
Shaw, Inc., E.R. (See Small Arms Mfg. Co.)
Shay's Gunsmithing, 931 Marvin Ave., Lebanon, PA 17042
Shell Shack, 113 E. Main, Laurel, MT 59044/406-628-8986
Shepherd Scope Ltd., Box 189, Waterloo, NE 68069/402-779-2424; FAX: 402-779-4010
Shilen Rifles, Inc., P.O. Box 1300, 205 Metro Park Blvd., Ennis, TX 75119/214-875-5318; FAX: 214-875-5402
Shiloh Creek, Box 357, Cottleville, MO 63338/314-447-2900; FAX: 314-447-2900
Shooter's Choice, 16770 Hilltop Park Place, Chagrin Falls, OH 44023/216-543-8808; FAX: 216-543-8811
Shooter's Edge, Inc., P.O.Box 769, Trinidad, CO 81082
Shooters Supply, 1120 Tieton Dr., Yakima, WA 98902/509-452-1181
Shootin' Accessories, Ltd., P.O. Box 6810, Auburn, CA 95604/916-889-2220
Shooting Chrony, Inc., 3269 Niagara Falls Blvd., N. Tonawanda, NY 14120/905-276-6292; FAX: 416-276-6295
Shooting Components Marketing, P.O. Box 1069, Englewood, CO 80150/303-987-2543; FAX: 303-989-3508
Shoot-N-C Targets (See Birchwood Casey)
Shotgun Shop, The, 14145 Proctor Ave., Suite 3, Industry, CA 91746/818-855-2737; FAX: 818-855-2735
Siegrist Gun Shop, 8754 Turtle Road, Whittemore, MI 48770
Sierra Bullets, 1400 W. Henry St., Sedalia, MO 65301/816-827-6300; FAX: 816-827-6300; WEB: http://www.sierrabullets.com
Sierra Specialty Prod. Co., 1344 Oakhurst Ave., Los Altos, CA 94024/FAX: 415-965-1536
Sightron, Inc., 1672B Hwy. 96, Franklinton, NC 27525/919-528-8783; FAX: 919-528-0995
Signet Metal Corp., 551 Stewart Ave., Brooklyn, NY 11222/718-384-5400; FAX: 718-388-7488
Sile Distributors, Inc., 7 Centre Market Pl., New York, NY 10013/212-925-4111; FAX: 212-925-3149
Silencio/Safety Direct, 56 Coney Island Dr., Sparks, NV 89431/800-648-1812, 702-354-4451; FAX: 702-359-1074
Silver Eagle Machining, 18007 N. 69th Ave., Glendale, AZ 85308
Silver-Tip Corp., RR2, Box 184, Gloster, MS 39638-9520
Simmons, Jerry, 715 Middlebury St., Goshen, IN 46526/219-533-8546
Simmons Enterprises, Ernie, 709 East Elizabethtown Rd., Manheim, PA 17545/717-664-4040
Simmons Gun Repair, Inc., 700 S. Rogers Rd., Olathe, KS 66062/913-782-3131; FAX: 913-782-4189
Simmons Outdoor Corp., 2120 Kilarney Way, Tallahassee, FL 32308/904-878-5100; FAX: 904-878-0300
Sinclair International, Inc., 2330 Wayne Haven St., Fort Wayne, IN 46803/219-493-1858; FAX: 219-493-2530
Siskiyou Gun Works (See Donnelly, C.P.)
Six Enterprises, 320-D Turtle Creek Ct., San Jose, CA 95125/408-999-0201; FAX: 408-999-0216
SKAN A.R., 4 St. Catherines Road, Long Melford, Suffolk, CO10 9JU ENGLAND/011-0787-312942
SKB Shotguns, 4325 S. 120th St., P.O. Box 37669, Omaha, NE 68137/800-752-2767; FAX: 402-330-8029
Skeoch, Brian R., P.O. Box 279, Glenrock, WY 82637/307-436-9655; FAX: 307-436-9034
Skip's Machine, 364 29 Road, Grand Junction, CO 81501/303-245-5417
SKR Industries, POB 1382, San Angelo, TX 76902/915-658-3133
S.L.A.P. Industries, P.O. Box 1121, Parklands 2121, SOUTH AFRICA/27-11-788-0030; FAX: 27-11-788-0030
Slug Group, Inc., P.O. Box 376, New Paris, PA 15554/814-839-4517; FAX: 814-839-2601
Slug Site Co., Ozark Wilds, Rt. 2, Box 158, Versailles, MO 65084/314-378-6430
Small Arms Mfg. Co., 5312 Thoms Run Rd., Bridgeville, PA 15017/412-221-4343; FAX: 412-221-4303
Small Custom Mould & Bullet Co., Box 17211, Tucson, AZ 85731
Smith, Art, 230 Main St. S., Hector, MN 55342/612-848-2760; FAX: 612-848-2760
Smith, Sharmon, 4545 Speas Rd., Fruitland, ID 83619/208-452-6329
Snider Stocks, Walter S., Rt. 2 P.O. Box 147, Denton, NC 27239
Sno-Seal (See Atsko/Sno-Seal)
Sonora Rifle Barrel Co., 14396 D. Tuolumne Rd., Sonora, CA 95370/209-532-4139
SOS Products Co. (See Buck Stix—SOS Products Co.)
Southern Ammunition Co., Inc., 4232 Meadow St., Loris, SC 29569-3124/803-756-3262; FAX: 803-756-3583
Specialty Gunsmithing, Lynn McMurdo, P.O. Box 404, Afton, WY 83110/307-886-5535
Specialty Shooters Supply, Inc., 3325 Griffin Rd., Suite 9mm, Fort Lauderdale, FL 33317

Speedfeed, Inc., 3820 Industrial Way, Suite N, Benicia, CA 94510/707-746-1221; FAX: 707-746-1888
Speer Products, Div. of Blount, Inc., Sporting Equipment Div., P.O. Box 856, Lewiston, ID 83501/208-746-2351; FAX: 208-746-2915
Speiser, Fred D., 2229 Dearborn, Missoula, MT 59801/406-549-8133
Spence, George W., 115 Locust St., Steele, MO 63877/314-695-4926
Spencer's Custom Guns, Rt. 1, Box 546, Scottsville, VA 24590/804-293-6836
S.P.G., Inc., P.O. Box 761-H, Livingston, MT 59047/406-222-8416; FAX: 406-222-8416
Sport Flite Manufacturing Co., P.O. Box 1082, Bloomfield Hills, MI 48303/810-647-3747
Sportsman Supply Co., 714 East Eastwood, P.O. Box 650, Marshall, MO 65340/816-886-9393
Sportsmatch U.K. Ltd., 16 Summer St., Leighton Buzzard, Bedfordshire, LU7 8HT ENGLAND/01525-381638; FAX: 01525-851236
Springfield, Inc., 420 W. Main St., Geneseo, IL 61254/309-944-5631; FAX: 309-944-3676
SSK Industries, 721 Woodvue Lane, Wintersville, OH 43952/614-264-0176; FAX: 614-264-2257
Stackpole Books, 5067 Ritter Rd., Mechanicsburg, PA 17055-6921/717-234-5041; FAX: 717-234-1359
Stalwart Corporation, 76 Imperial, Unit A, Evanston, WY 82930/307-789-7687; FAX: 307-789-7688
Stanley Bullets, 2085 Heatheridge Ln., Reno, NV 89509
Star Custom Bullets, P.O. Box 608, 468 Main St., Ferndale, CA 95536/707-786-9140; FAX: 707-786-9117
Starke Bullet Company, P.O. Box 400, Cooperstown, ND 58425/701-797-3431
Starkey Labs, 6700 Washington Ave. S., Eden Prairie, MN 55344
Starkey's Gun Shop, 9430 McCombs, El Paso, TX 79924/915-751-3030
Starline, 1300 W. Henry St., Sedalia, MO 65301/816-827-6640; FAX: 816-827-6650
Star Machine Works, 418 10th Ave., San Diego, CA 92101/619-232-3216
Star Reloading Co., Inc., 5520 Rock Hampton Ct., Indianapolis, IN 46268/317-872-5840
Stark's Bullet Mfg., 2580 Monroe St., Eugene, OR 97405
State Arms Gun Co., 815 S. Division St., Waunakee, WI 53597/608-849-5800
Stegall, James B., 26 Forest Rd., Wallkill, NY 12589
Stewart's Gunsmithing, P.O. Box 5854, Pietersburg North 0750, Transvaal, SOUTH AFRICA/01521-89401
Steyr Mannlicher AG, Mannlicherstrasse 1, P.O.B. 1000, A-4400 Steyr, AUSTRIA/0043-7252-896-0; FAX: 0043-7252-68621
Stiles Custom Guns, RD3, Box 1605, Homer City, PA 15748/412-479-9945, 412-479-8666
Stillwell, Robert, 421 Judith Ann Dr., Schertz, TX 78154
Stoeger Industries, 5 Mansard Ct., Wayne, NJ 07470/201-872-9500, 800-631-0722; FAX: 201-872-2230
Stoney Point Products, Inc., P.O. Box 234, 1815 North Spring Street, New Ulm, MN 56073-0234/507-354-3360; FAX: 507-354-7236
Storey, Dale A. (See DGS, Inc.)
Storm, Gary, P.O. Box 5211, Richardson, TX 75083/214-385-0862
Stratco, Inc., P.O. Box 2270, Kalispell, MT 59901/406-755-1221; FAX: 406-755-1226
Strawbridge, Victor W., 6 Pineview Dr., Dover, NH 03820/603-742-0013
Strutz Rifle Barrels, Inc., W.C., P.O. Box 611, Eagle River, WI 54521/715-479-4766
"Su-Press-On," Inc., P.O. Box 09161, Detroit, MI 48209/313-842-4222 7:30-11p.m. Mon-Thurs.
Svon Corp., 280 Eliot St., Ashland, MA 01721/508-881-8852
Swann, D.J., 5 Orsova Close, Eltham North, Vic. 3095, AUSTRALIA/03-431-0323
SwaroSports, Inc. (See JagerSport, Ltd.)
Swarovski Optik North America Ltd., One Wholesale Way, Cranston, RI 02920/401-942-3380, 800-426-3089; FAX: 401-946-2587
Swift Bullet Co., P.O. Box 27, 201 Main St., Quinter, KS 67752/913-754-3959; FAX: 913-754-2359
Swift Instruments, Inc., 952 Dorchester Ave., Boston, MA 02125/617-436-2960; FAX: 617-436-3232
Swivel Machine Works, Inc., 11 Monitor Hill Rd., Newtown, CT 06470/203-270-6343; FAX: 203-874-9212
Szweda, Robert (See RMS Custom Gunsmithing)

T

TacStar Industries, Inc., 218 Justin Drive, P.O. Box 70, Cottonwood, AZ 86326/602-639-0072; FAX: 602-634-8781
Tag Distributors, 1331 Penna. Ave., Emmaus, PA 18049/610-966-3839
Talbot QD Mounts, 2210 E. Grand Blanc Rd., Grand Blanc, MI 48439-8113/810-695-2497
Talley, Dave, P.O. Box 821, Glenrock, WY 82637/307-436-8724, 307-436-9315
Talmage, William G., 10208 N. County Rd. 425 W., Brazil, IN 47834/812-442-0804
Talon Mfg. Co., Inc., 575 Bevans Industrial Ln., Paw Paw, WV 25434/304-947-7440; FAX: 304-947-7447
Tamarack Products, Inc., P.O. Box 625, Wauconda, IL 60084/708-526-9333; FAX: 708-526-9353
Tank's Rifle Shop, P.O. Box 474, Fremont, NE 68025/402-727-1317; FAX: 402-721-2573
Taracorp Industries, Inc., 1200 Sixteenth St., Granite City, IL 62040/618-451-4400
Tasco Sales, Inc., 7600 NW 26th St., Miami, FL 33156/305-591-3670; FAX: 305-592-5895
Taylor & Robbins, P.O. Box 164, Rixford, PA 16745/814-966-3233
TCCI, P.O. Box 302, Phoenix, AZ 85001/602-237-3823; FAX: 602-237-3858
TCSR, 3998 Hoffman Rd., White Bear Lake, MN 55110-4626/800-328-5323; FAX: 612-429-0526
TDP Industries, Inc., 606 Airport Blvd., Doylestown, PA 18901/215-345-8687; FAX: 215-345-6057
Tecnolegno S.p.A., Via A. Locatelli, 6, 10, 24019 Zogno, ITALY/0345-91114; FAX: 0345-93254
Tele-Optics, 5514 W. Lawrence Ave., Chicago, IL 60630/312-283-7757; FAX: 312-283-7757
Tepeco, P.O. Box 342, Friendswood, TX 77546/713-482-2702
Testing Systems, Inc., 220 Pegasus Ave., Northvale, NJ 07647
Teton Arms, Inc., P.O. Box 411, Wilson, WY 83014/307-733-3395
Tetra Gun Lubricants, 1812 Margaret Ave., Annapolis, MD 21401/410-268-6451; FAX: 410-268-8377
Texas Platers Supply Co., 2453 W. Five Mile Parkway, Dallas, TX 75233/214-330-7168
T.F.C. S.p.A., Via G. Marconi 118, B, Villa Carcina, Brescia 25069, ITALY/030-881271; FAX: 030-881826
Things Unlimited, 235 N. Kimbau, Casper, WY 82601/307-234-5277
Thomas, Charles C., 2600 S. First St., Springfield, IL 62794/217-789-8980; FAX: 217-789-9130
Thompson Bullet Lube Co., P.O. Box 472343, Garland, TX 75047-2343/214-271-8063; FAX: 214-840-6743
Thompson/Center Arms, P.O. Box 5002, Rochester, NH 03866/603-332-2394; FAX: 603-332-5133
Thompson Precision, 110 Mary St., P.O. Box 251, Warren, IL 61087/815-745-3625
Thompson Target Technology, 618 Roslyn Ave., SW, Canton, OH 44710/216-453-7707; FAX: 216-478-4723
Thompson Tool Mount (See TTM)
3-D Ammunition & Bullets, 112 W. Plum St., P.O. Box J, Doniphan, NE 68832/402-845-2285, 800-255-6712; FAX: 402-845-6546
3-Ten Corp., P.O. Box 269, Feeding Hills, MA 01030/413-789-2086; FAX: 413-789-1549
300 Gunsmith Service, Inc., at Cherry Creek State Park Shooting Center,, 12500 E. Belleview Ave.,Englewood, CO 80111/303-690-3300
T.H.U. Enterprises, Inc., P.O. Box 418, Lederach, PA 19450/215-256-1665; FAX: 215-256-9718
Thunderbird Cartridge Co., Inc. (See TCCI)
Tiger-Hunt, Box 379, Beaverdale, PA 15921/814-472-5161
Timber Heirloom Products, 618 Roslyn Ave. SW, Canton, OH 44710/216-453-7707; FAX: 216-478-4723
Timney Mfg., Inc., 3065 W. Fairmont Ave., Phoenix, AZ 85017/602-274-2999; FAX: 602-241-0361
Tioga Engineering Co., Inc., P.O. Box 913, 13 Cone St., Wellsboro, PA 16901/717-724-3533, 717-662-3347

Tirelli, Snc Di Tirelli Primo E.C., Via Matteotti No. 359, Gardone V.T., Brescia, ITALY 25063/030-8912819; FAX: 030-832240
TM Stockworks, 6355 Maplecrest Rd., Fort Wayne, IN 46835/219-485-5389
TMI Products (See Haselbauer Products, Jerry)
Tom's Gun Repair, Thomas G. Ivanoff, 76-6 Rt. Southfork Rd., Cody, WY 82414/307-587-6949
Tom's Gunshop, 3601 Central Ave., Hot Springs, AR 71913/501-624-3856
Tombstone Smoke`n'Deals, 3218 East Bell Road, Phoenix, AZ 85032/602-905-7013; Fax: 602-443-1998
Tonoloway Tack Drives, HCR 81, Box 100, Needmore, PA 17238
Totally Dependable Products (See TDP Industries, Inc.)
TR Metals Corp., 1 Pavilion Ave., Riverside, NJ 08075/609-461-9000; FAX: 609-764-6340
Trafalgar Square, P.O. Box 257, N. Pomfret, VT 05053/802-457-1911
Traft Gunshop, P.O. Box 1078, Buena Vista, CO 81211
Trammco, 839 Gold Run Rd., Boulder, CO 80302
Trevallion Gunstocks, 9 Old Mountain Rd., Cape Neddick, ME 03902/207-361-1130
Trico Plastics, 590 S. Vincent Ave., Azusa, CA 91702
Trijicon, Inc., 49385 Shafer Ave., P.O. Box 930059, Wixom, MI 48393-0059/810-960-7700; FAX: 810-960-7725
Trilux Inc., P.O. Box 24608, Winston-Salem, NC 27114/910-659-9438; FAX: 910-768-7720
Trophy Bonded Bullets, Inc., 900 S. Loop W., Suite 190, Houston, TX 77054/713-645-4499; FAX: 713-741-6393
Trotman, Ken, 135 Ditton Walk, Unit 11, Cambridge CB5 8PY, ENGLAND/01223-211030; FAX: 01223-212317
Tru-Square Metal Prods., Inc., 640 First St. SW, P.O. Box 585, Auburn, WA 98071/206-833-2310; FAX: 206-833-2349
True Flight Bullet Co., 5581 Roosevelt St., Whitehall, PA 18052/610-262-7630; FAX: 610-262-7806
TTM, 1550 Solomon Rd., Santa Maria, CA 93455/805-934-1281
Tucker, James C., P.O. Box 15485, Sacramento, CA 95851/916-923-0571
Turkish Firearms Corp., 522 W. Maple St., Allentown, PA 18101/610-821-8660; FAX: 610-821-9049
Tuttle, Dale, 4046 Russell Rd., Muskegon, MI 49445/616-766-2250
Tyler Scott, Inc., 313 Rugby Ave., Terrace Park, OH 45174/513-831-7603; FAX: 513-831-7417

U

Uncle Bud's, HCR 81, Box 100, Needmore, PA 17238/717-294-6000; FAX: 717-294-6005
Uncle Mike's (See Michaels of Oregon Co.)
Unertl Optical Co., Inc., John, 308 Clay Ave., P.O. Box 818, Mars, PA 16046-0818/412-625-3810
United Binocular Co., 9043 S. Western Ave., Chicago, IL 60620
United States Ammunition Co. (See USAC)
United States Optics Technologies, Inc., 5900 Dale St., Buena Park, CA 90621/714-994-4901; FAX: 714-994-4904
United States Products Co., 518 Melwood Ave., Pittsburgh, PA 15213/412-621-2130
USAC, 4500-15th St. East, Tacoma, WA 98424/206-922-7589
USA Sporting Inc., 1330 N. Glassell, Unit M, Orange, CA 92667/714-538-3109, 800-538-3109; FAX: 714-538-1334
Uvalde Machine & Tool, P.O. Box 1604, Uvalde, TX 78802

V

Valor Corp., 5555 NW 36th Ave., Miami, FL 33142/305-633-0127; FAX: 305-634-4536
Van Gorden & Son, Inc., C.S., 1815 Main St., Bloomer, WI 54724/715-568-2612
Van Patten, J.W., P.O. Box 145, Foster Hill, Milford, PA 18337/717-296-7069
Vancini, Carl (See Bestload, Inc.)
Vann Custom Bullets, 330 Grandview Ave., Novato, CA 94947
Varner's Service, 102 Shaffer Rd., Antwerp, OH 45813/419-258-8631
Vega Tool Co., c/o T.R. Ross, 4865 Tanglewood Ct., Boulder, CO 80301/303-530-0174
Venco Industries, Inc. (See Shooter's Choice)
Vest, John, P.O. Box 1552, Susanville, CA 96130/916-257-7228
VibraShine, Inc., P.O. Box 577, Taylorsville, MS 39168/601-785-9854; FAX: 601-785-9874
Vibra-Tek Co., 1844 Arroya Rd., Colorado Springs, CO 80906/719-634-8611; FAX: 719-634-6886
Vic's Gun Refinishing, 6 Pineview Dr., Dover, NH 03820-6422/603-742-0013
Victory USA, P.O. Box 1021, Pine Bush, NY 12566/914-744-2060; FAX: 914-744-5181
Vihtavuori Oy, FIN-41330 Vihtavuori, FINLAND/358-41-3779211; FAX: 358-41-3771643
Vihtavuori Oy/Kaltron-Pettibone, 1241 Ellis St., Bensenville, IL 60106/708-350-1116; FAX: 708-350-1606
Viking Video Productions, P.O. Box 251, Roseburg, OR 97470
Vincent's Shop, 210 Antoinette, Fairbanks, AK 99701
Vintage Industries, Inc., 781 Big Tree Dr., Longwood, FL 32750/407-831-8949; FAX: 407-831-5346
Visible Impact Targets, Rts. 5 & 20, E. Bloomfield, NY 14443/716-657-6161; FAX: 716-657-5405
Vitt/Boos, 2178 Nichols Ave., Stratford, CT 06497/203-375-6859
Voere-KGH m.b.H., P.O. Box 416, A-6333 Kufstein, Tirol, AUSTRIA/0043-5372-62547; FAX: 0043-5372-65752
Volquartsen Custom Ltd., 24276 240th Street, P.O. Box 271, Carroll, IA 51401/712-792-4238; FAX: 712-792-2542
Vom Hoffe (See Old Western Scrounger, Inc., The)
Von Minden Gunsmithing Services, 2403 SW 39 Terrace, Cape Coral, FL 33914/813-542-8946
VSP Publishers (See Heritage/VSP Gun Books)
Vulpes Ventures, Inc., Fox Cartridge Division, P.O. Box 1363, Bolingbrook, IL 60440-7363/708-759-1229

W

Walker Mfg., Inc., 8296 S. Channel, Harsen's Island, MI 48028
Walnut Factory, The, 235 West Rd. No. 1, Portsmouth, NH 03801/603-436-2225; FAX: 603-433-7003
Walters, John, 500 N. Avery Dr., Moore, OK 73160/405-799-0376
WAMCO—New Mexico, P.O. Box 205, Peralta, NM 87042-0205/505-869-0826
Ward & Van Valkenburg, 114 32nd Ave. N., Fargo, ND 58102/701-232-2351
Warne Manufacturing Co., 9039 SE Jannsen Rd., Clackamas, OR 97015/503-657-5590, 800-683-5590; FAX: 503-657-5695
Warren Muzzleloading Co., Inc., Hwy. 21 North, P.O. Box 100, Ozone, AR 72854/501-292-3268
WASP Shooting Systems, Rt. 1, Box 147, Lakeview, AR 72642/501-431-5606
Watson Trophy Match Bullets, 2404 Wade Hampton Blvd., Greenville, SC 29615/803-244-7948
Watsontown Machine & Tool Co., 309 Dickson Ave., Watsontown, PA 17777/717-538-3533
Wayne Specialty Services, 260 Waterford Drive, Florissant, MO 63033/413-831-7083
WD-40 Co., 1061 Cudahy Pl., San Diego, CA 92110/619-275-1400; FAX: 619-275-5823
Weatherby, Inc., 3100 El Camino Real, Atascadero, CA 93422/805-466-1767, 800-227-2016, 800-334-4423 (Calif.); FAX: 805-466-2527
Weaver Arms Corp. Gun Shop, RR 3, P.O. Box 266, Bloomfield, MO 63825-9528
Weaver Products, Div. of Blount, Inc., Sporting Equipment Div., P.O. Box 39, Onalaska, WI 54650/800-648-9624, 608-781-5800; FAX: 608-781-0368
Weaver Scope Repair Service, 1121 Larry Mahan Dr., Suite B, El Paso, TX 79925/915-593-1005
Webb, Bill, 6504 North Bellefontaine, Kansas City, MO 64119/816-453-7431

Weber & Markin Custom Gunsmiths, 4-1691 Powick Rd., Kelowna, B.C. CANADA V1X 4L1/604-762-7575; FAX: 604-861-3655
Webster Scale Mfg. Co., P.O. Box 188, Sebring, FL 33870/813-385-6362
Weems, Cecil, P.O. Box 657, Mineral Wells, TX 76067/817-325-1462
Weigand Combat Handguns, Inc., P.O. Box 239, Crestwood Industrial Park, Mountain Top, PA 18707/717-474-9804; FAX: 717-474-9987
Wells Custom Gunsmith, R.A., 3452 1st Ave., Racine, WI 53402/414-639-5223
Wells, Fred F., Wells Sport Store, 110 N. Summit St., Prescott, AZ 86301/520-445-3655
Welsh, Bud, 80 New Road, E. Amherst, NY 14051/716-688-6344
Wenig Custom Gunstocks, Inc., 103 N. Market St., P.O. Box 249, Lincoln, MO 65338/816-547-3334; FAX: 816-547-2881
Werner, Carl, P.O. Box 492, Littleton, CO 80160
Werth, T.W., 1203 Woodlawn Rd., Lincoln, IL 62656/217-732-1300
Wessinger Custom Guns & Engraving, 268 Limestone Rd., Chapin, SC 29036/803-345-5677
West, Jack L., 1220 W. Fifth, P.O. Box 427, Arlington, OR 97812
West, Robert G., 3973 Pam St., Eugene, OR 97402/541-344-3700
Western Gunstock Mfg. Co., 550 Valencia School Rd., Aptos, CA 95003/408-688-5884
Western Nevada West Coast Bullets, 2307 W. Washington St., Carson City, NV 89703/702-246-3941; FAX: 702-246-0836
Westfield Engineering, 6823 Watcher St., Commerce, CA 90040/FAX: 213-928-8270
Westley Richards & Co., 40 Grange Rd., Birmingham, ENGLAND B29 6AR/010-214722953
Whildin & Sons Ltd., E.H., RR2, Box 119, Tamaqua, PA 18252/717-668-6743; FAX: 717-668-6745
White Flyer Targets, 124 River Road, Middlesex, NJ 08846/908-469-0100, 602-972-7528 (Export); FAX: 908-469-9692, 602-530-3360 (Export)
White Laboratory, Inc., H.P., 3114 Scarboro Rd., Street, MD 21154/410-838-6550; FAX: 410-838-2802
White Rock Tool & Die, 6400 N. Brighton Ave., Kansas City, MO 64119/816-454-0478
White Shooting Systems, Inc., 25 E. Hwy. 40, Box 330-12, Roosevelt, UT 84066/801-722-3085, 800-213-1315; FAX: 801-722-3054
Whitetail Design & Engineering Ltd., 9421 E. Mannsiding Rd., Clare, MI 48617/517-386-3932
Whits Shooting Stuff, Box 1340, Cody, WY 82414
Wichita Arms, Inc., 923 E. Gilbert, P.O. Box 11371, Wichita, KS 67211/316-265-0661; FAX: 316-265-0760
Wick, David E., 1504 Michigan Ave., Columbus, IN 47201/812-376-6960
Widener's Reloading & Shooting Supply, Inc., P.O. Box 3009 CRS, Johnson City, TN 37602/615-282-6786; FAX: 615-282-6651
Wideview Scope Mount Corp., 13535 S. Hwy. 16, Rapid City, SD 57701/605-341-3220; FAX: 605-341-9142
Wiest, M.C., 10737 Dutchtown Rd., Knoxville, TN 37932/423-966-4545
Wilderness Sound Products Ltd., 4015 Main St. A, Springfield, OR 97478/503-741-0263, 800-437-0006; FAX: 503-741-7648
William's Gun Shop, Ben, 1151 S. Cedar Ridge, Duncanville, TX 75137/214-780-1807
Williams Bullet Co., J.R., 2008 Tucker Rd., Perry, GA 31069/912-987-0274
Williams Gun Sight Co., 7389 Lapeer Rd., Box 329, Davison, MI 48423/810-653-2131, 800-530-9028; FAX: 810-658-2140
Williams Shootin' Iron Service, The Lynx-Line, 8857 Bennett Hill Rd., Central Lake, MI 49622/616-544-6615
Williamson Precision Gunsmithing, 117 W. Pipeline, Hurst, TX 76053/817-285-0064
Willow Bend, P.O. Box 203, Chelmsford, MA 01824/508-256-8508; FAX: 508-256-8508
Willson Safety Prods. Div., P.O. Box 622, Reading, PA 19603-0622/610-376-6161; FAX: 610-371-7725

Wilson Arms Co., The, 63 Leetes Island Rd., Branford, CT 06405/203-488-7297; FAX: 203-488-0135
Wilson, Inc., L.E., Box 324, 404 Pioneer Ave., Cashmere, WA 98815/509-782-1328
Winchester Div., Olin Corp., 427 N. Shamrock, E. Alton, IL 62024/618-258-3566; FAX: 618-258-3599
Winchester Press (See New Win Publishing, Inc.)
Windish, Jim, 2510 Dawn Dr., Alexandria, VA 22306/703-765-1994
Windjammer Tournament Wads, Inc., 750 W. Hampden Ave. Suite 170, Englewood, CO 80110/303-781-6329
Winkle Bullets, R.R. 1 Box 316, Heyworth, IL 61745
Winter, Robert M., P.O. Box 484, Menno, SD 57045/605-387-5322
Wiseman and Co., Bill, P.O. Box 3427, Bryan, TX 77805/409-690-3456; FAX: 409-690-0156
Wolf's Western Traders, 40 E. Works, No. 3F, Sheridan, WY 82801/307-674-5352
Wolfe Publishing Co., 6471 Airpark Dr., Prescott, AZ 86301/602-445-7810, 800-899-7810; FAX: 602-778-5124
Worthy Products, Inc., RR 1, P.O. Box 213, Martville, NY 13111/315-324-5298
Wosenitz VHP, Inc., Box 741, Dania, FL 33004/305-923-3748; FAX: 305-925-2217
Wright's Hardwood Gunstock Blanks, 8540 SE Kane Rd., Gresham, OR 97080/503-666-1705
Wyant Bullets, Gen. Del., Swan Lake, MT 59911
Wyoming Bonded Bullets, Box 91, Sheridan, WY 82801/307-674-8091
Wyoming Custom Bullets, 1626 21st St., Cody, WY 82414

X, Y

X-Spand Target Systems, 26-10th St. SE, Medicine Hat, AB T1A 1P7 CANADA/403-526-7997; FAX: 403-528-2362
Yearout, Lewis E. (See Montana Outfitters)
Yee, Mike, 29927 56 Pl. S., Auburn, WA 98001/206-839-3991
Yesteryear Armory & Supply, P.O. Box 408, Carthage, TN 37030
York M-1 Conversions, 803 Mill Creek Run, Plantersville, TX 77363/800-527-2881, 713-477-8442
Young Country Arms, P.O. Box 3615, Simi Valley, CA 93093
Yukon Arms Classic Ammunition, 1916 Brooks, P.O. Box 223, Missoula, MT 59801/406-543-9614

Z

Z's Metal Targets & Frames, P.O. Box 78, South Newbury, NH 03255/603-938-2826
Zanotti Armor, Inc., 123 W. Lone Tree Rd., Cedar Falls, IA 50613/319-232-9650
Z-Coat Industrial Coatings, Inc., 3375 U.S. Hwy. 98 S. No. A, Lakeland, FL 33803-8365/813-665-1734
Zeeryp, Russ, 1601 Foard Dr., Lynn Ross Manor, Morristown, TN 37814/615-586-2357
Zeiss Optical, Carl, 1015 Commerce St., Petersburg, VA 23803/804-861-0033, 800-388-2984; FAX: 804-733-4024
Zero Ammunition Co., Inc., 1601 22nd St. SE, P.O. Box 1188, Cullman, AL 35056-1188/800-545-9376; FAX: 205-739-4683
Zim's Inc., 4370 S. 3rd West, Salt Lake City, UT 84107/801-268-2505
Zonie Bullets, 790 N. Lake Havasu Ave., Suite 26, Lake Havasu City, AZ 86403/520-680-6303; FAX: 520-680-6201
Zriny's Metal Targets (See Z's Metal Targets & Frames)
Zufall, Joseph F., P.O. Box 304, Golden, CO 80402-0304

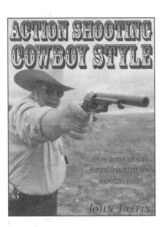

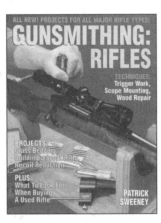

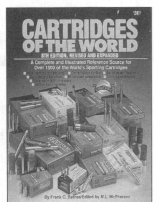

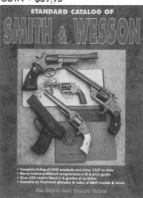
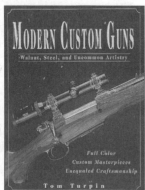
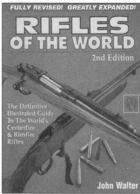